The North Carolina Atlas

Edited by

DOUGLAS M. ORR JR. & ALFRED W. STUART

Foreword by

JAMES B. HUNT JR.

THE UNIVERSITY OF NORTH CAROLINA PRESS · CHAPEL HILL AND LONDON

The North Carolina Atlas

PORTRAIT FOR A NEW CENTURY

Manufactured in Hong Kong

The paper in this book meets the guidelines for permanence
and durability of the Committee on Production Guidelines for Book
Longevity of the Council on Library Resources.
Designed by Heidi Perov

Library of Congress Cataloging-in-Publication Data
The North Carolina atlas: portrait for a new century /
edited by Douglas M. Orr, Jr., and Alfred W. Stuart.
p.   cm.
Includes bibliographical references and index.
ISBN 0-8078-2507-7 (cloth: alk. paper)
1. North Carolina—Maps.   I. Orr, Douglas Milton.
II. Stuart, Alfred W.
G1300 N7   1999   <G&M>
912.756—DC21   99-17353
                                              CIP
                                             MAPS

04 03 02 01 00   5 4 3 2 1

DEDICATION

In remembrance of Jim Clay (1933–94),
our friend, colleague, kindred spirit, and
coeditor for twenty-five years, and always a
loving critic of his adopted Tar Heel state.
Although he did not complete the journey
with us into a new century, his inspiration,
creativity, and vision were with us as we
completed this work. This book is
dedicated to his memory.

CONTENTS

FOREWORD

As the end of the twentieth century nears, North Carolina is at a crossroads in its history. Once a struggling southern state, it is now a national growth leader. A dedicated and hard-working labor force, an ideal location, honest government, and a choice environment are among the factors that are attracting businesses and people to our state in unprecedented numbers. At the same time, our progress brings with it change and challenges. We need to do more to make sure our rural communities and distressed urban areas are sharing in North Carolina's prosperity, and our beautiful environment that has made our state a great place to live and work in must not be compromised by growth.

This book provides a timely and objective analysis of these changes that is accessible to all interested North Carolinians. Informative and richly illustrated with colorful maps and charts, *The North Carolina Atlas* brings together in one place information that will help us all deal more effectively with a challenging future. This information will be useful to public officials, business decision makers, students, involved citizens, or those who simply love the "Old North State."

The North Carolina Atlas will benefit us all by reminding us of our history and inspiring us to look forward as we head into the next century.

James B. Hunt Jr.
Governor of North Carolina

ACKNOWLEDGMENTS

This book represents the culmination of many years of work, involving a multitude of colleagues and friends as well as a family tree of publications that preceded it.

In 1972 we collaborated with our colleagues at the University of North Carolina (UNC) Press, one of the nation's finest university publishers, to produce the groundbreaking *Metrolina Atlas*. It introduced a thematic, multifaceted perspective of the burgeoning two-state urban region around Charlotte. That phenomenon of regionalism is very much with us in today's American urbanizing society. The *Metrolina Atlas* was followed by the 1975 *North Carolina Atlas: Portrait of a Changing Southern State*, also published by the UNC Press, and then in 1989 we turned to the entire southern region with the release of *Land of the South*, utilizing the same thematic, multicolored graphics approach of earlier efforts. We are especially mindful that today we stand on the shoulders of the many participants, supporters, and readers throughout the years of those publications.

This turn-of-the-century *Atlas* was supported from the beginning by the University of North Carolina at Charlotte—its administration led by Chancellor Jim Woodward, the university's foundation, and the human and budgetary resources of the Department of Geography and Earth Sciences. The department has established a national reputation for its cartographic lab and pioneering work through the several *Atlas* projects as well as other publications. We are grateful for this partnership and ongoing support, particularly represented by a substantial contingent of student and staff cartographic and research assistants. They were the day-to-day colleagues who helped explore and sort through the immense amount of data that is contained within the boundaries of this complex and diverse state. Our thanks, then, go to the following people for their invaluable assistance.

Chief cartographers: Laurie Garo and Jeff Simpson
Computer systems administrator: Gary Addington
Administrative support: Kathy Gaskey, Becky Guy, Norma Redmond, Mary Robinette, and Debbie Scaporo
Cartographic technicians: Courtney Bazaire, Bo King, and Holly Orr
Cartographic assistants: Tricia Byrd, Scott Carpenter, Allen Compton, Denise Curtis, John Dewey, Fleming El-Amin, Antonia Gomez, Jesus Guteriez, Nathan Harp, Alex Manfrediz, Jason Ross, and Eric Swinson
Research assistants: Kim Schriefer, Danny Swicegood, and Allan Watson

We are also grateful to Rowena Pomeroy of Warren Wilson College for her administrative support.

We especially thank our colleagues who have authored chapters or sidebars throughout the book. Each is not only knowledgeable about his or her field but also has an abiding personal and professional affinity for North Carolina. We are grateful for their patience, perseverance, and insightful perspectives of the many aspects of North Carolina's profile and changes.

The early production costs of the book were offset by a generous grant from the Knight Foundation. We thank our friend and retired *Charlotte Observer* publisher Rolfe Neill for his support, as well as his ongoing encouragement for the overall effort. His onetime colleague at the *Observer*, former associate editor Jack Claiborne, who now serves as associate vice chancellor for university relations at UNC Charlotte, has been of invaluable assistance. Jack read and critiqued the entire text, made constructive suggestions about many facets of the book, and wrote one of the chapters.

Of particular significance has been the close cooperation and highly professional support provided by the staff of our publisher, the University of

North Carolina Press. We have been privileged by this working relationship over the years, and it has made all the difference.

Finally, we extend our heartfelt appreciation to our families, who were patient, supportive, and understanding as we worked over the long hours and years to put all the pieces together: our wives, Darcy Orr and Mary Louise Stuart, deserve a full share of the credit.

Douglas M. Orr Jr.
Alfred W. Stuart

The North Carolina Atlas

North Carolina

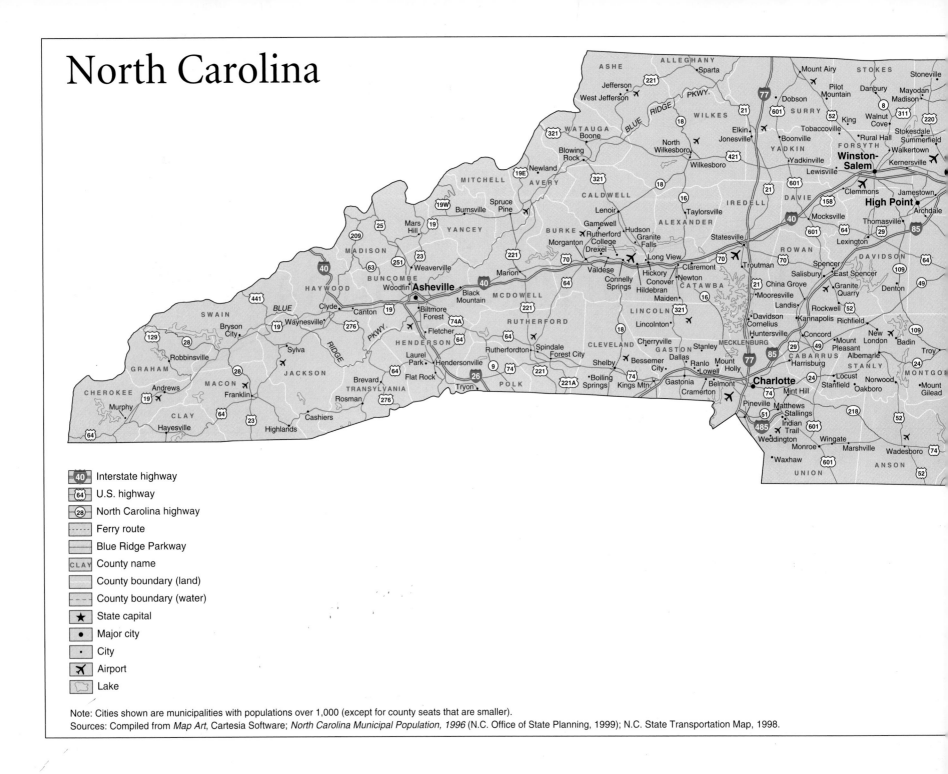

🛣 **40**	Interstate highway
🛣 64	U.S. highway
🛣 28	North Carolina highway
- - - - -	Ferry route
▭	Blue Ridge Parkway
CLAY	County name
▭	County boundary (land)
- - - - -	County boundary (water)
★	State capital
●	Major city
•	City
✈	Airport
▱	Lake

Note: Cities shown are municipalities with populations over 1,000 (except for county seats that are smaller).

Sources: Compiled from *Map Art*, Cartesia Software; *North Carolina Municipal Population, 1996* (N.C. Office of State Planning, 1999); N.C. State Transportation Map, 1998.

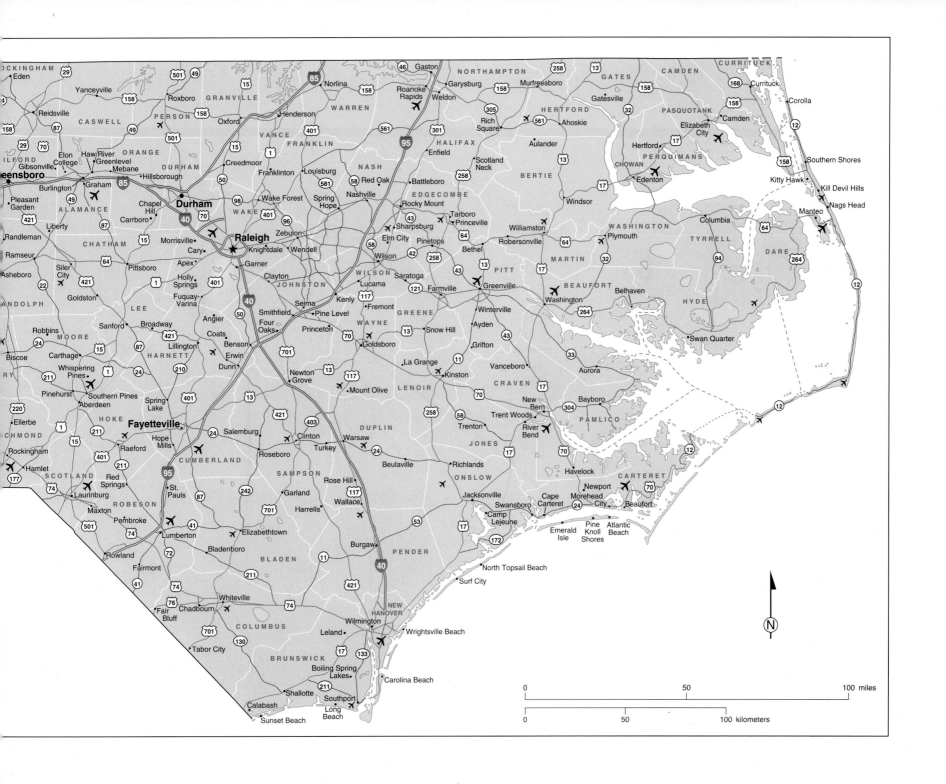

1. INTRODUCTION

No state is more difficult to understand—

to arrive at the essence of how it got to be

what it is—because it is vastly different not

only from states in other regions but from

other Southern states as well.

—John Herbers, The New Heartland

The forces of change, ushering in a

new post-industrial age, are coming at

a whirlwind pace to North Carolina, and

include the dynamics of globalization,

information technology and population

shifts on an unprecedented scale.

—Paul Hawken, author and

sustainable development advocate

As North Carolina comes to the confluence of two centuries, perhaps no southern state presents a more intriguing combination of challenges and opportunities. In many respects, North Carolina is a typical southern state, with an agrarian past, a legacy of slaveholding, and the experiences of Confederacy and the long, painful Reconstruction. Many contemporary challenges derive from that regional context, such as rural poverty, inadequate health care delivery, great disparities in public education, and inequality of opportunity for peoples of different backgrounds.

Yet North Carolina is unique in ways that set it apart from its southern setting and present reoccurring paradoxes: one of the nation's most industrialized states, it also has one of the nation's largest farm populations; home of one of the oldest and most distinguished systems of higher education, it has a public school system that lags behind our national standards; the high-technology complex of the Research Triangle area and Charlotte's rise to national prominence as a banking center have led those parts of the state to a prosperity that compares favorably with any metropolitan area in the country, whereas other counties, left out of the late-twentieth-century boom, are mired in grinding rural poverty; long a one-party state, current political voting behaviors contradict and defy prediction. Given these paradoxes, one challenge is simply that of understanding the state as we enter the new century. This search for understanding is critical if North Carolina is to realize the potential in its abundant human and natural resources.

Among the early colonies, North Carolina was settled relatively late. Shielded by a string of barrier islands and lacking the good natural harbors of neighboring states, early footholds were difficult and required European settlers to make inroads through long wagon road tracks from Pennsylvania and the Chesapeake Bay to the north and Charleston to the south.

This belated settlement and early physical—as well as psychological—isolation from the rest of the country was an ongoing pattern. Indeed, North Carolina remained so remote and uninvolved with the outside that, at one point in the early nineteenth century, it became known as the "Rip Van Winkle State." This stubborn streak of independence has been evidenced in many ways. The first formal sanction of independence from England by any American colony occurred in North Carolina, but then the colony steadfastly refused to join the new Union until the Constitution had a Bill of Rights. Later, secession from the Union was strongly resisted, and the state was the last to join the Confederacy in 1861. North Carolina became the last state to allow the governor veto power in 1996.

The state's physical diversity is usually expressed in four physiographic regions: the Tidewater (or Outer Coastal Plain), Inner Coastal Plain, Pied-

The Swannanoa Valley of the Blue Ridge Mountains

mont, and Mountains (Fig. 1.1). (These physiographic boundaries follow a path that crosses county lines; however, for displaying data by county throughout the *Atlas*, the boundaries are adjusted to conform to county lines.) But the differences are much more than merely physical. As early settlers funneled into each area by different routes and from different sources, human variances began to match the diversities in the physical landscape. Each region developed its own human imprint, socially, economically, politically, and culturally.

One of the most lasting legacies of the settlement pattern in North Carolina was that the population was highly dispersed. When industry finally did come to the state, principally through the textile mill campaigns of the late nineteenth and early twentieth centuries, the mills were scattered among the small agricultural market towns and rural crossroads, thereby reinforcing a dispersed population pattern that is unique in the nation as well as in the South.

It was particularly this pattern of dispersed population that John Herbers was referring to in the quotation that begins this chapter. According to Herbers, North Carolina is perhaps a prototype

Figure 1.1. Land Regions

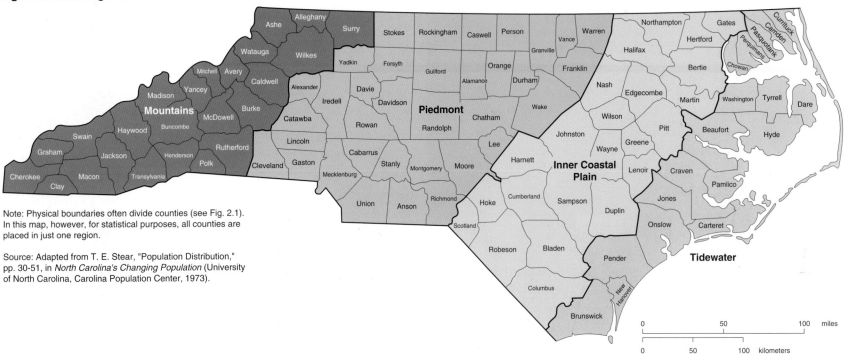

Note: Physical boundaries often divide counties (see Fig. 2.1). In this map, however, for statistical purposes, all counties are placed in just one region.

Source: Adapted from T. E. Stear, "Population Distribution," pp. 30-51, in *North Carolina's Changing Population* (University of North Carolina, Carolina Population Center, 1973).

state for the twenty-first century, with its few large cities and dispersed population and industry. North Carolina is the eighth largest manufacturing state in the United States, yet only a bare majority of its citizenry lives in an urban place. Charlotte, the largest city, had a population of over 500,000 by the end of the 1990s, giving North Carolina the distinction among all of the fifty states of having one of the smallest percentages of the state's total population residing in its largest city. This phenomenon has been described as North Carolina's "urban anomaly."

The dispersion of job-producing industries traditionally has given millions of North Carolinians the option of maintaining a rural, small-town lifestyle while having access to an industrial job and urban services. Rural values and perspectives persist despite heavy industrialization. However, dispersion also has perpetuated lower incomes, higher infant mortality, and other social problems in the widening gap between urban and rural areas.

In the last thirty or so years, broad shifts in regional, national, and global economies have had profound effects on North Carolina's demographic

and economic patterns. First among the changes was the growth and restructuring of the economy of the South that occurred after World War II. Until the late 1950s, farming was the leading employment sector in the region. It has continued to lose jobs while manufacturing, trade, and services, most notably, have grown rapidly. By the late 1970s, farming had fallen to last place among the major sectors, and the larger sectors each employed five or six times as many workers as did agriculture.

Following trends in the South, North Carolina farm employment fell from 26 percent of the total

Charlotte's urban skyline at dusk

in 1960 to only 2 percent by the end of the century. Manufacturing, which developed earlier in North Carolina than in most of the South, stood at 30 percent of the total in 1970 and, despite adding over 119,000 jobs, it fell to under 21 percent in the late 1990s. This happened because the nonindustrial sectors of the economy grew even more rapidly. The services sector expanded fourfold, and both trade and finance tripled. Most of this high growth was urban based, bypassing most of the more rural parts of the state.

Manufacturing grew strongly in both urban and rural areas through the early 1970s, reducing rural-urban disparities, but the rural part began to either decline or slow in its growth by the 1980s. With the internationalization of the economy, major transnational corporations moved aggressively to lower production costs by placing facilities in countries that offered the most comparative advantages. Imports from these and other offshore producers took markets away from domestic companies, especially the labor-intensive industries that tended to predominate in rural North Carolina.

Meanwhile, a third trend, the emergence of the information-processing economy, resulted in the growth of high-tech industry and office clusters in and around major metropolitan centers. The larger urban areas, in North Carolina and elsewhere, experienced boom conditions whereas economic growth stagnated in rural areas, a phenomenon that has been referred to as "Shadows in the Sunbelt."

Population change tends to follow economic change. For decades southerners had been leaving the region to seek greater opportunity elsewhere. This tendency began to reverse in the 1960s, and during the 1970s about 3.5 million more people moved into the region than left it. North Carolina experienced its first net in-migration (278,000) of the twentieth century in the 1970s and added another 792,000 between 1980 and 1998. Most of the recent immigrants settled in metropolitan areas, a trend that coincided with the growth of urban-oriented jobs. Conversely, a number of rural countries experienced net out-migration, particularly among younger adults.

So it is clear that regional, national, and global economic change is dramatically impacting the traditional pattern of population dispersion. As we begin a

A vacated farmstead in the Inner Coastal Plain region

new century and millennium, North Carolina is in a historic period of transition. A systematic analysis of the present state of the state is a necessary first step to meeting the future in a rational and informed manner. Taking stock in this way can provide a challenge to outmoded perceptions that are a poor, even dangerous, basis for future public policy decisions.

Long known as a strongly rural, small-town state, North Carolina is becoming increasingly urbanized with an economy that is more likely to be housed in an office tower than in a textile mill or on a farm. State policy struggles to divide attention between protracted rural issues and mounting urban concerns. What are the implications of these economic and other changes for the transportation network, educational programming, environmental protection, economic vitality, health care, and overall quality of life for all North Carolinians? These implications must be considered in the light of reality, not outdated perceptions. After all, the state motto is *Esse Quam Videri*, "to be, rather than to seem."

That is the rationale for this book: to present a critical analysis of the changing spatial order of a state at a pivotal time in its history. In that sense, the book is a work of geography, the social science that derives much of its subject matter from other social and physical sciences but which is, above all, focused on the issue of location as a primary consideration.

Emphasizing the geographic, or spatial, aspect of change requires first an explanation of the context in which change occurs. Thus, the first section of this book displays the physical environment, the stage on which the human story of North Carolina has been acted out. The next group of chapters deals with the overarching topics of history, population, and urbanization. History is the story of the evolution of the state out of its early past. In many ways, the

Carolina Memories

From where I sit, on the broad porch of my mother and father, I can see down Jean Guite Creek to Currituck Sound. The sun warms my shoulders, a breeze whispers through the pines, a great blue heron flaps across the water toward the marsh.

I have been gone a long time, but now I am home.

I have seen much of every state, and lingered on every continent, and always, always, I have been aware that I am merely a North Carolinian traveling outside my native borders. To come back to Dare County (300 square miles of land, 1,200 square miles of water), and to take off my tie (for a tie is necessary in tidewater North Carolina only for going to church), and to relax into the ministrations of my parents ("Better have one of those biscuits, Charles—they'll go to waste") is to return to innocence, to ease, to Eden.

From my earliest childhood, the names of Dare County places, those strange and evocative names—Kitty Hawk, Nag's Head, Kill Devil Hills, Whalebone Junction, Jockey's Ridge, and Seven Sisters—have thrilled me and filled me with wonder.

Not far from my parents' porch, a highway brings tourists from faraway places here to the beach. Their cars come loaded with ice chests and fishing poles, surfboards and children itching to build sand castles. They will bask in today's sun. But they have no memories of all the yesterdays that make North Carolina so precious to me, and to other North Carolinians like me. The reality of any place is what its people remember of it . . .

I'll always be glad I have seen the shrimp boats leaving Beaufort with the sun coming up. And I'll always remember the sudden chill of night coming early in the coves in the mountains, while the ridges above were still bright with day.

I remember the red gullies, the broomstraw, the fields of cornstubble in the Mecklenburg November, and in Spring, the daffodils that still bloom by the hundreds under a certain Orange County oak. I remember mills with blue windows, and monuments of Confederate soldiers in sleepy courthouse squares.

I remember the bobolinks and buntings, and mockingbirds mocking, loblolly pines and live oaks hung with moss, the taste of scuppernongs from vines my father planted.

I remember making a slingshot from the fork of a persimmon tree and hunting rabbits with it along the creek bed. Those rabbits were as safe as if they'd been in their mothers' arms. I never hit a one.

Of course, it is all changed, or changing. I lived in the country outside Charlotte for many years. The deep woods my brother and I explored, certain that we were the first human beings to know these rabbit paths and clear streams—except, perhaps, for the Indians long ago—these woods are gone, the rabbit paths are residential streets with sidewalks and fire hydrants, and the streams have vanished into culverts underground.

The cranes and bulldozers do their work. Those who look back on our state as it is becoming will have great cities to talk and sing about—skyscrapers, six-lane highways, microchips and megagrowth and jet planes leaving contrails in the sky of Carolina blue.

North Carolina is 503 miles from east to west, and 187 miles from north to south, so that leaves plenty of room for growth and change. Still, I am glad I know it as it is, and remember it as it was.

Charles Kuralt, North Carolina Is My Home *(Charlotte: East Woods Press, 1986)*

---

numbers and patterns analyzed in the population and urbanization chapters are both symptoms and a measure of many of the changes that are sweeping the state. The nature and extent of population growth and the organization of it into a peculiarly North Carolina pattern is driven by the state's economy, the subject matter of another section.

The sinews of farming, manufacturing, transportation, and trade are displayed in a succession of chapters that show both how and why so much change is reshaping the geography of North Carolina.

The final section of this book portrays other aspects of life that also are both symptom and cause.

Crime and impacts on both air and water quality are clearly symptoms of growth, and they present major concerns that must be addressed if the state's economic progress is not to be threatened. Government, politics, education, and health care are not only themselves affected by change, but in many cases they are where efforts to manage change are focused. In addition, they, along with the cultural arts and outdoor recreation assets, are parts of the quality of life that has long been appreciated by North Carolinians and need to be maintained. A last, retrospective chapter seeks to tie together the various threads that are found in all of the preceding chapters of the book and to consider their implications for the future of North Carolina as it stands on the threshold of the twenty-first century.

We hope that this volume also will serve as a basic reference work on the state, where, within a single cover, one can glean information about everything from early settlement routes to the location of interstate highways. It is as well an atlas, in that a primary emphasis is placed on graphic displays of information: photographs, charts, and, above all, maps. The map is the classic tool of the geographer, and it remains one of the most effective ways to simplify the understanding of complex sets of information. Modern computer and printing technology makes it possible to take advantage of this powerful conceptual tool to an unprecedented degree.

This is not an atlas in the conventional sense of simply a book of maps, however. The term "atlas" derives from the Greek word that means to bear or uphold. The mythological Titan, Atlas, was forced to hold up the earth and, from his perspective, was able to view it as a globe. His name became associated with other views of the earth, collections of maps. A more contemporary dictionary defines an atlas as "a book of tables, charts and illustrations of a specific subject." This volume both meets and extends that definition by adding an interpretive text that adds analysis to the visual displays of information. The editors prefer to describe this as an "analytic atlas" to distinguish it from the more conventional descriptive book of maps.

One problem that arises in producing a work of this nature is the timeliness of statistical data. Especially in areas such as population or economics, new data emerge on a regular basis but some sources materialize more quickly than others. For example, certain statistics, such as those for wholesale trade, come out only every five years in the economic censuses published by the U.S. Bureau of the Census. The last such reports cover 1992, but even those were not released until several years after the data year. Another series, containing 1997 data, will be issued about the time this book is published. On the other hand, the Census Bureau released county-level population estimates for 1998 in early 1999. In yet another instance, at press time some measures of air pollution were available only through 1990.

Perhaps the most troublesome example of this timeliness problem lies with the important banking industry, in which mergers and acquisitions change the corporate landscape suddenly and dramatically. All the authors can do is to provide the latest information available before the manuscript is put into production. Whatever the situation, every effort has been made to acquire, analyze, and process the most current data possible.

On the other hand, the primary purpose of this book is not necessarily to present absolutely current statistics. In this age of the Internet such data can be accessed on demand. Rather, the point of this book is to analyze longer-term trends, to consider the factors that drive them, and to determine what their implications are for now and for the future. Most socioeconomic processes operate over a long period of time, and one more year of data, although more current, will not necessarily sharpen the analysis of these trends.

It is our hope that the resulting graphics-rich analysis of the geography of North Carolina presented here will be of value to public officials, business decision makers, teachers, students, journalists, and members of the general public as they seek to understand the events that affect their lives and their futures. It is offered in the same constructive spirit as an observation made years ago by one of North Carolina's and the nation's great writers, Thomas Wolfe. In his day Wolfe wrote: "North Carolina needs honest criticism—rather than the false, shallow 'we-are-the-finest-state-and-greatest-people-in-the-country'-kind of thing. An artist who refuses to accept fair criticism of his work will never go far. What of a state?"

2. THE NATURAL ENVIRONMENT

The shape of the land, the climate, and related elements such as soil and vegetation comprise the stage on which the human drama has been enacted. Sometimes the natural environment of North Carolina was merely a backdrop, but more often it either had a profound influence on human events or was itself greatly affected by what people did.

Setting the Stage

When Native Americans occupied the land and as European settlers first arrived, the influence of nature was predominant. Food came from whatever hunters and gatherers could glean from nature's bounty; initial cultivation depended on level land that was naturally fertile. Travel was controlled by the lay of the land and natural fords in streams. Typically it was easier to traverse the rolling land of the Piedmont or to paddle up from the coast along Coastal Plain rivers than it was to climb across the western Mountains. And on the Coastal Plain the many swamps and marshes were barriers to travel away from the rivers.

Over time, the emergence and deployment of increasingly sophisticated technologies supported larger populations, changing the nature of production and vastly increasing mobility. Much of this growth and change involved an ability to modify, manipulate, and control the natural environment. Land could be leveled, swamps drained, rivers bridged, and soils maintained through the application of artificial fertilizers or roads built through the mountains. Inexorably, the relationship between culture and nature changed.

Today, natural conditions are still important, of course, but increasingly it is more a matter of people impacting nature rather than vice versa. Resources depletion, air and water pollution, soil erosion, destruction of natural habitats, draining of wetland ecosystems, and groundwater contamination are some of the issues that have emerged as a result of this changed relationship between culture and natural environment.

The focus of this book is on the nature, cause, and consequences of change in North Carolina. Vital to this story is understanding the natural setting that has influenced and been influenced by changes in human activities. That is the purpose of this chapter. It begins with an overview of the land, especially landform regions and the geologic conditions that shaped them. This treatment is followed by a portrayal of climatic conditions that are important for agriculture, recreation, and general living. Over time, weather elements such as precipitation and temperature have interacted with the lithospheric environment. This interaction between rocks and weather produced, directly or indirectly, both soil and vegetation. These also are important features on the human stage. In addition to describing them, consideration is given to human impacts on natural vegetation, wetlands, and other environmental elements.

An understanding of these environmental elements is critical to any explanation of the state's past, but, more important, such an understanding is essential to knowing how present and future growth will change the state. Later chapters, especially Chapters 12 ("Air Quality") and 13 ("Water Resources"), will deal with these complex issues.

Land Regions and Geology

ANDY R. BOBYARCHICK AND JOHN A. DIEMER

One of the most distinctive aspects of the North Carolina natural setting is the shape of the land. Topography helped forge the history of the state, and even today it is common for people to distinguish between the Piedmont, Mountains, or Coastal parts of the state when talking about politics or other events. These land regions thus have become historical and cultural divisions as well, but their fundamental basis lies in the nature of the land.

More specifically, these distinct and historically important regions are (1) the Appalachian Mountains of western North Carolina; (2) the Piedmont Plateau, a broad belt that cuts diagonally across the middle of the state; and (3) the Coastal Plain, a low-lying plain that comprises the eastern portion of North Carolina (Fig. 2.1). The latter is often subdivided into the Outer Coastal Plain, or Tidewater, section on the coast and the Inner Coastal Plain, farther inland and mostly removed from the direct influence of the ocean.

Geologic History

The geologic processes that formed this landscape have operated over a span of at least 1.2 billion years and have involved massive shifts in the plates that make up the earth's crust (Fig. 2.2). About 1 billion years ago the eastern margin of North America was situated where the Blue Ridge Mountains are today. To the east lay a wide ocean containing island arcs and microcontinents that were moving as the plates they rested on shifted. Beginning about 450 million years ago, the island arcs and microcontinents began to collide with, and add onto, eastern North America. These collisions generated heat and pressure that thrust the rocks up into great mountain ranges, often associated with the injection of molten magma into subterranean chambers and volcanic eruptions.

The last major mountain-building event was the result of Africa colliding with North America about 300 million years ago. The energy from this

Figure 2.1. Physical Regions

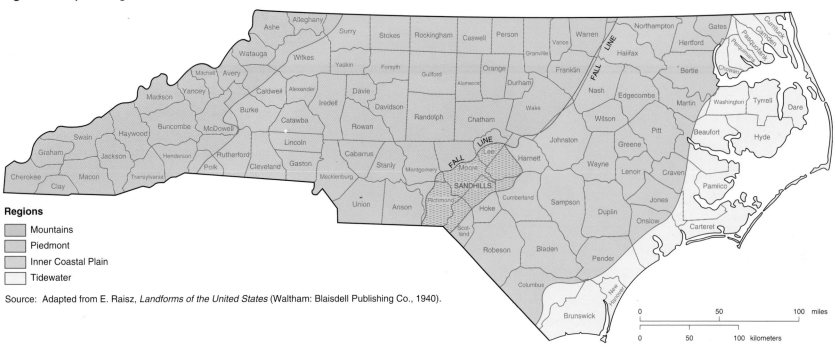

Regions

Mountains
Piedmont
Inner Coastal Plain
Tidewater

Source: Adapted from E. Raisz, *Landforms of the United States* (Waltham: Blaisdell Publishing Co., 1940).

collision was so great that a mountain range the size of the present Himalayas was built. The effects of the collision can be seen in the folded rocks as far west as central Tennessee. The eroded debris from those mountains built the widespread deposits of the Appalachian Plateau, which extends across Kentucky as far west as Cincinnati.

The supercontinent formed by the collision of North America and Africa is known as Pangea, and it persisted for about 100 million years. Pangea began to stretch apart about 225 million years ago,

and by 200 million years ago the Atlantic Ocean started to open. With the opening of the Atlantic Ocean, the Coastal Plain began to form. It was constructed mainly from the sediments that eroded from the nearby mountains and were carried to shore by rivers. These sediments were deposited in alluvial, coastal, and shallow marine environments as the ocean invaded far inland (Fig. 2.3). With time, these deposits built eastward, constructing an enormous wedge-shaped deposit of sediments and sedimentary rocks. The top of the

sedimentary wedge is nearly flat, whereas the base of the wedge increases from zero thickness along its inland margin to more than 10,000 feet under Cape Hatteras. Offshore, the wedge reaches a maximum thickness of 30,000 feet and begins to taper once more toward the ocean floor. The rocks within the wedge dip gently eastward, and progressively younger deposits can be seen on an eastward traverse across the Coastal Plain.

During the long interval of the construction of the sedimentary wedge, the sea level fluctuated

Figure 2.2. Continental Drift and the Completion of the Land of North Carolina

a. Silurian Period (395-435 million years ago)

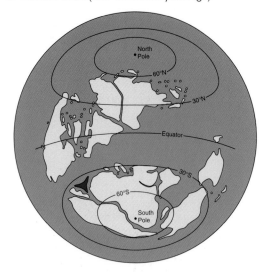

b. Devonian Period (345-395 million years ago)

c. Carboniferous Period (293-345 million years ago)

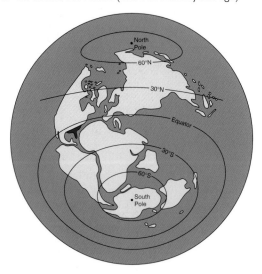

d. Cretaceous Period (65-136 million years ago)

Source: J. W. Clay, P. D. Escott, D. M. Orr Jr., and A. W. Stuart, *Land of the South* (Birmingham: Oxmoor House, 1989).

many times. Occasionally the shoreline was situated at least as far inland as the Fall Line (Fig. 2.3). At other times the shoreline was located farther east, at the edge of the continental shelf. Some of these fluctuations in sea level are recorded by terraces on the Coastal Plain, where the eroded edge of a terrace represents a temporary shoreline. About 18,000 years ago, the sea level dropped as much as 400 feet below its current level. This drop was caused by the growth of continental glaciers in North America, Europe, and Asia. As the glaciers grew, they removed vast quantities of water from the world's oceans. With the end of the Ice Age, the glaciers have largely melted and returned pent-up waters to the oceans, causing the sea level to rise once again. The sea level continues to rise today at a rate of about six inches per century.

The current geology of the state is illustrated in Figure 2.4. It is the result of these episodes of continental collisions, mountain building, fluctuations in sea level, and erosion. Although this land may seem constant to the human observer, it is in fact a very dynamic situation that is changing constantly, albeit slowly.

The Coastal Plain

The Coastal Plain forms the eastern edge of North Carolina, making up about 45 percent of the state's total land area (Fig. 2.5). It is bounded on the east by the Atlantic Ocean and on the west by the *Fall Line*, a broad zone where the soft rocks of the

Coastal Plain meet the hard crystalline rocks of the Piedmont. The Coastal Plain varies in width from 100 to 140 miles. It rises gently in elevation to the west, from about sea level at the coast to as much as 500 feet in the Sandhills district.

Wetlands are a dominant feature of the North Carolina Coastal Plain. Wetlands are defined as "those areas that are inundated or saturated by surface or ground water at a frequency and duration sufficient to support, and that under normal circumstances do support, a prevalence of vegetation typically adapted for life in saturated soil conditions." That is, the descriptive characteristics of wetlands are their hydrology, hydric soils, and wetland plants. The fact is, however, that they are creations of topography that causes land areas to drain poorly, whether because of terraces left along ancient shorelines or due to flat-lying deposits on floodplains.

Originally North Carolina had about 10.3 million acres of wetlands. As Figure 2.6 shows, the vast majority of this acreage lies on the Coastal Plain. Wetlands on the Piedmont or in the Mountains tend to lie along streams, whereas those near the Coast are products of that region's low elevation. About half of the state's earliest wetlands have been drained and converted to forestry, agriculture, or urban uses. Most of the remaining inventory is in freshwater wetlands. About 240,000 acres initially were in salt marshes, and more than 85 percent of that acreage remains undisturbed. Wetlands can provide valuable wildlife and aquatic life habitat,

shoreline stabilization, and flood storage. About two-thirds of North Carolina's rare, threatened, and endangered species of plants and animals live in wetlands. Wetlands often provide crucial water quality benefits by trapping sediment, nutrients, and toxic pollutants by filtering them from urban or agricultural runoff before they enter streams. The filling of wetlands requires permits from the U.S. Corps of Engineers and the North Carolina Division of Environmental Management. Currently only about 500 acres per year of freshwater wetlands are receiving permits to be filled.

An event in June 1998 illustrates the need for wetlands protection. In that month a federal court struck down controls on wetlands drainage. Developers took advantage of this lapse in restrictions and rushed in to drain over 10,000 acres in southeastern North Carolina before the state could impose controls on opening new drainage ditches.

The Coastal Plain is subdivided into two major subareas. The *Outer Coastal Plain*, or *Tidewater*, lies closest to the ocean, is extremely flat, averages less than 20 feet above sea level, and contains large swamps and lakes indicative of poor drainage conditions. Eleven of the twelve counties that have 55 percent or more of their areas in wetland soil areas are in the Tidewater section. Streams on the Outer Coastal Plain are brackish and subject to tidal fluctuations in level.

The Inner Coastal Plain is higher in elevation and better drained. Locally, however, there are distinctive wetlands or upland bogs known as *po-*

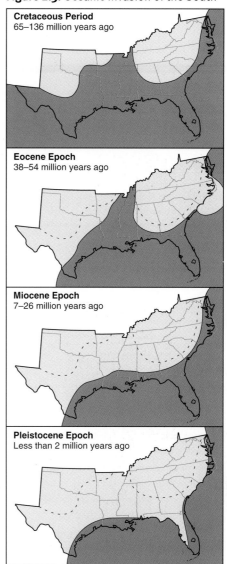

Figure 2.3. Oceanic Invasion of the South

Note: The dashed line represents the boundary of the sea during the Cretaceous period.
Source: J. W. Clay, P. D. Escott, D. M. Orr Jr., and A. W. Stuart, *Land of the South* (Birmingham: Oxmoor House, 1989).

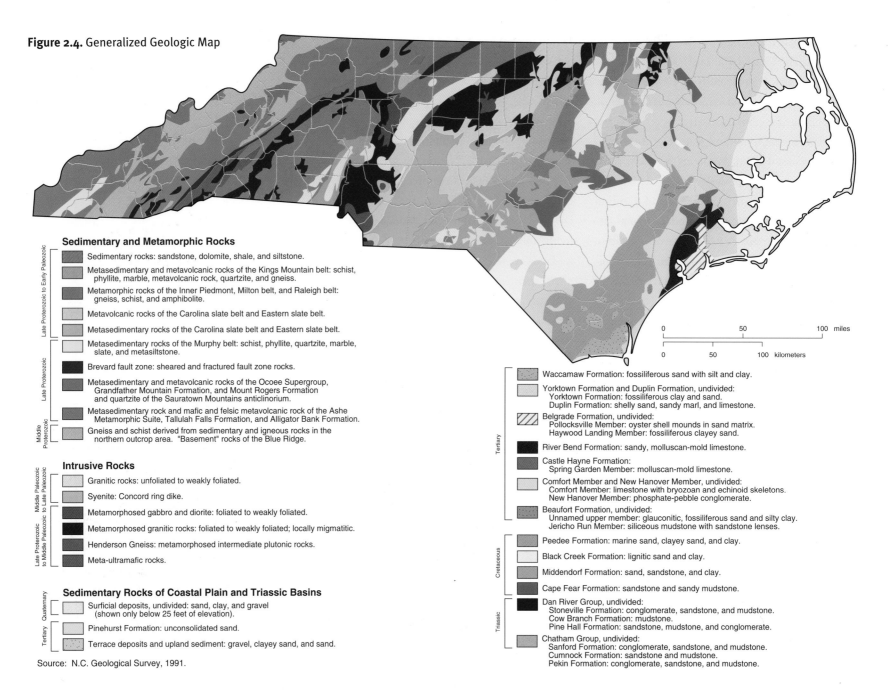

Figure 2.4. Generalized Geologic Map

Sedimentary and Metamorphic Rocks

Late Proterozoic to Early Paleozoic

- Sedimentary rocks: sandstone, dolomite, shale, and siltstone.
- Metasedimentary and metavolcanic rocks of the Kings Mountain belt: schist, phyllite, marble, metavolcanic rock, quartzite, and gneiss.
- Metamorphic rocks of the Inner Piedmont, Milton belt, and Raleigh belt: gneiss, schist, and amphibolite.
- Metavolcanic rocks of the Carolina slate belt and Eastern slate belt.
- Metasedimentary rocks of the Carolina slate belt and Eastern slate belt.

Late Proterozoic

- Metasedimentary rocks of the Murphy belt: schist, phyllite, quartzite, marble, slate, and metasiltstone.
- Brevard fault zone: sheared and fractured fault zone rocks.
- Metasedimentary and metavolcanic rocks of the Ocoee Supergroup, Grandfather Mountain Formation, and Mount Rogers Formation and quartzite of the Sauratown Mountains anticlinorium.

Middle Proterozoic

- Metasedimentary rock and mafic and felsic metavolcanic rock of the Ashe Metamorphic Suite, Tallulah Falls Formation, and Alligator Bank Formation.
- Gneiss and schist derived from sedimentary and igneous rocks in the northern outcrop area. "Basement" rocks of the Blue Ridge.

Intrusive Rocks

Middle Paleozoic to Late Paleozoic / Late Proterozoic to Middle Paleozoic

- Granitic rocks: unfoliated to weakly foliated.
- Syenite: Concord ring dike.
- Metamorphosed gabbro and diorite: foliated to weakly foliated.
- Metamorphosed granitic rocks: foliated to weakly foliated; locally migmatitic.
- Henderson Gneiss: metamorphosed intermediate plutonic rocks.
- Meta-ultramafic rocks.

Sedimentary Rocks of Coastal Plain and Triassic Basins

Quaternary

- Surficial deposits, undivided: sand, clay, and gravel (shown only below 25 feet of elevation).

Tertiary

- Pinehurst Formation: unconsolidated sand.
- Terrace deposits and upland sediment: gravel, clayey sand, and sand.

Source: N.C. Geological Survey, 1991.

Tertiary

- Waccamaw Formation: fossiliferous sand with silt and clay.
- Yorktown Formation and Duplin Formation, undivided: Yorktown Formation: fossiliferous clay and sand. Duplin Formation: shelly sand, sandy marl, and limestone.
- Belgrade Formation, undivided: Pollocksville Member: oyster shell mounds in sand matrix. Haywood Landing Member: fossiliferous clayey sand.
- River Bend Formation: sandy, molluscan-mold limestone.
- Castle Hayne Formation: Spring Garden Member: molluscan-mold limestone.
- Comfort Member and New Hanover Member, undivided: Comfort Member: limestone with bryozoan and echinoid skeletons. New Hanover Member: phosphate-pebble conglomerate.
- Beaufort Formation, undivided: Unnamed upper member: glauconitic, fossiliferous sand and silty clay. Jericho Run Member: siliceous mudstone with sandstone lenses.

Cretaceous

- Peedee Formation: marine sand, clayey sand, and clay.
- Black Creek Formation: lignitic sand and clay.
- Middendorf Formation: sand, sandstone, and clay.
- Cape Fear Formation: sandstone and sandy mudstone.

Triassic

- Dan River Group, undivided: Stoneville Formation: conglomerate, sandstone, and mudstone. Cow Branch Formation: mudstone. Pine Hall Formation: sandstone, mudstone, and conglomerate.
- Chatham Group, undivided: Sanford Formation: conglomerate, sandstone, and mudstone. Cumnock Formation: sandstone and mudstone. Pekin Formation: conglomerate, sandstone, and mudstone.

cosins. There are also the *Carolina Bays*, elliptical lakes of unknown origin. Many pocosins originated as Carolina Bays that have since filled with vegetation and sediment.

Pocosins, the name for which derives from an Algonquin Indian term for "swamp-on-a-hill," are really bogs that are located on relatively high ground. They contain peat, are acidic, and hold large quantities of water. Pocosins are perhaps best described as waterlogged areas covered by bushes and shrubs much more than by forest. The majority of North Carolina's pocosins have been drained since the 1960s and converted to other uses. Once drained and fertilized to counteract their natural acidity, the pocosin soils are highly productive in the cultivation of corn, soybeans, and vegetables. Similar treatment will yield good crops of high-quality timber, especially loblolly pine. In other instances, the peat, which is relatively low in sulfur and ash, has been extracted and used as an energy source. Unfortunately, the exploitation of such large pocosins has taken a natural sponge and filter out of the coastal ecosystem. The cultivation of pocosins introduces large quantities of fertilizers into coastal streams, polluting them and carrying the fertilizers into brackish estuaries and marshes where shrimp and other seafoods develop. Even if these chemicals were not released, the removal of pocosins increases the flow of freshwater into the estuary breeding grounds and the change in salinity can kill large numbers of juvenile sea animals.

The *Fall Line* marks the boundary between the

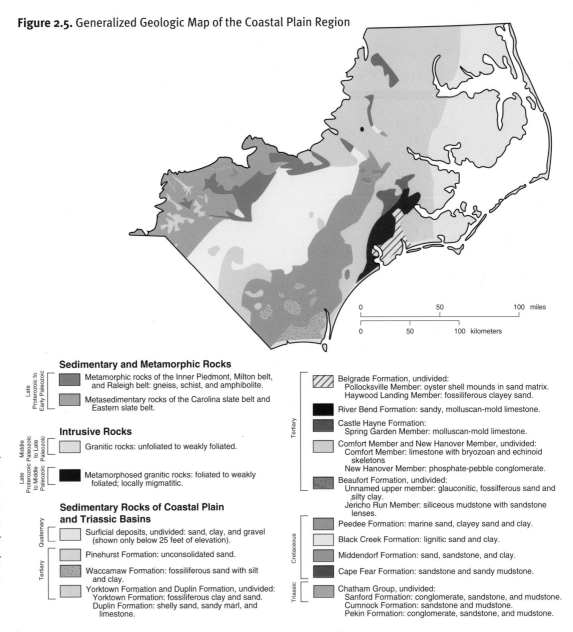

Figure 2.5. Generalized Geologic Map of the Coastal Plain Region

0   50   100 miles

0   50   100 kilometers

Sedimentary and Metamorphic Rocks

Late Proterozoic to Early Paleozoic

- Metamorphic rocks of the Inner Piedmont, Milton belt, and Raleigh belt: gneiss, schist, and amphibolite.
- Metasedimentary rocks of the Carolina slate belt and Eastern slate belt.

Intrusive Rocks

Late Proterozoic to Middle Paleozoic / Middle Paleozoic to Late Paleozoic

- Granitic rocks: unfoliated to weakly foliated.
- Metamorphosed granitic rocks: foliated to weakly foliated; locally migmatitic.

Sedimentary Rocks of Coastal Plain and Triassic Basins

Quaternary

- Surficial deposits, undivided: sand, clay, and gravel (shown only below 25 feet of elevation).

Tertiary

- Pinehurst Formation: unconsolidated sand.
- Waccamaw Formation: fossiliferous sand with silt and clay.
- Yorktown Formation and Duplin Formation, undivided: Yorktown Formation: fossiliferous clay and sand. Duplin Formation: shelly sand, sandy marl, and limestone.

Tertiary

- Belgrade Formation, undivided: Pollocksville Member: oyster shell mounds in sand matrix. Haywood Landing Member: fossiliferous clayey sand.
- River Bend Formation: sandy, molluscan-mold limestone.
- Castle Hayne Formation: Spring Garden Member: molluscan-mold limestone.
- Comfort Member and New Hanover Member, undivided: Comfort Member: limestone with bryozoan and echinoid skeletons New Hanover Member: phosphate-pebble conglomerate.
- Beaufort Formation, undivided: Unnamed upper member: glauconitic, fossiliferous sand and silty clay. Jericho Run Member: siliceous mudstone with sandstone lenses.

Cretaceous

- Peedee Formation: marine sand, clayey sand and clay.
- Black Creek Formation: lignitic sand and clay.
- Middendorf Formation: sand, sandstone, and clay.
- Cape Fear Formation: sandstone and sandy mudstone.

Triassic

- Chatham Group, undivided: Sanford Formation: conglomerate, sandstone, and mudstone. Cumnock Formation: sandstone and mudstone. Pekin Formation: conglomerate, sandstone, and mudstone.

Source: N.C. Geological Survey, 1991.

Figure 2.6. Wetlands

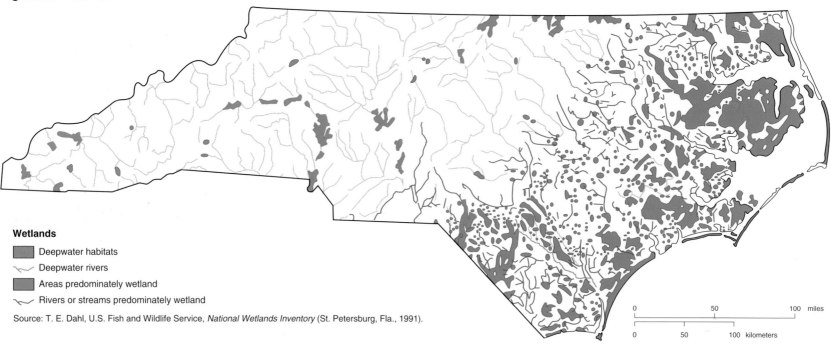

Wetlands

▓ Deepwater habitats

〜 Deepwater rivers

▒ Areas predominately wetland

〜 Rivers or streams predominately wetland

Source: T. E. Dahl, U.S. Fish and Wildlife Service, *National Wetlands Inventory* (St. Petersburg, Fla., 1991).

Coastal Plain and the Piedmont. Rivers that rise in the Blue Ridge Mountains flow across the Piedmont and enter the Coastal Plain at the Fall Line. This boundary is characterized by steep river gradients and rapids. Downstream of the Fall Line, the rivers flow to the southeast and have carved broad, low valleys in the soft, easily eroded sediments of the Coastal Plain. There the rivers have gentle gradients and are flanked by swamps and marshes. They are generally navigable all the way up to the Fall Line, an important factor in the early settlement of the region from the coast. A distinctive feature along the Fall Line are the *Sandhills* (Fig. 2.1). These deposits originally formed as windblown sand dunes. They are permeable, quartz-rich deposits that produce well-drained, acidic soils that are deficient in plant nutrients.

The coastal margin north of Cape Lookout is a "drowned coast," in which the sea level rise associated with the end of the last Ice Age and the continual melting of the ice caps have caused the ocean to invade the lower reaches of river valleys. This drowning has produced large embayments such as Albemarle and Pamlico Sounds. Associated with these embayments is a string of barrier islands that are separated from the mainland by as much as 20 miles, the *Outer Banks* (Fig. 2.7). These linear islands apparently were formed as the sea level rose over old beach ridges and sand dunes. Continued rises in sea level, accompanied by wave and wind action, cause these islands and their lagoons to slowly move inland. This steady inland migration, known as barrier island rollover, plus the exposure to hurricanes and other storms, makes the many developments along these attractive shores highly vulnerable to damage and destruction. The most famous example of this is the historic Cape Hatteras Lighthouse. In 1999, after much public debate, the old lighthouse was relocated about a half-mile inland in order to save it from the inexorable encroachment of the sea.

The lagoons and sea marshes along the coast near the Outer Banks are vital parts of the coastal ecosystem. The shallow shoals and sandbars that are associated with barrier islands are constantly shifting in location. They have presented sailors with very hazardous waters in which to navigate; indeed, this stretch of the Atlantic coast is so littered with shipwrecks that it is known as the "Graveyard of the Atlantic." These dangerous waters also made it difficult for early explorers and settlers to land on the northeastern coast of North Carolina.

South of Cape Lookout is the *Cape Fear Uplift*, where the coast was gently folded upward. Instead of drowning the river valleys, the uplift exposed an even coastline, along which have formed long stretches of broad beaches. The deep embayments found to the north are not present, nor are extensive barrier islands. Historically, this length of coast was somewhat more accessible, despite the Frying Pan Shoals that make the mouth of the Cape Fear River dangerous and that require dredging to maintain a navigable channel. Today this region is known for its miles of wide, sandy beaches that extend southward through the Grand Strand of South Carolina.

The Piedmont

West of the Fall Line is a geologically ancient region that is underlain by a complex of metamorphic and igneous rocks (Fig. 2.8). The rocks are remnants of the previously mentioned major Mountain system that was created over 300 million years. The associated upheaval involved volcanic activity as well as the folding and faulting of the preexisting rocks. After the uplift was over, erosion took hold and wore away the Mountain chain, leaving the contemporary, rolling plateau of the Piedmont. Here and there areas of more resistant rocks form hills or low mountains on the surface of the Piedmont. These hills are known as *Monadnocks*. Examples are the Uwharries, Sauratown Mountains,

Cape Lookout National Seashore and Barrier Island

Figure 2.7. Major Coastline Features of the Outer Banks

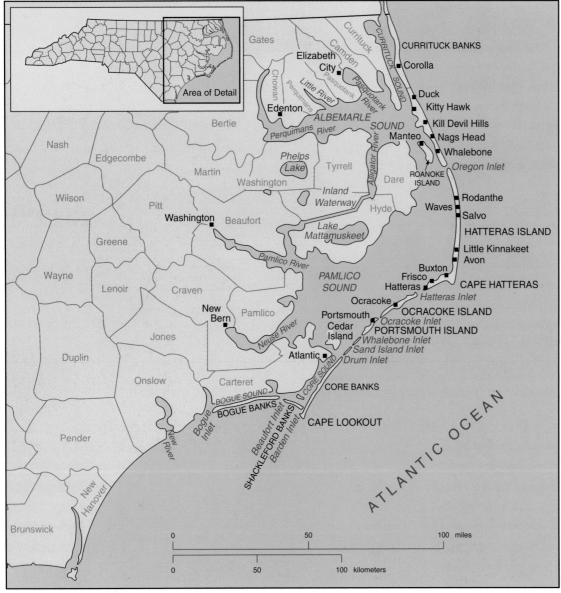

Source: J. W. Clay, D. M. Orr Jr., and A. W. Stuart, eds., *North Carolina Atlas: Portrait of a Changing Southern State* (Chapel Hill: University of North Carolina Press, 1975).

Kings Mountain, Brushy Mountains, and South Mountains. In other areas, such as the Carolina Slate Belt, somewhat softer rocks have eroded more deeply, forming lower areas that are often filled by lakes.

The Piedmont covers about the same amount of area as the Coastal Plain but it is higher in elevation, ranging from as low as 300 feet at the Fall Line to as much as 1,500 feet at the foot of the Blue Ridge Mountains. Seven major rivers and their tributaries (Dan, Tar, Neuse, Cape Fear, Yadkin, Catawba, and Broad) drain the eastern flanks of the Blue Ridge, carving narrow, deep valleys in the hard rocks of the Piedmont. These streams and their valleys are not navigable, but they have afforded numerous sites for waterpower uses.

The record of the early stretching of Pangea is seen where the crust of the Piedmont fractured and great blocks subsided (Fig. 2.9). These long lowlands, mainly along the southeastern edge of the Piedmont, are known as *Triassic basins* and they include the Durham, Sanford, and Wadesboro Basins. Rivers filled these valleys with sediments from the adjacent land. Some iron ore deposits formed in them, and these were important during colonial times but they are no longer of economic interest today. Swampy conditions within the basins led to the accumulation of small coal deposits that also were of some value during the colonial era.

Some of the Piedmont rocks contain gold and other valuable metals, and the area from Cabarrus

County south into Georgia was the site of the first U.S. gold rush. The area supplied most of the U.S. gold production from its discovery in 1799 until the California gold rush of 1849. Mines were operating in the city of Charlotte into the early twentieth century, and some other Piedmont mines were worked into the 1930s.

Topographically, the Piedmont forms a wide, rolling plateau between the low relief Coastal Plain to the east and the more rugged Mountains to the west. Historically, the Piedmont has been easier to cross than either of the other landform regions, and, until recently, most major transportation routes followed it. Thus, the Piedmont has acted as a natural corridor between the northeastern United States and the Deep South, from the time of Native Americans until today. Early colonial trails followed Indian paths, then came the North Carolina Railroad and later Interstate 85. All followed the natural corridor that was created by events that began millions of years ago.

Appalachian Mountains

The Piedmont ends and the Appalachian Mountains begin abruptly at a major fault line, the Brevard Fault, west of which rises a steep escarpment, the edge of the Blue Ridge Mountains (Fig. 2.10). That escarpment rises as much as 1,500 feet above the adjacent land, clearly visible at places such as where Interstate 77 crosses into Virginia and rises quickly to pass through Fancy Gap in

Figure 2.8. Generalized Geologic Map of the Piedmont Region

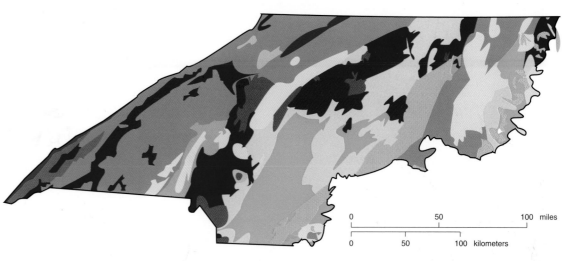

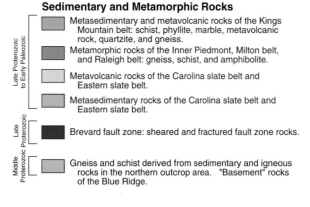

Sedimentary and Metamorphic Rocks

Late Proterozoic to Early Paleozoic

Metasedimentary and metavolcanic rocks of the Kings Mountain belt: schist, phyllite, marble, metavolcanic rock, quartzite, and gneiss.

Metamorphic rocks of the Inner Piedmont, Milton belt, and Raleigh belt: gneiss, schist, and amphibolite.

Metavolcanic rocks of the Carolina slate belt and Eastern slate belt.

Metasedimentary rocks of the Carolina slate belt and Eastern slate belt.

Late Proterozoic

Brevard fault zone: sheared and fractured fault zone rocks.

Middle Proterozoic

Gneiss and schist derived from sedimentary and igneous rocks in the northern outcrop area. "Basement" rocks of the Blue Ridge.

Intrusive Rocks

Middle Paleozoic to Late Paleozoic

Granitic rocks: unfoliated to weakly foliated.

Syenite: Concord ring dike.

Late Proterozoic to Middle Paleozoic

Metamorphosed gabbro and diorite: foliated to weakly foliated.

Metamorphosed granitic rocks: foliated to weakly foliated; locally migmatitic.

Henderson Gneiss: metamorphosed intermediate plutonic rocks.

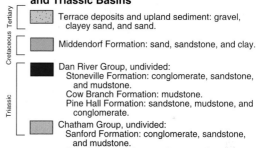

Sedimentary Rocks of Coastal Plain and Triassic Basins

Cretaceous Tertiary

Terrace deposits and upland sediment: gravel, clayey sand, and sand.

Middendorf Formation: sand, sandstone, and clay.

Triassic

Dan River Group, undivided:
Stoneville Formation: conglomerate, sandstone, and mudstone.
Cow Branch Formation: mudstone.
Pine Hall Formation: sandstone, mudstone, and conglomerate.

Chatham Group, undivided:
Sanford Formation: conglomerate, sandstone, and mudstone.
Cumnock Formation: sandstone and mudstone.
Pekin Formation: conglomerate, sandstone, and mudstone.

Source: N.C. Geological Survey, 1991.

Pilot Mountain: a sandstone-capped monadnock in Surry County

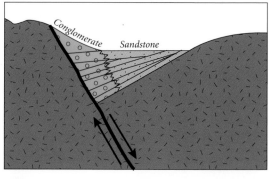

Figure 2.9. A Typical Triassic Basin

Older Piedmont rocks   Triassic Basin sediments

Source: J. W. Clay, P. D. Escott, D. M. Orr Jr., and A. W. Stuart, *Land of the South* (Birmingham: Oxmoor House, 1989).

the Blue Ridge Mountains. It is also visible in the Swannanoa Gap, where Interstate 40 crosses the Blue Ridge Mountains and enters the Asheville Basin. The Blue Ridge Mountains form the eastern continental divide, with waters draining off its western slopes into the Mississippi River system and those from its eastern slopes flowing into the Atlantic Ocean. Rivers that originate, at least in part, on the eastern flanks of the Blue Ridge in North Carolina include the Roanoke, Yadkin, Catawba, Broad, and Savannah Rivers. The major westward-flowing rivers are the New, French Broad, Little Tennessee, and Hiawassee. The New

River, despite its name, is very old, as indicated by the fact that its winding course has maintained itself despite flowing across hills and valleys. It is believed that this happened because at one time the river flowed over a plain that developed into mountains as the land was uplifted and erosion wore away the soft rocks faster than the harder ones. The strong flow of the New cut through both hard and soft rocks, thus maintaining its original valley.

The Appalachian Mountain system reaches its greatest width and elevation in North Carolina. The Blue Ridge Mountains are the eastern edge of a

highly dissected mountain plateau. This plateau is bounded on the west by the Unaka and Great Smoky Mountains, along the Tennessee border. In between are a number of cross ridges and broad intermontane valleys. Most prominent of these cross ridges are the Black Mountains, which include Mount Mitchell, at 6,684 feet the highest peak in the eastern United States. Other cross ridges are the Pisgah, New Found, Balsam, Cowee, Nantahala, Snowbird, and Valley River Mountains. Altogether, in North Carolina forty-three peaks exceed 6,000 feet in elevation and another eighty-two range between 5,000 and 6,000 feet.

The Mountains of North Carolina are made up of a variety of rock types, but the predominant type is a mass of *metamorphic* rocks. Metamorphic (Greek for "changed form") rocks are preexisting rocks of any type that have been changed by heat

Figure 2.10. Generalized Geologic
Map of the Mountain Region

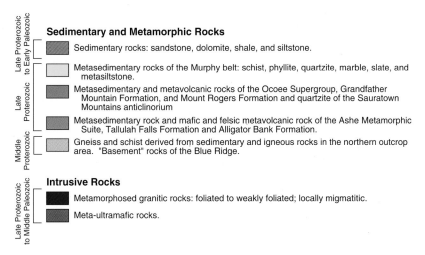

0   50   100 miles

0   50   100 kilometers

Late Proterozoic to Early Paleozoic

Sedimentary and Metamorphic Rocks

Sedimentary rocks: sandstone, dolomite, shale, and siltstone.

Metasedimentary rocks of the Murphy belt: schist, phyllite, quartzite, marble, slate, and metasiltstone.

Late Proterozoic

Metasedimentary and metavolcanic rocks of the Ocoee Supergroup, Grandfather Mountain Formation, and Mount Rogers Formation and quartzite of the Sauratown Mountains anticlinorium.

Metasedimentary rock and mafic and felsic metavolcanic rock of the Ashe Metamorphic Suite, Tallulah Falls Formation and Alligator Bank Formation.

Middle Proterozoic

Gneiss and schist derived from sedimentary and igneous rocks in the northern outcrop area. "Basement" rocks of the Blue Ridge.

Late Proterozoic to Middle Paleozoic

Intrusive Rocks

Metamorphosed granitic rocks: foliated to weakly foliated; locally migmatitic.

Meta-ultramafic rocks.

Source: N.C. Geological Survey, 1991.

and pressure but not so much that their original character is not discernible. Limestone became marble, for example. Usually the result was to create a rock that is relatively resistant to erosion. Associated with metamorphism has been faulting and the intrusion of molten (*igneous*) rocks into the area. Rocks in the Mountains range in age from over 1 billion years to about 400 million years.

The western Mountains contain the oldest rocks in North Carolina, and they are separated from slightly younger rocks in the eastern Mountains by several fault zones. The older rocks are referred to as *basement* rocks. They were mostly igneous in origin, prior to metamorphism, and they comprise a remnant of the original mass of ancient North America.

In the eastern Mountains the rocks are somewhat younger mixed volcanic and sedimentary rocks that were deposited on the continental margin and subsequently metamorphosed during the episodes of mountain building. These rocks make up the main mass of features such as Mount Rogers and Grandfather Mountain. Intermontane basins, especially the Asheville Basin, at the confluence of the French Broad and Swannanoa Rivers, have provided most of the level land on which people have settled in this region.

Weather and Climate

PETER J. ROBINSON

General Conditions

Weather and climate, the short- and long-term conditions of the atmosphere, respectively, affect one's comfort and powerfully influence the success of a season's crops. Despite society's ability to modify the weather through space heating, air-conditioning, irrigation, and the like, an area's climate is still an important economic aspect of the quality of life. Some of the indirect and direct effects of weather, such as floods, hurricanes, tornadoes, and droughts, are reminders that the ability to control the environment is, at best, limited.

North Carolina receives precipitation in all seasons. Summers are warm to hot, thundery, and humid, and winters are cool, mild, with little snow, except for the western Mountains, but with occasional severe cold spells. In between, spring and fall are noteworthy for unusually pleasant weather. Thus, unlike many parts of the nation, North Carolina has four distinct seasons, each with its characteristic climatic patterns. Wind speeds are generally low except on mountain peaks and along the coast. Occasional tornado outbreaks and hurricanes bring dramatic changes in the more typical pattern.

Table 2.1 provides a general summary of climatic conditions recorded at six weather stations scattered across the state. Collectively, they document both the mildness of the climate and the moderate levels of precipitation. There is some intrastate variation in these conditions, including a tendency for the highest temperatures to be along the Coast and the lowest in the Mountains. Related to this trend, snowfall is highest in the mountains. Overall precipitation levels are higher in both the Mountains and along the Coast. However, neither the midday reading of relative humidity nor the proportion of possible sunshine varies substantially from one weather station to the next.

Weather Factors

The state's latitude dictates that for most of the year the weather of North Carolina is dominated by that portion of the global air circulation known as the *Westerlies*—a broad band of eastward-moving air that encircles the globe throughout latitudes 30 to 60 degrees north. This general flow is marked by wavelike meanders that sometimes take the main areas of the Westerlies far to the north, only to sweep the air back to the south as the air moves eastward. These waves cover the whole depth of the weather-producing layer of the atmosphere, except for a thin layer right at the ground, where frictional effects modify the pattern. The simple movement of clouds, especially when several layers are present, will indicate the direction and complexity of this airstream.

The best-known portion of this westerly airflow is the *Jet Stream*, air currents that are generally 20,000 feet or more above the ground and that have wind velocities of 100 miles per hour or more. The day-to-day variability in location and strength of this feature is a familiar component of almost any television weathercast. Not only does the Jet Stream provide a good guide for weather forecasting, but also it can be used to describe the sequence and kinds of weather that taken together make up the climate. A major reason for this lies in the fact that the high elevation winds of the Jet Stream drag beneath them large segments of the atmosphere, known as *air masses*, that contain characteristics of the areas in which they form. As the air masses are dragged along by the Jet Stream, they carry these characteristics with them into other parts of the country. Figure 2.11 illustrates the major kinds of air masses that come through North Carolina. Much of the television coverage of weather conditions shows the movement through the state of these air masses as "highs" and "lows" and indicates the weather conditions that are associated with each.

The position of the waves in the Westerlies, epitomized by the Jet Stream, together with the strength of the winds in them, largely controls the weather North Carolina gets. The waves are responsible for the movement of rain-bearing atmospheric depressions (cyclonic storms), so when the waves are more or less overhead, rainy weather coming from a westerly direction is the result. The moisture from such depressions is commonly widespread, prolonged, and fairly gentle, giving the good soaking rains beloved of farmers and gardeners. Several depressions will pass over North Carolina in any winter, and the precipitation from them fills reservoirs and recharges the soil. In summer, in contrast, the average Jet Stream position is farther north, and only occasionally does it move south to allow a depression to cross North Carolina directly. Consequently, although the state usually gets some precipitation in the summer, depressions are by no means a reliable water source. And though other processes increase summer moisture, year-to-year variability in precipitation is much greater in summer than it is in winter.

When the Jet Stream is away to the north, North Carolina's weather is dominated by air masses that originate over the tropical Atlantic Ocean, slowly drifting in from a southerly direction. This is a warm, moist air mass. It is common in summer, giving the hot, humid, hazy conditions, with afternoon thunderstorms, so typical of that season. The thunderstorms produce intense, short-lived bursts of rain. They are highly localized and often widely scattered and so do not provide a reliable source of precipitation for agricultural or water supply purposes. Although this maritime tropical air mass

Table 2.1. Climatic Averages

Weather Station	Average Temperature (°F)			Possible Sunshine (%)	Annual Precip. (in.)	Annual Snowfall (in.)	Relative Humidity (% at 1 P.M.)
	Annual	Jan.	July				
Asheville	55.5	36.8	73.2	59	47.7	25.5	58
Cape Hatteras	61.9	45.1	78.2	59	55.7	13.5	66
Charlotte	60.0	40.5	78.5	63	43.2	19.3	63
Greensboro	57.9	37.5	77.2	61	42.5	22.9	55
Raleigh	59.0	39.6	77.7	59	41.8	17.2	54
Wilmington	63.4	45.6	80.3	63	53.4	15.3	56

Source: National Oceanic and Atmospheric Administration, *Climatic Averages and Extremes for U.S. Cities* (Asheville: National Climatic Data Center, Historical Climatology Series 6-3, 1991).

dominates summer conditions, it also occurs frequently in winter. At that season it is, naturally, cooler, but it is still warm and humid. Usually there is a low-level cloud deck associated with it, though not much rain from the clouds. Again, occasional thunderstorms occur.

Some of the most unpleasant weather to afflict the state occurs when the high-pressure region centered over Bermuda expands westward during the summer. Commonly referred to as the *Bermuda High*, it brings periods of hot, sticky weather that can last for many days. Because this is high pressure, it blocks out storm systems that might bring in precipitation. Air movement within the Bermuda High is minimal, and therefore there is little dispersion of any pollutants in the air. More is

said about these systems and other weather patterns that affect air pollution in Chapter 12, "Air Quality."

The opposite condition, when the Jet Stream is south of the state, gives very different weather. This situation occurs almost exclusively in winter. The jet is usually well developed and forces a strong northwest wind to bring air from the cold continental interior, frequently originating over the Canadian Arctic. Conditions under this polar continental air mass are very cold, dry, and cloudless. Indeed, almost all of the state's lowest temperatures and sunniest winter skies occur in this situation.

As a result of this interplay of air masses and Jet Stream movements, North Carolina gets rain,

from various processes, in all months, but the winter rains are more reliable than those of summer. For temperatures, summer is dominated by air from the tropical Atlantic, with high temperatures that vary little from day to day. In winter, temperatures depend on whether the air is coming off the warm Atlantic or from the cold interior and thus are much more variable. Extreme events will often disrupt this general progression. Hurricanes and ice storms can create chaos anywhere in the state, tornadoes are likely to have an impact over the southern Piedmont and Coastal Plain, storms giving violent northeast winds erode the coastline, and drought is a long-term, almost silent, extreme event. In addition, location in the state will influence the details of the weather and climate.

Temperature

The state's midlatitude position provides it with an abundance of sunlight, especially in summer. The sun is less intense and the days are shorter in winter, of course, meaning that temperatures are lower. The distribution of temperatures within the state, however, is influenced strongly by altitude. Temperatures commonly decrease with altitude, an effect apparent in Figure 2.12. At the higher elevations in the Mountains the mean annual temperature is around 52 degrees Fahrenheit, but it rises to the low 60s in the Piedmont and reaches well into the 60s on the low-lying Coastal Plain. In

Figure 2.11. Air Masses Responsible for North Carolina's Weather and Climate

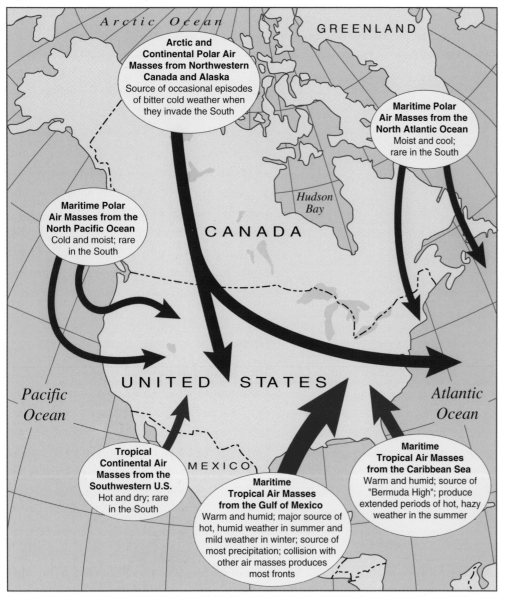

Source: J. W. Clay, P. D. Escott, D. M. Orr Jr., and A. W. Stuart, *Land of the South* (Birmingham: Oxmoor House, 1989).

the Mountains more complex topographic effects occur. For example, cold, high elevation air may drain down a slope and collect at the base. This gives both cold mountain tops and valley bottoms, but the slopes are warmer. Mountain slopes are known as *thermal belts*, and traditionally they have been favored locations for activities such as apple growing.

Of special interest to farmers and gardeners is the length of the frost-free season. Figure 2.13 shows that in the Mountains this season lasts from just under 160–180 days. It increases in length toward the east, exceeding 200 days over much of the rest of the state and 220 days along most of the Coast. The last killing frost typically occurs in the east in late March but may not take place in the Mountains until a month later. In the fall, the Mountains are likely to have a frost by the middle of October, whereas the Coast may not experience one before mid-November.

Precipitation

Precipitation levels are affected by the Mountains as well. They form what are known as *orographic barriers*, in which a mountain causes moving air to rise, cool, and yield precipitation as it passes over. On the downside of the mountain the descending air is compressed. It then becomes warmer and drier, and no rain occurs. The west-facing slopes of the Mountains receive the heaviest precipitation in the state, averaging over 80 inches per year along the border with Georgia (Fig. 2.14). The same effect works for east-facing slopes, but wind from the east is less frequent and precipitation levels are lower. Mountain valleys, sheltered on all sides, have some of the lowest annual precipitation totals in the state. The Asheville area, for example, averages only about 37 inches of precipitation a year. Outside the Mountains, the driest area in the state is over the Piedmont, where the average is less than 46 inches a year. Precipitation increases toward the east, exceeding 54 inches along the southeastern Coast, where moisture from the sea is able to penetrate a short distance inland.

The effects of elevation are especially apparent in the annual accumulation of snow. Accumulations of 14 inches or more are common in the western Mountains, but this level drops off sharply to less than 10 inches in the western Piedmont and less than 4 inches in the southeastern part of the state (Fig. 2.15). These averages are deceptive because areas east of the Mountains may get a foot of snow in one storm and then not see any significant accumulation again for several years.

Storms

Far more common than snow are the thunderstorms that bring substantial rain to North Carolina, along with occasional hail and high winds. Figure 2.16 shows that these storms are primarily a

Figure 2.12. Average Annual Temperature

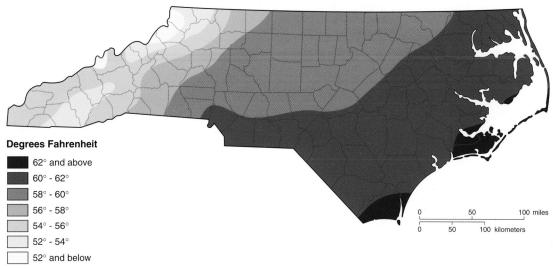

Degrees Fahrenheit

- 62° and above
- 60° - 62°
- 58° - 60°
- 56° - 58°
- 54° - 56°
- 52° - 54°
- 52° and below

Source: National Climatic Data Center, *Annual Climatological Data*, 1993, Asheville.

Figure 2.13. Median Length of Growing Season

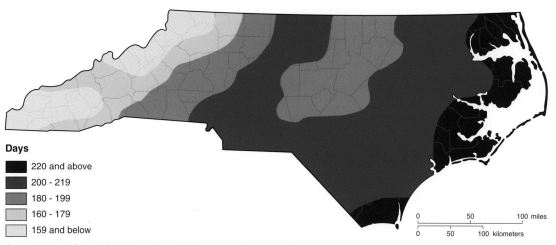

Days

- 220 and above
- 200 - 219
- 180 - 199
- 160 - 179
- 159 and below

Source: National Climatic Data Center, *Annual Climatological Data*, 1993, Asheville.

Figure 2.14. Average Annual Precipitation

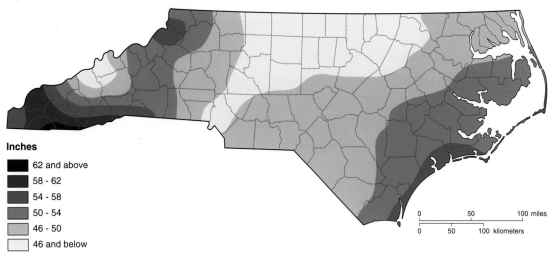

Inches

- ■ 62 and above
- ■ 58 - 62
- ■ 54 - 58
- ■ 50 - 54
- ■ 46 - 50
- □ 46 and below

0   50   100 miles
0   50   100 kilometers

Source: National Climatic Data Center, *Annual Climatological Data*, 1993, Asheville.

Figure 2.15. Average Annual Snowfall

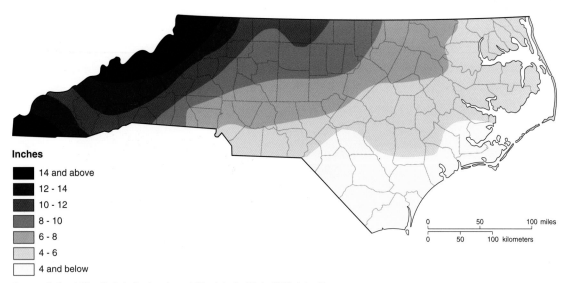

Inches

- ■ 14 and above
- ■ 12 - 14
- ■ 10 - 12
- ■ 8 - 10
- ■ 6 - 8
- □ 4 - 6
- □ 4 and below

0   50   100 miles
0   50   100 kilometers

Source: National Climatic Data Center, *Annual Climatological Data*, 1993, Asheville.

summer phenomenon, with the majority of them developing between May and August. But they can occur at any time, especially as strong frontal systems move through the state. Perhaps not surprisingly, there is a strong correlation between the outbreak of these storms and the number of flash floods. Again, the greatest occurrence of these rapid flooding episodes is between May and August (Fig. 2.17).

Sometimes associated with exceptionally strong thunderstorms or even hurricanes are the deadly twisters of tornadoes. Although North Carolina is not within the notorious "Tornado Alley" of the prairies of the central United States, it has recorded a large number of these frightening storms. Figure 2.18 shows that they can appear anywhere in the state, but the most frequent outbreaks have been along the eastern Piedmont and over much of the Coastal Plain. The worst tornado event in the state's history was an outbreak of tornadoes that moved over eighteen counties of the Inner Coastal Plain on March 28, 1984, accounting for forty-two deaths and substantial property damage. On April 3–4, 1974, a series of twisters killed seven people in the extreme western part of the state, illustrating how long-term averages can be misleading.

It is difficult to forecast tornadoes. However, in recent years the National Weather Service and local television stations have dramatically improved their ability to track such storms, especially through the use of Doppler radar, or at least to warn of conditions that are favorable to their formation. Such early warnings probably have saved many lives.

Though not as intense as tornadoes, hurricanes are probably the most fearsome to residents of North Carolina. While less frequent, they are larger and last much longer than tornadoes. Hurricanes originate over the warm tropical seas of the southern Atlantic or Caribbean and migrate northward or westward along often erratic paths during the summer or early fall. Hurricanes have minimum sustained wind speeds of greater than 74 miles per hour. They are graded on a scale of one to five on the Saffir/Simpson Hurricane Scale. Any storm that is graded three or higher is a major storm, meaning that it packs sustained winds of at least 110 miles per hour.

The very magnitude of hurricanes offers one advantage in that it is easier to see them and track their movements. The National Hurricane Center in Coral Gables, Florida, operated by the National Weather Service, uses satellite images to monitor hurricanes as they form over the southern oceans. Early warnings of their movements are reported in the media, and airplanes fly through them to measure wind speed, temperature, air pressure, and other critical aspects. The resulting data are used to estimate the strength of a hurricane and to enable meteorologists to project the likely movement pattern. This advance information allows communities to prepare for these storms by organizing evacuations, preparing buildings, and placing emergency crews on alert. Coastal commu-

Figure 2.16. Average Monthly Variation of Thunderstorm Activity, 1948–986

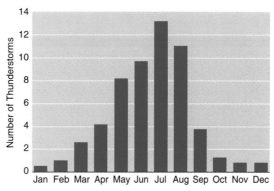

Source: D. L. Epperson, G. L. Johnson, J. M. Davis, and P. J. Robinson, *Weather and Climate in North Carolina* (Raleigh: N.C. Agricultural Extension Service, AG-375, 1988).

Figure 2.17. Average Occurrence of Flash Floods, 1961–1985

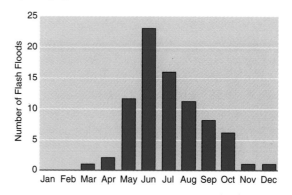

Source: D. L. Epperson, G. L. Johnson, J. M. Davis, and P. J. Robinson, *Weather and Climate in North Carolina* (Raleigh: N.C. Agricultural Extension Service, AG-375, 1988).

Figure 2.18. Number of Tornadoes Reported, 1950–1990

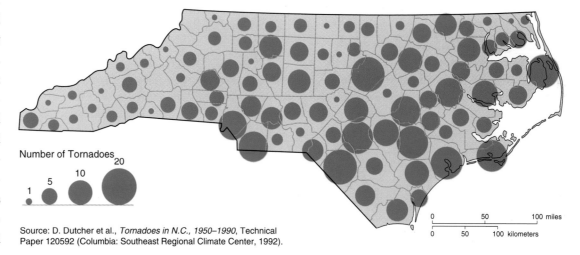

Source: D. Dutcher et al., *Tornadoes in N.C., 1950–1990*, Technical Paper 120592 (Columbia: Southeast Regional Climate Center, 1992).

Earthquakes in North Carolina

Most damaging earthquakes occur at plate boundaries such as the San Andreas fault or along the movement zone beneath the Japanese islands. Certainly during the earlier mountain-building episodes and during Triassic rifting, North Carolina must have been very active seismically. Today, however, North Carolina is a great distance from the nearest plate boundary, and no seismic activity due directly to plate motions is expected.

A second kind of earthquake activity that is still poorly understood by geologists is intraplate seismicity. This kind of earth movement is caused by earthquakes that occur within plates rather than at their margins. If North Carolina is to be affected by damaging earthquakes, it would be due to intraplate seismicity.

There are few recorded earthquake epicenters in North Carolina, and little of the seismicity can be correlated with specific mapped faults. A fault is a break in the crust along which two blocks of rocks have been displaced relative to each other. Earthquake faults are those faults that can be demonstrated to have been active with a certain frequency over a given time period. For example, a fault may be considered capable of generating an earthquake if it can be deduced that one event occurred on the fault within the last 100,000 years. Although there are hundreds, if not thousands, of faults in North Carolina, it appears that most of these faults have not been active for millions of years.

North Carolina, though, is not beyond possible seismic damage. As shown on the accompanying map, two intraplate seismic zones have the potential of generating ground shaking in North Carolina. One is the Charleston, South Carolina, seismic zone, where an earthquake of estimated 6.8 magnitude on the Richter scale occurred in 1886. Like most of the large earthquakes that occur in the eastern United States, the Charleston earthquake was felt over most of the country east of the Mississippi River. In addition to the better-known Richter scale, geologists use the Modified Mercalli (MM) intensity scale to estimate the degree of damage and destruction caused by an earthquake. During the 1886 Charleston earthquake, most of North Carolina would have been within MM intensity zones of VI to VII, high enough to cause considerable structural damage in some areas.

The second eastern seismic zone affecting North Carolina is the New Madrid zone in Missouri. That area experienced a series of three great earthquakes in 1811 and 1812 ranging in estimated magnitudes between 8.4 and 8.7. Again, most of North Carolina would be in MM zones VI–VII if an earthquake of equal magnitude occurred today in the New Madrid area.

Fortunately, eastern U.S. earthquakes are not nearly so frequent as those along active plate boundaries. On the other hand, infrequent seismicity means that geologists have a much smaller data set to use in understanding and possibly predicting intraplate earthquakes. This makes it all the more difficult to anticipate damaging events such as the 1886 earthquake in Charleston, for which there was no precedent in recorded history.

Andy R. Bobyarchick

Distribution and Intensity of Selected U.S. Earthquakes

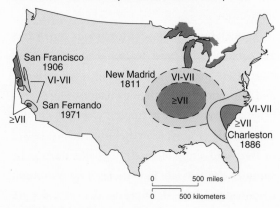

Modified Mercalli Intensity Scale

Intensity Value	Description / Damage
I.	Not felt except by very few people under especially favorable circumstances. No damage.
II.	Felt only by a few persons at rest, especially on upper floors of buildings.
III.	Felt quite noticeably indoors, especially on upper floors of buildings, but many people do not recognize it as an earthquake.
IV.	During the day felt indoors by many, outdoors by few. Some awakened at night.
V.	Felt by nearly everyone, many awakened at night. Disturbances of trees, poles, and other tall objects sometimes noticed.
VI.	Felt by all; many are frightened and run outdoors. Damage slight.
VII.	Damage negligible in buildings of good design and construction; slight to moderate in well-built ordinary structures; considerable in poorly built or badly designed ordinary structures.
VIII.	Damage slight in specially designed structures; considerable in ordinary substantial buildings, with partial collapse; great in poorly built structures. Sand and mud ejected in small amounts.
IX.	Damage considerable even in specially designed structures. Buildings shifted off foundations. Ground cracked conspicuously. Underground pipes broken.
X.	Most structures destroyed with foundation; ground badly cracked. Landslides considerable from river banks and steep slopes.
XI.	Few, if any, masonry structures remain standing. Bridges destroyed. Broad fissures in ground.
XII.	Damage total. Waves seen on ground surface. Lines of sight and level distorted. Objects thrown into air.

Source: Adapted from M. Schnell, and D. Herd, eds., *National Earthquake Hazards Reduction Program: Report to the U.S. Congress*, U.S. Geological Survey Circular 918, n.d. (c.1985).

nities have enacted building regulations that increase the probability that structures will withstand the destruction of high winds, waves, or flood waters. As a result of these regulations and early warnings, the damage to property and the loss of lives that resulted from past hurricanes has been reduced dramatically.

The North Carolina coast was hit by several major hurricanes during the middle 1950s (Hazel, Connie, Diane, and Ione). This was followed by a rather quiet period until the 1980s, when Gloria and Hugo landed (Fig. 2.19). Hurricane Hugo (September 1989) was unusual in that it maintained its major strength as it penetrated inland as far as Charlotte and beyond, causing extensive damage in its wake. Similarly, Hurricane Fran (September 1996) surprised residents of Raleigh and the northern Piedmont when it wreaked its havoc there. In September 1999, eastern North Carolina was hit by one of the most devastating natural disasters in the state's history. Hurricane Floyd came ashore near Wilmington on September 16 as a category 4 storm and dumped upward of 15 inches of rain over a wide area already saturated by Hurricane Dennis just two weeks earlier. The subsequent flooding of the Cape Fear, Neuse, Tar, and other rivers ruined crops, drowned livestock, destroyed homes, disrupted municipal water and waste treatment operations, and left more than 45 people dead. Waste spills and many thousands of dead animals created major threats to public health. Hundreds of roads, including interstate highways, were closed

Figure 2.19. Hurricanes with Landfall in North Carolina, 1989–1999

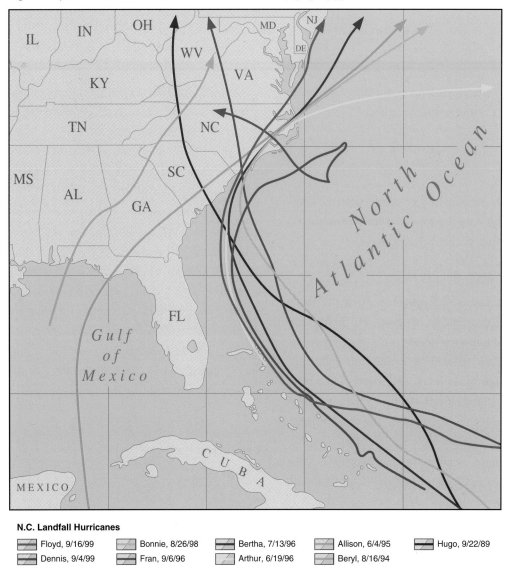

N.C. Landfall Hurricanes

Floyd, 9/16/99   Bonnie, 8/26/98   Bertha, 7/13/96   Allison, 6/4/95   Hugo, 9/22/89
Dennis, 9/4/99   Fran, 9/6/96   Arthur, 6/19/96   Beryl, 8/16/94

Source: U.S. Department of Commerce, National Hurricane Center.

for many days, as was the campus of East Carolina University.

Less dangerous than hurricanes are "nor'easters," storms that come ashore from a northeasterly direction during any season. Though less threatening than hurricanes, these storms can still cause heavy beach erosion and property damage.

Droughts

Individual years can depart radically from the long-term averages for precipitation. Most problematic are the droughts that periodically affect the state, when several months with below-normal precipitation lead to severe loss of soil water, creating crop losses, problems with livestock, shortages of water for urban distribution systems, and potentially severe economic problems for the state generally. The hardships created by periodic droughts are made all the more severe precisely because normally the state enjoys a humid climate in which there is no regular dry season. The temporal and geographic distribution of major droughts that have impacted North Carolina in recent decades is illustrated in Chapter 13, "Water Resources."

Outlook

There is growing concern that human actions, such as the emission of various substances including carbon dioxide and hydroflurocarbons from air conditioners, may be causing atmospheric temperatures to rise and other shifts in the climate. The National Climatic Data Center in Asheville, for example, reported that globally 1997 was the warmest year on record and that the first six months of 1998 set another record. Average high temperature records were set during nine of the preceding eleven years. The center estimates that, as of 1998, temperatures rose one degree during the twentieth century, and that, if that trend continues, global temperatures could rise three or four more degrees by the year 2100. Whether this increase represents human-caused "global warming" or is the result of long-term, natural climatic cycles is not entirely understood and is a subject of much controversy. However, if this trend does continue, for whatever reasons, it could have major implications for North Carolina, especially along the coast, as global warming could lead to significant melting of the polar ice caps and a subsequent rise in sea level.

Vegetation
ARTHUR W. COOPER

The natural vegetation of North Carolina, rich in species and varied in composition, constitutes one of the state's greatest natural resources. It not only supplies a large supply of timber and pulpwood for industry, but it also is an aesthetic resource of in-calculable value. The coastal live oak forests and the high mountain spruce-fir forests are but two extremes in a range of vegetation types unequaled in any other eastern state. Unfortunately, much of the state's vast forests and other areas of vegetation have been cleared by centuries of population growth and urbanization. Perhaps this removal has been the most extensive impact on the environment of growth, and it is destined to continue. On the other hand, major efforts are under way to protect and restore large areas of the state's natural vegetation. These efforts are reviewed in Chapter 19, "Outdoor Recreation."

Despite the removal of many areas of natural vegetation, enough still remain from which the essential features of the state's natural vegetation can be deduced. Forests comprise virtually the entire area of climax vegetation in North Carolina (Fig. 2.20). A climax community is one that will occupy its habitat continually in response to prevailing conditions of climate and geology if it is not disturbed by human intervention. Each vegetation type can be recognized by any observer who can, in turn, recognize the major plant species involved.

Outer Coastal Plain

The distribution of vegetation types on the coast is influenced primarily by the effects of saltwater ocean tides, windblown sand and salt spray, and the texture and drainage of the soil. In addition, the

Figure 2.20. Major Forest Types

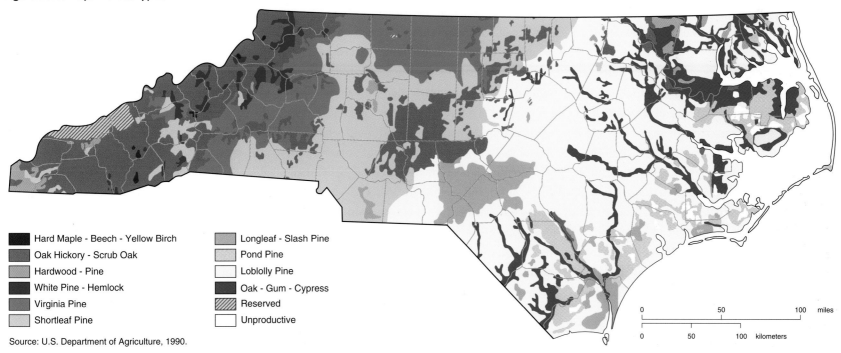

Legend:
- Hard Maple - Beech - Yellow Birch
- Oak Hickory - Scrub Oak
- Hardwood - Pine
- White Pine - Hemlock
- Virginia Pine
- Shortleaf Pine
- Longleaf - Slash Pine
- Pond Pine
- Loblolly Pine
- Oak - Gum - Cypress
- Reserved
- Unproductive

Source: U.S. Department of Agriculture, 1990.

0   50   100   miles

0   50   100   kilometers

effects of coastal development have, in many places, so severely altered the landscape that the natural pattern of vegetation is entirely obscured. Only in the national seashores and in isolated other locations can the natural pattern of coastal vegetation be observed.

Maritime forest varies from south to north along the coast. Forests of the southern coast are strongly dominated by live oak, with other species present, but only locally dominant. Palmetto is common on Smith Island, indicating an affinity of such forests with those farther south in the Sea Islands. From Bogue Banks north, remaining well-developed stands of maritime forest include an intermixture of other species more characteristic of inland areas such as beech, pine, hickory, and hophornbeam. Such areas are probably relics of hardwood forests that extended much farther seaward during geologically recent periods of low sea level. The best examples of such forests are preserved in the Nags Head Woods Preserve of the Nature Conservancy, at Hatteras Woods in Buxton, and in fragmentary locations on Bogue Banks.

Coastal marshes form in protected areas behind the barrier beaches and on the edges of sounds where the substratum is periodically flooded. North Carolina originally had over 200,000 acres of coastal wetlands, which constitute one of the state's most valuable natural resources. By the early 1970s, however, dredging and filling had destroyed as many as 50,000 acres.

Salt marshes occur where flooding waters are saline or brackish. Regularly flooded salt marshes are found primarily southwest of Beaufort Inlet. Smooth cordgrass dominates these marshes, growing very tall along tidal creeks where drainage is good but reduced to less than a foot in height in areas away from creeks where drainage is poorer and salinity increases. Clumps of black needlerush are scattered throughout the marsh and as narrow fringes between the marsh and high ground. Above the mean high-tide line, smooth cordgrass is replaced by saltmeadow cordgrass and salt grass in a zone called the "high marsh."

North of Beaufort Inlet and along the Outer Banks, regularly flooded salt marsh becomes much less common and is replaced by irregularly flooded salt marsh. Vast areas of these marshes, dominated by black needlerush, occur along the inner and outer edges of Core, Pamlico, and lower Currituck Sounds. Behind the black needlerush, beyond the effects of all but extreme storm tides, large expanses of saltmeadow cordgrass and salt grass occur, intermixed with brackish ponds and wet openings.

Extensive freshwater marshes are found in the upper Currituck Sound, along the fringes of Albemarle Sound, and along the Cape Fear River near Wilmington. Here the major species are bulrush, cattail, saw grass, and big cordgrass. The soils of these marshes are typically peaty and continually waterlogged with fresh to slightly brackish water.

All coastal marshes are valuable and productive natural systems. Regularly flooded salt marshes produce large amounts of plant material that is washed from the marsh by the tides and, while undergoing decay in the surrounding estuarine waters, serves as a major food source for many small forms of fish and shellfish. In addition, tidal creeks act as nursery areas for these small animals. It is estimated that over 95 percent of the fish and shellfish that are taken by commercial or sports fishers along the North Carolina coast depend in one way or another on coastal salt marshes and their adjacent waters. Irregularly flooded salt marshes serve as major waterfowl resting and feeding areas, as do fresh marshes. In many ways, the biological health of coastal waters depends on the natural activities that occur in its adjacent marshes.

Perennial grasses dominate the dunes. Sea oats are the most common of these, although American beach grass has become prevalent in recent years as a result of extensive planting for dune stabilization. There is a rich dune herb flora of which beach pea, croton, and dune elder are the most important species. Sea oats, croton, and dune elder occupy the slopes and crests of dunes, whereas other species such as broomsedge, spurge, and primrose occur in the more protected areas and on "blowouts" (wind-formed depressions) between dunes. This zonation is due primarily to the relative tolerance to salt spray of the various species. Low, moist areas within the dunes, which are influenced by freshwater accumulations through much of the year and by occasional accumulations of salt water, have a distinctive flora made up of saltmeadow cordgrass, yaupon, wax myrtle, and red cedar. They are usually interlaced with thick growths of catbrier. It is also not uncommon to find occasional stunted individuals of tree species characteristic of inland forests such as cypress and pine. These are undoubtedly relics of a time when forests occupied the site and are evidence of the general shoreline recession characteristic of the entire North Carolina coast.

Inland from the shrub zone, in areas where some protection from salt spray is afforded either by distance or by dunes, a maritime forest develops. Live oak is the characteristic tree of this forest, as it is markedly well adapted to withstand the effects of salt spray. In many areas active dunes are overwhelming the seaward edge of maritime forest as they migrate inland.

Inner Coastal Plain

The vegetation of the Inner Coastal Plain proper is characterized by a wide variety of plant communities of very different aspect and species composition. The distribution and ecology of these plant communities are determined primarily by the depth of the water table below the soil surface, soil texture, and fire. Superimposed on these natural variables are the effects produced by the activities of people.

Swamp forests of two major types occur along the major rivers and lesser streams of the Inner Coastal Plain. Gum-cypress swamps are best developed on floodplains of black water rivers and on flats associated with upland drainage channels. Cypress occurs in the wettest portions of such swamps where the soil rarely, if ever, dries out. Tupelo gum and swamp gum dominate the slightly drier sites, with tupelo gum typically able to survive longer periods of flooding than swamp gum. The cypress trees show development of "knees," structures once thought to aid in aerating the roots but now generally agreed to have no aerating capacity, thus representing a growth response by the tree roots to the wet soils. The floodplains of the major through-flowing rivers of the Coastal Plain and their tributaries are dominated by hardwood swamp forests. The major trees of these forests are willow oak, water oak, cherrybark oak, sweet gum, ash, sycamore, river birch, and elm.

One of the most fascinating and formidable wetland vegetation types of the Inner Coastal Plain is the pocosin (also called "bay" or "shrub bog"). Pocosins cover more than half of several eastern counties (Fig. 2.21). These consist of dense masses of evergreen shrubs, with scattered pond pine,

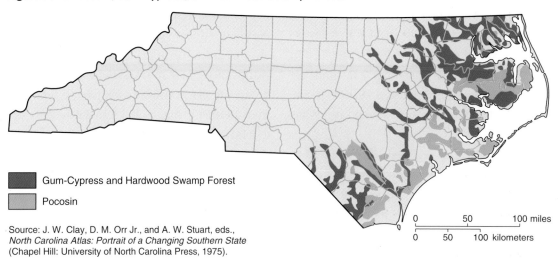

Figure 2.21. Pocosin, Gum-Cypress, and Hardwood Swamp Forests

Gum-Cypress and Hardwood Swamp Forest
Pocosin

Source: J. W. Clay, D. M. Orr Jr., and A. W. Stuart, eds., *North Carolina Atlas: Portrait of a Changing Southern State* (Chapel Hill: University of North Carolina Press, 1975).

growing on highly organic peat soils. The peat underlying the surface varies in depth from a few inches to 15–20 feet and, particularly in the extensive flats of the lower Coastal Plain, often has a distinct layer of buried logs. Pond pine is the only tree of any importance, and it is usually scattered in rather open stands. On the deeper, more acid peats its growth rate is very slow. Consequently, only the shallower peats and those where acidity can be controlled by drainage are productive forest soils. The universal occurrence of pond pine in pocosins is related to its capacity to sprout profusely at the root collar and in the crown following fire.

Although the water table is near the surface throughout much of the year, pocosins are not regularly flooded. Where the peat is deep and most regularly flooded, dwarf shrubs often dominate. Pocosins are very susceptible to fire and often burn extensively during dry periods. For many years the peat soils of pocosins were considered nonproductive for agricultural purposes. But, with the development of new heavy equipment and techniques for drainage, many of the shallower peats have been cleared and converted to agriculture. With proper water management and fertilization, such soils can be highly productive. However, the high costs of preparing and maintaining peat soils in agriculture as well as declining corn and soybean prices have led to the abandonment of virtually every peat farming operation in North Carolina. In fact, the largest of the operations was ultimately sold to the federal government and serves as the core of the Alligator River and Pocosin Lakes Wildlife Refuges.

Another important vegetation type of the lower Inner Coastal Plain is the pine flatwoods or savanna. As the name implies, these are dominated by scattered pines and usually have a continuous ground cover of grasses and herbs. Flatwoods form both on gently sloping sand ridges and on extensive, poorly drained flatlands. Pond pine and longleaf pine are the major trees. Shrubs vary considerably in their abundance, being common in some places and entirely absent in others. Gallberry, wax myrtle, and sweet bay are the most common. On the coarse, well-drained sandy soils wire grass is the common savanna grass. The savannas are very rich in wildflowers, and this community is perhaps the most showy of all North Carolina vegetation types. A number of species, including orchids, pitcher plants, lilies, goldenrods, sunflowers, and asters, may be in bloom at any one time from early March to late November. The unique Venus flytrap occurs in grassy, poorly drained habitats similar to those of savannas. Flytrap plants cannot survive extended competition from grasses and shrubs. Consequently, they thrive only in areas that are burned fairly regularly. Repeated fires destroy all accumulation of peat on the soil surface as well as the crowns of shrubs, thus favoring grasses. Repeated fires perpetuate grasses at the expense of shrubs and therefore permit the savanna to persist. Where savannas are protected from fire, they change rapidly into shrub- and tree-dominated stands with species of a composition similar to that of the drier pocosins.

Deep, well-drained, coarse sands in the Inner Coastal Plain typically are dominated by the longleaf pine–turkey oak–wire grass community. This vegetation type is confined principally to the southern half of the Coastal Plain, being best developed in the Sandhills region along the Fall Line, but also occurring on the deep sands of old dunes and terraces associated with ancient inland shorelines. These areas have a distinctive appearance, usually consisting of an open layer of scattered, large longleaf pines and a lower layer of scrub oaks, primarily turkey oak, bluejack oak, blackjack oak, and scrubby post oak. Dwarf huckleberry is the most common shrub, supplanting wire grass in areas where the turkey oaks are thickest. Although wire grass is the major herb, numerous other herbaceous species are present, many of which have showy flowers. Virtually all herbs show adaptations to the extreme dryness of the habitat, as do many of the woody plants.

This vast original longleaf pine forest was systematically eradicated by human activities. Much was destroyed by the naval stores industry, which peaked in the mid-1800s. Logging, which followed turpentining, completed this destruction, so that by the early 1900s the last of the virgin longleaf pine forests had been eliminated. Agriculture, the systematic exclusion of fire, and the effects of feral livestock prevented longleaf pine from recovering, and the type was thus virtually obliterated from the landscape except in those areas (such as the Sandhills) where extreme sandy soils and continued fire allowed the species to persist. It now occupies less than 5 percent of a landscape in which it was once the dominant species. Today the uplands of the North Carolina Inner Coastal Plain are dominated by a mixture of types of which loblolly pine–mixed hardwood stands resulting from abandonment of agriculture fields, exclusion of fire, and logging are the most common. Pine plantations and agricultural land make up virtually all of the remaining vegetation. The common hardwoods are white oak, southern red oak, post oak, blackjack oak, and hickory.

The status of the purely deciduous forests of the Inner Coastal Plain, which are very limited in their distribution, is unclear. These forests were probably more extensive in the northern half of the Coastal Plain, where soils are loamy and adequately, but not excessively, drained. There deciduous forests extended much closer to sea level. In the southern Coastal Plain, however, because of the preponderance of sandy soils, deciduous forests are found relatively near the Piedmont where the majority of the landscape was covered by longleaf pine forest. The deciduous forests on the drier sites of the Coastal Plain have a composition similar to that described above and are probably best considered as oak-hickory forests. Other stands, particularly those on moist but well-drained sites where beech was common in association with laurel oak, white oak, southern red oak, water oak, willow oak, post oak, swamp chestnut oak, hickories, sweet gum, tulip poplar, black gum, and red maple, are classified as Southern Mixed Hardwood Forest, a type that is more common farther south on the southeastern Coastal Plain.

The Piedmont

Perhaps more than in any other part of the state, the vegetation of the Piedmont shows the impact of society's treatment of the land. Three and one-half centuries of logging, farming, grazing, and increasing urbanization have converted a once forested landscape into patches of pine and deciduous forests mixed with fields in varying kinds of cultivation and in varying stages of abandonment. Despite these massive changes in the landscape, remaining patches of forest reflect the natural variability in soils and topography that influence the pattern of Piedmont vegetation. From this one can reconstruct what the original vegetation might have been like.

Oak-hickory forests undoubtedly covered all of the Piedmont uplands except for the extremely dry and extremely wet sites. Judging from the records of early explorers and from existing little-disturbed stands, these Piedmont forests were fine indeed, much more so than one might judge from observing the present, heavily disturbed woodlots now scattered through the area. On the rolling uplands of the Piedmont, oak-hickory forests were dominated by white, black, scarlet, southern red, and post oaks, mockernut and smooth hickory, black gum, tulip poplar, and occasional shortleaf and loblolly pines. Dogwood and sourwood were the common understory trees.

The great diversity of topography and soil in the Piedmont produces much local variation in forest composition. On steep, sheltered slopes, and on the more fertile and less eroded soils, beech, northern red oak, white oak, and tulip poplar are the major species. On such sites there is a great diversity of shrubs and low trees, and one may find large numbers of spring and summer flowering herbs. Upland sites, with soils that become very wet in winter and very dry in summer, are dominated by post and blackjack oak with some sand hickory and white and southern red oak. Carolina shagbark hickory is found on sites with similar moisture conditions, but only where such sites occur in the Carolina Slate Belt running through the center of the Piedmont. On dry, excessively drained ridges, scarlet oak and occasionally chestnut oak

are common. Such stands become much more abundant in the western Piedmont, rarer in the Blue Ridge. Hardwood swamp forests, similar to those of the Coastal Plain, occur on the floodplains of the major rivers and their tributaries. The major species of this community are sycamore, river birch, ash, elm, sweet gum, willow oak, swamp chestnut oak, and tulip poplar.

There are many isolated patches of vegetation on the Piedmont of limited distribution but of considerable interest. For example, an isolated stand of hemlock and one of white pine occur in Wake and Lee Counties, respectively, near the edge of the Inner Coastal Plain. Also, a number of stands of purple rhododendron can be seen in the Piedmont and on the Coastal Plain. Several areas of granite flatrock occur as well, and these have a number of interesting flowering herbs that appear in few other habitats. Pilot Mountain, Kings Mountain, Crowders Mountain, and isolated low hills in the eastern and central Piedmont are crowned with stands of chestnut oak and present a mountainous aspect on the otherwise subdued Piedmont landscape.

The sequence of communities that develops following abandonment of a cultivated field is so much a part of the Piedmont scene that one must understand it to understand the vegetation of the region. When a field is cultivated, crabgrass and other weeds dominate during the autumn after crops are harvested. In the first summer following abandonment, horseweed dominates, and in the second year its place is taken by whitetopped aster. Gradually, during the next few years, the field shifts to a cover of broomsedge that is rapidly invaded by pines. Different pines dominate in different regions of the Piedmont, with loblolly, shortleaf, and Virginia characteristic of the eastern, central, and western portions, respectively. As the pines mature, a layer of young hardwood seedlings develops beneath them. These mature as the growth of the pines slows, and in time the pines are replaced by hardwoods. Eventually, an oak-hickory forest is reestablished on the site. The stages from abandonment to a young pine forest may typically take place in fifteen years, but the entire sequence from farm field to a mature climax forest requires up to two hundred years.

The Mountains

Two major vegetation systems occur in the Mountains. Deciduous forests cover the valleys and slopes up to 5,000–5,500 feet, whereas boreal conifer forests and related types occur above 4,500–5,000 feet. Within each of these systems there are several major vegetation types, each with its own characteristic history and habitat relationships. The seasonal changes in the appearance of the vegetation make North Carolina's mountain scenery as beautiful as that found anywhere in the world.

Five major forest types can be found in the deciduous forests that cover the lower mountain slopes and valleys. Before the arrival of European settlers, cove hardwood forests (often called mixed *mesophytic* forests) occupied sheltered mountain valleys and clothed protected lower slopes and more open north- and east-facing slopes from 1,500 to 4,500 feet. Although many of these sites are now cultivated, large unbroken tracts still occur in the Great Smoky Mountains and in the national forests.

Cove forests are among the most magnificent deciduous forests found anywhere on earth. There are, for example, more tree species in the Great Smoky Mountains than in all of Europe, and most of these occur in cove forests. It is this richness in species, in fact, that characterizes cove forests. Although twenty-five to thirty species may occur in any given stand, towering specimens of six trees are especially typical: hemlock, silverbell, yellow buckeye, white basswood, sugar maple, and yellow birch. Huge tulip poplar and beech also grow in most stands. Other species frequently found are the cucumber tree, fraser magnolia, sweet birch, white ash, black cherry, red maple, northern red oak, and bitternut hickory. White oak, chestnut oak, and, before advent of the blight, chestnut from the adjacent oak forests are often present. Although low trees and shrubs do not form an evident layer, a number of kinds do occur. A luxuriant herb layer is present in all cove forests, and its beauty and seasonal variety is without equal in

North Carolina. In coves that have been logged, tulip poplar is the dominant tree. However, the original botanical richness of the vegetation can still be observed in herbs and tree reproduction. Toward the upper altitudinal limits of cove forests, the number of species decreases, and there is a gradual rise in importance of white basswood, yellow buckeye, and yellow birch. Toward the moisture limits of cove forests on drier open slopes, the proportion of oaks increases.

Dark and somber hemlock forests dominate creek bottoms and ravines at low elevation. Such forests also occur in moist sites at higher elevations in ravines and on valley flats. White basswood, sugar maple, silverbell, and fraser magnolia are the most common associates of hemlock. Perhaps the most characteristic feature of these forests where they occur along streams is the dense tangle of rosebay rhododendron with doghobble underneath. On hemlock slopes the shrub stratum virtually disappears, and a dense, varied layer of herbs and ferns is present.

Exposed slopes up to 4,500–5,000 feet are covered with forests dominated by various species of oak. These forests are continuous with those of the adjacent Piedmont. Oak-hickory forests, similar to those of the Piedmont, occur over the southern- and eastern-facing outer slopes of the Blue Ridge below 3,000 feet and in the interior mountain basins. These stands are typically dominated by white oak with chestnut; black and scarlet oaks are commonly the codominants. Red maple, black locust, black gum, sourwood, and dogwood are the other common trees. The shrub layer is dominated by mountain laurel and blueberries. Few herbs are present. In the Asheville Basin a mixture of oaks and pine, similar to that of the Piedmont, dominates.

The most extensive oak type of the middle and lower slopes is chestnut oak forest. In the early days, this was oak-chestnut forest because of the former codominant role of chestnut. Now, because of the death of chestnut due to the blight fungus that invaded the Mountains in the 1920s, it seems appropriate to use the more descriptive name based on the present leading dominant, chestnut oak. At lower elevations this vegetation type occurs on long, gradual east- and north-facing slopes, whereas at higher elevations it is continuous on exposed slopes facing in any direction. Chestnut oak dominates virtually all stands, but northern red oak becomes more important at higher elevations. Common associates are red maple, scarlet oak (particularly on drier sites), and sourwood. Dead snags of chestnut are commonly scattered throughout, indicating the important role this species once played in this forest community. The shrub layer is always well developed. Mountain laurel is the major species, and on the driest sites it often occurs as a dense, continuous tangle. Rosebay rhododendron is frequently important on more moist sites. The beautiful flame azalea is commonly scattered throughout these forests. At the extreme upper limits of chestnut oak forests, forests of northern red oak with dead chestnut snags occur widely. Such stands often have shrubs and herbs similar to those found in more moist cove forests at similar elevations.

Virtually all dry, open ridges (called "leads") and steep open south- and southwest-facing slopes are dominated by pine forests. Such forests are most common at low elevations but virtually disappear by 4,500 feet. Up to about 2,500 feet, Virginia pine dominates, with pitch pine often codominant. At mid-elevation, between 2,500 and 3,500 feet, pitch pine is the major species of leads. Table Mountain pine assumes dominance up to the limits of pine at about 4,500 feet. Shortleaf pine occurs throughout but in greatest numbers at lower elevations. Scarlet oak is almost always present in pine stands, and it frequently becomes dominant in the zone between the pine forest and the dry oak forest of adjacent slopes. Chestnut oak, red maple, black gum, and sourwood are virtually always present in small numbers. The shrub layer is usually a dense layer of mountain laurel and blueberry. The soils are usually shallower with higher contents of clay and rock than those downslope under hardwoods. Nutrient levels are low due to the steepness of slopes on which pine occurs. Fire appears to favor pines, and many pine stands are populations of pine that entered after fire. Once established, however, pines are self-maintaining on the steep, dry slopes and thus can be regarded as a climax type of the most extreme sites in the deciduous forests.

Boreal Conifer Forests and High-Elevation Types

The peaks and ridges of the mountains above 4,500–5,000 feet are usually clothed with spruce-fir forests of a distinctly boreal aspect. The most extensive stands of spruce and fir are in the Great Smoky Mountains, where they occur as low as 4,500 feet, and in the Black Mountains, the Balsam and Plott Balsam ranges where they begin at about 5,500 feet.

These forests, more reminiscent of Canada than North Carolina, are composed primarily of red spruce and Fraser fir. Spruce-fir forest is best developed over 6,000 feet, where spruce and fir make up over 95 percent of the canopy. The only other common trees are mountain ash, yellow birch, and fire cherry. Where these reach the canopy they are usually relicts of past disturbances such as fire or windthrow. In general, spruce dominates at lower elevations and fir increases in importance with rising elevation. Although shrubs are rarely important in mature spruce-fir forests, the herbaceous layer is well developed. Ferns and herbs are usually present. Mosses and liverworts are abundant.

Large areas within the spruce-fir region have been disturbed by lumbering, fire, storms, and windthrow. Lumbering began in the early 1900s and was followed by extensive fires. Fire cherry, and often yellow birch, become established immediately after fire. Such stands are usually very dense, and as they age many trees die and the canopy opens up so that blackberry forms a dense underlayer. Ultimately, the cherry–yellow birch stands are invaded by spruce and fir seedlings. Such invasion is slow, and after twenty years only occasional spruce and fir seedlings may be encountered in a badly burned area. Windthrows are common, particularly in high-elevation fir stands, where the trees are shallowly rooted and the soil thin and rocky. Following overthrow of canopy trees, dense stands of fir seedlings develop, leading to pole stands of even-aged trees. Thus reproduction of many high-elevation stands are cyclical. At lower elevations, however, individual trees are uprooted, broken off, or die and are gradually replaced, giving rise to uneven-aged stands.

Although spruce and fir dominate the high mountain peaks, climax stands of deciduous forest are also present. Such stands range in stature from true forest to scrubby stands of gnarled trees. The major trees of these forests are beech, yellow birch, sugar maple, and yellow buckeye. The most distinctive of these forests are dense stands of low, gnarled beech trees, regenerated from root sprouts, known as beech gaps or beech orchards. Such stands are best developed on steep south-facing gaps between ridges covered with spruce and fir.

The herbaceous flora of these forests is very rich, notably in spring, when dense layers of wildflowers carpet the forest floor.

The high-elevation spruce-fir and, to a lesser extent, deciduous forests have been the subject of intense study recently because of the death or decline of the leading dominants, Fraser fir and red spruce. Many heavily visited areas, such as Mount Mitchell, Grandfather Mountain, and Richland and Balsam, have in recent decades been converted from dense spruce-fir forests to a tangle of dead fir snags and dead or dying red spruce. The scene of devastation concerns everyone who sees it, and there have been many attempts to explain the reasons for this disaster.

The reasons that have been suggested include the balsam wooly adelgid, acid rain, ozone, climate change, and purely natural causes. The only fact that seems beyond debate is that the balsam wooly adelgid has been the major cause of death of Fraser fir. Although it is evident that the high-elevation southern Appalachian forests are subject to precipitation (rain, snow, fog) that is highly acidified, it is not clear that acid rain or any other pollutant is the sole cause of the decline and death of red spruce or any other tree. On the other hand, the combination of acid rain and climatic stress may be the cause of the demise of red spruce. Spruce-fir forests generally are cyclic in nature, with stands arising after natural catastrophes such as windthrow or fire and maturing as even-aged stands. It

may well be that some of the mortality observed in the southern Appalachians is the result of such natural cycles. Whatever the cause, the spruce-fir forests that have dominated the highest mountain peaks are undergoing rapid change, and neither the ultimate outcome of that change or its causes are entirely clear.

Two unique, naturally treeless, communities are also found in the same elevation zone as spruce-fir forests, heath balds and grass balds. Although both are called "balds," they are very different in appearance and species composition. Heath balds, or "laurel slicks," are treeless communities dominated by evergreen rhododendrons and mountain laurel. They cover exposed areas of steep, rugged topography at elevations from 4,000 to 6,000 feet. Although at a distance they appear smooth (thus the name "slick"), within they are extremely rough, tangled, and virtually impenetrable. While the shrubs may exceed ten feet in height, on exposed ridges they diminish to a few feet and, in places, consist of scattered mats and cushions.

The steepest and most dramatic heath balds occur in the Smoky Mountains, but the famous rhododendron "gardens" of the Craggies and Roan Mountains are such balds on more gentle summits. The heath balds of lower elevation are dominated by mountain laurel, rosebay rhododendron, and purple rhododendron, but at higher elevations mountain laurel drops out. Heath bald soils are thin, and balds almost always occur on relatively

Dead trees near the summit of Mt. Mitchell

origin of these high mountain pastures has been a matter of speculation for years; there are almost as many theories for their origin as there are people who have visited them. Four sorts of areas are called grass balds: (1) forested areas dominated by widely spaced dwarfed hardwoods, (2) areas recently cleared for fire towers, (3) grassland occupying recently deforested sites, and (4) the true balds presumably in existence prior to the advent of white people in the Mountains. True grass balds show no relationship to topography, as they occur on dome-shaped summits, in gaps, and on ridges. They are most common on southern, southwestern, and western exposures, and the majority occur between 5,200 and 5,800 feet. Most are either surrounded by deciduous forests or lie between deciduous and spruce-fir forests. Deciduous trees at bald margins are gnarled and stunted.

Mountain oat grass is the characteristic plant of all balds, forming a dense turf over the surface and extending into the adjacent open woods. Many weeds occur in the balds, as do a number of native herbs. Woody plants are common. Flame azalea, blueberry, and blackberry are common shrubs, with shadblow and hawthorn the most frequent small trees. Studies over the past thirty years show that the percentage of woody plants on the balds has increased and that forests have moved onto the balds themselves. It is difficult to suggest a satisfactory explanation for the formation and persistence of the grass balds. Some observers have hypothesized a catastrophic origin by fire, storm, or windthrow with grasses entering after elimination of the trees and persisting by excluding them through root competition. Another theory holds that they were formed by Native Americans who cleared and maintained them as hunting openings. Whatever their origin, it is evident they were expanded and maintained by grazing during the 1800s and early 1900s. Now, with reduced grazing, many balds are reverting to forest and, without maintenance, will disappear.

Soils

DONALD STEILA

Soil quality was a vital aspect of the environment for early subsistence farmers and for owners of large antebellum cotton plantations. And despite advances in fertilization and other production practices, it remains an important matter for contemporary farmers. In today's more urban society, various soil characteristics also are significant. The ability for water to percolate through the soil horizon determines whether septic tanks can be used in a new suburban housing subdivision, for example. Soil acidity is important to home lawn care and gardens. Slight acidity is preferred by roses; on the other hand, lime may be added to the lawn's soil to make it less acidic.

steep, exposed slopes. These factors combine to make the balds dry sites, thus virtually eliminating trees. These plant species are not confined to balds alone, and the bald flora are derived from that of the surrounding forest.

Beyond all doubt, the most enigmatic of all mountain vegetation types is the grass bald. The

Formation

No element of North Carolina's physical environment expresses the interrelatedness of environmental processes more than the soils of the state. Soil formation is controlled by interactions that take place between the atmosphere, geologic materials at the earth's surface, the shape of the land, and the type of vegetation that is present. These interactions differ in the Mountains, Piedmont, and Coastal Plain. Thus, North Carolina has a multitude of environmental settings, providing the state with diverse soil resources that support a wide variety of agricultural and timber products.

Practically all of North Carolina soils are acidic and relatively infertile due to a loss of soluble nutrients, especially nitrogen, potash, calcium, and magnesium. This loss results from a process referred to as *leaching*, in which downward percolating water takes the nutrients into solution and removes them from the topsoil. Leaching is a particularly active process in the warm, humid climate that prevails in North Carolina. Visitors to the state often remark on the red color of upland soils, a characteristic that is not generally found in northern and midwestern states. This is the result of long, hot summers, year-round weathering conditions, and the great length of time soils have been forming in North Carolina. These factors produce soils that are rich in clay and iron oxides, the latter accounting for the characteristic red clay. Yet the contrasting qualities of the black organic and white sandy soils of the lowlands or the varied traits of the Mountain soils seldom receive any comment.

Soil Characteristics and Patterns

Approximately three hundred types of soils (*soil series*) have been identified in the state. There are major differences on a regional basis, with soils ranging from light sands with little humus in the Sandhills to the heavy plastic clays of the Piedmont, and from the black, highly organic soils of the Coast to the brown loams of the Mountains. There is also considerable variability within

each of these regions and, in fact, within a single field or lot. These local and regional differences are due to a variety of causes—differences in native vegetation, which is in part related to climatic differences; differences in the kinds of rocks from which the soils have formed; variations in the degree of wetness (water saturation) resulting from the soils' topographic position; and variations in the age of soils.

Effects of vegetation differences on soils are mostly expressed in the nature of the humus (decaying organic debris) layers and in their upper mineral layers, or "A" horizons (topsoil). Soils under pines have raw undecomposed needle layers and very acidic, leached topsoils. Those formed under broadleaf forests, on the other hand, have well-decomposed rich humus layers and less acidic and leached A horizons. Soils of the cove forests in the Mountains are richer, browner, and much less acidic than those of the oak forests; they especially contrast with the lighter-colored acidic soils of spruce-fir forests.

A major reason for differences among soils is the kind of parent rock or sediment from which they have formed. This is the most important factor in understanding soil variations in the Piedmont. Soils formed from disintegration of light-colored, coarse granitic rocks have coarse sandy A horizons (topsoils), are yellowish in color, and are very acidic. In contrast, those formed from the weathering of the dark "basic" or "mafic" rocks have heavy loam horizons and dark red subsoils (if well drained) and are less acidic and infertile than those from granitic and gneissic rocks.

In the Coastal Plain, depositional environment is highly relevant to soil patterns. Soils formed from sediments deposited in former lagoons and sounds are heavy, plastic soils. Sediments from environments like offshore bars, beaches, and sandy floodplains form sandy, infertile soils.

The most important factor causing local soil differences in the middle and lower Coastal Plain, however, is the topographic position the soils occupy on the local landscape. Those of the higher points are lower in organic matter, are yellower or browner in color, have sandier surface layers, and ordinarily do not have high water tables. In contrast, those of low-lying swampy areas like swales and pocosins contain high amounts of organic matter (humus) with loamy surfaces, are gray and very acidic, and maintain high water tables much of the year unless artificially drained. The association of soils formed from similar geologic materials, but with gradation in soil properties, from highest point to lowest on a landscape, is called a *soil system*, which by definition is a recurring group of soils that occupies the landscape from the interstream divide to the stream. The soils that make up these systems normally occupy specific landscape positions.

Another reason for so many variations in Coastal Plain soils is the difference in the ages of the landscape on which they have formed. The Coastal Plain underwent several cycles of invasion and recession of the sea in the Pleistocene period (Ice Age). This period of sea invasion has left a series of sedimentary deposits of varying age—from more than a million to less than twenty thousand years—the oldest being in the upper Coastal Plain and the youngest in the lower Coastal Plain and Tidewater. If these sedimentary deposits have not been disturbed or eroded, the soils that have formed vary in their properties in accordance with the age of the sediments, with the older soils having experienced greater weathering and leaching. However, during periods in the Ice Age when sea level was much lower than it is now and when rainfall was possibly higher, there was much erosion and removal of sediments, especially from hillsides along streams in the upper Coastal Plain and to a lesser extent in the middle Coastal Plain. In these places, soils are much younger and less weathered than the undisturbed, uneroded soils of the adjacent smoother uplands and the broader ridge tops.

Rainfall and temperature have some influence on soil variety in North Carolina, but not nearly as much as parent material, local landscape position, and soil age. Soils of the southern portion of the Mountains receive larger amounts of rainfall and are more highly leached and weathered than others, even though they are on steep hillsides and are rather young soils. This is especially true for soils of the warmer south-facing slopes. These soils contain large amounts of gibbsite, an aluminum ore mineral generally found to a significant extent in the highly weathered soils of the warm humid tropics. In contrast, the soils of northeastern North Carolina are less leached, more fertile, and browner than other soils in the state. Differences in soils from place to place are not always obvious from casual examination of the land, but they may be important to environmental, engineering, or agricultural decisions. To show these differences, soils have been described, classified, and mapped throughout the state.

Soil Classification

The problem of classifying soils is extremely complicated. Soils are formed through the interaction of five variable factors—climate, vegetation and microorganisms, parent material, slope, and time. As these variables change from place to place, a great number of combinations can result. To accommodate these many possible combinations, a comprehensive soil classification system, the *soil taxonomy*, was published in 1975. This publication identifies ten broad kinds of soil, called soil orders. Each soil order is composed of soils with similar genetic layers of horizons, formed by the same kind and intensity of soil-forming factors. Six of these ten soil orders are common in North Carolina (Table 2.2). Each of these orders is subdivided into successively smaller, more narrowly defined classes. That is, each of them is subdivided into several subclasses or suborders. Each of the suborders is further subdivided into a number of great groups. A great group is composed of soils having similar profiles (the same kind, arrangement, and thickness of genetic layers—"A" horizons or topsoil, "E" horizons that lack the organic richness of the topsoil, and "B" horizons or subsoils).

The great groups are further subdivided into subgroups and these into families. Finally, each family is subdivided into several soil series, the basic soil taxonomic and map unit. Soil series are designed to illustrate and describe what soils are like in individual fields, tracts, and lots and are ordinarily used for detailed surveys and classifications.

Table 2.2. Soil Orders Represented in North Carolina

Soil Order	Characteristics
Alfisol	Well-developed subsoils, generally brown or yellowish in color, and not as acid, leached, and weathered as the more common Ultisols (formed from "basic" parent material that has more dense, clayey subsoils)
Entisols	Recent or juvenile soils with little or no soil development
Histosols	Organic soils, the peats, and the mucks of the Blacklands
Inceptisols	Modest subsoil development formed on rather young Coastal Plain landscapes or on steeper slopes where geologic erosion nearly keeps pace with soil development
Spodosols	Very acid, sandy soils with subsoil accumulations of humus and aluminum
Ultisols	Soils with prominent subsoils of clay accumulation—very acid, highly leached, and weathered

Note: The soil series are composed of soils similar in color, texture, reaction, consistency, and chemical layers and horizons. The characteristic county soil maps display soils at the series level of classification.

Soil Resources in North Carolina

The broad soil pattern of North Carolina is illustrated in Figure 2.22. This map has been generalized from county surveys to show broad soil resource areas (soil orders) composed of combinations of certain great groups that occur together. Soils belonging to the same great group generally have similar kinds of physical and chemical properties, vegetation associations, agricultural and nonfarm use potentials, and utilization problems. Therefore, soil orders are probably the most feasible units or classes for examining soil resources in broad general terms.

Soil Type and Vegetation

Histosols and Spodosols in the lower Coastal Plain are associated with pine flatwoods, pocosins, and savanna types of vegetation. Entisols of the Sandhills are associated with longleaf pine and oak-hickory vegetation types, whereas Entisols along the Outer Banks support maritime forests and salt marshes. Other great groups of the Coastal Plain are in wetland vegetation, upland oak-hickory, and pines. The great groups of the Piedmont are in old field pines and upland oak-hickory. Some cove forests of yellow poplar occur in the upper Piedmont and foothills. The Dystrochrepts of the higher mountains are associated with spruce-fir, heath balds, "beech gaps," and cove forests. Other great groups of the Mountains support oak forests, old field pine, and yellow poplar in the coves.

Soil Type and Agriculture

The smooth slopes, high organic-matter content, good moisture-supplying capacity, and responsiveness of the Umbraquult and Ochraquult soils of the southern Coastal Plain and Tidewater are in part responsible for the concentration of corn-soybean production in these areas. Sloping land, highly erodible soils with acidic clay subsoils, and low summer-moisture supply of the Hapludults and associated soils of the Piedmont are factors related to the greater specialization in pastures and small grain.

The North Carolina peach-growing industry is concentrated in the Sandhills, mainly on the Quartzipsamment soils such as the Lakeland soil type. The good air drainage of the rolling hills, plus the early warming, ease of root penetration, and good tilth of the sands are among the factors responsible for this localization. The North Carolina blueberry industry is concentrated on Haplaquod soils in the southern Tidewater region. The highbush type of blueberry now used for main production is adapted to these very sandy acidic soils with an organic pan or hardpan in the subsoil. (Rabbiteye blueberries are suited to a wider range of soil conditions.)

Figure 2.22. Soil Resources

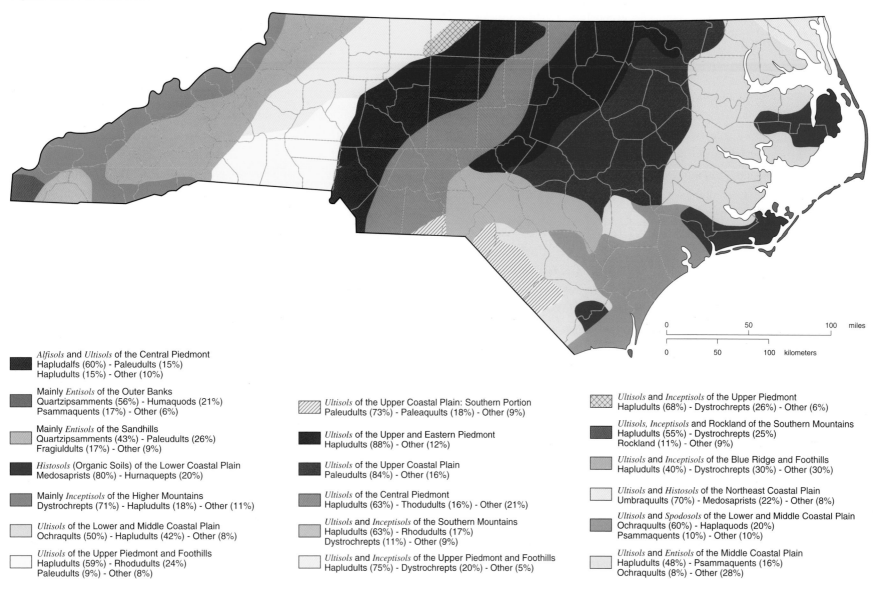

Legend:

Alfisols and **Ultisols** of the Central Piedmont
Hapludalfs (60%) - Paleudults (15%)
Hapludults (15%) - Other (10%)

Mainly **Entisols** of the Outer Banks
Quartzipsamments (56%) - Humaquods (21%)
Psammaquents (17%) - Other (6%)

Mainly **Entisols** of the Sandhills
Quartzipsamments (43%) - Paleudults (26%)
Fragiuldults (17%) - Other (9%)

Histosols (Organic Soils) of the Lower Coastal Plain
Medosaprists (80%) - Hurnaquepts (20%)

Mainly **Inceptisols** of the Higher Mountains
Dystrochrepts (71%) - Hapludults (18%) - Other (11%)

Ultisols of the Lower and Middle Coastal Plain
Ochraqults (50%) - Hapludults (42%) - Other (8%)

Ultisols of the Upper Piedmont and Foothills
Hapludults (59%) - Rhodudults (24%)
Paleudults (9%) - Other (8%)

Ultisols of the Upper Coastal Plain: Southern Portion
Paleudults (73%) - Paleaquults (18%) - Other (9%)

Ultisols of the Upper and Eastern Piedmont
Hapludults (88%) - Other (12%)

Ultisols of the Upper Coastal Plain
Paleudults (84%) - Other (16%)

Ultisols of the Central Piedmont
Hapludults (63%) - Thodudults (16%) - Other (21%)

Ultisols and **Inceptisols** of the Southern Mountains
Hapludults (63%) - Rhodudults (17%)
Dystrochrepts (11%) - Other (9%)

Ultisols and **Inceptisols** of the Upper Piedmont and Foothills
Hapludults (75%) - Dystrochrepts (20%) - Other (5%)

Ultisols and **Inceptisols** of the Upper Piedmont
Hapludults (68%) - Dystrochrepts (26%) - Other (6%)

Ultisols, **Inceptisols** and Rockland of the Southern Mountains
Hapludults (55%) - Dystrochrepts (25%)
Rockland (11%) - Other (9%)

Ultisols and **Inceptisols** of the Blue Ridge and Foothills
Hapludults (40%) - Dystrochrepts (30%) - Other (30%)

Ultisols and **Histosols** of the Northeast Coastal Plain
Umbraquults (70%) - Medosaprists (22%) - Other (8%)

Ultisols and **Spodosols** of the Lower and Middle Coastal Plain
Ochraqults (60%) - Haplaquods (20%)
Psammaquents (10%) - Other (10%)

Ultisols and **Entisols** of the Middle Coastal Plain
Hapludults (48%) - Psammaquents (16%)
Ochraqults (8%) - Other (28%)

Source: S. W. Buol, ed., *Soils of the Southern States and Puerto Rico* (Raleigh: Agricultural Experiment Station, N.C. State University, 1973).

Peanut production in North Carolina is concentrated in seventeen counties in the north-central Coastal Plain. This production is mainly on Paleudults and Hapludults, soils that have good natural drainage, a sandy loam topsoil, and a friable, sandy clay loam subsoil. The sandy loam surface soils are well suited to peanut "pegging," and the well-drained friable subsoils provide excellent soil moisture and physical conditions for peanut growth. Further, these soils occur on relatively smooth land suited for the machine cultivation of peanuts. Apple production is concentrated in the west, on shallow Hapludults and Dystrochrepts of the Blue Ridge and foothills. Here, the good air drainage provided by the slopes and the excellent growth and timely ripening permitted by the cooler climate combine with the good physical conditions of the soils to encourage this expanding enterprise.

Soil Type and Nonfarm Urban Uses

There is an increasing interest in nonfarm urban uses of soil resources. Although a store of information is available on soil from an agronomy viewpoint, little has been published concerning the compatibility of soils with various urban uses. In examining the compatibility of the land with nonfarm urban uses for specific sites, a map showing soil series should be consulted or even a field examination made. For more general planning purposes, however, soil association maps have proven useful. The soil association classification is derived by grouping together several similar soil series. In compiling the maps, county surveys of soil series are checked in the field for association boundaries.

The Mountains
The major soil characteristics affecting nonfarm land use in the Mountain region of North Carolina are slope and thickness of the soil mantle over rock or other impermeable layers. The most desirable soils for residential, industrial, and recreational purposes are those having slopes under 12 percent and a soil thickness greater than thirty-six inches. The greater the slope, the greater

the potential for excessive sediment and erosion losses from site clearing. The effectiveness of soil areas as waste treatment systems, where public sewage disposal is unavailable, is mainly associated with the thickness and permeability of the soil and slope gradient. Slope, depth to hard or bed rock, support and slippage potentials of the soil, and natural drainage are strongly related to problems associated with the construction of roads and parking facilities.

Although flood-prone land in the Mountains is not extensive, problems of sediment control and active erosion are serious where nonfarm uses would involve removal of vegetative cover. Further, watersheds are subject to flash flooding at low points within the watershed boundary. This flooding potential increases drastically as urban development increases. Thus, as in other regions of the state, hazards are involved in nonfarm uses of flood-prone areas. Considering these limitations, approximately 18 percent of the North Carolina Mountain region is suitable for nonfarm uses when public utilities (sewer lines) are unavailable. With widespread public sewer lines and minimal development expenses, approximately 32 percent of the areas might be compatible with nonfarm urban uses.

The Piedmont
Soil characteristics that affect nonfarm urban uses in the Piedmont include slope, the amounts and kinds of clay, the thickness of the soil mantle over hard rock, and the presence of any impermeable strata. Considering these limitations, about two-thirds of the soil resources of the Piedmont have one or more characteristics that impose moderate-to-severe limitations for urban-suburban use.

In urban-suburban development of Piedmont soils, the following considerations should be noted:

1. The control of erosion and the resulting sediment is closely related to slope and the erodibility of the Piedmont soil. Nonfarm developments that require removal of vegetation and that expose the soil for long periods of time lead to severe soil losses by erosion. Where slopes exceed 12

percent, nonfarm uses frequently require extensive grading, cutting, and filling.

2. The percolation of subsurface horizons in Piedmont soils is variable. Some soil areas are underlain by dense clays with low percolation rates and thus are unsuitable as waste sinks. Piedmont soils are not well adapted to high-density development unless waste treatment systems are available. Percolation rates of the soils restrict their use as waste sinks. But they are generally satisfactory if the quantity of waste is controlled and if soils are not subjected to saturation for long periods of time.

3. Some soil resource areas consist of clayey, plastic soils that create serious problems for foundations, streets, and all building appurtenances. The recognition and modification of these resource areas for urban-suburban uses are essential.

4. High-density development in and close to natural drainage ways is hazardous. Although flood-prone land areas are not extensive, they severely restrict urban-suburban uses and their use should be limited to recreation, green belts, and parks. As the hydrologic characteristics in watersheds are changed by urban development, the flooding potential is greatly increased.

The Coastal Plain

On the Coastal Plain, physical limitations on urban-suburban development are largely related to internal and external drainage, soil texture, and the organic content of the soil. For urban-suburban development in this region, the following soil characteristics are most significant:

1. Erosion and sediment control are not major problems and are confined to the more sloping lands of the northern Coastal Plain. But flooding is a problem, and floodplain land areas are generally best suited for recreational activities or farm uses.

2. Many soils are seasonally wet. This limits the usefulness of the land area as waste sinks and generally renders the land area unstable for foundations and traffic ways.

3. Soils of either slow or rapid percolation will contribute to pollution problems where soils are used as waste sinks. Both types are present in the Coastal Plain.

4. The organic soils and soils with organic hard pans present special problems in urban-suburban development in the Coastal Plain. These soils are poorly suited for many nonfarm uses. They are not suitable as waste disposal areas when intensively drained.

High water tables, clayey soils with slow percolation rates, organic soils, and soils with impermeable hard pans are the principal limitations on about two-thirds of the soils in the region. All nonfarm uses of these soils will encounter waste disposal and pollution hazards without extensive modification. Urban-suburban uses of these soils generally require that special measures be undertaken to correct soil limitations prior to development, for failure to correct results in environmental deterioration. The other third of soil resources is well drained and has characteristics very favorable for engineering uses. Percolation rates are favorable, providing good waste disposal areas where soils are not subject to continuous saturation.

Selected References

Beyer, F. *North Carolina: The Years before Man.* Durham: Carolina Academic Press, 1991.

Brady, N., and R. Weil. *The Nature and Properties of Soils.* 12th ed. Upper Saddle River, N.J.: Prentice-Hall, 1999.

Brown, C. *Vegetation of the Outer Banks of North Carolina.* Baton Rouge: Louisiana State University Press, 1959.

Cabe, S., and R. Reiman. "Sandhills of the Carolinas." In *Snapshots of the Carolinas: Landscapes and Cultures*, edited by G. Gordon Bennett, pp. 83–86. Washington, D.C.: Association of American Geographers, 1996.

Carpenter, P. A. I., ed. *A Geologic Guide to North Carolina's State Parks.* Bulletin 91. Raleigh: North Carolina Geological Survey, 1989.

Foth, H., and J. Schaffer. *Soil Geography and Land Use.* New York: John Wiley and Sons, 1980.

Hardin, J. *Poisonous Plants of North Carolina.* Raleigh: North Carolina State University, Agricultural Experiment Station, 1961.

———. *Guide to the Literature on Plants of North Carolina.* Raleigh: North Carolina Agricultural Extension Service, 1975.

Hidore, J., and J. Patton. "North Carolina Hurricanes." In *Snapshots of the Carolinas: Landscapes and Cultures*, edited by G. Gordon Bennett, pp. 69–72. Washington, D.C.: Association of American Geographers, 1996.

Horton, J. W., Jr., and V. A. Zullo, eds. *The Geology of the Carolinas.* Knoxville: University of Tennessee Press, 1991.

Jahn, L. *Forestry and Forest Products in North Carolina.* Raleigh: North Carolina Cooperative Extension Service, 1994.

Martin, W. "Storm Hazard Zones along the Outer Banks of North Carolina." *North Carolina Geographer* 2 (1993): 1–11.

Radford, A. E., H. E. Ahles, and C. R. Bell. *Manual of the Vascular Flora of the Carolinas.* Chapel Hill: University of North Carolina Press, 1968.

Robinson, P. "The Spatial Scale of Daily Precipitation in North Carolina." *North Carolina Geographer* 2 (1993): 12–20.

———. "A View of Western North Carolina's Climate." *North Carolina Geographer* 5 (1996): 11–20.

Ross, T. "Carolina Bays: Coastal Plain Enigma." In *Snapshots of the Carolinas: Landscapes and Cultures*, edited by G. Gordon Bennett, pp. 77–82. Washington, D.C.: Association of American Geographers, 1996.

Soule, P. "North Carolina's Climate." In *Snapshots of the Carolinas*, ed. Bennett, pp. 66–68.

Steila, D. *The Geography of Soils.* Englewood Cliffs, N.J.: Prentice-Hall, 1976.

U.S. Department of Agriculture. Natural Resources Conservation Service. *Soil Taxonomy: A Basic System of Soil Classification for Making and Interpreting Soil Surveys.* 2d ed. 1998.

Wells, B. *The Natural Gardens of North Carolina.* Chapel Hill: University of North Carolina Press, 1967.

Wilbur, R. *The Leguminous Plants of North Carolina.* Raleigh: North Carolina Agricultural Experiment Station, 1963.

3. HISTORY

David R. Goldfield

Through much of history, North Carolinians have perceived their state as an egalitarian haven of progressive farmers and small-town merchants. They have proudly distinguished themselves from their neighbors in haughty Virginia and pretentious South Carolina, a sort of "vale of humility between two mountains of conceit." North Carolinians have pointed to their state motto, *Esse Quam Videri* (to be, rather than to seem), as their guide for personal conduct as well. And in some periods this perception accurately reflected the facts.

But North Carolina is also a southern state and has shared the racial angst of the South and the corresponding ills that have flowed from a society based, until recent decades, on white supremacy. Rural and small-town implies an emphasis on hearth and kin and community responsibility; but it also has meant isolation, provincialism, and low educational attainment. Much of the North Carolina experience has involved attempts to break the negative aspects of the state's characteristic settlement pattern. The transformation to a thriving metropolitan, postindustrial economy centered in the Piedmont region at the end of the twentieth century played a major role in ratifying the perception of North Carolina as a progressive southern state. Today, North

Carolinians—natives and transplants alike—feel good about their state. More than 90 percent of them would not live anywhere else, the highest percentage of satisfaction with one's home state in the nation.

Beginnings

Such a destiny was hardly prefigured ten thousand years ago when the first arrivals hunted the incomparable forests of hardwood and pine. Gradually, the peoples of what would become North Carolina relied more on agriculture than on hunting for their sustenance. By A.D. 1200 small agricultural villages appeared along the rivers from the Coast to the Piedmont, and by 1500 the indigenous tribes had withstood an invasion of Creek Indians from present-day Alabama and Georgia. But they would not survive the next invasion.

The voyages of Christopher Columbus had fired the European imagination of a passage to the Orient. Italian navigator Giovanni da Verrazzano, under French employ, set sail for China in 1524 and landed along the Carolina coast just north of Cape Fear. Sailing northeastward to Ocracoke, he came upon his gateway to the Pacific, or so he thought. Verrazzano gazed to the northwest and confidently recorded in his log, "we could see the eastern sea from the ship. This doubtless is the one which goes around the tip of India, China, and Cathay." The

Figure 3.1. John White, *La Virgenia Pars*, 1585 MS A.

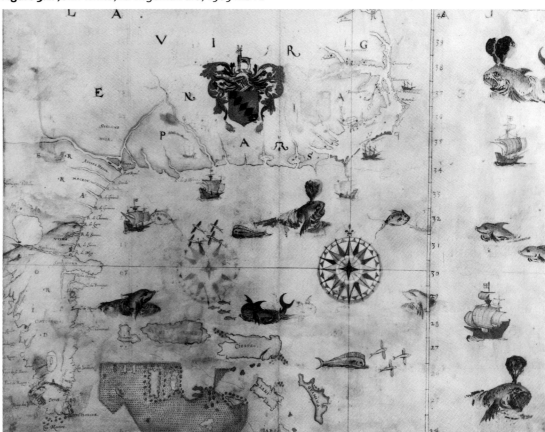

Source: British Museum, Department of Prints and Drawings, 1906-5-9-1(2).

navigator had confused Pamlico Sound with the Pacific Ocean. The mistake persisted on European maps and in the European consciousness for nearly a century. A map made by Englishman John White in the 1580s shows the coast extending due west from the Outer Banks toward southern California (Fig. 3.1). This placed most of North Carolina under water.

In the meantime, Spain renewed its quest for the elusive passage as Hernando de Soto led six hundred men on a futile mission through the Carolina backcountry. A few decades later Juan

Pardo extended de Soto's search and was similarly disappointed. By the 1560s the Spanish were convinced that North Carolina (or "La Florida," as they called that part of their domain) existed and the water route to the East did not.

But in those days word traveled slowly, and Spain and England were not on cordial speaking terms in any case. The English continued to believe in the existence of the "Sea of Verrazzano," as Sir Walter Raleigh's expeditions to the New World in the 1580s indicated. After a series of false starts along the Outer Banks, John White settled a colony on Roanoke Island in 1587. This became the famous "Lost Colony." Hostilities with Spain and internal political problems postponed further English attempts until 1607, when Captain John Smith established the first permanent English settlement at Jamestown, Virginia.

Although James I had included North Carolina as part of the Virginia grant, no permanent white settlement got under way there until the 1660s. By that time Virginia was well established, and its ambitious young men, many of them former indentured servants, sought land. They moved southward into the Albemarle frontier and settled along the Pasquotank, Perquimans, and Chowan Rivers, purchasing land from the Indians and planting the cash crop they knew best, tobacco.

These early settlers struggled because of North Carolina's difficult topography, a factor that would keep the colony's population modest, dispersed, and relatively poor. Albemarle Sound's shoals and the treacherous waters off the Outer Banks discouraged oceangoing vessels. Unable to ship their tobacco directly to England, early North Carolina farmers looked to Virginia outlets. But swamps and the lack of roads inhibited transportation. Nevertheless, Virginians continued to move south and in 1663 King Charles II granted the province of Carolina (which included present-day Florida north to the Virginia border) to eight supporters, the Lords Proprietors, thus ending North Carolina's apprenticeship as an appendage of Virginia.

For the remainder of the seventeenth century, settlement in North Carolina proceeded from Virginia migration, first into the Albemarle region, then into the Pamlico district. Eventually, such colonial towns as Edenton, Bath, New Bern, and Beaufort emerged. Another milestone occurred in 1689, when the Proprietors separated North and South Carolina. By 1710 the new, sparsely settled province had a capital at Edenton.

By that date the colony also had another cash crop: naval stores. England sought relief from its dependence on Sweden and Finland for tar, turpentine, pitch, and hemp, essential products for seagoing vessels. The Crown established a subsidy for these commodities, and the ample pine forests behind the North Carolina coast provided abundant and high-quality naval stores. Until 1710 the vast majority of the colony's population consisted of Indians and Virginians. But in that year, a group of Swiss and German immigrants arrived in the Pamlico district and established the town of New Bern. This was the first of many migrations that added to the growing diversity of North Carolina. The settlers were so successful in their new environment that the capital of the colony shifted to New Bern in 1770.

But the continued migration of Virginians, as well as the new settlement of Germans and Swiss, caused growing alarm among the Indian populations, already depleted by smallpox and the periodic skirmishes among themselves and with the English. In addition, white traders, mainly from South Carolina, periodically cheated the Indians and trafficked in Indian slaves. With their hunting lands diminishing and exploitation by white traders increasing, the Tuscarora launched an attack on white settlements near New Bern in 1711. The conflict raged on and off for four years, retarding white encroachment but also resulting in the loss of half the tribe and opening the remainder of its lands to future incursions. The surviving Tuscarora fled North Carolina and returned to New York.

The removal of the Indian threat encouraged further migration. But the key event that affected the colony's development until the time of the Revolution was King George II's takeover of North Carolina from the heirs of the Lords Proprietors in 1729. A decade earlier, the British Crown had assumed control of South Carolina, so the move was

Figure 3.2. The Development of the Frontier, 1657–1835

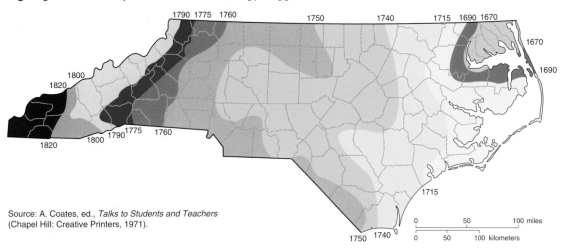

Source: A. Coates, ed., *Talks to Students and Teachers* (Chapel Hill: Creative Printers, 1971).

Figure 3.3. Avenues of Early Settlement

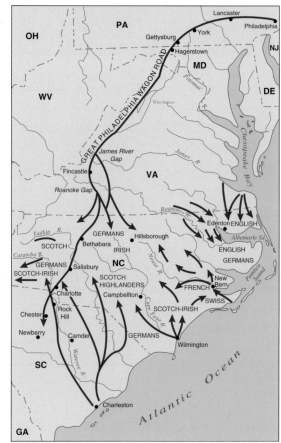

Source: C. Camp, ed., *Influence of Geography upon Early North Carolina* (Raleigh: Carolina Charter Tercentenary Commission, 1963).

not unprecedented. Besides exchanging a government with weak executive authority and frequent turnover for an administration that offered stability and continuity, the change generated a land bonanza in the colony as the Crown eased land purchase requirements and sent out the equivalent of real estate agents to drum up business.

Their work, and the encouragement of royal governors, touched off a boom in North Carolina that lasted from 1730 to the American Revolution. Forests along the Coastal Plain were leveled for farms, settlers poured into the backcountry, and the line of settlement extended to the Blue Ridge Mountains (Fig. 3.2). In addition to farms, newcomers built mills, constructed roads, and erected lighthouses along the coast.

The origins of the newcomers varied widely. South Carolinians moved north into the Lower Cape Fear area to establish pine plantations with African slave labor. As land grew scarce in Pennsylvania, Maryland, and Virginia after 1730, migrants trekked down the Great Wagon road that began near Philadelphia and extended southwestward to the Shenandoah Valley before veering east onto the North and South Carolina Piedmont (Fig. 3.3). These newcomers included a variety of ethnic and religious groups, among them Quakers, German Lutherans, German Moravians, Scots-Irish Presbyterians, and Baptists. Settling primarily on the Piedmont, they contrasted with the mostly English and African coastal areas and, in fact, had little contact with them. The rivers of the Piedmont

flowed into the South Carolina colony, and that is the route that commerce and communications followed as well. By the mid-eighteenth century residents of Piedmont North Carolina had more contact with Pennsylvania than they did with the coastal district of their own colony.

Hoi Toide: *The Ocracoke Brogue*

The Outer Banks of North Carolina are distinctive in a number of ways. This long chain of islands lies as much as 20 miles off the mainland coast. Wild ponies roamed at will. Hundreds of ships sank on the shallow, off-shore shoals. But perhaps most distinctive is a dialect spoken by longtime natives that is known as the "Ocracoke Brogue."

It is comprised of pronunciations that are likened by some to Elizabethan English. Odd pronunciations include calling a high tide a "Hoi Toide" and the word "town" comes out sounding more like "tain." Ocracokers are apt to say "People goes to the store" or "It weren' t me." Most difficult for a dingbatter *(an outsider) to understand are the many unusual words used. Examples include the following:*

Begombed—to be soiled
Doast—a cold or influenza
Fladget—a piece of something
Goaty—foul smelling
Meehonkey—a game of hide-and-seek
Mommuck—to bother someone
Pizer—a porch on a house
Quamished—sick to the stomach
Whipstitch—Every now and then, sporadically

Legend has it that the brogue is a relic of the seventeenth century when the area was first settled by English people, perhaps going back to Sir Walter Raleigh's Roanoke Island colony that disappeared so mysteriously in 1597. Linguists, such as Walt Wolfram and Natalie Schilling-Estes, however, attribute only some of its origins to the early English settlers. More likely is that the dialect emerged independently over the years as the inhabitants of the island remained isolated from their mainland compatriots, an example of the way a common language often develops in different ways when groups of speakers are isolated from each other for generations. Unfortunately, the quaint Ocracoke brogue seems to be disappearing fast as the Outer Banks are inundated by the thousands of dingbatter tourists and new residents who are pouring into the islands.

Walt Wolfram and Natalie Schilling-Estes, Hoi Toide on the Outer Banks *(Chapel Hill: University of North Carolina Press, 1997)*

In 1730 the colony consisted of 30,000 whites and 6,000 blacks, almost all of whom lived along the Coastal Plain; by 1775 the population had grown to 265,000 inhabitants, including 10,000 blacks, and settlement was scattered from the Coast to the Mountains (Fig. 3.4). By the latter year, North Carolina was the fourth most populous of the thirteen colonies. Moreover, its residents were among the most diverse, with some estimates placing the German settlers as high as 30 percent of the total.

The newcomers tended to sharpen distinctions between the Piedmont and Coastal regions of North Carolina. Similar geographic divisions existed in the other southern colonies, but Virginians had managed to soften conflict by creating new counties and providing them with self-governing political and religious institutions. This was not the case in North Carolina, where a narrow group of royal favorites headquartered in eastern towns such as Edenton and New Bern directed colonial policy and appointed officials in the backcountry areas.

Tight money, fluctuating crop prices, and a regressive tax structure threatened the independence of backcountry farmers. A few merchants, lawyers, and public officials with close connections to coastal elites controlled the financial and political machinery of these districts. By the mid-1760s, when colonists throughout North America reassessed the meaning of freedom within the British Empire, a group of North Carolina backcountry farmers resolved to "regulate" local officials. Led by a prosperous farmer and Quaker, Herman Husband, the "Regulators" sought an end to regressive taxes, official arrogance, and underrepresentation. Between 1766 and 1770 violence flared periodically between the royal government and the Regulators, culminating in the Battle of Alamance and the defeat of the backcountry partisans.

Although some of the backcountry leaders used the rhetoric of class conflict to incite their poorer neighbors, the Regulation was not a class struggle, nor was it a preview of the American Revolution in North Carolina. But it was indicative of a recurring theme in the colony's and later the state's history: the reluctance of mostly eastern elites to part with power.

The American Revolution in North Carolina took on the character of a civil war. The patriot cause was most prominent in the eastern part of the colony, where leaders were most involved in the Atlantic economy and hence most affected by British trade and tax policies. But serious obstacles to independence emerged in 1775. Although royal governor Josiah Martin (1771–75) had left the capital of New Bern for a safer haven offshore, he rallied Highland Scots and some former Regulators to the cause of the Crown. In addition, Lord Dunmore, Virginia's royal governor, encouraged slaves in the Albemarle region to revolt against their masters in exchange for freedom. From South Carolina, upcountry Tories threatened settlements in the North Carolina Piedmont. And in the western reaches of the colony, British agents stirred the enmity of Indian tribes against the patriots.

The Battle of Moores Creek Bridge in February 1776 was a critical patriot victory against an expatriate force of Scots Highlanders who were heading toward Wilmington to join up with the British army. The battle neutralized Tory efforts in the region and delayed British occupation of the South until 1780. But the euphoria over Moores Creek soon dissipated when the Creeks and the Cherokee launched a concerted attack along the western frontier in the spring of 1776. Coordinating with troops from other colonies, North Carolina's pa-

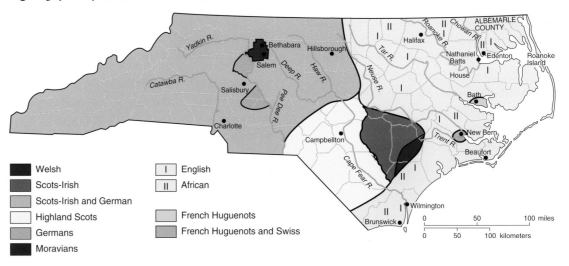

Figure 3.4. European and African Settlement

Welsh
Scots-Irish
Scots-Irish and German
Highland Scots
Germans
Moravians
I English
II African
French Huguenots
French Huguenots and Swiss

Source: A. Coates, ed., *Talks to Students and Teachers* (Chapel Hill: Creative Printers, 1971).

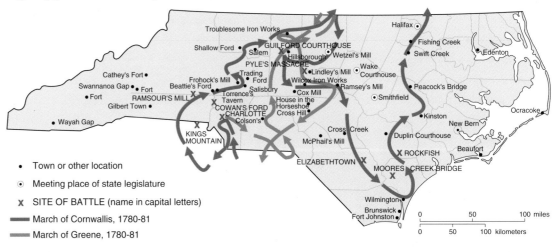

Figure 3.5. The Revolutionary War

• Town or other location
⊙ Meeting place of state legislature
X SITE OF BATTLE (name in capital letters)
— March of Cornwallis, 1780-81
— March of Greene, 1780-81

Source: R. E. Lonsdale, ed., *Atlas of North Carolina* (Chapel Hill: University of North Carolina Press, 1967).

triot forces defeated the Indian coalition by May 1777. Fortunately for the patriots, the British were occupied in the northern colonies during the conflict.

When the British finally turned their attention southward in early 1780, their lightning success in subjugating coastal South Carolina and much of Georgia alarmed North Carolinians. Troops led by General Charles Cornwallis hoped to conquer the colony by rallying loyal forces in the backcountry. Setting up headquarters at Charlotte in the midst of a "Hornets Nest" of hostile Scots-Irish Presbyterians, Cornwallis mapped out his campaign. But a smashing victory by patriot forces at Kings Mountain and later at Cowpens in South Carolina caused Cornwallis to retreat from the Carolinas, toward Yorktown (Fig. 3.5).

New State, New Nation

In the process of forming a new nation, North Carolina resembled most other states in establishing a weak executive and maintaining property-holding qualifications for officeholding. The new state constitution gave propertyless residents the right to vote, but eastern planters and merchants dominated the legislature.

The Revolution seems to have exhausted the citizens of North Carolina as they fell into a half century of decline. As early as 1786, a traveler who went from Edenton to Charlotte found the people "in a state of mental degradation." Forty years later, Governor Hutchins G. Burton (1824–27) noted that residents had been better educated in 1776 than they were in 1826. While other states expanded boundaries, built roads and canals, and made other internal improvements, as well as boosted their educational systems, North Carolina stood still.

Historian William Powell attributes the post-Revolutionary inertia to the isolation and individualism of the people. Most of the farms were self-sustaining, and few farmers had links to the outside world. A cosmopolitan out-

Figure 3.6. Historical Evolution of County Boundaries

a. 1760

b. 1800

c. 1912

Note: The current delineation of counties was completed in 1912.

Source: J. W. Clay, D. M. Orr Jr., and A. W. Stuart, eds., *North Carolina Atlas: Portrait of a Changing Southern State* (Chapel Hill: University of North Carolina Press, 1975).

look, a belief in improvement for the future, and a willingness to pay taxes to educate their children were lacking. The existence of slavery, which soaked up investments and encouraged planters to maintain a low tax base, also was part of the problem. The planters' profligacy with the soil and competition from new lands in Alabama, Mississippi, and Louisiana further depressed the state's economy and encouraged families to emigrate. Between 1815 and 1850 one-third of North Carolina's population left the state. During the early nineteenth century, neighboring states referred to North Carolina as the "Rip Van Winkle State," stuck in an earlier era and seemingly unable to wake up and respond to either a stagnant economy or the loss of its young people.

Still, the government, controlled by a minority of whites in the eastern counties who were jealous of their power and unwilling to share it with the rising population of the Piedmont, seemed content with the status quo. Each county had the same number of representatives to the legislature, regardless of population, and officeholding remained the privilege of property holders. Between 1790 and 1840 the counties east of Wake County experienced a 53 percent increase in population, compared with a 156 percent increase in the west. But the east controlled the legislature and only grudgingly created new counties (and hence representatives). As new counties were formed in the west, the legislature also increased the number of east-

ern counties by continually subdividing the existing ones. This ensured that the new western counties did not outnumber their eastern counterparts. This is illustrated in Figure 3.6, which shows county outlines in 1780, 1800, and 1912. By the latter year the current pattern was established.

Western legislators eventually convinced enough easterners that the best interests of the state required a revised political system. In 1835 the lawmakers framed a new constitution that based representation in the lower house of the General Assembly on population. The injection of energetic westerners into the state government touched

off a second boom period in North Carolina that lasted until the Civil War. In 1839 the General Assembly passed the state's first public school law, and the following year the first public school opened in Rockingham County. Within a decade more than 2,600 public schools appeared throughout the state.

North Carolina also invested in internal improvements such as roads and railroads and promoted the establishment of banks and industry, though communications between the state's geographic divisions remained poor through the 1840s. Many Piedmont farmers with agricultural

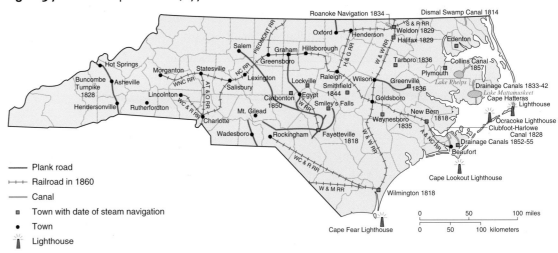

Figure 3.7. Internal Improvements, 1776–1860

Source: A. Coates, ed., *Talks to Students and Teachers* (Chapel Hill: Creative Printers, 1971).

Early North Carolina railroad in Elizabeth City

surpluses traveled the Yadkin and Catawba Rivers into South Carolina because the roads in North Carolina remained unreliable. A frustrated Governor John M. Morehead (1841–45) claimed in 1842 that it cost half the value of a farmer's crop "to transport the other [half] to market."

In the 1840s and 1850s the state plunged heavily into railroad construction to overcome geographic isolation (Fig. 3.7). State and private subscriptions constructed nine hundred miles of railroad by the time of the Civil War, and the treasury incurred a debt of $9 million. The North Carolina Railroad was the key facility as it connected the eastern portion of the state with the Piedmont, extending from Goldsboro to Raleigh to Charlotte in 1856. The railroad served as an early architect of the urban Piedmont Crescent that transformed the state's economy in the twentieth century. The cres-

Figure 3.8. Slave Population, 1850

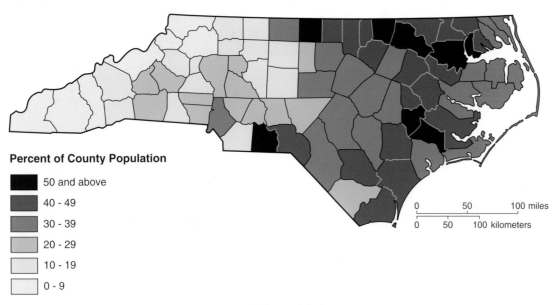

Percent of County Population

- 50 and above
- 40 - 49
- 30 - 39
- 20 - 29
- 10 - 19
- 0 - 9

0   50   100 miles

0   50   100 kilometers

Note: Total number of slaves in 1850 = 288,548 (33% of N.C. population).
County boundaries are shown as they were drawn in 1850.

Source: R. E. Lonsdale, ed., *Atlas of North Carolina* (Chapel Hill: University of North Carolina Press, 1967).

cent extended from Raleigh (and later Durham and Chapel Hill) to what would become the Triad (Winston-Salem, High Point, and Greensboro), and to Charlotte. More immediately, the North Carolina Railroad cut the farmers' transportation costs in half, although only those with substantial surpluses could use the railroad profitably. Most Tar Heel farmers did not send their produce to market via railroads, but they bore the heaviest tax burden to pay for the system.

Poor transportation and a subsistence agricul-tural economy limited capital formation and the prospect of manufacturing investments. Industrial development remained primitive and closely tied to the land. In 1860 turpentine production was the state's leading industry, with corn and wheat mill-ing a close second. By the same year North Caro-lina possessed thirty-nine textile mills, more than any other southern state, but most were small op-erations. Textile milling stood no better than fifth in the state's industrial output, and few firms com-peted on a regional or national scale. Whatever

transportation improvements occurred during the late antebellum era generally served to increase manufactured imports into the state and dampen industrial potential.

Despite the economic and transportation im-provements, the lives of most North Carolinians changed little from the end of the Revolution to the beginning of the Civil War. The cycle of farm-work determined their existence. Naval stores remained the primary cash "crop," with tobacco second, although corn was the most widely culti-vated, reflecting both home consumption and the growth of livestock farming. The average farm size declined as one moved westward in the state, as did the number of slaves. The few towns strung along the rivers paled in comparison with Charleston in South Carolina and Norfolk and Richmond in Vir-ginia. And residents lived most of their lives with-out venturing into other parts of the state.

For all their relative isolation from each other, North Carolinians shared some common features of life and economy. The typical antebellum North Carolina farm held less than one hundred acres. The average farmer lived in a three-room log or frame house, owned no slaves, and grew corn as his leading crop; his wife and children worked alongside him in the fields. He also cultivated squash, turnips, cucumbers, onions, and sweet po-tatoes, sometimes in sufficient abundance to mar-ket the surplus in the nearby town. Livestock pro-vided an important food source as well as some extra income. But usually the farmer barely earned enough to cover expenses at the town store for such staples as salt, sugar, and coffee. Storekeepers often marked up goods 100 percent, reflecting both high transportation costs and the fact that nearly everyone bought on credit, waiting for their crops to be sold. Purchasing the latest farm implements or work animals was unlikely, so farming methods remained as they were in the eighteenth century. Leisure activity revolved around family and church, and farm cycles such as corn-shucking time often dictated entertainment.

On the eastern plantations, such as Somerset Place, a different pattern emerged. There, white women rarely worked outside the house; the white master was the patriarchal leader of both his family and his slaves. Although the plantations of antebellum North Carolina were not as grand as in neighboring South Carolina, the slave's life did not differ significantly from that of slaves in other parts of the South.

Slave quarters were rudimentary; the surviving two-story structures at Horton Grove near Durham were unusual for their spaciousness. Slaves, organized into gangs, performed the backbreaking work of worming tobacco or chopping (weeding) cotton. Some slaves managed to perfect artisan skills, learn to read and write (although this was illegal), and grow garden crops that they sold in town with or without their masters' knowledge. After the "Second Great Awakening" during the early 1800s, some masters converted their slaves to Christianity. Slaves embraced Christianity, of-

A pioneer farmstead in what is now Great Smoky Mountains National Park

ten blending African and American customs and manipulating biblical parables for their own purposes.

But Christianity was not a saving grace for slaves. Few of them, even house servants, escaped the lash. And although family ties were important to slaves, the cruel fact of slavery meant that no matter how kind a master was, his sudden death, the marriage of one of his children, or economic misfortune often resulted in the breakup of slave families. Despite slaveholders' claims to the contrary, slaves could expect to be sold at least once in their lifetime.

Slaves had several means to register protest, most of them only temporarily effective. Because the white population of North Carolina outnumbered the black population by a two-to-one margin, armed slave rebellions were improbable. From

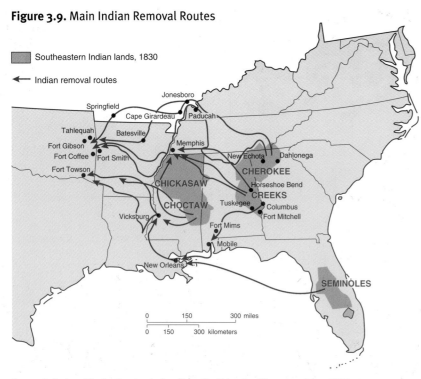

Figure 3.9. Main Indian Removal Routes

Southeastern Indian lands, 1830

← Indian removal routes

Jonesboro
Springfield
Cape Girardeau
Paducah
Tahlequah
Batesville
Fort Gibson
Memphis
Fort Coffee
Fort Smith
New Echota
Dahlonega
Fort Towson
CHEROKEE
CHICKASAW
Horseshoe Bend
CREEKS
CHOCTAW
Tuskegee
Columbus
Vicksburg
Fort Mitchell
Fort Mims
Mobile
New Orleans
SEMINOLES

0   150   300 miles
0   150   300 kilometers

Source: C. Hudson, *The Southeastern Indians* (Knoxville: University of Tennessee Press, 1976).

the white people's agriculture and religion, as well as the English language. Much of this adaptation occurred within the tribe in Georgia. But the success of the Americanized Cherokee aroused the hostility of covetous white neighbors, and, beginning in 1835, the federal government ordered the removal of the Cherokee from the Southeast to present-day Oklahoma along the infamous "Trail of Tears" (Fig. 3.9). A small band of Cherokee evaded federal authorities and hid deep in the North Carolina mountains, where their descendants remain today.

Civil War and Reconstruction

The state of small farms and towns was unprepared for the Civil War and, in fact, did not want to fight initially. Though divided by geography, social status, race, ethnicity, and religion, North Carolinians managed to agree that Abraham Lincoln's election in 1860 did not justify leaving the Union. But when Lincoln called upon North Carolina troops to put down the rebellion in South Carolina after the firing on Fort Sumter in April 1861, secession sentiment overwhelmed the caution of previous months. North Carolina did not finalize its decision until more than a month later, on May 20, 1861. A reluctant member of the Confederacy, North Carolina would lose forty thousand men to the cause, more than any other southern state, and better than one-third of its population would be freed from bondage.

North Carolina troops spent a good deal of their time fighting in Virginia, where many of the war's crucial operations occurred. Eastern North Carolina fell under Union control early in the war as Federal forces took the Outer Banks in August 1861; by March 1862 they had established headquarters at New Bern. The Yankee invasion had not united Tar Heels behind the Confederate war effort. As Confederate fortunes wavered in late 1862 and especially after the reverses at Gettysburg and Vicksburg in July 1863, dissident voices grew louder. In Washington County in eastern North Carolina, intermittent warfare erupted between yeomen and landless farmers and wealthy planta-

time to time, rumors surfaced of an impending slave uprising, as in 1800 in the aftermath of Gabriel's aborted conspiracy in Richmond, Virginia, when several alleged conspirators in North Carolina were hanged. But no concrete evidence of plots has surfaced. Rather, slaves resorted to more subtle forms of resistance like slowing the pace of work, sabotaging equipment or buildings, feigning illness, and running away.

While blacks and whites shared the eastern part of the state (Fig. 3.8), white yeomen farmers dominated the Piedmont and constantly pushed back the western frontier where the Cherokee resided. The Cherokee had undergone a remarkable transformation by the early 1800s. They had essentially adopted

tion owners. James Pettigrew, a prosperous land-owner, complained that those who lived "on the edge of the swamp thought that if the Yankees succeeded, the rich men would be forced to divide with them & all share alike." At Somerset Place, hundreds of landless men looted Josiah Collins's mansion.

Dissent was even greater in the Piedmont and the west where the Heroes of America, a pro-Union, pro-peace secret organization emerged, claiming a membership of ten thousand and using guerrilla tactics to disrupt Confederate operations and harass Confederate loyalists. As the desertion rate increased from Robert E. Lee's army after 1863, the mountains of North Carolina provided good hideouts for those seeking to avoid the authorities.

Women who sewed uniforms and flags, served in hospitals, and wrote inspirational poetry for the cause eventually succumbed to the futility of the war and the difficulties of maintaining households, cultivating crops, managing slaves, and living in the midst of lawlessness on both sides. Increasingly, beginning in 1863, their letters changed from encouragement to pleas to come home. Some women helped deserting husbands or relatives elude Confederate authorities. In Randolph County, two women allegedly torched a barn belonging to a state official in charge of rounding up deserters. A few Confederate leaders charged that women were primarily responsible for the high desertion rates during 1864. According to one North Carolina official: "Desertion takes place because

Figure 3.10. The Civil War

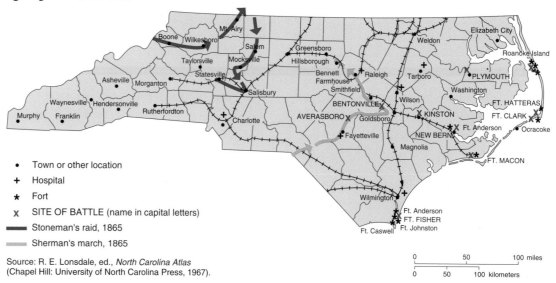

- ●   Town or other location
- +   Hospital
- ★   Fort
- X   SITE OF BATTLE (name in capital letters)
- ▬▬   Stoneman's raid, 1865
- ▬▬   Sherman's march, 1865

Source: R. E. Lonsdale, ed., *North Carolina Atlas*
(Chapel Hill: University of North Carolina Press, 1967).

desertion is encouraged. . . . And though the ladies may not be willing to concede the fact, they are nevertheless responsible . . . for the desertion in the army and the dissipation in the country."

But dissent from the war crossed gender lines. A growing number of North Carolina men spoke out against the curtailment of civil liberties, the large number of North Carolina soldiers killed defending other states, the grinding poverty that forced the state to provide relief for 20 to 40 percent of its white families, the so-called "twenty-nigger" law that exempted plantation owners from military service, and regressive tax laws. William Woods Holden's *North Carolina Standard*, published in Raleigh, became one of the strongest critics of

the Jefferson Davis administration in the South. Governor Zebulon B. Vance (1862–65, 1877–79), although a supporter of the war, guarded his state's sovereignty ferociously, withholding taxes and materiel from the central government in Richmond and at one point even threatening to secede from the Confederacy.

In January 1865 Federal forces took Fort Fisher and closed the Confederacy's last major port at Wilmington (Fig. 3.10). In March, General William T. Sherman crossed the Cape Fear River and established headquarters at Goldsboro to plan for a confrontation with Confederate General Joseph E. Johnston. The two armies clashed at Bentonville in the bloodiest conflict ever fought on North

Carolina soil. Although Johnston's army gave a good account of itself, Sherman prevailed. Once Lee surrendered, Johnston saw the futility of further struggle and in a meeting at Greensboro advised President Davis to fight no more. At the farmhouse of James Bennett near Durham Station on April 18, 1865, Johnston surrendered his army to Sherman. Except for a few bloody but meaningless raids in the western part of the state by Union general George Stoneman, the war in North Carolina was over.

As the Reconstruction era began, North Carolina faced many of the same daunting problems confronting other southern states. But the entry of freed slaves, one-third of the population, into a broader economic and political life, the discrediting of the eastern elites that had favored secession and war, and the influence of newcomers from the North all portended a new social and economic order for the state.

When congressional Reconstruction replaced President Andrew Johnson's conciliatory policies in 1867, North Carolina Republicans, led by William Woods Holden, organized a biracial party. The new state constitution of 1868, drafted under Republican leadership, was North Carolina's first truly democratic charter. County government positions were thrown open to the voters, and a public school system was established for both black and white youngsters. White yeomen and some blacks attained political office. However, the white supremacist Democratic Party, with strong assists

from paramilitary groups such as the Ku Klux Klan, used violence and intimidation to break the interracial coalition and overcome the Republicans. Reconstruction, for all intents and purposes, ended in 1870, when the Conservatives (Democrats) won control of the General Assembly. When Zebulon Vance was elected governor in 1876, the Democratic domination was complete.

New South Hopes, Old South Realities

As before the Civil War, agriculture remained at the center of the state's economy. The pattern of small farms and small towns persisted as well. But the lives of many Tar Heel farmers changed for the worse in the decades after 1865. Between 1865 and 1890 independent farming receded before sharecropping and tenantry (Fig. 3.11). Black freedmen and white landowners achieved a labor accommodation of sorts in the form of sharecropping. In exchange for one-half or one-third of the crop, black farmworkers usually received a house, farm implements, and the freedom to work the land as they saw fit. As cotton and tobacco became the major cash crops in a cash-poor region, more land was given over to them, resulting in overproduction, falling prices, and increasing debt. The economic situation not only ruined the fond hopes of blacks, but also forced numerous white landowners into dependence as well. By 1890 one of three white farmers and three of four black farmers were either

tenants or sharecroppers. Many others were in danger of losing their land. As merchants charged more for basic provisions (as larger merchants up North increased their prices to southern store owners) and as railroads increased freight rates, cotton and tobacco prices plummeted.

Beginning in the 1880s, farmers began to band together to press for political solutions to their economic hardships. The ruling Democrats did not address their problems. As the party of "Redemption"—that is, having redeemed the state from black and Republican rule—the Democrats maintained power by appealing to the patriotism of white southerners, a successful tactic that relieved them of taxing property owners to help poor farmers.

This is not to say that the Democrats reverted to the do-nothing politics of the early nineteenth century. They encouraged industrial development: North Carolina expanded its small textile industry and made significant strides in tobacco and furniture manufacturing. Urban banks and individual shareholders fueled this economic expansion; little investment came from outside the state. Railroad construction and consolidation supported industrial development. By 1900 more than 3,800 miles of track served the state. The Democrats had kindly provided railroad companies with relief from taxes and corporate regulations so that at the turn of the century three major lines connected North Carolina with the rest of the nation: the Seaboard Airline Railway, the Southern Railway, and

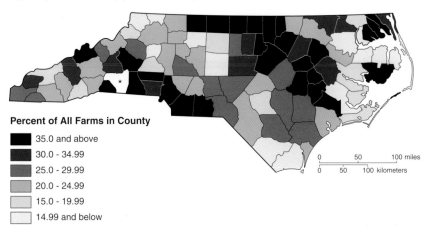

Figure 3.11. Sharecropped Farms, 1890

Percent of All Farms in County

- 35.0 and above
- 30.0 - 34.99
- 25.0 - 29.99
- 20.0 - 24.99
- 15.0 - 19.99
- 14.99 and below

*No data available for Rutherford County.

Note: County boundaries are shown as they were drawn in 1890.

Source: U.S. Census of Population, 1890.

the Atlantic Coast Line Railroad. All of these railroads ran, roughly, in a north-south direction (Fig. 3.12). The dream of a united eastern and western North Carolina, via a road or railroad, remained elusive.

The result of a business-oriented state government and the enterprise of industrialists was urban growth, especially in the Piedmont region. In 1870 only one town in North Carolina—Wilmington—possessed more than 10,000 inhabitants. By 1900 five additional towns had crossed that population threshold, four in the Piedmont (Charlotte, Winston, Raleigh, and Greensboro) and one in the Mountain region (Asheville). The urban growth reflected a shift in the state's economy to the towns and cities of the Piedmont, though North Carolina remained an overwhelmingly rural state (Fig. 3.13).

But in other policy areas, the Democrats faltered. Although Governor Vance led the way in chartering the Fayetteville Colored Normal School in 1877 to train black teachers, the first state-supported institution for blacks in the South, the General Assembly compiled a poor record on education be-

tween 1876 and 1900. Illiteracy was greater in North Carolina in 1880 than it had been in 1860, and the state held the dubious distinction of having the highest illiteracy rate in the nation. By 1900 only 37 percent of its children attended school regularly, even though the school term lasted only sixty days.

Democrats demonstrated considerably more vigor in putting down a political revolt of farmers that threatened to topple the ruling regime. By 1890 the Farmers Alliance, a national organization concerned about rising debt, tight credit, and high transportation costs, had grown to 90,000 members in North Carolina. The farmers formed cooperatives to exchange goods at wholesale prices. Items from seeds, to fertilizers, to cook stoves were sold through the co-ops, but the refusal of banks to extend credit limited their effectiveness. State legislators, primarily lawyers, merchants, and large landowners, would not ease credit restrictions, challenge railroad rates, or install a progressive tax structure. Beginning in 1890, a national political party, the People's or Populist Party, sought to articulate the concerns of workers and farmers around the country. Leonidas L. Polk, a Confederate veteran from North Carolina, became a leading spokesman for the new party and probably would have received its presidential nomination in 1892 were it not for his untimely death three weeks prior to the nominating convention.

North Carolina Populists openly challenged the dominant Democratic Party and joined with Republicans to oust the ruling elites from political office in 1894 on a platform of fair elections, improved education for all children, lower interest rates, and regulation of the railroads. The triumph of the "Fusion" ticket, as it was called, cut across class and race lines, and the Fusion legislature enacted a host of measures to ease the economic burdens and enhance the education and welfare of farmers and workers in the state, regardless of race. Fusion lawmakers restored much of the legislation from the Reconstruction era that Democrats had repealed. They increased funding for public education and social services, raised taxes on railroads and businesses, and enabled voters to choose their county governments again.

But race was the Achilles heel of the movement. Blacks holding office, challenging segregation and lobbying for economic relief, invited Democrats to

Figure 3.12. Railroads, 1899

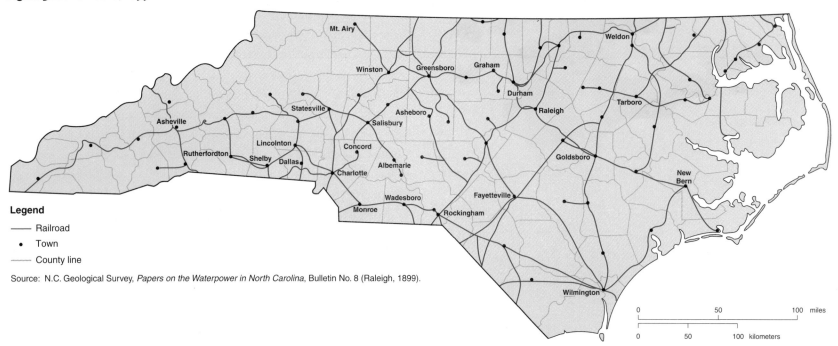

Legend

— Railroad

• Town

— County line

Source: N.C. Geological Survey, *Papers on the Waterpower in North Carolina*, Bulletin No. 8 (Raleigh, 1899).

raise the false specter of "Negro domination" and a return to the alleged abuses of the Reconstruction era. The Democratic Party launched a virulent white supremacist campaign in 1898. Well financed by the state's business leaders, the Democrats took control of the government and repealed the Fusion legislation. The bitter campaign and election incited a bloody race riot in Wilmington, where Democrats violently overthrew the legally elected Republican local government.

Democrats used the momentum from the 1898 election to ensure that the Fusion coalition of race and class would not recur. As had Democrats in most other southern states by this time, they successfully pushed for a state constitutional amendment in 1900 that effectively disfranchised black voters and some white voters. The *Charlotte Observer* promoted the amendment as "a struggle of the white people to rid themselves of the dangers of rule by Negroes and the lower class of whites." The amendment worked. In 1896, 87 percent of eligible blacks voted; in 1900, 67 percent; and by 1904, the figure dropped to less than 5 percent.

Meanwhile, white leaders pursued economic and political strategies to separate black and white interests further. As early as the 1880s, the white elite had expressed concerns about the growing dependence and desperate condition of whites on the farms. Some of the concern was genuine; some of it derived from the fear that discontented whites would shatter white solidarity and topple Democratic Party leaders. The events of the 1890s justified some of these fears.

North Carolina grew large amounts of cotton in the postwar decades, and large numbers of whites who struggled to make a living on the farm saw their lives degraded to the point where there was little social or economic distance between themselves and the former slaves. Charlotte entrepreneur D. A. Tompkins saw the social danger of an impoverished rural white population and the opportunities both the abundance of cotton and cheap labor would offer for textile manufacturing. Beginning in the 1880s, Tompkins became a leading proponent of the Cotton Mill Campaign to encourage the development of the textile industry in the Carolina Piedmont.

Textile milling had existed in North Carolina since before the Civil War. Michael Schenck, a German immigrant who had arrived from Pennsylvania around 1790, erected the state's first textile mill in Lincoln County in 1813. But by 1840 only twenty-five mills employing a total of 1,200 workers operated in the state. By the time of Tompkins's campaign, the number of spindles in North Carolina was barely 1 percent of the total for New England. And the mills manufactured almost exclusively for a local market.

But after 1880, the change was astonishing. The number of spindles operated in North Carolina nearly quadrupled between 1879 and 1889 and tripled between 1889 and 1899, reaching more than 1.1 million in the latter year. That total surpassed the number in either Connecticut, Maine, or Vermont. Although local entrepreneurs provided some of the capital and local workers all of the labor, external factors accounted for much of this increase. An urbanizing nation expanded the market for cloth. As millions of people moved from farms to cities, they lost both the opportunity and the time to make their own cloth or clothing. Also, established New England companies specialized in producing higher-quality cloth and were content to allow the fledgling southern industry to concentrate on producing cheaper cloth. Finally, northern capital rebuilt and expanded the southern rail network, connecting especially the Piedmont region with both the urban markets of the North and the western part of the South where most of the cotton grew. Railway lines extended into the river valleys of the Piedmont, opening numerous waterpower sites for mill development.

North Carolina mill developers followed the "Rhode Island model" by building isolated villages to house workers employed in one small water-

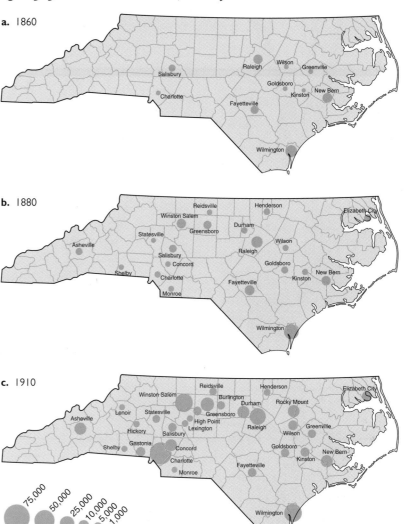

Figure 3.13. Urban Growth Patterns, 1860–1910

a. 1860

b. 1880

c. 1910

Urban Population

Source: J. W. Clay, D. M. Orr Jr., and A. W. Stuart, eds., *North Carolina Atlas: Portrait of a Changing Southern State* (Chapel Hill: University of North Carolina Press, 1975).

One of many early textile mill villages

powered mill. Entrepreneurs did not follow the "Waltham model," which concentrated a number of large mills along a series of canals that provided waterpower for each mill. In the Waltham model most workers lived in tenement housing, whereas the Rhode Island model featured small, company-owned homes, often including a garden plot, to house millworkers and their families.

Again borrowing from the experience of New England industrialists, the North Carolina mill owners used waterpower as their primary energy source. The fast-flowing streams of the Piedmont offered the greatest array of such energy sites in the state. Of the ninety-one cotton mills in North Carolina in 1890, at least seventy wholly or partially used waterpower. But nine years later, only 41 percent of the mills used waterpower and many of those supplemented their energy supply with the

more reliable and consistent steam engine (Fig. 3.14). By the early twentieth century improved technology for generating and transmitting electricity gave mill owners greater locational freedom. The industry continued to expand, and by 1929 southern textiles had surpassed New England in the number of spindles operating and the amount of cotton consumed. North Carolina led the South, accounting for over one-third of the spindles among the six leading southern states. More efficient southern mills, no longer satisfied with producing only cheap cloth, began taking markets away from the increasingly obsolete New England factories.

The textile industry reinforced the dispersed settlement pattern of North Carolina. In the North, industrialization reinforced urbanization. In the Carolinas, manufacturing enterprises, especially textiles, were located in mill villages and not in the cities of the Piedmont (Fig. 3.15). These modest towns were strung along the railroad line and seldom developed other economic functions. Workers moved from nearby farms to factories with relative ease and back again as their desires and pockets dictated. Mill owners consciously avoided the "bad influences" of the city, maintained control over the workforce, and located near the source of labor supply. Although subsistence wages and other forms of economic, religious, and social exploitation existed in the mill villages, a sense of camaraderie among the work-

Figure 3.14. Location of Cotton Mills, 1899

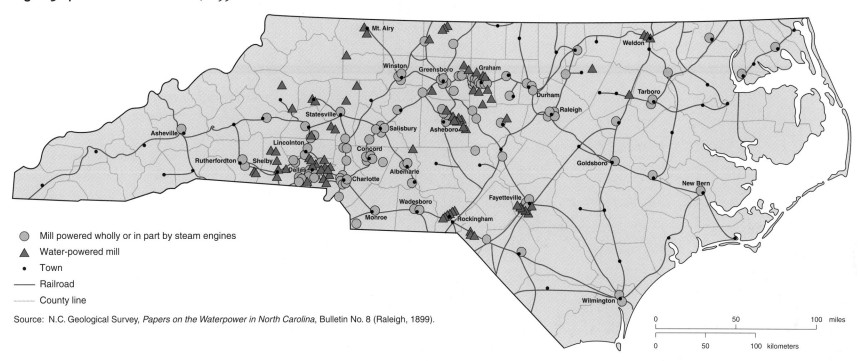

Mill powered wholly or in part by steam engines
Water-powered mill
Town
Railroad
County line

Source: N.C. Geological Survey, *Papers on the Waterpower in North Carolina*, Bulletin No. 8 (Raleigh, 1899).

force made life bearable. Family members often worked together at the mill, recruited kin for mill-work, and supported each other through difficult times. Low wages necessitated that everyone in the family work, including children and women. By the early twentieth century North Carolina led the nation in the percentage of its female workforce in manufacturing.

A smaller concentration of furniture plants in the northern Piedmont around High Point and Greensboro and in the western Mountains augmented the dispersion of people and jobs associated with textiles. By 1927 furniture manufacturing employed 15,000. Tobacco, textiles, and furniture comprised the "Big Three" of North Carolina industries that dominated the economy and leadership for decades.

Even today, barely half of all North Carolinians live within the boundaries of an incorporated municipality, though these "rural" residents may commute to a nearby city to work rather than to the local mill. Moreover, the values and attitudes associated with rural, small-town living, including strong antiunion attitudes, are still a major characteristic of North Carolina's culture and politics. Ironically, the state's strong rural character may owe more to its industrial history than to its agricultural heritage. And that rural character helped shape North Carolina politics in the twentieth century.

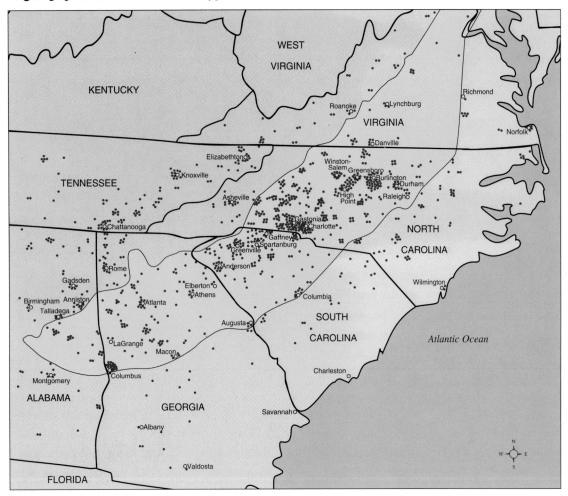

Figure 3.15. Location of Textile Mills, 1931

Piedmont region

• Manufacturing plant

○ Town

Source: Adapted from B. F. Lemert, *The Cotton Textile Industry of the Southern Appalachian Piedmont* (Chapel Hill: University of North Carolina Press, 1933).

The Democrats' second redemption, complete by 1900, inaugurated a period of almost seventy-five years of one-party rule in North Carolina. Recognizing the geographic divisions in the state, a gentleman's agreement prevailed during this era that Democratic governors would alternate, with one coming from the eastern part of the state one time and the western part of the state the next time. Governors could not succeed themselves. This practice continued until 1977, when an amendment to the state constitution permitted a governor to serve two successive terms.

The first Democratic governor of this second redemption was Charles Brantley Aycock (1901–5), who seized upon the new political stability to energize state government, particularly in the area of public education. Aycock became the first "education governor." He pressed for taxes to support education, arguing that educated children meant a better economy in the long run. The school term was extended to four months a year and the state gave more education money to poor counties, but many rural counties lacked high schools, even for whites, as late as 1910. Women's groups probably accomplished as much as the governor in upgrading facilities of public schools, although they focused on white schools.

Middle-class white women were also prominent in another early twentieth-century crusade in North Carolina, the prohibition of alcoholic beverages. Like the school issue, Prohibition emerged from women's church work. Southern men generally conceded the church's outreach activities to women. Because regional customs frowned on married middle-class white women working outside the home, church causes were one of the few avenues that ambitious and talented women could pursue. Although more black middle-class women worked outside the home (an economic necessity for them), they too became involved in school reform and Prohibition.

Prohibition in North Carolina, as school reform, was connected to race and class issues. As one Tar Heel Prohibition publicist noted in 1908, alcohol contributed to blacks' poverty and "fed their animalism." Alcohol also made "a considerable mass of the white population unable to resist the elemental impulse of lawlessness when racial antipathies are aroused." But the publicist's greatest fear was the possibility that blacks and whites might combine their forces. "The danger," he wrote, "is not in the upper but in the lower levels of both races. . . . [T]he lines of both races converge at the saloon. The intelligent white people of the South are . . . tired of the depraved and criminal Negro. They are tired of the irresponsible white man. The Liquor Traffic fosters and encourages both."

Despite the continuity in North Carolina's race and class relations during the half century after the Civil War, several changes occurred in the lifestyles of its citizens as well as in the state's economy. By 1920 North Carolina was the leading industrial state in the Southeast; its wealth had increased tenfold since 1900, and its bank resources jumped from $33 million to $456 million. The automobile was supplanting the horse, and paved roads were beginning to replace the muddy lanes that choked commerce and travel thanks to the tireless lobbying efforts of Harriet Morehead Berry, the "Mother of Good Roads." But the task of knitting together a geographically diverse state with a dispersed population living in scattered farms and small towns (although the outlines of future clusters of urbanization were evident in Charlotte, Raleigh-Durham, High Point, Greensboro, and Winston-Salem) would defy solution until well after World War II.

Nevertheless, during the 1920s the state made significant strides toward modernization. Governor Cameron Morrison (1921–25) became known as the "Good Roads Governor." As Aycock had touted education, Morrison's vision was to break the isolation of the rural parts of the state and begin to connect the disparate geographic divisions. He created a State Highway Commission and promoted bond issues totaling $65 million for the construction of state highways. Morrison also persuaded the legislature to increase funding for the struggling state institutions of higher education. Although upholding racial segregation, he was instrumental in establishing the North Carolina Commission on Interracial Cooperation, which opened an interracial dialogue for the first time since Reconstruction. Unlike many other southern politicians of the era, Morrison forcefully denounced lynching. His successor, Angus W. McLean (1925–29), continued the Good Roads program and streamlined state government. Figure 3.16 shows the state highway system in 1920 and its expansion under the federal highway system by 1962.

As North Carolina moved ahead, the rest of the nation advanced even more rapidly. And in some areas, the state regressed. Farm tenancy increased by 26 percent and per capita farm income declined to less than half the average for nonsouthern states during the first two decades of the twentieth century. A 1923 survey revealed that the average income of tenant farmers in Chatham County was nine cents a day. The amount of land devoted to cotton and tobacco increased from 21 percent to 31 percent between 1900 and 1920, which meant that Tar Heel farmers produced less food. A 1926 report concluded that "Drawing breath in the South and drawing rations from the West makes permanent farm prosperity well nigh impossible, no matter how large our tobacco and cotton crops, or how high the market prices."

The boost in manufacturing occurred on the backs of the men, women, and children who worked in the labor-intensive industries. North Carolina in 1919 ranked forty-fifth in the nation in the average factory wage. Even the Good Roads campaign was more promise than pavement. Scarce funds and the onset of the Great Depression limited road building. Not until the admin-

Figure 3.16. Highway Systems

a. State Highway System, 1920

b. Federal Highway System, 1962

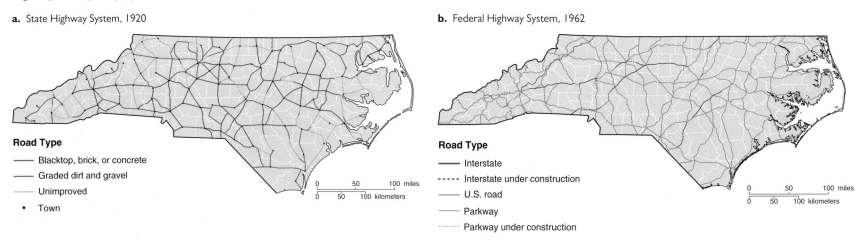

Road Type

—— Blacktop, brick, or concrete

—— Graded dirt and gravel

—— Unimproved

• Town

Road Type

—— Interstate

┅┅┅ Interstate under construction

—— U.S. road

—— Parkway

┄┄┄ Parkway under construction

Source: State Highway Commission, Raleigh.

istration of W. Kerr Scott (1949–53) did road building accelerate. Finally, the lives of black North Carolinians took a decided turn for the worse after 1900: not only were they deprived of political power, but also growing discrimination caused them to lose traditional occupations such as brick masonry to whites.

Yet blacks succeeded in making the most of a difficult situation by creating a community within the confines of a segregated society. That community began as early as the Reconstruction era, when several black colleges such as Freedman's College in Charlotte (later Johnson C. Smith University) and Shaw University in Raleigh were founded by northern ministers. By the 1890s black faculty and administrators staffed these institutions. In 1910 the first state-supported liberal arts college for blacks in the nation opened in Raleigh. The National Training School and Chautauqua later became North Carolina Central University.

The Wilmington riot of 1898 and the disfranchisement of blacks two years later redirected black efforts from politics to economic improvement. John Merrick of Durham concluded after the Wilmington riot that blacks must turn their "attention to making money. The almighty dollar is the magic wand that knocks the bottom out of race prejudice and all the humbugs that fatten on it." Merrick and six other black entrepreneurs and artisans formed the North Carolina Mutual Life Insurance Company in 1899 and within two decades developed it into a multimillion-dollar enterprise with a six-story building in the heart of "the Negro Wall Street of America" in Durham.

The Spirit of Enterprise

The entrepreneurial skills of Merrick and his colleagues reflected the growing economic opportunities available in the city even though only one in ten Tar Heels lived in an urban place in 1900. Perhaps the most significant urban success story of the late nineteenth and early twentieth centuries occurred in 1874, when Washington Duke gathered a predominantly black workforce and built a factory in Durham to produce cigarettes, an item of growing popularity in Europe but as yet untested in the United States. Duke revolutionized the nascent cigarette industry in the 1880s with a cigarette-making machine that turned out two hundred cigarettes a minute instead of four per minute by hand. Duke's son, James B. "Buck"

Duke, parlayed the family's achievement into the giant corporation, the American Tobacco Company, and other enterprises such as the Southern Power Company, incorporated in 1905, which powered numerous textile mills up and down the Piedmont. Willis Carrier, a young New Yorker, attracted by the reliability of Duke's hydroelectric power and the need for a controlled climate in textile plants, tested his invention that he called "air-conditioning" in a Belmont, North Carolina, textile mill in 1906, thus introducing to the South (and to America) an innovation that eventually changed the region dramatically.

Duke and Merrick were joined by several other entrepreneurs who used their urban settings to try out new ideas. Lunsford Richardson of Greensboro developed Vick's *Vaporub* in 1912; Edward Dilworth Latta introduced the electric streetcar to Charlotte in 1891 and went on to design the Carolinas' first planned suburb, Dilworth; Caleb Bradham, a pharmacist who dabbled with soft drinks, eventually came up with *Pepsi-Cola* in New Bern in 1896; and two Durham residents, German Bernard and Thomas Council, cured headaches after 1900 with their *BC Powder*. Richard Reynolds prospered with chewing and pipe tobacco until he decided to go into the cigarette business in 1914. That year he introduced *Camel* cigarettes, which, in the wake of a multimillion-dollar advertising campaign, became the nation's leading brand by 1920.

The fortunes generated by innovation and entrepreneurial skill in the late nineteenth and early twentieth centuries could be enormous. Reynolds invested some of his fortune in Reynolda House and Village in Winston-Salem, featuring a model farm designed by his wife, Mary Katherine Smith Reynolds. Entrepreneurs from outside North Carolina discovered the state and its salubrious climate and scenery as well. Asheville, whose pure air and water had attracted consumptives to America's first sanitarium in the 1870s, drew E. W. Grove, a St. Louis resident who had invented *Bromo-Seltzer* in 1896. He built the Grove Park Inn and advertised it as "the finest resort hotel in the world." George Vanderbilt, whose family made its fortune in the railroad and steamship industries, found Asheville and its environs so enchanting that he erected a country estate, the Biltmore, and turned the surrounding forest into a 100,000-acre laboratory that his heirs donated to the federal government to become part of the Pisgah National Forest. Finally, James Tufts, a soda fountain equipment manufacturer from Boston, wanted a place to play golf and heard about the healthful environment of the Sandhills in North Carolina. Pinehurst's first golf course was completed in 1898, and thereafter the resort became a mecca for wealthy easterners.

The spirit of enterprise placed North Carolina within (and sometimes ahead of) the national economic mainstream in the early twentieth century. Yet sometimes incidents would emerge that reminded progressive North Carolinians that their state still retained provincial attitudes with respect to race and dissent. In 1903 North Carolina native John Spencer Bassett, a professor at Trinity College (now Duke University), offered the opinion that next to Robert E. Lee, Booker T. Washington was the greatest southerner who ever lived. Bassett went on to suggest that blacks would eventually demand and be ready for equal rights. Under the blaring headline, PROF. BASSETT SAYS NEGRO WILL WIN EQUALITY AND SOUTHERN LEADERS SLANDERED, *Raleigh News and Observer* editor Josephus Daniels took Bassett to task. The professor weathered the resulting storm but soon left the state for a position at Smith College in Massachusetts.

The Spirit of Inquiry

By the 1920s more North Carolinians were willing to speak out on the state of their state. The University of North Carolina became the center for the state's critical self-analysis and sociologist Howard W. Odum its leading critic. Odum founded the Institute for Research in Social Science and a journal, *Social Forces*, which he and his colleagues used to investigate the human problems of North Carolina and the South. Previously taboo subjects such as lynching, sharecropping, child labor, and the teaching of evolution in the public schools came under Odum's social scientific scrutiny. His massive survey of southern resources and problems, *Southern Regions* (1936), became the standard reference work for a generation of southerners. Political and religious leaders pilloried Odum and his associates and demanded his ouster. But the university had friends in the legislature who had great respect for the president, Frank Porter Graham, and his efforts to bring the school into the front ranks of southern universities.

At the same time, at nearby Wake Forest College, President William L. Poteat provided a similar kind of progressive and inspirational leadership for the small Baptist-affiliated institution. By the 1930s Wake Forest, Duke, and the University of North Carolina were widely recognized as top universities in the South. Odum's major publisher, the University of North Carolina Press under the direction of W. T. Couch, achieved a national reputation for publishing the investigative work of the university's faculty.

Thomas Wolfe, a gifted writer from Asheville, was another major Tar Heel critic in the late 1920s and 1930s. In several of his novels, notably *Look Homeward, Angel* and *You Can't Go Home Again,* he railed against the mindless boosterism and religious hypocrisy of some of his neighbors.

Depression and War

Boosterism gave way in the 1930s to sometimes desperate attempts to restart the Tar Heel economy battered by the Great Depression. For farmers and textile workers, the depression was not news,

merely more of the same, as crop prices, especially for the two major crops, cotton and tobacco, had dropped steadily through the 1920s. North Carolina was still an overwhelmingly rural state in an urbanized and industrialized nation. In 1930 only one in four Tar Heels lived in the city. Family and church remained the focus of life in rural North Carolina.

Governor O. Max Gardner (1929–33) had the misfortune of being in office when the depression struck. The response it required from state government went considerably beyond both the philosophy and the practice of the ruling Democratic Party. One of Gardner's first acts was to call upon the Brookings Institution in Washington, D.C., to help him cut administrative expenditures while at the same time tending to the growing needs of a state in the midst of a national depression. One change involved the consolidation of the public university system. Frank Porter Graham became the first president of that consolidated system, which remains the model for many other states around the country.

Although administrative streamlining may have helped the state's bottom line, it did not address growing unemployment or the overtaxed resources of local government. Washington would do a better job. The depression coaxed some farmers back into cooperatives, but the big changes occurred on the cotton farms, where, under the Agricultural Adjustment Act (AAA), owners were paid for taking acres out of production. The landlords

took sharecroppers and tenants out of production as well, despite federal intentions to the contrary. The National Industrial Recovery Administration (NIRA) and, later in the decade, the Fair Labor Standards Act (FLSA) upgraded wages in such low-wage industries as textiles and furniture making, but the legislation also displaced blacks, who held the most menial jobs in these industries, as higher wage scales attracted whites.

Blacks and poor whites, however, reaped some benefits from Franklin D. Roosevelt's New Deal. Federal money, funneled through such agencies as the Public Works Administration (PWA), the Civil Works Administration (CWA), and the Works Progress Administration (WPA), built infrastructure such as water and sewer systems in some communities, funded the State Archives at Raleigh, and constructed the Blue Ridge Parkway.

But North Carolina's traditionally conservative leaders limited the amount of federal funds and therefore federal control. In rural areas, federal programs could have disrupted the landlords' economic power over tenants and sharecroppers. PWA wage rates, for example, exceeded average wage levels in the state, a situation that North Carolina's powerful textile and tobacco lobbies fought successfully. In Winston-Salem, local officials spurned a one-million-dollar slum clearance grant from the Federal Housing Administration (FHA) because of landlord opposition. Only Wilmington and Raleigh established housing authorities to secure federal loans, and they did so over vigorous protests from real estate interests. The lobbying efforts of real estate promoters proved more successful in Charlotte, Asheville, and Greensboro, though in Charlotte Piedmont Courts and Fairview Homes were constructed later in the decade.

In 1937, when the PWA lobbied the North Carolina legislature to remove restrictions on municipalities for raising matching funds for PWA projects, the Duke Power Company (successor to the Southern Power Company), fearful that localities would utilize these funds to construct power plants, opposed the measure. The bill finally passed a year later. However, when High Point moved to erect a plant on the Yadkin River, Duke Power hauled the city into court claiming that the Yadkin River was beyond the jurisdiction of the federal government, a position upheld by the court and Governor Clyde R. Hoey (1937–41).

North Carolina industrialists not only opposed higher wage levels, but also the protection offered by the 1935 Wagner Act to labor unions. When the militant Congress of Industrial Organizations (CIO) moved into the South to capitalize on the federal invitation to organize workers, business leaders counterattacked. In Charlotte, textile propagandist David Clark alluded darkly to alien influences in the CIO leadership, especially Lithuanian-born Sidney Hillman. Clark warned his readers that Hillman "was educated to be a rabbi" and had probably changed his name to confound his adversaries. In summarizing North Carolina's response to the New Deal, the *Raleigh News and Observer* lamented that the state did not participate in "some of the essentials of the nation's awakened sense of social responsibility."

The onset of World War II jolted North Carolina out of the depression. Roughly $2 billion in federal contracts came into the state. The ports of Elizabeth City, New Bern, and Wilmington received contracts for shipbuilding, and in the Piedmont the textile industry geared up to supply the armed forces. A federal official noted, "so wide is the variety of production . . . that every soldier and sailor in the service of the Nation either wears or carries some article manufactured in North Carolina."

Governor J. Melville Broughton (1940–44) carried the state through the war. His accomplishments included extending the school year to nine months and equalizing salaries for both black and white teachers, a rarity in the South at the time. The General Assembly also added a twelfth year to the curriculum.

But the war wrought greater changes in North Carolina. First, New Deal legislation and the war accelerated the movement of rural citizens to the cities, a trend that would dominate the last third of the twentieth century. Second, the state's black population expected more after the war. "Double-Victory," fighting fascism abroad and segregation at home, became a rallying cry. At an interracial meeting in Durham in 1943, delegates agreed to address black civil rights. A year later they provided the nucleus for a new civil rights organization, the Southern Regional Council, based in Atlanta and headed by Chapel Hill's Howard W. Odum. Also in 1944 the University of North Carolina Press published *What the Negro Wants*, an anthology edited by Howard University professor Rayford Logan, which explicitly called for an end to the South's segregated society. Finally, tens of thousands of young black and white North Carolinians had left the state for the first time in their lives. They had seen other parts of the country and the world. The victory over the Axis powers imparted a new sense of optimism, of possibility beyond the drudgery of subsistence agriculture and beyond race-tinged, one-party politics.

Few political leaders captured the postwar optimism better than W. Kerr Scott. Not closely allied to traditional Democratic Party leaders, Scott typified many progressive Democrats with his efforts to expand state government to serve a population energized by the war effort. Scott also appointed Harold Leonard Trigg as the first black to serve on the State Board of Education and named Susie Sharp as the first female superior court judge. But his most fateful appointment occurred early in his administration when he named Frank Porter Graham to fill out the senatorial term of J. Melville Broughton, who had died in office. This set the stage for a momentous senatorial election campaign in 1950 that demonstrated yet again that North Carolina progressivism stopped at the color line.

In the Democratic runoff primary to determine who would serve the full term, Graham faced Willis Smith, a prominent attorney and chair of the Duke University Board of Trustees. Smith's campaigners, including Jesse Helms, alleged that Graham favored race mixing and held communist sympathies. Graham lost.

The Civil Rights Era

When the U.S. Supreme Court ruled in *Brown v. Board of Education* that school segregation was unconstitutional, local educational boards either ignored the edict or, as in Greensboro, successfully evaded the spirit of the law through freedom-of-choice programs whereby school boards invariably denied most blacks their choice of school. But a lawsuit filed by Darius Swann against the Charlotte-Mecklenburg school system in 1965 eventually led to a federal district court ruling in 1969 that ended the dilatory pace of school desegregation in the South and sanctioned busing as a means to achieve integrated systems.

Other racial barriers fell as well. In 1960 four freshmen from North Carolina A&T in Greensboro sat at a Woolworth's lunch counter, ordered a hamburger, and were served a large portion of history. The sit-in demonstrations, which quickly spread throughout the South, ended the segregation of public facilities and led to the 1964 Civil Rights Act. In the wake of the sit-ins, civil rights activist Ella Baker helped to found the Student Nonviolent Coordinating Committee (SNCC) in Raleigh. Finally, the passage of the 1965 Voting Rights Act broke the waning grip of one-party politics on North Carolina as thousands of black voters, especially in rural counties, registered to vote for the first time and entered the ranks of the Democratic Party. The Republican Party, which experienced growing strength in the cities and maintained its attraction in some Mountain counties, grew rapidly among conservative white Democrats who identified the national Democratic Party with the cause of civil rights. The growth of the religious right during and after the 1970s provided a well-organized, activist cadre of Republican Party workers.

Four students from North Carolina A&T at Woolworth's white-only lunch counter in Greensboro

The 1972 election of Jesse Helms to the U.S. Senate and James E. Holshouser Jr. (1973–77) as governor, as well as the persistent vote of the state for Republican presidential candidates since 1968 (except in 1976), reflected the growth of two-party politics in North Carolina and the perpetuation of race as a defining issue of party affiliation (Fig. 3.17).

James B. Hunt Jr. (1977–85, 1993–2001), a Democrat, halted the Republican trend in 1977. He also managed to change the state constitution to allow governors to succeed themselves, and he did so, serving a second term, until the Republicans took back the office with Davidson College chemistry professor and former congressman James G. Martin (1985–93) in 1985. Martin also served two terms and was succeeded by Hunt, who was elected to two more

Freedom's Spring Stirring: When Jackie Robinson Came to Town

It was on an early spring day more than fifty years ago, at a baseball game in my North Carolina hometown of Greensboro, that I witnessed the stirring of the racial liberation of the South. Although Jackie Robinson had broken baseball's color barrier in 1947, the following year's spring exhibition schedule began his first visits to the baseball parks of the South, launching a series of annual springtime train journeys from Vero Beach, Florida, to New York.

Until then, the South's African Americans had been deprived of seeing their sports heroes firsthand. The television age was in its infancy. The great heavyweight boxing champion Joe Louis never entered the ring south of Washington, D.C., except for a little noticed bout in his career's twilight days.

Robinson had exploded upon the American baseball scene in 1947, called up from Montreal, leading the Brooklyn Dodgers to the National League pennant and changing forever the face of baseball and American society. In the process, he had become an instant celebrity, as well as a lightning rod for the old passions of racial separation. Nowhere were those feelings more deeply rooted than in the South, and as the Dodgers made their annual railroad odyssey from one southern city to another each April, attendance at the parks was overflowing, with the black fans in segregated sections usually making up half the crowd.

It was on April 11, 1950, at Greensboro's Memorial stadium, home of the Carolina League Patriots where, as a youngster, I had the opportunity to see this phenomenon unfolding. My father frequently would take me to a ball game there and, when the Dodgers rode into town, we were in our usual seats along the third base line. The crowd of 8,434 was announced as the largest in North Carolina baseball history and a subsequent newspaper account estimated "another 500 clinging perilously to tree branches and rooftops around the outside of the stadium." I especially remember the fans seated down the first base and right field line—Jackie Robinson's people, overflowing the "Colored Section" of the stadium and dressed as if they had come to church. In a way, they had.

Robinson was playing second base and batting fifth. The excitement in the air was electric as the National League champions had come to our town. But the sense of expectation centered on Robinson. Even before he came to the on-deck circle for his first at-bat, a steady murmur arose from those segregated seats beyond the Dodger dugout and down the right field line. Then number 42 emerged into view, with that characteristic pigeon-toed walk, gracefully taking practice swings. The gathering sound from the right field stands took on an ethereal quality, not really a cheer, but rather a deep-seated stirring, as if a collective human soul was speaking with a single voice. It began to spill onto the field in a rising crescendo. Their moment, one that generations before them had longed for, was occurring before their eyes.

Though I don't recall the outcome of that first at-bat, Robinson went three for seven that day, "fielding flawlessly" according to game accounts, and leading the star-studded Dodgers to a lopsided 22-0 win over the Patriots as Carl Erskine pitched a one-hitter. But the crowd reaction—that haunting, resonating sound—stayed with me although, as a child of the segregated South, I could not fully comprehend its essence at the time.

In subsequent years I always pulled hard for Brooklyn's "Boys of Summer" while most of my school friends rooted for those bitter rivals, the Yankees. A long-awaited World Championship came in 1955 against New York in seven games. Yet I never forgot that April day and that undefinable crowd response when Jackie Robinson first made his way to the plate.

By the 1960s I was grown, out of college, and the nation was awakening to an unfolding civil rights drama, including historic sit-ins at Woolworth's lunch counter in Greensboro, ironically enough; and the drumbeat of marches, demonstrations, the eloquent cadences of Martin Luther King Jr., and the songs of freedom and social justice. And at that moment in time, I finally understood what I had heard two decades earlier during that April day in Greensboro. The words to an old spiritual heard in the 1960s helped bring understanding: "It's the sound of freedom calling, calling up to the sky. It's the sound of freedom calling, you can hear it if you try."

As an impressionable youngster, witnessing baseball's panorama in a minor league park that warm spring day with my dad, the deep-throated wail we heard was no less than freedom's song, whose refrain extended back through time and place, as far back as the slave ships from West Africa. And its messenger, passing through the ballparks of our southern towns, was number 42, playing second base for the Brooklyn Dodgers.

Douglas M. Orr Jr.

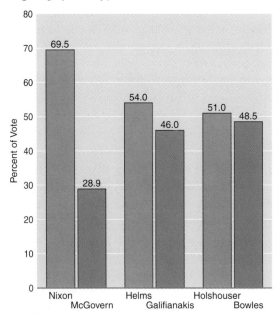

Figure 3.17. The 1972 Election in North Carolina

Political Party

- Republican
- Democrat

Source: *North Carolina Manual*, N.C. Secretary of State, 1973.

terms. Hunt was the latest chief executive to be called the "education governor," and during his four terms in office upgrading the state's lagging public school system became a high priority. That effort included bringing teacher salaries up to the national average by the beginning of the twenty-first century. A strong economy helped ease political friction.

A Sunbelt State

The civil rights movement in North Carolina occurred against the backdrop of economic change. Cotton gave way to the green revolution of pasture, soybeans, and peanuts, while tobacco cultivation revived. Much of agriculture was mechanized, and the number of farms and farmers continued to decline. In the twentieth century, employment in farming and farm-related activities plummeted from a majority of the workforce to less than 5 percent, much of the change occurring after 1945. While industry suffered in other parts of the country after 1960, North Carolina attracted a share of the footloose, low-wage manufacturers, particularly in the rural east where educational levels were low and employment options few. By the 1980s, however, many of these operations had been closed or cut back, as jobs were shifted to Mexico and other low-wage havens. The attraction of a low-wage, nonunionized labor force, plus relatively cheap land prices, tax incentives, and lax environmental and safety controls proved irresistible to the "captains of second-class industry and first-class extortion," as southern writer Robert Penn Warren called them. Whatever their initial benefits, they eventually left their communities poorer for their brief presence.

The textile industry faltered in the 1970s, just after it began to hire black workers in significant numbers. Overseas competition and outmoded

technology contributed to the demise of marginal firms, most of which were located in one-industry towns. But by the 1980s the textile industry had restructured and mechanized. Gone for the most part were the company towns, either closed down or bought up by multinational conglomerates, as occurred with Cannon Mills in Kannapolis in the mid-1980s.

A transformation of the state's economy accelerated the shifting settlement patterns in North Carolina, especially favoring the Piedmont region, although Coastal areas, particularly the Outer Banks, expanded from the tourist trade. The farm and the small town no longer held attractions for most young, ambitious Tar Heel residents. But North Carolina's growing cities offered numerous possibilities for talented citizens who no longer had to seek out their fortunes in the North; rather, they could remain in the state and contribute to its development. Increasingly after 1970, they were joined by migrants from the North and overseas who not only added to the diversity of the population but also further reinforced the concentration of people, jobs, and innovation in metropolitan areas.

These newcomers to the employment scene, from both within and outside the state, were attracted by an array of enterprises that differed from the labor-intensive, low-wage enterprises that had characterized North Carolina's economy since early in the century. Before his death in 1954,

Howard Odum convinced Governor Luther H. Hodges (1954–61) of the efficacy of a nonprofit, taxpaying corporation devoted to research and development apart from, but at times associated with, the three major universities in the capital area—the University of North Carolina at Chapel Hill, North Carolina State University, and Duke University. The Research Triangle Park was born in 1958 on an expanse of land donated by private sources. By the end of the 1970s nearly thirty research and development firms were located there, and another research park was blossoming near the campus of the University of North Carolina at Charlotte, an institution of post–World War II origins that became part of the UNC system in 1965 to serve the growing metropolitan area and its economic and demographic diversity.

Hodges proved to be an indefatigable promoter of economic development that transcended his work for the Research Triangle Park. His successor, Terry Sanford (1961–65), continued these efforts. Governor Sanford recognized that one of the prime reasons for the park's existence and early success related to the fine institutions of higher education in the area, and he supported funding to expand the university system. The state's excellent community college system also expanded during the 1960s and within two decades boasted fifty-eight institutions, the third largest community college system in the nation and a significant boost to the state's economic development policies as well as to a large population of first-generation college students. Sanford also understood that persistent poverty, particularly in the rural sections of eastern North Carolina, inhibited economic development in those areas beyond the footloose, low-wage industries that contributed little long-term benefit to local economies. He established a state antipoverty program, funded in part by private foundation money, that eventually served as a model for the federal War on Poverty later in the decade.

The efforts of leaders such as Hodges and Sanford to improve the economic, educational, and social foundations of North Carolina not only encouraged people from other parts of the country and the world to work in the state, but attracted retirees and tourists as well. The mailbox economy (created by retirees who receive pension and social security checks earned elsewhere but spend them in North Carolina) annually pours millions of dollars into the state. Tourists come to the beaches and the mountains to enjoy the natural environment, though at the same time placing more pressure on that environment. The state has a sound coastal zone management plan, but it is only beginning to seriously address the pollution of streams, the deteriorating quality of air in metropolitan areas, and the threat of acid rain in the mountains. State government since the end of Reconstruction has been a strong ally of business interests, particularly the development community. Although such support has been helpful in building the economy, the environment is one of North Carolina's greatest selling points for economic development in the future.

Perhaps the most important development in the state's growing economic diversity since the 1970s was the rise to national prominence of the banking industry in Charlotte, assisted by the legalization of interstate banking in the 1980s. As farmers of the 1890s realized, without credit it was difficult to get out from under debt and poverty. The South historically has been a net importer of capital. This fact has limited economic development, because entrepreneurs had to obtain credit, sometimes at unattractive terms, from lenders outside the region, especially in New York. The explosion of NationsBank and First Union onto the national banking scene in the 1990s relieved some of the problem of credit faced by an expanding economy. Moreover, a good deal of the profits earned by those banks have remained in the South and, more specifically, in North Carolina.

These changes brought with them thousands of new residents to the state. But it is not yet clear whether grits and bagels will get married or whether one will take over the other. Old patterns persist, and North Carolina, like the rest of the South, has had a habit of absorbing change rather than changing.

Selected References

Anderson, E. *Race and Politics in North Carolina, 1872–1901: The Black Second*. Baton Rouge: Louisiana State University Press, 1981.

Badger, A. *North Carolina and the New Deal*. Raleigh: North Carolina Department of Cultural Resources, 1981.

Cecelski, D. S. *Along Freedom Road: Hyde County, North Carolina, and the Fate of Black Schools in the South*. Chapel Hill: University of North Carolina Press, 1994.

Claiborne, J. *The Charlotte Observer: Its Time and Place, 1869–1986*. Chapel Hill: University of North Carolina Press, 1986.

Crow, J., P. Escott, and F. Hatley. *A History of African Americans in North Carolina*. Raleigh: North Carolina Department of Cultural Resources, 1992.

Escott, P. D. *Many Excellent People: Power and Privilege in North Carolina, 1850–1900*. Chapel Hill: University of North Carolina Press, 1985.

Flowers, L. *Throwed Away: Failures of Progress in Eastern North Carolina*. Knoxville: University of Tennessee Press, 1990.

Franklin, J. *The Free Negro in North Carolina, 1790–1860*. New York: Russell and Russell, 1943.

Gilmore, G. E. *Gender and Jim Crow: Women and the Politics of White Supremacy in North Carolina, 1896–1920*. Chapel Hill: University of North Carolina Press, 1996.

Kenzer, R. *Enterprising Southerners: Black Economic Success in North Carolina, 1865–1915*. Charlottesville: University Press of Virginia, 1997.

Leloudis, J. L. *Schooling the New South: Pedagogy, Self, and Society in North Carolina, 1880–1920*. Chapel Hill: University of North Carolina Press, 1996.

Pleasants, J. M., and A. M. Burns III. *Frank Porter Graham and the 1950 Senate Race in North Carolina*. Chapel Hill: University of North Carolina Press, 1990.

Powell, W. S. *North Carolina through Four Centuries*. Chapel Hill: University of North Carolina Press, 1989.

4. POPULATION

Sallie M. Ives and Alfred W. Stuart

The single most significant measure of any state's size, growth, and change is its population. With over 7.5 million residents, North Carolina in 1998 ranked as the eleventh most populous state in the nation. That total made it equivalent to ninetieth largest among the world's 223 nations. This status is the result of relatively strong growth in recent decades, with the state rank moving up from fourteenth in 1920 and twelfth as recently as 1970. Projections prepared by the North Carolina Office of State Planning call for the statewide total to approach 9.6 million people by the year 2020. The U.S. Census has identified North Carolina as one of eight states it expects to be growth centers that will account for 60 percent of net population growth for the entire nation between 1990 and 2020. This represents quite a change from just a few decades ago, when more people were leaving the state than moving in.

This pattern of sustained and vigorous growth has major implications for public services, environmental quality, economic opportunities, and virtually every other aspect of the quality of life for residents of this state. In addition to simple growth, the population has become older, more urban, more female, and ethnically more diverse. Perhaps the most distinctive aspect of population in North Carolina is its long-standing tendency to be widely dispersed in rural areas, small towns, and cities of modest size. It is only recently that the U.S. Census classified a bare majority of the state's population as living in urban places. This pattern is the basis for the perception that North Carolina is a small-town, rural state even though it is one of the nation's most populous and highly industrialized. The state is in the midst of a historic transition in which broad dispersion is giving way to a seemingly inexorable concentration of growth in metropolitan areas, especially the larger ones. Even more significant is the tendency for the great majority of recent and projected future growth to be the result of the net migration into the state of hundreds of thousands of people. That is, most of the state's growth comes from people moving in from other states and from overseas rather than from the native population.

Growth of the North Carolina Population

In a little more than two hundred years the population of North Carolina grew impressively—from just under 400,000 in 1790 to over 7.5 million in 1998. Although this growth was almost continuous, there were differences throughout the period in both numbers of people added and rates of increase (Fig. 4.1). This growth and its variations over time reflect both the rates at which women of

child-bearing age had children and the even more variable tendency for people to migrate into or out of the state.

North Carolina's population change is best understood in the context of the nation and the South as a whole (Fig. 4.2). In the colonial period, the state, along with most of the eastern United States, grew rapidly; by the time of the first census in 1790 it contained just over 10 percent of the new republic's total. It maintained steady growth for the next several decades but at much lower rates than for the country as a whole as more people moved into the western parts of the nation. Throughout the first half of the nineteenth century, the expanding nation added population at the rate of better than 30 percent every decade, whereas North Carolina's rate was around 15 percent, at least until 1830.

Between 1830 and 1840 the state grew by a paltry 2.1 percent. North Carolina had entered its "Rip van Winkle" period, when it became a backward state with a sluggish economy. During this decade, thirty-two out of sixty-eight counties actually declined in population. In many other counties, growth occurred only because the birthrate among the rural population was high enough to offset a net out-migration of people. Part of the loss was attributed to large slaveholders selling their property and moving into the Deep South in search of fertile virgin land after they had exhausted the soil through overcultivation and erosion. Little was known then about fertilization or practices that

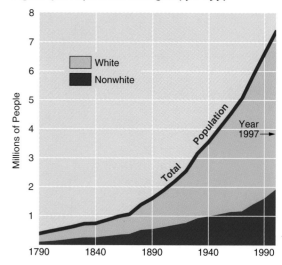

Figure 4.1. Population Change, 1790–1997

Sources: U.S. Census, Population Estimates Program, 1998; Census of Population and Housing, 1790-1990.

minimized erosion, such as contour farming. The lack of internal transportation and communications made it difficult for farmers to get their crops to market. General backwardness, indifference to education, neglect of resources, and resistance to taxation for any purpose drove many of North Carolina's more productive citizens to leave the state, a process known as *negative selectivity*. Those left behind were, by contrast, older, less educated, and not as productive. In 1840 the U.S. Census revealed that 31 percent of all native North Carolinians, or over 405,000 people, were living somewhere else.

A more active state role in improving infrastructure, including the building of the North

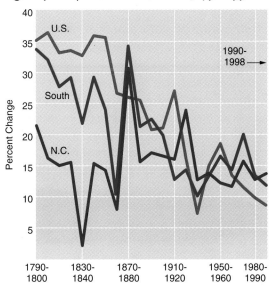

Figure 4.2. Population Growth Rates, 1790–1998

Source: U.S. Census, Population Estimates Program, March 1999; Census of Population and Housing, 1790-1990.

Carolina Railroad, led to increased growth, but by 1860, on the threshold of the Civil War, North Carolina's share of the national total had fallen to 3.2 percent. Growth was slow immediately after the war, then jumped by 30 percent between 1870 and 1880 and another 15 percent every decade thereafter through 1910, a period when the state's economy began to enjoy the fruits of industrialization. These increases reflected the high fertility rate in a population that was still 86 percent rural, with little or no net migration into the state. But the rest of the nation grew even faster, so that by 1910 North Carolina's share of the U.S. total dropped to an all-time low of 2.4 percent.

From 1910 through 1940, however, North Carolina grew faster than the rest of the nation. This trend could be attributed to the drastic slowing of emigration into the United States from overseas, which reduced national growth rates; the continuation of a high fertility rate in the state, which by 1940 was still 73 percent rural; and by the return of many native North Carolinians, at least temporally, during the national economic depression of the 1930s. This relatively strong growth occurred despite the fact that thousands of rural blacks and whites had left the state, primarily during the 1920s. By 1940 North Carolina's proportion of the national population had risen to 2.7 percent.

The period after World War II through the 1960s saw growth slow as rural residents continued to leave in search of better economic opportunities in the industrial cities of the North. Simultaneously, birthrates began to decline and were barely high enough to offset this out-migration. As a result, between 1940 and 1970 North Carolina once again grew more slowly than did the nation as a whole. Both white and black North Carolinians left initially, but beginning in the 1960s the state experienced a modest net in-migration of whites while African Americans were still leaving by the hundreds of thousands. At this point, the economy of the state was expanding vigorously, as it was in the rest of the South, especially in urban areas, but many of these jobs were unavailable to blacks. Although the civil rights movement of the 1950s and 1960s opened up employment to African Americans, the net out-migration continued, and between 1960 and 1970 about 94,000 more people left the state than moved in. This trend reversed sharply in the next decade, when North Carolina saw a net in-migration of over 278,000 people, including a modest number of blacks, their first net gain through migration in modern history.

From 1980 to 1990 in-migration swelled to over 374,000 people, including 31,090 nonwhites. Since 1970, North Carolina has grown faster than the nation; its proportion, which regressed to 2.50 percent in 1970, reached 2.79 percent in 1998. This relative gain was made possible by yet another surge of in-migrants between 1990 and 1998. According to U.S. Census estimates, new residents outnumbered those who left by a record-breaking total of 550,407 during the eight-year period. These in-migrants accounted for 60 percent of the state's net population growth during that period, far outnumbering natural increase.

Ethnic Composition

From 1790 to 1990 anywhere from two-thirds to three-quarters of the people who lived in North Carolina were white (Fig. 4.1). This proportion underwent some shifts, however. In 1790 the white proportion was a little over 73 percent, but from 1790 to 1870 it declined to about 62 percent; from 1870 to 1970 whites increased to a high of almost 77 percent, reflecting the massive out-migration of

A Changing Racial Climate

My family and I moved to North Carolina in 1970, a time of despair as well as hope about race relations. Two years earlier, after Martin Luther King Jr.'s assassination, violence had erupted in some communities. The governor ordered National Guard troops into Raleigh, Greensboro, Goldsboro, Wilmington, Wilson, and Durham to quell rioting. Local groups, reminiscent of the 1963 Good Neighbor Councils during nonviolent protests, sought to heal racial wounds. Meanwhile, the state was moving "with all deliberate speed" to enforce the civil rights for which King had died.

I also recall that a liberal spirit and community action quickened the pace of change. For example, my elementary and middle school Parent Teacher Associations pushed repeatedly for "equal educational opportunity." Among other things on behalf of our children, we demanded a timely and fair desegregation plan; equitable teaching and learning resources; and intercultural studies. We advocated and practiced interracial cooperation. Black and white teachers, with whom I worked as a consultant, designed the pilot Afro-American history course for Durham's high schools.

Racial changes since the 1970s, in my opinion, comprise a good omen for North Carolina. There is no question that we have made remarkable progress. We are beyond the foothills of segregation in public education and accommodations, electoral politics, much of the workplace, and other venues. But the "mountaintop" of freedom and justice for all, which King frequently invoked in his speeches, still beckons us. Now we need policies and strategies to end institutional racism and ensure equality.

I would welcome a statewide conversation on overcoming inequality. Suffice it to say that African Americans, Native Americans, Hispanics, and Asians, among others once enslaved or excluded by custom and law, participate widely in Tar Heel civic life. Yet citizens of color more frequently are illiterate, poor, and powerless. Meantime, powerful interests in the economy and government undermine opportunities and protections for minorities and women, including many new immigrants. Racism permeates popular and political culture. Issues such as affirmative action, welfare reform, and majority-minority congressional districts remain

racially coded in the media. Race hate crimes proceed apace, as does "white flight" from urban school districts.

We should bridge the divide by building on the foundation of our "best practices." These include curricula in classrooms K-12 and exhibits at the North Carolina Museum of History that promote knowledge of North Carolina's multiracial past and present. They encompass church and school-led dialogues in support of the President's Initiative on Race and Reconciliation. These discussions continue in neighborhoods and on college campuses, promoting tolerance and understanding between the races. Critics of the race initiative label it as mere talk. However, through frequent and honest dialogue, I believe that we can build solidarity on policies and programs to eradicate illiteracy, poverty, and powerlessness. North Carolina's future compels us to try.

Raymond Gavins, professor of history, Duke University

---

blacks. In the 1980s and 1990s the white proportion of the population remained at about 76 percent. Since 1790, the nonwhite portion of residents has been dominated by African Americans. Blacks made up 33 percent of the total population in 1900, but their numbers declined steadily thereafter; in 1997 they comprised 22.1 percent of the state's population.

The recent growth in the nonwhite population other than by African Americans is a measure of North Carolina's increasing ethnic diversity. This is reflected in more languages heard on the street, restaurants specializing in different cuisines, and bilingual programs in schools. Once almost entirely a biracial state dominated by African Americans and whites, the state has experienced a dramatic rise in other population groups. Between 1990 and 1997 the white population grew by 11.1 percent and African Americans by 12.4 percent, compared with an overall state increase of 12 percent. Several other ethnic groups grew even faster. Although Native Americans have been relatively insignificant numerically at the state level (1.3 percent of the population in 1997), their total rose by 16 percent between 1990 and 1997.

Table 4.1. Ethnic Populations in North Carolina

Group	Growth, 1990–1997		
	1990	1997	Change (%)
Total population	6,632,448	7,425,183	12.0
Total white	5,036,941	5,594,769	11.1
White Hispanic	61,549	128,661	109.0
White non-Hispanic	4,975,392	5,466,108	9.9
Black	1,461,579	1,642,980	12.4
Native American	80,826	95,398	18.0
Asian	53,102	92,036	73.0

Leading Counties, 1997			
County	Hispanics	County	Asians*
Cumberland	23,411	Wake	16,467
Mecklenburg	14,409	Mecklenburg	15,605
Wake	12,648	Cumberland	9,313
Onslow	12,587	Guilford	6,309
Guilford	5,564	Durham	5,275
Forsyth	4,048	Onslow	4,673
Durham	3,842	Forsyth	2,780
Craven	3,327	Gaston	1,504
Johnston	2,844	Catawba	1,439
Wayne	2,625	Wayne	1,372
Buncombe	2,425	Burke	1,363
Subtotal	87,730		66,100
Other counties	61,660		29,298
N.C. total	149,390		95,398
Leading counties as proportion of N.C. total	61.0%		76.3%

Source: U.S. Census, Population Estimates Program, September 1998.
*Includes Pacific Islanders

Hispanic migrant farm workers in a cabbage field

Asians increased even more dramatically, by 63 percent, between 1990 and 1997 and totaled over 92,000 persons in 1997 (Table 4.1). Hispanics, 85 percent of whom are white, grew by 95 percent between 1990 and 1997, to over 149,000 persons, and constituted 2 percent of the North Carolina total. The non-Hispanic white population was the slowest-growing group of all, gaining by just under 10 percent, whereas the white Hispanic group more than doubled, rising 109 percent.

Hispanics and Asians, unlike Native Americans, are found predominantly in urban areas. Almost 58 percent of the Hispanic population and 69 percent of Asians live in the eleven metropolitan counties listed in Table 4.1. However, even the vigorous growth rates shown in the U.S. Census estimates may actually understate the case. In Charlotte, for example, the local International House, based on reports from various organizations and support groups, estimated that by 1998 the Hispanic population in Charlotte was at least 50,000, in contrast to the 14,000 that the U.S. Census reported for 1997.

This trend toward ethnic diversity is expected to continue. U.S. Census projections indicate that by the year 2020 the Asian population will rise to over 260,000 and Hispanics will make up another 224,000, 2.4 percent of the total. However, the recent accelerated growth of these population segments suggests that these projections may be rather conservative. Whites will still be in the great majority, but their share of the state total is expected to decline to just over 72 percent, and blacks are projected to increase their share to 23.5 percent.

Age

Like the rest of the nation, the population of North Carolina is getting progressively older. The median age, for example, rose from 26.5 years in 1970 to 33.0 in 1990, and by the year 2020 it is expected to reach about 39 years. The recent and future projected increases are slightly higher than those for the nation as a whole. This increase in age reflects greater life expectancies for older people, smaller families, and the tendency for more of the population growth to come from people moving into the state, many of whom are retirees.

Figure 4.3 indicates population growth by age group between 1980 and 1997 and projections to the year 2020. All age groups show a substantial increase through the entire period, but there have been some significant variations among groups. Whereas residents of preschool age (0–4 years) have increased in number and are expected to continue this trend, those of school age (5–18 years) have been less consistent. They actually declined

between 1980 and 1990, and the estimated total for 1997 is only slightly above that recorded in 1980. Yet a sharp increase is projected between 1997 and 2010. These fluctuations have major implications for school systems across the state. The college/early working age group (19–24 years) declined even further—a drop of over 50,000 residents in 1997 from 1980. However, numbers will rise sharply as the five- to eighteen-year-olds come of age.

The middle working age group (25–44 years) grew steadily through 1997, but its total is expected to decline in the early twenty-first century before slowly rising again. It is this age group that, in great measure, has supplied the employees for North Carolina's robust economy. Its anticipated decline or slow growth raises serious questions about future labor supplies.

All of these age groups have declined markedly in their share of the state's population, another pattern that is expected to continue. The two groups representing ages 5–18 and 19–24 together fell from 35 percent of the total in 1980 to 27.5 percent in 1997, and they are expected to drop to 25 percent by 2020. The middle working age group, 12 percent of the state total in 1980, is projected to barely exceed 8 percent by 2020.

The reason for the falling shares of younger people has been the strong increase in the older population, which is expected to grow even faster in the future. The older working age group (45–64 years) has grown steadily in number even though

Figure 4.3. Growth of the North Carolina Population by Age Group, 1980–2020

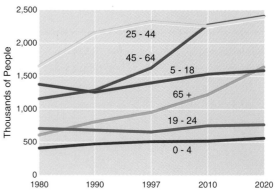

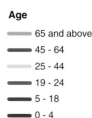

Age

— 65 and above
— 45 - 64
— 25 - 44
— 19 - 24
— 5 - 18
— 0 - 4

Sources: U.S. Census of Population and Housing, 1980 and 1990; N.C. Office of State Planning, Estimates and projections, 1998.

its statewide share declined slightly between 1980 and 1990—from 19.6 to 19.3 percent. But the numbers in this group are projected to nearly double between 1990 and 2020, and their share of the state total is expected to rise to almost 26 percent.

The fastest-growing group in the population is the elderly, those 65 years and older. Rising numbers caused their share of the state total to increase from 10.2 percent in 1980 to 12.5 percent in 1997, and their proportion is expected to reach 17.7 percent by 2020. The number of elderly people is expected to double between 1990 and 2020. In 1980 there were twice as many people aged 5 to 18 years as there were 65 or older. By 2020 the elderly will outnumber the younger group by 50,000 people. This growth has enormous implications for health care (including Medicare and Medicaid), other support services, housing, and many other sectors of life.

One reason for the rapid growth of the elderly population is that North Carolina has become a major destination for retirees. In 1990 about 65,000 people who were aged 60 or older between 1985 and 1990 moved to North Carolina. This ranked the state fifth highest in the nation in the in-migration of retirees, trailing only Florida, California, Arizona, and Texas—in contrast, it ranked twenty-seventh in 1960, seventeenth in 1970, and seventh in 1980. This sharp rise led *American Demographics* magazine (November 1994) to designate North Carolina as "the rising star" among those states that have become more popular destinations for the elderly. A major source of these retirees has been the state of New York. About 222,000 people aged 65 or older left New York between 1985 and 1990, and nearly 9,000 of them moved to North Carolina.

Urban

North Carolina has long been known as a relatively underurbanized state, but the proportion of the population that lives in urban areas has gradually increased. According to the U.S. Census, only 39.5 percent of the population lived in urban places in 1960, when the South had a comparable proportion of almost 59 percent (Fig. 4.4). By 1970 the North Carolina proportion had increased to 45 percent and by 1980 to 48 percent, whereas the South's share for those periods was nearly 65 and 67 percent, respectively. This divergence continued into 1990, when approximately 50.4 percent of the population in North Carolina was classified as urban compared to almost 68.6 percent of the South. Only five other states (Maine, Mississippi, South Dakota, Vermont, and West Virginia) have smaller urban proportions than North Carolina and none are as populous. Another measure of North Carolina's underurbanization is provided by a 1997 estimate prepared by the North Carolina Office of State Planning. According to the estimate, only 51.0 percent of the total population lived within the boundaries of one of the state's 536 incorporated municipalities, of which at least 13 had fewer than one hundred residents. This was the first year in the state's history in which incorporated towns and cities contained a majority of the population.

Somewhat paradoxically, in 1997, 68 percent of the state's inhabitants lived within a federally rec-

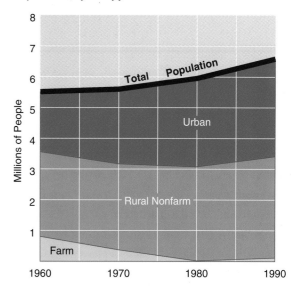

Figure 4.4. North Carolina's Urban and Rural Population, 1960–1990

Source: U.S. Census of Population and Housing, 1960-90.

ognized Metropolitan Statistical Area (MSA), not far behind the South's 74.3 percent and the national mean of 79.7 percent. This indicates that although many North Carolinians do not reside within an incorporated place, they do live close to a city, including the outer margins of metropolitan areas. The relatively high proportion of people living outside towns and in unincorporated parts of MSA counties reflects the historic tendency for the population of North Carolina to be rather dispersed, typically residing in a rural setting and working in a nearby town.

Rural

North Carolina has long had a large rural population, which has represented a majority of its total residents throughout all but its most recent history. And even though it has declined in recent decades, the rural component has increased in actual numbers, from 2.7 million in 1960 to nearly 3.3 million in 1990 (Fig. 4.4). Nevertheless, these numbers mask a substantial restructuring within the rural population. The U.S. Census distinguishes between a rural "farm" and a rural "non-farm" population, based on whether or not the rural population actually lives on a working farm. The 1990 census defined a farm as a place from which $1,000 or more of agricultural products were sold, certainly a minimal definition. Those people classified as nonfarm thus do not live in an incorporated place of at least 2,500 people and they sell less than $1,000 worth of agricultural products, if any. More likely, they live outside a town but hold a factory or urban job. They truly represent the dispersed population that is such a hallmark of North Carolina.

Between 1960 and 1990 the rural population increased 19.6 percent as part of the total population increase of 45.5 percent. However, the rural nonfarm component grew by a robust 63.2 percent, whereas the rural farm total plummeted by nearly 86 percent during the same thirty-year period. The number of people living on farms fell by over 690,000, and their share of the state total declined from 17.7 to just 1.8 percent. In 1960 North Carolina had the largest farm population of any state in the nation, but by 1990 it had fallen to fifth place. On the other hand, the rural nonfarm segment increased its share of the population from 42.7 in 1960 to 47.9 percent in 1990. In many cases, of course, the shift from farm to nonfarm represented a change in employment rather than residence. Many farmers gave up tilling the soil for a factory or other wage job but still lived on the original farm. Some kept a garden, and many leased out or sold their fields to other farmers. This switch in employment was facilitated by the spread of manufacturing facilities to rural areas and led to extensive intercounty commuting by the displaced farmers. Other rural nonfarm residents, probably the great majority, were never farmers but simply chose to live in a rural setting and, like the ex-farmers, commuted to jobs at rural factories or in town. They are found in the outer fringes of the metropolitan areas as well as in the more rural parts of the state.

Gender

In the last thirty years, women have continued to increase both in number and in proportion to the total population. From 1960 to 1990 the number of women grew from about 2.3 million to over 3.4 million. During the same time the male population rose by about 45 percent compared to the female total of about 48 percent. As a result, the male per 100 females ratio declined steadily—from 97.3 in 1960 to 95.9 in 1970, 94.3 in 1980, and 91.2 in 1997. This trend is not surprising because of two factors that influence sex ratios. First, women generally live longer than men and have higher survival rates than men at most ages. And second, net migration to North Carolina has not been particularly gender-specific for either males or females, as it has been in the past in true "boom areas," such as Alaska during the construction of the Alaskan pipeline by a predominantly male labor force, or in "bust areas," such as parts of Appalachia when mostly men left the region to find work elsewhere.

These trends may be seen more clearly in population pyramids of the state for 1990, which show the distribution of the population by age and gender, a snapshot of the result of the processes just described (Fig. 4.5). Several generalizations can be made about the pyramid for the population as a whole. In 1990 females outnumbered males by 51.5 to 48.5 percent, but the female proportion was particularly high after age 50. The state is attractive to both men and women in their early to middle working years (ages 20 to 44). This is likely to be a function both of the aging of the children born during the higher-fertility years of the 1950s, 1960s, and early 1970s and the age-selective migration that has occurred particularly in the urban areas of the state. That is, the people who are most likely to move into an area are young adults or, if older, still of working age. The pyramid of the urban popula-

Figure 4.5. North Carolina Population Pyramids by Age and Gender, 1990

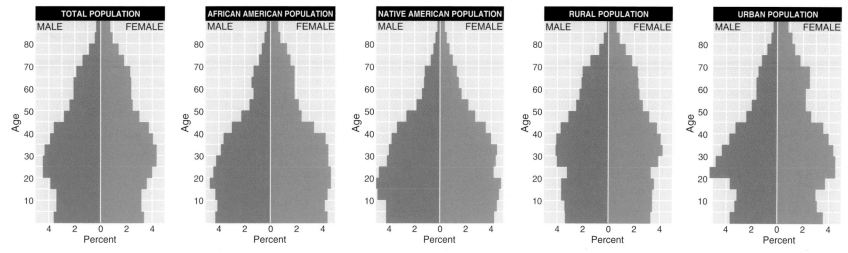

Source: U.S. Census of Population and Housing, 1990.

tion clearly shows this tendency. A considerable portion of the urban population is in the 20-to-39-year-old group and another only slightly less important portion is aged 40 to 49. These young and middle-aged adults are also more likely to have young children (under 5 years) or older children (15 to 19 years). In urban areas, there is also a tendency to find significantly more women than men aged 55 and older.

The pyramid of the rural population displays the results of the negative selectivity of the out-migration process. The rural population does not have the larger proportion of younger adults that formed the dominant bulge in the urban population. Consequently, the proportion of children is also smaller in rural areas. This contrasts with the larger proportion of residents aged 55 years and older. That is, rural areas tend to have fewer young adults, fewer children, and more older adults.

Differences in population structure are apparent in the pyramids of the two dominant nonwhite subgroups. The broad bases of the pyramids of African Americans and Native Americans indicate that the fertility rates of these two ethnic groups are higher than that of the population at large. The narrow peaks formed by older adults reflect the groups' relative "youth," although this is actually the product of a much higher mortality rate after age 50, especially for men.

One concern is the general aging of women of all races in all settings. Older women tend to be less well off economically than men for various reasons, including smaller or no retirement resources. Meeting the needs of this group may become in-creasingly difficult in rural areas, where the out-migration of younger workers can lead to a declining tax base, a static economic climate, and the disruption of family support networks. Even in communities where the elderly are better off economically, there may be more and more demands for services geared to this group, including nursing care, in-home services, and adult day care. This may occur at the same time that pressures are being placed on the state to emphasize the child care and educational needs of the younger portions of the population, including everything from day care, public schools, colleges and universities, and community colleges to the technical training facilities that are needed to retrain workers to meet the changing demands of employers.

Regional Population Growth

The division of North Carolina into four land regions—Tidewater (or Outer Coastal Plain), Inner Coastal Plain, Piedmont, and Mountains (Fig. 1.1)—is a conventional practice that derives not only from variations in the nature of the land but also from different patterns of occupancy and use. These regions are as much historical as they are physiographic. European settlement in the Tidewater and on the Inner Coastal Plain was predominantly from English stock from Virginia or in from the coast. Originally these areas had an Old South culture driven primarily by slave-based plantation systems of production. More recently, the Inner Coastal Plain became the state's agricultural heartland and its most rural area. Most of the region's recent growth has been in and around its larger cities, especially Greenville, Fayetteville, Goldsboro, Jacksonville, and Rocky Mount. A good part of this growth has been associated with nearby military facilities. The Tidewater has grown vigorously in recent decades due to the attraction of the beaches especially along the Outer Banks and the southeastern coast. Historic cities such as New Bern and Wilmington are booming as service centers for nearby beach areas.

The Piedmont was settled mainly by Europeans of Scots-Irish and German stock who migrated southward from Pennsylvania in the eighteenth century. Most of these farms have been replaced by all of North Carolina's largest cities and a highly industrialized countryside. Nearly all of the settlement in the coves and valleys of the Mountains by Scots Highlanders, Scots-Irish, Germans, and other Europeans took place a little later, and these communities remained isolated until the recent investment in transportation facilities. Today the scenic beauty of the region attracts thousands of tourists and retirees.

In the colonial period and the early decades of the republic the Coastal Plain contained the majority of North Carolina residents. This began to change in the early nineteenth century in favor of the Piedmont, and for some time the eastern part of the state, which contains 41 of its 100 counties, included about one-third of the people. Since about 1960 both the absolute and the relative population of the Piedmont has increased from 51 percent of the state total in that year to 56 percent in 1998 (Fig. 4.6). Perhaps more telling, the region accounted for nearly 64 percent of North Carolina's net growth between 1960 and 1998. The Coastal Plain counties collectively declined to 30.5 percent of the state total by 1998, but there was a significant shift within the region. Whereas the Tidewater increased its share from 9.4 to 10 percent, the counties of the Inner Coastal Plain saw their share fall from 24.6 to 20.5 percent between 1960 and 1998. Meanwhile, the twenty-four Mountain counties experienced a drop from 14.8 to 13.5 percent of the state total. Despite these relative

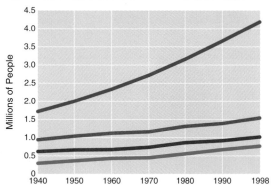

Figure 4.6. Regional Growth Trends, 1940–1998

Region
- Mountains
- Piedmont
- Inner Coastal Plain
- Tidewater

Sources: U.S. Census, Population Estimates Program, March 1999; Census of Population and Housing, 1940-90.

shifts, the Inner Coastal Plain's actual population rose from 1.309 million in 1960 to 1.523 million in 1998. The Tidewater had a sharper growth rate, from 552,000 to 745,000, during the same time. The Mountain counties increased their total from just over 673,000 to 1 million in 1998. The Piedmont total—2.309 million in 1960—reached 4.167 million in 1998. In other words, growth occurred throughout the state, but it was strongest in the most urban and industrial areas.

The Piedmont also contained 52 percent of North Carolina's nonwhite population, but the region remained 79 percent white in 1990. A rapidly growing share of the nonwhite population in Piedmont cities is Asian, and some of the white portion is Hispanic. The Inner Coastal Plain contains 35 percent of the state's nonwhite population, and these ethnic groups comprise almost 40 percent of the region's total population. Most of these nonwhites are African Americans, but they also include the large Native American population in Robeson and nearby counties. The Tidewater is 24 percent nonwhite, contributing 10 percent to the state total. The Mountain region is the state's "whitest," containing just over 2 percent of the total number of nonwhites.

County Patterns

Within each region there are variations in the patterns of population change. Three primary factors account for most of the growth in individual counties. The first is the influence of the several urban centers, which act as magnets to economic activities and subsequent population expansion. Charlotte, Raleigh-Durham, Greensboro–Winston-Salem, and smaller metropolitan areas such as Asheville, Fayetteville, Greenville, Hickory, Jacksonville, Rocky Mount, and Wilmington have attracted economic growth in today's highly competitive global economy. These urban centers influence population dynamics in two ways. One is that the employment opportunities they provide tend to draw large numbers of people both to their core counties and to adjacent counties that are under their influence. The second influence relates to the type of people urban centers tend to attract. Net migration to these areas is often age-selective in that larger numbers of young adults of a child-rearing age settle in and near urban centers. This type of selectivity tends to set the stage for the area's future growth through natural increase.

The second factor affecting the patterns of change across counties is the presence of certain amenities that also serve as magnets to in-migrants. In the case of the Mountains, the net migration flows may also be age-selective in that they tend to attract proportionally higher rates of older people who seek retirement homes in areas that are likely to offer the types of services they need in smaller communities. Another amenity area is the coast, which tends to be more age-selective in its year-round population. Particularly important are the coastal beaches, the Intracoastal Waterway, or areas in the immediate vicinity. The golf courses developed in the Southern Pines/Pinehurst area have attracted a large retirement community as well.

The third factor influencing population change at the county level is the presence of large institutions, such as colleges and universities or military installations, that grow or decline by administrative action. There are fifteen counties whose age structure is significantly affected by these institutions. These include the university/college-impacted counties of Alamance, Durham, Guilford, Harnett, Jackson, Mecklenburg, New Hanover, Orange, Pitt, Wake, and Watauga and the military-impacted counties of Craven, Cumberland, Onslow, and Wayne. Colleges and universities differentially attract younger adults who typically do not age in place but, instead, are regularly replaced by other adults. Hence, they are places where population turnover is common. The military bases tend to draw large civilian workforces to support their missions. Both the civilian and military populations of these areas can be affected dramatically by shifts in national defense policies. For instance, Cumberland and Onslow Counties have experienced strong outmigrations that are attributable to recent downsizing of the military establishment nationally. The university/college counties offer special amenities associated with the schools that interest large numbers of new residents, especially retirees. Examples include collegiate sports and a host of cultural activities.

Growth Patterns

As shown in Figure 4.7a, the decade of 1970–80 was a boom time for many North Carolina counties, especially those in the Piedmont. Three counties in the Mountains, four in the Piedmont, and four in the Tidewater grew by 30 percent or more during that decade. The Mountain counties of Swain

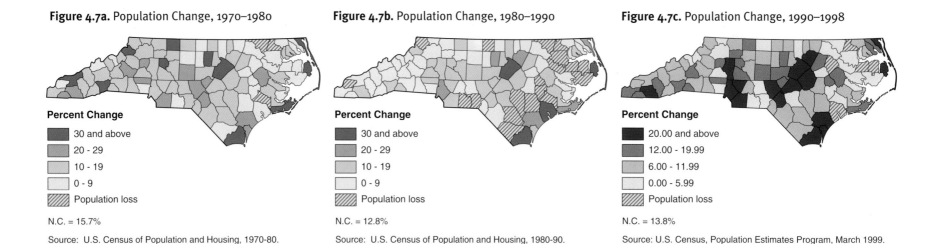

Figure 4.7a. Population Change, 1970–1980

Percent Change

- 30 and above
- 20 - 29
- 10 - 19
- 0 - 9
- Population loss

N.C. = 15.7%

Source: U.S. Census of Population and Housing, 1970-80.

Figure 4.7b. Population Change, 1980–1990

Percent Change

- 30 and above
- 20 - 29
- 10 - 19
- 0 - 9
- Population loss

N.C. = 12.8%

Source: U.S. Census of Population and Housing, 1980-90.

Figure 4.7c. Population Change, 1990–1998

Percent Change

- 20.00 and above
- 12.00 - 19.99
- 6.00 - 11.99
- 0.00 - 5.99
- Population loss

N.C. = 13.8%

Source: U.S. Census, Population Estimates Program, March 1999.

(Fontana Lake), Henderson (Hendersonville), and Watauga (Appalachian State University) had started to attract retirees in the late 1970s, as did Brunswick, Carteret, Dare, and Currituck Counties along the coast. Currituck and Brunswick also benefited from spillover development from the Norfolk–Virginia Beach–Newport News area and Myrtle Beach, South Carolina, respectively. During this period Orange, Durham, and Wake Counties were beginning to benefit from the attraction of high-tech research facilities to the Research Triangle Park.

The interplay of urban centers, amenities, and large institutions was also evident in those counties that grew 20–29 percent in the 1970s. Lincoln and Union Counties benefited from their proximity to Charlotte, growth in Wilmington impacted the rest of New Hanover and (adjacent) Pender Counties, and Randolph County gained from its proximity to Winston-Salem and Asheboro. Amenities influenced the high rate of change for Clay and Macon Counties (mountains), Burke and Alexander (lakes), and Moore (golf retirement communities). Nearby military institutions played a major role in the growth of Hoke and Pitt Counties. Only three counties recorded population declines: Hertford and Northampton on the northeastern Inner Coastal Plain and Jones County in the central Tidewater region.

From 1980 to 1990 growth patterns changed significantly (Fig. 4.7b). The greatest differences appeared in the Tidewater, where overall growth was 21 percent, well above the statewide rate of 12.6 percent. However, there was considerable variation among the counties in that region. Four (Hyde, Jones, Tyrrell, and Washington) lost population, and seven (Beaufort, Camden, Chowan, Craven, Pamlico, Pasquotank, and Perquimans) grew at rates slower than the state average. The others, in contrast, experienced strong growth. Dare was the fastest-growing county in the state, expanding by two-thirds. Brunswick increased by over 42 percent, and Currituck and Pender had growth rates of 23 percent and 29 percent, respectively. New Hanover County, though it grew by "only" 16 percent, had the Tidewater's largest absolute gain of over 16,000 people.

The twenty-three counties on the Inner Coastal Plain, away from the beaches, are rural, and most do not have the advantage of large institutions. Collectively they grew at a slow rate of 6.1 percent, and ten of them actually lost population.

The Piedmont demonstrated less variability in rates, but there were clearly "winners" and "losers." Anson, Caswell, and Richmond Counties lost population. At the other extreme, Wake County, even with its large population base in 1980, grew over 40 percent and generated growth that spilled over into nearby Durham, Franklin, and Orange Counties. Other counties that were tied to the several urban centers in this region achieved rates of at least 20 percent. Mecklenburg grew faster than any other county in its region, adding over 105,000 people at a healthy 26 percent clip. In fact, only Wake and Mecklenburg grew by more than 100,000 people during the decade. The other large Piedmont counties, Forsyth and Guilford, expanded more modestly at 9.1 and 9.5 percent, respectively, slower than the rate statewide; together, they added just over 52,000 people to their totals.

In the Mountains, the flurry of growth that had characterized the 1970s either slowed or disappeared. Three counties (Ashe, Graham, and Swain) lost population, and overall the region grew by only 6.3 percent between 1980 and 1990. Henderson, Macon, and Watauga were the only counties to grow by more than 16 percent. Buncombe, site of Asheville, the regional capital, added nearly 14,000 people to its population, at a growth rate of 8.6 percent.

Between 1990 and 1998 growth was again the general rule (Fig. 4.7c). The eight-year statewide growth rate of 13.8 percent was higher than that of the previous decade. Five counties lost population—three of them (Hertford, Tyrrell, and Washington) in the northeastern part of the state. The remaining two are eastern metropolitan counties. One, Edgecombe, is part of the Rocky Mount met-

Figure 4.8. Total Population, 1998

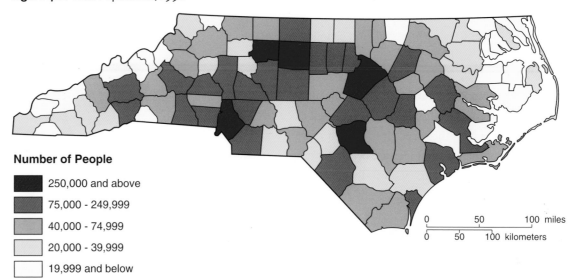

Number of People

- 250,000 and above
- 75,000 - 249,999
- 40,000 - 74,999
- 20,000 - 39,999
- 19,999 and below

Source: U.S. Census, Population Estimates Program, March 1999.

ropolitan area, and the other, Onslow, is the site of Jacksonville. Onslow may have lost population because of reductions in personnel at its several military facilities. Wake County accelerated its phenomenal growth, adding over 144,000 people in the eight-year period at a rate of almost 34 percent. It gained on Mecklenburg as the state's largest county, which grew by "only" 23 percent and added over 120,000 people. Six other counties had growth rates of 30 percent or more, five of which are in or adjacent to metropolitan areas. Two—Brunswick and Pender—surround Wilmington. Currituck is part of the Norfolk, Virginia, area; Hoke borders Fayetteville; Johnston is immediately east of Raleigh; and Union is suburban to Charlotte. Dare

County lost its pride of place as the fastest-growing county in the state but still recorded a strong 27 percent increase.

Growth was somewhat slower but still above the statewide average in a number of other suburban metropolitan counties, especially Cabarrus, Chatham, Franklin, Harnett, Stokes, and Yadkin. In the meantime, the high growth rates experienced in the Tidewater seemed to have peaked, with that region growing by only 11.5 percent, less than the statewide average. Figure 4.8 displays total population ranges produced by these growth trends as of 1998.

Migration

The most dynamic cause of population change is migration. This is the net difference between the number of people who move into an area and those who leave. By definition, migration involves a change of residence. It can also be regarded as "people voting with their feet." It is a much more volatile factor than natural increase because it can change suddenly and is driven by individual decision-making rather than by generally more predictable demographic factors. Figure 4.9 is a map of total net migration for North Carolina between 1980 and 1990. Many counties experienced net out-migration, but they still managed to show a little growth because the loss due to migration was offset by a positive natural increase. For example, Edgecombe and Lenoir, on the Coastal Plain, lost over 3,000 people due to migration but produced enough babies to little more than break even in population growth for the decade. Many other counties on the Coastal Plain, with significant concentrations of African Americans and Native Americans, who tend to have higher fertility rates than the general population, had net gains through natural increase that also were large enough to offset losses due to migration. Cumberland County, with its ties to the military, was a huge loser (-12,377) in migration but a big gainer from natural increase (39,783).

In the Mountains and the Piedmont, counties

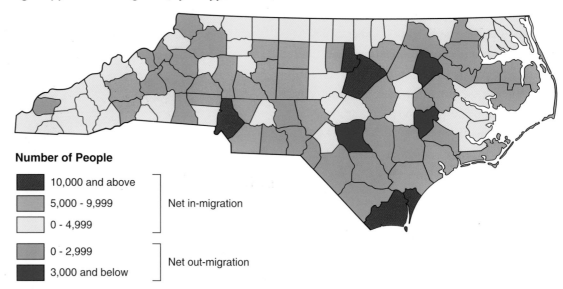

Figure 4.9. Total Net Migration, 1980–1990

Number of People

⬛ 10,000 and above	
◼ 5,000 - 9,999	Net in-migration
◻ 0 - 4,999	
◼ 0 - 2,999	Net out-migration
⬛ 3,000 and below	

Source: U.S. Census of Population and Housing, 1990.

that did not benefit from the presence of urban centers lost people in greater numbers than were attracted to those areas. Henderson County, a major destination for retirees, had a net growth of 10,705 people between 1980 and 1990, all but 643 of whom were in-migrants. The influence of urban centers as magnets for growth is also apparent on the map. Gains of over 10,000 people were found in Mecklenburg (Charlotte), Durham (city of Durham), Guilford (Greensboro–High Point), Wake (Raleigh), and New Hanover (Wilmington) Counties. Wake (91,969) and Mecklenburg (68,835) were the only counties to record a net in-migration of 20,000 or more. Other counties that attracted

net in-migrations of 10,000 or more were Brunswick, containing the coastal amenity area adjacent to Wilmington; Onslow (Jacksonville), whose economy is military-driven; and two university counties, Orange (Chapel Hill) and Pitt (Greenville). Forsyth (Winston-Salem) and Buncombe (Asheville) barely missed a net in-migration of 10,000 people.

No fewer than thirty-five of North Carolina's one hundred counties experienced net out-migration between 1980 and 1990 (Fig. 4.9). Although a number of them managed to grow slightly in spite of it, the effects could still be harmful. Because out-migration tends to be *negatively selective* (i.e., it is usually the younger adults, who are more skilled, energetic, and ambitious, who leave), those who remain are more likely to be elderly, the very young, and the least capable. The loss becomes a downward spiral as the funds needed to correct the problem through investments in education, health, and infrastructure must be extracted from a smaller population and a declining economy.

Of the thirty-five counties that experienced net out-migration, twelve lost 2,000 or more residents and only one, Cleveland, is not in the eastern part of the state. Similarly, most of the smaller net losers were in the east and some were in the Mountains. A few of the more rural counties in the Piedmont also had small net out-migrations. Another way of looking at the pattern of migration is to note that Wake and Mecklenburg Counties alone accounted for 43 percent of the state's total net in-migration.

Figure 4.10 displays U.S. Census estimates of migration totals between 1990 and 1998. These estimates affirm the tendency for in-migration to be strong in and around major metropolitan areas and in recreational-retirement areas along the coast and in the mountains. A possibly important change from the previous decade is that far fewer counties recorded net out-migration. In the earlier decade some thirty-five counties, mostly on the Coastal Plain or in the Mountains, had net out-migration, but that number dropped to only twelve during the 1990–98 period. Significantly, two of the losers, Cumberland and Onslow, are eastern metropolitan counties that contain large military facilities. Of the rest, all but one are along the Coast or on the Inner Coastal Plain. Montgomery County, in the Piedmont, was the lone exception to this eastern trend. All other Piedmont and Mountain counties had net in-migrations. This reversal of rural migration patterns may indicate an increased movement of retirees and other persons who are attracted to the environmental amenities that many rural areas provide.

Although these patterns do communicate important information about the relative ability of counties to attract and sustain numbers of people within their borders, they also mask the dynamics of population turnover. In those

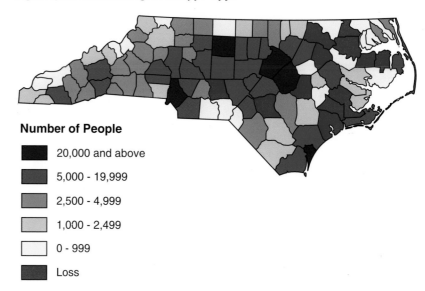

Figure 4.10. Total Net Migration, 1990–1998

Number of People

- 20,000 and above
- 5,000 - 19,999
- 2,500 - 4,999
- 1,000 - 2,499
- 0 - 999
- Loss

Source: U.S. Census, Population Estimates Program, March 1999.

counties where the net loss or gain may number in the thousands, it is easy to understand the gain in terms of demand for new services or the loss of people in the labor force or those who make up a market for goods. But even in counties where the net change due to net migration is relatively small, there may be substantial upheaval as people move out and others replace them. This is particularly a problem in areas affected by large institutions where turnover and replacement are common, such as on military bases, or in areas where long-term residents are replaced by newcomers who may have different needs, social characteristics, and political ideas. Both numerical change as well as structural change may have significant impacts on local areas.

Population Density

A key characteristic of population is its density, or the concentration of people per unit of area—in this case, the number of people per square mile. Density serves as a crude measure of crowdedness. It is crude in that it does not take into account the land in a county that may not be available for residential development either because of the competition of other types of land use (industrial, commercial, institutional), because of topographic features that make development unsuitable, or because of restrictions imposed by the public sector (protection for parks, national and state forests, cultural sites, or military bases). But water bodies are excluded from Figure 4.11, which displays density only in terms of total land area. From the map it is apparent that there is considerable variation in the density of population across the state. The obvious "empty" counties are low-amenity rural, coastal counties and counties deep in the mountains. Twenty-three counties have fewer than forty-nine persons per square mile. Hyde County, in northeastern North Carolina, is the lowest in the state with only nine persons per square mile.

The obvious high-density areas, not surprisingly, are core counties in the larger metropolitan areas, led by Mecklenburg County's 1,164 persons per square mile, the only county to have more than 1,000 per square mile. Most of those in the 150–399-persons-per-square-mile range are either cen-

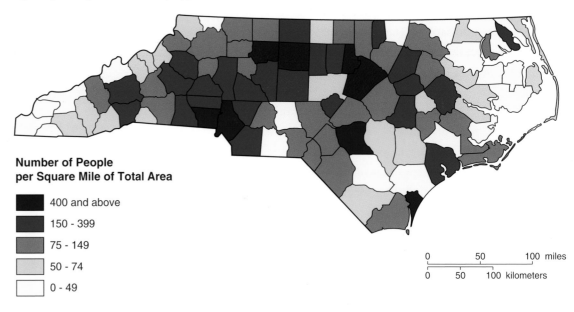

Figure 4.11. Population Density, 1998

Number of People per Square Mile of Total Area

- 400 and above
- 150 - 399
- 75 - 149
- 50 - 74
- 0 - 49

N.C. average, 1980 = 111.7
N.C. average, 1997 = 152.0

Source: Calculated from U.S. Census, Population Estimates Program, March 1999.

tral to smaller metropolitan areas or suburban parts of larger metro areas. An exception to this trend is New Hanover County, the site of Wilmington. That county is the second most densely settled in the state with 742 persons per square mile. This density is due in part to the fact that New Hanover has the second smallest land area of all North Carolina counties.

Although these measures of crowding are crude, they do reveal several issues that may be of increasing concern. The areas with high densities are already facing the dilemmas of water and air pollution, reduction of open space, traffic congestion, and other quality-of-life issues. In mainly rural areas where density levels are relatively moderate, there is already concern for the need to preserve farmland. On the other hand, it may seem beneficial to have decreasing levels of population density, except where the provision of services is concerned. It may become increasingly more difficult to provide medical, educational, and social services to places where the population is dispersed over broad areas. In these places the volume of the need may be relatively small but the severity of the problems may be great simply because the density is so low.

Key Racial and Ethnic Groups

Another important demographic pattern is that of key racial or ethnic groups in counties across the state. North Carolina is 75.4 percent white, a proportion that has remained fairly stable in recent decades. This is also true in metropolitan areas. In the thirteen largest counties that are central to metropolitan areas, the white proportion declined slightly between 1980 and 1990, from 75.2 to 74.2 percent. In the other eighty-seven counties the white proportion increased during the same time from 76.2 to 76.7 percent. In sixty-one one of these eighty-seven counties, the nonwhite population recorded net out-migration.

The single largest minority group in North Carolina is composed of African Americans. Their relative strength in counties of the Coastal Plain is evident in Figure 4.12. Except in the beach amenity areas along the coast, they made up a third or more of each county's population in 1997. Many of those counties are poor and have limited economic opportunities. The Piedmont is mixed in terms of the

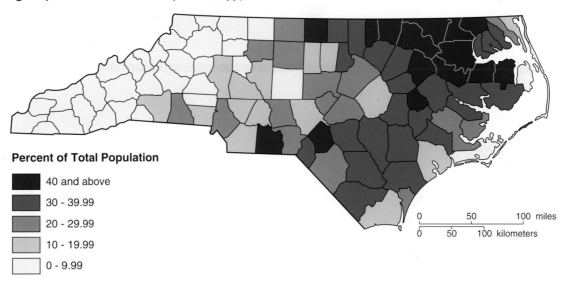

Figure 4.12. African American Population, 1997

Percent of Total Population

- 40 and above
- 30 - 39.99
- 20 - 29.99
- 10 - 19.99
- 0 - 9.99

Source: U.S. Census, Population Estimates Program, September 1998.

proportion of blacks. In the counties with larger urban centers, the number of African Americans may be significant, but their proportions are diluted by the larger numbers of nonblacks there. In several parts of the Piedmont and virtually all of the Mountain counties, less than 10 percent of the population is black. Within the municipalities that comprise the state's ten largest cities, the number of blacks increased marginally between 1980 and 1990, from 32.4 to 32.7 percent of the population.

Whereas blacks make up a significant portion of the population of the state and of several counties, such is not the case for Native Americans. In 1997 there were only 95,398 Native Americans in North Carolina, 1.3 percent of the state total. The majority of them resided in Robeson County alone (Fig. 4.13). Robeson County lies at the center of the large coastal core area for the Lumbee people that also includes Columbus, Cumberland, Hoke, and Scotland Counties. About 63 percent of the state's Native American population lived in this cluster of five counties in 1997. A second core area was in the western Mountains, home of the Cherokee. Jackson and Swain Counties contained 6,739 Native Americans, 7.1 percent of the state total. The largest remaining numbers were found in the larger

A Lumbee Indian tobacco farmer in Robeson County

well as in the urban, industrial counties of the Piedmont.

The rapidly increasing Asian population was concentrated principally in the state's urban areas. In 1990 about 77 percent resided in the thirteen largest metropolitan counties, where they increased by over 157 percent between 1980 and 1990. The rate of increase in the other eighty-seven counties was also high (117 percent), but the total change involved only 6,491 persons of Asian descent, whereas the thirteen metropolitan counties gained 24,597 persons. By 1997 over 76 percent of the Asian population resided in the eleven metropolitan counties shown in Table 4.1. By far the largest numbers were in the two largest counties, Wake and Mecklenburg. Collectively, they accounted for over one-third of the state total.

A similar pattern was followed by Hispanics except that they tended to concentrate more heavily around military bases. Hispanics' numbers increased by 55.5 percent in the thirteen largest metropolitan counties and only 13 percent in the rest of the state between 1980 and 1990. By 1997, 61 percent were located in the eleven counties listed in Table 4.1, led by Cumberland. Together, Cumberland and Onslow, another site of major military facilities, accounted for one-quarter of the state total. Otherwise, the leaders were in six metropolitan areas, including the three largest in the state.

metropolitan areas. Nearly 2,600 lived in Mecklenburg, almost 2,000 in Guilford, and another 1,600 in Wake County.

The demographic patterns of the two ethnic groups present some interesting insights. Most of the Native American population resides in rural areas where their influence may be felt and in relative isolation where they may be better able to preserve their way of life. On the other hand, they are predominantly located in poorer parts of the state where the lack of economic opportunities may force younger adults to leave the area to find work. Blacks, on the other hand, are more divided in their proximity to economic opportunities in that they are found in large numbers both in the poorer, rural areas of the Inner Coastal Plain, as

Figure 4.13. Counties Containing Greatest Number of Native Americans, 1997

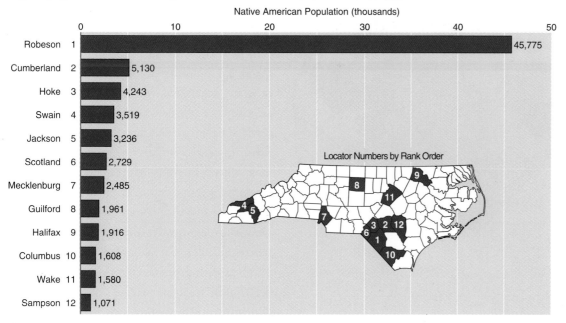

Native American Population (thousands)

County	Rank	Population
Robeson	1	45,775
Cumberland	2	5,130
Hoke	3	4,243
Swain	4	3,519
Jackson	5	3,236
Scotland	6	2,729
Mecklenburg	7	2,485
Guilford	8	1,961
Halifax	9	1,916
Columbus	10	1,608
Wake	11	1,580
Sampson	12	1,071

Locator Numbers by Rank Order

Source: U.S. Census, Population Estimates Program, March 1998.

The Elderly

A final characteristic to be considered is the distribution of the population that was 65 years or older as of 1997 (Fig. 4.14). The pattern of higher proportions of older people may reflect the results of two types of selective migration. The first is that there has been a net out-migration of younger age groups to places that offer more opportunities for work and education. This may describe the situation in several counties in the predominantly rural Inner Coastal Plain that are located away from the attractions of beach amenities or metropolitan areas. The same pattern also may be true for some Piedmont and Mountain counties that do not have a sufficient economic base to keep younger segments of the population in place.

On the other hand, some counties with high proportions of older people are actually destinations of older migrants who seek amenity-type areas that also have adequate services to meet their needs. In particular, Clay, Henderson, Polk, Macon, and Moore Counties fit into this category, each with 20 percent or more of its population aged 65 or older in 1997. Even there, the proportions listed by the U.S. Census may be significant underestimates of the 65-or-older population in these counties who are seasonal residents. Because the Census Bureau reports only full-time residents, and because being a resident of Florida as opposed to North Carolina supposedly has tax advantages, this seasonal population is not always counted. But its effects may be felt in several ways. First, on the negative side, this quasi-transient population may put a strain on existing medical and other services for that portion of the year that it is present. On the positive side, retirees often have more income to spend on discretionary items, such as works of art, antiques, crafts, and expensive meals. Hence, they may make an important contribution to the economic well-being of the community.

In addition to those who move to the Mountains as full- or part-time residents, a substantial but unmeasured number of retirees have migrated to metropolitan areas to which an adult child has been drawn by economic opportunities. Another group, military retirees, choose to retire near the military bases where they spent years in service, have a network of friends, and are close to military stores and medical facilities. These retirees are often relatively young and start new careers before truly retiring.

All one hundred counties in North Carolina

Figure 4.14. Population Age 65 and Over, 1997

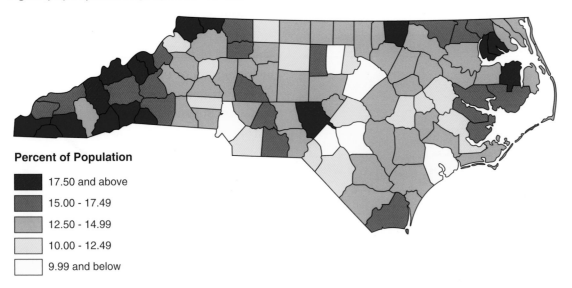

Percent of Population

- 17.50 and above
- 15.00 - 17.49
- 12.50 - 14.99
- 10.00 - 12.49
- 9.99 and below

Source: U.S. Census, Population Estimates Program, March 1998.

had populations that contained at least 8 percent or more of the 65-and-older age group, and in ninety-four of them this proportion reached at least 10 percent (Fig. 4.14). Those that had fewer than 10 percent were either large metropolitan areas (Mecklenburg, Orange, and Wake) or close to military bases (Cumberland, Hoke, and Onslow). Others that were below the statewide average of 12.5 percent were either metropolitan, contained military bases, or had sizable university campuses. Interestingly, eighty counties had proportions higher than the state average. This was statistically possible because most of the larger counties, which accounted for a disproportionate share of the total population, had low proportions of elderly residents. Thus, their numbers skewed the state average to a level lower than it was for most counties.

As the population of the state ages, the implications of this dispersed pattern are both sobering and important. Even in counties that are comparatively well off economically, there likely will be significant numbers of people who will demand specialized goods and services, ranging from nursing homes, in-home care, and adult day care to larger lettering on road signs to compensate for inevitable changes in physiology. This group may also be resistant to reversals in entitlements, such as reduced property and income taxes for older residents, or increases in taxes, at a time when their demand for services from various levels of government is likely to escalate and run counter to demands made by other groups for schools, adult day care, and other services. On the other hand, the elderly may create new markets for businesses and services. Counties that have not already done so may consider recruiting affluent retirees to supplement other forms of economic development. This type of targeting seems to be particularly successful in areas with amenity appeal (coastal beaches, mountains, lakes, golf courses) and those that offer sports and cultural activities (college towns).

In more rural, poorer counties where the number of older residents may be small, there will be difficulty both in finding sufficient resources to meet the needs of older citizens and in providing services in the locale they may have lived in for many years. For example, there may be increasing pressure to build a single nursing facility to serve the needs of several counties, which may result in the severance of social networks of which the elderly have been a part because the commute would be problematic for their families and friends.

Housing

North Carolinians have an even stronger preference for home ownership than do other Americans. In 1990 about 68 percent of all housing units in the state were occupied by their owners, compared with a 64 percent share in the country as a whole. Perhaps this was helped by the fact that average house values in North Carolina were 17 percent below the national median of $79,100. Home ownership rates in the Mountains exceeded 75 percent, and both on the Coastal Plain and in the Piedmont it was about 67 percent. These rates also varied among ethnic and racial groups: for whites, 73 percent; Native Americans, 66 percent; African Americans, 50 percent; Asians, 48 percent; and Hispanics, 42 percent. Over 65 percent of all units were for single families, but the share of multifamily units is expected to rise, especially in the state's burgeoning urban areas.

The quality of housing has improved to some extent in recent years. In 1980, 4.4 percent of all units lacked complete kitchen facilities, but by 1990 this proportion had fallen to 1.2 percent. Similarly, the number of units that lacked complete plumbing dropped from 4.0 to 1.3 percent. In 1990 most of the housing was relatively new—only 9.9 percent was fifty years old or older. By the year 2000, however, about 21 percent was projected to be between forty and sixty years old. The Mountain region had the highest share of older housing, and the Piedmont had the lowest.

Significantly, in 1990 fully 15 percent of all housing units in North Carolina were mobile homes, compared with a national share of 7.2 percent. It is small wonder that mobile homes are such a common feature on the landscape, especially in rural

Figure 4.15. Mobile Homes, 1990

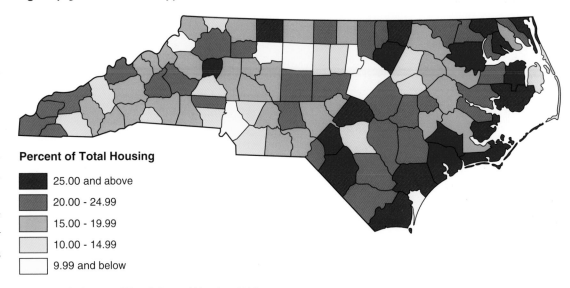

Percent of Total Housing

- 25.00 and above
- 20.00 - 24.99
- 15.00 - 19.99
- 10.00 - 14.99
- 9.99 and below

Source: U.S. Census of Population and Housing, 1990.

areas. Mobile homes are generally less expensive than "stick built" houses and thus make single-family housing more affordable for lower-income people.

Unfortunately, mobile homes tend to depreciate rather than appreciate in value, so their buyers are unable to build equity in their homes. Thus, even though this housing is less expensive, mobile home buyers find it difficult to "trade up" into more expensive houses. The correlation between income levels and mobile home preference is inferred from Figure 4.15, which displays the proportion of mobile homes in the total housing stock in 1990. All nineteen counties that had mobile home

shares of 25 percent or more had per capita income levels well below the state average and were largely rural in nature. On the other hand, the areas that had shares of less than 10 percent were among the state's most populous, higher-income counties, including Durham, Forsyth, Guilford, Mecklenburg, New Hanover, and Wake. Another factor in mobile home ownership is their use as second homes, as appears to be the case in the eleven counties on the coast.

The only comprehensive data available on mobile home housing come from the 1990 census. However, building permit data collected in the Charlotte area suggest that the preference/need for

Table 4.2. Mobile Homes as a Percentage
of Total Housing Units in the Charlotte Area

County	Mobile Home Units, 1990 (%)	Mobile Home Units Permitted, 1990–97 (%)
Anson	15.4	84.4
Cabarrus	13.5	28.2
Cleveland	15.6	60.2
Gaston	11.9	35.9
Iredell	19.2	41.9
Lincoln	23.5	47.0*
Mecklenburg	2.7	2.8
Rowan	18.1	45.6
Stanly	13.8	35.2
Union	12.9	22.4
Total	14.7	40.4

Source: Centralina Council of Governments.
*1990–96

mobile homes is growing. Table 4.2 shows that mobile/modular homes constituted 40 percent of the new housing units authorized in the period 1990–97, compared with an average share of 14.7 percent in 1990 in the ten-county region surveyed. Union County had the highest unit value for a mobile/modular home, $28,012, but this was still only 36 percent of the average single-family house value in that county, a strong indicator that mobile homes are a matter of affordability.

Affordable housing units are defined as "units for which a family would pay no more than 30 per-cent of their income for rent and no more than 2.5 times their annual income to purchase." By that standard some 12.5 percent of North Carolina households, nearly 315,000, were too poor to afford housing in 1990. The 1996 North Carolina Consolidated Plan has proposed a host of actions to address this need, including low-interest–low-down-payment loans, rent subsidies, and housing rehabilitation programs.

Another, nongovernmental, response to this need is Habitat for Humanity, a Christian-based organization that uses volunteer labor to build homes for qualifying low-income families, many of them minorities. The houses are priced below market values and mortgage loans are interest free. In 1997 Habitat built 253 homes in North Carolina, and Charlotte had one of the most active Habitat programs in the country. The program is so popular and the need so great that in 1998 there were eighty-two Habitat groups in the state. Every metropolitan area had one or more Habitat affiliates, including seven in the Greensboro–Winston-Salem–High Point area, eight in Charlotte-Gastonia, and seven in Raleigh-Durham. All together, there were thirty-eight Habitat affiliates in the state's metro areas and forty-four in smaller cities or rural areas. The number of affiliates and their geographic dispersion indicate that the need for more affordable housing is widespread.

The rapid growth of population and housing has had an inflationary impact on housing prices, especially housing that is affordable for more affluent households. The National Homebuilders Association calculates a Housing Opportunity Index (HOI) that expresses the percentage of home sales that a family earning an area's median income could afford. Table 4.3 summarizes the HOI report for the 5 North Carolina metropolitan areas that were included in the national total of 191 areas for the first quarter of 1998. All five metro areas had index values that were only a few points above or below the national index. Three of them had sale prices that were below the national median, and two had index values higher than the national HOI of 67.6 percent. This means that in those two areas a household with an income at or above the local median could afford better than two-thirds of all the houses sold there. In Asheville, median sales prices were below the national median, but lower income levels caused the index to be slightly below the national average. In the state's two largest metropolitan areas, Raleigh-Durham and Charlotte, the HOI values were several points below the national level because of higher sales prices. The average sales price in Raleigh-Durham was higher than Charlotte's but so were median incomes.

Outlook

Although North Carolina has continued to grow relatively consistently over the last several decades, the sorting process across regions and across coun-

Table 4.3. Housing Affordability,
First Quarter, 1998

Metropolitan Area	HOI*	Median House Sales Price ($ thousands)
Asheville	66.7	105
Charlotte-Gastonia	63.0	136
Fayetteville	70.5	90
Greensboro/Winston-Salem/High Point	69.9	116
Raleigh-Durham	65.9	144
U.S. (191 areas)	67.6	129

Source: National Home Builders Association.
*HOI (Housing Opportunity Index) is the percentage of families who could afford the median sales price of a home.

ties has presented both opportunities and problems. As can be seen in the patterns at both regional and county levels, this sorting process has been influenced strongly by the presence of urban centers. These centers tend to act as magnets both for people and for economic activities that in the best of circumstances provide new resources for the centers and the areas within their influence. These resources may involve anything from the influx of new ideas, to additional sources of revenue to support the provision of services, to diversity in employment opportunities. More rural areas along the Coast, in the Mountains, or even in the Piedmont have not fared as well, in that their population characteristics describe places where the productive workforce has left for opportunities in growth areas. Unless circumstances change substantially, the aging of the population in place as well as the selective out-migration of younger people will continue to empty these small towns and rural areas. These population dynamics have significant implications for the provision of services across the state as well as the sources of funding for local, county, and state government.

Not all rural areas are experiencing these types of patterns. Places that have some type of amenity, like barrier islands along the Atlantic Coast, mountains, lakes, or good golf course environments, continue to attract people and economic activities to sustain their communities. The popularity of these areas is of interest both locally and at the state level—not only for the tourist dollars that come in, but also for the pressures that seasonal concentrations of visitors may place on these often environmentally sensitive areas. Care must be taken that their popularity does not destroy the very qualities that attracted the visitors in the first place. Seasonal visitors not only help to maintain the economic and social viability of these environmentally advantaged places, but they also form the pool from which future residents are drawn, as people often retire to places where they vacationed in earlier periods of their lives. This type of "showcasing" of amenity sites in rural areas is another reason why parks, campgrounds, and other recreational facilities should be treated as more than just frills but as resources. This may be especially true in those areas with amenity potential that have not yet been "discovered" by tourists and other visitors.

A third significant force in the sorting process across the counties of North Carolina has been the influence of large institutions, in particular, military installations and colleges and universities. Military installations such as Fort Bragg, Camp Lejeune, and Pope Air Force Base, and colleges and universities, such as those in the Research Triangle area and in the Mountains (Appalachian State University, Western Carolina University, and the University of North Carolina at Asheville) influence their home counties and adjacent counties by the selective populations they contain and by the types of economic services that they attract to serve these populations. Moreover, they are not affected by the same economic forces that operate elsewhere in North Carolina. They truly stand out in more isolated parts of the state that do not have other advantages to attract people and economic activities. Their well-being is critical to the vitality of those areas.

In the past, North Carolina's population often grew slowly. But in recent years growth has exceeded national averages and people are moving into rather than leaving the state. The North Carolina Office of State Planning projected that in the year 2000 the state would have 7,713,383 residents, a total to be achieved through a record-shattering net in-migration of 698,038 people between 1990 and 2000. The state planners foresee a population of over 9.3 million by 2020. The projected growth between 1990 and 2020 includes nearly 1.8 million net in-migrants, a level that is expected to be exceeded only by California, Florida, Texas, and Washington State. These in-migrants will account for at least two-thirds of North Carolina's net growth between 1990 and 2020.

Figure 4.16 presents a striking picture of the nature of population growth between 1940 and 1990 and projections to the year 2020. It shows that from 1940 to 1970 the North Carolina population grew only because natural increase, the excess in the number of births over deaths, exceeded out-migration. But since the 1950s the amount of natural increase has been declining, and it is projected to continue to decline through 2020. For the first time, between 1980 and 1990 in-migration equaled natural increase; it is expected to far exceed it in the near future, by over 300,000 in each succeeding decade.

Two-thirds or more of the state's net growth is expected to come from in-migration. In short, North Carolina previously grew only because of high birthrates and large families, but families have grown much smaller as the state has become more urban and more prosperous. Now the state must depend for most of its growth on attracting large numbers of new residents. Appealing to such large numbers is generally a function of a strong economy and an inviting quality of life. If the economy falters or the environment seriously deteriorates, it is likely that growth will drop sharply,

Figure 4.16. Components of North Carolina Population Change, 1940–2020

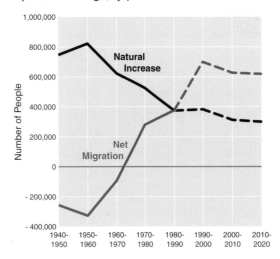

Sources: U.S. Census of Population and Housing, 1940-90; N.C. Office of State Planning, 1998 (for 2000-2020), http://www.ospl.state.ncus/demog/.

perhaps abruptly. Further, dependence on in-migrants for growth will favor the larger metropolitan areas and selected rural high-amenity areas. For many other small towns and rural locations with a limited economic base or few if any amenities, it will be difficult to attract new residents.

In addition to the danger posed by depending on newcomers for growth, the recent floodtide of new residents is bringing with it major cultural change. There is more ethnic diversity, of course, but there also are more subtle changes as people from all over the country, and indeed the world, move to North Carolina in increasing numbers. Daily newspapers witness this in a steady stream of letters complaining about rude "Yankees" or crude "Rednecks." People from the Northeast bring a love for ice hockey, a sport unknown to most native North Carolinians, whereas NASCAR races are new to recent in-migrants. Roman Catholic churches grow faster than the Presbyterian churches that were founded by Scots-Irish settlers. Mexican and Thai restaurants stand next to Bubba's barbecue pit. Migrants from Texas think barbecue should be made from beef, and they completely miss the distinction between "Down East" and "Lexington" styles of barbecuing pork.

The list goes on, but the point is that both native North Carolinians and their new neighbors are undergoing a period of social and cultural change unprecedented in the state's history. Although most of the examples of this change may seem inconsequential, the adjustments are real and promise to both threaten and improve the quality of life in the state. Perhaps the most disturbing fact about in-migration is its apparent association with rising crime rates, as shown in Chapter 14, "Crime."

Equally as important as the projected statewide growth is the question of how it will be distributed in the state between 1990 and 2020. The North Carolina Office of State Planning breaks its projections down to the county level and reveals some very significant trends (Fig. 4.17). These projections can be compared with the distribution shown in Figure 4.8.

Elsewhere in this book it has been observed that the state's largest metropolitan areas—those cen-

International restaurant signs along Central Avenue in Charlotte

tering on Charlotte, Raleigh-Durham, and Greensboro–Winston-Salem—are increasingly dominating the North Carolina economy. This is especially true for Charlotte and Raleigh-Durham and the counties proximate to them. The core of the Charlotte area is made up of Mecklenburg, Cabarrus, Gaston, and Union Counties. Mecklenburg will add 398,319 residents on a 78 percent growth rate. Raleigh-Durham is focused on Durham, Franklin, Johnston, Orange, and Wake Counties. Wake County alone is expected to add 528,023 residents. Its growth rate—124 percent—will be the highest in North Carolina, propelling it past Mecklenburg to be the state's most populous county by 2020. Central to the Triad area are Davidson, Forsyth, Guilford, and Randolph Counties. Collectively, these thirteen counties in the Charlotte, Raleigh-Durham, and Greensboro–Winston-Salem areas contained 38.2 percent of the state's population in 1990, but between 1990 and 2020 they are projected to capture the majority (55.8 percent) of the net statewide growth of 2,925,762 people, raising their collective share of the state total to 44 percent.

Eight more counties (Buncombe, Catawba, Cumberland, Nash, New Hanover, Onslow, Pitt, and Wayne) that are central to the state's other metropolitan areas are projected to account for another 14.9 percent of the 1990–2020 increase, leaving just 29.3 percent (857,551) to be divided among the re-

maining seventy-nine counties. Clearly, then, unless some major unexpected shifts occur, growth in this state will be dominated to an unprecedented extent by its metropolitan areas, especially the larger ones. Between 1990 and 2020 the Raleigh-Durham cluster of counties is projected to grow by 93 percent and the Charlotte cluster by 65 percent. But the seven smaller metropolitan counties, at 39 percent, are expected to grow faster than the Greensboro–Winston-Salem area, which is projected to gain by just 36 percent, less than the statewide increase of 44 percent. All four groups of metropolitan counties are expected to outperform the remaining seventy-nine counties, those that are not central to one of the state's metropolitan areas, as they will grow only 28.9 percent during the thirty-year projection period. Thus, their share of the state total will drop from almost 45 percent to barely 40 percent.

Within this group of seventy-nine counties, eleven are projected to experience absolute population losses between 1990 and 2020, and as many as sixteen are expected to have net out-migrations sometime during that period. By the end of the period about twenty-one counties are expected to record more deaths than births, a reflection of the increasing median age of their populations. This group includes the Mountain and Coastal counties that are major destinations for retirees. All together, the counties that are both losing population and growing older are primarily nonmetropolitan and in the east, with most of the rest in the Mountains and a few in the Piedmont.

These estimates of growth and losses are not infallible, of course, but they do represent the best judgments of professional demographers. In essence, the projections portray a future that is substantially different from the past. Until recently North Carolina was a state that, despite being the eleventh most populous and the eighth largest in manufacturing, was characterized by a relatively dispersed, rural, small-town population and a lack of large cities. By contrast, the Raleigh-Durham and Charlotte areas are emerging as million-plus core urban areas, and their full metropolitan areas will be even larger. The Triad area and the smaller metropolitan areas will claim still more shares of the growth. The remaining seventy-nine counties will grow less vigorously except for a few along the Coast, in Mountain recreation areas, or in proximity to metropolitan areas. Many of the smaller ones, especially on the Inner Coastal Plain, are returning to classic southern rural patterns of past decades, marked by net out-migration and the downward cycle that comes with it. Only counties that are within commuting distance of the metropolitan jobs centers or that have significant recreational resources can hope to escape this negative trend.

The historic basis for the perception of North Carolina as a rural, small-town state is rapidly disappearing. In its place is a new reality in which the state's population and economy are dominated by its metropolitan areas, especially Raleigh-Durham and Charlotte. In many respects this means that the state is moving toward a pattern that is more typical of other states. Many may understandably mourn the loss of North Carolina's predominantly rural, small-town character, but this new reality provides a more accurate basis for managing the future of the state. Ironically, the best chance for helping the left-behind rural areas is to ensure that the metropolitan areas, both large and small, are able to function properly and compete successfully in the high-tech, information processing, global economy of the future. If this happens because of wise business leadership and supportive public policies, then the state may have the resources to look after those areas that are not getting their share of the growth.

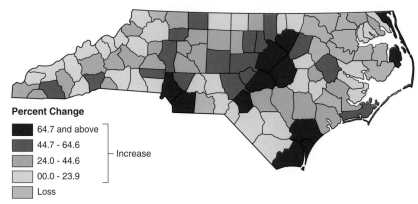

Figure 4.17. County Population Projections, 1990–2020

Percent Change

- 64.7 and above ⎤
- 44.7 - 64.6 ⎟
- 24.0 - 44.6 ⎬ Increase
- 00.0 - 23.9 ⎦
- Loss

Note: Projected growth rate for the total state is 44.6%.

Sources: N.C. Office of State Planning, 1998, http://www.ospl.state.ncus/demog/.

Selected References

Bennett, D., and J. Florin. "The Population of the Carolinas." In *Snapshots of the Carolinas: Landscapes and Culture*, edited by D. Gordon Bennett, pp. 105–8. Washington, D.C.: Association of American Geographers, 1996.

North Carolina Office of State Planning. *County Growth Patterns 1990–2000, 2000–2010, 2010–2020*. June 1998. Available on the Internet at http://www.ospl.state.nc.us/demog/.

U.S. Bureau of the Census. Population Division. Population Estimates Program. *Estimates of the Population of Counties for July 1, 1997, and Population Change: April 1, 1990 to July 1, 1997*. CO-97-1, March 1998.

U.S. Census of Population and Housing, 1790–1990. Summary data contained in the *Statistical Abstract of the United States, 1997*. National, regional, and state data available on the Internet at http://www.census.gov/prod/www/abs/cc97stab.html.

U.S. Department of Housing and Urban Development. Office of Community Planning and Development. *Consolidated Plan for the State of North Carolina for 1996–2000*. 1996.

5. URBANIZATION

Gerald L. Ingalls

North Carolinians are accustomed to growth and change. They have characterized the economy and population of the state and of most of its larger cities over the past three decades. Such developments have included a steady restructuring of the places where North Carolinians live. There is strong evidence that the population is consolidating into higher-density, urban landscapes.

As recently as the mid-1970s, North Carolina was dominated by what one writer called "dispersed urbanism"—where most of the residents lived in smaller towns that were, more often than not, established around the ubiquitous textile or furniture mills where many people still worked. Whereas North Carolina ranked among the most industrialized states in the country, it was, unlike the classic examples of high-density urban development in Europe and the northern and midwestern United States, one of the least urbanized states. Its population was dispersed across hundreds of small towns and villages rather than concentrated into a few dominant metropolitan places.

Although lower levels of urbanization have been characteristic of the American South generally, North Carolina's urbanization has been unlike that of even most of its southern cousins. And in North Carolina no urban center has played a crucial role in the economic or historic development of the state, as have New Orleans, Atlanta, Richmond, and Charleston in their respective states. In fact, North Carolina had little appreciable urban development until the beginning of the twentieth century. Urban development in North Carolina moved at a slower pace than in other southern states and considerably slower than much of the rest of the nation.

The last three decades of this century have seen significant change in North Carolina's urban landscape. By 1998 population estimates indicated that most residents had assembled into one of eleven major metropolitan areas, and this consolidation into fewer urban places seems to be accelerating. Current estimates suggest that people are moving into the counties that comprise Metropolitan Statistical Areas (MSAs) at a rate three times that of nonmetropolitan counties. Of the fifty-one fastest-growing municipalities in North Carolina during 1990–97, thirty-four were in MSA counties and seventeen were either in the two largest counties, Wake and Mecklenburg, or immediately adjacent to one of their boundaries.

As this century closed, North Carolinians were witnessing an era of urban expansion unprecedented since the turn of the last century. Current urban restructuring will establish the landscape of the twenty-first century, just as the explosive urban growth of the late nineteenth century set the urban pattern for the twentieth. This chapter describes the existing urban pattern and explores the social,

economic, and political forces that created it. Operating on the premise that an understanding of the past will guide us into the future, it is helpful to examine the state's urban development, past and present.

The urbanization of North Carolina can be divided into three distinct periods. The first, "Rural North Carolina," saw little or no development of cities. This period extended roughly from the first census in 1790 to the beginning of industrialization in 1880. The middle period, "Dispersed Urbanization," extended from 1880 to roughly 1970 and was characterized by strong industrial and economic growth, particularly in industries that sought out a more rural, small-town setting. Finally, in the decades since 1970, North Carolina has entered a period of "Urban Concentration" in which the population is consolidating into larger urban places.

Rural North Carolina, 1790–1880

Small towns and villages have dominated the settlement pattern in North Carolina for most of its history. The state emerged from the colonial era and entered the decade after the first U.S. Census in 1790 with a few tiny trading centers to serve its population of planters and farmers. Despite a substantial population base (10 percent of the nation's total in 1790), North Carolina had no urban population as late as 1820 (Table 5.1 and Fig.

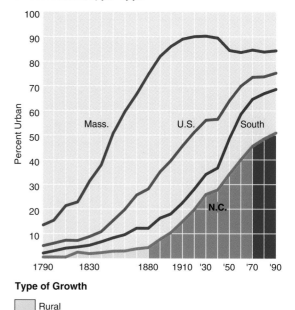

Figure 5.1. Growth of Urbanization in North Carolina, the South, Massachusetts, and the United States, 1790–1990

Type of Growth

- Rural
- Dispersed urban
- Urban concentration

Source: U.S. Census of Population and Housing, 1790-1990.

5.1). Wilmington, the principal port and largest city during the latter part of this period, never rivaled the development of other ports of the east coast. Neighboring Charleston co-opted its North Carolina competitors as the major port city of the Carolinas. As late as 1860, what passed for urban development was concentrated primarily on the Coastal Plain.

During this period North Carolina, like most

of the South, was a rural, agrarian society quite different from the rapidly developing, highly competitive market and urban societies emerging in the rest of the nation. When states such as Massachusetts urbanized early and quickly on the strength of substantial industrialization, the South chose to maintain a steadfastly rural, agricultural, antiurban/antiindustrial attitude. Despite vocal advocates of urbanization like J. D. B. De Bow and North Carolinian Hinton Helper, the dominant southern voices parroted that of Thomas Jefferson, who equated cities with "vice and wretchedness" and labeled them "sores on the national body."

The Civil War left what southern urban infrastructure there had been largely in ruins, and Reconstruction stifled what little incentive for urban development there had been before 1860. As late as 1880 the South remained a rural, agrarian society. In North Carolina, urbanization hovered below 4 percent until the 1880s, when it began to edge upward, following, but not necessarily keeping pace with, the South as a whole (Table 5.1 and Fig. 5.1).

In the antiurban setting of the South before 1880, an elite class composed chiefly of planters and merchants dominated both the economy and society. Government was a vehicle by which professional politicians acted as custodians for the small rural elite that strove to maintain the established order. This system discouraged interparty competition because voter mobilization might jeopardize the stability of the status quo. Industrialization and urbanization, which might well have served to empower a nonelite sector of society to compete for leadership, were viewed with suspicion as, indeed, was any change. This was a South unprepared to compete with the emerging economic dominance of cities such as New York, Chicago, St. Louis, and Cincinnati.

Between 1820 and 1860 the nation's population expanded by 226 percent and its cities grew at a

Table 5.1. Two Hundred Years of Urbanization in North Carolina, 1790–1997

	Year	Population	Urban (%)	Rural (%)	Largest City	Population
Rural North Carolina	1790	393,751	0.0	100.0	NA	NA
	1800	478,103	0.0	100.0	New Bern	2,467
	1810	555,500	0.0	100.0	NA	NA
	1820	638,829	2.0	98.0	New Bern	3,663
	1830	737,987	1.4	98.6	New Bern	3,796
	1840	753,419	1.8	98.2	Fayetteville	4,285
	1850	869,039	2.4	97.6	Wilmington	7,264
	1860	992,622	2.5	97.5	Wilmington	9,552
	1870	1,071,361	3.4	96.6	Wilmington	13,446
	1880	1,399,750	3.9	96.1	Wilmington	17,350
Dispersed urbanization	1890	1,617,947	7.2	92.8	Wilmington	20,056
	1900	1,893,810	9.9	90.1	Wilmington	20,976
	1910	2,206,287	14.4	85.6	Charlotte	34,014
	1920	2,559,123	19.2	80.8	Winston-Salem	48,395
	1930	3,170,276	25.5	74.5	Charlotte	82,675
	1940	3,571,623	27.3	72.7	Charlotte	100,899
	1950	4,061,929	33.7	66.3	Charlotte	134,042
	1960	4,556,155	39.5	60.5	Charlotte	201,564
Urbanization	1970	5,082,059	45.5	54.5	Charlotte	241,420
	1980	5,881,766	48.0	52.0	Charlotte	314,447
	1990	6,628,637	50.4	49.6	Charlotte	395,934
	1997	7,431,161	NA	NA	Charlotte	516,341

Sources: U.S. Census, 1790–1990; *North Carolina Municipal Population, 1997* (N.C. Office of State Planning, 1998).

A Reminiscence of My Old Home Town

Hamlet—the small community where I grew up a half-century ago—was a working man's town, a division point for "the road," as everyone called the Seaboard Air Line Railway (as a company, it disappeared several mergers ago). Train smoke dropped soot and cinders everywhere and steam whistles blew long and lonely in the night.

Six miles west along Highway 74, Rockingham, the Richmond County seat, was Old South—big houses, old families and a history dating to antebellum days. A surrounding ring of textile mills could not detract from its blueblood aura. Two less similar communities, joined only in heated baseball and football rivalries, could hardly be imagined.

Nevertheless, it was locally believed that as the modern era progressed Hamlet and Rockingham inevitably would grow together. Fat chance, most of us thought. But contemporary economic development, a county union high school on neutral ground, and a large shopping mall that now sprawls across Highway 74 between the two towns make the idea less ludicrous than it once seemed.

No doubt the amalgamation of two towns is far less likely than the growth of one, the kind of economic growth businessmen usually welcome, but that can also lead a community right out of the "small town" category. I don't live in North Carolina any longer so perhaps I have no right to protest the aspirations, economic and otherwise, of those who do. But enough such "growth" will change the face and nature of the state—in some ways it already has—not necessarily for the better. The urban monstrosities that dominate elsewhere have until recently been mostly avoided, but growth happens and enough of it could make the small towns that once flourished in North Carolina an endangered species. In an age of development, after all, the industrial base is king and the shopping mall is queen.

We all know what follows industrial development—a gigantic nightmare on the edge of town where they used to grow cotton and cantaloupes, a contraption of steam and chimney and conveyor belts and parking lots, Rube Goldberg gone mad, prosperity in the saddle. And we know, too, what happens when businesses move to the mall—customers follow, old familiar sidewalks are as empty as the store buildings they once fronted, and in not a few cases grass literally grows through the pavement. Old streets turn unkempt, the houses that line them look dilapidated.

The center of activity moves somewhere reachable only by automobile.

Decades ago, an earlier time of "development" robbed the southern small town of one of its most practical and graceful amenities—the wooden roofs that used to cover and shade downtown sidewalks. Not too long afterwards, home television converted the old movie theater—central to the magic visions of my youth—into an empty cavern of dusty dreams, and all too often into a funeral parlor or a discount store.

Years after I finished high school in Hamlet (Class of '44), I encountered a former classmate, who tearfully declared how fortunate we had been to grow up in a "perfect" little town. I didn't remember it or our youth quite so fondly. Still, she was right that in Hamlet, undistinguished though it surely was, we knew little and thought less about crime (maybe a watermelon theft now and then), drugs (nobody considered tobacco just as dangerous), murder (anybody who might have wanted to kill a teacher wouldn't have known how), suicide, and teen pregnancy. A game of "spin the bottle" was pretty racy (though I remember one girl who went to visit her aunt in another state and somehow never came back).

The only danger on the streets was a growing num-

rate of 797 percent. North Carolina's rural population grew by 94 percent, and its urban population grew only from 12,777 (2 percent of the total) to 24,816, 2.5 percent of the total (Fig. 5.1). In 1880 the South still claimed only 30 of the 227 U.S. cities with a population over 10,000. In North Carolina, only Wilmington held that distinction (Fig. 5.2 and Table 5.2).

But change was in the wind. The South and North Carolina were poised to begin a period of industrialization, economic development, and urbanization, albeit in a manner much unlike, at least initially, that of its northern counterparts.

ber of cars, plus a local hazard—to get almost anywhere in Hamlet, you had to cross railroad tracks—grade crossings on every major street, menacing to cars and pedestrians alike. I suppose shopping, like most activities, was limited, though for sophisticated purposes the big cities of Charlotte and Raleigh were only an hour or two away by train. We had a Belk department store, three drug stores (in one of which air conditioning first heralded the age of technology), several pre-supermarket grocery stores, an ice plant, two pool halls (of particular interest to me), and the aforesaid movie theater (three first-run films a week, Bank Night on Wednesday, and a double feature including a cowboy picture on Saturdays).

Despite these Hollywood riches, the centers of social activity still were the churches—dominantly Baptist, but Presbyterians and Methodists were prominent too. Sunday mornings, in any denomination, folks were ordained. Adult social lives were dominated by church socials and "suppers," at which my mother was in great demand for her Parker House rolls. For younger worshipers, Sunday nights were reserved for junior choir practice and heavy dating afterwards. In summer, young people of decent parentage, having bravely survived nine months of regular school,

were sent to Vacation Bible School—which, with the ever present threat of infantile paralysis, was the recurring horror of my youth.

Throughout those days I never once saw a firearm in the old red brick, flat-roofed Hamlet High or sniffed the odor of pot in the basement boys' room. At least half the student body rode in from the countryside on yellow buses Norman Rockwell made famous on a Saturday Evening Post cover. Of course, we seldom thought about the black people who lived in the other part of town. They went to different schools and their mothers came to wash our clothes on Monday mornings. We heard them moving about in the balcony over our heads in the movies.

I occasionally was allowed the privilege of a railroad man's son—to ride my Seaboard "pass" on an early Diesel-powered train known locally as the Boll Weevil—for a day in Charlotte. There I would always lunch on mashed potatoes and gravy at the memory-enriched S & W cafeteria. There, too, on a glorious day at the old Carolina theater I saw Gone With the Wind and on an even more glorious day, Hedy Lamarr in Ecstasy and the altogether.

On these memorable journeys, as the Boll Weevil stopped to take on an occasional passenger, allowing

me to gaze at even smaller communities along the way—Lilesville, Marshville, Indian Trail—I would always be thankful that I lived in and would return to a "big town" like Hamlet. I knew it wasn't New York or Chicago or even Charlotte, but it had life and activity—sports, movies, junior choir, Bank Night. Yet Hamlet had the virtues of a small town too. It was quiet and the pace of life was easy; it was not too big you couldn't find your way around, and it was small enough so that you could know everyone you wanted to know. Someday it would grow together with Rockingham and that would be development, growth, progress.

Well, someday may be a great deal nearer than I ever really thought, in those long ago reveries on the road to Charlotte. And now that I remember it, my weepy classmate's recollection of the small North Carolina town in which she and I grew up was pretty good. Not perfect, of course, but then what is?

Tom Wicker, nationally syndicated newspaper columnist

Dispersed Urbanization, 1880–1970

Change came in the form of a cry by New South advocates for industrialization. J. D. B. De Bow, along with fellow industrial promoters such as Charlotte's D. A. Tompkins, worked in a more receptive climate in the defeated and humiliated South of the 1880s. This time actions followed words and nowhere as swiftly or comprehensively as in North Carolina, which boasted the "greatest native southern industrialist"—James Buchanan Duke of Durham. From a small inherited tobacco company Duke parlayed one of the largest trusts of the period—the American Tobacco Company.

Table 5.2. North Carolina's Ten Largest Cities, 1880–1997

Year	City	Population	Year	City	Population
1997	Charlotte	516,341	1940	Charlotte	100,899
	Raleigh	266,530		Winston-Salem	79,815
	Greensboro	203,342		Durham	60,195
	Winston-Salem	172,763		Greensboro	59,319
	Durham	159,030		Asheville	51,310
	Fayetteville	113,406		Raleigh	46,897
	Cary	80,751		High Point	38,495
	Jacksonville	73,746		Wilmington	33,407
	High Point	73,332		Rocky Mount	25,568
	Asheville	68,133		Fayetteville	17,428
1980	Charlotte	314,447	1910	Charlotte	34,019
	Greensboro	155,642		Wilmington	25,798
	Raleigh	150,225		Winston-Salem	22,700
	Winston-Salem	131,885		Raleigh	19,218
	Durham	100,831		Asheville	18,762
	High Point	63,380		Durham	18,241
	Fayetteville	59,507		Greensboro	15,895
	Asheville	53,583		New Bern	9,961
	Gastonia	47,333		High Point	9,525
	Wilmington	44,000		Concord	8,715
1970	Charlotte	241,178	1880	Wilmington	17,350
	Greensboro	144,076		Raleigh	9,265
	Winston-Salem	132,913		Charlotte	7,094
	Raleigh	121,577		New Bern	6,443
	Durham	95,438		Winston-Salem	4,194
	High Point	63,204		Fayetteville	3,485
	Asheville	57,681		Goldsboro	3,286
	Fayetteville	53,510		Salisbury	2,723
	Gastonia	47,142		Asheville	2,616
	Wilmington	46,169		Elizabeth	2,315

Sources: U.S. Census, 1880–1990; *North Carolina Municipal Population, 1997* (N.C. Office of State Planning, 1998).

Urbanization in North Carolina accompanied a pattern of industrial expansion that came initially in the form of Duke's tobacco factories, followed closely by textile mills. This type of industrialization moved quickly and pervasively into small towns and even rural settings. The textile mills and the towns that surrounded and serviced them came to dominate the settlement pattern of the state in a "dispersed urban pattern." The result of this development in North Carolina was a sprawling, semirural pattern. Jacquelyn Dowd Hall and her colleagues described it in their book, *Like a Family: The Making of a Southern Cotton Mill World*, as "loose patterns of unincorporated mill villages joined by central business districts."

While North Carolina and the South in general were poised to speed this new era of industrial and urban development, social and economic conditions dictated a uniquely southern form of urban-industrial development. As Wilbur Cash argued in his 1941 classic, *The Mind of the South*, southern industrialization blended a Yankee form of manufacturing with southern traditions of a "color line" and an elite political and economic dominance of the workforce whether it was black or white. Between 1870 and 1900 the center of political gravity in North Carolina shifted from farm and plantation to town and small city.

As the economic focus and residence of workers changed, political influence shifted into the thousands of small towns, and particularly into the county seats, across the South. A new system of

Figure 5.2. Urban Growth Patterns, 1910–1997

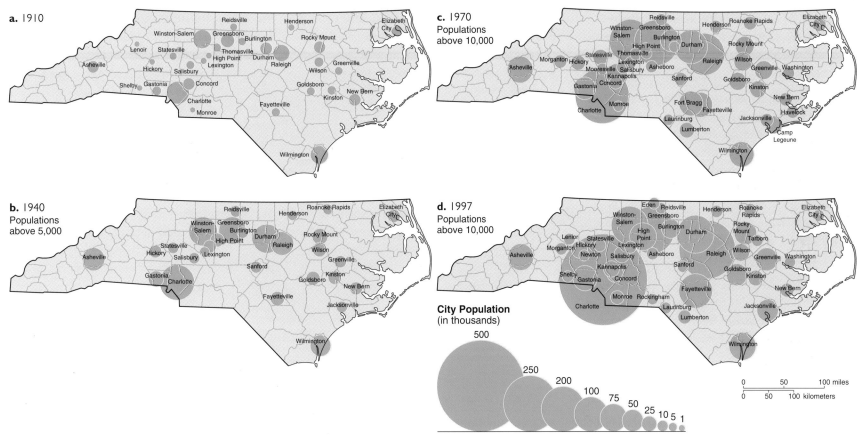

a. 1910

b. 1940
Populations above 5,000

c. 1970
Populations above 10,000

d. 1997
Populations above 10,000

City Population (in thousands)
500
250
200
100
75
50
25
10 5 1

0   50   100 miles
0   50   100 kilometers

Sources: U.S. Census of Population and Housing, 1910, 1940, and 1970;
N.C. Office of State Planning, 1998.

elite control developed whereby local elites "steered" their county vote to the "right" candidates. In this new political system big-business money, which underwrote campaign financing, was firmly wedded to the grassroots support of the county seat crowd. It was a marriage of prosperous large farmers and the economic and social elite of the small towns and cities. This is what Jasper Shannon called the "banker-merchant-farmer-lawyer-doctor governing class,"

a group, he argued, that was "caught between the agrarian and industrial mores" and one whose values dictated a firm commitment to the accumulation of wealth as a measure of success and worth, "a necessity and desirability of white supremacy, elitist control of all vital local and state political institutions, and allegiance to the conservative wing of the Democratic party." According to Earle and Merle Black, this marriage of political power and control pro-

Urban Terminology

In speaking of matters urban, several widely used terms or concepts have legal or bureaucratic meaning as well as geographic delineations. The major ones are as follows:

• Incorporated City/Municipality. *This is the corporate city as recognized under rules established by the General Assembly of North Carolina. The boundaries, or corporate limits, are specifically defined but are subject to change through annexation. The city is the official, legally incorporated entity that is empowered to govern its specific geographic area. It is assigned to administer services such as police, fire, water, sewerage, and the like, and it is authorized to levy and collect taxes in support of these services.*

• Urban. *For statistical purposes, the U.S. Census defines* urban *as those places that have a population of 2,500 or more people. They may be either legally incorporated municipalities or Census Designated Places (CDPs). CDPs are similar concentrations of people that may have locally recognized names but that lack legal status and jurisdictional authority. Just as corporate boundaries are subject to change over time, the CDPs may change as settlement patterns change. Any area or population that does not fall into an urban place is defined as* rural.

• Urbanized Areas. *In many cases the true or functional city extends beyond its corporate limits. Recognizing this, the U.S. Census has created a somewhat larger urban definition that includes an incorporated city of at least 50,000 residents plus any surrounding, higher-density, settled area that is contiguous to the incorporated place. Though potentially useful, this urban definition is rarely used, primarily because it changes as the city expands, but there is no clear physical evidence of its extent, such as a city limits sign.*

• Metropolitan Statistical Areas (MSAs). *MSAs are defined by the U.S. Office of Management and Budget. The county is the basic building block of the MSA. Each MSA is comprised of at least one county, typically one that contains an incorporated city of at least 50,000 people. Other adjacent counties that meet specific criteria of population, metropolitan character, and functional integration with the central county may be included. These criteria are reviewed after every decennial census, and, as a result, counties are added or deleted and MSAs are created or deleted. The MSAs have no jurisdictional authority and are used almost exclusively for reporting statistical information by the U.S. Census, other public agencies, and a host of private businesses. They are widely recognized as the definition of metropolitan areas.*

Gerald L. Ingalls

---

duced governors and senators who were "acutely sympathetic and attentive to the interests of both the small-town elites and leading industries." Equally important were the veteran politicians who returned time and again to leadership positions in the legislature and who could from that powerful vantage point control the distribution of state resources.

In North Carolina this political and socioeconomic system coupled with a highly decentralized urban network led to, indeed necessitated, a considerable investment in infrastructure. In 1921 the governor and the legislature embarked on an ambitious $50 million road-building program that produced 5,500 miles of paved and improved highways linking all county seats, principal towns, and major institutions. Eventually over $115 million was invested in roads during the 1920s. In 1931 the state assumed responsibility for 40,000 miles of county roads and over 15,000 bridges. This move helped maintain the extensive highway network that the dispersed urban pattern required. It was also consistent with the county seat origin of the political system that undertook this investment. It was sound politics. It was sound economics. The roads went to the small towns and rural areas that were the lifeline of the state's economic and political systems.

The American South and North Carolina had modernized, industrialized, and urbanized in their own way. A newfound interest in money moderated the southern elite's perspectives on change. Clearly, the Old South attitude of opposition to any change was a barrier to economic revival of the South so it was simply modified. Once economic development was embraced, economic change was startlingly rapid. But there were limits to how much change the elite would tolerate, especially if one consequence might be a societal restructuring. Consequently, the initial shift from farm to mill was accomplished with little if any challenge to the social and political system. The traditionalistic elite fostered radical economic, but a conservative social and political modernization. As a result many whites exchanged rural poverty for a slightly more secure form of industrial poverty. For blacks, nothing changed.

Industrial and economic changes exploded across the South, bringing corresponding changes in the rural landscape. North Carolina—indeed, most of the Piedmont between south-central Virginia and northern Georgia—enjoyed valuable locational advantages in abundant waterpower, nearby cotton fields, and, above all, cheap labor. All that was needed was capital and the blessings of the heretofore recalcitrant elite. Accumulation of capital by small-town merchants led directly to mill construction, and the competition among towns for mills and railroad lines was fierce. The result was a wave of industrial construction that began slowly in the 1870s but mushroomed in the 1880s. More than six new mills were built each year between 1880 and 1900, and by 1900 there were 177 mills in the state, with over 90 percent of them in the Piedmont.

In North Carolina, the center of economic and political gravity began a migration from the Coastal Plain to the Piedmont, where industrialization had begun. Until 1870 the Piedmont had been the economic periphery to the Coastal Plain's core. But powerful political, social, and economic forces such as the devastation and economic dislocation of the Civil War, the introduction of higher taxes, and fence laws that led to cash cropping and liens on those crops induced a shift from farmer to millworker. The Piedmont moved from agriculture to industry and became the economic core of the state.

Between 1880 and 1910 urbanization spread steadily across the Piedmont. Existing centers such as Charlotte, Raleigh, and Winston-Salem grew rapidly.

And many new centers such as Durham, Greensboro, High Point, and Concord exploded on the scene (Table 5.2 and Fig. 5.2). They were centers of sprawling, semirural industrial districts.

By 1930 the Piedmont had become the economic hearth of North Carolina. In textile, furniture, and tobacco manufacturing, the economic mainstays of the state, there was little of consequence elsewhere. Within the Piedmont, however, industrialization remained quite ubiquitous and well dispersed across a wide area, although decidedly rural and small-town in character.

From 1880 to 1930 the state gained substantial urban population, from 3.9 percent of the total to over 25 percent (Table 5.1). The relative rate of urbanization in North Carolina was greater than in either the South or the United States as a whole. In the nation, the level of urbanization increased approximately twofold between 1880 and 1930; in the South, there was almost a threefold increase; and in North Carolina, there was a sixfold increase, albeit from a rather small initial urban population. Figure 5.3 graphically depicts the percentage increase in North Carolina's urban population during key periods, such as 1880–90, when the rate of increase was over 100 percent. In fact, in each decade from 1880 to 1930 the rate of increase in urban residents was always above 50 percent.

North Carolina witnessed the explosive growth of a "new" system of cities (Table 5.2). Three of the eighteen southern cities that passed the 10,000 population mark during the decade of the 1880s were in North Carolina. Charlotte had a 63 percent growth spurt, Raleigh grew by 37 percent and Asheville recorded a remarkable rate of 291 percent. Charlotte by 1910 had became the largest city in the state (Tables 5.1–5.2 and Fig. 5.2). In large measure Charlotte, Raleigh, and others such as Greensboro and Winston-Salem emerged as financial and service centers to the plethora of small mill towns founded during the industrial boom.

The pattern of urbanization that emerged during this era is important to the appreciation of North Carolina's urban landscape in the 1990s. The urban consolidation of the 1980s and 1990s was built on a low-density foundation established during this middle or "Dispersed Urban Period." When the larger cities of the middle period—particularly Charlotte and Raleigh—began to grow rapidly in population and areal extent during the recent or "Consolidation Period" after 1970, most of the small mill towns created during the state's industrial development lay within easy commuting distance of major growth centers. They were in a position to serve as satellite, suburban, bedroom communities to Raleigh and Charlotte during their explosive growth from 1980 to 2000. Thus, the urban pattern begun in 1880 became the base for the development of a new urbanization that began one century later.

Urban Concentration, 1970–Present

As before, in the transition from rural North Carolina to dispersed urban, the urban changes that are sweeping the state into a new era are predicated on broad-based shifts in the economy. Beginning as early as 1970, North Carolina has witnessed massive economic change away from agriculture and manufacturing toward a service-based economy. In response to the demand by a service economy for increased agglomeration, the state's population has steadily concentrated into a higher-density, metropolitan settlement pattern.

As the service sector has expanded, larger, higher-density urban centers have developed massive office concentrations. In Charlotte alone, multi-tenant office space expanded from about 2.0 million square feet in 1970 to 7.2 million in 1974 and almost 30 million by the end of the century. Of the 338 largest multi-tenant buildings in Charlotte in 1998, 199 were built after 1980. Of the state's five largest concentrations of leasable office space, the top three are in Charlotte. This expansion of office capacity has been matched by corresponding growth in the retail sector.

The growth of retail and office clusters is indicative of the shift occurring within the state toward higher-density living and working environments. In most instances office concentrations have developed initially in traditional central business districts (CBDs) of regional centers, especially Charlotte, Raleigh, Greensboro, and Winston-Salem. For the most part these central city (CBD) office centers still dominate the major urban areas of the state. More recently, secondary centers have developed in major suburban concentrations such as South Park, the University of North Carolina at Charlotte Research Park, and the Interstate 77 corridor, all in Charlotte, and the Research Triangle Park on the outskirts of Raleigh, Durham, and Chapel Hill.

Urbanization in North Carolina is not unidimensional; it has at least three faces. First, there is the urbanization characterized by the growth of the major cities, the engines that are powering the state's economic growth. Because most of the state's service sector employment remains focused on its largest cities, most are growing rapidly (Fig. 5.3). Of course, within these central cities the

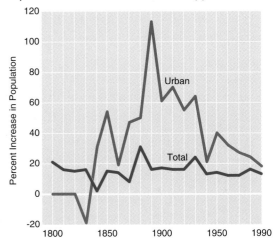

Figure 5.3. Percentage Change in Urban and Total Population in North Carolina, 1800–1990

Source: U.S. Census of Population and Housing, 1800-1990.

majority of the population has chosen to reside in rapidly developing, automobile-dominated, lower-density, suburbs and commute to their workplace. Second, there are the villages, towns, and cities—vestiges of another, Dispersed Urban Period—that dot the landscape around major regional centers. In such suburban, bedroom settings, part of the regional center's workforce has chosen to maintain residence within reasonable commuting distances of the major centers of employment. For example, in 1990 over 103,000 of the 350,000 employees in Mecklenburg County commuted in daily from surrounding counties. Finally, the third face is the urbanization characterized by consolidation into larger Metropolitan Statistical Areas (Fig. 5.4). Since 1980, MSA counties have led the state in population growth (Table 5.3). Most people recognize or experience the first two faces of urbanization—the growth of the major cities or suburban towns where people work and play. Seldom do they consider the extended cities or metropolitan places.

Several municipalities with populations over 50,000 (Table 5.4) have experienced explosive growth during the 1980s and 1990s. Jacksonville grew over 300 percent and Cary expanded over 270 percent; Fayetteville almost doubled (91 percent); Raleigh increased by over three-quarters; and Charlotte, Durham, and Greenville added half or more population to their 1980 bases. The explosive growth of cities such as Jacksonville and Cary has introduced new names to the list of the state's ten largest cities, supplanting Gastonia and Wilmington as longtime occupants of the top ten list (Table 5.2). Together, the fourteen cities in Table 5.4 acquired more than 700,000 new residents and now account for almost 27 percent of the state's population. Charlotte, Raleigh, and Jacksonville alone accounted for almost half of the total statewide increase in population. Cary, suburban to Raleigh, more than doubled its population in every decade since 1950 and grew by more than 50 percent from 1990 to 1997.

A significant factor in the growth of North Carolina's cities has been a relatively liberal annexation law. Under it cities can annex any contiguously built-up areas that meet minimum density standards. Areas to be annexed can influence such

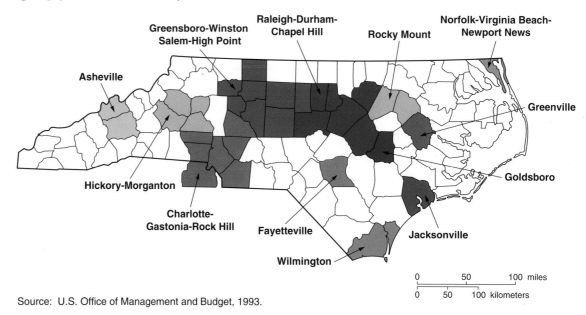

Figure 5.4. North Carolina Metropolitan Statistical Areas

Source: U.S. Office of Management and Budget, 1993.

actions only through negotiation. Some voters and legislators are beginning to question this authority because it does not allow property owners in areas to be annexed to have a formal voice in the decision. This concern is heightened by the fact that, even though those who are annexed must pay increased property taxes, some cities have been slow or negligent in providing promised new services to the annexed areas. Proponents of this annexation policy argue that it is very beneficial in that it allows cities to grow in an orderly manner. Urban authorities cite it as model legislation that is envied by many other states. They contrast it with Virginia, where cities are totally separate political

entities from their surrounding counties. Annexation there is difficult to achieve, and the cities are seriously constrained in their ability to grow. The importance of annexation to North Carolina cities is measured by the fact that 68 percent of the net population growth between 1980 and 1997 in these fourteen cities was through annexation.

It is noteworthy that most of the state's population growth in the last three decades of the twentieth century has been absorbed either by its largest cities (Fig. 5.3) or the county in which they are located. The twelve counties in which these fourteen cities are located added more than 831,000 people from 1980 to 1997. Wake and Mecklenburg,

Table 5.3. Population Change by Area of the State

Area	Total Population			Change (%)	
	1997	1990	1980	1980–90	1990–97
North Carolina	7,431,161	6,632,448	5,880,095	12.8	12.0
MSA counties	4,985,945	4,379,639	3,749,118	16.8	13.8
Non-MSA counties	2,445,216	2,252,809	2,130,977	7.7	8.5
Forsyth-Guilford	670,340	613,298	569,858	9.3	9.3
Mecklenburg	608,567	511,481	404,270	26.5	21.0
Wake	556,853	426,301	301,429	41.4	30.6

Sources: U.S. Census, 1980–90; *North Carolina Municipal Population, 1997* (N.C. Office of State Planning, 1998).

the state's two largest counties, accounted for more than 55 percent of this total. Combined, their populations equaled 11.5 percent of the total state population in 1970 and 12.0 percent in 1980. The overall population growth rate of these two counties from 1970 to 1980 had been a relatively modest 12.1 percent, or about 1.2 percent per year.

In 1990 and 1997, however, Mecklenburg and Wake together contained 14.1 percent and 15.7 percent of the total state population, respectively. More important, these two counties grew by about 30 percent from 1980 to 1990. At this rate—almost 3 percent per year—these two populations would double in twenty-three years. Yet from 1990 to 1997 their rate of growth accelerated and the net growth between 1980 and 1997 exceeded 65 percent—almost 4 percent per year. If that rate were sustained, the population of the two counties could double in less than two decades. The North Carolina Office

of State Planning projected that by the year 2000 the combined population of Wake and Mecklenburg would total approximately 1.25 million, and they would contain about 16 percent of the state's total population. That would represent a strong growth rate of nearly 3.3 percent per year over the last decade of the twentieth century. Recent experience suggests that even that vigorous growth rate may be conservative. Clearly, a considerable part of the total population growth of the state is centered in the two largest cities and counties. How can these two counties sustain such growth rates without substantial increases in service provision, especially transportation infrastructure? How might failure to provide such support impact their own and even the state's economic and urban health?

Much of the population growth in regional centers such as Charlotte and Raleigh comes as new

suburbs spill out into the rural areas that surround them, expanding the geographic city beyond its municipal limits. As growth accelerates, so do the problems that attend it. Although relatively good roads provide, at least initially, reasonable commuting corridors for long-distance commuting to jobs in the major cities, as growth accelerates, if the automobile remains the only alternative for commuting, these roads will clog, requiring substantial investment to maintain the flow of commuters. Eventually, growth spills over into adjacent municipalities as bedroom communities. Initially these will be the smaller towns in the same county as the regional centers, but increasingly there is longer-distance commuting from surrounding suburban counties, continuing a synergy established in the previous urban period. But will the transportation network designed to service a dispersed urbanization serve the higher densities of consolidation taking place since 1970?

North Carolina has seventeen urbanized areas that have been delineated by the U.S. Census. They are incorporated municipalities plus adjacent built-up areas that have populations of at least 50,000. As such, they are larger than cities but smaller than metropolitan areas. The estimated populations, their density, and data on transportation for the North Carolina areas are provided in Table 5.5. The total daily vehicular miles traveled (DVMT) in these urbanized areas show that two cities, Charlotte and Raleigh, far exceeded the other fifteen. Charlotte's totals are double that of

Table 5.4. Growth of All Cities of at Least 50,000 Population in 1997

| | Total Population Annexed | | | | | | Growth, 1980–97 | | |
	1997	1990	1980	1980–90	1990–97	Total 1980–97	Total (%)	By Annex. (%)	1997 City Share of State Pop. (%)
Charlotte	516,341	395,934	315,474	45,303	67,957	113,260	64	56	7.1
Raleigh	266,530	212,092	150,255	48,879	27,981	76,860	77	77	3.6
Greensboro	203,342	183,894	155,642	25,982	12,060	38,042	31	80	2.8
Winston-Salem	172,763	143,485	131,885	13,605	24,657	38,262	31	94	2.4
Durham	159,630	136,612	101,149	20,817	12,167	32,984	58	56	2.2
Fayetteville	113,406	75,850	59,507	16,078	33,526	49,604	91	92	1.5
Cary	80,751	44,397	21,763	15,620	12,457	28,077	271	48	1.1
Jacksonville	73,746	30,398	18,259	10,638	42,393	53,031	304	96	1.0
High Point	73,322	69,428	63,479	5,805	1,521	7,326	16	74	1.0
Asheville	68,133	61,855	54,022	9,134	3,995	13,129	26	93	0.9
Wilmington	64,513	55,530	44,000	8,901	0	8,901	47	43	0.9
Gastonia	62,204	54,725	47,218	7,021	5,550	12,571	32	84	0.8
Rocky Mount	57,340	49,961	42,158	5,479	4,133	9,612	36	63	0.8
Greenville	55,877	46,305	35,740	7,496	8,872	16,368	56	81	0.8
Total city population	1,967,298	1,560,466	1,240,551	240,758	257,269	498,027	59	68	26.5

Source: Computed from data in *North Carolina Municipal Population, 1997* (N.C. Office of State Planning, 1998).
Note: Growth by annexation is the percentage share of total growth that was achieved through annexation.

any other urbanized area and four to five times that of most of them. Yet the number of miles of roadway per 1,000 population in the Charlotte urbanized area was the lowest on this list after Jacksonville. This raises the issue of whether transportation infrastructure is keeping pace with population growth.

Herein lies the difficulty for state and local planners. Because cities such as Raleigh and Charlotte are sustaining their peak growth during the automobile era, it is possible to anticipate that suburbanization will continue to sprawl into adjacent rural areas and surrounding counties, providing residential alternatives farther and farther from the workplace. How long will it be before increased commuting and congestion threaten the livelihood of central city workers? How attractive will the state's principle economic engines be if they are choked by traffic?

Again, there is no reason to believe that such sprawl will be contained by arbitrary political boundaries such as county or state lines. Sprawl may well be reinforced, indeed accentuated, by the availability of attractive small towns

Table 5.5. Urbanized Areas

Urbanized Area*	Estimated Population (thousands)	Number of Persons per Square Mile	Total DVMT** per 1,000 Population	Miles Roadway per 1,000 Population	Total DVMT** per Capita
All 392 areas in U.S.	—	2,080	—	3.8	21.5
Pop. over 500,000	—	2,543	—	3.3	21.4
Charlotte	571	1,909	14,378	4.2	25.1
Raleigh	399	1,445	12,910	4.6	32.3
Fayetteville	279	1,354	5,923	4.8	21.2
Durham	230	1,074	6,999	5.3	30.4
Winston-Salem	222	1,254	6,825	6.4	30.7
Greensboro	207	1,269	7,188	6.1	34.7
Asheville	125	694	5,462	7.9	43.6
Gastonia	118	983	4,220	7.1	35.7
Wilmington	118	1,092	2,856	5.1	24.2
High Point	114	682	4,107	8.7	36.0
Jacksonville	109	1,238	1,429	2.4	13.1
Kannapolis	97	808	3,026	7.7	31.1
Burlington	82	1,261	3,068	7.1	37.4
Hickory	79	766	3,272	8.7	41.4
Goldsboro	71	934	1,711	5.0	24.0
Greenville	62	1,319	1,287	5.1	20.7
Rocky Mount	57	1,676	1,207	6.2	21.1
New York City	16,320	4,119	246,964	2.2	15.1
Chicago	7,961	2,915	152,256	2.9	19.1
Los Angeles	12,222	5,490	264,941	2.1	21.6

Source: U.S. Department of Transportation, Federal Highway Administration, *Highway Statistics, 1996.*
*An urbanized area, as defined by the U.S. Census, is the incorporated city with a population of at least 50,000 plus any contiguously built-up areas. It is thus larger in area and population than just the city itself.
**DVMT = Daily vehicular miles traveled

and cities within relatively easy commuting distances from the state's economic growth engines. Once more, the Charlotte area is a case in point. Urban sprawl has spilled over into the cities and towns in the counties surrounding Mecklenburg County. From 1990 to 1997 the number of new residential building permits issued was equivalent to 24 percent of the total housing stock that was in place in 1990. Although the largest number of new units was going into Mecklenburg itself, neighboring counties saw high gains in residential units as well. Cabarrus County issued permits totaling 31 percent of the existing housing stock, Iredell experienced increases of 34 percent, Mecklenburg recorded a 26 percent increase, and Union would sustain a 45 percent growth in the number of units. All other counties recorded increases of less than the area's average. As shown in Figure 5.5, most of the high-growth census tracts were concentrated in the areas on either side of the Mecklenburg County line, where expansions of 50 percent or more in the housing stock from 1990 to 1997 were common. Many of the other high-growth areas were either suburban to other urban centers or around several of the lakes. Conversely, the more rural parts of the area and the central part of Charlotte recorded slow growth or no activity at all.

There are 322 census tracts in the twelve-county area, but only 24 of them (7.5 percent) recorded increases of 55 percent or more (Fig. 5.5). But these 24 tracts reported permits for 46,723 new housing units, one-third of the entire area total. About

Suburban sprawl in the Fayetteville area

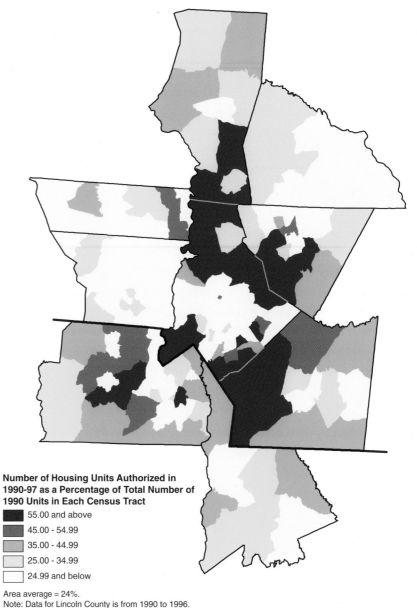

Figure 5.5. Suburban Sprawl in the Charlotte Area, 1990–1997

**Number of Housing Units Authorized in
1990-97 as a Percentage of Total Number of
1990 Units in Each Census Tract**

- 55.00 and above
- 45.00 - 54.99
- 35.00 - 44.99
- 25.00 - 34.99
- 24.99 and below

Area average = 24%.
Note: Data for Lincoln County is from 1990 to 1996.
Source: Centralina Council of Governments, Charlotte.

59 percent of the units were in 14 high-growth tracts in suburban Mecklenburg County, and the remaining 10 high-growth tracts were in four adjacent counties.

Suburban expansion into counties adjacent to regional centers will constitute an increasing part of the state's growth, and an ever-increasing proportion of its population will assemble in these clusters. In 1997 Wake and Mecklenburg and the counties that surrounded them contained almost one-third of the state's total population.

Of course, not all of the total area of these adjacent counties is equally impacted. As seen in the example of Mecklenburg County, those parts of the adjacent counties nearest the central city will initially sustain the highest rates of growth, in part because they are nearer. However, commuting distances are less critical than commuting times. The national average for travel from home to work is about thirty minutes. In most of North Carolina's regional centers, especially the largest, fifteen miles in thirty minutes, even along interstate highways, is probably nearer the norm. Figure 5.6 depicts those areas within fifteen miles of an interstate highway that are among the state's most attractive commuting routes and that link virtually all of its metropolitan centers.

In 1990 over 70 percent of the state's population lived within the thirty-mile bands depicted in Figure 5.6 (within fifteen miles on either side of one of the state's five interstate highways). Over 32 percent lived within fifteen miles of Interstate 85, which traverses the state from northeast through the Raleigh-Durham area toward the southwest into the area around Charlotte and Gastonia. Using this network of interstates and improved connectors that tie into them, it is possible for residents of smaller towns and villages, often vestiges of the mill town landscape, to commute daily into larger cities. The massive highway construction projects of the previous urban era and the continued commitment by successive state government administrations to maintain, indeed expand, the highway network may be contributing to long-range commuting patterns that serve to maintain much of the dispersed urban pattern of the past.

The corridors shown in Figure 5.6 coincide well with the state's metropolitan areas. The state's interstate highway system runs through most of the MSA counties. In 1997, 67 percent of state's population lived in the thirty-five counties that comprise the eleven MSAs in North Carolina (Fig. 5.4 and Table 5.3). Between 1980 and 1990 these thirty-five counties grew at a rate of 16.8 percent; from

Figure 5.6. Land Area within 15 miles of an Interstate Highway

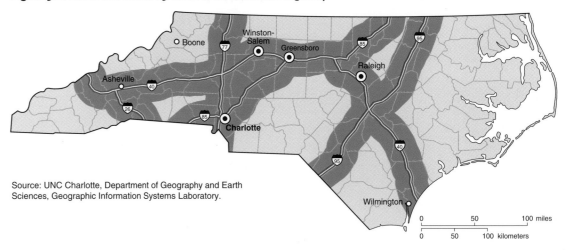

Source: UNC Charlotte, Department of Geography and Earth Sciences, Geographic Information Systems Laboratory.

1990 to 1997 the population of these counties grew by nearly 14 percent (Table 5.3). From 1990 to 1997 the nonmetropolitan counties of the state grew at a rate of 8.5 percent, less than the statewide growth of 12 percent.

Over the last century the population has consolidated into less of the total area of the state. Consequently, with each passing decade fewer counties account for increasingly more of the state's population. In 1997 over half of all North Carolinians lived in the seventeen most populous counties (Fig. 5.7). In 1890, after more than a decade of mill building, it would have taken more than one-third of the state's one hundred counties to account for 50 percent of the total population. Even with such continued consolidation, no single city has grown sufficiently to dominate the state.

Charlotte has grown steadily during the past three decades and still ranks first among the state's cities in population size. But unlike other states where one city and the county in which it is situated dominates the state (Hawaii and Delaware in Fig. 5.8), the Charlotte urbanized area contains a relatively smaller (8.1 percent in 1996) portion of the state's total population. While North Carolina cities are growing in population and in density, the outlets for population growth are so numerous that the higher-population densities of northern and midwestern cities are seldom seen. (Table 5.5 also gives comparative population densities for the New York, Chicago, and Los Angeles urbanized areas as a whole.)

It is easier to appreciate why North Carolina's urban picture is different by recalling the two im-

Figure 5.7. Counties Containing over 50 Percent of the Total Population, 1997

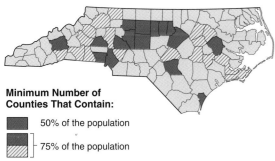

Minimum Number of Counties That Contain:

▓ 50% of the population

▨ 75% of the population

Source: U.S. Census, Population Estimates Program, March 1998.

portant building blocks in the state's urban growth. First, the foundation on which the current urban system is constructed is the dispersed, low-density, urban-industrial pattern of the 1880–1970 period. Second, current urban growth is firmly rooted in the classic low-density, automobile-oriented, Sunbelt urbanization of the late twentieth century. However, the realities of such low-density urbanization confront the state with serious policy implications. In the classic model of economic development, most of the economic growth and most of the jobs are centered in the largest urban centers of the state. Unless investments in transportation systems in those urban centers keep pace with urban and economic growth, the result could not only choke transportation arteries that feed the cities but also discourage further investment (job creation and relocation) in those centers. What are the prospects that the current poli-

tical and social systems of North Carolina will see either the need or the urgency for such investments? During the middle or Dispersed Urban Period, the state's elite changed its stance on urban and industrial development and rallied to encourage economic change and to provide the infrastructure necessary to support it. Now, as then, there is evidence that increased urbanization has brought a changing attitude among elites, and this time there is substantial social and political change.

The Social and Political Context for Urban Growth

Beginning in the 1960s in North Carolina and across the South, both the form and the character of the traditional social and political culture came under challenge from what Daniel Elazar labeled the "individualistic culture." Individualists stress the making and keeping of wealth and view government as a means of achieving marketplace efficiency. Earl and Merle Black summarized the individualistic culture of the southern elite: "The South's entrepreneurial individualists were willing to take bigger risks with traditional southern values to dream and then construct urban landscapes far beyond the imagination of the traditionalists."

For southern individualists, the purpose of government was to subsidize institutional and indi-

Figure 5.8. Proportion of the Population Contained in Each State's Largest Urbanized Area, 1996

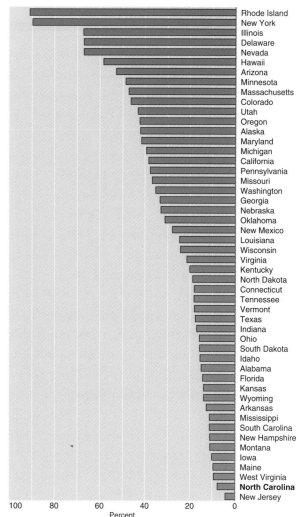

Source: Federal Highway Administration, *Highway Statistics, 1996,* November 1997.

vidual producers of wealth by creating services such as roads, airports, and universities that foster the production of additional wealth. Government thus became an instrument of investment, particularly in the infrastructure needed to successfully compete for higher-paying, higher-quality jobs. To many southern individualists, the Old South's low-wage structure and waste of human resources restricted economic development and needed restructuring regardless of the potential impact on the highly structured social system of the South. Although southern-born individualists were products of a color-line society, change in racial relations was viewed as an economic and social necessity; according to the Blacks, by the 1960s this individualistic culture gave "reluctant assent to modifications of the caste system."

Of course, the second front in the war against the Old South caste system, and perhaps its most open, direct, and vocal assault, came from southern blacks—a disenfranchised segment of southern society increasingly intolerant of an oppressive status quo. This two-prong challenge produced startling new directions in southern politics and society, and nowhere can one see this more clearly than in North Carolina.

Entrepreneurial individualism was a product of the cities. It began in larger cities and diffused down the urban hierarchy; its diffusion and adoption was more rapid in Texas, Florida, Virginia, and Georgia and came later to states like North Carolina, South Carolina, Alabama, and Mississippi. By the 1960s Houston, Dallas, Fort Worth, San Antonio, Atlanta, and Miami were its urban centers; it emerged by the 1970s in cities of less population. With no cities in the top tier of the southern urban hierarchy during the 1960s and 1970s, the impact of this new individualistic culture came somewhat later in North Carolina.

Once again, another decisive shift in the center of southern political gravity was apparent. Power moved from the courthouse to the office towers of emerging metropolitan centers. The influence of the county seat–based political system was severely restricted as the population and financial centers shifted. Even the style of "politicking" changed as cost efficiencies in television and radio advertising seriously eroded the old courthouse grassroots tradition of "pressing the flesh" and increasingly provided political clout and leverage to large media markets in higher-density urban concentrations. If the courthouse crowd lost control, however, it did not lose all influence. In state legislatures the ability of lawmakers to return year after year has allowed the county seat crowd to maintain a formidable influence on state politics in most southern states. Rural interests are still large enough to compel statewide politicians to give attention to their problems and concerns. Even today, few politicians are foolhardy enough to run campaigns touting their urban roots. A recent two-term Republican governor of North Carolina, who fit well the individualistic mold, named always as his "home" county the more rural Iredell, where his suburban lake home was located, rather than Mecklenburg (Charlotte), where, before public office, he had worked and lived and where he had won his first election.

The far-reaching social, economic, and political changes of the past three decades have produced a highly complex and eclectic system where elements of the politics of two separate political and urban eras overlay one another. If anything, the political and social picture is increasingly more complex, as illustrated in Chapter 14 ("Crime").

There are several reasons for this complexity. First, there are more players in the political game. With many more institutional actors who are concerned about the division of governmental resources, the competition for limited state resources has been intense. All too often elected officials appear not to understand how to respond to a state in economic, social, and political transition.

A second factor in the complexity of social, economic, and political systems is increased partisan competitiveness. No longer does one party dominate on election day. However, in this competitive environment political partisanship often produces different responses to economic development strategies. The state's political leadership, sharply divided along party lines, follows different, often highly contentious and competitive paths. Republicans and Democrats, sharing the state legislature since 1986, have been ineffectual in establishing and implementing their party agendas.

Finally, both parties respond to pressure from

what remains of the old courthouse crowd to protect the economic interests of small-town and rural North Carolina, the textile industry, and tobacco. The majority of the state legislature and the governor's office are too willing to dissipate precious state funds on a multitude of politically expedient projects rather than marshal resources to compete effectively. Evidence of this comes in the form of policies such as "balanced growth." This policy would, in effect, take increasingly scarce state resources (particularly in transportation) and allocate them by a formula that is highly favorable to rural areas. In 1992, for example, some state leaders were suggesting that transportation funds be used to pave every road in the state that carries more than fifty cars per day. Although this is sound county seat politics, it fails as a strategy to prepare the state for participation in the global economy. Directing these funds to the needs of the more competitive, largely urban, economic core of the state might prove to be a wiser future investment that would benefit what has become the overwhelming majority of the state's population.

Outlook

It is clear that the pattern of consolidation and increasing urbanization is irrevocable. The state's cities are the major engines of its growth, and as such they will continue to serve as the primary magnets for economic development and jobs. Their population growth will continue to lead the state, and the result will be increasingly larger, ever more dominant urban centers.

To service its economic engines the state must be prepared to invest heavily in the infrastructure of the urban regions of which they are the center. This will require a measure of political change. And the state is at the point where, once again, economic and social changes have set in motion political change. Unfortunately, the climate for decisive and immediate action is not good. In this climate of economic and social change the political system remains in flux. A new political framework has not yet been established.

Undoubtedly, North Carolina's future is an urban future. This trend is driven not by internal circumstances so much as by the national and global economy, of which the state must play a part if it is to prosper. It is imperative that North Carolina's leaders recognize this and implement policies that are consistent with it.

Selected References

Black, E., and M. Black. *Politics and Society in the South*. Cambridge: Harvard University Press, 1987.

Cash, W. J. *The Mind of the South*. New York: Vintage Books, 1941.

Clay, J., and A. Stuart. *Charlotte: Patterns and Trends of a Dynamic City*. Charlotte: Department of Geography and Earth Sciences, 1990.

Hall, J. D., J. Leloudis, R. Korstad, M. Murphy, L. A. Jones, and C. E. Daly. *Like a Family: The Making of a Southern Cotton Mill World*. Chapel Hill: University of North Carolina Press, 1987.

Hanchett, T. W. *Sorting Out the New South City: Race, Class, and Urban Development in Charlotte*. Chapel Hill: University of North Carolina Press, 1998.

Key, V. O. *Southern Politics in State and Nation*. New York: Knopf, 1949.

Larsen, L. *The Rise of the Urban South*. Lexington: University Press of Kentucky, 1985.

———. *The Urban South: A History*. Lexington: University Press of Kentucky, 1990.

Mills, E., and J. McDonald, eds. *Sources of Metropolitan Growth*. New Brunswick, N.J.: Center for Public Policy Research, 1992.

Shannon, J. *Toward a New Politics in the South*. Knoxville: University of Tennessee Press, 1949.

Svara, J. "Regional Councils as Linchpins in North Carolina." *Popular Government*, Spring 1998, pp. 21–28.

Tindall, G. *Emergence of the New South*. Baton Rouge: Louisiana State University Press, 1967.

6. THE ECONOMY

Harrison S. Campbell Jr.

Growth and change best describe recent trends in the North Carolina economy. Prior to World War II, settlement and economic activity were highly dispersed throughout the state. Relatively small farms characterized much of agriculture, particularly in the Piedmont and Mountain regions, and the state's major industries—textiles and furniture—also supported dispersed settlement patterns. Textile production initially evolved along rivers and waterways that could be harnessed as a source of power. Even after textile mills modernized, replacing waterpower as the source of energy, textile manufacturing remained relatively dispersed as the labor force continued to live in the mill villages established by the larger mills. The geography of furniture making was shaped, in part, by the North Carolina Railroad, which transported heavy, bulky raw materials and helped to establish the pattern of an industry that stretched from Durham to Marion, a pattern that persists to this day. The inherent uncertainty associated with agriculture, coupled with falling cotton prices and competition in tobacco markets, persuaded many families to leave their farms in search of other employment. Thus began the transformation of the North Carolina economy.

Growth and Diversification

Although textile and furniture production flourished into the early 1970s, the "Big Three" manufacturing industries of textiles, furniture, and tobacco had begun to decline in terms of their domination of the state's economy. In the early 1970s the textile industry was in crisis as competition in the global economy began to erode its markets. Declines in the real cost of transportation for both finished products and raw materials meant that many textile products no longer had to be produced domestically. Industrial technology had become highly standardized and work routinized to permit the profitable utilization of less expensive sources of labor available in other parts of the world. Some North Carolina mills modernized plant equipment to enhance worker productivity, but others, unable to compete, closed down. The combined effects of globalization, productivity improvements, and mill closures caused employment in textiles to decline even if the remaining mills enhanced their competitive positions. Likewise, mergers, imports, and the rising cost of lumber provided the ingredients for structural change to take place in furniture manufacturing. Similarly, intensive automation led to declines in cigarette factory employment even though output increased. Now, rising national concerns over health issues associated with tobacco use threaten to erode markets for these products. Thus, a host of factors have led to changes in North Carolina's Big Three industries and helped set the stage for transformation of the state's economy.

Agriculture, textiles, and furniture are still important components of the state's economic base. But construction of the interstate highway system, advances in telecommunications and information processing, lower-than-average wage rates, and a favorable business climate have connected North Carolina, and, indeed, the entire South, to the rest of the United States like never before. Relatively low wages have made North Carolina an attractive location for new and expanding businesses. Today, much of the economy's expansion is taking place in business and financial services and information processing. Telecommunications have allowed some of these activities, particularly lower-level, back-office operations, to take advantage of lower wages, especially on the fringes of metropolitan areas.

At the same time, a larger trend in North Carolina has emerged—the urbanization of economic activity and, consequently, population. Finance and banking, professional and technical services, and corporate headquarters are particularly prone to centralized, urban locations. As these sectors have grown, they have attracted population to urban centers and metropolitan areas at increasing rates. Urbanization of economic activity has served to redistribute the state's population away from rural areas and between different metropolitan areas. Although levels of urbanization in North Carolina are still below national averages, population migration has reinforced this pattern of urban growth as the state attracts people from all over the world in search of better employment, leisure, and recreational opportunities. As the urban population has grown, so too have service, retail, and construction activities that are required to serve this population. These activities further stimulate growth in the urban sector, attracting still more people to metropolitan areas. Though state and local governments struggle to meet expanding infrastructure needs, this process of cumulative causation continues. For good or for bad, the evolution and diversification of North Carolina is reflected in the structure of the state's economy, which increasingly resembles that of the nation.

Changing Economic Structure

One way to reveal structural change in the state's economy is to examine trends in the gross state product (GSP), a measure analogous to the nation's gross domestic product (GDP). Both measure the market value of all domestic goods and services produced in a single year. Table 6.1 presents data on GSP for selected years between 1977 and 1996 to illustrate one perspective on the changing state economy. In 1996, for example, the North Carolina economy produced over $204 bil-

Table 6.1. North Carolina Gross State Product as a Percentage of U.S. Gross Domestic Product, by Sector, 1977–1996

Sector	1977		1980		1985		1996	
	N.C.	U.S.	N.C.	U.S.	N.C.	U.S.	N.C.	U.S.
Farming	3.35	2.58	2.97	2.45	2.28	1.90	1.85	1.17
Agricultural services*	0.37	0.43	0.42	0.44	0.39	0.42	0.48	0.53
Mining	0.23	2.56	0.36	4.02	0.28	2.88	0.13	1.49
Construction	4.27	5.00	3.97	5.16	4.03	4.70	4.19	4.01
Manufacturing	34.80	23.77	33.43	21.76	30.94	19.91	26.97	17.44
Durable	11.40	14.18	12.43	13.18	11.95	11.57	10.22	9.81
Nondurable	23.40	9.59	21.00	8.58	18.99	8.34	16.74	7.64
TCPU**	8.22	9.14	8.29	9.02	8.83	9.43	7.90	8.45
Wholesale trade	6.30	7.14	6.49	7.26	6.44	7.08	6.41	6.77
Retail trade	9.76	9.86	9.24	9.17	9.88	9.52	8.93	8.75
FIRE***	9.91	14.32	11.37	15.00	13.14	16.12	14.55	18.97
Services	9.79	12.95	10.45	14.00	11.53	16.34	15.38	20.16
Government	13.00	12.26	13.00	11.72	12.26	11.70	13.20	13.05
Total ($ millions)	44,148	1,957,608	59,110	2,670,330	94,622	3,966,280	204,229	7,636,000
N.C. % of U.S.	2.26		2.21		2.39		2.67	

Source: U.S. Department of Commerce, *Survey of Current Business*.
*Agricultural services include forestry and fishing.
**TCPU = transportation, communications, and public utilities
***FIRE = finance, insurance, and real estate

lion in goods and services. Nearly 27 percent of the state's output came from the manufacturing sector; the financial sector (finance, insurance, real estate) added 14.6 percent and the service sector another 15.4 percent to GSP in 1996. More important, however, were structural changes in production as suggested by each sector's changing share of output. In both the state and the nation, manufacturing's share of output declined significantly while services gained in their share of output. In 1977 manufacturing accounted for nearly 35 percent of North Carolina GSP. At the national level, manufacturing's share of output dropped from almost 24 percent to 17.4 percent between 1977 and 1996. The concurrent rise in the financial and service sectors illustrates their grow-

Figure 6.1. North Carolina Gross State Product and U.S. Gross Domestic Product: Real and Projected Growth 1977–2005

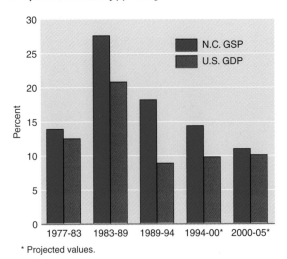

* Projected values.

Source: U.S. Bureau of Economic Analysis, Regional Information System, http://www.bea.doc.gov/bea/dn2.htm, December 1998.

Figure 6.2. Growth Rates in Total Employment for North Carolina and the United States, 1970–1997

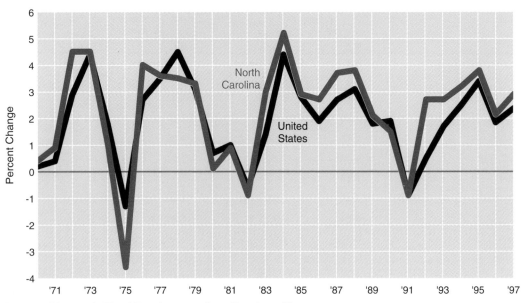

Percent Change in Total Employment from Previous Year

North Carolina

United States

Source: U.S. Bureau of Economic Analysis, Regional Information System, http://www.bea.doc.gov/bea/dn2.htm, December 1998.

ing importance to both the state and the nation. In fact, at the national level, services and finance both edged out manufacturing as the leading sector by 1996. Though manufacturing is still the dominant sector of North Carolina's economy, its share of the total has declined significantly over time. Despite its long and important history in the state, farming by 1996 contributed less than 2 percent of GSP, slightly more than was the case nationwide.

Another perspective on the state's growth is illustrated by its contribution to the national GDP, which rose from 2.3 percent in 1977 to 2.7 percent

by 1996. As illustrated in Figure 6.1, North Carolina has consistently grown faster than the U.S. economy since 1977 and is projected to outpace the nation in the beginning of this century. Rapid growth was particularly evident between 1983 and 1994, although growth of the state's economy is expected to more closely resemble national rates by 2005.

Overall, data on GSP reveal North Carolina's robust economy, which despite movements toward greater emphasis on services and finance, remains more industrial than national averages. This picture is reinforced by data in Table 6.2 depicting the structure of nonfarm employment in the state. Clearly, manufacturing is a dominant source of employment in the state, though growth since 1970

Table 6.2. North Carolina Nonfarm Employment, by Sector, 1970, 1980, and 1996

Sector	1970			1980			1996		
	Jobs	(%)	Index	Jobs	(%)	Index	Jobs	(%)	Index
Agricultural services*	6,645	0.3	0.78	12,214	0.5	0.80	50,875	1.2	0.92
Mining	3,766	0.2	0.23	5,199	0.2	0.19	5,316	0.1	0.21
Construction	104,827	5.1	1.10	124,080	4.8	1.03	283,796	6.5	1.19
Manufacturing	723,012	35.4	1.42	827,059	32.1	1.52	866,354	19.8	1.54
TCPU**	93,610	4.6	0.79	118,116	4.6	0.85	189,650	4.3	0.90
Wholesale trade	85,143	4.2	0.85	123,780	4.8	0.87	192,841	4.4	0.95
Retail trade	248,964	12.2	0.82	361,000	14.0	0.87	748,552	17.1	0.99
FIRE***	70,309	3.4	0.71	98,271	3.8	0.69	255,838	5.8	0.77
Services	295,535	14.5	0.82	384,494	14.9	0.72	1,092,581	25.0	0.86
Government	410,559	20.1	0.96	524,625	20.3	1.05	691,000	15.8	1.09
Federal	46,185	2.3	0.61	49,796	1.9	0.61	60,970	1.4	0.72
Military	134,272	6.6	1.58	115,154	4.5	1.76	125,307	2.9	1.91
State and Local	230,102	11.3	0.86	359,675	13.9	1.01	504,723	11.5	1.04
Total	2,042,370			2,578,838			4,376,803		

Source: U.S. Bureau of Economic Analysis.
Note: The job index measures the concentration of employment relative to that of the United States. It is equal to the share of North Carolina jobs in a sector divided by the U.S. share in that sector.
*Agricultural services include forestry and fishing.
**TCPU = transportation, communications, and public utilities
***FIRE = finance, insurance, and real estate

was modest (less than 1 percent per year) and its share of the total fell from 35.4 percent in 1970 to less than 20 percent in 1996. As of 1996, however, North Carolina's share of employment in manufacturing was still the highest among all states in the nation. Retail Trade and Services, on the other hand, showed strong rates of growth during this period, together accounting for over 42 percent of state employment. The fact that the share of employment in the retail and service sectors was far greater than their share of GSP indicates that output per employee in both sectors was far less than that found in manufacturing.

The state's relationship to the United States as a whole is implied in the job index presented in Table 6.2. This index measures the concentration of employment in a given sector relative to the national average. An index of 1.00

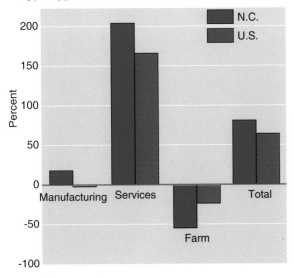

Figure 6.3. Employment Growth Rates for North Carolina and the United States, by Major Sector, 1970–1996

Source: U.S. Bureau of Economic Analysis, Regional Information System, http://www.bea.doc.gov/bea/dn2.htm, December 1998.

indicates that North Carolina has the same share of employment in an industry as the nation, whereas an index above (below) indicates heavier (less) concentration. The point to be made here is that, with a few important exceptions, the structure of North Carolina's employment increasingly resembles the national structure as the index has moved toward a value of one. This is particularly true in Retail Trade, for example, as its index increased from 0.82 in 1970 to 0.99 in 1996, indicating an almost identical concentration of em-

ployment with the United States. Similar patterns are found in Transportation, Communications, and Public Utilities (TCPU), Wholesale Trade, and State and Local Government. Interestingly, the manufacturing job index increased substantially even though job growth in this sector was modest. This reflects the fact that, although manufacturing employment as a whole has been fairly stable in North Carolina, U.S. employment in manufacturing has declined over the twenty-six-year period. Also noteworthy is the exceptionally high index in the Military sector, reflecting the state's disproportionate share of military bases and operations, even though military employment declined as a percentage of the statewide total.

In most cases, employment has grown faster in North Carolina than it has nationally. Figures 6.2 and 6.3 show overall employment growth and growth rates by major sector, respectively, for North Carolina and the United States. Figure 6.2 illustrates how employment growth has fluctuated over recent years. As evident in the chart, it was common for state economies to oscillate more widely than the national economy. Although the peaks and troughs of employment growth swung more widely in the state, Figure 6.3 indicates that North Carolina generally outperformed the nation. With the exception of farming, rates of growth in total employment and the major sectors of manufacturing and services exceeded national averages during the 1970–97 period.

This analysis demonstrates that the state's economy has grown in diversity while maintaining a solid industrial base. In broader terms, North Carolina has participated in the general restructuring of the U.S. economy, a trend that has been described as deindustrialization, the rise of the information-processing economy, or the shift toward a more service-based economy. Although the state has participated in this restructuring, it has maintained a relatively strong manufacturing base, which some analysts feel is an advantage because wealth that is generated by the production of physical commodities drives much of the service sector economy.

The Geographic Distribution of Employment

The spatial distribution of employment has also changed significantly. Figures 6.4a and 6.4b show the distribution of total employment by county in 1997 and changes in this distribution since 1970. Not unexpectedly, employment is highly concentrated in a few counties of the state. In 1997 there were nearly 4.4 million jobs in North Carolina, 36 percent of which were found in five counties—Durham, Forsyth, Guilford, Mecklenburg, and Wake. These are the central counties of the state's three largest metropolitan areas, and together they provided over 1.5 million jobs in 1997. The share of total employment jumps to 51 percent when the suburban counties of these three metro areas are

Women in the Workforce

One of the major changes that has occurred in the national labor force has been the increasing number of women who work outside the home. This is expressed in the participation rate, *the percentage of adult women who are in the labor force. Female participation in the national labor force rose from 31.5 percent in 1970 to 59.3 percent in 1996, compared with a male participation rate of 51.2 percent in 1970 and 74.9 percent in 1996. The working woman is not a new trend in North Carolina. In 1976 fully 54.3 percent of adult women were in the labor force, and that proportion grew slowly, reaching 61.5 percent in 1996. Thus, the spread between North Carolina and the nation has narrowed in recent years. Put another way, in 1976, among all the states, North Carolina trailed only Nevada, Alaska, and Hawaii in terms of highest female participation rates. By 1996, though still ahead of the national average (59.3 percent), North Carolina ranked only twenty-third among the fifty states and the District of Columbia.*

The high level of working women has its roots in the nature of one of the state's historically dominant industries, textile manufacturing. From the outset, in the late nineteenth century, the mills were located mostly in largely agricultural areas and whole families left the farm to work in the new industry. Men, women, and children all were given jobs, but women were soon channeled into sex-typed positions. As something of a carryover from the farm, men received assignments involving heavy work and authority. They were also expected to be long-term workers, justifying the expense of longer training for more complex, higher-wage tasks. Women were considered to be more patient and neat, better suited for working on fast-moving, repetitive machines. Winding and spinning operations were almost always limited to

females, for example. In 1880 women constituted only 18 percent of all "gainfully employed" people, but by 1910 this proportion reached nearly 29 percent as some 186,000 women joined the ranks. An early "glass ceiling" existed for women. Some low-level managerial positions opened up in the 1930s, when new management techniques called for more precise record keeping. But one report indicated that there was only one known female overseer in the entire South in 1935. Typically, women's wages were about 60 percent of those paid to males.

Initially, many female mill hands were young and unmarried or widows, but this changed after child labor was outlawed. In 1930 less than half of the female millworkers in North Carolina were married, whereas by 1940 the proportion had risen to 72 percent The average age also rose, and by 1940 nearly 64 percent were between twenty-five and forty-four. The primary reason that so many women worked was that wages were low for men and for women. Everybody who could had to work in order for the family to exist. According to Jacquelyn Dowd Hall's history of the North Carolina textile industry, Like a Family, *"As long as mill work paid ' Just a niff to Keep Sole and Body to gather,' families could survive only by pooling the wages of everyone over the legal working age of sixteen." Moreover, women were expected to run their households and nurture their children even after putting in long hours at the mill. Thus, having a "career" and a family is nothing new to the women of North Carolina.*

Alfred W. Stuart

included in the calculation. Though banking and finance, information processing, biotechnology, software development, higher education, and health care are high-profile sources of employment, much of the employment in these and other counties also reflects retail and service functions required to meet the state's changing population distribution.

Central counties of metropolitan areas tend to serve as regional centers of commerce, but the role of government as a source of employment should not be overlooked. Obviously, the city of Raleigh serves as the seat of state government. But local governments are also an important source of employment, particularly in rural areas. It is common, for example, for the public school system to be the largest employer in a county, and current demographic trends in the number of school-age children suggest that this trend will continue. Other demographic trends include a growing retirement population that increasingly seeks the recreational and leisure opportunities available in

Figure 6.4a. Total Wage and Salary Employment, 1997

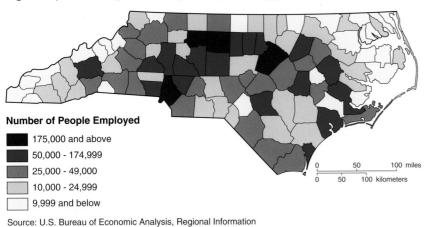

Number of People Employed

- ■ 175,000 and above
- ■ 50,000 - 174,999
- ■ 25,000 - 49,000
- ■ 10,000 - 24,999
- □ 9,999 and below

Source: U.S. Bureau of Economic Analysis, Regional Information System, http://www.bea.doc.gov/bea/dn2.htm, December 1998.

Figure 6.4b. Change in Wage and Salary Employment, 1970–1997

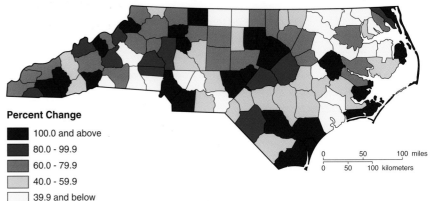

Percent Change

- ■ 100.0 and above
- ■ 80.0 - 99.9
- ■ 60.0 - 79.9
- ■ 40.0 - 59.9
- □ 39.9 and below

Source: U.S. Bureau of Economic Analysis, Regional Information System, http://www.bea.doc.gov/bea/dn2.htm, December 1998.

the state. Similarly, the federal government, particularly the military in counties such as Cumberland, Onslow, and Wayne, directly and indirectly contribute to the local employment base.

Consistent with previous observations, urban growth has dominated the employment picture over the last quarter century. Mecklenburg County alone accounted for 12 percent of state employment in 1997, up from 9.3 percent in 1970. The five central counties of the three largest metropolitan areas similarly increased their share of state employment from 30 percent in 1970 to 38 percent in 1997, together growing by 132 percent over this period. Between 1970 and 1997 about six of every ten net new jobs were found in these three areas. Among the suburban counties of these large metropolitan areas, Orange and Union recorded especially large gains.

Growth has not been confined to the largest counties, however, as other, smaller metropolitan areas and some rural counties posted substantial job gains. For example, the highest rate of employment growth in the state was reported in Dare County (508 percent). The Greenville and Wilmington Metropolitan Statistical Areas (MSAs) more than doubled in employment, as did nine nonmetropolitan counties, including the retirement communities of Moore County and mountain recreation/retirement counties such as Jackson, Macon, Watauga, and Yancey. The only county to lose employment over this period was Northampton. The sources of employment change in these counties reflect trends taking place in the larger economies of the state and nation. For instance, among those counties that lost workers, declines in farm and manufacturing employment ac-

counted for the lion's share of job losses. In Gates and Hertford Counties, these losses were partially offset by modest growth in services and state/local government. Although some of these counties did add jobs in manufacturing, much of the growth was attributable to the service sector. Service employment in both Dare and Cumberland Counties, for example, grew by over 532 percent between 1970 and 1997. Similar gains in retailing were recorded in Cumberland, Dare, and New Hanover.

Structural changes in production are manifest in the changing economic sectors in which North Carolinians find employment. Employment growth in the major metropolitan areas implies a corresponding change in the urbanization of the population. To the extent that agriculture or manufacturing is spatially concentrated in the state, these structural changes have pronounced impacts on localities. The employment base of some Coastal and Mountain regions has benefited from these changes particularly as they relate to recreation and tourism, though many such service and retail positions are characterized by relatively low wages. On the other hand, shifts in manufacturing and the declining role of the agricultural sector as a source of employment have had a severe impact on communities specializing in these sectors.

Occupations

Structural changes in production have affected the availability of jobs in different sectors and occupations. Although North Carolina has experienced a significant change in output and sources of employment, the state remains more industrial than the nation. This is reflected not only in the industry of employment, but also in the occupations of residents. Figure 6.5 compares the occupational profiles of North Carolina and the United States in 1980 and 1990. Because of its relatively large manufacturing base, North Carolina has a larger proportion of its labor force in occupations directly involved in production activities. Compared to the national average of 31.7 percent in 1980, 40.7 percent of the state's labor force held positions classified as *precision production workers, fabricators, operators, and laborers.* As other sectors of the state's economy grew relative to manufacturing, so too did occupations utilized in those sectors. Be-

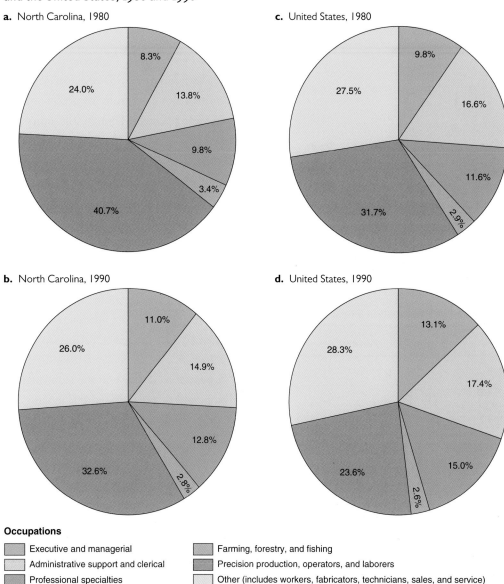

Figure 6.5. Occupational Composition of the Labor Force in North Carolina and the United States, 1980 and 1990

a. North Carolina, 1980

8.3%
13.8%
9.8%
3.4%
40.7%
24.0%

c. United States, 1980

9.8%
16.6%
11.6%
2.9%
31.7%
27.5%

b. North Carolina, 1990

11.0%
14.9%
12.8%
2.8%
32.6%
26.0%

d. United States, 1990

13.1%
17.4%
15.0%
2.6%
23.6%
28.3%

Occupations

Executive and managerial
Administrative support and clerical
Professional specialties
Farming, forestry, and fishing
Precision production, operators, and laborers
Other (includes workers, fabricators, technicians, sales, and service)

Source: U.S. Census of Population and Housing, 1980-90.

Table 6.3. Composition of the Civilian Labor Force, 1990 (proportion of the total, 16 years and older)

	Percentage of Total	
	N.C.	U.S.
Male	52.4	54.7
Female	47.6	45.3
White	78.2	85.9
African American	19.6	10.8
Other races	2.2	0.3
Hispanic	0.9	7.7

Source: U.S. Census of Population and Housing, 1990.

Table 6.4. Labor Force Participation Rates, 1990

	Percentage	
	N.C.	U.S.
Total	68.7	66.5
Male	77.7	76.4
Female	60.4	57.4
White	69.1	66.7
African American	66.9	64.2
16–19-year-olds	56.7	55.9

Source: U.S. Census of Population and Housing, 1990.
Note: Participation rates represent the proportion of the population 16 years and older that is in the labor force.

tween 1980 and 1990 the state share of the labor force holding *executive and managerial* positions grew from 8.3 percent to 11.0 percent while the national average moved in a similar direction, from 9.8 percent to 13.1 percent. *Professional specialties* (medicine, law, consulting, architecture, etc.) in North Carolina also grew from 9.8 percent of the labor force to 12.8 percent. Though still somewhat less white-collar than the nation, occupational shifts in the state reflect sectoral shifts in employment. *Farming* and other agricultural occupations declined in both the state and the nation to below 3 percent of the labor force.

Not only does North Carolina's labor force hold more production-related jobs, but also it is proportionately more female and less white than that of the nation as a whole (Table 6.3). Similarly, North Carolinians participate more actively in the labor force than does the rest of the nation (Table 6.4). Of persons age sixteen and over in 1990, nearly 69 percent were active in the labor market (either employed or unemployed but looking for work), compared to 66.5 percent in the United States.

Labor Unions

One of the more striking characteristics of North Carolina's labor force is that it is relatively nonunionized. One reason for this may be that the state is one of only twenty-one with a right-to-work law, which prohibits requiring all workers in a company to join a union if some workers are represented by organized labor. More likely, the scarcity of unions has to do with the memories of bitter, violent, and unsuccessful strikes in the 1920s and 1930s that left many workers disenchanted with organized labor. Union membership has never been high in the state, and between 1983 and 1996 the number of workers who belonged to a union fell from 179,000 to 134,000. This 25 percent drop was far greater than the nationwide decline of 8 percent. In 1996 only 4.1 percent of all North Carolina workers belonged to a union, the second lowest level among all U.S. states, ahead only of South Carolina. Among manufacturing employees, the North Carolina rate was just 2.5 percent, the lowest in the nation, and a sharp drop from the 6.9 percent level of 1983.

Participation Rates

Figure 6.6 illustrates the rate of labor force participation in 1995 countywide. As a general rule, average or above-average rates of participation are found in the Piedmont region, whereas the Coastal Plain and Mountain regions exhibit a lower, patchwork pattern of participation. Participation in the workforce appears to be highest in large urban counties that have also experienced high rates of employment growth. For example, in 1995 Mecklenburg and Wake Counties had the highest par-

Figure 6.6. Labor Force Participation, 1995

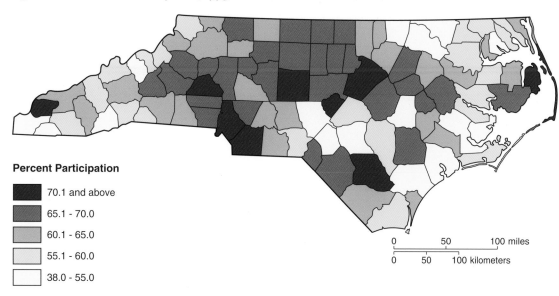

Percent Participation

- 70.1 and above
- 65.1 - 70.0
- 60.1 - 65.0
- 55.1 - 60.0
- 38.0 - 55.0

0   50   100 miles

0   50   100 kilometers

Sources: Derived from data of the N.C. Employment Security Commission; N.C. Office of State Planning, 1997.

ticipation rates (72.8 percent and 72.3 percent, respectively), whereas counties that experienced stagnation or long-run declines in employment generally had lower rates.

When comparing labor force participation to long-term trends in employment growth, there are several important dynamics to consider. First, participation can fluctuate from year to year as young people enter the labor market or persons previously not active (re)join it. Thus, short-term fluctuations in workforce participation will not necessarily mirror long-term trends in employment growth. Second, participation is partly determined by individuals' expectations about the re-

wards of work. Consequently, current wage levels and unemployment rates are apt to affect participation in the short run. Most important, however, labor force participation is measured according to where people live, whereas these employment data represent where people work. The prevalence of intercounty commuting means that members of the labor force do not always live and work in the same county. It is entirely possible, for example, that high labor force participation in Lee County was related to economic conditions in Wake County. It should be noted that civilian participation in the workforce is related to a host of variables, including a person's age, education, oc-

cupation, and prior work experience. Thus, counties with large military installations or retirement populations are likely to have relatively low rates of labor force participation.

Unemployment

North Carolina's economy not only has grown faster than the national rate (Fig. 6.1) but also typically has experienced lower rates of unemployment—3.6 percent, compared to the national mean of 5.0 in 1997 (Fig. 6.7). The data in Table 6.5 reflect intrastate variations in labor force and unemployment rates. Generally, larger metropolitan areas experienced unemployment rates below the state average, whereas most of the smaller and other labor market areas exceeded the state average. Figure 6.8 also illustrates unemployment patterns across the state in 1998. Orange County, a suburban component of the Raleigh-Durham MSA, had the lowest rate of unemployment at 1.9 percent in 1995 and 1.2 percent in 1998. But on the whole, the central counties of the larger MSAs had lower rates than did their suburban fringes, which, in turn, had lower rates than the smaller MSA group. However, several of seven nonmetropolitan counties that contained cities of at least 15,000 not only fared worse than other metropolitan areas, but also their unemployment rates were frequently higher than those for more rural counties.

It is instructive to note that patterns of unem-

Figure 6.7. Unemployment Rates in North Carolina and the United States, 1975–1997

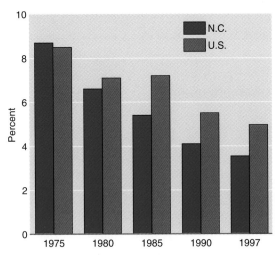

Source: U.S. Bureau of Labor Statistics, 1998.

ployment loosely resemble patterns of labor force participation. That is, participation in the workforce tends to be higher in counties with low unemployment rates and vice versa. Comparison of Figures 6.6 and 6.8 reveals that economic conditions were generally better in the central Piedmont, whereas indicators of relative distress were found in the northeastern Coastal Plain. But this pattern does not strictly hold for all counties. For example, Moore, Polk, and Watauga simultaneously had low rates of both labor force participation and unemployment. All three counties contain popular retirement communities. Retirees do not take part in the labor force and thus damp-

Table 6.5. Annual Average Labor Force and Unemployment in North Carolina, 1998

	Labor Force	Workers Unemployed (%)
Metropolitan statistical area		
Asheville	111,100	2.6
Charlotte/Gastonia/Rock Hill*	658,760	2.5
Fayetteville	114,520	4.1
Goldsboro	48,550	4.3
Greensboro/Winston-Salem/High Point	631,500	2.7
Greenville	64,810	4.3
Hickory/Morganton/Lenoir	172,090	2.7
Jacksonville	45,710	3.5
Raleigh/Durham/Chapel Hill	617,200	1.7
Rocky Mount	68,250	6.8
Wilmington	107,250	4.2
Subtotal	2,639,740	2.7
Multicounty labor areas		
Elizabeth City/Hertford	22,570	4.1
Henderson/Warrenton	25,920	6.9
Kinston/New Bern	112,460	4.8
Murphy	13,240	5.9
Nags Head	18,530	5.9
Roanoke Rapids	30,860	8.1
Southern Pines/Raeford	39,730	4.3
Subtotal	263,310	5.4
Remainder of North Carolina	914,750	5.0
N.C. total	3,817,800	3.5

Source: North Carolina Employment Security Commission, 1999.
*North Carolina portion only

Figure 6.8. Unemployment Rates, 1998

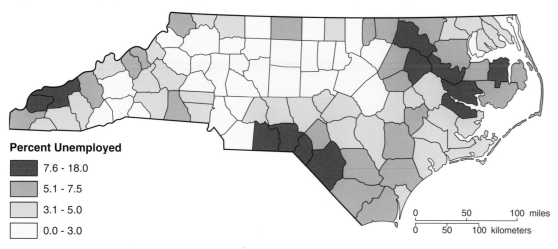

Percent Unemployed

- 7.6 - 18.0
- 5.1 - 7.5
- 3.1 - 5.0
- 0.0 - 3.0

Source: N.C. Employment Security Commission, 1999.

Figure 6.9. Average Wage, 1997

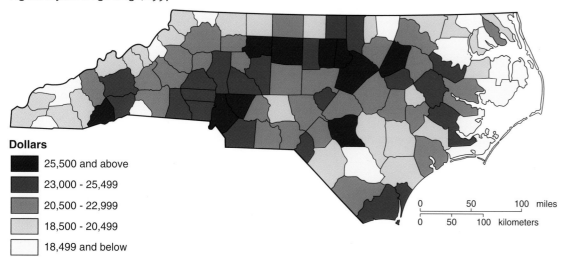

Dollars

- 25,500 and above
- 23,000 - 25,499
- 20,500 - 22,999
- 18,500 - 20,499
- 18,499 and below

Note: The average wage in North Carolina was $26,285.
Source: U.S. Bureau of Economic Analysis, Regional Information System, http://www.bea.doc.gov/bea/dn2.htm, December 1998.

en the participation rate, yet they have substantial consumer and service demands that are a source of local employment and thereby help to keep unemployment rates low. There also is a substantial seasonal variation among the recreation counties. Dare County, in the Outer Banks, had a 5.7 percent unemployment rate for all of 1998, but in January 1998 its off-season rate soared to 18.3 percent.

Earnings

In 1997 the average North Carolina worker earned $26,285, just over 88 percent of the national average. This average is highly skewed by a handful of urban counties that employ vast numbers of people (Fig. 6.9). Durham and Mecklenburg registered the highest average with $37,704 and $34,296, respectively, the only counties to record $30,000 or more. The lowest wages were found in Tyrrell ($15,868) and Perquimans ($16,353). Clearly, wages are higher in and around major urban areas that serve as regional centers of commerce and finance. The low wages of counties in the extreme east and west reflect their remote positions in the state and, to some extent, their reliance on tourism for their economic base. Brunswick and Transylvania Counties are minor exceptions to this pattern largely due to prominent manufactures in the area, particularly paper mills.

Per Capita Income

For most of its history, North Carolina has been a poor state, one that was part of the South that Franklin D. Roosevelt described in the 1930s as "the nation's number one economic problem." Despite major industrial growth during the previous fifty years, in 1930 the state's per capita income was only 47 percent of the national average. By the end of World War II, per capita income had increased to two-thirds of the national average (Fig. 6.10). Over the last fifty years, North Carolina has made tremendous progress in improving per capita incomes. In the 1950s, when economic expansion was fueled by relatively low-wage textile and other

Figure 6.11. Per Capita Income, 1996

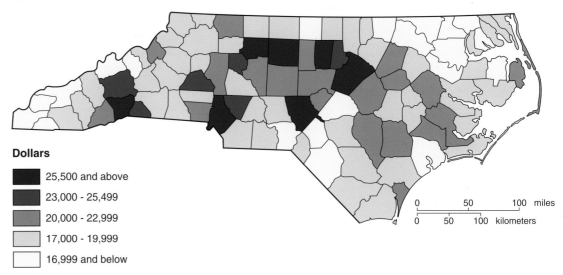

Dollars

- 25,500 and above
- 23,000 - 25,499
- 20,000 - 22,999
- 17,000 - 19,999
- 16,999 and below

Note: Per capita income in North Carolina was $22,205.

Source: U.S. Bureau of Economic Analysis, Regional Information System, http://www.bea.doc.gov/bea/dn2.htm, December 1998.

Figure 6.10. North Carolina per Capita Income as a Percentage of U.S. per Capita Income, 1945–1997

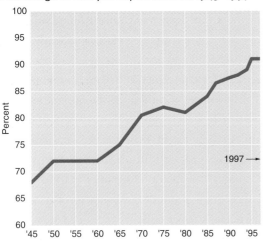

Source: U.S. Bureau of Economic Analysis, Regional Information System, http://www.bea.doc.gov/bea/dn2.htm, December 1998.

labor-intensive industries, the state's per capita income remained at about 72 percent of the national mean. Since the early 1960s sustained growth and diversification in the economy have driven a sustained rise in per capita income, despite a slight drop in the 1980s, to reach a high of 91 percent in 1997.

Of course, not all counties have shared in income growth to the same extent. In 1996 the highest income levels were found in the larger urban counties in the Piedmont, roughly following the corridors of Interstates 77 and 85, and some of the lowest were on the Coastal Plain and in the western tip of the state (Fig. 6.11). The 1975 *North Carolina Atlas* reported that rural-urban disparities in income had diminished. It noted: "One of the most encouraging developments in the North Carolina income situation is a significant trend toward equalization of income over the state. In 1929, the urban-rural contrast was very pronounced but since then many of the rural counties have experienced higher income gains than have the larger urban areas. . . . The populous metropolitan counties still have the highest levels of income in the state but their gains were slow in relation to the state average during the 1929–70 period."

Yet seventeen poorer counties actually fell further behind the state average during that period.

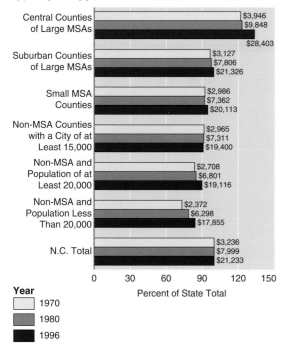

Figure 6.12. North Carolina per Capita Income, 1970, 1980, 1996

Central Counties of Large MSAs: $3,946 / $9,848 / $28,403

Suburban Counties of Large MSAs: $3,127 / $7,806 / $21,326

Small MSA Counties: $2,986 / $7,362 / $20,113

Non-MSA Counties with a City of at Least 15,000: $2,965 / $7,311 / $19,400

Non-MSA and Population of at Least 20,000: $2,708 / $6,801 / $19,116

Non-MSA and Population Less Than 20,000: $2,372 / $6,298 / $17,855

N.C. Total: $3,236 / $7,999 / $21,233

Percent of State Total (0, 30, 60, 90, 120, 150)

Year
- 1970
- 1980
- 1996

Note: Metropolitan and population status as of 1995.
Source: Compiled from data from the U.S. Bureau of Economic Analysis, Regional Information System, http://www.bea.doc.gov/bea/dn2.htm.

Although many counties have improved their economic position, great disparities still exist: per capita income in Graham County, for example, is about half of that in Forsyth or Mecklenburg.

Figure 6.12 portrays the relative income performance of groups of counties between 1970 and 1996. The five core counties of the three largest metropolitan areas continued to gain on the state average, rising from 122 to 134 percent of the mean during the twenty-six-year period. The suburban counties of these larger metro areas also gained, going from 97 to just over 100 percent. The other, smaller metropolitan area counties also rose, from 92 to 95 percent. But the nonmetro counties that in 1996 contained a city of at least 15,000 people declined slightly, from 92 to 91 percent. Interestingly, the least urban categories, while still the poorest in the state, showed substantial improvement. Counties with a population of at least 20,000 people but without a city of at least 15,000 people rose from 84 to 90 percent, and the most rural group, with fewer than 20,000 people and no city of at least 15,000 people, jumped from 73 to 84 percent of the average. These gains are all the more impressive when seen from the perspective of the state mean gaining compared to the national average. One reason for the relative improvement of the more rural counties is that several of them have become major destinations of affluent retirees. Henderson ($23,562), Moore ($26,242), and Polk ($25,304), for instance, had per capita income levels that were substantially higher than the statewide average despite their largely rural status.

In terms of total personal income, probably the best measure of aggregate purchasing power, the three largest metro areas are clearly dominant. The twenty-one counties that comprised the Charlotte, Greensboro–Winston-Salem, and Raleigh–Durham urban regions accounted for 52.6 percent of the income of all North Carolina residents in 1996.

Unearned Income

Wages account for the majority of personal income. Increasingly, however, "unearned" income is becoming an important component of total personal income. This includes dividends, interest, rent, government retirement benefits, unemployment insurance payments, income maintenance benefits, and the like. For both North Carolina and the nation as a whole, the proportion of income that comes from sources other than wages has increased over time (Fig. 6.13). As illustrated in the graph, the importance of unearned income has risen from about 17 percent to almost 30 percent of personal income in the state. At the national level, unearned income was about 35 percent of total personal income in 1995. In general, the largest components of nonwage income are (1) government payments for social security and disability and (2) earnings from interest, dividends, and rent. Social security and government retirement payments are affected by the age composition of counties, whereas dividends, interest, and rent are largely related to wealth accumulated over long periods of time. Income maintenance payments, on average, account for only 1.5 percent of personal income in North Carolina.

Several factors help to explain the trends presented in Figure 6.13. Among the most important is aging of the national and state population, which obviously contributes to growing social security payments and their importance to personal

Figure 6.13. Unearned Income as a Percentage of Total Personal Income in North Carolina and the United States, 1969–1995

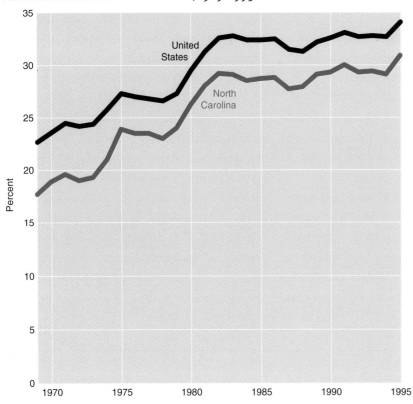

Source: Compiled from data from the U.S. Bureau of Economic Analysis, Regional Information System.

Figure 6.14. Unearned Income as a Percentage of Personal Income, 1995

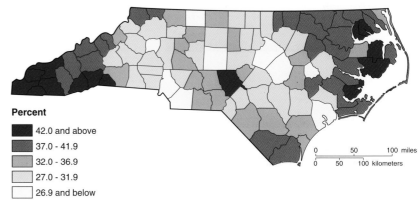

Percent

- ■ 42.0 and above
- ■ 37.0 - 41.9
- ■ 32.0 - 36.9
- □ 27.0 - 31.9
- □ 26.9 and below

Source: U.S. Bureau of Economic Analysis, Regional Information System, http://www.bea.doc.gov/bea/dn2.htm, December 1998.

income. At the same time, those who are retiring, or near retirement, have spent their working lives during the most prosperous period in our nation's history, and North Carolina has shared in that prosperity. Income derived from interest, dividends, and rent reflect the past earnings and wealth that have been accumulated and invested during times of economic expansion.

Just as income and employment are not evenly distributed across the state, the components of unearned income are also unevenly distributed (Fig. 6.14).

Unearned income is a high proportion of total personal income in the extreme western portions of North Carolina and, to a somewhat lesser extent, on the Coastal Plain. In these cases, government retirement payments in 1995 (Fig. 6.14) were higher than the statewide average, reflecting an older resident population. However, there were differences between counties in this group. For example, both Polk and Swain Counties in the west had high proportions of unearned income. But in Polk, income from interest, dividends, and rent was more than twice the statewide average, whereas income maintenance payments were relatively high in Swain. It would appear that retirement communities in Polk have attracted relatively well-to-do retirees who raise the county's per capita income but who are not active in the labor force. This also helps to explain why average wages (Fig. 6.9) are relatively low. A similar set of circumstances applies to Moore County and its communities around Pinehurst and Southern Pines. Swain County, on the other hand, had low per capita income in 1995 largely due to lower-than-average wages and few other sources of income. In most cases, the existence of a large elderly population tends to elevate values in this variable as many people age in place. But some communities have been successful in attracting migrant retirees who typically have higher-than-average sources of income.

Among the counties with low proportions of unearned income were those in and around the urban areas of Charlotte, Greensboro, and Raleigh. In these counties, unemployment has been low, labor force participation high, and job growth strong. These are also some of the areas that have attracted large numbers of migrants to their local workforces. All of these factors tend to create populations that are relatively young, well educated, and more heavily reliant on wages as a source of income.

Cost of Living

A commonly held myth in North Carolina is that lower incomes and wages are offset by lower living costs. This may be true in some cases, particularly in rural areas, but that may be more of a tendency for expectations to be different rather than lower costs for specific items. Housing may cost more in cities, for example, not just because land, labor, and materials are more expensive but also because urban residents prefer homes that are larger, newer, or more prestigious over other goods. Whatever the cause, the American Chambers of Commerce Research Association (ACCRA), a nonprofit research organization, has published a

Figure 6.15. Cost of Living, First Quarter, 1998

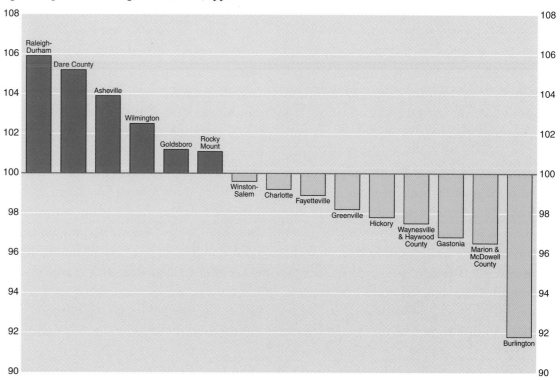

Composite Index*

■ Above average

□ Below average

* The national index value for cities and other reporting areas is 100. Composite index reflects cost of grocery items, utilities, housing, transportation, health care, and miscellaneous goods and services.

Source: ACCRA Cost of Living Survey, 1998.

composite cost-of-living index that compares over three hundred metropolitan and nonmetropolitan U.S. locations to a national average. Presented in Figure 6.15, the data for the first quarter of 1998

indicate that the cost of living in various North Carolina areas did not vary much from the national average. Interestingly, Dare County, a sparsely populated but major coastal recreation area, was one of the most expensive sites in the North Carolina sample, trailing only the fast-growing Raleigh-Durham area. Other places with relatively high living costs were Asheville, Goldsboro, Rocky Mount, and Wilmington. Conversely, Charlotte, Winston-Salem, and the remaining other urban areas had indices that were below the national average. The nonmetropolitan areas of McDowell and Haywood Counties, the most rural places that participated in the survey, had indices that were 96 percent or more of the national mean. In all areas surveyed, utility costs were uniformly higher, miscellaneous goods and services were higher or near parity, and groceries were slightly less than the national average. Typically, housing costs determined whether a place's index was above or below the national mean. Overall, the ACCRA survey tends to belie the myth of lower living costs by showing that (1) costs of living in North Carolina are not far behind those nationwide and (2) the urban-rural disparity is not as great as is commonly believed, and in some cases it is nonexistent.

International Business

The internationalization of the economy has had substantial implications for North Carolina. Especially in manufacturing, there is a tendency for some industrial firms to maintain a competitive position in international markets by locating production facilities wherever the most favorable production costs can be achieved. This is explored in more depth in Chapter 8 ("Manufacturing"), where it is shown that global shifts and a concomitant acceleration of foreign competition have underlain a sharp decline in several major industrial groups in the state. The rise of the global economy means that international trade is more important than ever. Whereas the United States recently has tended to import more than it exports, creating a trade deficit, this is generally not the case in North Carolina. It has been reported, for example, that the value of North Carolina's exports exceeded the value of its imports by 1.3 percent during the late 1980s, when it ranked fourteenth in both imports and exports. In 1996 the state's exports totaled $15.7 billion, ranking it tenth among all the states in that measure (Table 6.6). By 1997 the North Carolina total reached $18.1 billion, divided among a host of industries exporting goods to many parts of the world (Table 6.7).

About 60 percent of the state's exports were accounted for by 7 metropolitan areas: Greensboro–Winston-Salem–High Point, Raleigh–Durham–Chapel Hill, Charlotte-Gastonia, Hickory-Morganton, Wilmington, Asheville, and Fayetteville, in that order. Total exports by these areas collectively increased by about 13 percent between 1995 and 1996. In 1996 the 7 areas ranked in the top 253 metro areas nationally in the value of exports. The three largest (Greensboro–Winston-Salem–High Point, Raleigh–Durham–Chapel Hill, and Charlotte-Gastonia) were in the top 50 nationally, with combined exports of $8.4 billion. That was the bulk of the $9.4 billion in exports generated by all 7 nationally ranked North Carolina metro areas. It is estimated that those sales supported nearly 180,000 jobs.

The state's strong economic environment has also attracted foreign firms (Table 6.8). Since the early 1980s, North Carolina has experienced a fourfold increase in the value of foreign direct investment, amounting to $22.7 billion in 1994 and providing 222,000 jobs. By 1995 this total had reached 225,000, 7.5 percent of total private industry employment in the state. This proportion ranked North Carolina third highest among all the states. Over 124,000 of these employees worked in manufacturing, representing 14.3 percent of all factory workers in the state.

Table 6.6. Total Exports from North Carolina and the United States, 1988, 1992, and 1996 ($ millions)

	1988	1992	1996
U.S.	235,956	379,542	555,960
N.C.	5,373	8,540	15,374
N.C. % of U.S.	2.27	2.25	2.77
N.C. rank	14	14	10

Source: U.S. Department of Commerce, 1998.

Table 6.7. North Carolina Exports, 1997

Industry	Value ($ millions)	Share (%)
Industrial machinery/ equipment	3,179	17.5
Chemicals	2,179	12.0
Electronic/ electrical equipment	1,726	9.5
Apparel	1,373	7.6
Textiles	1,325	7.3
Transportation equipment	1,313	7.2
Crops	1,306	7.2
Tobacco products	902	5.0
Primary metals	888	4.9
Instruments	613	3.4
Total	18,167	100.0

Destination	Value ($ millions)	Share (%)
Canada	4,424	24.4
Japan	1,749	9.6
Mexico	1,218	6.7
United Kingdom	1,069	5.9
Germany	805	4.4
Saudi Arabia	658	3.6
Belgium	625	3.4
Netherlands	478	2.6
Brazil	392	2.2
Hong Kong	378	2.1

Source: Wachovia World Trade Index, 1997.

A freight crane handling South Korean and Taiwanese containers at the Port of Wilmington

In 1998 there were 738 foreign-owned companies from 35 countries in North Carolina, mostly from Germany, the United Kingdom, Japan, Switzerland, Canada, France, and Italy (Fig. 6.16). Three-quarters of these firms were located in the state's larger metropolitan areas, with one-third in Mecklenburg County alone. Of the 738 firms, about 300 were exclusively in sales, services, distribution, or research and development or were headquarters/administrative offices. The remain-

Table 6.8. Foreign Direct Investment in North Carolina

	Property, Plant, Equipment ($ millions)	Percentage of U.S.	Employed (thousands)
1981	5,543	3.1	89.0
1990	15,160	2.6	180.8
1994	22,718	3.2	221.8

Source: U.S. Bureau of Economic Analysis.

Figure 6.16. Number of International Firms Operating in North Carolina, 1998

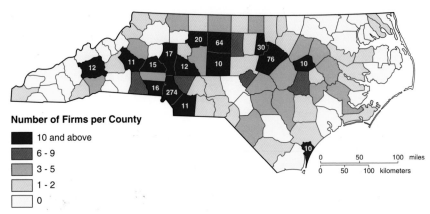

Number of Firms per County

- 10 and above
- 6 - 9
- 3 - 5
- 1 - 2
- 0

Source: N.C. Department of Commerce, *International Firms Directory*, Raleigh, 1998.

ing firms were almost totally manufacturing operations. Significantly, 90 percent of the non-manufacturing operations were located in the five core counties of the largest metropolitan areas: Durham, Forsyth, Guilford, Mecklenburg, and Wake. In contrast, the manufacturing facilities were scattered among sixty-six of the state's counties.

According to a 1994 study by KPMG Peat Marwick, a national accounting firm, 326 of these companies were the U.S. headquarters for their parent companies. A survey of 238 of these headquarters revealed that 147 of them in-

vested over $2.6 billion in the state, with sales and sales/distribution facilities (49 percent) being the leading types of business, followed by manufacturing (40 percent). The 238 headquartered companies reported employing 70,390 people in the state, with about 58 percent in manufacturing.

Primary locational attractions for foreign-owned firms at the state level are proximity to a key industry or market, access to air transportation, acquisition/joint venture opportunities, personal preference, quality and cost of labor, and living conditions/climate. At the local level, important factors include strategic location, local transportation, and personal preference. No doubt, the presence of major airports in Charlotte and Raleigh-Durham, both of which offer nonstop service to most other U.S. cities and some international destinations, were significant considerations for these international firms.

Financial Incentives

Economic development has been a major emphasis of state government at least since the 1950s. Aggressive recruiting of prospective businesses has helped to create more jobs for North Carolinians. Other states, especially in the South, have followed a similar course, and at times the competition among them has become heated. In recent years this competition has taken the form of incentives, whereby states and communities offer new businesses a host of financial concessions. Perhaps the most famous example of this was Alabama's $253 million package to entice Mercedes Benz to locate an automobile assembly plant in the state. Incentives take on many forms such as offering tax rebates, providing free sites, training workers, or even, as in the Alabama case, buying some of the company's product. The largest incentives package offered by North Carolina in the 1990s was the $155 million inducement to get Charlotte-based Nucor to build a $300 million steel plant in rural Hertford County. The plant is expected to create three hundred relatively high-wage jobs in one of the state's most impoverished counties. Nearly $69 million of the tax credits offered to Nucor will offset the cost of building a port on the Chowan River. Federal Express was granted another $145 million in incentives to construct a facility in Greensboro that will create about 1,500 new jobs.

These examples are representative of a competition that has become something of a bidding war among the states. South Carolina is one of the most competitive, offering tax abatements, free land, and worker training to companies such as BMW. North Carolina has taken a more conservative approach, feeling that its many economic advantages already offer a sound environment for long-term business success. Although some states offer tax abatements as an incentive, most analysts think doing so is poor public policy. Instead, North Carolina invests principally in worker training, infrastructure development, and other forms of capital assistance that will benefit the state even if the recipient firm leaves after a few years.

The central feature of North Carolina's business incentives program is to grant tax credits to both new and expanded businesses for worker training, building renovation, investment in machinery, or employment of workers at pay levels equal to or greater than the average wage in the county. To ensure accountability, the tax credits may be taken only in the year after a new or expanded business actually begins operating. In most cases, credits against either the state income tax or the business franchise fee are limited to no more than 50 percent of the total tax liability. The state will provide training for new employees at a nearby community college or on site at no cost and will even pay company employees as instructors.

In 1996 the North Carolina General Assembly passed the William S. Lee Quality Jobs and Business Expansion Act, which was amended by the 1997 legislature. A key feature of this act is that it applies to new or expanded businesses that create at least forty new jobs. Manufacturing, warehousing, air courier, distribution, and data processing businesses qualify for these benefits. Central administrative offices also are eligible under this act, as are increases in research and development activities. Another major feature of the program is that the level of per-worker tax incentives a company may re-

ceive is determined by the relative economic status of the county in which it locates. This provision is a straightforward attempt to attract economic growth to the state's poorer, rural counties. All counties are classified into one of five "enterprise tiers" that are determined by the county's per capita income, unemployment rate, and recent population growth rate. Tax credits are limited to $500 per new job in the most affluent counties and $12,500 per new job in the most economically distressed. In addition, qualifying companies can receive a tax credit for 7 percent of the value of new machinery and equipment. The credit applies to amounts above the threshold level established for each enterprise tier, ranging from zero in tier one to $1 million in tier five. Membership in the five tiers is periodically reviewed and is subject to modification. Figure 6.17 shows the enterprise tier classification of all counties that was effective in 1998.

The 1998 General Assembly amended the William S. Lee Act by adding the Economic Opportunity Act, which authorized tax credits of $4,000 per job created in forty-four "state development zones." These zones are comprised of census tracts that the 1990 U.S. Census indicated had poverty rates of at least 20 percent. Most are found in rural areas, but also included are portions of metropolitan areas, such as two zones in Charlotte.

Upon application, the North Carolina Department of Transportation will install access roads to a facility and provide necessary traffic controls. Assistance also can be provided for installing a railroad spur. Local communities may choose to extend water and sewerage services at reduced rates. Electric utility companies will generally offer a phased rate reduction for a period of years. For example, Duke Power Company will reduce the power bill for qualifying companies for four years, beginning at 20 percent the first year and dropping to 5 percent in the final year. Natural gas utilities can offer reduced rates as well.

No universally accepted standards exist to measure the relative benefits of these incentive programs, but it is widely believed that without them North Carolina would lose jobs to other states. Growth in the state's economy and population has been so vigorous, though, that it raises a question as to the

Figure 6.17. Enterprise Tiers, 1998–1999

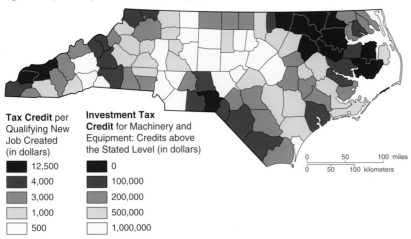

Tax Credit per Qualifying New Job Created (in dollars)

- ■ 12,500
- ■ 4,000
- ■ 3,000
- ▨ 1,000
- □ 500

Investment Tax Credit for Machinery and Equipment: Credits above the Stated Level (in dollars)

- ■ 0
- ■ 100,000
- ■ 200,000
- ▨ 500,000
- □ 1,000,000

0   50   100 miles
0   50   100 kilometers

Source: N.C. Department of Commerce, Finance Center, 1999.

wisdom of continually promoting even more growth. Without a doubt, the more economically distressed parts of the state need more and better economic opportunities, but it is in these very places that it is most difficult to generate more and better jobs. Incentives alone are unlikely to offset the lack of supporting business services, inadequate school systems, poor infrastructure, limited access to markets and raw materials, or minimal amenities that are desirable for professional employees of sophisticated companies.

Economic Growth and Urbanization

Dramatic growth in the number of foreign-owned firms is a noteworthy trend in the North Carolina economy. However, the rapid movement of many U.S. headquarters to the state's larger metropolitan areas is also an important trend. It not only has promoted business activity in those areas, but it also has increased the diversity of their population and generally brought them more fully in touch with the rest of the world. The larger cities are now more visible

and better known in the international business community, and as these local companies succeed in North Carolina, others will follow. The location of headquarters in larger cities is the most visible trend that will further widen growth disparities between these larger counties and the rest of the state. This is not to say that nonmetropolitan areas are losing business, but that the metro areas are receiving an increasingly disproportionate share of it. Metropolitan growth is taking place nationwide because a large share of economic growth in the United States is in office-related information processing, services, finance, health care, and high technology. These businesses tend to be attracted to, and cluster in and around, larger metropolitan areas where they can access well-educated labor, major airports, business and technical services, amenities, and each other. This is the economic reality at the beginning of the twenty-first century.

The continued urbanization of the state's population and employment is also expected to extend well into the new century. Structural change in the economy has shifted the location of employment growth, causing larger metropolitan areas to emerge as job magnets. Between 1980 and 1990 the five largest counties (Durham, Forsyth, Guilford, Mecklenburg, and Wake) accounted for nearly half of the state's net nonagricultural job growth, yet they contained just 26 percent of the population. Despite an overall population increase of 21.5 percent, job growth in the five counties outstripped population growth. While 306,328 people were added to their populations, net job growth totaled 347,350—over 41,000 more jobs than people. This is made all the more remarkable by the fact that typically just over half of the population holds a job.

Where did these workers come from? Some came from the ranks of the unemployed, and some were women who entered the labor force for the first time. However, much of the new demand for labor was met by a dramatic increase in the number of workers commuting into these job magnet counties from other counties.

An instructive example of this is provided by the relationship between Mecklenburg and adjacent Cabarrus County. Between 1980 and 1990 Mecklenburg added 17,486 more jobs to its labor force than it did to its population. During the same period, according to U.S. Census data, commuting into Mecklenburg increased from about 45,000 to over 103,000 people. Another 18,000 Mecklenburg residents traveled daily to jobs in one of the suburban counties. Meanwhile, employment in Cabarrus County rose by only 5.7 percent with the addition of just 2,200 jobs but population grew by 13,040, or 15 percent. Commuting to work from Cabarrus into Mecklenburg almost doubled, from 8,463 to 16,603 people between 1980 and 1990. Thus, Cabarrus became more heavily dependent on its neighbor for employment, raising concerns that it, like other suburban counties, was becoming a bedroom community.

Conversely, Mecklenburg was equally dependent on its neighbors for workers, without whom its economy could never have grown as vigorously. In fact, 1990 census records indicate that over one-quarter of all full-time employees in Mecklenburg County were commuters from another county. Unfortunately, data on intercounty commuting are provided only in the decennial census. But all indications are that, since 1990, the strong growth of these core counties has continued and the flow of commuters into them probably has increased.

As the major metropolitan counties emerge as the state's primary growth centers, they experience various growth problems, not the least of which are massive traffic flows that result from both their own population growth and increased intercounty

commuting. Looking further into the future, if North Carolina's metropolitan areas follow the path of most other urban areas in America, the pattern of large-scale urbanization at the state level will be accompanied by decentralization at the local level, when central cities become more congested and new businesses seek lower-density suburban green-field sites. The multibillion-dollar, long-term highway construction package adopted by the North Carolina General Assembly might actually accelerate this process through the construction of beltways and the expansion of other four-lane highways.

Certainly, efficiency gains from improving accessibility, and ease of transportation lowers costs and makes the state more productive. However, beltways, in particular, tend to pull economic activity away from the core areas they surround, especially at access points. These highways will contribute to localized decentralization within urbanized areas, pulling activity to suburban nodes and urban fringe jurisdictions. A positive aspect of this prospect is that it might bring increasing opportunities and better job access to those living in more rural areas. Conversely, it can also limit access to employment for inner-city dwellers, particularly those who rely on public transportation.

Does this mean that central cities of urban areas will fall into decline? Probably not. In North Carolina, central cities are apt to remain strong as they serve as administrative centers for both the public and private sectors. It does mean that suburban ju-

risdictions may begin to experience a growing share of employment growth, however. To the extent that suburban growth will reflect current trends, it is likely that much of the new employment will be found in sectors that are information-intensive.

Technology and Regional Development

For centuries, technological change has driven economic growth and development. Technology has been central to regional economic change in its use to both create and destroy jobs and alter the geography of production. Edward Malecki, an expert in the field of technology and economic development, describes technology as encompassing knowledge in all of its forms, from simple and routine procedures of everyday life, to the methods of organization and management in large and small business enterprises alike. From the machines that produce enormous quantities of what formerly required many workers, to the complex scientific investigations that create ever newer inventions and products, technology has been the principal source of change for firms, regions, and nations.

What is less understood about technology, its innovation and its adoption, is how it changes the location of economic activity on the landscape and the mix of labor skills required by firms that employ advanced technological systems. Importantly, the adoption and use of technologies is an inherently social process. Technology does not exist in a vacuum, but it is used and adopted to varying degrees by people who work in factories and offices, who combine to form businesses and corporations, and who use different technologies to manufacture products and produce services that are delivered to a marketplace. People and regions that are at the forefront of technological innovation and adoption are at a continual advantage over those that are not. Increasingly labor markets are being segmented along lines of "primary" and "secondary" labor defined by the active use of technology. Though overlapping geographically, these labor markets are beginning to have a spatial expression on the landscape, with technology-intensive primary markets being national in scope and secondary markets, characterized by lower wages and less job security, being mostly local.

One, more recent form of technological change that is permeating modern societies is *information technology* (IT). Information technology consists of the tools and techniques required to collect, generate, and record data. More important from the perspective of development and urbanization, however, is the role of IT and the use of computers and telecommunications that are integrated into a single system of information processing and exchange. According to Peter Dicken, the accumulative effect of IT adoption is to both reinforce certain communication routes and enhance the importance of significant nodes (cities) on those

routes. In the process, IT affects both workers and workplaces.

One popular example of IT use is telecommuting—workers using telecommunications to do many office-related tasks at home, or in some other remote location, and transmitting their work over lines via facsimiles, E-mail, and the Internet. Though they represent a small proportion of the workforce, the number of workers who telecommute at least some of the time has grown substantially in recent years. A survey by Telecommute America revealed that the number of Americans who telecommute from their homes increased 30 percent between 1995 and 1997. In the latter year, approximately 11 million people—8 percent of the labor force—telecommuted; by 2000 the number was expected to be 14 million. This represents a substantial increase over the 4 million Americans who did so in 1990.

In theory, telecommuting should allow some workers to live farther from their employers and possibly help spur development in fringe and rural areas. But it is likely that such prophecies are easily exaggerated. Though the fraction of workers who telecommute is growing, it still comprises a relatively small proportion of the workforce. Among those who do telecommute, most only do so a few times per week, which requires that they still choose residential locations that facilitate commuting by standard means. Most important, however, is that even if workers telecommuted every

day, most would still demand the amenities urban areas have to offer. This is especially true because telecommuters are typically white-collar professionals with incomes to spend.

From the perspective of firms, IT also has changed the way and location in which business is conducted, at least among those that utilize advanced information technology. There are two faces to IT that have opposite, yet reinforcing, impacts on the location of businesses and jobs. Specifically, IT is thought to allow both separation of production and concentration of administrative control. For example, many newspapers with a national circulation now print the newspaper near the major market areas where it is sold (separation of production), whereas their news copy is written and edited in the paper's headquarters location (concentration of administrative control) before it is transmitted via satellite or the Internet to printing facilities in other regions. An example is the southeastern edition of the *Wall Street Journal*, which is composed in New York and printed in Charlotte.

Likewise, most headquarters and decision-making units of manufacturers, financial institutions, and high-level service providers continue to be located in core cities of metropolitan areas, whereas branch plant production and routine data processing take place in locations where wages and other production costs can be minimized. Although IT facilitates extremely high access to information from around the globe at almost any location, firms continue to locate in proximity to one another, which further promotes the process of urban growth and development. This is due in part to the fact that as firms become more specialized, they increasingly establish client-supplier linkages where the costs of doing certain kinds of business are minimized by locating in close proximity to one another. Labor is less mobile than information or finance capital, and members in the primary segment of the workforce continue to find employment alternatives in urban areas. These facts imply that the impact of IT is to make the location of less mobile factors of production, such as skilled labor, more important in the location decisions of firms. In other words, advanced technology accelerates urban growth rather than slowing it.

What does this mean for North Carolina? First, it is likely that although some technologies may bring new jobs to rural areas, those areas will be increasingly tied to activities in urban areas of the state. This, according to journalist Neil Pierce, is because metro America is "where the action is" and will continue to drive regional and global competitiveness in the new century. Also, it should not be forgotten that access to markets is still an important consideration for many services and manufacturers. Although many goods can now be ordered over the Internet, many service functions, both high-end (e.g., health, legal, architectural,

specialized repair) and low-end (dry cleaners, day care, haircuts) require face-to-face contact that is possible only through proximity. Because humans are inherently social creatures and urban growth has been the hallmark of recent development in North Carolina, technology, in general, and IT, in particular, will reinforce the patterns of urban growth in the state.

Outlook

Although technology has been used to deskill certain kinds of work, the technological and educational requirements of most jobs are increasing. This is the bad news for North Carolina as its K-12 system of public education and levels of educational attainment still lag behind national averages. From a policy perspective, this means that state policymakers must carefully balance investments in physical capital with investments in human capital.

Metropolitan areas are the economic engines of the state. As these areas continue to grow, their integration with the other parts of the state will intensify. As engines of growth, it is necessary that they remain well tuned or the entire state will suffer. The economic growth they generate will help deal with problems of rural North Carolina, and properly designed networks of transportation and telecommunications will allow more businesses to

locate in the periphery of metropolitan centers, thereby bringing more jobs within reach of the rural population. The state's changing economic and spatial structures favor metropolitan areas, and efforts to more fully integrate and connect rural areas with their urban counterparts will assure North Carolina's continued success.

The chapters that follow deal in more detail with the major components of the economy, especially agriculture and related activities (Chapter 7), manufacturing (Chapter 8), transportation and utilities (Chapter 9), and trade, finance, and tourism (Chapter 10). In all of these chapters the reader will find further evidence of the trend away from the state's historic pattern of geographic dispersion and toward more centralization of growth in larger metropolitan areas. Other chapters, such as those covering population (Chapter 4), urbanization (Chapter 5), politics (Chapter 11), and health care (Chapter 17), deal with the implications of a changed economic geography. The tension between economic forces that favor centralization, on the one hand, and a prized rural, small-town lifestyle, on the other, will compel North Carolinians and their policymakers to face some difficult decisions in the years to come. These decisions will require careful analysis and recognition of the forces that shape the state's economy.

Selected References

Campbell, H., and A. Stuart. "Foreign Direct Investment in North Carolina." *North Carolina Geographer* 6 (Summer 1998): 37–49.

Dicken, P. *Global Shift: Transforming the World Economy.* 3d ed. New York: Guilford Press, 1998.

Downs, A. *New Visions for Metropolitan America.* Washington, D.C.: Brookings Institution, 1994.

Furuseth, O. "The North Carolina Business Landscape View through Foreign Eyes." In *Snapshot of the Carolinas: Landscapes and Cultures,* edited by G. Gordon Bennett, pp. 159–64. Washington, D.C.: Association of American Geographers, 1996.

Malecki, E. *Technology and Economic Development.* New York: John Wiley and Sons, 1991.

U.S. Department of Commerce. Bureau of Economic Analysis. Regional Economic Analysis Division. Regional Information System. [Source of employment, earnings, and income data]

7. AGRICULTURE, FORESTRY, FISHING, AND MINING

North Carolina has a long tradition of extracting raw materials from nature and then converting them into finished products. Agriculture, forestry, fishing, and mining have always been important contributors to the state's economy and have played a substantial role in maintaining its economic diversity. Now these industries comprise a steadily declining share of the state's economic output and employment. They do, however, indirectly support many other jobs in the construction, manufacturing, processing, and service industries. Indeed, in many cases such industries owe their existence to these suppliers of basic materials.

As we enter the twenty-first century, agriculture, forestry, fishing, and mining in North Carolina are all experiencing tumultuous times. Traditional crops and farming practices are changing with the greater use of labor-saving technologies and a consequent rise in the size of farms. The shift from emphasis on the family farm to larger but fewer industrial farms is undermining a cherished way of life. Controversy is swirling around tobacco allotment programs and the threat of smoking to public health. The pollution of groundwater and streams by hog waste lagoons has provoked a public outcry against the big hog farms and a call for tighter controls.

People who fish for a living view the regulation of commercial fishing, intended to conserve the seafood supply, as a threat to their livelihood. Concern abounds over the use and possible misuse of the state's historically bountiful forest resources. Controversies periodically surround proposed mining projects, especially near urban areas where residents object to the dust, the damage to homes caused by blasting, and the traffic of heavy trucks. All of these changes are direct consequences of rapid growth and the shift to a more urban economy.

Agriculture

TOM ROSS AND ROBERT REIMAN

Farms and Farming

Farming historically not only has been a pillar of the economy but also has helped to shape North Carolina's unique character as a predominantly rural, small-town state. Tobacco farming, with its unusually high-dollar yields per acre, has been especially prominent in supporting a relatively dispersed population pattern. More recently, both population and economic activities in the state have taken on a distinctly urban pattern. This has paralleled a decline of agriculture's role in the economy. Today, farming accounts for only about 2.5 percent of both employment and gross state product (GSP). In 1969 farm employment of 201,138 accounted for 8.3 percent of the statewide employment total, but by 1996 it had dropped to about 86,000. As would be expected, most nonowner or nonoperator agricultural workers are employed seasonally. In 1995, the last year for which data were gathered, 56,000 farmworkers were employed in the July–September quarter, compared to 17,000 in the January–March quarter. As the farm labor force has declined, so has the contribution of agriculture to total GSP, down significantly from 3.7 percent of the North

Carolina total in 1977. Nevertheless, agriculture still gives character to the rural landscape, and the values and attitudes associated with it are pervasive, particularly in politics, even though farming is no longer the defining element of the North Carolina economy.

Now one of the most diverse agricultural states in the country, North Carolina produces an extensive list of farm items from both crops and livestock. For many years it has been first nationally in the output of tobacco (both burley and flue-cured), sweet potatoes, and turkeys and first in farm forest receipts. The state has long ranked either second or third in the country in the production of cucumbers for pickles, number three in poultry receipts, and either third or fourth in the production of peanuts. In 1997 it ranked among the top ten states in such diverse farm commodities as trout, Christmas trees, and hogs on farms (second); greenhouse and nursery products (third); commercial broilers and strawberries (fourth); burley tobacco, livestock, dairy products, and blueberries (sixth); cotton, poultry, watermelons, and rye (seventh); pecans and apples (eighth); and chickens (excluding broilers) and eggs (ninth). In 1997 North Carolina was in third position in net farm income, and since 1984 it has ranked annually between eighth and twelfth in total cash receipts from farming. But its national rank in receipt of government payments has ranged from twenty-fourth to thirty-second, an indication that North Carolina depends less heavily on federal farm subsidies than do more than half of the other states. In fact, 1997 government payments to North Carolina farmers constituted less than 1 percent of total receipts.

All of this diversification and production is being carried out on a relatively small amount of land. In 1997 farms in North Carolina occupied only 9 million acres, about 27.3 percent of the state's land area and 1 percent of the country's total farmland. Average farm size is also much smaller than in the United States generally, only 159 acres—about one-third the size of the 471-acre average American farm. In 1981 there were about 2,434,000 farms in the United States, of which 90,000 (or about 3.7 percent) were located in North Carolina. By 1997, when the number of farms nationwide had declined by about 15.5 percent to 2,058,000, the North Carolina total dropped by almost 37 percent and accounted for about 2.8 percent of all U.S. farms.

Farming occupies relatively more land in eastern North Carolina, especially the northeastern part (Fig. 7.1). Fifteen counties, all of them in the east, have at least 25 percent of their total land area devoted to harvested cropland, led by Pasquotank with 54 percent and by Greene, Lenoir, Perquimans, Washington, Wayne, and Wilson each with 35 percent or more.

Average farm size in the United States in 1981 was 424 acres. By 1997 the average had risen to 471 acres, a gain of 10 percent. In North Carolina the increase was from 127 acres to 159 acres, a 25 percent jump. In other words, farm acreage and the number of farms are declining, but the average size of farms is increasing at a greater rate in North Carolina than in the United States overall.

In 1997 cash receipts from farm commodities in North Carolina totaled nearly $8.3 billion. About 43.5 percent of this amount was from the sale of crops and the balance from sales of livestock, dairy, and poultry products. Not surprisingly, tobacco overshadowed all other contributors in the crops category, with receipts of more than $1 billion. Meat animals (hogs, cattle, sheep) led the livestock category with receipts of $2.40 billion, followed by poultry and eggs with $2.21 billion. The next most important sector consisted of oil crops (soybeans, peanuts, and canola) with sales nearing $345 million. Feed grains accounted for more than $202 million, but they were surpassed by greenhouse

and nursery products, which amounted to more than $943 million, and sales of vegetables accounted for another $343 million. Fruits and nuts brought in $45 million, with apples being the most important with sales of $16.7 million. Peaches earned only $3.5 million, whereas blueberries and strawberries accounted for a total of $22.7 million. As might be expected, the top ten counties in receipts from the production of crops were among the larger counties of the Inner Coastal Plain, whereas the top ten counties in sales of livestock ranged farther across the state (Table 7.1).

In 1997 more than 53 percent of the state's farms

averaged sales of less than $10,000. About 27 percent had sales of between $10,000 and $100,000. Twenty percent (10,146 farms), with more than one-half of the farm acreage, registered sales of more than $100,000 (Fig. 7.2).

Farming is not a lucrative business in North Carolina (Fig. 7.3). Between 1969 and 1997 total gross farm income expanded from about $1.7 billion to more than $8.3 billion, but much of this increase was attributable to inflation. Perhaps of greater significance is that net income has risen more slowly than gross income. This reflects the higher rate of capitalization necessary for land,

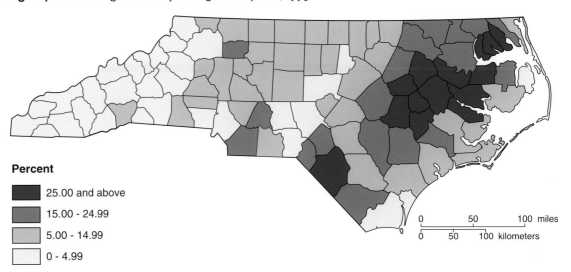

Figure 7.1. Percentage of County Acreage in Cropland, 1995

Percent

- 25.00 and above
- 15.00 - 24.99
- 5.00 - 14.99
- 0 - 4.99

Note: Total state acreage in Cropland = 11.94%.

Source: N.C. Dept. of Agriculture, *N.C. Agricultural Statistics*, 1996.

Table 7.1. Top Ten North Carolina Counties in Farm Cash Receipts, 1996

Rank	All Crops		Livestock, Dairy, and Poultry		Total*	
	County	$000	County	$000	County	$000
1	Johnston	162,271	Duplin	602,050	Duplin	679,964
2	Henderson	139,505	Sampson	509,473	Sampson	623,659
3	Wilson	129,947	Union	269,650	Union	324,120
4	Mecklenburg	120,866	Wayne	231,152	Wayne	310,936
5	Sampson	114,186	Wilkes	190,463	Johnston	217,046
6	Pitt	104,975	Moore	148,861	Robeson	209,734
7	Robeson	101,187	Randolph	146,764	Wilkes	199,560
8	Nash	88,723	Bladen	146,649	Bladen	189,055
9	Columbus	87,293	Chatham	117,717	Randolph	179,216
10	Wayne	79,784	Robeson	108,547	Pitt	177,023

Source: North Carolina Agricultural Statistics, 1998.
*Includes government payments

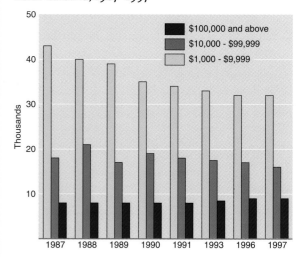

Figure 7.2. Number of Farms, by Sales Class, in North Carolina, 1987–1997

Source: N.C. Dept. of Agriculture, *N.C. Agricultural Statistics*, 1998.

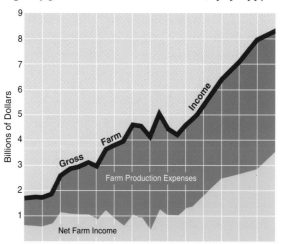

Figure 7.3. North Carolina Farm Income, 1969–1997

Source: N.C. Dept. of Agriculture, *N.C. Agricultural Statistics*, 1998.

farm machinery, and equipment and the higher prices for and expanded use of energy. The net effect is that small farmers either stay small or are forced out of farming. Farmland located near growing urban areas becomes increasingly more valuable as potential housing or shopping areas than as farms. Higher taxation, based on potential urban use, then makes the cost of farming prohibitive.

Farm income is also tied directly to the vagaries of market conditions and weather. When favorable weather allows high yields, markets become saturated and prices depressed. Net profit suffers as a result. Periods of unfavorable weather produce shortages of commodities and accompanying high prices. However, many farmers have nothing to sell during such times.

Profile of Farmers

North Carolina has one of the country's largest rural farm populations, even though many rural people do not farm or farm only on a part-time basis. In fact, 51 percent of all farm operators pursue a primary occupation other than farming. This helps explain the large number of farms that had sales of less than $10,000 per year. The highly dispersed nature of manufacturing plants provides the opportunity for many farmers to hold down a wage job while specializing in tobacco, fruits, and vegetables, or even aquaculture, on the side. Ironically, loss of many rural industrial jobs noted in Chapter 8 ("Manufacturing") may also undercut the economic prospects of many of these part-time farmers.

Farm operators also must be assisted in many cases by hired labor, most of which is seasonal. According to data provided by the North Carolina Growers Association, during peak harvest in 1995, some 67,000 seasonal farm workers were employed. Of those, 35,000 were migrants, most of whom were Spanish speaking. Counties with more than 2,000 migrant farmworkers included Sampson (3,500), Duplin (2,700), Nash (2,350), and Pitt (2,000). Five additional counties employed between 1,000 and 1,999 migrant workers.

North Carolina farm owners and operators in 1997 were mostly white, with only 4.8 percent belonging to nonwhite ethnic groups, and they utilized only 2.7 percent of the total farmland in the state. Between 1954 and 1997 the average age of farm operators rose from 48 to 55 years, an indication that farming appeals to fewer young people. About 92.4 percent of farm operators in the state were male.

The predominant farm management type in North Carolina is the individual or family (sole proprietorship). The 87.3 percent of farms so classified is a little higher than the national average. According to the 1997 U.S. Census of Agriculture, the partnership style prevails on 9.1 percent of farms, and the rest are operated by tenants, down from 16.7 percent in 1978.

At the time of the 1997 U.S. Census of Agriculture, the total market value of North Carolina's farmland and buildings was estimated to be nearly $19 billion, or an average of $376,000 per farm. Although this figure was somewhat lower than the national average, it should be remembered that North Carolina farms are considerably smaller than the national mean. Moreover, the average figure is somewhat misleading in another sense. The 6,400 farms in the value group $1 to $40,000 were 10.6 percent of all farms in the state. The 4,500 farms in the value group over $1,000,000 comrpised 7.7 percent of all farms. The estimated average value of machinery and equipment for all farms in 1997 was $49,106.

North Carolina farmers help to keep the country's balance of foreign trade from being even more negative than it already is by contributing heavily on the export side. In 1997 the state's farm exports totaled more than $1.5 billion, with raw tobacco furnishing 39.5 percent of the total, down from 59.0 percent in 1989. But cotton, poultry, and meat products furnished ever-increasing shares. Cotton exports soared from almost $18 million in 1989 to over $128 million in 1997. During the same period poultry products moved from fourth to second place among North Carolina's agricultural exports by climbing from $65 million to more than $327 million.

Crop Production

North Carolina produces a wide variety of crops, of which tobacco generates the largest cash farm income, followed by cotton, soybeans, corn, wheat, peanuts, sweet potatoes, fruits, and vegetables. Other than farmland devoted to woodland, soybeans occupy more land than any other single crop, replacing corn in recent years. However, because some of the corn and other grains are fed directly to livestock and poultry, all feed grains that are produced do not enter the cash market. Figures 7.4 and 7.5 reveal production patterns for the state's most important crops.

Figure 7.4 shows the quantity of production and the location of two major field crops, corn and wheat, that in grain alone brought in combined receipts in 1997 of about $290 million. Corn is used as a cash grain commodity and also for silage. The heaviest concentration of corn grown for grain is in the counties of the Coastal Plain. Corn for silage, on the other hand, has more of a Piedmont and Mountain orientation, mainly because it is used as fodder for cattle. In 1997, 77.4 million bushels of corn for grain were produced on 870,000 acres, down about 10 percent from the year before. The yield per

Figure 7.4. Grains Production, 1997

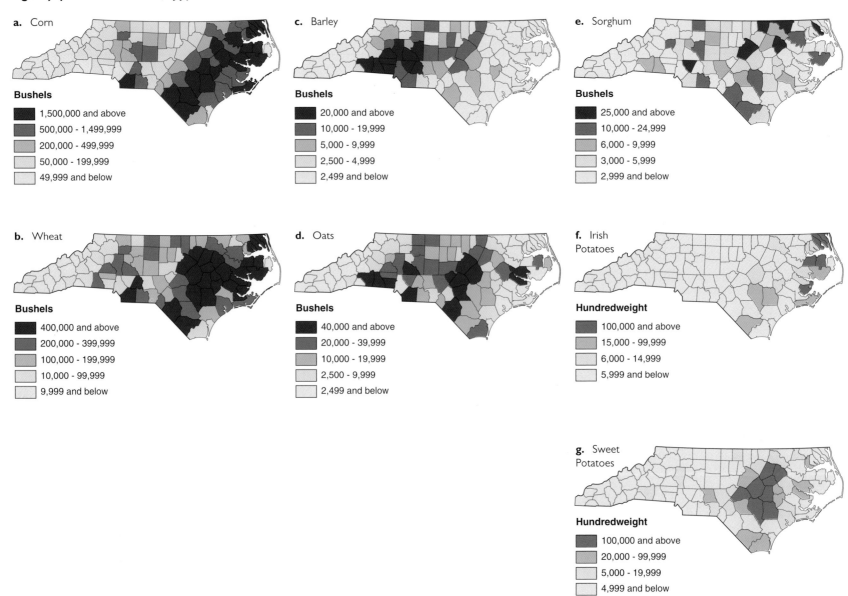

a. Corn

Bushels
- 1,500,000 and above
- 500,000 - 1,499,999
- 200,000 - 499,999
- 50,000 - 199,999
- 49,999 and below

b. Wheat

Bushels
- 400,000 and above
- 200,000 - 399,999
- 100,000 - 199,999
- 10,000 - 99,999
- 9,999 and below

c. Barley

Bushels
- 20,000 and above
- 10,000 - 19,999
- 5,000 - 9,999
- 2,500 - 4,999
- 2,499 and below

d. Oats

Bushels
- 40,000 and above
- 20,000 - 39,999
- 10,000 - 19,999
- 2,500 - 9,999
- 2,499 and below

e. Sorghum

Bushels
- 25,000 and above
- 10,000 - 24,999
- 6,000 - 9,999
- 3,000 - 5,999
- 2,999 and below

f. Irish Potatoes

Hundredweight
- 100,000 and above
- 15,000 - 99,999
- 6,000 - 14,999
- 5,999 and below

g. Sweet Potatoes

Hundredweight
- 100,000 and above
- 20,000 - 99,999
- 5,000 - 19,999
- 4,999 and below

Source: N.C. Dept. of Agriculture, *N.C. Agricultural Statistics*, 1998.

Figure 7.5. Production of Industrial Raw Materials and Foods, 1997

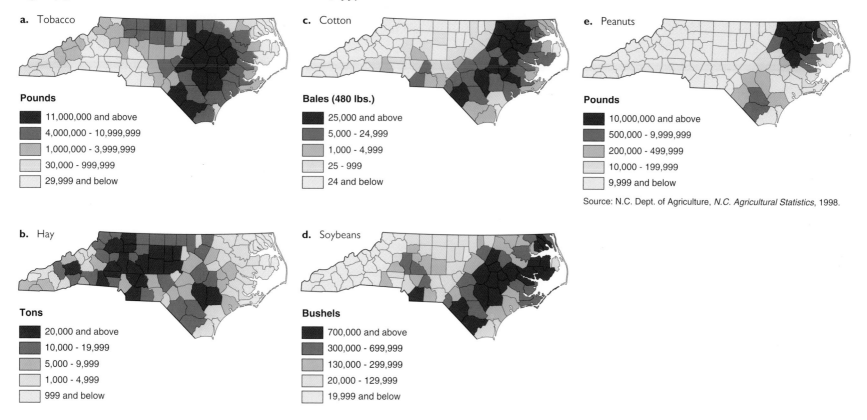

a. Tobacco

Pounds
- 11,000,000 and above
- 4,000,000 - 10,999,999
- 1,000,000 - 3,999,999
- 30,000 - 999,999
- 29,999 and below

c. Cotton

Bales (480 lbs.)
- 25,000 and above
- 5,000 - 24,999
- 1,000 - 4,999
- 25 - 999
- 24 and below

e. Peanuts

Pounds
- 10,000,000 and above
- 500,000 - 9,999,999
- 200,000 - 499,999
- 10,000 - 199,999
- 9,999 and below

Source: N.C. Dept. of Agriculture, *N.C. Agricultural Statistics*, 1998.

b. Hay

Tons
- 20,000 and above
- 10,000 - 19,999
- 5,000 - 9,999
- 1,000 - 4,999
- 999 and below

d. Soybeans

Bushels
- 700,000 and above
- 300,000 - 699,999
- 130,000 - 299,999
- 20,000 - 129,999
- 19,999 and below

land unit (89 bushels per acre) was lower than the United States average of 138.

The wheat produced in North Carolina is of the soft, winter-wheat variety, used primarily in cake flour and pastry and for bakery products other than bread. Although nearly as important as corn, wheat makes a good rotation crop and can be "multiple-cropped," that is, planted in the fall and harvested early enough in the summer to allow an-

other crop to be grown in the same field. Wheat is grown mainly on the Coastal Plain, multiple-cropped with soybeans. The yield in 1997 was almost 35 million bushels on 730,000 acres—about 52 bushels per acre.

The production of small grains—barley, oats, and sorghum—amounts to less than one-twentieth of that accounted for by wheat and corn (Fig. 7.4). Nevertheless, these crops are important in

that they add diversity. They can be used in rotation with wheat and corn or in multiple-cropping situations. Moreover, they can often be grown on agriculturally marginal land that is not as suitable for wheat or corn. In 1997 total value for the three crops was $7.4 million. Piedmont counties showed a larger proportion of the small grains than they did of corn or wheat.

Irish potatoes and sweet potatoes, with a 1997

gross value of $76.2 million, are grown mostly on the Coastal Plain, with ancillary production in the Mountain counties. Sweet potatoes, for which North Carolina is the leading producer in the United States, accounted for almost three-fourths of the potato income. They do well in the sandy loam soils of the Coastal Plain (Fig. 7.4). Irish potatoes like those same soils and also make a good cash crop in some of the cooler Mountain counties.

In North Carolina, favorable soils, moisture conditions, temperatures, and a long growing season combine to make the planting of tobacco a lucrative economic activity—it overwhelms the production of all other crops and is grown in almost every county of the state (Fig. 7.5.a). Tobacco cultivation in the state goes back to the seventeenth century, when the lucrative crop spread southward from Virginia. In the nineteenth century it was discovered that the loamy soils of the northern Piedmont produced a desirable bright, yellow tobacco leaf, and production shifted to that area. However, in the late nineteenth century declining cotton prices and the development of various fertilizers attracted the interest of farmers in the east, and the center of production shifted to Nash, Pitt, and other counties on the northern Inner Coastal Plain. It was not long before small tobacco patches, associated barns, and warehouses where the crop was auctioned off became a distinctive feature on the landscape of the state.

Today, flue-cured varieties are raised in the Piedmont and on the Coastal Plain and air-cured burley in very small fields in the lower-temperature regime of the western Mountains. Burley accounts for only about 2 percent of the total crop, but it brings a somewhat higher price and fills an important niche as a flavoring ingredient in the production of tobacco products. Total value of the 1997 tobacco crop exceeded $1.258 billion, about the same as in 1992. Much of the raw product is processed in the state, providing additional jobs in manufacturing.

Tobacco farmers have suffered income losses from the growing controversy surrounding the health impacts of smoking. A major legal settlement was reached between the cigarette companies and a number of states that is intended to ameliorate these losses. North Carolina is to receive an estimated $4.6 billion from this settlement over twenty-five years, in addition to a $1.9 billion trust fund established by the companies to cover losses in income by tobacco growers and allotment holders.

The 1999 General Assembly established several other nonprofit trust funds to manage the distribution of the $4.6 billion allocation. Under one trust, half of the money will aid farming communities that are expected to suffer financially as cigarette sales drop. The remaining $2.3 billion is to be divided equally between two other funds, one for smoking-related health programs and the other for payments sent to tobacco growers and allotment holders.

In 1997 hay crops worth about $99 million were harvested from fields throughout the state. Heaviest production was in the central and northern Piedmont, in areas where cattle production was also high (Fig. 7.5.b). Yield per acre was 2.22 tons, about 10 percent lower than the 1995 average of 2.59.

Cotton, soybeans, and peanuts—all high-value crops—contributed nearly $682 million to the state's farm economy in 1997. Cotton was the most important of the three, at more than $335 million (Fig. 7.5.c). The cotton production area increased to 665,000 acres, up sevenfold from the 97,000 acres harvested in 1984, as cotton made a modest comeback as a desired fiber. But this is still a marked contrast with the 829,000 acres harvested in 1940. Cotton is concentrated mainly in a few counties on the Coastal Plain.

Peanut production has fluctuated in the recent past between a high of 485 million pounds in 1994 and a low of 329 million pounds in 1997 (Fig. 7.5.e). Production is centered on the northern counties of the Coastal Plain. Soybeans, a versatile crop with both food and industrial uses, are especially desirable because they can be used as a second crop on the same fields and in the same season after grains are harvested (Fig. 7.5.d). The climate and soils of North Carolina are well enough suited to soybeans to provide reasonable yields per acre, but not nearly as high as yields in the midwestern states. Again, in North Carolina heaviest production is on the Coastal Plain, but a considerable amount of soybeans is produced on the Piedmont. Production in 1997 was 39 million bushels, down from 42 million in 1994.

The Flue-Cured Tobacco Program in North Carolina

North Carolina, with its fields of golden leaf and cities built by tobacco barons, may well be the "Hub of the Tobacco Universe," but its role in that universe depends in part on one of the New Deal's most durable programs.

By the time the Great Depression hit North Carolina in 1929, tobacco was the predominant cash crop in the rural state, and cigarette manufacturing was the most lucrative industry. But glutted markets meant low and unstable prices for farmers, many of whom were sharecroppers struggling just to stay on the farm. In 1933 the Farm Relief bill gave birth to the federal Agricultural Adjustment Administration (AAA), which responded to the tobacco crisis by proposing a program of voluntary crop reductions. After a few false starts, farmers overwhelmingly approved a schedule of price supports and allotments for the 1940 season, and the federal tobacco program was born.

The AAA awarded acreage allotments based on farmers' past history of production, and though some shifts have occurred, the geographic pattern of tobacco cultivation in the state has remained essentially frozen ever since. A quota can now be sold and ownership transferred permanently, but otherwise a quota is still tied to the farms themselves (similar allotments based on poundage were added in 1966 and now are the main mechanisms for controlling supply). Because a quota can only be sold within county lines, each county has its own separate markets, and quota prices vary widely from county to county.

In exchange for limiting production, farmers can depend on a minimum support price when they get to market. Any tobacco that does not bring at least the support price at auction can be sold to the Tobacco Cooperative Stabilization Corporation, which then stores the tobacco for later sale. An assessment paid by tobacco growers covers all but some general administrative costs of the program.

There have been periodic attempts to abolish the tobacco program, both by tobacco and cigarette opponents and by some tobacco-state legislators. A growing number of tobacco-state representatives believe doing away with the quota system would actually increase profits by making domestic tobacco competitive on the world market. Although the program has thus far survived numerous attempts to kill it, its future is by no means certain, and the impact of its possible demise is unknown.

Tom Ross

A tobacco farm in Robeson County

Livestock and Poultry Production

Livestock, dairy, and poultry products accounted for 56.5 percent of North Carolina's total sales of farm commodities in 1997, generating cash receipts of more than $4.6 billion. Of this amount, $2 billion came from poultry and eggs, twice the value of the tobacco crop.

Figure 7.6 displays livestock production on North Carolina farms in 1997. There were about 1.2 million head of cattle, valued at $534 million (Fig. 7.6.b). Milk cows produced cash receipts for sales of milk and cream amounting to $188 million. Output per cow in that year was 16,566 pounds. Both milk cows and beef cattle are produced mostly in the Piedmont. Small herds of brood cows fit the conditions on many North Carolina farms, especially as a source of supplementary income. The gross income from cattle and calves in 1997 was $227 million.

The most dramatic growth in livestock has been in swine production, which is now the leading source of farm income in North Carolina (Fig 7.6.e). Hog farming generated $2.02 billion in farm income in 1997, more than even broilers and tobacco combined. That was up more than 55 percent from 1994.

The number of swine in North Carolina is truly staggering. About 9.8 million head were counted in December 1997, more than the number of people in the state. The all-time record was 10.1 million head in September 1997. Since 1982 the number of

A large hog farm complex in Robeson County, showing the waste lagoon and related buildings

swine has increased by more than 7.5 million head. The leaders in hog production are the eastern counties of Duplin, Sampson, Robeson, Wayne, and Pitt (Fig. 7.6.e).

More than 18 million hogs were bred in North Carolina in 1997, up 12 percent from 1996. Of the approximately 5,800 hog operators that year, 4,000 were farrow-to-finish operators, 1,000 farrow only,

and 1,400 finish only. But fewer than eight hundred farms produced more than 90 percent of the hogs in 1997. The independent farmer is rapidly passing from the hog production scene as these large corporate farms continue to expand. Currently 82 percent of North Carolina's hogs are grown by contract growers.

But this massive increase in production has not

Figure 7.6. Livestock Production, 1997

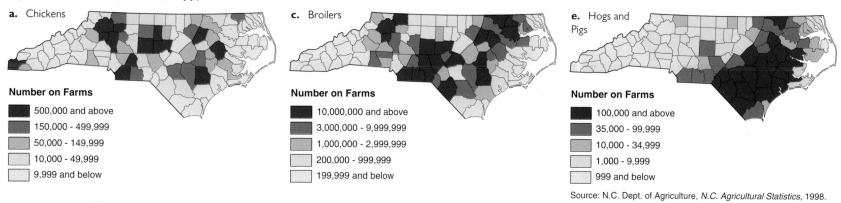

a. Chickens

Number on Farms

- 500,000 and above
- 150,000 - 499,999
- 50,000 - 149,999
- 10,000 - 49,999
- 9,999 and below

c. Broilers

Number on Farms

- 10,000,000 and above
- 3,000,000 - 9,999,999
- 1,000,000 - 2,999,999
- 200,000 - 999,999
- 199,999 and below

e. Hogs and Pigs

Number on Farms

- 100,000 and above
- 35,000 - 99,999
- 10,000 - 34,999
- 1,000 - 9,999
- 999 and below

Source: N.C. Dept. of Agriculture, *N.C. Agricultural Statistics*, 1998.

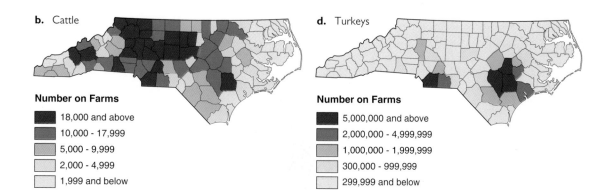

b. Cattle

Number on Farms

- 18,000 and above
- 10,000 - 17,999
- 5,000 - 9,999
- 2,000 - 4,999
- 1,999 and below

d. Turkeys

Number on Farms

- 5,000,000 and above
- 2,000,000 - 4,999,999
- 1,000,000 - 1,999,999
- 300,000 - 999,999
- 299,999 and below

occurred without controversy. Since 1994 eastern North Carolina has experienced a boom in industrial hog farming, as well as an increase in environmental and social problems associated with the industry. The largest industrial hog farming complex in the United States is located in the eastern part of the state, and many additional industrial hog farms are being constructed or planned through-

out the more rural parts of the Coastal Plain. The concentration in a relatively small area accentuates the environmental and social problems and has led to a backlash against large hog farms. This has been prompted by objections to the odor associated with these farms, but also by concern about groundwater and surface water pollution when farm "lagoons" break and discharge their

hog wastes into streams and rivers. Thousands of fish have been killed in the recent past as a result of lagoon spillage. The hog industry claims that it can resolve the odor problem, and that with time it can also ensure that groundwater and surface waters are not polluted. The industry also claims that the problem is exaggerated because so many other polluted substances are dumped into streams by municipal waste treatment plants and other point sources.

In response to the public outcry and despite intense lobbying by the hog growers, the 1997 North Carolina General Assembly declared a two-year moratorium on new hog farms; it also put in place tougher water quality standards that are more stringent than those of the U.S. Environmental Protection Agency. Even though several companies had applications on file before the moratorium was effective and thus may yet get to open new plants, it appears that the rapid growth of this industry has slowed. Falling prices for pork contributed to this.

The map of chicken production (Fig. 7.6.a) includes hens, pullets, and other chickens but not commercial broilers. In 1997 these chickens were responsible for the production of about 3 billion eggs, which sold for more than $203 million.

Broiler production has increased steadily— from 482 million birds in 1982 to 540 million in 1990 and 665 million in 1997. Much of the broiler production is in the Piedmont, where the amount of farmland suitable for row cropping is relatively limited (Fig. 7.6.c). A distinguishing characteristic of the broiler industry is its high degree of vertical integration, a production system in which farmers growing broilers operate under contracts with feed companies, broiler processors, and hatcheries, all three of which are sometimes under the same ownership. Turkeys are produced in much the same way as broilers (Fig. 7.6.d). North Carolina retained its number-one national ranking in turkey production during 1997 with a total of 54 million birds raised. Cash receipts were a record high $528 million.

Forest Resources

TOM ROSS AND ROBERT REIMAN

The forests of North Carolina are among its most valuable natural resources and have long been used in a number of ways. Woodlands are not just a source of lumber; they serve a multitude of other purposes. Forests are an important element in the environment. They provide food and cover for an abundance of wildlife and freshwater fish, many of which are sought by hunters and fishers. Forests are also a critical factor in the development of soils. Water quality and stream flow are directly tied to the forests. Vegetation slows the speed at which water moves over the land and hence is an agent of erosion control; it eventually works to stabilize stream flow and reduce the potential for flooding.

Forests provide nonlumber products such as medicinal plants and vegetation used for landscaping. In some regions, pine needles, desirable for mulch, are harvested from the loblolly and longleaf pine forests. Recreation is another use for which forested land is valuable. A broad expanse of trees is visually appealing and enhances activities such as hiking, bird watching, wildflower identification, horseback and bicycle riding. In other instances, forests are simply places to which people can retreat for times of reflection and solitude. Nevertheless, in an economic sense, forest products are the single most important use of the forest. It is estimated that in 1995 landowners in North Carolina earned almost half a billion dollars from timber sales. This timber was used in the manufacture of lumber, furniture, and paper. The value added at the point of first processing of the timber is calculated at another half billion dollars. Additional value added occurs as the lumber and timber is further manufactured into furniture, veneers, or paper or used in construction.

Historical Background

When Europeans arrived in North Carolina they found a heavily forested region. Most of the state was forested, although there were extensive areas where Native Americans had burned the forest to create better hunting conditions and to farm. Most of the southern Coastal Plain was dominated by longleaf pines, whereas in the northern Coastal Plain mixed pines and hardwoods were the predominant species. Hardwood forests of oak, hickory, and pine sheathed the Piedmont, and oak and chestnut grew on mountains up to an elevation of 4,500 feet. Spruce and fir were found above the oak and chestnut.

Soon after European settlement began, the forests became a source of economic activity. Major impediments to the development of the forest industry, however, were the weight and bulkiness of forest products and the distance to potential European markets. Nevertheless, from the earliest settlement, timber and lumber were shipped to Europe and the West Indies. By the early eighteenth century the forests were a significant source of commerce for North Carolina, but the forest products sold were not the trees themselves but the naval stores products of tar and turpentine.

By the turn of the century the naval stores industry had become a major revenue source for many landowners. It reached such proportions in North Carolina that legend has it that the nickname "Tar Heels" was applied to North Carolinians because of the amount of tar extracted from the state's pine trees. In 1840 North Carolina produced 96 percent of the country's naval stores, but in the latter part of the nineteenth and early twentieth centuries overproduction and mismanagement led to the demise of this extractive industry. By 1929 the naval stores industry had ceased to exist. Naval stores today are generated as by-products of the paper manufacturing industry.

The more traditional forest product, lumber, was also important during the early history of North Carolina. Most of the lumber was used locally or regionally and was produced by operators of small sawmills. Lumber production peaked in the early 1900s. In 1914, 2.2 billion board feet were produced, but by the 1930s production had slipped to less than 800 million board feet. In the late 1990s production was back to about 2 billion board feet.

Forest Types and Resource Base

A number of major commercial forest types are found in North Carolina. Loblolly pine, shortleaf pine, Virginia pine, and oak-hickory types are the most important, covering about 60 percent of the state. Hardwoods are the dominant species in 53 percent of the forests, mixed stands of oak and pine total 14 percent, and about 33 percent consists of pine and other conifers.

Another classification divides the state's forests into five categories: upland hardwoods, lowland hardwoods, pine-hardwoods, natural pine, and plantation. The upland hardwoods account for almost 39 percent of the forestland and are found in all physiographic regions. But they are most common in the Mountains, where they represent the dominant type. Species include various oaks, yellow poplar, red maple, hickories, sugar maple, ash, birch and shortleaf, and Virginia pines. The second largest type is natural pine, occupying about 22 percent of all forestland. It too occurs in all regions but is most prevalent on the Coastal Plain, usually thriving on abandoned agricultural lands. At one time it was the most extensive forest type, but its acreage continues to shrink as it is being replaced by pine-hardwoods (natural regeneration) and pine plantations. Some land formerly home to natural pine is being transformed into nonforest uses. Lowland hardwoods cover a little more than 14 percent of North Carolina's forestland and are found in or near floodplains of streams and swamps. For the most part, they comprise a Coastal Plain forest that includes species such as sycamore, tupelo gum, elm, sweetgum, cypress, ash, birch, and oak. Pine-hardwoods grow on 14 percent of the forestland, more than half of which is found on the Coastal Plain. The smallest in acreage is the plantation type. It includes several pines and softwoods, including longleaf, loblolly, and eastern white pine. Since 1950 plantation forest area has been steadily expanding.

The size of the resource base for forestry products is constantly changing. In 1995 about 62 percent of the state—19.3 million acres—was forested, and about 18.7 million of those acres, or 60 percent of the state, was commercial timberland (Fig. 7.7). In 1885, 48 percent of the state's land area was forested. The acreage increased to about 18 million acres in 1938. The increase continued until the 1960s, when it reached 64 percent. The present proportion is about the same as in 1938. Forests cover approximately 77 percent of the Mountains, 54 percent of the Piedmont, and 52 percent of the Coastal Plain.

About 67 percent of the forestland is owned by 300,000 individuals or families, of whom 27 per-

Figure 7.7. Percentage of Land in Forests, 1995

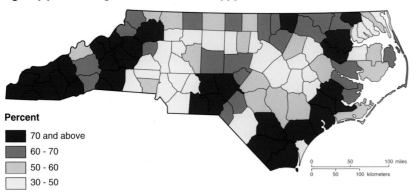

Percent

- ■ 70 and above
- ■ 60 - 70
- ■ 50 - 60
- □ 30 - 50

Source: N.C. Dept. of Agriculture, *N.C. Agricultural Statistics*, 1996.

cent are farmers. Timber or forest companies own or lease about 13 percent, and the balance is owned by federal, state, and local governments (11 percent) and other corporations (9 percent). Approximately thirty thousand owners of 100 acres or more control about 64 percent of the total forest acreage. Trends in forest ownership will have a significant effect on the utilization of forests as a source of raw materials in the future. The consistent increase in the number of owners of forested land reduces the size of the holdings; therefore, they are not managed as effectively as larger tracts. In 1996 the Governor's Task Force on Forest Sustainability, which studied the future of the state's forests, reported: "Concomitant with smaller ownerships is the growing importance of aesthetics as justification for land ownership. In the minds of many, conventional harvesting practices are incompatible with sylvan beauty. This fact, coupled with the rapid rise in the number of 10 to 20 acre tracts serving as residences or second homes, tends to eliminate many acres from organized timber production." The most popular reason for owning land was aesthetic enjoyment, selected by 25 percent of the people who owned about 10 percent of the state's individually owned forestland. Thirty-five percent of all owners indicated that they did not intend to harvest their forestland.

Forestlands remain a major North Carolina resource, but their viability is threatened. Data collected in the early 1980s by the U.S. Forest Service revealed problems with timber resources throughout the South, including North Carolina. It was concluded then that (1) many acres of southern forestlands were being lost, (2) there was a growing tendency toward inadequate regeneration of desirable species following harvest cuts, and (3) there was an unexpected slowdown in timber growth and an increase in mortality, particularly of southern pines. The 1996 report of the Governor's Task Force followed up with additional warnings about the future of the state's forests. According to the report, the major factors affecting forests are (1) a sharply reduced timber harvest in forests nationwide, (2) an accelerating demand for timber harvests in North Carolina, (3) a rapidly increasing population, (4) increasing development of home sites in traditionally rural areas, (5) increasing fragmentation of forested landscapes, and (6) a growing perception that forest management may harm the environment.

What caused these changes that are affecting North Carolina's forests? The reduced timber harvest on national forestlands is not because of a shortage of timber but rather because public policies have reduced the volume of timber taken from federally owned forests, mostly in the western states. To make up the shortfall, southern forests, including North Carolina's, have witnessed a dramatic increase in harvesting to meet the demands for wood products of a rapidly expanding population in North Carolina and elsewhere. The increase in North Carolina's population has also put more pressure on forested land as it is cleared for homesites, schools, factories, shopping centers, and highways. Although considerable forested acreage remains, in many areas it is fragmented or otherwise removed from the commercial timberland category. For example, in many resort areas, in the mountains and at the coast, the people being attracted to these settlements are likely to be more interested in the amenity value of forests than in their economic value. Also, more wood products are being exported from North Carolina. And finally, many people are beginning to regard timberland harvesting as a source of environmental destruction that should be limited or banned.

The Forest Products Industry

In 1996 the North Carolina Department of Agriculture estimated that the state's forest products industry earned more than $1.4 billion. Figure 7.8 displays the sources of this income. The industry includes lumber (hardwood and softwood), hardwood veneer, pulpwood, furniture lumber, flooring, plywood (hardwood and softwood), pressure-treated timbers, shipping pallets, wafer board, particle board, wood chip mulch, and paper and allied products. The value added by the manufacture of these and other forest-based products is more than $6 billion, ranking them fourth behind tobacco, chemicals, and textile mill products.

Several industries closely tied to the availability of forest products once were significant but are no longer economically viable. They include tanneries, manufacture of shuttles for textile mills, and insulator pins for telephone and electric lines. As noted above, in twentieth-century North Carolina other industries using forest products were developed. Forestry and these forestry product–dependent industries employ about 140,000 workers and generate payrolls of about $3 billion per year.

The demand for forest products is affected by shifts in population, economic activities, and technology. Tables 7.2 and 7.3 show inventory, net annual growth and drain for the past several decades, and projections drawn from the baseline assumptions for the next five decades for hardwoods and softwoods. The baseline projection indicated that in 1990 the annual removal of softwood from growing stock exceeded net annual growth by 23 million cubic feet. The projected shift in the year 2010 to a positive growth-drain position for North Carolina is based on the assumption that landowners and growers will invest sufficient capital to ensure proper forest management. It also requires that current trends in plantation establishment, technical innovation, financial assistance and incentives to landowners, and research and education in forest protection continue at current rates.

Between 1952 and 1984 the volume of North Carolina's softwood growing stock almost doubled. Most of this increase resulted from the establishment of

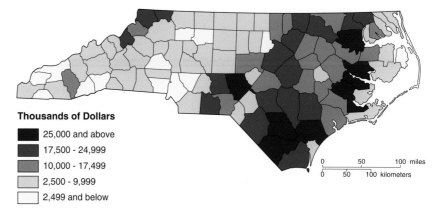

Figure 7.8. Forest Products Income, 1995

Thousands of Dollars
- 25,000 and above
- 17,500 - 24,999
- 10,000 - 17,499
- 2,500 - 9,999
- 2,499 and below

Source: N.C. Dept. of Agriculture, *N.C. Agricultural Statistics*, 1996.

millions of acres of young pines on abandoned agricultural lands between 1945 and 1965. It is unlikely that this will occur again, although there are areas in the Coastal Plains counties where well over one-third of the forestland is in saplings and seedlings. The extensive acreage devoted to saplings and seedlings is closely tied to regeneration and plantation activities and is a good indicator of future production.

Hardwood growing stock is another story. The absence of saplings and seedlings in the Mountain region, and hence the probable decline of marketable timber in the next generation, is unmistakable. With much of the present-day growth protected by environmental and aesthetic concerns, it is conceivable that the hardwood industry of the Mountains will suffer a dramatic decline by the middle of this century.

The growth-removal status of hardwoods in North Carolina generally parallels that for softwoods, but the shortfall is predicted to increase dramatically in the early part of the century. Reserves of hardwood growing stock are, however, much greater than that of softwood. The deficits that are projected to begin in 2010 represent an average of only 0.23 percent of growing stock volume, and thus greater utilization of the hardwood resource is possible. A seri-

Table 7.2. Hardwood Growing Stock, Annual Removals, Annual Growth, and Inventory: Recent and Projected (in billion cubic feet)

Year	Removals	Growth	Inventory
1976*	0.185	0.253	15.39
1984*	0.315	0.510	17.71
1990*	0.428	0.570	20.21
1990	0.439	0.573	17.92
2000	0.494	0.499	18.89
2010	0.489	0.480	19.03
2020	0.557	0.487	18.46
2030	0.543	0.494	17.68

Source: *Report of the Governor's Task Force on Forest Sustainability*, 1996.
*Actual survey results

Table 7.3. Softwood Growing Stock, Annual Removals, Annual Growth, and Inventory: Recent and Projected (in billion cubic feet)

Year	Removals	Growth	Inventory
1976*	0.413	0.545	10.74
1984*	0.431	0.501	11.24
1990*	0.511	0.590	12.53
1990	0.464	0.441	10.56
2000	0.496	0.520	10.29
2010	0.505	0.599	10.56
2020	0.544	0.630	11.64
2030	0.552	0.644	12.50

Source: *Report of the Governor's Task Force on Forest Sustainability*, 1996.
*Actual survey results

ous problem, though, is the shortage of high-quality hardwood trees. Most of the higher-quality and easily accessible trees have already been taken. Another problem or threat to production that must be considered is that of environmental constraints in several areas, including the mountains and wetlands. In the mountains, U.S. Forest Service administrative decisions concerning land use will impact the availability of forest for commercial use. Nevertheless, if the demand for wood as an energy source increases significantly, hardwoods most certainly will continue to be used, although probably with much more attention being given to environmental concerns.

A relatively new development in the forest products industry is the rapid growth of the wood-chipping process. The U.S. Forest Service reports that in 1995 North Carolina processed about 2 million cords of timber into chips. About 2 percent of these chips were exported, mostly to Japanese paper mills, but the level of exports increased by over 500 percent between 1989 and 1995. In 1997 seventeen chipping mills were operating in North Carolina and two more were under construction. Chipping mills are located in areas that have profuse stands of natural growth, marginal trees, and saplings. Many of these are low-quality pine trees, unsuitable for lumber or paper because they have hollow centers. Thus, the chips are made primarily from scrap timber, but in some instances large

areas are clear-cut and most of the timber is converted to chips. With the chipping process, otherwise useless trees become economically important. The downside is that the land that has been cutover has a scarred appearance because pines are the only trees used for chipping; straggly hardwoods are left standing. Another problem is that because many of these operations occur on small, privately held tracts, ecological disturbances are greater than in large-scale commercial operations. For example, few chippers will install silt fences or other devices to lessen environmental damage or replant with trees. The unattractive appearance of these areas leads the general public to perceive that too much of the region is being cleared of trees.

North Carolina is one of the country's largest producers of Christmas trees. In the late 1990s the state was harvesting 5 to 6 million trees valued at more than $85 million. The most important tree is the Fraser fir, a native of the Appalachians. The state provides about one in five of the live trees used nationally and has the potential to expand production to 7 to 8 million trees annually.

The outlook for North Carolina's forest resources is cautiously optimistic. However, the forested acreage most certainly will decline, especially with the increased pressure from urban areas. The value of forest products will continue to be important to the economy, but not at the same scale as today.

A partial solution to the many pressures being exerted on existing forestland is to increase the

Clearcut wetland forest along the Neuse River

productivity of the forest. A doubling of annual growth would, in addition to meeting the demands for raw materials, have a positive effect on soils and water. About 2 million acres of existing farm and pasture lands that are of marginal value for the production of food crops would be of greater value to their owners if planted in softwood trees. These lands could produce about 200 million cubic feet of annual growth and would do much to control prices. Finally, extending the years between regeneration and harvest would improve overall quality of the timber being grown.

The Fishing Industry

TOM ROSS AND ROBERT REIMAN

North Carolina's 320 miles of coastline provide abundant opportunity for fishing. In addition to the ocean, the shallow waters offshore and the numerous sounds, bays, river mouths, marshlands, and tidal creeks create an area of about 2,500 square miles that are well suited to a wide variety of fish and marine invertebrates. Many of the species are native to the state's waters, and others appear as transients during migratory movements at different seasons of the year. Some species use the shallow waters for nursery areas, feeding, or spawning grounds. The latitudinal position of North Carolina and the presence offshore of the Gulf Stream combine to make the northeastern coast near Cape Hatteras function as a natural boundary between subtropical and cold-water species. This boundary marks the southern limits of some fish forms and the northernmost distribution of others.

Commercial fishing is one of the state's oldest economic activities, dating to the early European settlements in the seventeenth century. More than two hundred years later, in 1890, North Carolina's commercial fishers experienced their first million-dollar year. In that year they netted almost 52 million pounds of seafood with a value, in 1890 dollars, of $1,028,000. By 1908 the catch had almost doubled, reaching 101 million pounds. In 1918 more than 210 million pounds were harvested. The largest annual catch on record was reported in 1959, when more than 342 million pounds were netted. Since then the harvest has fluctuated between that high and a low of 112 million pounds in 1973. In the last decade the annual finfish catch was, with one or two exceptions, between 115 and 118 million pounds. The shellfish catch, however, was up 340 percent from 1975. Total catch in the period grew from 17.2 to 59.1 million pounds. It is unlikely that such increases in the shellfish industry can continue as overharvesting and pollution take their toll.

Although currently not a major statewide industry, fishing is important regionally, especially

Figure 7.9. Income from Fish and Seafood, 1996

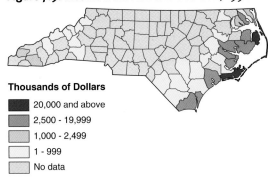

Thousands of Dollars

- 20,000 and above
- 2,500 - 19,999
- 1,000 - 2,499
- 1 - 999
- No data

Note: N.C. total income from fish and seafood in 1996 = $122 million.

Source: N.C. Dept. of Agriculture, *N.C. Agricultural Statistics*, 1998.

along the coast and, to a much lesser extent, in the Mountains (Fig. 7.9). In 1995 fishery products statewide were valued at about $122 million. The marine fisheries along the Atlantic coast accounted for about 92 percent of this total. Much of the remainder was generated by several inland counties through aquaculture—the raising of fish in ponds. Trout production is the principal aquacultural activity in the Mountains and the largest single source of agricultural revenue in at least three Mountain counties. On the Coastal Plain, catfish and hybrid bass, as well as crawfish, are the major sources of income for aquaculturalists. The absence of fishing income in the Piedmont will probably disappear as aquaculture becomes more established in the state.

Shellfish accounted for about 59 percent of the dollar value of marine seafood landings in 1995. Until the late 1960s, the dollar value of the finfish

catch exceeded that of shellfish. The increase in the relative economic importance of shellfish during the past twenty years has resulted mainly from the combined effect of a decline in the finfish catch, an increase in the shellfish catch, and the rising prices of shellfish. The total 1995 shellfish catch was more than 3.4 times the 1975 catch, whereas finfish decreased by about 45 percent during the same period.

Menhaden has traditionally been the principal finfish catch, but recently flounder has taken the leading position, making up approximately one-third of the total dollar value of the finfish catch. Nine types of finfish accounted for about 74 percent of the total value of the 1995 catch (Fig. 7.10). Blue crabs and shrimp are commercially the most important shellfish, constituting 52 and 30 percent, respectively, of the dollar value of the 1995 shellfish catch.

The effect of overfishing on marine fisheries can be illustrated by studying the catch of individual fish types over the past quarter century. Excessive fishing pressure has been the major cause of the decline in several species, including striped bass and flounder. The alewife catch shrank from more than 11 million pounds in 1972 to about 435,000 in 1995. Many other fish, including carp (191,000 to 81,000), catfish (2.4 million to 878,000), herring (21.4 million to 6.4 million), and menhaden (84.7 million to 58.4 million), also declined. But catches for some fish types were up, including bluefish (1.2 million to 3.0 million pounds), croaker (4.1 million

Icing down the catch off Pamlico Sound

Figure 7.10. North Carolina Fishery Income, 1995

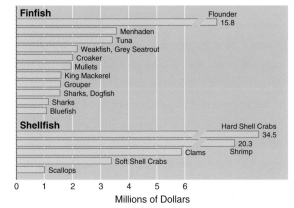

Source: N.C. Division of Marine Fisheries, *Commercial Landing Statistics*, February 26, 1997.

Aquaculture

Aquaculture acreage in North Carolina expanded dramatically over the past decade, but this advance halted in 1997. It has the potential to become a significant factor in fish production in the state. With sales increasing from $247,000 in 1987 to $8.4 million in 1997, aquaculture has been one of the fastest-growing sectors of the state's primary economy. Since 1996, however, some retrenchment has occurred. Future growth is still possible because of the large amount of marginal land that is suitable for conversion to ponds. The potential for expansion mostly depends on market conditions.

Most of the aquacultural acreage is on the clay-based soils of the Atlantic Coastal Plain and is devoted mostly to catfish, with secondary offerings of hybrid bass and crawfish. In 1997 total catfish sales from sixty producers totaled $2.2 million, up from $1.38 million in 1994 but down from a high of $2.47 million in 1996. Eastern or Coastal Plain operators produce crawfish on some of the poorly drained lowlands. In the Mountains, artificially constructed facilities combine with abundant clear, cold water to create superb conditions for trout production; in 1997 fifty-four producers generated sales of $6.2 million, down from $7.1 million in 1996. Trout production has increased much more rapidly than catfish and crawfish production, primarily because the latter two face stiff competition from growers in other southern states.

Although the industry currently is treading water in terms of growth, the future appears bright for the aquacultural segment of the fishing industry. In the 1990s more than 10 percent of the fish consumed in the United States came from fish farms. That is expected to increase as marine fisheries confront problems of overfishing and pollution.

Tom Ross

---

to 6.0 million), flounder (4.7 million to 8.8 million), and harvestfish (51,000 to 222,000). The shark catch increased to almost 3 million pounds from none reported in 1972. Just recently, though, a moratorium was placed on fishing sharks because overfishing was threatening their survival. In the past two decades moratoriums or fishery management plans have been put in place to protect several fish, including striped bass, Atlantic menhaden, summer flounder, red drum, weakfish, spot, bluefish, Spanish mackerel, and, recently, shrimp. These moratoriums and management plans have met with criticism from both recreational and commercial fishers. And in most cases, conservationists, some of whom fish, claim that many of the management programs are not effective in saving the fish. There is evidence, however, that management plans do work. One example is the Atlantic mackerel, which was overfished by foreign fleets during the 1960s–70s but has recovered dramatically as a result of a management plan. A recent study found the estimated stock size to be the highest on record, and the species is now underexploited. Sea herring, King mackerel, Spanish mackerel, and striped bass have also recovered through management programs. The reason for management plans is to ensure the long-term survival of both the fish and the fishing industry, whereas some members of the industry are more concerned with the short term. That is, they say they need to fish to survive economically now.

Although marine fisheries—both commercial and recreational—have long been an important component of the state's coastal economy and way of life, it is apparent from examination of catches data that some fish types have greatly reduced populations. Although fisheries stocks are not fixed (normally changes would be expected based on various physical phenomena), most of the changes are short-term. But the human influence is the greatest threat to the continued existence of fish in quantities suitable for commercial and, to a lesser extent, recreational fishers. The intense pressure on the stocks, the taking of mature, egg-laying fish and harvesting of smaller fish, and overfishing have all contributed to extreme population reductions of some fish types. Such actions, if permitted to continue, could lead to the eventual demise of commercial and recreational fishing along the coast.

Mining Industries

JOHN F. BENDER

North Carolina is endowed with an abundance of rocks and minerals, many of which are important to an industrial economy. Of the over three hundred varieties of rocks and minerals known to occur in the state, over seventy have commercial or industrial uses. As a result, mining has been of economic interest to the state since colonial days. In the colonial period emphasis was placed mainly on the search for base and precious metals. An iron industry, consisting of many small furnaces scattered throughout the central and western parts of the state, flourished during the eighteenth and nineteenth centuries and was a stabilizing factor in the early development of North Carolina. It derived most of its ores from small deposits found in the Triassic basins along the eastern edge of the Piedmont. But it was the discovery of gold in Cabarrus County in 1799 that is credited with ushering in the first period of major mining activity in the United States. Copper, lead, silver, and coal were also mined during this time.

The discovery of large deposits in other parts of the country resulted in a rapid decline in metal mining in North Carolina around the turn of the century. In contemporary times, only relatively small amounts of metallic ores have been produced, whereas the production of nonmetallic or industrial minerals has increased steadily to dominate the mineral industry of the state.

Nonmetallic Minerals

Minerals and rocks not classified as metallic ore that are used in their natural state, after suitable processing, are referred to as industrial minerals. Industrial minerals have dominated the North Carolina mineral industry since the turn of the century. In 1994 the state's total mineral production was valued at approximately $706 million, an increase of 21 percent over the 1992 figure. Crushed stone accounted for over half of the total value produced in 1994 (Fig. 7.11). In that year North Carolina ranked seventeenth nationally in total value of mineral production, and just over 3,600 people were employed in the industry in 1995.

Figure 7.11. Industrial Mineral Production in North Carolina

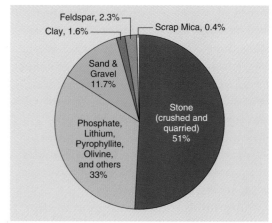

Source: U.S. Geological Survey, "The Mineral Industry in North Carolina," *Minerals and Mineral Information*, Compact Disc, June 1997.

Figure 7.12. Principal Mineral-Producing Areas

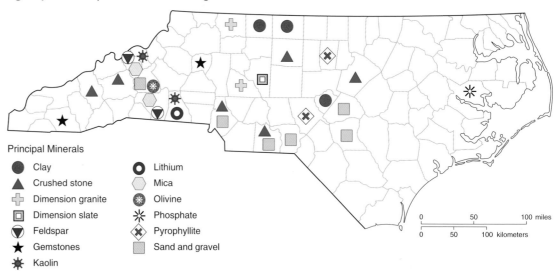

Principal Minerals

- ● Clay
- ▲ Crushed stone
- ✚ Dimension granite
- ▣ Dimension slate
- ▽ Feldspar
- ★ Gemstones
- ✳ Kaolin
- ◍ Lithium
- ⬡ Mica
- ✸ Olivine
- ✳ Phosphate
- ⊗ Pyrophyllite
- ▨ Sand and gravel

Source: U.S. Geological Survey, "The Mineral Industry in North Carolina," *Minerals and Mineral Information*, Compact Disc, June 1997.

In 1993, 816 mines, involved in the production of thirteen industrial minerals, were permitted to operate in the state. The locations of the principal mining regions and the minerals produced at these sites are illustrated in Figure 7.12. North Carolina ranks first nationally in the production of feldspar, first of two states in lithium and olivine, first in mica, second in phosphate rock, third in common clay, and fifth in talc and pyrophyllite. It also ranks fifth in the production of industrial sand and gravel and sixth in dimension stone. Most of this clay is used to make bricks, and for over thirty years North Carolina has led the nation in the production of building bricks.

Feldspar

The granite pegmatites of the Spruce Pine district in North Carolina annually produce more than 70 percent of the nation's feldspar. This area, located within the Blue Ridge geologic belt, has been mined actively since 1911. Currently nine mines, owned by six companies, operate throughout this district. The largest of these companies is the Feldspar Corporation, which is capable of producing 180,000 tons of feldspar from its two active mines and two flotation plants located in Spruce Pine. In 1994 the state produced 448,000 tons of feldspar with a value of $16.4 million. The feldspar that is mined in this area, which is the sodium-rich feldspar variety, albite ($NaASi_3O_8$), is used to make glass and ceramics. Quartz and muscovite, which occur along with feldspar in the pegmatite, are recovered during the processing and are sold separately.

Mica

Muscovite, the transparent form of mica, as opposed to biotite which is black, is usually found along with feldspar and quartz in granite pegmatites. It is fairly common to find muscovite pieces in pegmatites that are several feet in diameter and almost a foot thick. These large crystals of sheet mica, called books, were at one time highly sought after by the electronics industry as electrical insulation. Until the late 1950s, North Carolina was one of the world's largest producers of sheet mica. With the development of the transistor, however, the demand for large pieces of sheet muscovite quickly ebbed, and the state has not produced any significant quantities of sheet mica since then. But there is still a high demand for scrap of finely ground or scrap mica that is used in the manufacture of wallpaper, in making paint and lubricant, and as a fireproofing material. North Carolina accounts for more than 60 percent of the scrap mica produced annually in the United States both in terms of value and total production. Almost all the scrap mica in the state is produced either as a co-product or a by-product of feldspar, lithium, and industrial sand operations principally at five separate locations in western North Carolina. Production in 1993 amounted to approximately 56,000 tons, valued at just under $3 million.

Lithium

Occurring within the Kings Mountain Geologic Belt is the Carolina Tin-Spodumene District, an area one mile wide by some forty miles long extending from Gaffney, South Carolina, to Lincolnton, North Carolina. It is characterized by discontinuous outcroppings of 350-million-year-old spodumene-bearing granite pegmatite. Two major deposits within this belt have accounted for approximately 80 percent of the nation's lithium reserves and over 70 percent of the lithium produced annually in the United States. These deposits are in the Foote lithium mine operated by Cyprus Foote Mineral Company (FMC) just south of Kings Mountain and the FMC-owned Hallman-Beam Mine near Cherryville. At these two localities the spodumene-bearing granite dikes are comprised on average of 20 percent spodumene, a lithium-bearing pyroxene mineral; the open pit mining technique is used to remove the spodumene-bearing ore. However, the Foote mine was closed in the mid-1990s. The FMC mine near Cherryville is currently about 525 feet deep and measures approximately three-quarters of a mile long by one-half mile wide. More than 700,000 tons of spodumene-bearing ore is removed annually from this mine, where it is crushed and separated and then transported to the world's largest lithium-processing facility located in Bessemer City. At this chemical facility the lithium metal is removed from the spodumene and is concentrated as either lithium carbonate or lithium chloride and shipped to other manufacturers. Lithium metal is also produced by electrolysis at the plant. This lightest of all metals is then used to produce high energy, long-life, lightweight batteries that are now commonly used in watches, calculators, cameras, and pacemakers. Products made from lithium also include ceramics, a wide variety of lithium chemicals, lubricants, and pharmaceuticals.

Olivine

Olivine is an olive green–colored silicate mineral found concentrated in igneous rocks such as gabbro and peridotite that are sporadically found throughout the North Carolina Mountains. Currently, only the states of Washington and North Carolina are producing olivine, with North Carolina's olivine production valued at twice that of Washington's. AIMCOR Minerals is mining olivine from two open pit sites, one in Yancey County, the other in Avery. The olivine recovered from these mines is used by the steel industry as a refractory in its blast furnaces. A small percentage of olivine is used as an industrial sand blasting aggregate.

Pyrophyllite

This relatively rare aluminum silicate mineral is found in metamorphic rocks in Alamance, Orange, and Moore Counties. North Carolina produces 99 percent of the U.S. total pyrophyllite from four mining sites in the three counties. Pyrophyllite quarried from sites in the Carolina Slate Belt is used in the manufacture of ceramics and refractories and as a filler in various products.

Phosphate

North Carolina ranks only second to Florida in the production of sedimentary phosphate rock, which is used primarily in the manufacture of fertilizers. In terms of economic value, North Carolina phosphate is the second leading industrial mineral commodity, ranking only behind crushed stone. For over thirty years phosphate has been mined by Texasgulf, Inc., from a single large open pit mine located near Aurora in Beaufort County. The estimated reserves of phosphate ore in this area are about 2 billion tons. A phosphoric acid plant recently built by Texasgulf in Aurora is designed to produce approximately 120,000 tons of purified phospheric acid annually.

Sand, Gravel, and Stone

Crushed stone and sand and gravel annually account for over one-half the total value of industrial minerals produced in North Carolina. Of the 816 mines in the state that are permitted to operate by the Land Quality Section of the Division of Land Resources, about 73 percent are involved in the production of these particular construction and industrial materials. The Sandhills in Anson, Moore, Lee, Harnett, and Richmond Counties is the principal production area of sand and gravel, but sand is mined from practically every county in the state. Construction sand and gravel are used mainly as concrete and asphalt aggregate, and road base cover. At Marston in Richmond County, a mine and processing plant operated by Unimin Corporation produces most of the silica sand used by the glass and foundry markets in the southeastern United States. Industrial sand and gravel are also mined near Lilesville in Anson County. Sand and gravel are the fourth most valuable industrial mineral product mined in North Carolina, ranking just behind crushed stone, phosphate rock, and lithium. Production in 1993 amounted to over 12 million tons and had an estimated value of approximately $72 million.

Crushed stone is the leading mineral commodity produced in North Carolina in terms of both volume and value. In 1994 approximately 52 million tons of crushed stone, valued at almost $338 million, were produced from 131 quarries operating in sixty-four counties. Although more than thirty-five companies are involved in the production of crushed rock, Martin-Marietta and Vulcan are the two largest producers. Almost 70 percent of all crushed stone is directed to the construction industry, where it is used chiefly as an aggregate for concrete and railroad ballast and as roadbeds. The leading rock types used as crushed stone in the state are—in order of decreasing abundance—granite, limestone, trap rock, slate, quartzite, and sandstone. Granite and related crystalline rock quarries are located in the Piedmont and Mountain regions, and the Carolina Slate Belt is the major supplier of fine-grained, high-density crushed stone. The Castle Hayne limestone located on the Coastal Plain is the source of calcareous crushed rock.

In North Carolina, granite, sandstone, and quartzite are quarried as dimension or building stone. This type of stone, as opposed to crushed stone, is usually cut and finished to a predetermined size and finish. The cut stone is used in retaining walls, seawalls, and bridgework, and as a decorative facing on buildings both within and outside North Carolina. Fourteen different companies own twenty-four active dimension stone quarries located in eight counties of the state. The largest of these companies is the North Carolina Granite Company, which operates the world's largest open-face granite quarry at Mount Airy in Surry County. Stone from this quarry has been used to build many public buildings in Washington, D.C., and many other east coast cities. The Mount Airy granite was selected by the Amoco Corporation as the replacement facing stone for the eighty-story Amoco Building in Chicago. It is estimated that approximately 600,000 square feet

Dredging crane and phosphate ore at the Aurora phosphate mine, Beaufort County

of dimension stone were required to replace the 43,000, 1.5-inch-thick Italian marble panels that originally adorned this skyscraper.

Clay

The term "clay" implies an earthy, fine-grained material that develops plasticity when mixed with water. Clay consists of hydrous aluminum silicates of extremely small grains. Nearly all clays are the products of weathering of rocks exposed near the earth's surface. The principal clay minerals include kaolinite, the illites, and the montmorillonites. High-purity kaolinite, or kaolin, is used in the manufacture of fine china and dinnerware. It is also used as a filler in paper and in making ceramic refractories that can withstand high temperatures. Kaolin occurs in the Spruce Pine mining district, and these deposits are currently being partially worked by the Unimin Corporation at its Bushy

Creek mica operation in Avery County. By-product kaolin is also being recovered at the Moss Mica Mine in Cleveland County.

Low-purity kaolin, or common clay, is found in varying amounts throughout the state. This type of clay provides the raw material from which over one billion bricks are produced annually in North Carolina. Common clay was mined by thirty-eight companies from sixty-four pits located in twenty-nine counties. Lee, Chatham, Rockingham, and Stokes Counties are the largest producers. In addition to building bricks, clay is used as a lightweight aggregate and in the fabrication of sewer pipes and structural tiles.

Gemstones

North Carolina has long been famous for the variety of precious and semiprecious stones found in the Piedmont and Mountain regions. In 1994 fifteen companies operated thirteen mines in three counties. Almost all of these mines are operated to attract mineral collectors who are seeking to recover emeralds, rubies, sapphires, hiddenite, and garnet from crushed ore. These tourist mines provide each amateur prospector with a bucket of potentially gem-bearing ore and sluicing facilities with which to recover any possible gemstones.

Emeralds, the official state gemstone, are found in both Hiddenite in Alexander County and southwest of Spruce Pine in Mitchell County. The two largest emerald crystals recovered in North America were found in North Carolina. The 1,438-carat Stephenson emerald was recovered from the Rist Mine at Hiddenite in 1969 and the 1,686-carat LKA emerald was taken in 1989, also from Hiddenite. The famous Carolina Emerald, a 13.1-carat gemstone owned by Tiffany and Company in New York, was cut from an emerald also found at the Rist Mine. In 1998–99 James Hill, working in the Hiddenite area, dug up several thousand carats of emeralds, including one high-quality 71-carat gemstone. In addition to emeralds, North Carolina lays claim to the two largest star sapphires ever found, the 1,445-carat Star of the Carolinas and the 1,154-carat Star of the Americas.

Metallic Minerals

Metallic minerals, or metallic ores, are mined principally for the valuable metal or metals that they contain. Ores of gold, silver, iron, copper, chrome, lead, zinc, manganese, molybdenum, nickel, tin, titanium, and tungsten all occur in North Carolina. Noteworthy amounts of gold, copper, iron, and tungsten have been produced in the recent past, and over 1 million ounces of gold were mined from 1799 to 1962. Until 1849 the Reed Gold Mine in Cabarrus County produced approximately 75 percent of the nation's gold, and one of the largest gold nuggets ever recorded was found at this site. A replica of this 28-pound specimen is on display in the Smithsonian Institution. In the 1950s the Queen Mine in Vance County was the largest operating tungsten mine in the United States, but it was closed in 1971.

In contrast to its illustrious past, North Carolina has reported no significant metallic ore production in recent years. However, substantial amounts of metals are refined from ores shipped into the state or from recycled materials. These include aluminum, chromium, cobalt, copper, ferroalloys, steel, titanium, and tungsten.

Mining and the Environment

Because of the nature of mining, great environmental damage can result in the form of water, air, and land pollution unless proper restraints are exercised. Parts of the country have suffered these damages, particularly areas where coal has been mined by contour strip-mining methods. Fortunately, relatively small areas have been affected by the mining industry in North Carolina.

Recognizing the dangers that can result from uncontrolled mining practices, the 1971 North Carolina General Assembly enacted a surface mining control bill that requires every mining operation in the state that disturbs more than one acre of land per year to obtain a permit. The issuance of this permit is predicated on the submission of a reclamation plan that meets the requirements of the act and the posting of a surety bond to guarantee that the mining operation will be conducted in accordance with the terms of the permit. The act was revised by the General Assembly in 1994, primarily regarding various procedures to be followed in its implementation.

In 1994 the state issued permits for 816 mines involving a total of approximately 28,000 acres of land. Phosphate, crushed stone, and sand and gravel account for almost 90 percent of the total state lands affected by mining operations. Although the total amount of land affected by mining rose by 2,659 acres between 1989 and 1993, another 13,614 acres of former mining land were reclaimed during the same period.

Outlook

TOM ROSS AND ROBERT REIMAN

Agriculture

Despite its diminished role in the economy, agriculture will continue to be a significant element in the North Carolina economy. Even though blue mold—in addition to legal and health questions—continually threatens the tobacco crop, cash receipts in 1997 exceeded $1 billion for the eighth year out of nine. Cotton acreage has quadrupled since 1989, and poultry sales exceed $2 billion. The big news, though, is the explosive growth of the hog industry, with cash receipts up more than 500 per-

cent since 1986 to over $2 billion in 1997 and still expanding rapidly in 1998. But public concern about water quality, manure treatment, and hog farm odor pollution may lead to more restrictive regulations on the growth of the industry.

The export market for farm products is steadily increasing. Japan is North Carolina's number-one market. It buys soybeans, poultry, lumber, and copious amounts of seafood. England is buying bottled water, sweet potatoes, and poultry products. Canada is North Carolina's number-one fresh fruit and vegetable market. Expectations are high for Russia and China to substantially increase their purchases of American agricultural products. Exports of meat and poultry products increased rapidly in the 1993–97 period. Meat exports grew from $28 million in 1993 to $117 million in 1997, and poultry increased by $173 million from sales of $154 million in 1993.

Nevertheless, if agriculturalists are to maintain their competitive edge, and if North Carolina is to remain one of the largest and most diverse agricultural states in the country, new crops must be introduced that can furnish the high income per acre that tobacco presently returns. Some horticultural crops, such as fruits and vegetables, and some new oil crops, like canola, may be substituted for tobacco in some instances. Recent research even suggests possibilities for using tobacco as a food product, but its value as food will certainly be much less than it is as a smoking product. The search for new

dietary products may intensify the diversity. Increased activity in aquaculture is also promising. Integrated pest management practices, biological and genetic engineering, and improved varieties have and will continue to contribute substantially in increased food and fiber production. Computers will be used increasingly to control operations and systems like pest management and irrigation with great precision. High-value cash crops will be grown in sophisticated greenhouses where computers will control environments and plant services.

The greatest gains for North Carolina agriculture, however, are expected to be made by improving marketing efficiency and productivity. Off-farm productivity growth in marketing farm products has not kept pace with the on-farm productivity gains realized during the 1990s. By concentrating on value-added techniques, as industry does, more innovative and better-quality products, perhaps commanding higher prices, can be marketed. One such way to do this might be in the establishment of "agricultural parks," defined as a collection of complementary farms located in facilities near each other that are devoted primarily to agriculture and agribusiness. The common element among park tenants would be their participation as a link in the producer-to-consumer chain. Value-added techniques such as precooling perishable commodities, along with storing, trucking, and brokerage services also would be available.

An agricultural park offers an agricultural community a viable method to organize its economic advantages in changing marketplaces and improve local agriculture's ability to compete in national markets. The concept seems ideal for improving agriculture in North Carolina as the twenty-first century opens.

Forestry

Technological and scientific advances in the growing, harvesting, and processing of timber have historically been an important factor in how timber is used. But such advances have had less impact on the total volume of timber consumed. Thus, the assumption is made that future technological and scientific changes will affect production and consumption rates comparable to those of the past.

Consumption could be significantly affected by changes in the cost of energy. The demand for crude oil will most likely reach capacity early in the twenty-first century, and the price for crude will rise dramatically as a consequence. The increase in the cost of oil will be offset by increased use of alternative energy sources. Conversion of woody biomass to energy, already being done by a significant number of manufacturers and institutions, will be one of the alternative sources. Extensive development of wood as an energy source would have a great impact on the forest industry in North Carolina.

The timberlands of North Carolina are in a state of flux. The most recent data show that the available supply of both hardwoods and softwoods has declined recently and that the amount of timber harvested is rapidly approaching the amount grown. It is obvious that without better forest management and additional regeneration efforts, a serious problem is facing the state as forestlands are converted to uses, mainly urban and recreational, that prevent the full recovery of the resources produced in the forest. A pair of significant factors is that only 38 percent of the forestland in the state is owned by people who intend to harvest forest products and that the average size of forest ownership tracts is declining. The 20 to 30 percent of the timberland that is located in the urban fringe is another factor that points to decreased availability of forest products.

On the plus side, many former agricultural sites and degraded forestlands have the potential to be restored to productive timberland. Scientific forestry, such as the use of species selection and management practices based on site characteristics, is another means to enhance production. These are some factors that will shape the timber industry of the twenty-first century. The loss of products from the forests that are so vitally important to the economy of North Carolina would be a major challenge for the state to overcome. Overall, however, the outlook for the timber industry is not as positive as is that of the forest itself.

Fishing

The marine fisheries industry faces serious challenges in the new century. Pollution and the dwindling stocks that result from overfishing are the two biggest threats to the seafood industry. Shellfish are especially vulnerable to water pollution, and it seems that every year considerably more areas of water are ruled off-limits to fishers because of high levels of pollution of one kind or another. Pollution also threatens some North Carolina rivers. In the summer of 1994, for example, high mercury levels in the Lumber and Waccamaw Rivers led the state to issue a warning to avoid consumption of fish taken from those rivers. In March 1997 the national media addressed the "red tide" problem in the Neuse River and suggested that fish taken from the Neuse and other rivers in eastern North Carolina were a potential cause of illness. The State Department of Health, though not denying the charges, called for additional scientific study of the effects of pollutants in the Neuse and other rivers. Although health-conscious Americans are eating more fish, they tend to look for fish that portray an image of cleanliness, and that leads more and more of them to consume fish produced in farm ponds under controlled conditions, not fish from rivers and oceans.

Overharvesting is another problem facing the marine fisheries. Many fishers claim that regulations put in place to protect the resource are depriving them of their livelihood. Regardless, overfishing of the Atlantic waters, including the taking of mature breed stock and the harvesting of young immature stock, will in the long run create a shortage of marketable catch. Moratoriums do work, based on data available from restrictions enforced on some fish types in the early 1980s. But the future does not look particularly promising for North Carolina's marine fishers in the early twenty-first century.

A bright spot for the seafood industry—aquaculture—is far from the coast and the ocean. The raising of trout in the Mountains has been rapidly increasing, and all projections point to continued growth of the industry. The Coastal Plains also have a vibrant trade in aquaculture, one based primarily on catfish. It too has experienced healthy gains over the past few years, and, though its growth is not expected to rival that of the trout industry, it will grow in the twenty-first century.

In summary, North Carolina's marine fisheries in the last half decade of the twentieth century experienced much turmoil. But perhaps out of this period of conflict and bitterness plans will evolve to ensure the existence of a commercial seafood industry in this new century.

Mining Industries

The North Carolina mineral industry is relatively small yet vital to the state's economy. Given the steadily rising demand that is generated by growth, especially for building materials, it appears to have a bright future. Large inventories of stone, gravel, and clay will ensure this. However, this assumes that the industry will be able to operate successfully in an era of rising concerns over environmental quality management issues. Noise, dust, blasting shocks, and vibrations from mining operations and from the vehicles that move the products will be closely monitored, and in some cases nearby residents will protest plans for new or expanded production sites. If these issues can be managed, the industry should remain a vital part of the economy.

Selected References

Furuseth, O. "Restructuring of Hog Farming in North Carolina: Explosion and Implosion." *Professional Geographer* 49, no. 4 (1997): 391–403.

Jahn, L. *Forestry and Forest Products in North Carolina.* Raleigh: North Carolina Cooperative Extension Service, 1994.

Johnson, T., and D. Brown. *North Carolina's Timber Industry: An Assessment of Timber Product Output and Use, 1994.* U.S. Department of Agriculture, Forest Service, Southern Research Station Resource Bulletin SRS-4, 1996.

North Carolina Agricultural Statistics. *North Carolina Agricultural Statistics, 1998.* Raleigh: North Carolina Agricultural Statistics, 1998.

North Carolina Forestry Association, Inc. *Landowner Guide to Forestry in North Carolina.* Raleigh, n.d.

North Carolina Growers Association, Inc. *1995 Estimate of Migrant and Seasonal Farm Workers during Peak Harvest by County.* Vass: North Carolina Growers Association, 1997.

Office of the Governor. *Report of the Governor's Task Force on Forest Sustainability.* Raleigh: North Carolina Governor's Office, 1996.

Street, M., and D. Spitsbergen. *Review of Commercial Fisheries Landings Projections and Status of Fishery Management Plans for the Oregon Inlet, North Carolina Area.* Morehead City: North Carolina Department of Environment, Health, and Natural Resources, Division of Marine Fisheries, 1994.

U.S. Geological Survey. "The Mineral Industry in North Carolina." *Minerals and Mineral Information.* CD-ROM, June 1997.

8. MANUFACTURING

Alfred W. Stuart

Since the late nineteenth century, manufacturing has been the backbone of the North Carolina economy. Plentiful low-wage labor, a strategic location between the markets of the urban North and raw material supplies from the Deep South, and a strong probusiness, sociopolitical environment helped the state to move into industrialization ahead of most other southern states. As noted in Chapter 3 ("History"), real industrialization in North Carolina did not begin until the 1880s with the rapid expansion of the cotton textile industry. Soon afterward, the wood furniture industry began to develop in the northern Piedmont, around High Point and Greensboro. By the early twentieth century Durham and Winston-Salem emerged as major centers in the making of cigarettes. These "Big Three" industries, along with farming, dominated the state's economy at least through the time of World War II. The mill villages that were built up and down the length of the Piedmont to house textile workers became a unique feature on the North Carolina landscape. This scattering of industrial job sources led to a similar dispersion of people that is still a distinctive aspect of the state's geography.

As recently as 1966, for example, nearly 53 percent of all nonfarm jobs were in factories. And even though that share had fallen to less than 20 percent in 1996, it still ranked North Carolina first among all the states in that regard. In recent years factories have tended to locate more heavily in and around metropolitan areas, and this has been a major reason for the shift in population growth from rural to urban areas. Thus, not only is manufacturing a vital part of the state's economy but also it has played and continues to play a pivotal role in shaping the very nature of North Carolina and its people.

National Status

By national standards North Carolina is a major industrial state, ranking eighth among the fifty states by several widely used measures such as the value of output and employment. North Carolina also ranks first in the proportion of the total population that works in a factory: over 11 percent. By this and other measures, then, North Carolina is the most industrialized state in the nation. Not only is it an important industrial state, but also its relative importance nationally has increased in recent years. For example, between 1970 and 1997 the state added about 122,000 factory jobs whereas the national total decreased by over 427,000; consequently, North Carolina's share of the national total rose from 3.7 to 4.4 percent. This happened in the face of a national trend that has been called *deindustrialization*, represented by a steady decline in industrial jobs, especially in large industrial states such as New York, Pennsylvania, and Ohio.

Employment and Value Added

Employment is a widely used measure of industrial activity, primarily because it involves jobs and because statistics on it are more readily available. In some respects, however, employment is an inadequate measure because not all jobs are equal in terms of the skill levels that are involved or the wages that are paid. In North Carolina, for instance, although less than 20 percent of nonfarm jobs are in factories, manufacturing accounted for nearly $25 billion in wages and salaries, representing 26 percent of the earnings of all nonfarm workers in 1996. Another statistic that better measures the full economic impact of manufacturing is *value added*, a dollar figure that expresses the extent to which the worth of a material is increased through industrial processing. Value added is calculated by subtracting the cost of materials, contract labor, and several other incoming expenses from the sales price of the commodity as it leaves the factory. What is left that goes into value added are wages and salaries, along with the services of capital equipment. Thus, it represents the contributions of both capital and labor that occur at particular places. Contributions to value that are made before the material reaches the factory in question thus are excluded from the calculation.

Value added probably is the best single measure of the amount of manufacturing that takes place in a factory, county, state, or region. Its major drawback is that it is reported only by the U.S. Census and even then only after a delay of several years. The data are often not reported for small areas because of legal requirements that prohibit disclosing information about an individual company. Table 8.1 summarizes the value added totals for North Carolina industries between 1963 and 1996.

Historically, North Carolina factories have accounted for a higher proportion of national employment than they have value added. In 1972, for instance, their share of national value added was only 3.1 percent whereas employment's proportion was 3.9 percent. This disparity has been reduced substantially since then as the nature of manufacturing in the state has changed. Growth has been greater in those industries that are more highly mechanized or automated, increasing value added faster than employment. As a result, the spread between national shares of employment and value added (4.4 percent and 4.1 percent, respectively, in 1996) has narrowed. This narrowing represents an important shift away from lower-wage, lower-skill industries that

Table 8.1. Value Added by Manufactures in North Carolina, 1963–1996

SIC Industry	Percentage of State Total				
	1963	1971	1982	1987	1996
20 Food	7.1	6.5	6.8	6.0	6.6
21 Tobacco	19.0	12.9	14.9	15.2	13.7
22 Textiles	30.9	28.2	17.5	14.8	11.0
23 Apparel	5.1	6.0	4.9	4.1	3.2
24 Wood	2.8	2.5	2.6	2.8	2.7
25 Furniture	7.2	7.0	6.1	5.7	4.3
26 Paper	3.7	2.8	NA*	3.8	3.1
27 Printing/publishing	1.8	1.9	2.3	2.5	3.1
28 Chemicals	5.9	7.6	9.1	11.8	17.9
30 Rubber/plastics	0.7	2.0	4.0	4.6	4.7
31 Leather	0.3	0.4	0.4	0.3	0.2
32 Stone/clay/glass	2.0	2.1	2.0	2.6	2.9
33 Primary metals	0.9	1.2	1.3	1.3	1.8
34 Fabricated metals	1.8	4.9	3.8	3.3	3.3
35 Industrial machinery	2.5	4.4	7.2	7.0	6.7
36 Electrical equipment	6.0	6.4	NA*	8.7	9.3
37 Transportation equipment	0.8	1.2	2.1	2.7	2.9
38 Instruments	NA*	1.1	NA*	2.0	2.0
39 Miscellaneous	0.7	NA*	0.7	NA*	0.5
Total ($ millions)	4,618	9,824	28,510	47,007	77,577**

Sources: U.S. Census of Manufactures, 1977–87; Annual Survey of Manufactures, 1996.
*NA = Not available
**Estimated

characterized the state's industrial past and toward those that use more sophisticated machinery, require more skilled or better trained labor, and pay higher wages. Table 8.2 shows the amount of value added per employee for major industry groups in North Carolina and the entire United States for 1977 and 1996. Value added per employee is in part a measure of productivity per labor unit, but this productivity is also attributable to the technology that the workers use. In fact, high-value-added-per-employee averages generally indicate that an industry is *capital intensive*, that is, highly mechanized or automated. On the other hand, low-value-added-per employee averages indicate *labor-intensive* industries, in which the process is less mechanized and wages are a relatively large part of operating costs. In labor-intensive industries, the education, skills, and wages of workers tend to be below average.

Table 8.2 shows that between 1977 and 1996 value-added-per-employee levels in North Carolina rose sharply relative to the national average. From 21 percent below it in 1977, the state mean climbed to less than 5 percentage points below the U.S. average in 1996. The state average is significantly impacted by the cigarette industry, one of the nation's most highly automated industries. Removing the cigarette industry from the state statistics would cause the ratio to the national figure to drop to 69 percent for 1977, but it climbed sharply after that, reaching 83 percent of the national mean by 1996. Thus, although the cigarette industry skewed the state average upward, other industrial groups also contributed to this impressive gain on the national mean. As Table 8.2 indicates, other North Carolina industries were more capital-intensive than their U.S. counterparts in 1996, notably chemicals, rubber-plastics, leather, industrial machinery, stone-clay-glass, fabricated metals, and electrical equipment.

The large presence of the low-wage textile and apparel industries is the major reason the statewide value-added figure is below the national mean. If those two industries were subtracted from the state totals, the value-added-per-employee averages of the remaining industries would be nearly 6 percent higher than the comparable national figure. This fact highlights the sig-

Table 8.2. Value Added by Manufacturing, per Employee, 1977 and 1996

SIC Industry	1977		1996		N.C. % of U.S.	
	N.C.	U.S.	N.C.	U.S.	1977	1996
20 Food	$25,005	$36,876	$87,178	$117,902	67.8	73.9
21 Tobacco	90,333	71,518	911,077	823,564	126.3	110.6
22 Textiles	17,397	18,397	50,805	65,480	94.6	90.0
23 Apparel	11,049	14,968	45,913	44,355	73.8	103.5
24 Wood	17,908	23,430	48,864	56,161	76.4	87.0
25 Furniture	16,470	19,236	43,447	52,867	85.6	82.2
26 Paper	36,892	35,265	101,063	114,637	104.6	88.2
27 Printing/publishing	23,070	29,280	75,402	86,379	78.8	87.3
28 Chemicals	50,415	64,441	309,241	235,781	78.2	131.2
30 Rubber/plastics	28,224	27,367	80,611	73,627	103.1	109.5
31 Leather	14,814	15,335	53,889	61,377	96.6	87.8
32 Stone/clay/glass	27,601	31,171	100,423	88,498	88.5	113.5
33 Primary metals	47,085	33,736	90,051	101,163	139.6	89.0
34 Fabricated metals	35,278	29,255	77,920	72,819	120.6	107.0
35 Industrial machinery	29,039	32,267	90,205	95,494*	90.0	94.5
36 Electrical equipment	32,959	29,230	129,519	118,222	112.8	109.6
37 Transportation equipment	27,690	36,360	80,839	120,870	75.2	66.9
38 Instruments	32,905	33,558	109,124	119,395	98.1	91.4
39 Miscellaneous	20,684	23,351	44,728	68,014	88.6	65.8
All industries	$23,822	$31,603	$89,392	$93,776	75.4	95.3

Sources: U.S. Census of Manufactures, 1977–87; Annual Survey of Manufactures, 1996.
*Estimated

nearly one-quarter of all earnings paid to nonfarm workers, far more than services or any other sector. This income stream derived from over $55 billion in product worth (gross state product) that was attributed to North Carolina manufacturers in 1996, a sum that also contributed to public revenues, purchased great quantities of raw materials and various business services, and generally drove many other sectors of the economy. In dozens of communities a nearby factory was the foundation that supported the local economy.

Growth and Diversification

As demonstrated in Table 8.3, over the years North Carolina's industrial employment has grown slowly but steadily, in contrast with a national decline. However, this seemingly slow rate of growth has masked some fundamental shifts in the industrial sector of the economy. That is, some industries have been declining while others have been growing, with the net overall result being a modest rate of increase.

The Big Three of tobacco, textiles, and furniture continued to dominate the North Carolina industrial economy after World War II. In 1947 these three groups made up 70 percent of total manufacturing employment (Fig. 8.1). That proportion has fallen steadily since then, even though textiles did not peak, at 296,000 jobs, until 1973 and furniture continued adding jobs until the late 1980s. By 1996

nificance of the growing diversification of the industrial sector in North Carolina, a trend that involves both the absolute and relative decline of several more labor-intensive, low-wage industries

and, conversely, the growth of more capital-intensive industries.

Even though manufacturing now trails services as the state's leading employer, it still accounts for

Table 8.3. Manufacturing Employment in North Carolina, 1973–1996

SIC Industry	Number of Workers			Change (%)	
	1973	1984	1996	1973–84	1984–96
20 Food	40,190	44,978	57,445	11.9	27.7
21 Tobacco	28,371	24,503	17,586	-14.7	-28.2
22 Textiles	295,951	224,595	185,521	-24.1	-17.4
23 Apparel	80,860	92,388	58,037	14.3	-37.2
24 Wood	29,243	37,938	47,079	29.7	24.1
25 Furniture	80,372	85,628	78,341	6.5	-8.5
26 Paper	19,490	22,134	24,934	13.6	12.7
27 Printing/publishing	16,449	25,227	36,105	53.4	43.1
28 Chemicals	36,616	38,972	49,332	6.4	26.6
29 Petroleum	219	716	779	226.9	8.8
30 Rubber/plastics	17,673	29,388	40,559	66.3	38.0
31 Leather	4,002	4,350	2,402	8.7	-44.8
32 Stone/clay/glass	16,640	19,236	23,974	15.6	24.6
33 Primary metals	6,482	11,027	16,863	70.1	52.9
34 Fabricated metals	19,210	27,534	34,450	43.3	25.1
35 Industrial machinery	36,748	56,288	71,639	53.2	27.3
36 Electrical equipment	47,909	60,807	62,372	35.2	2.6
37 Transportation equipment	13,465	21,377	33,779	58.8	58.0
38 Instruments	6,222	10,315	14,917	65.8	44.6
39 Miscellaneous	6,253	6,120	10,204	-2.1	66.7
Total	802,391	843,521	866,354	5.1	2.7

Source: U.S. Bureau of Economic Analysis.

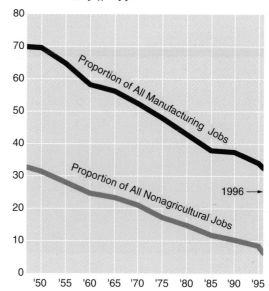

Figure 8.1. Big Three Manufacturing Industries in North Carolina, 1947–1996

Note: Big Three = Tobacco products, furniture, and textiles.
Source: N.C. Employment Security Commission.

ment, and transportation equipment industries collectively added nearly 154,000 jobs between 1973 and 1996. The remaining thirteen major industry groups thus recorded a net loss of almost 90,000 jobs.

In 1996 the textile industry was still the leading industrial employer, but in a broader economic sense its dominance was less apparent. By 1996 the chemicals manufacturing industry led the state with nearly $14 billion in value added. This represented over 17.8 percent of the state total but only

the Big Three share was down to just 32.5 percent of all manufacturing jobs. This drop has been due both to losses in the Big Three industries and the impressive diversification that has resulted from growth in other, newer components of the state's industrial base. The chemicals, rubber and plastics, primary metals, fabricated metals, industrial machinery, printing-publishing, electrical equip-

The old Gibson textile mill in Concord, part of which has now been demolished

the national figure. Among North Carolina industries, only employees in the paper, miscellaneous, and plastics industries earned more than their counterparts across the nation. And only two industry groups in the state (tobacco and chemicals) had higher average annual employee earnings than the overall national average of $34,561. By late 1997 manufacturing production workers in North Carolina earned $11.37 an hour, 86 percent of the national figure of $13.15. Six other states had lower wage levels. This was quite a jump over 1975, when the state's production workers earned $3.52 an hour, just 73 percent of the national average of $4.83 an hour, and when North Carolina ranked dead last among the fifty states. Despite these relatively steady increases, however, industrial wage levels have remained low compared with other states. Lower labor costs, though not necessarily beneficial to workers, probably contributed to North Carolina's success in continuing to add industrial jobs at a time when other states were losing them.

Not only are labor costs relatively low, but also North Carolina workers are rather productive. This is highlighted by the fact that, although average payroll per employee was just 81 percent of the national figure, value added per employee exceeded 95 percent of the U.S. average. In simple terms, industrialists get more "bang for their buck" in North Carolina factories. Another attraction for many employers is that only 5.1 percent of North Carolina's factory employees belong to a labor union, one of the lowest rates in the nation.

Industrial Dispersion

The 1950s not only ushered in an era of sustained industrial expansion for North Carolina but it also began a period of geographic redistribution. Between 1950 and 1970 factory employment advanced by nearly 310,000 jobs, a surge of over 75 percent. In describing the 1956–72 span, the 1975 *North Carolina Atlas* showed that manufacturing was remarkably dispersed throughout the state and that this dispersion was increasing. Significant growth occurred

5.7 percent of manufacturing employees (Tables 8.1 and 8.3). The highly automated tobacco products group, with $10.6 billion in value added, accounted for 13.7 percent of value added but just 2 percent of factory jobs. In 1963 the textile industry led the state with a 31 percent share of value added, a proportion that fell to about 11 percent by 1996. Conversely, the chemicals, industrial machinery, and electronic equipment industries' collective share of value added rose from 14.4 to 34 percent between 1963 and 1996, even though their proportion of employment rose only from 10 to 20 percent of the industrial total during the same time period.

Diversification of the North Carolina manufacturing sector not only has increased the state's share of national value added but also has had an upward effect on employee earnings. In 1977 the average total payroll per employee—$9,824—was just 75.2 percent of the U.S. mean (Table 8.4). By 1996 the North Carolina figure stood at $27,815, which was equivalent to almost 81 percent of

Table 8.4. Payroll per Employee in Manufacturing, 1996 and 1977

| | 1996 | | | 1977 | | |
SIC Industry	N.C.	U.S.	N.C. % of U.S.	N.C.	U.S.	N.C. % of U.S.
20 Food	$22,189	$26,625	83.3	$9,962	$12,200	81.7
21 Tobacco	46,376	48,455	95.7	13,179	12,388	106.4
22 Textiles	21,953	22,926	95.8	8,534	9,003	94.8
23 Apparel	16,525	17,250	95.8	6,281	7,239	86.8
24 Wood	22,284	23,438	95.1	8,521	10,723	79.5
25 Furniture	21,309	24,128	88.3	8,278	9,591	86.3
26 Paper	36,391	36,388	100.0	13,763	14,224	96.8
27 Printing/publishing	26,060	30,478	88.5	10,618	12,841	82.7
28 Chemicals	36,310	44,051	82.4	13,076	15,723	83.2
30 Rubber/plastics	29,473	27,936	105.5	10,694	11,834	90.4
31 Leather	19,741	20,725	93.9	7,326	7,669	95.5
32 Stone/clay/glass	27,644	30,471	89.9	10,797	12,943	83.4
33 Primary metals	30,904	37,306	82.8	12,339	16,833	72.6
34 Fabricated metals	28,156	31,106	90.5	11,468	13,522	84.8
35 Industrial machinery	28,880	35,714	80.9	12,906	14,668	88.0
36 Electrical equipment	32,102	34,892	92.0	11,025	13,084	84.3
37 Transportation equipment	31,750	43,358	73.2	10,522	17,347	60.7
38 Instruments	30,972	41,163	75.2	12,095	13,451	89.9
39 Miscellaneous	26,902	25,275	106.4	8,908	9,999	89.1
All industries	$27,815	$34,561	80.6	$9,824	$13,072	75.2

Sources: Calculated from data in the U.S. Census of Manufactures, 1977–78; Annual Survey of Manufactures, 1996.

turing employment multiplied almost fivefold and in Pitt County it nearly quadrupled. This episode of rural industrialization was led by the textile and apparel industries, which moved into the outlying parts of the state in search of pockets of farm laborers who would accept lower wages than workers in the already more industrialized Piedmont areas (Fig. 8.2). By the early 1970s the growth in textile employment was not so much in the already heavily industrialized Piedmont counties as in previously less industrial areas of the Piedmont and on the Coastal Plain. Apparently the labor-intensive textile industry had begun to move into less urbanized areas to avoid competing for labor with employers who paid higher wages in the larger cities. Textile employment was still heavy in the Piedmont counties, but most of the workers were in related fields such as the manufacturing of textile machinery and chemicals or in nonmanufacturing sectors like banking, wholesaling, research, and administration. The expansion of the apparel industry, which only began in the 1950s, was also mostly rural in location, concentrating on the Coastal Plain and some of the Mountain counties and tending to avoid the Piedmont.

What was happening was that the machinery, electrical equipment, and other nontextile industries were moving into and around the larger urban areas, where manufacturers found supporting business services, distribution centers, airports, amenities, and a better-educated supply of labor.

in the Piedmont, especially the southern part and in some of the nearby Mountain counties. But the strongest relative growth was on the Coastal Plain, from Raleigh eastward, and in many parts of southeastern North Carolina. For example, between 1956 and 1972 Robeson County's manufac-

Figure 8.2. Share of Growth in Textiles Employment, 1956–1972

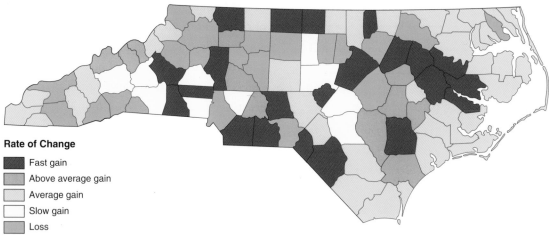

Rate of Change

- ◼ Fast gain
- ◼ Above average gain
- ◻ Average gain
- ◻ Slow gain
- ◼ Loss

Source: J. W. Clay, D. M. Orr Jr., and A. W. Stuart, eds., *North Carolina Atlas: Portrait of a Changing Southern State* (Chapel Hill: University of North Carolina Press, 1975).

Industrial development along Little Sugar Creek in Charlotte

More labor-intensive industries having less need of well-educated workers began to relocate to rural areas, and new entrants to the industrial economy, such as apparel plants, began to locate there in the first place. This movement generated something of an economic boom in rural areas that were losing farm jobs and facing population out-migration.

This dispersion of more labor-intensive industries supported a rural, small-town lifestyle that many North Carolinians preferred. But no matter how folksy or charming it may have been, this lifestyle came at a cost. In the late 1960s Richard Lonsdale found that most plants that located in rural North Carolina "are usually labor-oriented, low-profit margin operations wherein lower labor costs are considered essential to maintain a competitive market position." Barry Moriarity, in a study of all new plants that located in North Carolina between 1969 and 1974, came to a similar conclusion. He went further, stating: "The analysis supports the argument that along with the state's traditional industry mix, it is the dominance of industry in small urban places and rural areas that is mainly responsible for the state's low manufacturing wage rate rather than the low level of unionization. Consequently, the supply of low-skilled surplus labor in small towns and rural areas is an important factor contributing to the state's low economic situation."

Figure 8.3 shows just how dispersed manufac-

Famous Labor Disputes

A downturn in economic conditions beginning in the 1920s led to the biggest labor disputes in North Carolina history. As markets tightened, mill owners instituted the infamous stretch-out, a practice employing fewer workers to operate more machines, sometimes for less pay. Increased workloads may have raised productivity, but it also increased fatigue and stress and lowered morale. The desperate workers became open to the blandishments of labor organizers while equally desperate owners bitterly opposed efforts to form union chapters.

Perhaps the most sensational episode was a strike at the giant Loray mill in Gastonia in 1929. This mill, purchased by the Jenckes Spinning Company of Pawtucket, Rhode Island, in 1919, was the first mill in Gaston County "to be owned and operated by outside capital." In 1927 the new owners established a stretch-out and eliminated 1,300 of 3,500 jobs. Leaders of the National Textile Workers Union (NTWU), an affiliate of the American Communist Party, seized on the discontent of the Loray workers to act out their "class against class" rhetoric and sent organizers to Gastonia to initiate a strike. In the resulting confrontation, the local police chief was murdered, as was Ella May Wiggins, a folk-singing striker. No one was ever prosecuted for Wiggins's death nor were the vigilantes who abducted and severely beat some other strikers. Seven local NTWU leaders were tried in Charlotte for the murder of the police chief, but, when the prosecution introduced an effigy of the slain police chief in his blood-stained uniform, one of the jurors had an emotional breakdown. The judge ordered a mistrial, and soon afterward five of the defendants jumped bail and fled to the Soviet Union, confirming public suspicions that the strike was a communist plot to disrupt the economy and promote class struggle rather than a simple labor dispute. The strike ended and the workers returned to the mill, except for the known strikers who no longer had jobs.

The national depression of the 1930s hit mill owners even harder than before, leading to increased pressure on workers to raise productivity. In July 1933 the Roosevelt administration instituted the "Textile Code," which lowered the work-week to forty hours, set a minimum wage of twenty-five cents an hour for millworkers, banned child labor, and gave workers the right to organize unions. Managers frequently ignored these standards, and the United Textile Workers Union, a unit of the American Federation of Labor, used this reaction as the centerpiece of a major push to organize southern textile workers. This led to one of the largest strikes in U.S. history, on Labor Day 1934, involving hundreds of thousands of textile employees throughout the South. "Flying Squadrons" of volunteers descended on one mill after another, shutting off the machinery and calling out the workers. The owners retaliated by persuading the several governors to call out the National Guard to restore the peace, and some of the Flying Squadrons were thrown into prison camps. The mill owner and mayor in Honea Path, South Carolina, posted gunmen in the windows of his plant, and they killed seven strikers out on the street, several of whom were shot in the back. A settlement negotiated by the federal government soon ended the strike with no concessions to the workers except that none of the strikers were to be blackballed by their employers. The owners ignored this agreement as well. Thousands of workers were turned away from their jobs and their families abruptly evicted from their mill houses. Workers blamed the union for the brutality and hardship of the strike and its aftermath, not the mill owners.

These labor disputes became part of a secret history in North Carolina, and to this day many people are reluctant to talk about them. Intimidated workers did not discuss these events with their families or friends. Years later, the children of former strikers were afraid to admit the family association for fear of losing their jobs. Returning veterans from World War II would talk about the killing and carnage that they had seen in the war but would never mention the strike. When a Charlotte television reporter went to Gastonia in 1979 to do a story on the fiftieth anniversary of the Loray strike, no one would talk about the event on camera. In 1996 several Carolinas Public Television stations either showed a documentary film on the 1934 strike late at night or did not air it at all. Consequently, most North Carolinians are totally unaware of this crucial episode in their history. For others, the fearful memories of these strikes are probably a major reason for North Carolina's low rate of union membership, even though its factory workers are, on average, among the lowest paid in the nation.

Alfred W. Stuart

Figure 8.3. Manufacturing Employment, 1995

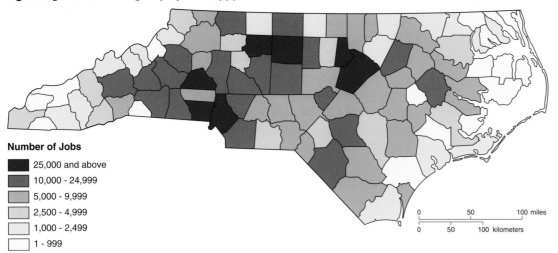

Number of Jobs

- 25,000 and above
- 10,000 - 24,999
- 5,000 - 9,999
- 2,500 - 4,999
- 1,000 - 2,499
- 1 - 999

Source: U.S. Bureau of Economic Analysis, Regional Information System, http://www.bea.doc.gov/bea/dn2.htm.

turing has been in North Carolina. In 1995 all one hundred counties recorded some industrial employment, and two-thirds of them counted 2,500 or more industrial jobs. But the figure also demonstrates that manufacturing employment has been dominated by the larger metropolitan counties. Guilford and Mecklenburg were the largest factory employers in the state, and they, together with Catawba, Durham, Forsyth, Gaston, and Wake, were the only counties to report 25,000 or more manufacturing jobs.

Specialization

Figure 8.4 presents a remarkably different pattern by revealing the degree to which each county's nonfarm employment is devoted to manufacturing. In 1995, of the thirty-three counties in which at least 30 percent of all jobs were in factories, only Gaston and Catawba represented the seven counties that had at least 25,000 industrial workers. Another nine of these industrially specialized counties were in the suburbs of metropolitan areas, and the remaining twenty-two were nonmetropolitan in nature. Most of these heavily industrialized counties also had 60 percent or more of their populations classified as rural. Some of them had

40 percent or more of all jobs in factories; they also had nearly 70 percent of their populations living in rural areas. In short, manufacturing is an important part of the economy in a host of predominantly rural counties. In contrast, most of the industrial counties with large numbers of industrial employees also have diversified metropolitan economies in which manufacturing comprises a small share, whereas manufacturing is relatively more important to many rural areas.

Growth Patterns

Figure 8.5 displays the change in manufacturing employment that began in 1973. For rural counties it was a mixed picture. Both in the Mountains and on the Coastal Plain, many counties lost jobs, a painful development for rural economies that depended on factory employment. On the other hand, a number gained jobs, especially those where 30 percent of the workforce was in manufacturing. Nineteen of these more specialized manufacturing counties added factory jobs between 1973 and 1995, and only six suffered losses. The picture was similarly mixed in the larger metropolitan counties. Counties in the Charlotte, Hickory, and Raleigh-Durham areas were among the seven that added 5,000 or more factory jobs. They were joined by Randolph County, part of the Triad area, and Lee County, just south of Raleigh-Durham.

Figure 8.4. Manufacturing Specialization, 1995

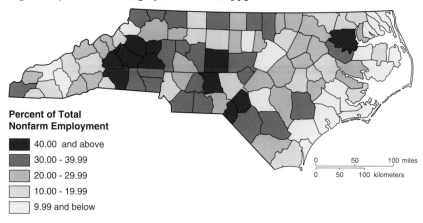

Percent of Total
Nonfarm Employment

- 40.00 and above
- 30.00 - 39.99
- 20.00 - 29.99
- 10.00 - 19.99
- 9.99 and below

0   50   100 miles
0   50   100 kilometers

Source: U.S. Bureau of Economic Analysis, Regional Information
System, http://www.bea.doc.gov/bea/dn2.htm.

Figure 8.5. Change in Manufacturing Employment, 1973–1995

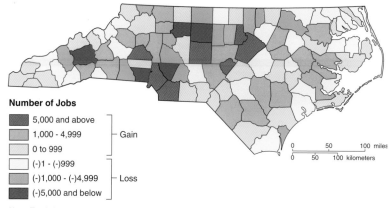

Number of Jobs

- 5,000 and above   ⎫
- 1,000 - 4,999   ⎬ Gain
- 0 to 999   ⎭
- (-)1 - (-)999   ⎫
- (-)1,000 - (-)4,999 ⎬ Loss
- (-)5,000 and below ⎭

0   50   100 miles
0   50   100 kilometers

Note: Total change = 59,899.

Source: U.S. Bureau of Economic Analysis, Regional Information
System, http://www.bea.doc.gov/bea/dn2.htm.

However, some suburban counties in metropolitan areas, especially those that traditionally specialized in textiles, recorded substantial losses. Cabarrus County, for example, lost over 13,000 textiles manufacturing jobs from the mid-1970s through the mid-1990s, nearly two-thirds of its total in the industry.

The 1975 *North Carolina Atlas* addressed the issue of continued dependence on labor-intensive industry in a somewhat prophetic statement: "The future of the textile industry is clouded by the severe competition for labor that it faces within the state and the equally severe competition for markets it faces from foreign producers." The author observed then that either the industry would become more capital-intensive or it would lose business in the face of this double-sided pressure. Either outcome would lead to reduced employment. The labor-intensive, low-wage nature of North Carolina manufacturing left the state's economy vulnerable to largely unexpected changes that seemed to be ushered in with the OPEC oil embargo of 1973. That embargo in itself did not produce the change, even though it caused industry to rethink its energy use patterns and it put a surcharge on driving costs for its workers.

The more profound change occurred as Newly Industrializing Countries (NICs) in Asia, Latin America, and elsewhere became major exporters of certain products, especially those emphasizing labor-intensive, low-wage industries. In this the NICs were assisted by Trans National Corporations (TNCs), many of them U.S.-based, which sought to relocate production to sites with lower operating costs even if this meant going to foreign locations. This *global shift* produced a rising tide of imports at the expense of American products. Many industries were affected, notably textiles and apparel, the two largest industrial employers in North Carolina. The furniture and some other labor-intensive industries were impacted less, at least in part because the product cost too much to ship from overseas. The textile industry has lost one-quarter of its jobs since its record high level in 1973, and the apparel group has lost 10 percent from its 1984 peak level. Some of the larger textile corporations have invested hundreds of millions of dollars in more efficient equipment, allowing them to compete more effectively in global and domestic markets, but the inevitable consequence has still been the loss of thousands of jobs. Other companies, unwilling or unable to become more capital-intensive, have

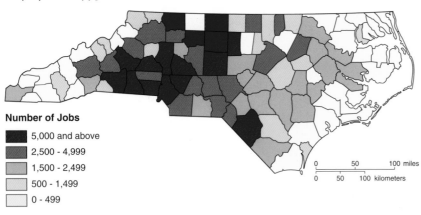

Figure 8.6. Textiles and Apparel Manufacturing Employment, 1995

Number of Jobs
- 5,000 and above
- 2,500 - 4,999
- 1,500 - 2,499
- 500 - 1,499
- 0 - 499

Source: U.S. Bureau of Economic Analysis, Regional Information System, http://www.bea.doc.gov/bea/dn2.htm.

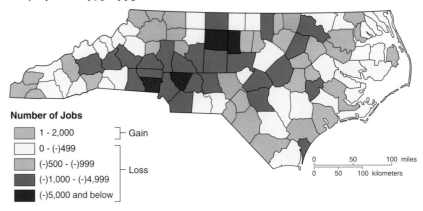

Figure 8.7. Changes in Textiles and Apparel Manufacturing Employment, 1973–1995

Number of Jobs
- 1 - 2,000 ⎱ Gain
- 0 - (-)499 ⎰
- (-)500 - (-)999 ⎱
- (-)1,000 - (-)4,999 ⎰ Loss
- (-)5,000 and below

Note: Total change = (-)115,178.

Source: U.S. Bureau of Economic Analysis, Regional Information System, http://www.bea.doc.gov/bea/dn2.htm.

slowly lost their markets, and many have ceased to exist.

The global shift has also benefited North Carolina. As shown in Chapter 6 ("The Economy"), North Carolina has been a major target for foreign investors and a host of foreign-owned businesses have located here, many of them manufacturers. Between 1990 and 1997 the state attracted 122 foreign-owned plants, to rank first in the nation in this regard. A striking aspect of this development is that the vast majority of foreign-owned plants have located in the larger metropolitan areas, especially Charlotte, Greensboro, and the Research Triangle Park.

The Textile and Apparel Industries

The cloth industries are still heavily represented in most Piedmont counties, but the 1950s–early 1970s era of rural industrialization brought major concentrations of its jobs to a host of Coastal Plain and Mountain counties (Fig. 8.6). And though the totals remained substantial in the Piedmont, the more urban areas had economies that were substantially diversified and therefore relatively less dependent on the textile and apparel industries. In contrast, in the more rural areas, which were more specialized in manufacturing, the jobs in a textile or apparel mill may have represented the backbone of the local economy. Consequently, they were more vulnerable to recent changes in the global economy.

Figure 8.7 shows how the pattern of textile and apparel employment changed between 1973 and 1995. Traditional centers of the cloth industries were the heaviest losers, especially Alamance, Cabarrus, Gaston, and Guilford Counties, which each lost more than 5,000 jobs, led by Gaston at just over 15,000. Most of the others that lost 1,000 or more cloth industry jobs were also located in the traditional Piedmont heartland of the industry. The twenty counties that gained textile or apparel jobs were predominantly rural and located either in the Mountains or on the Coastal Plain, notably in a southeastern corridor that included Richmond, Robeson, and Columbus Counties.

Major studies were conducted to determine the effects of these and other changes on the entire South, including *Shadows in the Sunbelt*, prepared

Figure 8.8. Changes in Nontextiles and Apparel Manufacturing Employment, 1973–1995

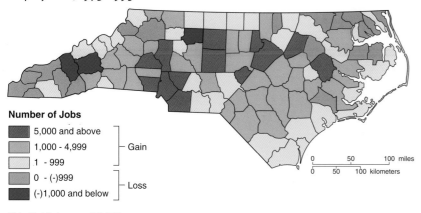

Number of Jobs

■ 5,000 and above	
■ 1,000 - 4,999	⎤ Gain
□ 1 - 999	⎦
■ 0 - (-)999	⎤ Loss
■ (-)1,000 and below	⎦

Note: Total change = 175,077.

Source: U.S. Bureau of Economic Analysis, Regional Information System, http://www.bea.doc.gov/bea/dn2.htm.

by MDC in Chapel Hill, and *Halfway Home and a Long Way to Go*, published by the Southern Growth Policies Board. Both of these analyses, released in 1986, address the plight of rural southern economies, which lagged, in part, because of the loss of traditional labor-intensive jobs—once the bulwark of their economies. This pattern is amply represented in North Carolina.

Geographic Distribution

The geographic distribution of manufacturing employment in North Carolina (Fig. 8.3) generally supports the contention of these studies that industry favors the larger urban centers, and this is reinforced by the growth patterns shown in Figure 8.5. Most of the larger industrial counties, particularly Durham and Wake, had impressive growth, but so did a scattering of rural counties in both the mountains and the east. The difference is that these rural counties had small totals to begin with. Their high growth rates typically involved few new jobs.

The statistics displayed in these maps seem to suggest that the 1986 reports were correct—insofar as North Carolina was concerned—to the extent that most of the growth has focused on the larger, more metropolitan counties; the rest, especially the smaller counties, have not shared proportionately in this industrial expansion. It is not so much that the smaller ones lost a great deal. After all, they now have far more industrial jobs than they did several decades ago. It is just that they have ceased to have the often spectacular growth that they became accustomed to in the 1960s and early 1970s. From a longer view, this may signal the end of an era of rural industrialization and a shift in focus to more technologically sophisticated industries that tend to meet their locational requirements more often in and around metropolitan areas, notably the larger ones.

Between 1973 and 1996 over 200,000 jobs were added in manufacturing industries other than textiles or apparel. This stands in stark contrast to the net loss of over 133,000 jobs in the two cloth industries. The growth in the noncloth industries centered heavily in the Charlotte, Hickory, Greensboro, Raleigh-Durham, Rocky Mount, and Greenville areas (Fig. 8.8). The Winston-Salem and Asheville areas, by contrast, led the big losers, primarily because of downsizings by several major employers.

Industrial Mix

Further insight into these nontextile/apparel sectors is provided by examining the mix of the state's high-growth industries: chemicals, rubber/plastics, primary metals, industrial machinery (including computers), electrical/electronic equipment, and instruments. These "newer" industries not only exhibited strong growth but also tended to pay relatively high wages: in 1996 their annual payrolls per employee averaged $31,440, fully 13 percent higher than for all manufacturing industries, including the newer group.

Equally as significant as this overall shift was its geographic distribution in the state. Figure 8.9 and Table 8.5 demonstrate that the growth of the

Nortel (Northern Telecom, Inc.), a Canadian manufacturer of telephone equipment, located in the Research Triangle Park

Figure 8.9. Employment Change in Newer Manufacturing Industries by County Type, 1973–1995

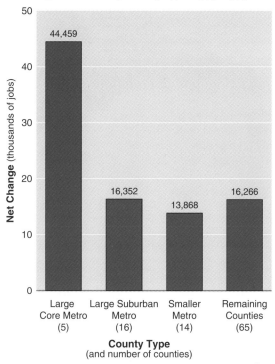

Note: Newer industries include chemicals, rubber/plastics, primary metals, machinery, electrical/electronic equipment and instruments.

Source: U.S. Bureau of Economic Analysis, Regional Information System, http://www.bea.doc.gov/bea/dn2.htm.

Newer Industries was concentrated heavily in the five counties that comprise the core of the state's three largest metropolitan areas: Durham, Forsyth, Guilford, Mecklenburg, and Wake Counties. Collectively, these industries expanded by almost 89 percent in those counties even though Forsyth lost several thousand jobs in this group. In addition,

Table 8.5. Manufacturing Employment by Type of County, 1973 and 1995

County Type	Total Manufacturing			Newer Industries[*]			Other Industries[**]		
	1973	1995	% Change	1973	1995	% Change	1973	1995	% Change
Core large MSA (5 counties)	182,219	206,887	13.5	50,141	94,600	88.7	132,078	112,287	-15.0
Suburban large MSA (16 counties)	185,713	183,467	-1.2	24,438	40,790	66.9	161,275	142,677	-11.5
Smaller MSA (14 counties)	158,261	167,860	6.1	35,007	48,875	39.6	123,254	118,985	-3.5
Non-MSA counties (65 counties)	276,198	304,076	11.1	42,011	58,277	38.7	234,187	245,799	5.0
Total N.C. (100 counties)	802,391	862,290	7.5	151,597	242,542	60.0	650,794	619,748	-4.8

Source: U.S. Bureau of Economic Analysis.
[*]Newer industries: Chemicals, rubber and plastics, primary metals, industrial machinery and equipment, electrical and electronic equipment, and instruments
[**]Other industries: Food, tobacco, textiles, apparel, wood, furniture, paper, printing and publishing, stone/clay/glass, leather, fabricated metals, transportation equipment, and miscellaneous

the suburban counties of the three largest metropolitan areas grew by a vigorous 67 percent. The twenty-one counties that collectively make up these three metro areas accounted for two-thirds of the entire statewide growth in the Newer Industries, and the other nine metropolitan areas accounted for another 15 percent of the net growth. That left less than 18 percent of the job gains in these high-growth industries to be distributed among the remaining sixty-five, nonmetropolitan counties. By 1995 the metropolitan areas dominated these industries to the extent that they accounted for over 75 percent of the state's total employment.

The Other Industries moved in a different direction. Even though some industries grew, especially printing-publishing, paper products, and transportation equipment, overall this group declined by 4.8 percent statewide. The greatest losses were recorded in the metropolitan areas, with the five large metropolitan counties declining by 15 percent. On the other hand, the sixty-five nonmetro counties actually increased 5 percent, gaining over 11,000 jobs. Clearly, then, while the more rural parts of the state continued to share in the expansion of the industrial sector of the economy, the urban areas attracted most of the growth in the more sophisticated, higher-wage industries. The more rural areas, by contrast, continued to load up on lower-skill, lower-wage industries, some of which, such as textiles and apparel, are especially vulnerable to competition from off-shore producers.

Major Industries

Figure 8.10 displays the distribution of jobs in major manufacturing industries other than textiles and apparel. Collectively, these maps illustrate the general concentration of manufacturing in the Piedmont and around urban centers, where a host of manufacturers form a complex of buyers and suppliers for each other, as well as for the construction industry, retailers, and other businesses. (SIC is the Standard Industrial Classification used in most statistical reports.)

Food Products (SIC 20)

Bakeries, bottling plants, and processors of agricultural products have a dual locational pattern. On the one hand, bottlers of soft drinks and beer, bakeries, and dairy plants tend to be close to urban markets. On the other hand, poultry plants, producers of cucumber pickles, such as the Mount Olive Pickle Company, and other facilities that handle perishable farm products tend to locate close to the rural areas where their raw materials are grown.

Tobacco (SIC 21)

North Carolina is the nation's leader in the making of cigarettes, and this industry is dominated by large, highly automated cigarette plants historically concentrated in the northern Piedmont and by the more recent Philip Morris plant in Cabarrus County. Stemming and redrying operations,

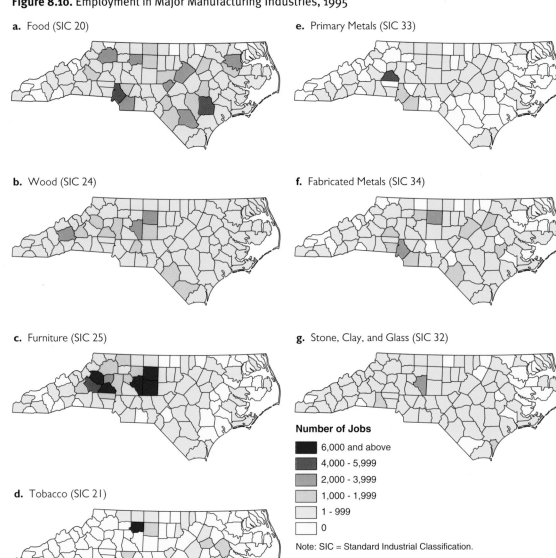

Figure 8.10. Employment in Major Manufacturing Industries, 1995

a. Food (SIC 20)

b. Wood (SIC 24)

c. Furniture (SIC 25)

d. Tobacco (SIC 21)

e. Primary Metals (SIC 33)

f. Fabricated Metals (SIC 34)

g. Stone, Clay, and Glass (SIC 32)

Number of Jobs

- 6,000 and above
- 4,000 - 5,999
- 2,000 - 3,999
- 1,000 - 1,999
- 1 - 999
- 0

Note: SIC = Standard Industrial Classification.

Source: U.S. Bureau of Economic Analysis, Regional Information System, http://www.bea.doc.gov/bea/dn2.htm.

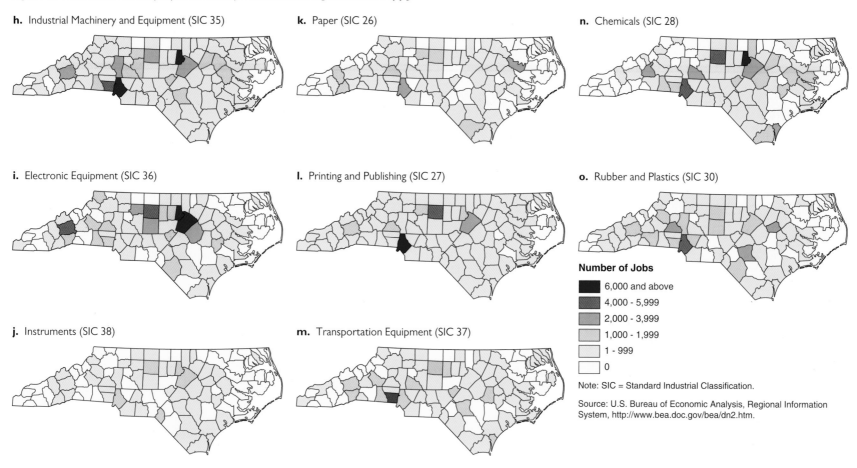

h. Industrial Machinery and Equipment (SIC 35)

k. Paper (SIC 26)

n. Chemicals (SIC 28)

i. Electronic Equipment (SIC 36)

l. Printing and Publishing (SIC 27)

o. Rubber and Plastics (SIC 30)

j. Instruments (SIC 38)

m. Transportation Equipment (SIC 37)

Number of Jobs

- 6,000 and above
- 4,000 - 5,999
- 2,000 - 3,999
- 1,000 - 1,999
- 1 - 999
- 0

Note: SIC = Standard Industrial Classification.

Source: U.S. Bureau of Economic Analysis, Regional Information System, http://www.bea.doc.gov/bea/dn2.htm.

which are a smaller part of the industry, tend to be closer to the tobacco-growing areas in the eastern part of the state.

Lumber and Wood (SIC 24)
This industry includes suppliers to the furniture industry, such as frame makers, and a large part of it is clustered close to that industry in the northern

Piedmont. Sawmills and logging operations are another part of this group, and many are scattered in rural areas close to forest resources.

Furniture and Fixtures (SIC 25)
North Carolina is a national leader in this industry, and most of its factories are in the northern Piedmont and Mountain foothills. The plants are some-

what scattered in these regions, but much of the industry focuses on Hickory, Greensboro, and High Point, with the latter serving as a major market center.

Paper and Allied Products (SIC 26)

This industry is somewhat like the food products group in that it has a major urban component and another part that is mostly rural. The urban part includes the fabricators of boxes and packaging materials for other manufacturers and for retailers. These typically bulky products are found mostly close to their markets. The other part of the industry is comprised of large paper mills that are found on rural sites in both eastern and western North Carolina, close to the forests that supply their basic raw material and to the streams that provide water for both processing and waste discharge.

Printing and Publishing (SIC 27)

Publishers of newspapers and books and printers of business forms, brochures, and similar products have a strong orientation in urban areas, where they can maintain close contact with their customers.

Chemicals (SIC 28)

This is a large, varied industry in North Carolina. Traditionally it has involved mostly various chemicals and dyes for the textile industry and the manufacture of synthetic fibers. These specialties remain important, and their plants are found mostly in the Piedmont. Major producers include Hoeschst Celanese in Rowan County and other areas. More recently, there has been strong growth in pharmaceutical companies such as the Glaxo Wellcome facility in the Research Triangle Park. A subset of the industry supplies paints and other finishing materials to the furniture industry and is located close to the furniture group in the northern Piedmont.

Rubber and Plastics Products (SIC 30)

An important part of this industry is comprised of automotive tire plants in Charlotte, Fayetteville, and Wilson and the Michelin aircraft tire plant in Stanly County. Another major part of the industry consists of a host of producers of various plastics products.

Stone, Clay, and Glass (SIC 32)

This is another varied industry. It includes glass plants, brickworks, ready-mixed concrete, and pottery. North Carolina is recognized as the nation's leading producer of bricks, an industry built on the good brick clays from the Piedmont. Some of the facilities are located close to raw materials such as glass sands, but those parts that supply the construction industry are typically close to their urban markets.

Primary Metals (SIC 33)

The Alcoa aluminum plant on Badin Lake has long been the site of North Carolina's most famous primary metals operations. Despite cutbacks at the Alcoa facility, this group is growing rapidly, primarily in support of a host of metals-using industries in the Piedmont. The group also includes foundries, but the major part involves the rolling and drawing of copper and aluminum. In addition, several small electric steel furnaces in North Carolina produce reinforcement rods and other products for the construction industry. In 1998 Nucor was induced by a large package of financial incentives from the state to build a steel plant in Hertford County that will offer high-wage jobs to six hundred workers.

Fabricated Metal Products (SIC 34)

This is another basic industry that supplies products to other manufacturers and the construction industry. In fact, its largest component is the making of structural steel for the construction of buildings and bridges. The industry is an important part of the industrial infrastructure of the Piedmont.

Industrial Machinery and Equipment (SIC 35)

This is one of North Carolina's fastest-growing and important newer industries. It encompasses everything from Westinghouse's steam turbine plant in Charlotte to the making of garden machinery. Probably its most noted representatives are the large IBM computer facilities in the Research Triangle Park and in Charlotte's University Research Park.

Electronic and Electrical Equipment (SIC 36)

Another fast-growing sector, this industry covers an array of products that include industrial apparatus, household appliances, and communications equipment. One of its largest facilities is the Northern Telecom plant in the Research Triangle Park.

Transportation Equipment (SIC 37)

This industry includes shipbuilding operations on the coast and High Point's Thomas Built producer of school buses. The concentration of the industry in Gaston County is accounted for mainly by the large Freightliner truck manufacturing facility. That company operates in nearby Rowan County as well.

Instruments and Related Products (SIC 38)

This group includes another host of Piedmont facilities that make medical instruments, measuring devices, photographic equipment, and clocks.

Outlook

North Carolina continues to be highly regarded in business circles as an attractive location for manufacturing plants. The substantial diversification of the state's industrial base achieved in recent decades is clearly a very positive trend. A 1990 survey of more than five hundred North Carolina manufacturing establishments found that over 93 percent were satisfied with their current locations. They gave their locations a mean rating of 3.21 on a 1-to-4 scale, with 4.0 the most positive rating. All industry groups in the survey responded in the affirmative, with newer durable goods industries rating their locations slightly higher than did the traditional labor-intensive industries such as textiles, apparel, wood, and furniture. Plant managers in metropolitan, suburban, and rural locations were overwhelmingly supportive as well. The most favorable locational factors had to do with labor cost, supply, and attitudes and with transportation and accessibility. This positive response bodes well for the continuation of North Carolina's strong industrial economy.

In looking to the future, however, the manufacturers who participated in the 1990 survey expressed considerable concern over labor issues: availability of qualified workers, quality of the public schools, worker attitudes and trainability. They saw a looming labor/education crisis that could threaten the viability of the state's largest economic sector. This concern was consistent among all industry groups from across the state. Previous surveys had found industrialists more concerned about traditional economic factors, such as markets, input materials, and transportation. Thus, their emphasis on educational issues is relatively new. Unfortunately, it is much easier to build new highways or airports than it is to successfully address the seemingly intractable, nationwide crisis in education. The problem may be even deeper in North Carolina because of its historical specialization in low-skill, low-wage industries, especially in rural areas and small towns.

The state has upped the ante in terms of the economic incentives that it offers to potential employers as part of an interstate war to attract new jobs. In contrast with states such as South Carolina, these incentives are modest but they are deemed necessary to keep up with the competition. The incentive program is weighted heavily in favor of economically distressed (rural) counties. This strategy, which represents an effort to help those areas that are not experiencing much of the current growth in higher-wage industries, appears to have worked in attracting Nucor to Hertford County.

North Carolina has made a multibillion-dollar commitment to expand its highway network. The state government is well along with plans to invest millions of dollars in an air cargo facility near Kinston (Lenoir County) that will seek to attract manufacturers who process materials flown in on huge cargo jets and ship the resulting products to global markets in the same aircraft. Targeted to bring tens of thousands of jobs to a largely rural part of the state, this complex is being hailed as a means of ensuring North Carolina's place in the global economy and of rejuvenating the somewhat stagnant industrial economy of a large rural segment of the state. Whether it will achieve this or not remains to be seen, of course, but in the meantime the concerns about the quality of the labor force and the educational system that will prepare it for work in a more highly technological age will remain and grow unless addressed soon and effectively. Not long ago North Carolina was a poor state compared to the rest of the nation, and failure to remain competitive could lead to a backward move. This could be true especially in rural areas, where the education-technology gap is widest.

American manufacturing is undergoing organizational and technological shifts that are intended to improve its competitive position in global markets, and these shifts will have an impact on its location. An emphasis on just-in-time deliveries of materials and products tends to favor places that have excellent intercity accessibility. Automated production, robotics, and various high-tech industries play more to the strength of the U.S. economy than do traditionally labor-intensive industries. These companies require a well-educated labor force and accessibility to national and global markets, whether via interstate highways or air service.

Another major change is the emergence of flexible manufacturing systems that depend heavily on computer-integrated processes. Production runs are smaller, and the uncertainties of volume associated with this are shifted to subcontractors and suppliers. These small, specialized producers do similar work for many different customers, to the advantage of all. Inevitably this arrangement leads to a clustering of related industries, especially in metropolitan areas. In contrast, the rapid changes associated with developing technologies and markets put any plant that specializes in the manufacture of a single product or product line at considerable risk. "Flexible" plants are better prepared to weather the turmoil of uncertainty. This favors smaller, flexible operations, including those that are affiliated with corporate headquarters and research and development functions. Labor forces that are amenable to cross-training for a number of tasks also are advantageous. This kind of manufacturing tends to favor small, innovative firms that are involved in denser supplier/producer networks and where cooperation among allied businesses is possible. These operations and the related skilled jobs in research and development, innovation, marketing, and finance tend to be located in the dominant urban centers.

These factors may make the current era rank with other major historical turning points in the state's industrial history, comparable to the first and second cotton mill campaigns of the 1880s and 1920s and the boom of the post–World War II period. This new era promises a continuation of factory growth in and around larger metropolitan areas, especially in the more suburban parts where manufacturers can access central city advantages while avoiding their higher costs. Conversely, a progressively smaller share of industrial growth, especially in high-growth, high-wage industries, will go to the more rural parts of the state, despite the use of state and local economic incentives intended to reverse this trend. Industrial employment in rural areas typically is associated with lower wages, fewer fringe benefits, and less attractive working conditions than in urban areas. The workers in these locations generally have the skills needed only for routine, inflexible tasks. Mostly they work in branch plants where no decision-making or innovation takes place. All of these factors limit the plant's ability to respond to rapid changes in technology and markets.

The seemingly inexorable growth of more desirable industries in metropolitan areas will result in a further widening of earnings gaps between their counties and the rest of the state. This, in turn, will erode the general pattern of geographic dispersion that has so strongly characterized the state throughout much of its history.

Selected References

Dicken, P. *Global Shift: Transforming the World Economy*. 3d ed. New York: Guilford Press, 1998.

Glass, B. *The Textile Industry in North Carolina: A History*. Raleigh: Division of Archives and History, North Carolina Department of Cultural Resources, 1992.

Lonsdale, R. "Barriers to Rural Industrialization in the South." Association of American Geographers, *Proceedings*, 1969, pp. 84–88.

Malecki, E. *Technology and Economic Change*. London: Longmans Scientific and Technical, 1991.

Manpower Development Corporation. *Shadows in the Sunbelt*. Chapel Hill, 1986.

Moriarity, B. "Manufacturing Wage Rate, Plant Location and Plant Location Policies." *Popular Government*, Spring 1977, pp. 48–53.

Salmond, J. A. *Gastonia 1929: The Story of the Loray Mill Strike*. Chapel Hill: University of North Carolina Press, 1995.

Southern Growth Policies Board. *Halfway Home and a Long Way to Go*. Research Triangle, 1986.

Stuart, A. "Manufacturing." In *North Carolina Atlas: Portrait of a Changing Southern State*, edited by J. Clay, D. Orr Jr., and A. Stuart, pp. 202–13. Chapel Hill: University of North Carolina Press, 1972.

Stuart, A., D. Hartgen, J. Clay, and W. Walcott. *Locational Satisfaction of North Carolina Manufacturers*. Charlotte: University of North Carolina at Charlotte, Department of Geography and Earth Sciences, 1990.

Stuart, A., D. Hartgen, W. Walcott, and J. Clay. "Role of Transportation in Manufacturers' Satisfaction with Locations." *Transportation Research Record*, no. 1274, pp. 12–23. Transportation Research Board, National Research Council, 1990.

U.S. Bureau of the Census. 1996 Annual Survey of Manufactures, M96(AS)-3. *Geographic Area Statistics*, April 1998.

9. TRANSPORTATION AND UTILITIES

David T. Hartgen and Wayne A. Walcott

Transportation

Few services are more important in fostering growth and prosperity than transportation and utilities. Transportation systems permit daily personal travel, delivery of goods and services, and access to land. In all of these aspects, transportation service has changed drastically in the past three decades. But the relationship between transportation and land use is fundamental to understanding growth. In North Carolina, development historically occurred in numerous relatively small cities and was dispersed throughout the state. But this trend has altered in the last two decades, as the larger metropolitan areas, particularly Charlotte and Raleigh-Durham, have emerged as the state's first truly large urban regions. A key factor in this more concentrated growth was the completion of the interstate highways and beltways serving the larger regions. Because of the investment required to support large transportation systems, it is vitally important to understand these changes.

Privately owned vehicles and freight and air passenger service have profoundly affected transportation in North Carolina and will continue to do so. But in the past, lack of intercity road systems encouraged dispersed, isolated cities and local economies. Now the larger metropolitan areas depend on regional highway access and intercity connections for labor and markets.

As the state's structures become more concentrated, transportation systems developed primarily for low-volume traffic are becoming overloaded. Suburban road systems are particularly inadequate. Meanwhile, rapidly rising personal mobility has changed how cars are used, where people live and work, and where they shop. It has also forever changed the role and function of public transportation services.

On a national level, North Carolina's role as a corridor state on the U.S. eastern seaboard is increasing the amount of traffic passing through the state and thus increasing the need for better intercity connectivity. This is related to changes in transportation's role in economic growth, shifting the emphasis from local access to interstate and international competition.

Historical Development

The first settlements in North Carolina were established along the coast. In the 1700s Wilmington, Edenton, and Beaufort were major trading sites. Inland development was dependent on navigable rivers that connected with the ports, especially the Cape Fear, Neuse, Tar, and Roanoke Rivers. Water transportation allowed the uninterrupted movement of goods to occur as far inland as the Fall Line that separates the Piedmont from the Coastal Plain. Early inland settlements often emerged to serve the change in transportation required at the Fall Line (ship to wagon). This *break of bulk* function was a major factor in the initial growth of cities along the Fall Line, including Raleigh.

In the late 1700s and early 1800s wagon roads from Virginia and Pennsylvania were improved, but intercity travel was slow and difficult, undertaken only when necessary. People generally stayed close to home, and most movement was local, within the immediate area of the settlement. Railroads appeared on the scene in the 1830s and 1840s, providing speedy connections between the settlements along the Fall Line and those on the coast. Railroads were faster and more reliable; they could handle more cargo than waterway transportation and increased accessibility to the interior of the state. Perhaps most important, they connected North Carolina with other states and cities. New settlement patterns evolved along the rail lines to take advantage of their technological capabilities. Perhaps the most important link in this network was the North Carolina Railroad, built by the state between Goldsboro and Charlotte and completed in 1856. This important link between transportation and development continues even today.

As population increased, connections between small urban places became more important. In the 1870s plank roads were built to offer toll-paid access to more places, but most failed economically because the builders underestimated the deterioration of wood due to heavy wagon loads and weather. As textile mills were opened all over the Piedmont and other parts of the state in the late nineteenth century, the mill owners found it necessary to build housing around their mills because rural workers lacked the means to commute to work from any significant distance. Railroads were not well suited for serving a large number of such connections all across the state.

A new technology, the automobile, in the early 1900s began to provide the means to develop these connections. Thus, it was not long before local government and the citizenry were requesting better roads. Initially, the Good Roads movement focused on the need for each county to build and maintain its own roads, serving primarily to connect county seats. By the 1920s, however, state officials recognized that development of a high-quality highway system for the state was beyond the capabilities of local government. As a result, the State Highway System was formed to connect the major urban places of the state, as well as many of the smaller towns. The political slogan that justified the development of this system was the need for "getting the farmers out of the mud." This highway system strengthened the dispersed nature of the urban population, permitting close-to-home employment in small industrial centers. It also helped farmers get their products to market. This pattern of clusters of smaller places well connected to one another, with one larger place operating as a focus, precluded the development of very large cities, even though the state was becoming more urbanized and industrialized.

During the period 1930–60, the federal government became involved in planning and building roads. The Federal Aid Highway System, including the interstate highway system, began by improving existing roads. But the federal system, particularly interstates, also connected urban places across state boundaries. State routes and national routes emerged as a large web tying North Carolina to the eastern United States. This connectivity today is permitting North Carolina's older dispersed pattern to give way to an urbanization pattern that favors the growth of major cities. Air service connectivity is having a similar effect nationally.

How is it that a transportation system can have such a far-reaching impact? When a transportation technology greatly reduces travel times and costs, it extends influence over longer distances. Figure 9.1 illustrates the dramatic changes that have taken place in ground transportation in North Carolina since the mid-1800s. Prior to the advent of the railroad, two-hour travel distance (by horse or carriage) was only a few miles from the point of origin. With the railroad, the distance covered in two hours increased to about 40 miles. By the 1950s, pre–interstate highway systems enlarged the two-hour distance to about 80 miles. Now, with the interstate highway system, the average distance trav-

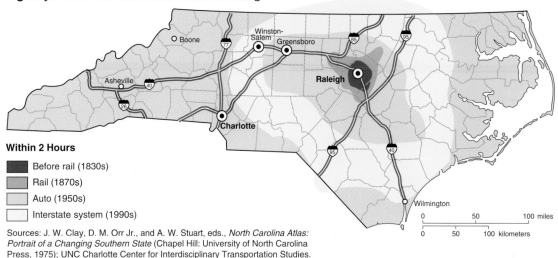

Figure 9.1. Two-Hour Travel Distances from Raleigh

Within 2 Hours

- Before rail (1830s)
- Rail (1870s)
- Auto (1950s)
- Interstate system (1990s)

Sources: J. W. Clay, D. M. Orr Jr., and A. W. Stuart, eds., *North Carolina Atlas: Portrait of a Changing Southern State* (Chapel Hill: University of North Carolina Press, 1975); UNC Charlotte Center for Interdisciplinary Transportation Studies.

eled in two hours has increased to 120–140 miles. This permits the spread of land uses that rely on urban areas and allows geographic connectivity. A trip from Raleigh to Asheville that took over a week in the 1700s now takes about four hours or less by car. Airline service reduces travel time still further, particularly between distant places.

Personal Mobility

Perhaps the greatest change in transportation in North Carolina over the last thirty years has been the rapid rise of private vehicle ownership and personal travel. Since 1970, vehicle registrations and licensed drivers in North Carolina have in-

creased about 100 percent (Table 9.1). Total travel increased 176 percent from 1970 to 1997. Meanwhile, road miles increased just 6.1 percent. Travel has expanded because North Carolina's population is expanding and because a higher proportion of people are driving. Not surprisingly, congestion in cities also has accelerated.

Increases in vehicle registrations have been caused by a growing population and rising incomes and economic activity, but these increases have not been uniform in all counties. Figure 9.2 shows that counties experiencing the greatest increases in registrations are generally metropolitan and suburban counties and a narrow strip of coastal counties. Rising incomes result in higher

A familiar symptom of growth—traffic congestion and highway construction

Table 9.1. North Carolina Selected Highway Statistics

Item	1970	1980	1990	1997	Change from 1990 (%)
Total road miles under state control	73,993	75,904	77,646	78,503	1.1
Vehicle registrations (millions)	2.825	4.532	5.162	5.785	12.1
Licensed drivers (millions)	2.743	3.777	4.551	5.399	18.6
Vehicle miles of travel (billions)	29.624	41.346	62.752	81.893	30.5
Fuel consumption (billions of gallons)	2.539	3.212	3.911	4.170	20.4
State fuel tax rate					
Gasoline (cents per gallon)	9	9	21.5	22.6	5.1
Diesel	9	9	21.5	22.6	5.1
Total receipts for state highways ($ billions)	NA	NA	1.424	1.937	36.0
Total disbursements for state highways ($ billions)	NA	NA	1.346	1.986	47.5
System performance					
Rural interstates in poor condition (%)	—	—	1.0	14.6	1,360.0
Rural primaries in poor condition (%)	—	—	1.6	2.8	75.0
Bridges deficient (%)	—	—	41.8	33.9	-18.9
Urban interstates congested (%)	—	—	80.3	45.7	-40.1
Urban other freeways congested (%)	—	—	23.7	33.2	40.1
Fatal accidents/100 million miles	5.98	3.64	1.99	1.56	-21.6

Source: N.C. Department of Transportation, Highway Division.

auto ownership levels. Automobile ownership offers the private mobility that allows people to commute to city jobs from suburban areas.

The average North Carolina household makes about eight vehicle trips per day. Most of these are short (less than 30 minutes), and most are for work or work-related, family, shopping, or school/church, social activities (Fig. 9.3). North Carolina's household travel patterns are similar to U.S. patterns.

Highway System

Responsibility for North Carolina's highway system rests primarily with the North Carolina Department of Transportation. Of the total 98,039 miles of highways in the state (1997), fully 78,503 miles are under state control, the second largest state-owned system in the nation. North Carolina differs from most other states in that it has no county-owned road system. Since the state took over the county roads in the early 1930s, North Carolina's state-owned highway system has

Figure 9.2. Percentage of Vehicle Registration Increase by County, 1980–1990

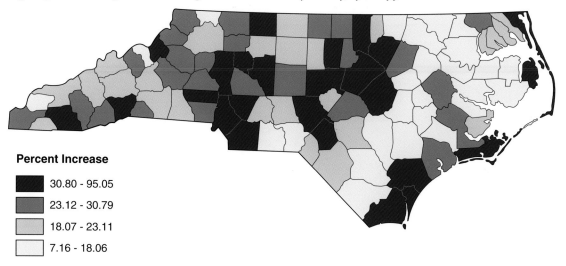

Percent Increase

- 30.80 - 95.05
- 23.12 - 30.79
- 18.07 - 23.11
- 7.16 - 18.06

Source: U.S. Census of Population and Housing, 1980-90.

Figure 9.3a. Trips by Time in North Carolina MSAs

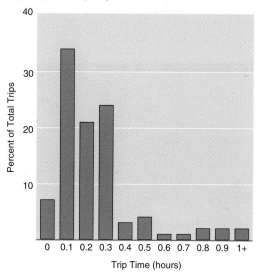

Figure 9.3b. Trips by Purpose in North Carolina MSAs

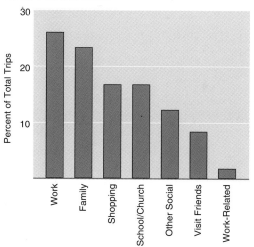

Note: MSAs = Metropolitan Statistical Areas.

Source: National Personal Transportation Study, 1990.

grown steadily from about 54,000 miles up to the present level. The major roads shown in Figure 9.4 constitute the primary highway system, which includes the interstates, U.S.-numbered, and N.C.-numbered highways. The interstates and U.S.-numbered highways generally serve longer-distance travel, whereas the secondary and local road system provides direct access to residences, shopping locations, and businesses. Local governments also participate in road planning. Federal law requires cooperative transportation planning in the state's seventeen urbanized areas.

The completion of the interstate system made North Carolina an integral part of the eastern sea-board road system. Important interstate routes run along the eastern seaboard from New England to Florida, often carrying greater than 40,000 vehicles daily, exceeding traffic counts on all but a few other state roads. The 1995 traffic counts (Fig. 9.5) show the impact of the interstate system on travel patterns. Interstate 40 (I-40) from Raleigh to Wilmington was completed in 1990, and by 1995 it carried an average of 10,000 vehicles daily through rural Duplin County, for example. North Carolina's interstate system is also used for the shipment of commodities and manufactured goods. Further, interstates serve as major radials and loops for commuter travel in urban areas.

Figure 9.4. Major Highways, 1997

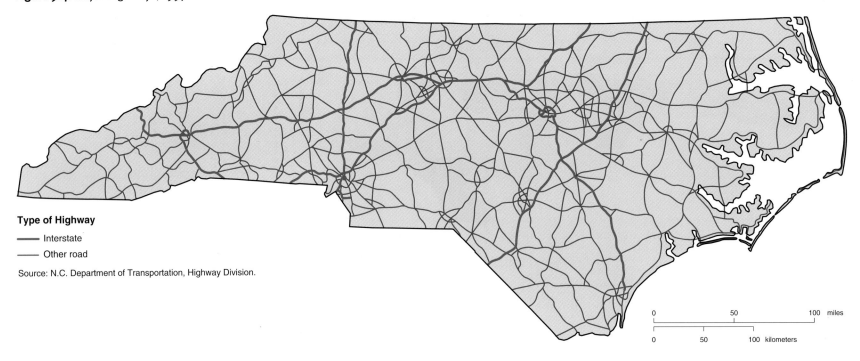

Type of Highway

—— Interstate

—— Other road

Source: N.C. Department of Transportation, Highway Division.

Statistics on the condition and performance of the state highway system have been kept only since the early 1980s. Changes in measurement methods cloud the trends, but North Carolina's system generally has been improving (Table 9.1). The percentage of substandard bridges has decreased, although North Carolina still ranks low compared with other states, and the condition of many roads has worsened. The state's fatal accident rate, although higher than the U.S. average, has also shown considerable improvement. Even urban congestion has been declining.

In spite of these statistics, highway conditions are not uniform. Bridge conditions vary from a high of 60.9 percent of bridges in substandard condition in Currituck County to a low of 15 percent substandard in Washington County (Fig. 9.6). Pavement conditions also vary substantially and are generally poorer in the Mountain counties (Fig. 9.7). With several exceptions, bridge conditions seem more uniform than pavement conditions.

North Carolina also manages an extensive highway construction program. In 1990 the General Assembly approved an expanded program to develop a 3,100-mile intrastate highway system that would place 90 percent of the population within ten min-

Figure 9.5. Volume of Traffic, 1995

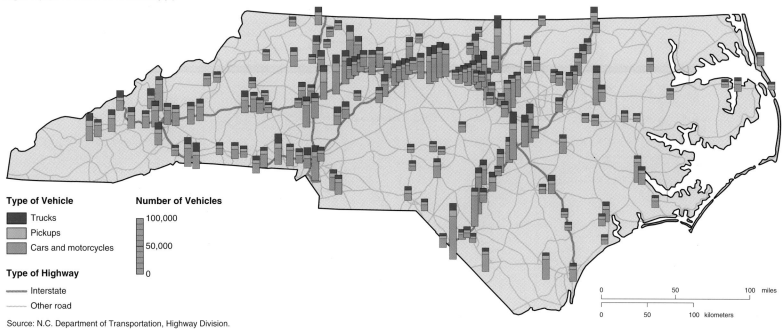

Type of Vehicle

- Trucks
- Pickups
- Cars and motorcycles

Number of Vehicles

- 100,000
- 50,000
- 0

Type of Highway

- Interstate
- Other road

| 0 | 50 | 100 | miles |
| 0 | 50 | 100 | kilometers |

Source: N.C. Department of Transportation, Highway Division.

Figure 9.6. Bridge Conditions, 1996

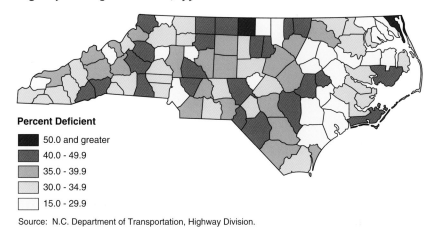

Percent Deficient

- 50.0 and greater
- 40.0 - 49.9
- 35.0 - 39.9
- 30.0 - 34.9
- 15.0 - 29.9

Source: N.C. Department of Transportation, Highway Division.

Figure 9.7. Pavement Conditions, 1996

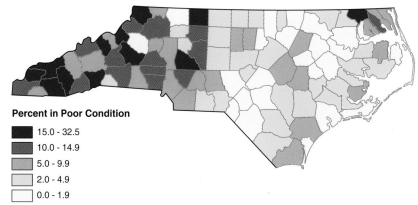

Percent in Poor Condition

- 15.0 - 32.5
- 10.0 - 14.9
- 5.0 - 9.9
- 2.0 - 4.9
- 0.0 - 1.9

Source: N.C. Department of Transportation, Highway Division.

Figure 9.8. Highway Improvements, 1995–2001

Project Status

〰〰〰 Existing interstate

──── Other road

Intrastate Highways

━━━ Completed project

━━━ Under construction (completed by 2001)

━━━ Accelerated for construction by 2001

━━━ Programmed project, 2002-2007

Other Roads

──── Under construction (completed by 2001)

──── Accelerated for construction by 2001

──── Programmed project, 2002-2007

┝┿┿┥ High-speed rail corridor

Source: N.C. Department of Transportation, Highway Division.

utes of a four-lane road. This system (Fig. 9.8) also includes the construction of major loops around metropolitan areas and the paving of 20,000 miles of North Carolina's dirt roads. Funded initially at $9.1 billion, the building program was expected to take between fifteen to twenty years to complete. In 1996 the fund was augmented by an $800 million bond issue to speed up construction of urban loops. The U.S. National Highway System also will improve North Carolina's connectivity to other states.

Trucking

North Carolina's trucking operations are extensive, reflecting the state's access to major eastern markets and favorable operating conditions. The entire east coast is within two days' travel time from North Carolina on the interstate system (Fig. 9.9). This makes North Carolina an ideal location for siting transportation terminals and operations.

For-hire transportation (commercial trucks) represents almost 20 percent of truck ton-mileage. The average for-hire travel per truck is about

Figure 9.9. Truck Delivery Time from the Geographic Center of North Carolina

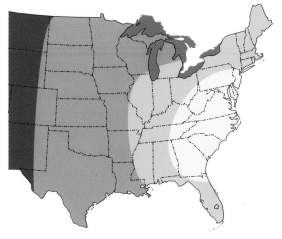

Number of Days

- 4 and above
- 3
- 2
- 1

Source: J. W. Clay, and A. W. Stuart, eds., *Charlotte: An Analytical Atlas of Patterns and Trends* (Charlotte: UNC Charlotte, Department of Geography and Earth Sciences, 1992).

Figure 9.10. Total Truck Volume, 1995

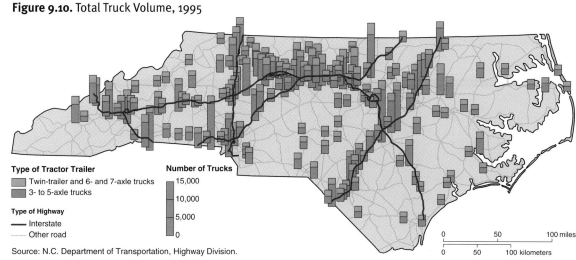

Type of Tractor Trailer
- Twin-trailer and 6- and 7-axle trucks
- 3- to 5-axle trucks

Type of Highway
- —— Interstate
- ------ Other road

Number of Trucks
- 15,000
- 10,000
- 5,000
- 0

Source: N.C. Department of Transportation, Highway Division.

63,000 miles annually, compared with 9,500 miles annually for personal-use trucks. North Carolina has a large number of personal trucks, primarily pickups and minivans.

Perhaps no mode so clearly shows the profound impact of changes in North Carolina's transportation system over the last decade than does commercial truck traffic. As shown in Figure 9.10, which displays typical truck classification information for selected sites in North Carolina, the high-est percentage of trucks is generally on the interstate and major primary systems. The Surface Transportation Assistance Act of 1982 permitted twin-trailer operations for the interstate system and other key roads. In 1991 the Intermodal Surface Transportation Efficiency Act restricted double trailers to these routes and banned triple trucks from eastern states. Weights also were limited to 80,000 pounds. Service between rail, air, and truck intermodal terminals has greatly expanded. North Carolina truck traffic has been influenced by these rapid changes in technology, road system access, and the completion of the interstate system. In the future, automated truck administration, electronic communications advances, and sophisticated just-in-time delivery and intermodal truck-rail and truck-water systems will further blur the distinction between warehousing, transportation, and distribution.

Commuting to Work

An important trend in North Carolina has been the increase in multicar households (Table 9.2). In 1980 there were 2.043 million households in North Carolina, of which 420,000, or about 20.6 percent, owned three or more cars. By 1990 the number of households had grown to 2.517 million, and the percentage of households owning three-plus cars had increased to 21.1 percent. In 1990 over twice as many households (530,107) owned three or more vehicles as owned no vehicle (241,711).

The number of workers in North Carolina increased about 24.4 percent in the 1980–90 de-

Table 9.2. Travel-Related Statistics for North Carolina

| | 1980 | | 1990 | | |
	Total	%	Total	%	Change (%)
Population	5,881,166	—	6,628,637	—	+12.7
Workers (16+)	2,652,593	—	3,300,481	—	+24.4
Drove alone	1,756,417	66.2	2,528,168	76.6	+43.9
Carpool	653,985	24.7	531,377	16.1	-18.7
Public transit	40,100	1.5	33,005	1.0	-17.7
Other means	34,468	1.3	39,606	1.2	+14.9
Walk/work at home	167,623	6.3	168,325	5.1	+4.1
Total daily person-trips	12,938,000	—	15,246,000	—	+17.8
Approx. no. of daily trips per person	2.2	—	2.3	—	+4.5
Median travel time to work (min.)	19.1	—	19.8	—	+3.7
Household auto ownership					
Total no. of households	2,043,291	—	2,517,026	—	+23.2
No. of vehicles per household					
0	219,700	10.8	241,711	9.6	+10.0
1	657,898	32.2	786,080	31.22	+19.5
2	745,112	36.5	959,128	38.1	+28.7
3+	420,490	20.6	530,107	21.1	+26.1
Total no. of household-owned vehicles	3,409,683	—	4,294,657	—	+26.0
Average no. of vehicles per household	1.67	—	1.71	—	+2.4
Total no. of vehicles registered	3,871,840	—	4,919,592	—	+27.1

Source: U.S. Census of Population and Housing.

cade, compared with a 12.7 percent increase in the population (Table 9.2). There also have been large changes in commuting patterns caused by increasing automobile ownership. Most of the change has been in the "drive alone" category, which rose from 66.2 percent of commuters in 1980 to 76.6 percent in 1990. Perhaps surprisingly, the percentage of workers in carpools has dropped markedly, from 24.7 percent to 16.1 percent. Public transit's share also dropped by about a third, from 1.5 percent to 1.0 percent. These trends are slowing, but not reversing, in the 1990s. Thus, the most dramatic changes in commuting patterns have been an increase in car ownership and a reduction in carpooling, coupled with substantial increases in solo driving. These trends, also observable nationwide, have been called the "democratization of mobility." They are partly attributed to rising incomes and cheap fuel, which have put automobiles within the reach of more workers, but the greatest influence has been growing labor force participation by women, who have increased both car purchasing and solo driving. Other factors, such as slowly declining costs of transportation relative to incomes and generally rising accessibility, also have contributed to these trends.

It is commonly believed that urban areas have a higher percentage of carpooling and public transit use than rural, more isolated areas. In fact, just the opposite is true in North Carolina. Solo driving commuting is highest in the Piedmont and the larger metropolitan areas (Fig. 9.11), which have generally higher income and auto ownership levels. Carpooling, on the other hand, is greatest in rural, relatively isolated counties where incomes are usually lower (Fig. 9.12).

More than 2 percent of commuters use public transportation in only four North Carolina counties: Durham, Forsyth, Mecklenburg, and Orange.

Figure 9.11. Percentage of Workers Commuting Alone, 1990

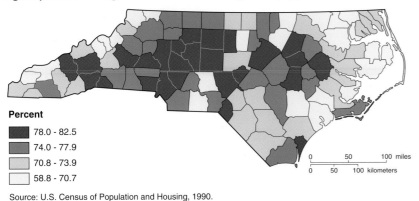

Percent
- 78.0 - 82.5
- 74.0 - 77.9
- 70.8 - 73.9
- 58.8 - 70.7

0 50 100 miles
0 50 100 kilometers

Source: U.S. Census of Population and Housing, 1990.

Figure 9.12. Percentage of Commuters Carpooling, 1990

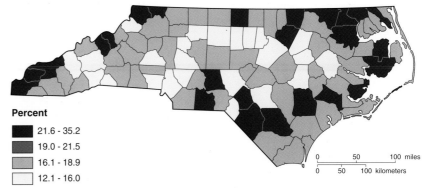

Percent
- 21.6 - 35.2
- 19.0 - 21.5
- 16.1 - 18.9
- 12.1 - 16.0

0 50 100 miles
0 50 100 kilometers

Source: U.S. Census of Population and Housing, 1990.

Two other urban counties, Buncombe and New Hanover, reported between 1 and 2 percent of commuters using public transit, along with four rural counties: Avery, Hertford, Pasquotank, and Washington.

Although North Carolina has experienced considerable changes in the mode of commuting, the overall effect on travel time has been surprisingly small. The average travel time to work has risen only slightly, from 19.1 minutes in 1980 to 19.8 minutes in 1990. Commuting times are generally longest in suburban counties on the outer reaches of large metropolitan regions (Fig. 9.13). The longest commuting times in North Carolina ranged from 22.3 minutes to 33.4 minutes. Gates (at 33.4 minutes) and Currituck were the only counties in the state with an average commuting time greater than 30 minutes. These two counties send commuters primarily to Virginia Beach and Newport News, Virginia. Shorter commuting times are associated both with isolated rural economies, where most commuting is local, and with a few urban areas that draw from expansive regions. The two counties with the lowest average travel times to work were Scotland (16.4 minutes) and Dare (16.8 minutes). These counties have relatively self-contained economies.

Cross-county commuting to work is closely related to the economic struc-

Figure 9.13. Median Travel Time to Work, 1990

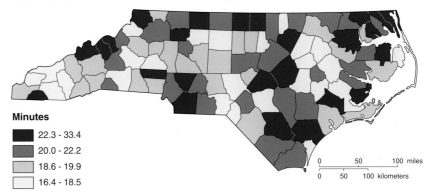

Minutes
- 22.3 - 33.4
- 20.0 - 22.2
- 18.6 - 19.9
- 16.4 - 18.5

0 50 100 miles
0 50 100 kilometers

Source: U.S. Census of Population and Housing, 1990.

Figure 9.14. County-to-County Work Trips, 1990

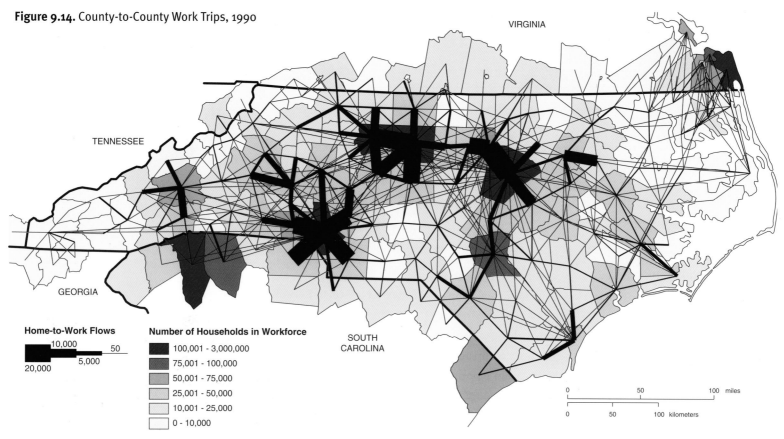

Home-to-Work Flows

10,000
20,000
5,000
50

Number of Households in Workforce

- 100,001 - 3,000,000
- 75,001 - 100,000
- 50,001 - 75,000
- 25,001 - 50,000
- 10,001 - 25,000
- 0 - 10,000

0   50   100 miles

0   50   100 kilometers

Source: U.S. Census of Population and Housing, Special Tabulation, 1990.

ture of each county and its neighbors. Higher wage levels in larger metropolitan counties attract workers from surrounding counties, thereby increasing commuting times and distances and resulting in significant net in-commuting (Fig. 9.14). In North Carolina, five large metropolitan areas account for most in-commuting: Catawba (Hickory), Durham (city of Durham), Guilford (Greensboro and High Point), Mecklenburg (Charlotte), and Wake (Raleigh). The greatest cross-commuting comes from counties adjacent to these large metropolitan areas, exemplified by Cabarrus, Davidson, Gaston,

Randolph, Rowan, and Stokes. Davidson led all counties in net out-commuting, with over 17,000 workers daily in 1990.

Public Transportation

Although about 50 percent of North Carolina's population is urban, its cities are fairly small and widely dispersed, population density is low, and automobile ownership is high. Urban transit services are limited compared to those in more concentrated metropolitan regions. Sixteen cities in North Carolina presently operate public transportation systems, typically on fixed schedules at fixed base fares and within the confines of urbanized areas (Table 9.3). The largest system serves the Charlotte area, handling about 11.7 million passengers annually (Fig. 9.15). In 1995, all sixteen systems carried a total of 31.8 million passengers, 13.9 million bus-miles, and 1,040,000 bus-hours. The passenger traffic was approximately 0.5 percent of the total annual person-trips. The 17.163 million annual trips of the estimated 33,005 workers in North Carolina who used public transit to commute to work amounted to about 60 percent of urban transit travel.

Typically, urban public transit services throughout the United States, including North Carolina, operate at a deficit. That is, it costs more to operate the service than the fare charged. Transit ridership trends are mixed, with transit work travel declining as a percentage of total trips and ridership slowly increasing in some cities and declining or remaining stable in others. But new services also are being offered. A regional transportation authority has been established in the Raleigh-Durham area, funded through a $5.00 tax on vehicle registrations. Limited bus service between area hubs is attracting about 1,200 riders per day, and longer-range plans call for light rail service in the area. A number of cities, notably Charlotte, Greensboro, Raleigh, and Durham, operate long-distance car-pooling and vanpooling services on a limited basis from outlying communities to city centers. In 1996 Governor James B. Hunt's Transit 2000 Commission called for a substantial increase in the state's transit funding to support expanded services in rural and urban areas and high-speed train service between Raleigh and Charlotte. In 1998 Mecklenburg County voters approved a half-cent increase in the sales tax for more buses, a network of new bus stations, and rapid bus and rail service in five radial corridors.

Table 9.3. Urban Public Transit Statistics, 1995

City	Passengers	Revenue Bus Miles	Revenue Bus Hours	Total Expenses ($)	Farebox Revenue ($)	Net Operating Deficit ($)
Hickory	142,121	165,993	10,483	432,726	74,980	357,746
Salisbury	203,676	156,814	11,895	436,711	103,057	333,654
Wilson	240,083	160,625	11,662	560,698	96,681	457,661
Greenville	258,788	155,711	11,026	430,299	104,477	317,866
Rocky Mount	329,104	146,724	11,265	367,171	104,696	245,273
Gastonia	370,258	237,287	17,984	666,413	162,962	493,064
High Point	898,129	388,934	30,573	966,689	393,257	562,979
Asheville	957,545	520,569	38,959	1,664,986	428,471	1,207,383
Wilmington	1,206,204	423,609	33,546	1,338,853	405,291	914,688
Fayetteville	1,427,340	536,143	44,983	1,948,241	508,882	1,416,988
Greensboro	1,698,784	1,046,291	71,453	3,666,785	755,022	2,911,763
Chapel Hill	2,590,537	1,116,699	84,142	4,256,576	1,402,231	2,853,456
Durham	2,977,180	1,218,384	92,092	3,944,048	1,130,329	2,811,964
Winston-Salem	3,296,072	1,297,160	110,054	4,283,393	1,373,016	2,786,728
Raleigh	3,426,530	1,621,637	116,847	5,934,083	1,327,533	4,586,333
Charlotte	11,797,948	4,707,163	342,814	18,167,648	6,148,927	11,808,891
Total	31,820,299	13,899,743	1,039,778	49,065,320	14,519,812	34,066,437

Source: N.C. Department of Transportation, Division of Public Transportation and Rail.

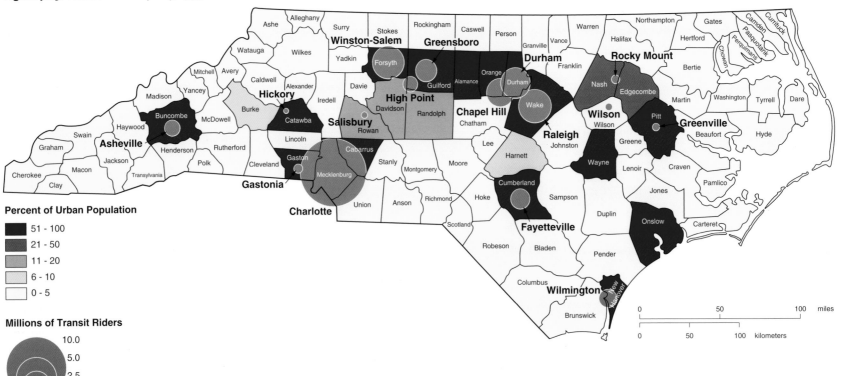

Figure 9.15. Transit Riders by City, 1995

Percent of Urban Population

- 51 - 100
- 21 - 50
- 11 - 20
- 6 - 10
- 0 - 5

Millions of Transit Riders

- 10.0
- 5.0
- 2.5
- 1.0

Source: N.C. Department of Transportation,
Public Transportation and Rail Division.

Railroads

North Carolina has an extensive network of freight railroad systems (Fig. 9.16). A total of twenty-five railroads serve the state. Two Class I railroads ($50 million or more in annual operating revenues)—CSX Transportation and the Norfolk Southern Railway—operate large rail networks in the Southeast and Midwest. North Carolina owns four railroads, including the North Carolina

Railroad between Charlotte, Raleigh, and points east. Of approximately 4,115 track-miles operating in North Carolina, 79 percent are controlled by CSX and Norfolk Southern.

Railroad freight volumes in North Carolina are substantial. CSX Transportation operates two major tracks through the Carolinas, one between South Carolina and Virginia, running roughly parallel to Interstate 95; the other from Laurinburg-Maxton west through Wadesboro and Charlotte, then

Figure 9.16. The Railroad System and Freight Traffic Density, 1996

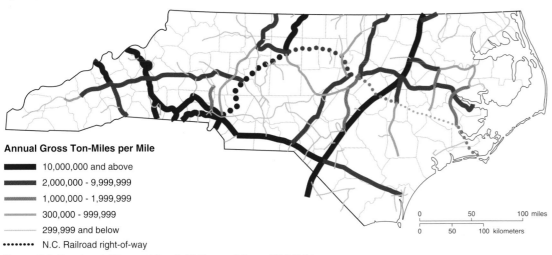

Annual Gross Ton-Miles per Mile

▬▬▬ 10,000,000 and above
▬▬ 2,000,000 - 9,999,999
▬ 1,000,000 - 1,999,999
— 300,000 - 999,999
— 299,999 and below
••••••• N.C. Railroad right-of-way

Source: N.C. Department of Transportation, Public Transportation and Rail Division.

through Shelby, Bostic, and Spruce Pine into Tennessee (Fig. 9.16). Both of these routes carry substantial traffic: over 10 million gross ton-miles per mile annually. Norfolk Southern Railway operates a high-volume line between Charlotte and Greensboro, continuing on north into Virginia and continuing south of Charlotte through Gastonia into South Carolina. This line also carries over 10 million gross ton-miles per mile annually. Supporting the three primary routes are a number of feeder and spur routes carrying 2–10 million tons per mile annually. Primary routes in this category include the CSX routes from Pembroke to Wilmington and Hamlet to Raleigh, and Norfolk Southern's routes from Chocowinity to Greensboro and from Asheville to Salisbury.

In 1993 rail shipments from North Carolina totaled 14.7 billion tons, about 7.2 percent of total freight tonnage, but railroads accounted for 18.5 percent of all ton-miles moved. About 87 percent of the tonnage was carried by CSX and Norfolk Southern. Recently, intermodal (truck-rail) services have also increased. The primary commodities carried are chemicals (20.2 percent), wood/lumber (15.3 percent), and minerals (11.9 percent). To ensure the availability of railroad rights-of-way in the future, the North Carolina Department of Transportation has pursued an active railroad right-of-way purchase and route preservation program, under which a number of private and publicly owned railroads have been supported.

Rail passenger service through North Carolina

is provided by Amtrak between New York and New Orleans via Greensboro and Charlotte, between New York and Florida via Fayetteville and Raleigh, and between New York and Charlotte via Raleigh. State funds support the New York–Charlotte (Carolinian) and the Raleigh-Charlotte (Piedmont) services. As of 1999, two trains daily in each direction operate between Charlotte and Raleigh. This new service was established in 1991 after a hiatus of about five years (Fig. 9.17). High-speed rail service is being considered for the future.

It is difficult to predict the future of rail transportation in North Carolina. Passenger service depends largely on service to other states on the eastern seaboard. Although railroad ridership has been stabilized, even slightly increased, Congress is reconsidering a permanent solution to the industry's fiscal problems. Discussions concerning the possibility of expanded northeastern corridor rail service and high-speed rail service also may impact the Carolinas positively. On the freight side, a general trend toward increased containerization and intermodal services between truck and rail has stabilized rail systems throughout the United States. Given the dependence of the national economy on reliable rail freight service, it is likely that this service will continue to be provided. The merger of ConRail into the CSX and Norfolk and Southern systems, completed in 1999, is expected to provide North Carolina shippers with better service into the northeastern United States.

In 1998 the state reacquired full ownership of

Figure 9.17. Annual Amtrak Ridership, 1996

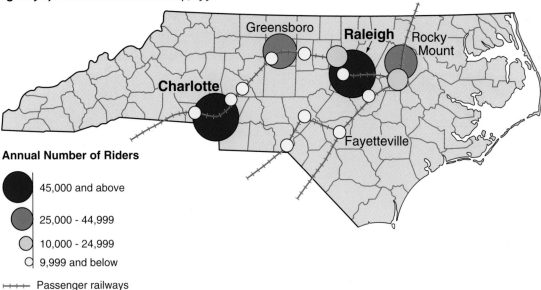

Annual Number of Riders

- 45,000 and above
- 25,000 - 44,999
- 10,000 - 24,999
- 9,999 and below
- ⊢┼┼┼⊣ Passenger railways

Source: N.C. Department of Transportation,
Public Transportation and Rail Division.

Figure 9.18. Navigable Waterways and Ports

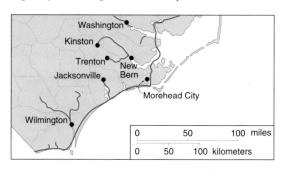

the North Carolina Railroad line from Goldsboro to Charlotte. This act is expected to facilitate transit service between and within the larger urban regions in the Piedmont.

Water Transportation

Historically water transportation has served a vital role in the economy of the state, particularly in the east. Figure 9.18 shows the two major state ports (Morehead City and Wilmington) and navigable waterways. Shipping activities occur at the mouth of each of the rivers and at some points upstream. The North Carolina State Ports Authority manages the ports. The primary commodities moved through the state ports are tobacco, phosphates, lumber, logs, plywood, fiber, urea, scrap metal, wood pulp, paperboard, chemicals, concrete products, and petroleum. Users of the state port in Wilmington are heavily concentrated in Charlotte and Wilmington. The state port at Morehead City is frequently used by industries in or near Hender-

son, Rocky Mount, Wilson, New Bern, and Greenville.

The Port of Morehead City is mainly a bulk cargo facility, with 89 percent of its cargo being bulk shipments. In the Port of Wilmington, by contrast, one-third of the cargo shipments in fiscal year 1996 involved containerized freight. In 1996 the Wilmington Customs District recorded moving 2.12 million tons, up 12 percent from 1991, and Morehead City reported 2.87 million tons, up 15 percent from 1991. These values trailed those for the nearest competing districts, Norfolk and Charleston. In 1997 the two state ports together handled about $3 billion in cargo. However, Charleston and Norfolk each handled three times that much. These differences reflect the difficulties that the North Carolina ports face in seeking to compete with the larger ports in South Carolina and Virginia. Part of the problem is that Wilmington has only a 38-foot channel, shallow by today's standards. In addition, the General Assembly has not always been willing to invest substantially in improving the ports and their facilities. That began to change in 1997, when the legislature allocated $6 million to the Ports Authority, an almost sevenfold increase from 1996; it was scheduled to raise that amount to $10 million in 1998.

Aviation and Airports

Of North Carolina's seventy-four public airports, fourteen offered scheduled air carrier passenger service in 1996 (Fig. 9.19). The Federal Aviation Administration assigns "hub" classifications based on the percentage of total domestic enplanements. North Carolina has one large hub (Charlotte), one medium hub (Raleigh-Durham), and three small hubs (Greensboro, Asheville, and Fayetteville). The largest airport service in the state is operated at Charlotte/ Douglas International (CLT), which in 1998 handled about 11.4 million enplanements. This places the Charlotte airport at seventeenth in size nationwide, compared with that city's thirty-third ranking in population. The state's second largest airport, Raleigh-Durham (RDU), serves about 3.4 million passengers, placing it approximately thirtieth nationwide, substantially above Raleigh-Durham's fifty-fourth ranking in population. In terms of connectivity, the number of other cities served by direct flights, Charlotte ranked eighth highest among the nation's sixty largest airports in 1992 and RDU was thirty-first. CLT's connectivity rose from thirtieth in 1978, RDU from forty-fifth. Overall, North Carolina enplanements increased 13.6 percent from 1990 to 1996.

Perhaps the most significant recent event in airline service has been the deregulation of the airline industry, which freed airlines to compete openly for passengers, expand domestic operations, and enter new markets. Overall, airline traffic statistics in North Carolina have generally followed national patterns, with some important exceptions. In the early 1970s enplanements from North Carolina totaled about 3.8 million passengers. This figure soared to 8.5

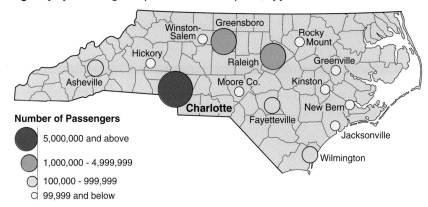

Figure 9.19. Passenger Enplanements at Airports, 1996

Number of Passengers

● 5,000,000 and above

● 1,000,000 - 4,999,999

○ 100,000 - 999,999

○ 99,999 and below

Source: N.C. Department of Transportation, Aviation Division.

Charlotte/Douglas International Airport

million passengers by 1985 and 17.1 million by 1997. Particularly rapid growth was observed at Charlotte and at RDU, emerging hubs for Piedmont Airlines (later US Airways), and American Airlines/Midway, respectively. Growth slowed at RDU during the early 1990s, when American Airlines closed its hub operation, but it has returned. Increasing service concentrations have also occurred within airlines, as carriers have recognized the economic advantages of hub-and-spoke structures. Essentially, hubs are profitable because they permit carriers to retain passengers on all legs of a journey (Fig. 9.20). At Charlotte, almost 80 percent of the enplanements are "transfers" from other flights. Even more important changes have taken place at smaller airports that affiliated with hub airports—under the old structure they served as little-used stop-off points on a larger route system. More recently, new no-frills services between city pairs have emerged as a competitive strategy.

Air cargo operations are closely tied to passenger operations as most air cargo goes along with passengers. North Carolina's three largest airports carry significant air cargo tonnages. Charlotte/Douglas International processed 209,842 tons in 1996, up 49.6 percent from 1991. It was followed by RDU at 108,723 tons, up 40.8 percent, and Piedmont Triad at 76,052 tons, up 78.3 percent. North Carolina also is developing a major air cargo industrial airport at Kinston, the "Transpark." It is intended to attract large companies that will pro-

cess materials at the airport site, with both final products and raw materials moving in from and out to international markets via jumbo jets. Moreover, package express services have expanded substantially. Federal Express has committed to opening a major eastern hub at the Piedmont Triad airport in Greensboro.

Military aviation in North Carolina is also extensive. Camp Lejeune, Fort Bragg and adjacent Pope Air Force Base, Seymour Johnson Air Force Base, Cherry Point, the Elizabeth City Coast Guard station, and other military airports create one of the largest proportions of restricted air space areas in the nation.

Aviation is of obvious importance in providing transportation services for people and commodities. It is also a major contributor to the state's economy. In 1995 a study conducted at the University of North Carolina at Charlotte for the North Carolina Department of Transportation found that the seventy-four publicly owned airports in North Carolina contributed $9.1 billion to the economy through expenditures by airlines, passengers, supporting services, and major business users. In addition, aviation directly or indirectly supported 181,000 jobs, with payrolls that totaled $4.6 billion. Nearly 98 percent of the total expenditures were attributed to the fourteen airports that provide regularly scheduled passenger service. In fact, 90 percent of expenditures, jobs, and earnings were associated with three airports: Charlotte/Douglas,

RDU, and Piedmont Triad. The sixty General Aviation airports were relatively small contributors to the state economy and did not offer regularly scheduled flights. Nonetheless, they are important local providers of air service for individuals and businesses.

Utilities

The rapid growth of population in North Carolina's cities and the rising affluence that has accompanied it have substantially increased the demand for electricity and natural gas for space heating, air-conditioning, water heating, and other residential uses. Economic growth adds to this demand as offices, factories, and stores air-condition their spaces or use electricity and natural gas in their operations. The burgeoning tourism industry means energy uses for hotels or beach cottages for the benefit of business and recreational travelers. As a result of these changes, between 1990 and 1996 the number of electricity and natural gas customers in the state increased by 13.6 percent and 33 percent, respectively.

Currently this demand is met by five natural gas and four electric companies that offer regulated service in North Carolina (Figs. 9.21 and 9.22). Additionally, municipal utilities reported having seventy-one electric and eight gas operations. Employment in these industries accounted for about

Figure 9.20. Daily Nonstop and Single Plane Air Service from Charlotte/Douglas International Airport, 1997

Nonstop Flights

— Domestic

— International

Single Plane Flights

— Domestic

— International

Source: Latest timetables
of carriers, May 1997.

Top Ten Destinations	Flights/day
1. New York-Newark	22
2. Atlanta	17
3. Washington	15
4. Philadelphia-Camden	15
5. Pittsburgh	12
6. Boston	12
7. Dallas-Fort Worth	11
8. Raleigh-Durham	10
9. Greenville-Spartanburg	10
10. Baltimore	10

Figure 9.21. Private Power Company Service Areas

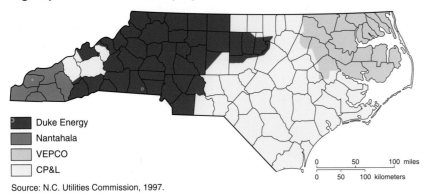

Duke Energy
Nantahala
VEPCO
CP&L

Source: N.C. Utilities Commission, 1997.

Figure 9.22. Natural Gas Companies

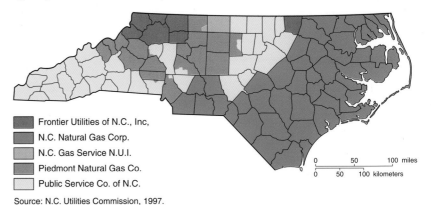

Frontier Utilities of N.C., Inc,
N.C. Natural Gas Corp.
N.C. Gas Service N.U.I.
Piedmont Natural Gas Co.
Public Service Co. of N.C.

Source: N.C. Utilities Commission, 1997.

0.7 percent of all employment in North Carolina; about 87 percent of those jobs were in the electric power industry.

Natural Gas

North Carolina does not produce natural gas but uses it extensively. A major pipeline system running through the state brings in the gas from Gulf Coast fields. About 637,000 residential customers consume about 28 percent of the total, and 87,000 commercial customers use 23 percent. Another 3,204 industrial users consume the largest portion, about 45 percent. Overall costs to consumers in the Carolinas are about 16 percent lower than the U.S. average. Total revenues were about $989 million in 1996, up 80 percent from 1990.

Some rural areas in North Carolina are not served by natural gas pipelines because, in the view of the utilities, the potential demand does not justify the cost of extending the pipelines into them. Efforts have been made in the General Assembly to require this service because its absence is seen as a deterrent to economic development. In 1998 voters approved a bond issue that will pay for extending natural gas service into some of these rural areas.

Electricity

Most of the electricity consumed in North Carolina is produced by four utility companies: Carolina Power and Light, Duke Energy, Virginia Electric Power Company (VEPCO), and Nantahala Power and Light (Fig. 9.23). Together they served nearly 2.5 million customers in 1996, 55 percent by Duke Energy and another 38 percent by Carolina Power and Light (CP&L). The four companies provide power directly to their own customers; they also sell it to twenty-eight electric membership corporations and seventy-one municipalities that operate electric distribution systems in various parts of the state. In 1996 electric power consumption per residential customer was 13,301 kilowatt hours, about 38 percent above the U.S. average. This compares with the average customer consumption of 12,130 kilowatt hours in 1990. Average usage has been growing about 2 percent per year, and the rate of usage for North Carolina residential consumers remains considerably above the U.S. average. This higher rate of consumption is primarily due to the extensive use of air-conditioning during the state's long and hot summers. Nevertheless, the electric bills of residential customers were about 8 percent lower than those of residential customers nationally, reflecting the lower unit cost of electricity in North Carolina.

Most of the state's electric-generating capacity

Figure 9.23. Customers of the Major Power Companies, 1996

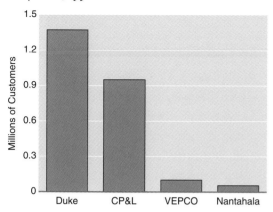

Source: N.C. Utilities Commission, 1997.

Duke Power's Allen Steam Plant along Lake Wylie

comes from coal, but nuclear power plants are also an important source of energy. Duke Energy Company, for example, operates three nuclear plants (seven units) that produce about 60 percent of the company's total power generated. Similarly, CP&L gets about 45 percent of its power from nuclear plants and VEPCO about 35 percent. On balance, about 35 percent of North Carolina's total generating capability comes from nuclear sources.

Additions to the state's generating capacity have slowed considerably in recent years. This has happened partly because the rate of demand has increased and partly because of serious environmental objections to both coal-fired and nuclear plants. As a result, utilities are increasingly considering alternatives such as cogeneration, pump storage, and other, more environmentally acceptable fuels. Cur-

rently, however, these do not account for a significant portion of the total generating capacity in the state, nor are they likely to do so in the immediate future. The search, then, for more acceptable large-scale generation technologies continues as electricity becomes an increasingly important source of energy for the citizens of North Carolina.

Another noteworthy change in the energy industry has been deregulation, which has loosened

geographic constraints on where a company can sell its power. The intent is to increase competition among energy producers. The ultimate effects of this policy shift on growth and development in North Carolina is difficult to predict. There is some concern that deregulation will equalize costs among the states, thereby reducing the competitive advantage of low power costs that North Carolina has been able to offer both residents and businesses. What impact this may have on the state's future economic and population growth remains to be seen.

Deregulation and the increased competition that goes with it are also changing the ways in which utilities see themselves. For instance, Duke Power recently became an arm of Duke Energy, a company that was formed after a merger with PanEnergy, a Houston-based gas pipeline company. As examples of other national and international expansion, Duke Power has bought three California generating plants; become co-owner of a generating plant in Bridgeport, Connecticut; acquired a half interest in American Ref-Fuel, a company that generates electricity in the New York–New Jersey area by burning waste; obtained U.S. Department of Energy approval to sell electricity to Canada; and participated in a venture to build an electric power plant in Indonesia.

Outlook

Transportation—whether by highway, rail, or air—and utilities provide critical infrastructure for growth and change. North Carolina has placed great emphasis on its highway system, which both supported and caused the state's unique pattern of dispersion. That is, as mills were constructed on scattered sites, roads were built to connect them, as well as to help farmers get their products to mar-

ket. The development of an extensive road network permitted further dispersion of industry. Overall, the state's highway system has served its citizens and businesses well. An extensive rail network and several strong airports have capitalized on North Carolina's strategic location between the industrial Northeast and the rapidly growing Deep South.

Along the way, many people, especially elected officials, came to see highways as a major determinant of economic growth, a view encouraged by the North Carolina Department of Transportation. It was thought that the way to fix a lagging local economy was to build or improve a highway. Many studies have shown that highway access is no longer the powerful attraction for economic development that it once was, primarily because now so many places are connected by good roads. Labor supplies, costs, and skill levels; market access; good air service; proximity to related business services and suppliers; amenities and the general quality of life; and a host of other factors have taken on greater importance in the modern economy. But the emphasis on highway development in rural areas remains strong within the Department of Transportation and the General Assembly.

In the meantime, urban areas have become the focal point of much recent and probable future growth. Their transportation needs include not only expensive expressways but also a greater commitment to mass transit and perhaps even light rail systems. Nowhere is the tension between percep-

tions of North Carolina as a rural, small-town state, on the one hand, and more contemporary views that properly functioning urban areas are the key to the state's future prosperity, on the other hand, more apparent.

But it is not just a matter of alternative transportation technologies. In North Carolina's urban areas, which collectively sprawl over two-thirds of the state, it is apparent that the various counties and municipalities need to develop more effective means of planning and coordinating transportation systems. Each jurisdiction and the Metropolitan Planning Organizations (MPOs) that are responsible for transportation planning tend to act mostly in their own interests, without due regard for the rest of the region of which they are a part. Coordinating transportation and related land use planning over these large areas will be both imperative and difficult.

The need to give a higher priority to transportation other than highways is a growing concern in North Carolina's burgeoning metropolitan areas, especially Charlotte and Raleigh. Portions of a new outerbelt highway in Charlotte were choked with traffic the day they opened. I-40 around Raleigh is a commuter's nightmare during rush hour.

Traffic congestion and the associated deterioration of air quality are complex issues that, if not dealt with effectively, threaten the future viability of the state's economy and quality of life. They will be difficult enough to deal with without imposing further limitations from an outdated perspective that emphasizes highways and rural economic development. Transportation has supported the state's growth to this point. In the future, if not developed realistically, it may actually put a brake on growth.

North Carolina power companies have been able to offer residential and business customers relatively low-cost energy. Deregulation of the industry, which will remove geographic monopolies as well as controls on rates, threatens to eliminate this competitive advantage. In anticipation of this change, the state's power companies, especially Duke Energy, are diversifying their activities and moving into new markets in the United States and other countries. This aggressive response to unprecedented changes in the industry may well position the North Carolina industry to be even stronger in the future.

Selected References

Brown, C. *The State Highway System of North Carolina: Its Evolution and Present Status*. Chapel Hill: University of North Carolina Press, 1931.

Clay, J., A. Stuart, and W. Walcott. *Jobs, Highways, and Regional Development in North Carolina*. Charlotte: University of North Carolina at Charlotte Department of Geography and Earth Sciences and University of North Carolina Institute for Transportation Research and Education, 1988.

Debbage, K. "Air Transportation in the Carolinas." In *Snapshots of the Carolinas: Landscapes and Culture*, edited by G. Gordon Bennett, pp. 197–202. Washington, D.C.: Association of American Geographers, 1996.

North Carolina Utilities Commission. *1997 Report*, vol. 28, June 1998.

Pisarski, A. *Commuting in America II*. Landsdowne, Va.: Eno Transportation Foundation, 1996.

Stuart, A., and D. Hartgen. *Economic Impact of Publicly Owned Airports in North Carolina*. Raleigh: North Carolina Department of Transportation, Aviation Division, 1996.

U.S. Army Corps of Engineers. Water Resources Support Center. National Waterways Study. Huntsville, Ala., 1994.

U.S. Department of Transportation. Federal Highway Commission. *Highway Statistics*, 1997.

U.S. Department of Transportation. *National Personal Transportation Study, North Carolina*, 1993.

———. *Transportation Statistics Annual Report, 1997*, 1998.

10. TRADE, FINANCE, AND TOURISM

The rapid increase in North Carolina's population, wealth, and cities is reflected in the equally strong growth of the broad services sector of the economy. This sector includes retail and wholesale trade, finance, insurance, real estate, and other services. North Carolina citizens and businesses are the primary consumers of these services, of course, but an important part is supported by the expenditures of tourists and other visitors to the state. Between 1970 and 1997, a period when statewide nonfarm employment doubled, the share of jobs accounted for by these service sectors shot up from 34.4 to 50 percent of the nonfarm total. In 1997 these service sectors contributed $43 billion in nonfarm wages, 44.3 percent of the state total.

Providing such services is more of an urban activity than is manufacturing. This is true even of tourism; though much of it occurs in rural Coastal and Mountain recreation areas, the highest levels of expenditures by travelers actually appear in the larger urban counties, in part because they attract many business travelers. Almost inevitably, as North Carolina continues to grow and become more urban, the services sector can be expected to comprise an even larger part of the state's economy, a pattern that is consistent with national trends.

Perhaps the most dramatic example of urban-oriented services expansion has been the rise of banking. Situated in Charlotte and Winston-Salem are the headquarters of three of the nation's largest banks, which support not only thousands of their own workers but also a host of other related businesses as well. In the movement toward larger financial institutions and an information-processing economy, North Carolina is a national leader.

Retail Trade

J. DENNIS LORD

The location of retail trade activities corresponds closely to the distribution of population (Fig. 10.1a). Because retailers sell goods directly to ultimate consumers, it is important that they be located in close proximity to the consuming population. Because consumers do not desire to travel long distances for goods, the geographic reach of most retail establishments is quite limited. The result is a close association between the population size of a market (city or county) and the dollar volume of retail trade. An illustration of this close association is provided by the rankings of North Carolina's largest counties in retail sales and population (Table 10.1). Mecklenburg County is the state's largest county in both retail sales and population with figures in 1998 of $8.2 billion and 613,310, respectively. In fact, nine of the ten largest counties in retail sales are among the state's ten largest counties in population, and often the respective

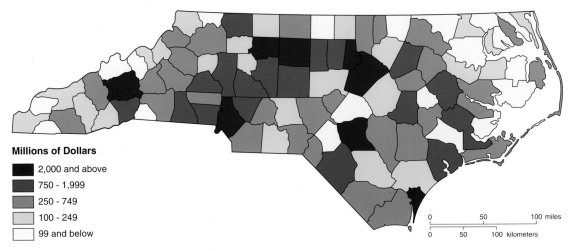

Figure 10.1a. Total Retail Sales, 1998

Millions of Dollars

- 2,000 and above
- 750 - 1,999
- 250 - 749
- 100 - 249
- 99 and below

Sources: *1998 Editor and Publishers Market Guide* ©.

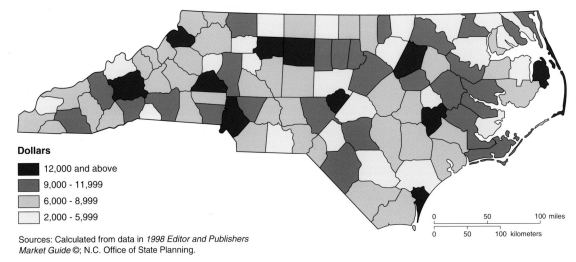

Figure 10.1b. Retail Sales per Capita, 1998

Dollars

- 12,000 and above
- 9,000 - 11,999
- 6,000 - 8,999
- 2,000 - 5,999

Sources: Calculated from data in *1998 Editor and Publishers Market Guide* ©; N.C. Office of State Planning.

rankings are similar. This pattern is also found for the smallest retail sales counties, where seven of the ten smallest counties in retail sales are among the ten smallest counties in population. In 1997 Camden was the smallest county in retail sales with only $19.8 million and the third smallest in population with 6,681 residents.

Trade Leakage

Factors other than population also influence the magnitude of retail trade. These include the income level of the population and retail *leakage*. Income level has an obvious influence on the retail expenditure potential of the population and a positive effect on the volume of retail sales. Retail leakage involves the flow of retail expenditures into or out of an area, thereby resulting in a net gain or loss of sales for the local economy. This can happen when residents of one area (city or county) make retail expenditures in another area, thus causing a loss of potential retail sales for the local economy. In other cases, retail dollars may flow into an area as a result of local purchases by people who are not residents of the area. The latter process enlarges the size of the retail economy and provides important economic benefits for the inflow community. In some cases, the inflow is from residents of the surrounding areas who travel to larger trade centers nearby to buy goods. The primary reason for this outshopping behavior is the greater selection of merchandise in the larger centers. In other cases, the inflow can result from expenditures in the retail sector by tourists or business travelers. The economic impact of retail leakage can be considerable for the affected communities. The loss of retail dollars to other localities has an adverse effect on the real estate tax base of a community, on retail sales tax collections, and on retail employment. The sales tax effect occurs because a portion of the local option sales tax in North Carolina is returned to counties based on the location of sales tax collections.

The influence of income level and retail leakage on retail sales is most obvious when per capita sales figures are examined (Fig. 10.1b). Counties with the highest retail sales per capita include several types of markets: (1) large urban

Table 10.1. Largest North Carolina Retail Trade Counties, 1998

County	Sales ($000)	County	Population (1997)
Mecklenburg	8,176,251	Mecklenburg	608,567
Wake	6,417,220	Wake	556,853
Guilford	5,402,269	Guilford	383,186
Forsyth	4,137,254	Cumberland	295,255
Cumberland	2,683,937	Forsyth	287,160
Buncombe	2,403,163	Durham	197,710
Durham	2,247,024	Buncombe	191,122
New Hanover	2,076,651	Gaston	180,082
Gaston	1,867,123	Onslow	147,352
Catawba	1,837,852	New Hanover	146,601

Sources: Retail Sales, *1998 Editor and Publishers Market Guide* ©; Population, N.C. Office of State Planning, 1998.

counties that benefit from both high income levels and the inflow of retail trade from surrounding counties (e.g., Guilford, Wake, Mecklenburg, and Forsyth); (2) small counties whose retail economies are boosted by tourist expenditures (e.g., Dare, Henderson, and Watauga); and (3) small or moderate-size counties that act as regional trade centers (e.g., Catawba, Pasquotank, Nash, and Pitt). Low-sales-per-capita counties are characterized by low income levels or loss of retail sales to nearby areas. Camden, one of the state's lowest-retail-sales-per-capita counties, is located adjacent to Pasquotank, one of the highest retail-sales-per-capita counties in the state. Similarly, Caswell, also a low-per-capita-sales county, no doubt loses sales to such larger nearby counties as Alamance and Guilford.

The total expenditure potential of a county's residents is largely a function of total income. The total income of the county can therefore be used to estimate the magnitude of the net inflow or outflow of retail sales (i.e., retail leakage). This can be calculated by estimating the amount of retail sales expected for a county if there were no inflow or outflow of retail expenditures, and by comparing this estimated sales to the actual sales in the county. Counties whose actual sales exceed expected sales are net *inflow* counties, whereas those whose actual sales are less than expected sales are net *outflow* counties.

Based on 1997 sales data, fifteen counties each had a net inflow exceeding $250 million. Many of these counties contained a large city that served as the dominant retail center for the surrounding region (Fig. 10.2). Guilford (Greensboro), Mecklenburg (Charlotte), Forsyth (Winston-Salem), and Wake (Raleigh) illustrate this situation. Mecklenburg had the largest net inflow retail trade in the state with a value of over $1.246 billion, followed closely by Guilford County with $1.206 billion. Other large net inflow counties either contained a smaller city that served as an important retail trade center for its region or attacted numerous tourists. Examples of the former include New Hanover (Wilmington), Cumberland (Fayetteville), and Buncombe (Asheville).

Pasquotank County is one of the state's best examples of where retail sales from the surrounding region and tourism have combined to produce a large net inflow of retail dollars. Although a relatively small county itself with Elizabeth City as its largest community, it still functioned as the major retail center for residents in the northeastern counties, as well as for tourists who visited the area. Pasquotank's net inflow in 1997 was estimated at nearly $178 million, the twenty-fifth highest county figure in the state despite its relatively small size.

Figure 10.2. Net Inflow or Outflow of Retail Sales, 1997

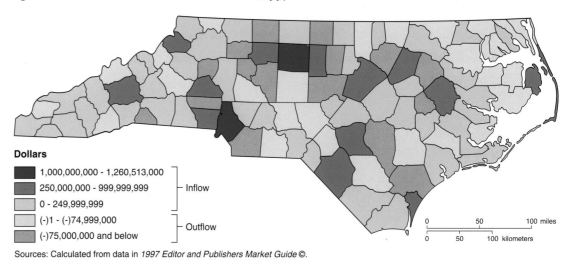

Sources: Calculated from data in *1997 Editor and Publishers Market Guide* ©.

If Pasquotank had depended solely on its own residents for retail sales generation, its sales would have been only $246 million instead of its actual total of $424 million. Thus, sales to tourists and to residents of surrounding counties have significantly increased the size of the county's retail economy.

Dare County is the state's best example of a tourism-inflated retail economy. In 1997 Dare's 27,875 residents would have likely generated only $209 million in sales. However, actual sales were $512 million, for a net inflow of $303 million. This influx of retail dollars more than doubled the size of the retail economy and, in so doing, expanded the tax base, increased receipts from sales taxes, and expanded retail employment levels.

Although some counties gain from intercounty retail trade flows, others lose. Many large net inflow counties are surrounded by other counties that experience sizable net outflows of sales. This pattern is well illustrated by the tier of counties that surround large net inflow counties such as Guilford, Forsyth, Alamance, Buncombe, Catawba, Mecklenburg, Wake, New Hanover, and Pasquotank. Large outflows were recorded by Chatham, Davidson, Davie, and Stokes Counties, close to Greensboro–Winston-Salem; Franklin and Orange Counties, next to Raleigh-Durham; Pender County, next to Wilmington; and Union County, adjacent to Charlotte. In each case, actual retail sales are well below the retail expenditure potential of county residents.

Commercial development around the Park Road shopping center in Charlotte

Urban Dominance

The intercounty movement of consumers and retail expenditures has accelerated as the population has become more mobile. This had led to subtle but significant changes in the retailing importance of different groups of counties. The metropolitan core counties, the largest in each of the state's metropolitan areas, have increased their share of retail sales. These counties traditionally have garnered a much larger share of retail sales than either population or income. But in recent decades the disparity has become even more pronounced. In 1970 the metropolitan core counties accounted for 38.4 percent of the state's population and 45.5 percent of its retail sales; by 1997 the corresponding figures increased to 41.5 and 50.3 percent, respectively. The greater share of retail sales than population cannot be attributed entirely to higher incomes in the metropolitan core counties, as their share of state income in 1997 was only 46.1 percent. Conversely, the remaining metro areas contained a

higher proportion of population than retail sales: 25.7 percent and 20.1, respectively.

Nonmetropolitan counties with less than 50,000 population have experienced a decline in their share of population, income, and retail sales over the past two decades. Nonmetro counties with more than 50,000 population have seen their share of retail sales decline less than their share of population, as many of these counties still function as important smaller regional trade centers. The increasing concentration of retail sales in large urban counties is likely to continue. It remains to be seen whether the entry of retailers such as Wal-Mart into smaller markets will slow or reverse this trend.

Geographic shifts have also taken place in the location of retailing in cities. The major shift has been a decline in the retailing role of the downtown area or central business district (CBD) as a result of the extensive decentralization or suburbanization of retail trade activity. This trend, which began in the 1950s and 1960s, has taken place in cities of all sizes both in North Carolina and across the nation. Coincident in time and also causally related to this decentralization has been the emergence of the planned-shopping-center form of retailing. Other factors contributing to the CBD's decline in retailing include population decentralization and the deterioration of downtown shopping facilities and infrastructure.

Shopping Centers

Planned shopping centers have captured an increasingly larger share of retail sales in North Carolina cities. Approximately 50 percent of all retail sales now occur in these centers. But if sales of gasoline stations and automobile dealerships are removed from the total, planned shopping centers account for approximately two-thirds of retail sales. Planned shopping centers range in size from less than 50,000 square feet to more than 1,000,000. The majority of centers are relatively small: 66 percent, or 1,006, of North Carolina's 1,524 shopping centers in 1996 measured less than 100,000 square feet (Table 10.2). Larger centers, although fewer in number, account for a substantial share of

Suburban shopping mall in Fayetteville

Table 10.2. Size of North Carolina Shopping Centers, 1996

Size (sq. ft.)	No. of Centers	Percentage of Total Centers
Less than 100,000	1,006	66.0
100,001 to 200,000	375	24.6
200,001 to 400,000	105	6.9
400,001 to 800,000	24	1.6
800,001 to 1,000,000	5	0.3
More than 1,000,000	9	0.6
Total	1,524	100.0

Source: NRB [National Research Bureau] Shopping Center Census, 1997.

shopping center floorspace. The size of shopping centers in North Carolina is relatively high compared to national standards. In 1996 the state had 21.9 square feet per capita compared to the national average of 19.2 square feet. This larger size is a trait of many Sunbelt states where the retail market has grown rapidly during the planned shopping center era. It is also a reflection of these states' dispersed population and the absence of major urban centers. In North Carolina, the largest shopping centers exist in larger metropolitan markets. For example, the Raleigh–Durham–Chapel Hill metropolitan area ranked tenth nationally in 1995 in terms of the amount of shopping center floorspace per capita.

Many types of shopping centers can be found in the state. Neighborhood centers are usually less than 100,000 square feet, provide mostly convenience goods, and are anchored by a supermarket. Community centers range from 100,000 to approximately 300,000 square feet, provide a mix of frequently purchased goods such as food and less frequently purchased items, such as clothing or appliances, and are typically anchored by a discount department store. Regional centers exceed 300,000 square feet, sell primarily shopping goods, and are anchored by department stores. The larger regional centers, those exceeding 750,000 square feet and containing at least three department stores, are referred to as super-regional. North Carolina has eleven centers that equal or exceed 900,000 square feet in floorspace (Table 10.3). The centers are found only in the state's largest cities and counties because of the large population base required for their support. Nine of the eleven largest centers were built during the 1970s. Recent construction of large centers has been low due in part to the saturation of markets. Another trait of the large centers is a commonality of department store anchors with such familiar names as Belk, Dillard's (formerly Ivey's), Hecht's (formerly Thalhimers), Sears, and JC Penney.

Two new types of shopping centers have appeared on the North Carolina landscape in recent years. These include the outlet, or off-price center, and the power center. The outlet/off-price center contains mostly manufacturers' out-

Table 10.3. Largest Shopping Centers in North Carolina, 1997

Center	Location	Size (sq. ft.)	Year Opened	Anchor Tenants
Hanes Mall	Winston-Salem	1,798,823	1975	Belk, Dillard's, J. C. Penney, Sears, Hecht's
Crabtree Valley	Raleigh	1,325,000	1972	Belk, Sears, Hecht's, Lord & Taylor
Four Seasons	Greensboro	1,300,000	1974	Belk, Dillard's, J. C. Penney, Hecht's
Southpark	Charlotte	1,300,000	1970	Belk, Dillard's, Sears, Hecht's
Eastland	Charlotte	1,215,170	1975	Belk, Dillard, J. C. Penney, Sears
Cary Towne Center	Cary	1,112,450	1979	Belk, Dillard's, J. C. Penney, Sears, Hecht's
Carolina Place	Charlotte	1,093,000	1991	Belk, Dillard's, J. C. Penney, Sears, Hecht's
Independence Mall	Wilmington	1,000,000	1979	Belk, J. C. Penney, Sears
Asheville Mall	Asheville	960,000	1973	Belk, Dillard's, J. C. Penney, Sears
Oak Hollow Mall	High Point	937,048	1995	Belk, Dillard's, Sears, J. C. Penney
Cross Creek	Fayetteville	905,328	1975	Belk, J. C. Penney, Sears, Hecht's

Source: NRB [National Research Bureau] Shopping Center Directory, 1998.

lets or off-price chains. The power center is dominated by a few large stores, known as "big boxes," that are strung along a large parking lot together with a few smaller stores.

Retail Companies

A number of large retail chains in the Southeast are headquartered in North Carolina. The list includes Belk (department store), Family Dollar (variety store), Pic N Pay (shoe store), Harris Teeter (supermarket), and Food Lion (supermarket). Most are headquartered in the Charlotte area, but some are based in relatively small cities. One example is Food Lion, whose corporate offices are located in Salisbury. This chain has exhibited massive growth and has become a familiar face on the retailing landscape in several states (Fig. 10.3). Food Lion (formerly Food Town) was started in 1957 by Salisbury businessman Ralph Ketner. The firm grew slowly for the first two decades and by 1977 had only fifty-five stores in operation, with all but three of those in North Carolina. Growth quickened in the latter half of the 1970s and became especially rapid during the 1980s.

By 1997 Food Lion had grown to 1,102 stores and its national ranking among supermarket chains had increased dramatically. In 1975 the firm ranked as only the 122d largest supermarket chain in the country in total sales. Ten years later, in 1985, it had moved to the 16th position with $1.9 billion in sales from 317 stores. By 1995 Food Lion was the eighth largest supermarket chain in the country and had expanded well beyond North Carolina's borders (Fig. 10.4). In 1997 the chain operated new stores in fourteen states. The largest number of stores was still in North Carolina (386), but the chain had more than 50 stores in each of five other states. Despite a late 1997 decision to close 61 stores in Texas, Oklahoma, and Louisiana, Food Lion announced plans to add another 62 stores in its traditional core market area in the Southeast and mid-Atlantic re-

Figure 10.3. Growth of Food Lion Stores, 1975–1997

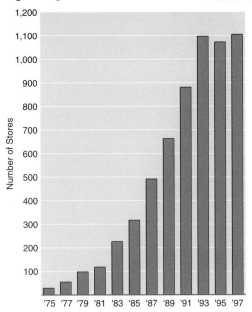

Sources: *Progressive Grocer Marketing Guidebook*, various years; Food Lion Annual Report, 1997.

Figure 10.4. Number of Food Lion Stores, mid-1997

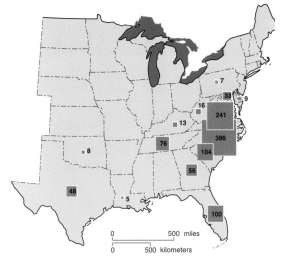

Source: Food Lion Real Estate Department, 1997.

gion. The withdrawal from relatively distant markets in the Southwest represented a return to the company's strategy of incremental growth in established market areas, especially in small towns.

Technology is having an impact on how consumers shop and has contributed to the growth of nonstore retailing. Avenues available to the consumer include catalog, cable television, and Internet shopping. However, it seems unlikely that these new forms will capture a major share of the retail market; that is, stores as we know them will not disappear in the foreseeable future.

Wholesale Trade

J. DENNIS LORD

The distribution of wholesale trade activity is much less closely associated with the distribution of population than is retail trade. There are several reasons for this difference. First, wholesalers serve a diverse set of markets and are therefore not limited to dealing with retailers who then sell to ultimate consumers. Thus, population distribution does not represent the market for some forms of wholesaling. The location of the market may instead be related to the distribution of an industry that consumes the wholesale product. Second, scale economies in the size of wholesale trade establishments permit these businesses to serve much larger geographic markets than can the retailer, with the result being a much greater geographic concentration of wholesaling than is the case for either retailing or population distribution. This pattern can be seen at the national level where the twenty largest metropolitan areas in wholesaling account for 60 percent of the nation's wholesale trade, whereas the twenty largest metropolitan areas in retailing account for less than 45 percent of retail sales. Finally, the location of wholesaling for some products is more closely tied to the location of the commodity's production than to its market and consumption, as in the wholesaling of farm products.

Geographic Concentration

One of the most obvious features of wholesale trade in North Carolina is its extreme geographic concentration (Table 10.4 and Fig. 10.5). In 1992 the seven largest counties in wholesale trade accounted for 72 percent of the state's total wholesale trade. By comparison, the same counties accounted for only 31 and 40 percent of the state's population and retail sales, respectively. Wholesale trade was even more concentrated than these figures indicate. Mecklenburg County alone accounted for 37 percent of the state's total wholesale trade, whereas its shares of population and retail

Figure 10.5. Volume of Wholesale Trade, 1992

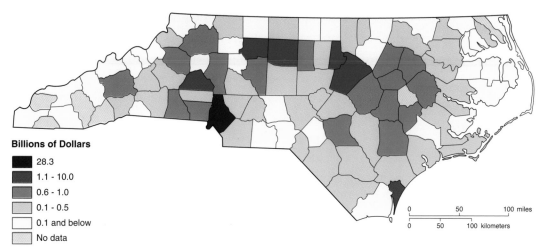

Billions of Dollars

- ■ 28.3
- ■ 1.1 - 10.0
- ■ 0.6 - 1.0
- ▨ 0.1 - 0.5
- □ 0.1 and below
- ▨ No data

Source: *U.S. Census of Wholesale Trade*, 1992.

Figure 10.6. Mecklenburg County's Share of North Carolina Wholesale Trade, Retail Trade, and Population, 1992

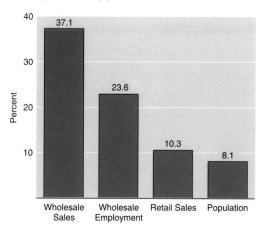

Sources: *U.S. Census of Wholesale Trade*, 1992; *U.S. Census of Retail Trade*, 1992.

Table 10.4. North Carolina's Largest Wholesale Trade Counties, 1992

County	Sales ($ billions)	Employment
Mecklenburg	28.357	35,598
Guilford	9.552	17,455
Wake	7.992	15,082
Forsyth	3.760	7,031
Durham	2.239	3,754
Catawba	1.983	5,429
New Hanover	1.115	3,025
N.C. total	76.365	131,131

Source: U.S. Bureau of the Census, Census of Wholesale Trade, 1992. These data are reported only in the census of wholesale trade, which is taken every five years. Results from the 1997 census of wholesale trade will not be available until after the publication of this book.

trade were only 8.1 and 10.3 percent, respectively (Fig. 10.6). It is obvious from these comparisons that Mecklenburg County provides the wholesale trade function for many areas well beyond its own boundaries. Charlotte and Mecklenburg County serve as the dominant wholesale trade center not only for North Carolina but for South Carolina as well. Their importance as a wholesaling center for the Carolinas can be seen in high wholesale/retail sales ratios and wholesale trade per capita values. The 1992 wholesale/retail ratio for Mecklenburg County was 5.51, compared with the state ratio of 1.50. North Carolina wholesale trade per capita was $11,170, whereas the value for Mecklenburg County was $52,735.

Specialization and Market Areas

Wholesale trade tends to have much greater product specialization by locality than does retailing because of its greater diversity of markets (many of which are concentrated geographically) and the greater scale economies and geographic reach of wholesale trade establishments, and because manufacturers consciously structure the geographic pattern for the distribution of their products. Although the product structure of wholesale trade for North Carolina does not differ dramatically from the pattern in the nation as a whole, the same cannot be said for individual wholesale trade centers in the state. Consider, for example, the product structure of Mecklenburg County. On a national level, the 1992 U.S. Census of Wholesale Trade reported that motor vehicles and chemicals accounted for 12.2 percent and 4.1 percent of total wholesale trade, respectively, whereas in North Carolina the values were 10.5 and 10.1 percent. However, motor vehicles accounted for 14.1 percent of the total wholesale trade volume in Mecklenburg County, whereas chemicals contributed an additional 20.8 percent. Thus, these two categories of wholesaling were more important to the wholesale structure of Mecklenburg County than to the state and nation and illustrate the product specialization that can occur by locality.

The geographic scale of the market served by wholesalers can be local, regional, or national. Although North Carolina's wholesalers do not typically serve national markets (such as New York's wholesalers of apparel), there are many instances when wholesalers' markets extend well beyond the local level. This is especially the case for Charlotte and Mecklenburg County. The geographic reach of Charlotte's wholesale trade function varies significantly by product type. For example, the wholesaling of motor vehicles serves a larger geographic area than does the wholesaling of grocery products. Mecklenburg accounts for half of the state's total motor vehicle sales. This level of dominance reflects the existence of regional sales offices of automobile manufacturers in the county that wholesale automobiles from the manufacturer to retail dealers throughout the Carolinas. By comparison, Mecklenburg's share of state wholesale trade in grocery products is much less. Although the market for grocery products is also regional in scope, it is not as extensive geographically as the market for motor vehicles.

The wholesaling of chemicals provides an example of a product that serves a regional industrial market rather than retailers and ultimate consumers in the region. Mecklenburg County accounts for over 75 percent of the state's total sales of chemicals. The major market for these chemicals is the textile industry found in the Piedmont region of the two Carolinas. Charlotte is centrally located to serve this industrial market.

Employment

Wholesale trade employment in North Carolina exhibits slightly less geographic concentration than sales. For instance, in 1992 Mecklenburg County accounted for 23.6 percent of employment compared to its 37.1 percent of sales. There were large differences in the sales/employment ratios for various product categories. Both motor vehicles and chemicals, two of Mecklenburg's largest product categories, generate large sales volumes per employee. Due to the importance of products like motor vehicles and chemicals in the structure of wholesaling in Mecklenburg, their share of state sales is much higher than their share of employment.

Banking

J. DENNIS LORD

Branch Banking

One of the major features of North Carolina's financial landscape is the presence of several large banks across the state. This reflects the state's long history of statewide branching. Every state in the nation determines the permissible level of branching within its boundaries. Some states do not permit statewide branching (unit banking states), whereas others allow only limited branching (e.g., branching only within a specified area such as a city, county, or metropolitan area). The most liberal state branching laws permit banks anywhere in the state by either de novo expansion (building new branches) or acquisition of other branches. In 1929 North Carolina was a pioneer in this area as one of only nine states with statewide branching legislation. Since then the practice has gradually increased, with the number of states engaged in statewide branching doubling from eighteen in 1961 to thirty-six by 1990. Now it is found in all but a few states.

Statewide branching has two important consequences for the banking

From Small-Town to International Banking

Often when I look back and think about growing up in Albemarle, in Stanly County, it seems a kind of idyllic place, where things were "real" and the people were uncomplicated, warm, and unspoiled by the excesses of today's world.

Albemarle is truly off the beaten path—it is not a place you run into by accident. There is no Interstate nearby. So even today it is still somewhat isolated, even though it is only about 40 miles from Charlotte.

In that time and place—the 1940s and 1950s, in a small mill town in North Carolina—you had to live up to a lot of community expectations, and I mean the entire community—parents, neighbors, teachers, preachers, scoutmasters, and coaches all made sure that you toed the line. You couldn't get by with anything— sassing a teacher, not trying your best, or not showing up for church on a Wednesday night or a Sunday morning. Most of all, if you had any size and ability, you'd better go out for football. Because if you had athletic skill and did not play for the team, you were looked upon as a kid who turned down a chance to go to college, or worse—someone who would not even become a good citizen.

That's because part of the magic about Albemarle in the 1950s was that the whole town was behind the football team. Whether you had kids on the team or not, large crowds turned out for scrimmages, daily practices, and, of course, away games.

We learned a lot of life's lessons on that football field, not the least of which was to live up to your potential and to apply maximum force to small openings—just give it everything you've got.

When I think about it, that's the lesson First Union applied in the mid-1980s, when regulatory restrictions were lifted that had kept the banking industry limited by geography and by product. Of course, we had been aided earlier by the progressive banking laws of North Carolina, so we already knew how to manage widespread banking operations. We also benefited from a strong economy, with a growing population, personal income, and employment. And we just poured into every small opening that the laws would allow, and applied maximum force.

We had been waiting for our chance for many years before the federal laws changed, because even as early as 1978, we had looked over the horizon and seen a world of significant change and industry consolidation coming. By the mid-1980s, banking in North Carolina was at a pivotal place in its history. Not only was the landscape changing rapidly through bank consolidation, but the competitive field, the regulatory environment, and even our customers were changing.

As a $7 billion asset bank in only one state, First Union was too small to compete with the encroaching competition from Wall Street, and we were too small to offer the new products that our customers were demanding to help them provide for longer retirements and other life needs. We had a choice: (1) sell the company—but in those days, there weren't many buyers interested in a $7 billion North Carolina bank; (2) wait to be bought—but that seemed passive and defeatist, and not what we were about as a company; or (3) pursue an active strategy of growth by acquisition ourselves. And that's what we did.

It is fair to say that a certain amount of southern pride supplied some of the impetus for the growth of North Carolina's banking industry. Today it is gratifying to be able to attract some of the best and brightest people in the nation to our state, and to see the vibrancy growing here.

Most important to me, personally, is the sense of accomplishment at seeing First Union live up to its potential—that we leave nothing on the playing field but sweat as we give our customers, communities, employees, and shareholders our absolute best.

*Edward E. Crutchfield, chairman of the board
and CEO, First Union Corporation*

structure of a state. First, it results in far fewer, but much larger banks than in states with more restrictive legislation. Second, liberal branching laws lead to a much greater number of branches on a per capita basis than in more restrictive states. The situation in North Carolina and Georgia, a state that permits only limited branching, illustrates these contrasts. North Carolina's three largest banks are on average almost twice as large in asset size as Georgia's three largest banks. North Carolina has only 0.84 banking firms per 100,000 population compared to 5.94 firms per 100,000 in Georgia. Yet the number of branches per 100,000 population is 33.2 in North Carolina, compared to only 22.8 per 100,000 in Georgia.

In terms of deposits held in the state, banking in North Carolina is dominated by seven large banks: Wachovia, First Union, BB&T, First Citizens, Bank of America, Central Carolina, and Centura, in that order. Collectively, they accounted for 83 percent of the $74 billion in deposits held by federally insured institutions in the state as of September 30, 1997.

Bank Mergers

Acquisitions and mergers have accounted for a decline in the total number of banking firms in the state. Between 1960 and 1970 the number of banks dropped from 183 to 97. This downward trend continued until the mid-1980s, when it was suddenly reversed by the creation of several community banks to fill the void left by the larger banks (Fig. 10.7). Since the early 1990s, however, the number of banks has once again decreased as additional mergers and acquisitions have taken place. During this period the number of branches continued to increase, and by 1995 the state's 61 banks had 2,140 branches. Consumers in the largest counties had available to them both more bank firms and more branches. Because of North Carolina's liberal branching laws, the state has one of the highest ratios of branches to population anywhere in the United States.

Restrictions on geographic expansion were placed on the U.S. banking industry beginning in the 1930s. The Glass-Stegall Act of 1933 and later the Bank Holding Company Act of 1956 (Douglas Amendment) established the state boundary as the limit for the geographic expansion of banks with national charters. Specifically, the Douglas Amendment prohibited bank holding companies (BHCs) from expanding across state lines to acquire an existing bank or charter a new one unless the laws of the state permitted such entry. Because no states had such laws at the time, the legislation in effect provided a barrier to interstate expansion.

Interstate Banking

For many years following the Douglas Amendment, states did not take any action to allow the entry of out-of-state bank holding companies. Faced with increased competition from other financial institutions, commercial banks started to push for geographic deregulation in the early 1980s. In response, states began to pass interstate banking laws that permitted the entry of out-of-state banks, usually by acquisition or merger but not by de novo expansion. The most common type of law passed in the early phase of interstate legislation was a regional reciprocal measure whereby entry was permitted only by BHCs from within the region. North Carolina, with a law in 1984, was one of the first states to pass legislation that was reciprocal with thirteen other southern states. The number of states with interstate banking legisla-

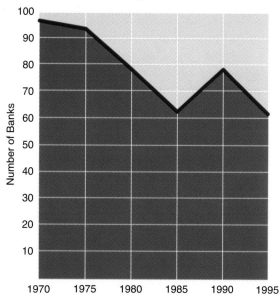

Figure 10.7. Number of Banks in North Carolina, 1970–1995

Source: N.C. Banking Commission.

tion rose from twenty-three in 1985 to forty-eight in the early 1990s. More recent laws passed nationwide permit BHCs to acquire banks in any state. But de novo branching across state lines is allowed only if specifically authorized by the states.

North Carolina banks have lobbied for interstate legislation and have been quick to seize the opportunity to expand across state lines. The state's long history of statewide branching has produced large banks with the resources needed for expansion and with the experience of operating geographically dispersed networks of branches (Fig. 10.8). These conditions, along with an aggres-

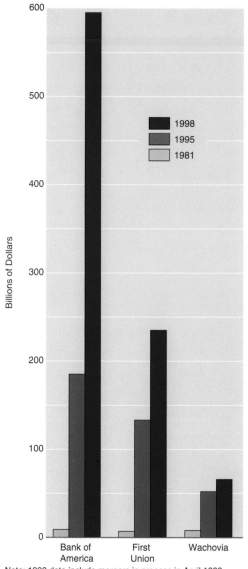

Figure 10.8. Growth in Asset Size of North Carolina's Largest Bank Holding Companies, 1981–1998

■ 1998
■ 1995
□ 1981

Billions of Dollars

Bank of America
First Union
Wachovia

Note: 1998 data include mergers in process in April 1998.

Source: SNL Securities ©.

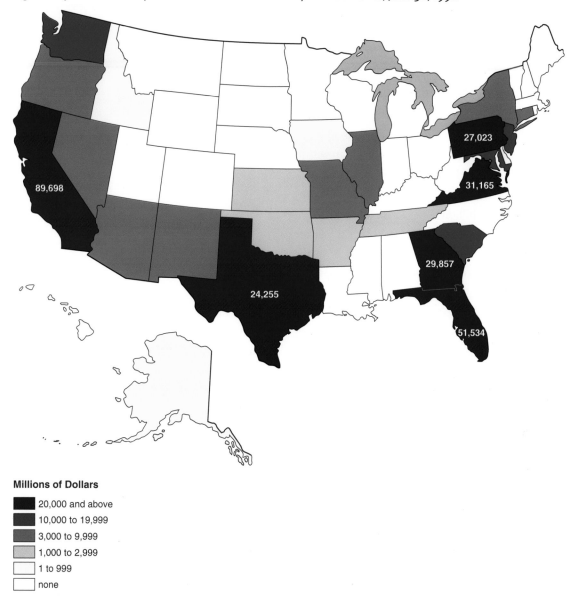

Figure 10.9. Interstate Deposits of North Carolina–Headquartered Banks, June 30, 1998

27,023
31,165
89,698
29,857
24,255
51,534

Millions of Dollars

■ 20,000 and above
■ 10,000 to 19,999
■ 3,000 to 9,999
□ 1,000 to 2,999
□ 1 to 999
□ none

Source: Calculated from data provided by the Board of Governors, Federal Reserve System, Financial Services Section, February 1999.

sive acquisition posture, have helped make North Carolina banks among the most active in the country in interstate acquisitions. Two principal economic incentives for these acquisitions have been risk reduction via geographic diversification of operations and the potential scale economies of larger banking companies.

Each of these bank holding companies now has more deposits outside North Carolina than within the state. In 1998 North Carolina–headquartered BHCs had deposits of $460.9 billion. Of this amount, $372.7 billion, or 80.9 percent, was located outside the home state. This was the largest volume of interstate deposit controlled by any state in the nation. North Carolina banks controlled 40.0 percent of the deposits in Virginia, 37.6 in South Carolina, and 33.8 percent in California. By comparison, few BHCs from other states have acquired North Carolina banks: less than 1 percent of the state's deposits were controlled by banks headquartered outside North Carolina. Examination of the geography of the interstate deposits of North Carolina–headquartered banks reveals not only a significant presence in several southeastern states but in several other states as well (Fig. 10.9). The largest absolute volume of interstate deposits in 1998 was located in California, Virginia, and Georgia with $89.7, $31.2, and $29.9 billion, respectively.

In recent years these multistate banking companies have grown tremendously in asset size, primarily through a number of mergers, and they now rank among the nation's largest banks. At the end of 1981, prior to the beginning of interstate banking expansion, NationsBank, Wachovia, and First Union ranked as the twenty-eighth, thirty-sixth, and forty-ninth largest banks in the nation with assets of $7.7, $6.3, and $5.3 billion, respectively. By December 1998 NationsBank (Bank of America) had become the country's second largest bank with assets of $595 billion (Table 10.5). During the same period First Union rose to sixth place with assets of $235 billion. Wachovia, although not as active in interstate acquisitions, saw its national ranking climb to sixteenth position on assets of $66 billion. In total deposits, Bank of America ranked first with $346 billion and First Union ranked fifth with $135 billion among the nation's largest banks.

North Carolina banks continued to expand through additional mergers in the late 1990s. In 1997–98 the three largest banks announced a number of acquisitions that added substantially to their out-of-state asset holdings. The most dramatic of these was NationsBank's merger with California's Bank of America, soon after its acquisition of Florida's largest bank, Barnett Banks and its $44 billion in assets. Although the bank headquarters will remain in Charlotte, the bank holding company has been renamed Bank of America Corporation. First Union gained a major presence in the Northeast by acquiring Philadelphia's CoreStates

Table 10.5. Largest North Carolina Banks

National Rank (deposits)	Bank	City	Assets ($000)	Deposits ($000)
2	Bank of America	Charlotte	594,673,000	345,756,000
6	First Union	Charlotte	234,580,000	134,528,000
16	Wachovia	Winston-Salem	65,574,008	38,807,144
24	BB&T	Winston-Salem	35,956,440	23,326,009
62	First Citizens	Raleigh	9,194,842	7,771,093
64	Centura	Rocky Mount	8,413,640	5,985,343
70	CCB	Durham	7,407,269	6,216,989

Source: SNL Securities.
Note: The banks listed are among the 300 largest U.S. banks. Assets and deposits are adjusted for completed and pending mergers and acquisitions as of December 10, 1998.

Financial, holder of nearly $48 billion in assets. Wachovia picked up four smaller institutions, two in Florida and two in Virginia, adding nearly $14 billion in assets. By mid-1998 North Carolina had seven of the nation's one hundred largest banks, trailing only New York and Ohio in that regard. Winston-Salem's BB&T continued the merger trend in 1999 with its acquisition of Premier Bancshares of Atlanta and its $2 billion in assets.

The state's two largest BHCs, Bank of America and First Union, are headquartered in Charlotte. Because of the magnitude of interstate acquisitions by these two banks, Charlotte has become an important command and control center in the banking industry not only for the Southeast but also for the nation. It is now the second largest metropolitan area in the country in the dollar volume of headquartered banking assets, ranking well ahead of several much larger population centers, including Chicago, Los Angeles, Boston, Pittsburgh, Detroit, Philadelphia, and Atlanta. The establishment of an area as a prominent corporate headquarters center, such as Charlotte in the case of the banking industry, can have important economic consequences for the city and its region. These include additional jobs in the expanding corporation and in related service companies, increased demand for office space in the local market, and greater attraction of the area for other businesses due to the city's enhanced status as a banking center.

Deposits and Population

The geography of bank deposits in North Carolina closely corresponds to the distribution of its population. The largest counties in population are also the largest counties in total bank deposits. Yet bank deposits per capita are quite variable across counties (Fig. 10.10). This variation reflects a number of factors, including differences in income levels among counties and the headquarters locations of banks (some deposits from nonlocal sources may be credited to the headquarters location of a bank). Some people may bank in a county other than their home county, perhaps because they work there, or banks in

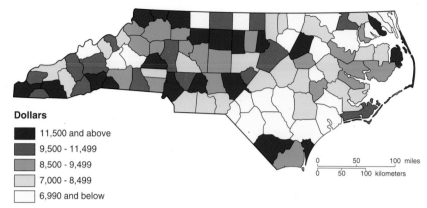

Figure 10.10. Per Capita Bank Deposits, June 30, 1997

Dollars

- ■ 11,500 and above
- ■ 9,500 - 11,499
- ■ 8,500 - 9,499
- ■ 7,000 - 8,499
- □ 6,990 and below

Note: N.C. average per capita bank deposit = $10,850.

Sources: Calculated from data provided by SNL Securities ©; N.C. Office of State Planning.

an adjacent county may be more accessible. Forsyth ($31,383 per capita), home to Wachovia, and Mecklenburg ($19,686 per capita) were the only counties to exceed $15,000 in per capita deposits in June 1997. Some counties that had many affluent retirees, such as Polk and Moore, also had high levels of per capita deposits. Statewide, North Carolina banks held $10,850 in deposits per resident. Certain coastal recreation counties, notably Dare, had high per capita deposits, perhaps because some owners of second homes used local banks while living there.

Trends in Banking

The banking industry is experiencing a number of trends that have implications for the location and provision of banking services. One of these trends is the continuing consolidation of the industry as a result of mergers and acquisitions. The number of bank firms is declining, not only in North Carolina but also in the nation as a whole. Banks are even merging with insurance companies and other financial institutions. Undoubtedly this will continue, but less clear is how this trend will affect the location of corporate headquarters of the big banks. NationsBank insisted as part of its merger agreement with Bank of America that the headquarters remain in Charlotte, but future changes in the corporate leadership of this or other large North Carolina banks could well lead to a relocation to some other city.

There has been something of a backlash to the creation of ever larger banks in the form of smaller community banks. Between 1995 and 1997 charters were issued for fourteen community banks in North Carolina, nine of them organized in 1997 alone. A number of these banks have enjoyed auspicious startups, achieving profitability well ahead of expectations. Analysts attribute much of this success to consumer rebellion against big banks and an emphasis on personal service. It remains to be seen how well these community banks will fare if the state's strong economy slows down.

An advantage of the big banks is their ability to make increasing use of technology in the provision of services. Many routine transactions previously handled by full-service branches can now be done on automated teller machines (ATMs). More and more transactions will be performed by consumers on their home computers. As a result of this technology, the number of branches will decline and those that remain will act as financial service centers for the sale of various bank products. Reportedly, Bank of America was preparing to invest $500 million in computer software and hardware to permit its customers to bank directly via their home computers, a service that Nations-Bank was already providing. Given the start-up costs, many smaller banks cannot afford this technology.

Within a few years many consumers will carry an electronic card that includes debit accounts, credit cards, ATM access, driver's license, social security card, insurance data, and other personal information. Cash will be less necessary, and no one will have to tote a multitude of cards in their wallets or purses.

A potential and even more fundamental change in the banking industry is *disintermediation*—the removal of intermediaries, such as banks, from financial transactions. This would happen as investors used software and computer networks to gain direct control over their finances. Microsoft and other large software firms could replace today's institutions as the leading "banks." On the other hand, some analysts see the future of personal finance being controlled by huge financial institutions that offer investors a greater range and variety of services. Both approaches are based on sophisticated, expensive technologies, the high costs and large-scale efficiencies of which are already helping to drive the formation of large banks. It is uncertain how these trends will affect this important industry in North Carolina.

Newspapers, Television, and Telephone Service
ALFRED W. STUART

Newspapers

Table 10.6 summarizes the average daily circulation of the twenty largest daily newspapers published in North Carolina in 1998. Reflecting the broad dispersion of people, all but two of the ten largest had at least 30 percent of their paid circulation going outside their home counties. Four papers distributed 40 percent or more outside their home counties, including the state's two largest, the *Charlotte Observer* and the *Raleigh News and Observer*. By contrast, the smaller dailies mostly served their home counties: the ten smallest had 20 percent or less of their circulation in other counties.

These proportions, especially the high percentage of the larger dailies sent to outside counties, are a measure of the influence that the larger cities have in the state. The *Charlotte Observer* is circulated in thirty-six North Carolina counties, and it is the leading paper in four counties outside Mecklenburg. Nearly 122,000 of its total circulation was outside Mecklenburg County, more

Table 10.6. Circulation of Daily Newspapers in North Carolina (20 Largest), 1998

Newspaper	Daily Circulation	Percentage Outside Home County	Newspaper	Daily Circulation	Percentage Outside Home County
Charlotte Observer	245,829	49.6	*Burlington Times-News*	27,545	7.8
Raleigh News and Observer	161,920	43.4	*Salisbury Post*	25,376	12.5
Winston-Salem Journal	90,523	36.7	*Jacksonville Daily News*	22,361	17.8
Greensboro News and Record	89,240	28.2	*Goldsboro News-Argus*	21,903	9.3
Fayetteville Observer-Times	69,757	34.5	*Hendersonville Times-News*	20,070	11.7
Asheville Citizen-Times	59,360	44.1	*Greenville Daily Reflector*	19,790	13.4
Wilmington Morning Star	56,015	39.5	*Hickory Daily Record*	18,924	20.0
Durham Herald-Sun	50,361	34.3	*Wilson Daily Times*	16,860	17.7
Gaston Gazette	39,736	17.9	*Asheboro Courier-Tribune*	16,625	13.2
High Point Enterprise	30,319	43.2	*Shelby Star*	15,249	0.9

Sources: Audit Bureau of Circulations, FAS-FAX Report, March 31, 1998; Audit Bureau of Circulations/County Penetration Report, March 10, 1998.
Note: The national newspaper, *USA Today*, had a daily circulation of 58,349 copies in 64 counties.

than the combined circulation of the six smallest dailies in the table. The *Raleigh News and Observer*'s reach in North Carolina is even more extensive, with circulation reported in fifty counties, and it is has the largest circulation of any newspaper in four counties in addition to Wake.

Television

Television viewing areas are known in the industry as designated market areas (DMAs). These market areas are so designated according to the TV stations that capture the highest percentage of viewer hours. Figure 10.11 shows that ten DMAs are recog-

Figure 10.11. Designated Market Areas for Television, 1998

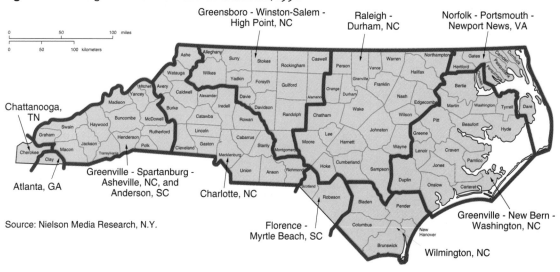

Source: Nielson Media Research, N.Y.

nized in North Carolina but only six are associated with stations, or groups of stations, located in the state. The other four are associated with broadcast centers in Georgia, Tennessee, South Carolina, and Virginia. Even the Asheville DMA is shared by stations in that city with those in Greenville and Spartanburg, South Carolina. The most centralized DMAs are in Charlotte and Wilmington, in that all of the major commercial stations are located in the vicinity of those cities. The Greensboro–Winston-Salem–High Point stations are scattered among the latter three cities, and the Raleigh-Durham DMA includes Fayetteville. The three most populous DMAs, which collectively cover fifty-three counties, are based in the Piedmont, but their reach extends well into both the Mountains and the Coastal Plain as well as blanketing the Piedmont. Thus, TV coverage and the extensive coverage of the big Piedmont daily newspapers are major indicators of the powerful influence of the state's major metropolitan centers.

Telephone Service

One of the surest symptoms of North Carolina's growth has been the subdivision of existing long-distance area code zones to create more zones to handle the rapid upsurge in the number of lines and the consequent increase in long-distance calling. In the 1990s new area codes were created on several occasions, the latest being in 1998. In the middle part of the decade the 919 zone was split to create a 910 zone that cut diagonally across the state from the northern mountains southeastward to the coast. More recently (Fig. 10.12), three new zones were added, one to serve the western part of the state, another for the northern Piedmont, and a third for the northeastern portion. Thus, in less than ten years coverage went from two to six zones.

For many years local telephone service in North Carolina was provided by regulated companies. Beginning in 1996 the industry was deregulated. At the time seventeen companies offered local service in the state, but by 1998 an additional forty-six new companies began competing for this business, primarily to commercial establishments or to residential customers with credit

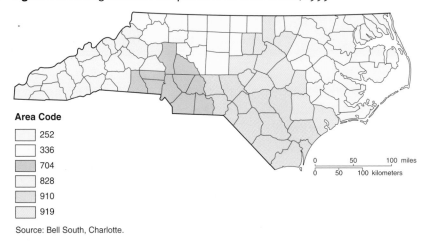

Figure 10.12. Long-Distance Telephone Area Code Zones, 1999

Area Code

- 252
- 336
- 704
- 828
- 910
- 919

Source: Bell South, Charlotte.

problems. By mid-1998 these new telephone companies controlled just 43,600 of the 4.5 million telephone lines in the state, and all but about 1,000 were business lines.

Tourism and Travel

LARRY D. GUSTKE

Traveler Expenditures

Tourism and travel in North Carolina are big business. They are composed of sectors of the state's economy that provide recreational opportunities, leisure pursuits, and a high quality of life for North Carolina residents and visitors. They involve both recreational and business travel. These sectors often are defined as, but not limited to, public transportation, private automobile transportation, lodging, food service, entertainment and recreation, general retail sales, and travel planning. At the state level, tourism is supported by the Division of Tourism, Film, and Sports Development of the North Carolina Department of Commerce. In 1997–98 the state's total travel budget was about

Figure 10.13. Estimated North Carolina Travel Expenditures, 1987–1997

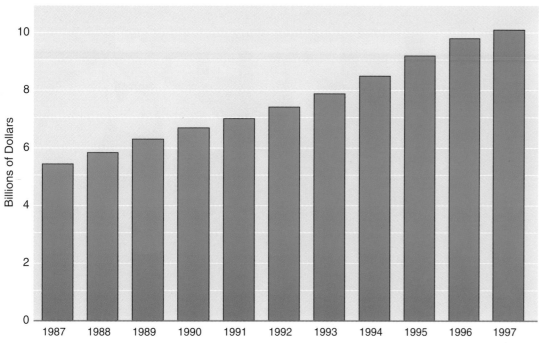

Source: Travel Industry Association of America, expenditure data. Summarized by Office of Park and Tourism Research, Parks, Recreation, and Tourism Management, N.C. State University.

Figure 10.14. Visitors to North Carolina, 1994–1996

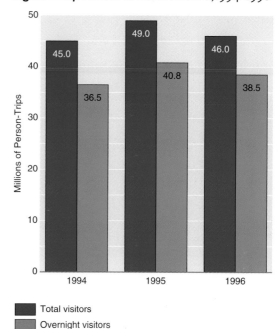

Source: Travel Industry Association of America, expenditure data. Summarized by Office of Park and Tourism Research, Parks, Recreation, and Tourism Management, N.C. State University.

$10.4 million, a 15 percent increase over the previous year and equivalent to about $1.35 for every resident. The most recent total ranked the state eighteenth among the forty-eight states reporting comparable data.

In 1997 the Travel Industry Association of America (TIA) estimated that the tourism-related sectors contributed $10.1 billion in expenditures to the North Carolina economy. According to TIA, these expenditures grew from $5.44 billion in 1987 to the 1997 level, a jump of some $4.66 billion. Figure 10.13 illustrates the steady rise in these expenditures, at an average annual rate of 8.5 percent, well above the average inflation rate for much of the period.

The latest available data for all states (1994) indicate that North Carolina ranked twelfth nationally in level of traveler expenditures and fourth among twelve southeastern states, trailing only Florida, Georgia, and Virginia in that region. The North Carolina expenditures represented 2.58 percent of the national total, an increase from 2.33 percent in 1987.

Visitors

Recent increases in tourism and travel expenditures have been associated with a rise in the number of visitors to the state. This is measured in terms of person-trips, and the data are available only for the 1994–96 period. In those years the total number of person-trips increased from 45 million in 1994 to 46 million in 1996 (Fig. 10.14). This total fluctuated from year to year, rising to 49

Figure 10.15. Overnight In-State and Out-of-State Visitors to North Carolina, 1994-1996

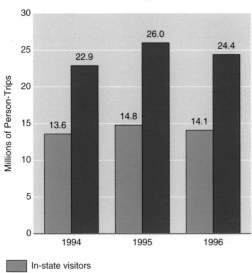

Source: Travel Industry Association of America, expenditure data. Summarized by Office of Park and Tourism Research, Parks, Recreation, and Tourism Management, N.C. State University.

The Sanitary Restaurant in Morehead City

million in 1995 but dropping back by 3 million in 1996. Those person-trips that involved an overnight stay rose by 2 million during the three-year period.

Visitors include both travelers from out of state and residents traveling within the state. Of those who stayed overnight in their travels, the total rose from 36.5 million in 1994 to 38.5 million in 1996. Of perhaps greatest significance in that trend was that whereas out-of-state, overnight visitors made up about two-thirds of the total visitors, a good three-quarters of the net growth between 1994 and 1996

was from these nonresident visitors (Fig. 10.15). That is, apparently increasing numbers of nonresidents are visiting North Carolina's beaches, mountains, and cities. This may help explain the recent rise in the state's share of national visitor expenditures, as long-distance travelers tend to spend more than those traveling closer to home.

Employment and Tax Revenues

Important benefits of traveler expenditures are the jobs they support and the tax revenues they gener-

ate. It is estimated that in 1997 travel and tourism provided 171,000 jobs in North Carolina, which represented over 4.8 percent of all nonagricultural wage and salaried employees in the state. That makes it a larger employer than all of the state's many manufacturing industries except for textiles. The state coffers were enriched by over $490 million in 1997, and travelers added over $271 million to local tax collections. It is small wonder that the state and many communities are eager to promote the tourism industry. Figure 10.16 shows the number of jobs that are supported by travelers in each

Figure 10.16. Employment Supported by Travel and Tourism, 1997

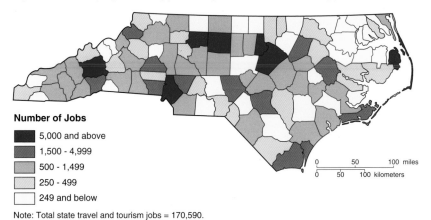

Number of Jobs

- 5,000 and above
- 1,500 - 4,999
- 500 - 1,499
- 250 - 499
- 249 and below

Note: Total state travel and tourism jobs = 170,590.

Source: Travel Industry Association of America, 1997.

Figure 10.17. Total Travelers' Expenditures, 1997

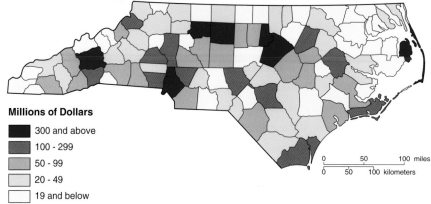

Millions of Dollars

- 300 and above
- 100 - 299
- 50 - 99
- 20 - 49
- 19 and below

Note: Total travelers' expenditures = $10,117,450,000.

Source: Travel Industry Association of America, 1997.

county. Mecklenburg tops the list with nearly 40,000, followed by Wake (17,000) and Guilford (12,000). In Mecklenburg, travel-related jobs constitute about 9.5 percent of nonagricultural wage and salary jobs. But in Dare County, travel-related jobs comprise more than half of all nonfarm employment, 56 percent. This is a mixed blessing, however, as the average weekly wage for private-sector workers in Dare was only $294 in late 1996, less than two-thirds of the statewide average. Moreover, many tourism-supported jobs are seasonal. They may be attractive for vacationing college students, but they do not always provide a living wage for permanent residents.

Figure 10.17 displays the distribution of travelers' expenditures among North Carolina counties in 1997. The largest single recipient was Mecklenburg, the only county to record more than $1 billion in travelers' expenditures. Its $2.2 billion represented no less than 22 percent of the entire state total. Mecklenburg was followed by the other central counties of the state's largest metropolitan counties, Wake and Guilford. Another four counties, Forsyth, Buncombe, Dare, and Durham, each accounted for more than $300 million.

Figure 10.18. Per Capita Travelers' Expenditures, 1997

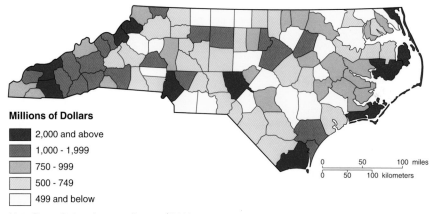

Millions of Dollars

- 2,000 and above
- 1,000 - 1,999
- 750 - 999
- 500 - 749
- 499 and below

Note: Per capita traveler expenditures = $1,363.

Sources: Travel Industry Association of America, 1997; U.S. Census, Population Estimates, 1998.

These seven counties had total expenditures of $5.41 billion, over half of the state sum. All are metropolitan counties except for Dare, testimony to the ability of the larger urban areas to attract both personal and business travelers.

To measure their impact on the local economy, Figure 10.18 shows these expenditures in 1997 on a per capita basis, calculated by dividing the total expenditures by the number of people in the local population. By this approach, Dare County was as far ahead of the rest of the state as Mecklenburg was in total expenditures. With expenditures of $14,189 per person, Dare was not closely rivaled by the second highest county, Avery, at just $4,217. The striking thing about the high per capita counties is that they are mostly rural. Of the six that reported per capita expenditures of at least $3,000, only Mecklenburg is part of a metropolitan area. The others (Swain, Carteret, Hyde) are either mountain or coastal recreation areas. In these three, travelers supported between 12 and 19 percent of all nonfarm jobs. Clearly, visitor expenditures are vital to the economies of a number of rural counties even if the total amounts of these expenditures are small in comparison with those of the more populous urban areas.

Outlook

The national trend toward a more service-based and information-processing economy focuses heavily on metropolitan areas, a pattern that appears in North Carolina. As the state has become more urbanized, there has been a steady concentration of services, retailing, wholesaling, and finance in cities, especially in the larger metropolitan centers. The dominant role of the major metro areas is also evident with both the print and electronic media.

As this trend continues, it will be a major factor in rearranging the geography of North Carolina away from a pattern of dispersed population and economy toward one that is increasingly dominated by metropolitan areas. Even though tourism has provided a major boost to the economies of selected rural areas, its continuation may be threatened by its very success. Overdevelopment of attractive coastal and mountain environments may damage those prized settings to the point where fewer visitors will be drawn to them. Clearly, if a more positive balance is not struck between tourism and its negative impacts, this source of economic growth for some rural areas may be lost.

Selected References

Audit Bureau of Circulations. FAS-FAX. *United States Daily Newspapers: Circulation Averages for Six Months Ended, March 31, 1998.*

Calem, P. S. "The Impact of Geographic Deregulation on Small Banks." *Business Review* (Federal Reserve Bank of Philadelphia), November–December 1994, pp. 17–31.

Lord, J. D. "Intercounty Retail Leakage Patterns in North Carolina." *Southeastern Geographer* 22, no. 1 (May 1982): 52–67.

———. "Charlotte's Role as a Major Banking Center." In *Snapshots of the Carolinas: Landscapes and Cultures,* edited by G. Gordon Bennett, pp. 209–13. Washington, D.C.: Association of American Geographers, 1996.

North Carolina Department of Commerce. Division of Tourism. Film and Sports Development. *1997 Annual Report.* Raleigh, 1998. (Source of data on travelers, by county)

Savage, D. T. "Interstate Banking: A Status Report." *Federal Reserve Bulletin 79,* 1993, pp. 1075–89.

11. GOVERNMENT AND POLITICS

Schley R. Lyons

The formidable public agenda generated by the changing economic, demographic, and social conditions in North Carolina is being addressed by a state government that is in transition. A stronghold for the Democratic Party for most of the twentieth century, the state is now firmly Republican at the presidential level and competitive for other offices. The pages that follow examine North Carolina's evolution from a one-party to a vigorous two-party system and the consequences of this transition on institutional behavior and public policy.

In reviewing the activities and powers of North Carolina government, it must be remembered that state and local governments in the United States function within the constraints of the American federal system. A common view of federalism is that it resembles a layer cake with local government at the base, state government in the middle, and the national government at the top. In practice, American government has never been structured in this fashion. The federal system always has been characterized by far more cooperation and shared responsibilities than by separation.

Another view of the American system portrays national and state powers at

A New Political Climate

For the first two-thirds of the twentieth century, the distinctive feature of southern, hence North Carolina, politics has been the enduring mandate of one-party rule. The most profound change in the modern political climate of North Carolina, just as in the entire South, has been the emergence of a stronger, healthier, more competitive two-party system. One-party competition might be viewed as the inevitable outcome of the redefinition but would still be deferred were it not for the popular appeal of a vigorous minority Republican Party.

There have been pervasive issues, some of which have commanded center stage throughout most of the century and have shaped (and been shaped by) both the earlier one-party monopoly and the two-party rivalry that replaced it. These include the policy objectives of education, economic development, transportation, and public works, as well as the underlying themes of race, poverty, illiteracy, taxation, and regional differences. My political slogan of "Better Schools, Better Roads, Better Jobs" may well characterize the goals of any state administration, but they cannot be achieved without careful attention to the latter, more personal, issues of condition and location.

Race has been a powerful, motivating factor of southern politics since our very earliest days. Beginning with the morbid institution of slavery, the Old South brought upon itself the reformist enmity of the rest of the nation and the destruction delivered by the Civil War. Our society certainly has made progress away from the inhumanly cruel slaveholding practices, reinforced by then prevalent notions of racial superiority, but not without periods of retrogression, typified by Ku Klux Klan activity and various expressions of intolerance.

To its credit, the Democratic Party, which began this century with the infamous Red Shirt movement which purged Republicanism in North Carolina, has now gained the reconciliation of uniting itself with the aspirations of African American voters. The party of Lincoln, on the other hand, has won the allegiance of many white voters who have resented what they view as excessive racial catering by the Democrats. Are such issues today just exercises in basic coalition building played out upon perceptions of racial overtones? Is either side, or both, justified in their use of racial cues? Is it possible to rise above racial politics in a society so imbued with it? Does it best serve the interests of any group to be aligned forever with one party?

Poverty has held back North Carolina and other states of the Old South ever since and as a direct consequence of the Civil War. So much of the economic strength of the Confederacy was torched by the advancing Union armies. The old plantations could no longer be managed and operated profitably. Investment capital dried up. Southern states were on the bottom rungs of any comparisons of per capita income. For a hundred years, the defeated Old South was an economic wasteland, mired in poverty from which it has only recently begun to rise.

That it has done so is a tribute to the vision and determination of many business and political leaders who rose above the paralysis of one-party politics. After World War II, there were opportunities to attract new industries and a greater diversity of jobs, most notably with the Research Triangle Park, which transformed older industries like textiles and furniture and generated new, high-technology industries. Today, both political parties challenge the ingenuity and commitment of the other to support economic development initiatives.

Illiteracy has been another seemingly ingrained part of southern culture, attributable partially to racial factors and partially to poverty. Early industrialization brought an abundance of entry-level jobs that illiterate

opposite ends of a seesaw. If national powers are increased, then state powers decline. Evidence also refutes this belief. For most of the twentieth century the power and scope of the national government expanded exponentially, but the size and activities of North Carolina government during the same period also increased. Most of the governmental services that really matter to the average citizen continue to be managed by state and local agencies, but often according to guidelines imposed by the national government.

The Evolution of Two-Party Politics in North Carolina

North Carolina politics have followed the southern pattern of presidential Republicanism emerging first, with Republican success in congressional

workers could handle. These are now relocating in developing countries. Newer industries offer jobs with more technologically demanding qualifications, making our relative backwardness a severe handicap. Community colleges were established to provide remedial, job-oriented education and training. Later in the 1970s and 1980s public schools began to win larger shares of the state budget, thanks to a keen rivalry between Democrats and Republicans, each striving to outdo the other. Education had long been the theme of an unbroken series of "education governors," but only with the advent of two-party competition did schools really take first priority.

Taxation will always be a battleground between those who want more government to fund more public programs and those who want less government and less interference with our economic engine of capitalism. Democrats and Republicans in North Carolina share a desire to minimize taxes, but in general Democrats advocate more state spending and Republicans favor more restraint coupled with lower taxes. Whether to achieve policy objectives within the existing tax structure, or with enactment of higher and/or different taxes, frequently finds strong partisan differences. It is readily arguable that the

balance of strength on opposing sides of these issues gives voters more influence over the outcome. Politicians are compelled to seek creative ways either to do more with less or to make choices among conflicting priorities. This is a genuine blessing of two-party politics.

Regional differences have long been a basis for hard-nosed political and economic rivalries between and among North Carolinians. Issues of secession, location of a railroad or an innovative industrial complex or a new medical school, distribution of essential educational funding, and less essential "pork barrel" largesse, for example, have fractured North Carolina into East and West and Piedmont.

Here again, our two parties have fought over relative advantages within regions in which each party had its strongest and most loyal following. With the rise of two-party competition, the Democrats have retained a powerful base in the Coastal Plain "Down East," while the Republicans have built upon their historic base in Mountain counties. Both parties have fought to make inroads into the other's territorial base, while the central Piedmont Crescent has become the major battleground for strategic advantages or statewide parity.

Conclusion: *This, then, is the present framework of North Carolina politics. We have become a competitive two-party state. Each major party holds the upper hand in certain regions and with racial or ethnic coalitions. Each is genuinely committed to improving education, economic development, and transportation for the benefit of the people. Each brings a distinctive flavor and philosophy in how it approaches the themes of poverty, illiteracy, and taxation, although there are as many similarities as differences.*

The outcomes of most North Carolina elections, then, depend on how well each party succeeds in recruiting able candidates and motivating its loyal voters, and on how well each appeals to the large blocks of swing voters and ticket splitters. Four decades ago, these factors did not matter much in general elections, because any Democrat who survived the primary would beat any Republican almost every time. With today's two-party system, debates and personalities and issues do matter a great deal, because they can swing the margin from defeat to victory, and vice versa. That is good for North Carolina.

*James G. Martin,
governor of North Carolina, 1985–93*

and state elections coming later (Fig. 11.1). At midcentury, V. O. Key noted that the Republican Party in North Carolina was a major electoral force of relatively constant strength, approximately one-third of the vote in gubernatorial and presidential elections, strong enough for many of the earmarks

of a two-party state yet not strong enough to threaten Democratic supremacy. But conditions changed over the next two decades, and two-party competition began in earnest in 1968, when Richard Nixon won the presidential election with 40 percent of the vote in a three-way race. Since then,

GOP candidates have carried the state's electoral votes in every presidential contest except 1976, when Jimmy Carter, a southerner running in the aftermath of Watergate, led the Democratic ticket. Republican milestones along the way to a competitive two-party system include the election of

Figure 11.1. Voting Trends by Elected Offices, 1968–1996

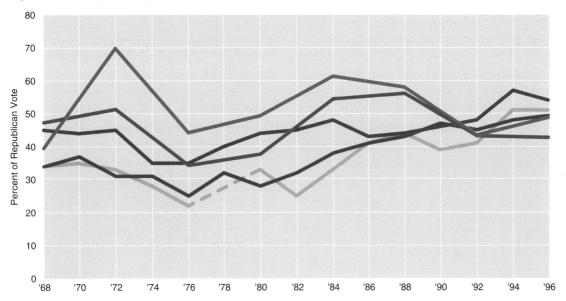

Elected Offices

━━━ President
━━━ Governor
━━━ U.S. House
━━━ N.C. Senate
━━━ N.C. House

Note: No data were available for the 1978 N.C. House election results. Elections for president and governor are held every fourth year.

Source: *N.C. Data Net*, June, October 1997.

Jesse Helms to a U.S. Senate seat and James E. Holshouser Jr. to the governorship in 1972, James Martin to the governor's office in 1984 and again in 1988, James Gardner to the lieutenant governorship in 1988, and the GOP winning control of the North Carolina House in 1994.

Factors Contributing to Partisan Competition

The resounding 1994 Republican victory in North Carolina was neither an aberration nor a sudden conversion on the part of the voters to the GOP. Rather, it was fashioned from the convergence of many factors that had been gaining strength for years. The mood of Tar Heel voters had become increasingly conservative. Businesses that moved to the state brought employees who were accustomed to casting ballots for Republican candidates. New voters who came of age during the Reagan era disproportionately identified with the Republican Party. Moreover, the state had become home to an increasing number of affluent retirees who preferred, on balance, lower taxes and a more restricted role for government—central themes in the Republican agenda. Even though the GOP made significant gains in registering citizens as Republicans, up from 541,916 in 1972 (23 percent) to 1,598,901 in 1998 (33 percent), the registration statistics understate the GOP vote in North Carolina. Exit polls over the last two decades documented the slowly expanding pool of Republican voters and the contracting pool of Democrats. By using self-identification as the measure of partisanship, a much more closely divided electorate is revealed: 41 percent Democrat, 39 percent Republican, and 20 percent independent in 1998 exit polls.

The consistent success of the GOP in winning presidential contests and a more competitive balance between the two major parties in "safe" electoral districts, which is partly the product of redistricting following the 1990 census, also contributed to the overall success of Republicans. The outcome of this convergence of factors was that citizens began to vote in congressional, state, and local races as they had been doing for many years in presidential elections. Other short-term factors that helped push Tar Heel voters in the direction of the GOP in 1994 were the unpopularity of President Bill Clinton and an unusually low voter turnout among Democrats.

A Brief History of Party Competition

Before making a closer examination of factors that contributed to the current competitive partisan environment in North Carolina, it should be acknowledged that the foundation for the sea change in North Carolina politics had its beginnings in the World War II years. For the first half of the twentieth century, Republican territory tended to be restricted to a few counties wedged in along the spine of the Blue Ridge Mountains. With few exceptions, the rest of the state's voters embraced the Democratic Party. The Democratic Party primary was the crucial election, because in most parts of North Carolina there would be little or no Republican opposition in the general election. Although not as prominent as in the states of the Deep South, Democratic power in North Carolina rested in part on white supremacy, a bargain struck between white constituents and their political leaders resulting in removal of blacks from the political process. World War II seriously interrupted the equilibrium of the one-party system by mixing up the population, moving people in and out of the

region, but mostly away from rural areas to the cities. After 1945, but especially since the mid-1960s, the in-migration of people from other parts of the country to mostly urban North Carolina accelerated. The 1970s became the first decade in more than a century when more people moved into North Carolina than out of it. The vast majority of these newcomers settled in metropolitan areas, and as a group they were more Republican in orientation than the citizens in the communities they were joining (Fig. 11.2).

About the time the in-migration was beginning in North Carolina, African Americans in virtually every city in the South were organizing political clubs for the expressed purpose of registering and turning out black voters on election day. It was these urban political clubs in the years after 1950 that provided African Americans the organization and the media markets for carrying on protests against the political exclusion of other African Americans living in rural parts of the South. The protests and the reaction of white supremacists to them eventually led to violence that, in turn, triggered the passage of the 1965 Voting Rights Act, the single most important event this century in the rise of black political power in the South. The act guaranteed the right of African Americans to register and vote and ensured that techniques employed to dilute or negate the black vote through changes in electoral procedures would come under the scrutiny of the U.S. Justice Department or the Federal

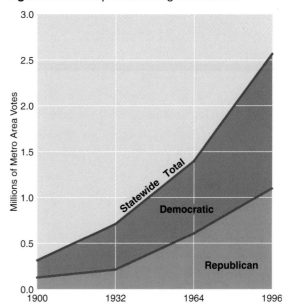

Figure 11.2. Metropolitan Voting for Governor

Note: Metro area counties include Buncombe, Cumberland, Durham, Forsyth, Gaston, Guilford, Mecklenburg, New Hanover, and Wake.

Source: *N.C. Data Net*, March 1997.

District Court in the District of Columbia. The 1965 Voting Rights Act forever changed the face of southern and North Carolina electoral politics.

The rise of black political power coincided with the beginning of the demise of one-party control in North Carolina. The Republican Party began its transformation into a serious contender for political power in the southern region with the presidential campaign of Senator Barry Goldwater and the implementation of the GOP's southern strategy. That strategy was based on two premises:

(1) national Republican candidates would not receive the vote of northern urban blacks under any political scenario and historically only a small minority of southern blacks turned out to vote, and (2) because the national Democratic Party was adopting civil rights and social policies that were objectionable to traditional white southern Democratic voters, these voters should be responsive to many traditional Republican appeals. Although the 1964 candidacy of Goldwater did not trigger a massive defection of southern white voters to the GOP outside the Deep South, he won Alabama, Georgia, Louisiana, Mississippi, and South Carolina. What many white southern voters learned in 1964 was that there was life after voting Republican, a lesson that they took to heart in subsequent years. One year later African Americans began to register to vote in large numbers, and in one of the great ironies of southern history, they joined the party of white supremacy, the Democratic Party.

Republicans made steady electoral gains during the late 1960s, but in 1972 North Carolina appeared to have turned the corner and become a genuine two-party state. Not only had the GOP captured the governorship and a U.S. Senate seat, but 50 Republicans—35 in the 120-member house and 15 in the 50-member senate—won seats in the General Assembly and four of the state's eleven U.S. House districts were carried by Republicans. Two years later the effects of the Watergate scandal and a recession wiped out these gains: U.S. Senate and attorney general candidates running on the Republi-

can ticket received less than 40 percent of the statewide vote, two incumbent U.S. House members were upset by Democrats, and Republicans lost 40 of their 50 seats in the General Assembly.

In the aftermath of President Nixon's resignation and throughout the rest of the 1970s, the GOP struggled to regain voter trust and to recover from the electoral devastation of Watergate. During the 1980s there was a surge-and-decline pattern to Republican successes. The biggest victories were registered during presidential years, when the party had the benefit of Ronald Reagan at the top of the ticket. Off-year elections were more favorable to Democrats. Terry Sanford, former Democratic governor of North Carolina, won a U.S. Senate seat in 1986, and Democrats recaptured two congressional seats from the GOP in both the 1982 and 1986 off-year elections. But within the surge-and-decline pattern of their electoral advances, Republican candidates were beginning to hold on to a larger share of the offices they had won (Fig. 11.3).

The 1994 Election

In a great national tide, Republicans in 1994 were swept into office everywhere, but particularly in the South. For the first time in forty-two years, Republicans captured control of the U.S. House of Representatives and did so in part by winning a majority of U.S. House seats in the South for the first time since Reconstruction. The Republicans also took control of the U.S. Senate. Across the na-

tion, the GOP picked up 450 state legislative seats as well as hundreds of local offices. In North Carolina, the long-awaited parity in partisan fortunes at the lower levels of the ballot finally arrived.

The Republican takeover of North Carolina was one of the most dramatic examples of not only how wide but also how deep was the GOP victory in 1994. The congressional delegation was transformed from an eight-to-four Democratic majority to an eight-to-four Republican majority as GOP candidates won two open Democratic seats (the Second and Fifth Congressional Districts) and defeated two Democratic incumbents (Martin Lancaster in the Third Congressional District and David Price in the Fourth). The Republicans gained thirteen seats in the state senate, surging to within two of a majority, and twenty-six seats in the state house, allowing the GOP to take control of that chamber for the first time in over one hundred years. Republicans won every contested statewide judicial race even though these usually low-visibility, low-turnout races were typically captured by Democrats. In counties where the Republican Party bothered to run candidates for sheriff, they frequently won. Republicans gained majorities on forty-two of the one hundred county commissions, an all-time high. The magnitude of the GOP tidal wave surprised even the most optimistic Republican partisans.

Conditions proved to be perfect for the North Carolina Republicans in 1994. Stagnant middle-class incomes, declining public services, fear on the

Figure 11.3. Seats Won in the U.S. House of Representatives and North Carolina General Assembly, by Party, 1968–1998

a. North Carolina Members of the U.S. House

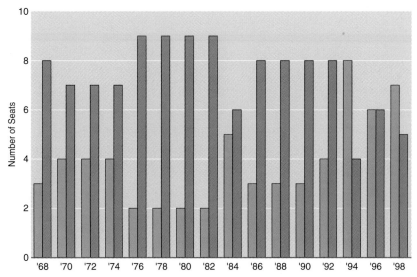

b. Members of the North Carolina House

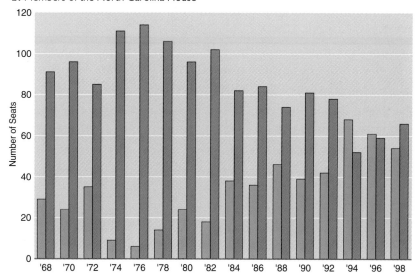

c. Members of the North Carolina Senate

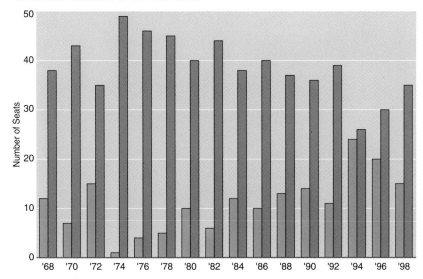

Party Affiliation

Republican
Democratic

Source: *N.C. Data Net*, 1998.

part of many citizens of being touched by crime, a national government paralyzed by gridlock, and a rising crescendo of sexual and illegal personal gain scandals in official Washington produced a large pool of dissatisfied voters. The cultural symbolism of the Clinton administration's actions was anathema to socially conservative white men, particularly in the South. The conspicuous attention to race and gender diversity in making appointments called to mind affirmative action programs white men believed disadvantaged them in the marketplace. Support for gays in the military and gun control reminded these swing voters of the cultural liberalism that was at the core of what they did not like about the Democratic Party.

Exit polls on election day showed that many white Tar Heel voters found President Clinton a perfect caricature to symbolize their antipathy toward big government and liberal social policies. In an election year when there was a widespread desire among voters for a more restricted federal government and lower taxes, Clinton reinvigorated the perception that Democrats were associated with liberal policies and big-government spending. In the tobacco-growing areas of North Carolina, the Clinton health care plan, which called for a steep hike in tobacco taxes as a financing mechanism, was an albatross for all Democrats on the ballot. Sensing Clinton's unpopularity, many Republican candidates deliberately sought to nationalize state and local races. In the course of the campaign, large numbers of voters became convinced that the way to punish the U.S. Congress and President Clinton was to vote against their own Democratic congressmen, state legislators, and even local officials. As a consequence, there was an extraordinary level of straight-ticket Republican voting in all sections of the state, particularly among working-class, white males.

It is easy to understand how exhilaration over the election results caused Republicans to overinterpret the verdict of 1994, but in hindsight the election was not the end of an era but another milestone on the road to two-party competition. Although it was true that an unusually large number of white men voted Republican, other demographic groups maintained their historical political loyalties. Democrats lost in 1994 for basically two reasons: (1) they received less support from crossover Republican voters than was typical, only about 7 percent in U.S. House races, and (2) close to one-half of traditional Democratic supporters decided to stay home and not vote at all—the largest two-year decline in voter turnout in recent memory. Contrary to election-night commentary, the election returns did not signal a political right turn on the part of a majority of Tar Heel voters, only a rightward shift among Republican voters, partly driven by negative reactions to the Clinton agenda. Poll data are consistent with this conclusion and document the fact that nonvoters in 1994 were less likely to be Republican and more likely to be sympathetic to government than those who voted. Therefore, turnout patterns provide a better explanation of the GOP's smashing victory than more complicated voter realignment themes.

Paradoxically, high abstention rates in voting have been occurring at the same time that record numbers of new citizens are being registered to vote. Nationally, the new motor voter law, which allows citizens to register by mail or while renewing a driver's license, added about 3.4 million Americans to the voter rolls. Voters also are bombarded by more political messages than ever before—an estimated $2 billion worth by candidates for the White House, the U.S. Senate, and the U.S. House during the 1996 campaign. Nevertheless, fewer than 39 percent of voting-age Americans cast ballots in the 1994 midterm election. In North Carolina, only 36 percent showed up at the polls, continuing the state's long history of trailing most of the country in voter turnout.

Until 1994, North Carolina Democrats were able to maintain control of the congressional delegation, despite Republican dominance of presidential contests, by persuading voters to use different criteria for making presidential and congressional choices. Research on U.S. House elections has long noted that incumbents, particularly Democratic incumbents in the South, attempted to insulate themselves from adverse national political trends by focusing on local issues, performing constituency services, and nurturing a personal, candidate-oriented following. Southern Democrats also improved their electoral prospects by portraying themselves as fiscal and social conservatives, despite the liberal and free-spending image of the national Democratic Party. Even

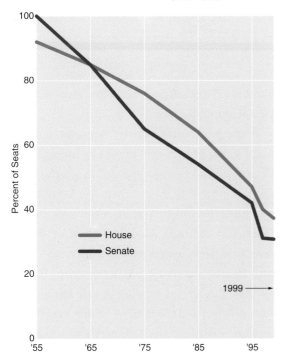

Figure 11.4. Democratic Strength in the South: U.S. House and Senate Seats, 1955–1999

Percent of Seats

— House
— Senate

1999 →

Sources: G. M. Pomper, *The Election of 1996: Reports and Interpretations* (Chatham: Chatham House Publishers, Inc., 1996); N.C. State Board of Elections.

though many of their constituents were voting Republican at the presidential level, congressional Democrats won by keeping the voters' attention focused on them and the district rather than on the national party. This strategy allowed North Carolina Democrats to survive in a political world that was increasingly embracing the logic and rhetoric of the GOP. But in 1994, the "all politics is local" strategy was turned on its head as many southern voters reacted to a national agenda by either staying at home or voting a straight Republican ticket, thus removing from office incumbent congressional Democrats in record numbers (Fig. 11.4).

Uncontested Legislative Races and Racial Districting

In their march to partisan parity, one of the most serious obstacles the Republican Party had to overcome was finding candidates to run for office at the lower levels of the ballot. Because the Democrats' electoral success for most of the twentieth century had been so impressive, finding Republican candidates to challenge entrenched Democrats in the General Assembly was especially difficult. Between 1968 and 1990, twenty to forty Democrats won seats in the North Carolina House each election without facing competition in the general election (Fig. 11.5). Conversely, relatively few Republicans won office without opposition. Democrats thus won on average about 25 percent of the seats in the General Assembly by default. Not only did this give the Democrats a tremendous advantage in the state legislature, it seriously skewed voting statistics because no Republican candidates on the ballot translated into no Republican votes. The result was an inflated Democratic split of the votes statewide. For example, in 1984 GOP candidates for the North Carolina House garnered 751,000 votes, 33 percent of the total vote. But the Republican vote tally was achieved in only 79 of the 120 races. In the contested races, the Republican-Democratic split was about 50-50.

The increasing number of safe seats at the congressional, state legislative, and even city council/county commission levels was partially due to the vigorous application of the federally mandated principle that legislative districts must provide greater opportunities for African American candidates. Following the 1990 census, the U.S. Department of Justice and Republican organizations worked with civil rights groups to secure the creation of as many new minority-dominated electoral districts as possible. North Carolina, along with other southern states, was required by the U.S. Justice Department and federal courts to create in their redistricting plans the maximum feasible number of majority minority districts. As a result, in 1992 two African Americans from North Carolina were elected to the U.S. House of Representatives for the first time in the twentieth century (Eva Clayton in the First Congressional District and Mel Watt in the Twelfth Congressional District), and the number of African Americans in the General Assembly increased to twenty-five.

Racial districting is beneficial to the GOP in two ways. First, by reducing the number of African Americans, who are generally loyal Democratic supporters, in electoral districts surrounding minority districts, Republicans improve their chances of winning in these districts. Second, by increasing

Figure 11.5. Number of Uncontested Races in the North Carolina General Assembly, 1968–1998

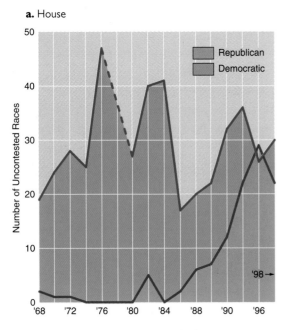

a. House

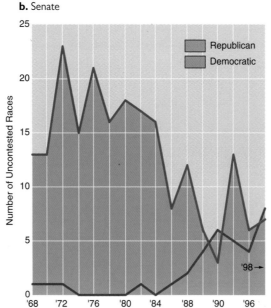

b. Senate

Note: No data were available for 1978.

Sources: *N.C. Data Net*, August 1995; N.C. Board of Elections.

Sources: *N.C. Data Net*, September 1995; N.C. Board of Elections.

the size of the Republican base in districts already held by Republicans, it makes it more difficult for Democratic challengers to win in these GOP districts, thus producing a larger number of safe seats for Republican candidates. Even though the goal of racial districting was to provide for greater minority representation, incumbents usually tried to protect themselves in the process by creating districts that favored their reelection. This impulse was shared by Democrats and Republicans alike; thus there was generally a bipartisan conspiracy to create the maximum number of safe districts and reduce partisan competition in these districts to a minimum.

Throughout the 1980s, when about 60 to 70 percent of the total vote in state legislative races went to Democrats, Republicans received about 45 percent of the vote in contested elections—further evidence that the so-called abrupt shift of 1994 voters toward the GOP was an illusion. More Republicans winning uncontested seats in GOP "safe havens" plus a below-average turnout of

Democratic voters had more to do with the "historical" transfer of power in the North Carolina House than voter conversion to the GOP. In 1994, 48 percent of the house seats (58) were uncontested; Democrats won 36 and Republicans 22. What was unique in that election was the large number of Republicans who won seats without Democratic opposition.

In the state senate, 18 of 50 races were uncontested in 1994. From 1968 to 1984 an average of 17 Democrats had been unopposed in general elections, compared to the relatively few Republicans who won uncontested seats. Over this period Democrats captured about one-third of the 50 seats by default, approximately 41 percent of the total Democratic contingent in the senate. But after 1986, the average number of safe Democratic seats declined and the number of safe Republican seats increased. In 1994 Democrats won thirteen uncontested senate races, 50 percent of the party's total wins, and Republicans took five uncontested seats. Overall, 76 out of 170 lawmakers in the General Assembly, or about 45 percent of the membership, faced no opposition in the general election of 1994.

Republican Parity in Perspective: The 1996 and 1998 Elections

In 1996 and 1998 the political scales tipped slightly in favor of the Democrats. The 1996 election was a good test of the competitiveness of the GOP in

North Carolina because all statewide executive offices were on the ballot and voter anger against Democrats had subsided. The economy was healthy, the performance of the Republican majority in Congress was beginning to disappoint some citizens, and there was growing awareness that throwing political scapegoats out of office would not automatically resolve all the problems confronting society. The two presidential candidates virtually ignored North Carolina and spent their time in other, more closely contested states. Robert Dole carried North Carolina by about five percentage points, and the resilient Jesse Helms returned to the U.S. Senate for a fifth term, defeating Harvey Gantt for the second time in a row in a highly visible and expensive race. In U.S. House races, Democrats recaptured the Second and Fourth Congressional Districts, creating an even division of six congressional seats for each party.

The popular Democratic incumbent, James Hunt, won a fourth term as governor. He began the race with significant advantages: an 80 percent voter approval rate, a healthy state economy, and a platform calling for tax cuts, welfare reform, and increased state spending for public education. Hunt's opponent was Robin Hayes, a conservative state legislator who had defeated the more moderate Richard Vinroot, the former mayor of Charlotte, in the Republican primary. Hayes was advantaged in the primary by low voter turnout and the support of the Christian Coalition (Fig. 11.6).

Campaign election signs at a Durham polling place

Although Hayes's campaign themes—opposition to Smart Start, abstinence-only sex education in the public schools, and phasing out the 4 percent state sales tax on food—hit the right chord for Christian Coalition voters in the primary, they played less well for the larger, more diverse electorate in the general election. Needing a more moderate message, one that focused more on economic rather than social issues, Hayes was unable to shift his campaign strategy fast enough to win against a popular governor. Two groups of voters who supported President Clinton and Harvey Gantt, African Americans and women, also backed Hunt, and to this base Hunt added about two-thirds of the political moderates and about one-third of the political conservatives. Democrats in the General As-

sembly regained lost ground by winning back seven house and four senate seats. Again, overall turnout declined. Only 49 percent of voting-age Americans cast ballots in 1996, the lowest presidential year turnout since 1924 and the second lowest turnout since 1824. In North Carolina, 45.6 percent of voting-age citizens showed up at the polls.

In the 1998 midterm election, prospects were promising for significant Republican gains in North Carolina and the nation. Historically, the president's party loses seats in the Congress and had done so in every election since 1934. Also, the nation was preoccupied with the President Clinton–Monica Lewinsky scandal and the possibility of impeachment proceedings. The popular Republican scenario was that Democratic voters

Figure 11.6. North Carolina Voter Turnout at Primaries, 1976–1996

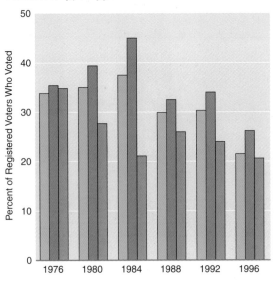

Registered Voters

- ☐ All registered voters
- ☐ Democrats
- ☐ Republicans

Note: All registered voters include nonaffiliated voters as well as Democrats and Republicans.

Source: *N.C. Data Net*, September 1996.

would be so discouraged by the president's personal problems that they would stay home on election day and thus deliver a great victory to the Republicans. Predictions of a low turnout were accurate; at the national level, only 36.1 percent of eligible voters cast a ballot, the lowest midterm election turnout since 1942. Although Tar Heel voters turned out at higher rates than in many other southern states, only 34.5 percent of the eligible

electorate voted. The better-than-expected turnout helped Democrats. John Edwards, a newcomer to politics who contributed almost $6 million to his campaign, upset Republican senator Lauch Faircloth; Democrats recaptured the state house and picked up five additional seats in the state senate. The Republican highlight was winning an open seat in the North Carolina Eighth Congressional District, which shifted the partisan balance in the congressional delegation to seven Republicans and five Democrats. Overall, the 1998 midterm election produced a good outcome for Democrats but not a surge back to dominant party status.

In the 1994 midterm election, 514 seats in the U.S. Congress and state legislatures had switched from Democrat to Republican; in 1998, fewer than a dozen incumbent governors and members of Congress were defeated, an extraordinary endorsement of the status quo. All incumbent members of Congress from North Carolina, except for Faircloth, were returned to office. Only 11 of 162 incumbents seeking another term in the General Assembly were defeated, a reelection rate of 93 percent. Three members of the state's congressional delegation won without major party opposition; 62 members of the General Assembly, 36 percent of total membership, were returned to office without major party opposition. Nevertheless, shifting even a handful of seats in the North Carolina House dramatically altered the balance of power in that chamber and the political priorities of the state.

The GOP agenda of stalemate and investigation proved to be self-destructive to congressional Republicans. The Lewinsky scandal did not cause voters to rise up against Democratic candidates; instead, it damaged Republicans more because of the negative reaction of voters to the GOP handling of the Starr Report and television "attack ads" on the president. On the other hand, the Democratic "get-out-the-vote" strategy was successful in getting traditional Democratic voters to the polls. African Americans, Hispanics, union members, gays, women, and Jews turned out in larger numbers than had been the case in 1994. Nearly a quarter of the Christian Coalition voters who had supported Republicans in 1994 switched to Democratic candidates in 1998. In North Carolina, African American voters were apprehensive about the GOP's plans for impeaching the president and pleased that the nation's growing economy had improved their status. In the battleground states of the South, including North Carolina, African Americans comprised a larger share of the total electorate than they had in 1994, and they delivered their votes to Democratic candidates by a nine-to-one margin. In close races, the black vote for Democrats was frequently the difference between winning and losing.

As the new century opens, North Carolina is firmly allied with the GOP at the presidential level, but further down the ballot partisan competition is intense. Redistricting has contributed to this more competitive status. Democrats continue to

Figure 11.7a. Competitiveness of North Carolina Senate Districts

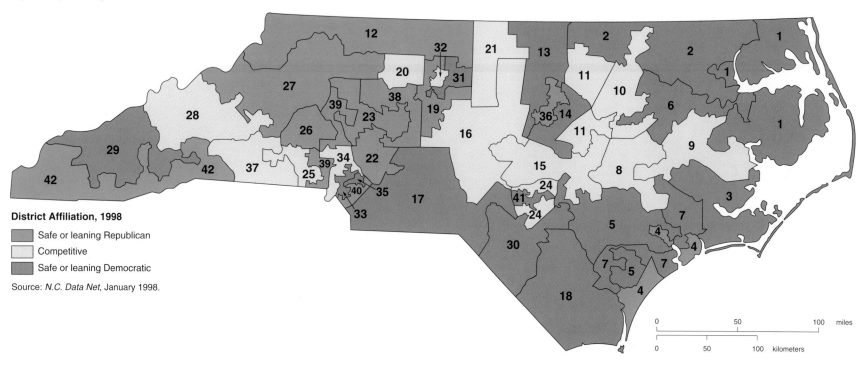

District Affiliation, 1998

- Safe or leaning Republican
- Competitive
- Safe or leaning Democratic

Source: *N.C. Data Net*, January 1998.

be elected from their party's safe districts, and Republicans are consolidating gains in their strongholds. The state has evolved into an electoral system where about thirty North Carolina House districts are solidly Democratic and close to thirty others are solidly Republican. In the state senate, ten districts are solidly Democratic and nine solidly Republican. This translates into 47 Democrats and 41 Republicans representing safe districts, 51 percent of the total membership of the state legislature. Thus, over the next few years control of the

General Assembly will be determined by the outcome of contests in toss-up districts, a distinct minority of the total number of districts but the true partisan battleground in North Carolina politics. In the 1996 and 1998 elections, 20 of the 25 seats (13 of 16 in the house and 7 of 9 in the senate) that changed from Republican to Democratic control or vice versa were in toss-up districts. Democrats captured 12 of the 13 house seats and all of the senate toss-up seats (Figs. 11.7a and 11.7b).

Both major parties have a formidable base of

safe electoral districts, an arrangement that assures survival even in the occasional "tide" elections such as 1974 and 1994. Competition in the toss-up districts—about 25 percent of the districts in the General Assembly—is keen and partisan control fragile. In the new political era, one-party domination of the state is a relic of the past; control of the governor's office, the General Assembly, the congressional delegation, and selected county commissions and city councils are now within the reach of both major parties. As to whether this heightened

Figure 11.7b. Competitiveness of North Carolina House Districts

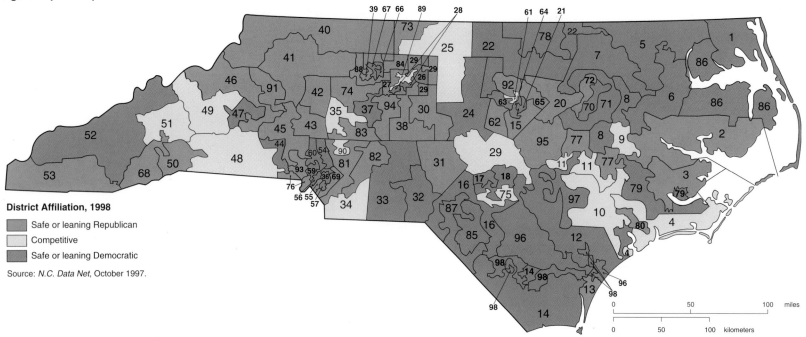

District Affiliation, 1998

- ▓ Safe or leaning Republican
- ░ Competitive
- ▓ Safe or leaning Democratic

Source: *N.C. Data Net*, October 1997.

partisan competition will benefit the state by producing more bipartisan cooperation in the management of executive and legislative power centers or result in stalemate and delay is yet to be determined.

Political Campaigning and Money in North Carolina Politics

In contemporary politics, money has become so indispensable in running for political office that cash has replaced supporters as a measure of the candidate's electoral strength. Money and the services it buys—pollsters, media consultants, direct mail advisers—have replaced volunteer canvassers, precinct organizers, and local party leaders. Few citizens today are asked to volunteer their time and labor in campaigns; instead, they are asked to make or solicit contributions. As a consequence of the state's new competitive environment, a flood of money by North Carolina standards flowed into the 1996 political campaigns. State legislative candidates spent a record $14 million in 1996, up from

$7.9 million in 1994. The average winner in the state senate spent $82,000, more than double the expenditure in 1994—$36,000; the average house winner spent $41,600, up from $25,000. The cost of winning a seat in the General Assembly in 1998 increased by nearly a third over 1996, rising to $53,000 for successful house candidates and $112,172 for winners of senate seats. Before 1994, only five members of the General Assembly had ever raised more than $100,000 in campaign funds; seven raised that amount in 1994, twenty-three and thirty-six topped it in 1996 and 1998, respectively.

Also, money had a very positive relationship with winning; those who spent the most money won nearly 85 percent of the time.

Escalating Campaign Costs and the Role of "Soft" Money

The amount of money spent on political campaigns has become so large that "soft money" contributions are now an issue in North Carolina politics. Soft money is defined as a political donation not subject to federal and state contribution limits. Under current law, individuals and political action committees (PACs) can give North Carolina candidates up to $4,000 per election and federal candidates up to $1,000. By contrast, individuals, PACs, and corporations can give political parties unlimited amounts of money for issue advertising and for party-building activities. The national parties share the donations they receive with their state organizations. In 1996 the Democratic National Committee gave the North Carolina party $2.9 million; the Republican National Committee gave the North Carolina GOP $2.8 million (Fig. 11.8). In addition, state party organizations receive large amounts of soft money directly. Because the size of the donations to political parties is not subject to legal limits, a large fraction of the money spent by selected candidates for the U.S. Congress and the North Carolina General Assembly in 1994 and 1996 came from soft money donations that were filtered through party organizations (Fig. 11.9).

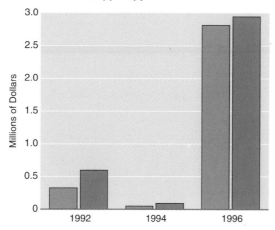

Figure 11.8. Soft Money Contributions to North Carolina Parties, 1992–1996

Party Organization

- GOP National Committee
- Democratic National Committee

Source: *Charlotte Observer*, March 2, 1997.

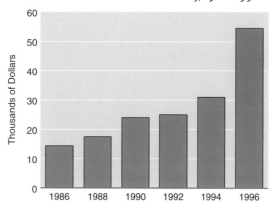

Figure 11.9. Average Campaign Contributions to Candidates for the General Assembly, 1986–1996

Note: Dollar amounts are not adjusted for inflation.

Source: *Charlotte Observer*, March 2, 1997.

As a result of the heightened partisan competition in the state and the lax rules on soft money contributions to parties, the Democratic and Republican organizations have begun to play a more significant role in funding campaigns at the state level (Fig. 11.9). North Carolina Republican Party spending for General Assembly races jumped from $1.3 million in 1994 to $5.2 million in 1996; Democratic Party spending soared from $2.1 million to $8.7 million. The flood of new money paid for professional consultants; television, radio, and newspaper ads; polling, mailings, phone banks, and other assorted campaign activities. Although candidates typically are pleased to receive financial assistance from any source that offers it, many candidates for office in North Carolina are beginning to feel that they are caught up in something akin to an arms race. If they do something novel in campaigning, the opposition responds in kind or in a new way, and they in turn must retaliate. These moves and countermoves constantly escalate the cost of campaigning. In the state's new political environment, a campaign for public office in a competitive district becomes a vicious cycle that consumes ever increasing amounts of money and requires the candidates to invest ever increasing amounts of time to raise it.

The widespread use of soft money in political campaigns raises serious ethical questions. First of all, the extensive use of soft money makes it impossible to impose any meaningful limit on political contributions. To the typical citizen, soft money transfers seem to be only a form of money laundering. Corporations, PACs, and individuals who want to support a particular candidate can avoid contribution limits by sending donations to a political party, which, in turn, can forward the contributions to the candidate. More significant than avoiding the legal limits on campaign contributions is the dilemma of big donors buying too much political influence. Relatively few elected officials would act contrary to their concept of the public interest because of a modest contribution of several thousand dollars, but a contribution in the $50,000 to $100,000 range raises questions about wealth taking unfair advantage of the public decision-making process.

Political Action Committees

PACs, virtually unknown before the Watergate "reforms," have proliferated and are now a source of significant campaign contributions for candidates at all levels of the ballot. Over the years, the attention of people who manage PAC funds has shifted from highly visible statewide races to congressional and state legislative contests. The movement of PAC money down the ballot makes political sense in that fewer dollars will gain greater access to the levels of government that directly impact the "balance sheet" of many corporations and public sector constituencies. For example, the salaries of educators are determined primarily by the state legislature; doctors, lawyers, and other professionals are licensed and regulated by state agencies; utility and insurance companies look to Raleigh to approve rate structures; and wholesalers of alcoholic beverages are dependent on the taxing and regulatory policies of the state.

The biggest spending PACs in North Carolina are affiliated with the medical industry, bankers and lenders, electric utilities, contractors and real estate salesmen, insurance firms, telephone companies, and trial lawyers. Other PACs that regularly make contributions to political candidates represent schoolteachers and state employees; agribusiness, tobacco, and timber interests; beverage companies; retailers and small businesses; organized labor; the textile industry; pharmaceutical and chemical manufacturers. Even though political contributions still come from "friends" of the candidates and often from the candidates themselves, an increasing share of the cost of seeking public office is paid for by the individuals and groups who have a big stake in the outcome of public policy deliberations.

Business, professional, and trade group PACs invest in candidates to gain access to friendly officeholders once the election is over. Consequently, there are patterns in the way PACs contribute money to those candidates. More goes to incumbents than to challengers because incumbents are more likely to win elections. Many PACs give contributions to both Democratic and Republican candidates running for the same seat to ensure access to the winner. PACs routinely donate significant amounts to persons holding leadership positions in the General Assembly even if they represent safe districts and are unopposed for office. Although unopposed, Marc Basnight, the Democratic leader in the state senate, raised a record $487,926 in 1996 and $732,994 in 1998. Republican speaker Harold Brubaker, also unopposed, raised a house record $304,213 in 1996 and $477,205 in 1998. Both Basnight and Brubaker shared their campaign wealth with fellow partisans. In 1996 Basnight gave $274,000 to a fund that paid for consultants, polling, mailings, and other assistance for Democratic state senate candidates, and Speaker Brubaker gave $126,000 to the Randolph County GOP, which helped elect Republicans to the North Carolina House.

Campaign Finance Reform Efforts

There is much unhappiness on the part of citizens—and even on the part of lawmakers—about the expanding role of money in North Carolina elections. Fund-raising by lobbyists for legislators' campaigns has been described as a parasitic but common relationship in the General Assembly. Legislators increasingly depend on lobbyists and special interests to raise money to meet skyrocketing campaign costs, and lobbyists engage in these fund-raising activities because they need bills before the General Assembly either passed or defeated. Given these conditions, campaign reform legislation is a popular topic, although little effective legislation has been enacted into law.

Nevertheless, various proposals have been advanced to curb the role of political money. One proposal that has not received a friendly reception either by lawmakers or by rank-and-file citizens is using tax money to fund political campaigns. Previous attempts to obtain public funding have not been encouraging. The North Carolina Candidate Financing Fund, for instance, by 1996 had raised less than $200,000 since its establishment in 1988. Nevertheless, publicly funded elections have their enthusiastic supporters. The North Carolina Alliance for Democracy, a forty-group coalition promoting campaign finance reform, claims that public funding of campaigns is the only constitutional way to make it possible for candidates who are not wealthy or dependent on wealthy backers or special interest groups to be elected. Critics of this particular reform refer to public financing of campaigns as "political welfare." A more serious criticism is that the public financing of campaigns probably would benefit incumbents by limiting how much lesser-known challengers could spend. In addition, there are practical problems. Should public monies go only to Democrats and Republicans? Would their use in only general elections just push more money into primaries? Are all primary candidates, even the marginal ones, eligible for public monies?

Another reform that enjoys some support among members of the General Assembly is to reduce the legal amount of money that individuals and PACs can donate to candidates. Currently, the maximum legal contribution is $4,000 per election, which translates into $8,000 for a primary and a general election and up to $12,000 if there is also a runoff primary. Proposals for a new maximum limit for donations range from $2,000 per election to as low as $500. A lower limit on donations would have the effect of reducing the influence of wealthy contributors, but, again, such a reform would make it more difficult for challengers to unseat incumbents and would increase the workload for all candidates who sought to raise campaign funds. The burden of raising monies

from a wider circle of contributors to pay for rising campaign costs might shrink even further the pool of willing candidates for public office in North Carolina.

Other proposed reforms would require candidates to report the occupations of their biggest contributors, setting limits on what a candidate's family can donate to a campaign, and offering incentives such as free advertisements to candidates who voluntarily limit campaign spending. The reality of political reform is that few, if any, of these proposals will be enacted into law. Most incumbents, regardless of party affiliation and the burden of political fundraising, prefer the system that elected them rather than any untested scheme that may replace it. Another reality is that it is extremely difficult to reduce the role of money in politics without violating the constitutional right of free speech. Although the public is looking for easy solutions to remove special interest money from state politics and elections, new campaign reforms are likely to be only cosmetic in practice.

The General Assembly

The North Carolina General Assembly is a part-time or citizens legislature struggling to cope with the problems of a large, complex state. It is the oldest governmental body in North Carolina, consisting of a senate and a house of representatives. Both bodies are apportioned by population with members elected biennially. Although some legislators are still elected from multi-member districts, increasingly they come from single-member districts of approximately equal populations. Since 1835, 50 senators and 120 representatives have comprised the General Assembly. A state senator must be at least twenty-five years old, a resident of the state for two years, and a resident of the district represented for one year immediately preceding the election. A member of the house of representatives must be a qualified voter and a resident of the district represented for one year immediately prior to the election.

Much of the work of the legislative branch is done in committees that are organized around different policy areas—for example, education, health, banking, and agriculture. The purpose of the committee system is to bring as much expertise as possible to bear on subjects under consideration and to reduce the legislative workload to manageable proportions through a division of labor. Bills approved at the committee level are ultimately voted on by the entire membership of the house and senate. Although service in the General Assembly is challenging, the legislator's paycheck is small ($13,951 annually, plus $559 per month expense allowance, $104 a day while the legislature is in session for food and lodging, and 29 cents per mile for round-trip drives between home and Raleigh). The turnover rate is relatively high, and only people who can afford to be away from their jobs for six to seven months every odd-numbered year and for two to three months in even-numbered years can apply. As the work of the General Assembly becomes more time consuming because of annual sessions and the failure of the house and senate leadership to bring legislative sessions to timely adjournments, only persons who have jobs with flexible work schedules, are independently wealthy or retired, or do not have a family to support find service in the legislature possible or attractive.

Nevertheless, the culture of a citizens' legislature is strongly entrenched in North Carolina. When asked in 1997 to identify their occupations, only 3 out of 170 members of the General Assembly stated that they were legislators; instead, they called themselves bankers, doctors, educators, farmers, lawyers, businesspeople, or retired persons. Even though the cost of winning a seat is escalating and the heavy burden of constituent demands gives a full-time character to a legislator's job, the vision of the General Assembly as populated by full-time, well-paid careerist legislators seems strangely out of place.

The North Carolina General Assembly has frequently been referred to as the most powerful state legislature in the nation. That reputation is derived from the fact that until 1997 the governor of North Carolina was the only state chief executive denied veto power. With the addition of relatively weak veto power, the North Carolina chief executive officer still ranks among the weakest governors in the nation in terms of formal powers; thus the will of the legislature is seldom thwarted. Also, the contemporary General Assembly is a far more complex institution than it was at midcentury. Its legislative and budgetary powers have been enhanced, professional research and clerical support staff added, and dependency on the governor and executive branch agencies for information, policy analysis, and policy alternatives diminished.

Changing Leadership Patterns in the General Assembly

In North Carolina, the road leading to a General Assembly where political power is widely dispersed was a long one with many twists and turns. Today, African Americans and women are prominent in leadership roles, and cooperation between Democrats and Republicans and between the governor and legislative leaders is commonplace. The new electoral parity between the Democratic and Republican Parties explains much of the change, but other factors also contributed to the legislature's newfound diversity and more collaborative leadership style. The decision to shift from biennial to annual sessions triggered unanticipated changes in the demographic makeup of the General Assembly. The court-imposed requirement that redistricting plans had to reflect the shift in population from rural to urban areas had an enormous impact on the legislature's demographic profile.

Prior to the 1970s, state legislatures in the United States were commonly depicted in government and politics textbooks as inept organizations that suffered from few staff assistants, rapid turnover of members, short legislative sessions, and low pay. In a 1971 study conducted by the Citizens Conference on State Legislatures, the North Carolina General Assembly seemed to endure these ills more than most, ranking forty-seventh among the fifty state legislatures in terms of efficiency and effectiveness. Although the report was not well received by North Carolina legislators, they implemented virtually all of its recommendations within a decade. The more important legislative reforms included the addition of four new staff divisions—Fiscal Research in 1971,

General Research in 1973, Bill Drafting in 1977, and Automated Systems in 1984. In addition, the membership decided to shift from biennial to annual sessions in 1973.

The move to annual sessions was consistent with national trends, but cynical observers of state politics claimed that the election of James E. Holshouser Jr. as governor in 1972, the first Republican in that office since 1901, had more to do with this reform than the findings of the Citizens Conference. Even though the state budget was more complex, expanding threefold between 1963 and 1973, the presence of a Republican in the governor's mansion provided Democrats in the legislature with an incentive to meet more often and to employ staff outside the executive branch to review the budget.

The rather modest procedural shift from biennial to annual sessions ushered in far-reaching changes in the composition of the General Assembly (Fig. 11.10). In 1971 lawyers occupied 40 percent of the seats (68 members), but by 1997 their share had dwindled to 21 percent (36 members). Individuals who earned their living in business, sales, and manufacturing also became less numerous, declining from 78 to 57 over the same period. Seats once occupied by lawyers and businesspeople were now filled by retirees and individuals employed in the real estate industry.

Census data collected in 1970 reveal how massive the rural-to-urban migration in North Caro-

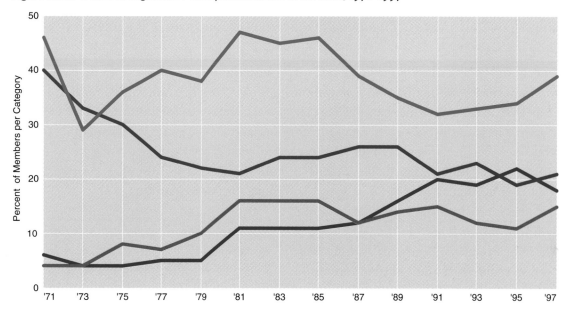

Figure 11.10. Trends in Legislators' Occupations in North Carolina, 1971–1997

Occupations

 Business/sales
Law
Real estate
Retired

Source: N.C. Center for Public Policy Research.

lina had become, a population shift that, according to constitutional requirements, had to be reflected in the 1971 redistricting plan. As a consequence, more legislators representing cities and towns and fewer representing farms and rural areas assembled in Raleigh for the 1973 session—a result that would be repeated in 1983 and 1993.

During the 1970s African American candidates

for the state legislature experienced great difficulty in winning elections because they usually were required to run for office in multimember districts. With such an electoral arrangement, black voting strength was diluted because a concentrated core of black voters in a multimember district would usually be surrounded by a larger white population. The white voters would regularly cast their ballots for white candidates, thus denying African Americans access to elective office.

African Americans who wanted to reform the multimember election system found unlikely allies among Republicans. Many Republicans believed that multimember districts worked against them in much the same way it disadvantaged black candidates. Republican pockets of strength were diluted when combined with voters from a larger region in a multimember district, thus ensuring in most cases the election of white Democrats. African Americans and many Republicans wanted a system of single-member districts, with some of the districts containing a majority of black voters. Such an arrangement would split the large, urban counties—Cumberland, Durham, Forsyth, Guilford, Mecklenburg, and Wake—into single-member districts and guarantee the election of at least a few African American candidates. Even though the "Helms" wing of the GOP remained opposed to the concept of "minority districts," other Republicans encouraged the concentration of black voters into a few districts because that meant that all other districts would become whiter, less Democratic, and fertile ground for electing Republican officeholders.

Between 1981 and 1985 African American representation increased fourfold in the General Assembly, from four to sixteen. These electoral successes were due largely to the creation of single-member districts that included a majority of black citizens. White Democrats in the assembly typically opposed the creation of single-member districts during the early 1980s, but a redistricting plan including single-member districts was eventually imposed by a three-judge federal court, whose judgment was affirmed in 1986 by the U.S. Supreme Court in *Thornburg vs. Gingles.* By 1996 black representation had increased to seventeen members in the house and seven in the senate, a coalition of sufficient size to influence the legislative agenda, particularly when Democrats controlled the General Assembly.

With increased numbers and growing political clout, African American legislators began to win legislative battles. The black coalition prevailed in making Dr. Martin Luther King's birthday a paid state holiday for state employees. It played a key role in the 1989 rewriting of the state's seventy-four-year-old primary law (a candidate now needs to receive 40 percent plus one vote in a primary to win outright rather than 50 percent plus one vote). Black voters contended for many years that the majority vote requirement made it extremely difficult for minority candidates to be elected. An African American candidate might be able to lead a field of white candidates in the first primary election but usually would be defeated in a one-on-one runoff with a white candidate in the second primary because of the voter tendency to cast ballots along racial lines.

The combined effect of redistricting to reflect rural-to-urban population migration patterns and court-imposed single-member districts in most urban areas transformed both the house and senate from chambers dominated by members from multiseat districts to those from single-seat districts (Fig. 11.11). In 1991, 80 house members were elected from multimember districts and 40 from single-member districts; in 1993, 39 were elected from multimember districts and 81 from single-member districts. On the senate side, 28 members were elected from multiseat districts and 22 from single-seat districts in 1991, but by 1993, 16 senators represented multimember districts and 34, single-seat districts. As a result of these changes, more African American legislators were elected from "safe minority" districts and more white Republicans from affluent suburban areas. The uneasy alliance between black and Republican legislators in the General Assembly disadvantaged white Democrats, whose numbers dwindled from 134 in 1983 to 74 in 1997.

While the fortunes of white male Democrats declined, those of female lawmakers ascended. In 1971 only two women served in the North Carolina General Assembly, but by the end of that decade their numbers had increased more than tenfold to twenty-two and reached a record thirty-one in the 1993 session. Although women failed to achieve ratification of the Equal Rights Amendment in North Carolina, their number-one goal in the 1970s, they won other important legislative battles. Female legislators unanimously supported the change in the state's marital rape law to allow prosecution of husbands living separately from their

Figure 11.11. Turnover Rate in the North Carolina General Assembly, 1981–1999

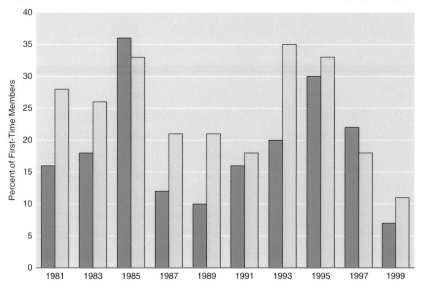

Legislative Offices

- ▮ Senate
- ▯ House

Source: N.C. Center for Public Policy Research.

Figure 11.12. Trends in the Demographics of the North Carolina General Assembly, 1971–1999

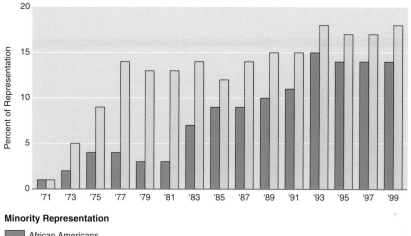

Minority Representation

- ▮ African Americans
- ▯ Women

Source: N.C. Center for Public Policy Research.

wives; they were a significant factor in the passage of a measure requiring insurance companies to pay for mammograms and pap smears and provide more than twenty-four hours of hospital coverage following childbirth. Women legislators generally played key roles in acquiring state funding for domestic violence centers and childhood initiatives and in strengthening laws against child abuse. But women typically had relatively little clout in the money committees, appropriations and finance, until the 1995 legislative session, when several female Republican lawmakers received major committee assignments.

After the 1994 election, the number of female Republican lawmakers nearly doubled, jumping from ten to eighteen. In the house, several Republican women were appointed as cochairs of the appropriation, finance, and welfare reform and human services committees—committees assigned the task of cutting taxes, initiating welfare reform, and drafting the state budget. Although women have never totaled more than 18 percent of the membership, they have become a significant, though not a monolithic, force in the legislature. Like their male counterparts, female Democrats and Republicans typically split their votes on partisan issues. For twenty years women have had a strong presence in the General Assembly and are now well integrated into the day-to-day activities of that body, indistinguishable from males in terms of committee assignments and influence (Fig. 11.12).

The increased presence of female legislators has had interesting side effects on the demographic profile of persons registering as lobbyists with the General Assembly. With the election of more African Americans, women, and Republicans, power in the state legislature is not as concentrated as in the past. Lobbyists, to be effective, must contact larger numbers of lawmakers on each piece of legislation. To accomplish this end, many lobbyists employ a team approach, and female lobbyists are increasingly being added to the team to maximize access to the growing number of women legislators who are well positioned on committees.

Current Leadership Patterns in the General Assembly

The General Assembly is much more complex today than it was just three decades ago. In the early 1960s the state's chief executive officers and members of the legislature were all located in the small state capitol that had been in service since 1829. One large Democratic caucus and a much smaller Republican caucus attempted to direct and control events within state government. In the late 1990s the number of Democrats and Republicans serving in the General Assembly was more evenly divided, and the professional staff supporting the state legislature was spread out over two modern office complexes. But even this space occasionally becomes inadequate when filled with legislators, staff, lobbyists, journalists, and citizens interested in various pieces of legislation. Members of the General Assembly now have loyalties beyond that of party alone; they may be members of a black caucus, women's caucus, urban caucus, or assorted and shifting regional, environmental, and educational alliances. All of these caucuses and alliances plan strategies, develop goals, and establish specific initiatives. They have enormous influence due to their ability to focus public attention on issues that

the governor and legislative leadership in former times might have chosen to ignore or manage behind closed doors. Persons selected for leadership positions in the General Assembly today generally enjoy longer tenure in those positions, are less dependent on the governor and executive branch officials for information and policy direction, and are more inclined to promote their own policy preferences.

The 1995 Legislative Session

When the General Assembly convened in January 1995, 30 percent of the senate and about one of every three house members were newcomers. Republicans controlled the house and were pledged to a contract with the people of North Carolina that called for term limits and veto power for the governor, budget and tax cuts, educational and welfare reform, and tough measures to deal with crime. For decades, Democrats had used the organizational and procedural powers that accompanied majority status in the legislature to humiliate the Republican minority; in 1995 house Democrats experienced the GOP's revenge as their protests were brushed aside when the Republicans assumed leadership. The new house leaders demonstrated their ability to keep GOP legislators under control and to deliver on selected campaign promises. Even though sharp-elbowed partisanship was evident during the session, including a budget standoff at the end, Speaker Harold Brubaker, Governor

James Hunt, and Senate Democratic leader Mark Basnight usually found ways to collaborate with one another. They collectively endorsed a budget-cutting, fiscally conservative approach to state government. In the probusiness atmosphere of the General Assembly, arguments that ran counter to provisions in the GOP contract were ignored. To the surprise of many veteran Democrats, there was little blundering on the part of the Republican leadership as it singlemindedly pursued the GOP agenda.

By the end of the 1995 legislative session, Republicans, with the help of Democratic sympathizers, enacted many of their campaign promises. The General Assembly passed a $413.8 million tax cut package, which included a $235 million reduction in income taxes and the repeal of the $124.4 million tax on intangible property. Employers in the state saved $51 million as a result of a cut in unemployment insurance taxes. Assuming that "what is good for business is good for the state," the assembly further shifted the tax burden in North Carolina from business and industry to individuals and families.

The record-breaking lowering of taxes on business and industry was not a reversal of state tax policy but a continuation of over fifty years of legislative practices. The individual income tax rates established during the 1930s, when local governments faced bankruptcy and the state assumed primary responsibility for funding public schools and highways, exempted all but the most wealthy citizens. Business taxes accounted for 60 percent of

General Fund revenues in 1934-35, sales taxes 31 percent, and individual income taxes 6 percent. Over time, primarily due to bracket creep, the relative shares of business and consumer taxes changed dramatically; citizens who originally were exempt from the income tax eventually became a major source of state revenues. Between 1935 and 1997, the business share of General Fund taxes dropped from 60 percent to 18.8 percent while the personal income tax share climbed from 6 percent to 50.7 percent. After all the 1995 tax cuts are fully implemented in the years 2000 and 2001, business and industry will enjoy a 16 percent cut in taxes and individuals will experience a 7 percent reduction, even though in actual dollars most of the savings will go to individuals.

Other contract provisions enacted into law during the 1995 session included the repeal of the limit on the state's prison population, the overhaul of the state's governing structure for education by shifting power from the superintendent of public instruction and the North Carolina Department of Public Instruction to the State Board of Education and local school boards, and the agreement to place on the ballot in 1996 a constitutional amendment to give the governor limited veto power. Parts of the GOP contract were approved in the house but defeated by the Democratic majority in the senate. Term limits for state legislators failed in the senate after they were linked in a "cynical manner," according to Republicans, with voluntary campaign spending limits, a combination that prompted every Republican present to vote against the legislation. The welfare reform package failed passage because of sharp disagreements between the house and senate versions of the bill and remained highly controversial throughout the 1996 session. The Taxpayer Protection Act, an effort to tie the growth of the state budget to inflation and population growth, also failed passage due to the inability of house Republicans and senate Democrats to find common ground.

The 1997 and 1998 Legislative Sessions

After the 1996 election the GOP margin in the house shrank to two votes, 61-59. Democrats expanded their majority in the senate to a more comfortable 30-20 edge. Surviving a failed attempt by the Democrats to take over the speakership by wooing Republican defectors into their camp, Speaker Brubaker squeaked back into office. The speaker was able to maintain the support of Republican colleagues partly by appointing a record seventy-four committee chairships, even though this action diluted the value of the appointments and made some of the Republicans unhappy with their assignments. Overall, 60 of 61 house Republicans chaired a committee during the 1997 session, and on the senate side all but 6 newcomers among the Democrats were appointed to either a leadership position or the chair of a committee.

With the partisan division less favorable and legislative power more dispersed, the new leadership style in the house emphasized bipartisan initiatives, compromise, and cooperation, at least on most issues. Even the governor with his brand-new legislative weapon, the veto, was careful not to make any overt threats. As a consequence, the Excellent Schools Act, which raised kindergarten-through-twelfth-grade (K-12) teacher pay as well as standards and accountability requirements for teachers, passed early and easily in the 1997 session. The governor, the senate majority leader, and the speaker of the house worked out their differences privately before announcing the agreement. Nevertheless, contentious issues remained, most notably the welfare reform plan. The GOP version of welfare reform returned enormous powers to counties and allowed them to set their own standards for welfare payments. Governor Hunt and most of the Democrats in the General Assembly opposed the establishment of one hundred separate county welfare systems with varying standards of eligibility.

In the final hours of the session and following months of often angry debate between Democrats and Republicans, the legislature passed a welfare reform plan that made North Carolina the first state in the nation to test whether local government could do a better job of managing welfare than the state. House Republicans tenaciously advanced the proposition that all one hundred counties should be authorized to determine eligibility for benefits, the size of the benefits, and the length of time recipients could collect them. Advocates for the poor, many social service directors, and nonprofit workers, as well as Democrats in the General Assembly and Governor James Hunt, feared that a carte blanche delegation of authority to counties would result in administrative chaos and perhaps "a race to the bottom" in the level of welfare benefits provided. Opponents to the Republican plan argued that if the welfare system allowed for one hundred different sets of rules and regulations, some counties might slash benefits to encourage recipient families to relocate to counties with higher benefits. The legislative logjam over welfare reform was eventually resolved by a compromise that limited "the reform" to no more than 15.5 percent of the state's 84,000 welfare families. Pilot counties were authorized to cut welfare spending by as much as 10 percent during the first year of the program and by 20 percent during the second year and use the savings for other purposes if they satisfied certain goals, mainly moving welfare recipients into jobs. Selected North Carolina counties will have the opportunity to fully manage the welfare program, but only as an experiment and not as a permanent change in policy.

Due largely to the rancorous debate over welfare reform, the 1997 General Assembly earned the dubious record of holding the second longest legislative session in North Carolina history (Fig. 11.13). The session provided excellent examples of partisan legislators learning to cooperate with one another on important public policy matters. Examples of this kind of cooperation included the bipartisan alliance that produced the Excellent

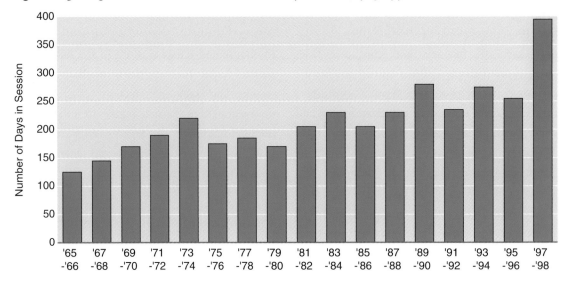

Figure 11.13. Length of North Carolina General Assembly Sessions, 1965–1998

Note: Includes special sessions.

Source: *Charlotte Observer.*

Schools Act and the redrawing of the North Carolina congressional district plan in time to satisfy a federal court–imposed deadline (Fig. 11.14). The state's sales tax on food was shaved by one cent, the second one-cent reduction in two years. Lawmakers also enacted the most significant environmental legislation in at least two decades. The measure imposed a two-year moratorium on new hog farms, established new nutrient discharge limits on municipal wastewater plants, restored authority to county commissioners to zone large animal operations, and enhanced the authority of state and local governments to control stormwater runoff into the state's waterways. The General Assembly expanded

Smart Start into unserved counties and enacted patronage reform legislation requiring state government agencies to hire "the most-qualified" job candidates rather than employing applicants with political connections. Late in the session, legislators passed a new campaign contribution disclosure law that required contributors of more than one hundred dollars to list the names of their employers or occupational category, an important step in allowing the public to know more about who has contributed money to the state's officeholders.

The 1997 legislative session also provided exasperating examples of unwillingness on the part of partisan legislators to compromise, thus producing legislative logjams and in some cases failure to take any action at all. Aside from the protracted logjam on the welfare bill, one of the General Assembly's most serious shortcomings was its failure to enact court reforms, even though the state courts were overburdened with cases and not taking advantage of new technologies to improve efficiency. (For more on the North Carolina judiciary, see "The Judicial Branch of State Government" later in this chapter.)

The General Assembly convened in May 1998 for a "short budget" session to "fine tune" the state's biennial spending plans. Exhausted legislators did not adjourn until a few days before the November off-year elections, ending the longest two-year session in state history. The unwillingness of house Republicans and senate Democrats to compromise on a long list of tax cuts and legislative initiatives produced total gridlock and frustration on the part of lawmakers and citizens alike. Of the forty-one part-time legislatures nationwide, North Carolina's is only one of four without constitutional or statutory limits on the length of sessions; it seemed possible in the latter part of the 1998 session that the legislature would leave Raleigh without agreeing on a new budget for fiscal year (FY) 1999. The primary reason for gridlock was the strategy of the house Republicans to insert into the budget dozens of "special provisions"—essentially GOP proposals that senate Democrats had either failed to consider or act on in earlier sessions. By inserting these pro-

Figure 11.14. Congressional Districts

a. Districts after Redistricting in 1992

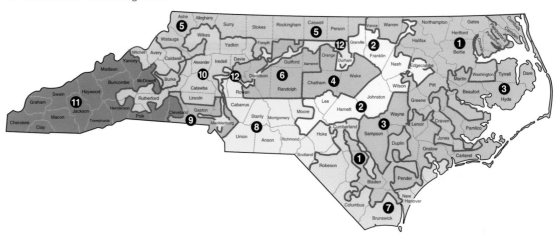

b. 1997 House and Senate Plan A Districts

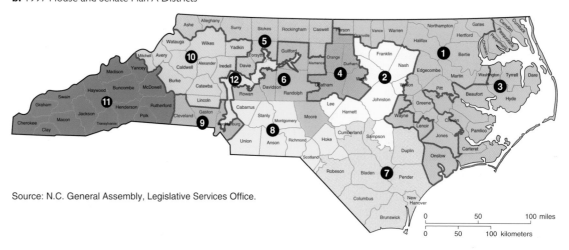

Source: N.C. General Assembly, Legislative Services Office.

visions into the budget, house Republicans planned to force senate Democrats to consider their agenda. Stalemate and frustration were the outcomes. In an attempt to break the deadlock, senate Democrats late in the session agreed to repeal the state's inheritance tax, which coupled with other tax cuts, including the repeal of the remaining two-cent sales tax on food, reduced state revenues by another $166 million in FY 1999 and a projected $531 million in FY 2000.

The four years of divided control of the General Assembly ended with the 1998 midterm election. Democrats regained the house by a 66-54 majority. In assessing the GOP's leadership legacy, it should be noted that house Republicans enlivened political debate and introduced many new ideas into the state's political dialogue. House Republicans demonstrated an unexpectedly high level of party discipline in 1995 and 1996, but with the GOP's working majority shrinking to only two legislators in 1997, Speaker Brubaker presided over a disorganized and frequently divided house during his last two years in office. With only a 61-59 majority, the Republican leadership occasionally saw the most carefully negotiated agreement with the Democratic-led senate derailed or frustrated by the most extreme or crankiest member of the majority party. Divided control of the house and senate produced many benefits and examples of partisan cooperation, but also excessive politicking, delays, stalemates, and legislative ineffectiveness.

Following the 1998 election, Democrats regained control of the North Carolina House and returned the General Assembly to its long history of single-party control. But the politicking and partisan maneuvering that characterized the previous four years continued. In a surprise move on opening day of the 1999 General Assembly, stealth candidate Dan Blue, an African American and former speaker of the house, almost won the office of speaker with the help of 5 other African American legislators and all but 3 house Republicans. This unlikely alliance failed by one vote—60 to 59—of denying James Black, the former house minority leader and the unanimous nominee of the Democratic caucus, the speakership. The black caucus members who supported Blue justified their action on the ground that the speaker of the North Carolina House should be an African American in recognition of the strong backing African American voters provided Democratic candidates in the 1998 elections. All but 3 of the 54 house Republicans supported Blue because of a "deal" with the dissident Democrats that promised the appointment of Republicans to one-half of the committee chairmanships. Speaker Black won with the votes of 57 Democrats, including 10 of the 17 African American house members (one was ill and did not participate), all but 2 of the 49 white Democrats, and 3 Republicans. The closeness of the vote for speaker highlighted the deep schism within the ranks of the North Carolina House, the increasing tendency among legislators to pursue personal influence and power, and a growing potential for unexpected coalitions to form around controversial issues confronting the legislature.

The Executive Branch

The governor of North Carolina serves as the state's chief executive officer and supervises the work of state employees, helps to identify the policy agenda for the state, influences the legislative and budgetary decisions of the General Assembly, promotes intergovernmental cooperation among officials at the national and state levels to improve program outcomes, acts as commander-in-chief of the National Guard during state emergencies such as natural disasters and civil disturbances, and is a leader of his or her state party organization. Due to the spectacular growth in the size of the state budget and the broad scope of governmental programming, the powers and responsibilities of the state's chief executive officer have been significantly enhanced over the last half century. Elected every four years, the governor has appointive and review power over nine departments—Administration, Corrections, Crime Control and Public Safety, Cultural Resources, Commerce, Environment and Natural Resources, Health and Human Services, Revenue, and Transportation. Other administrative departments are led by independently elected executive

Observations about Gubernatorial Power

Most people have little understanding of how our government functions, the powers and duties of elected and appointed officials, or how a seemingly insignificant decision or event can greatly impact their livelihood or environment. The title of governor itself creates a misconception. The phrase "the governor of North Carolina" implies great authority and the ability to rule. To the average citizen it means the governor can get things done. In a democracy, of course, it is not so straightforward.

Candidates for governor campaign throughout the state telling voters that if elected he or she can be counted on to do certain things such as improve the schools, roads, environment, the economy, etc. Pressure comes from special interest groups and the media—that is, what percentage salary increases for teachers and state employees, environmental regulations, tax reduction (how much and where), aid to the elderly, and so forth.

Since the purpose of campaigning is to win the election, which must happen before anything can be done, commitments are often made to gain support from blocks of voters. No one is keeping score and often the costs of all the commitments are beyond the ability of the state to fund, even though the individual promises may be feasible and worthwhile. Upon being elected, the governor-elect is faced with the reality that there are major limitations to delivering the commitments made.

Candidates for governor themselves are often unaware of some of the constraints on the powers of the office. Even though I had served four years (1965–69) as lieutenant governor and had grown up in a political family, I was sometimes surprised at what I was unable to do. My predecessor in office, Governor Dan Moore, had warned me by saying, "Bob, there is no training ground for governors." He was right.

We are taught in school that in our system of government the three branches (executive, legislative, judicial) are equal. In North Carolina, the legislative branch is the "most equal" of the three, even with the recently bestowed gubernatorial veto power. Increasingly legislators inject themselves into traditionally executive turf by adding footnotes to the budget, requiring legislative approval of the governor's appointees, and appointing themselves to executive boards and commissions.

It is surprising and incongruous to many that the governor has the constitutional authority to free every inmate in the state correctional system but cannot restore a person's revoked driver's license. Only the courts can do that. I was always surprised at how many people wrote me asking that I help them get their license returned.

In addition to formal constitutional and statutory constraints on the governor's ability to get things done, there are informal, and sometimes powerful, constraints as well. One of these is the history and traditions of the state. The governor is expected to do certain things. Examples might be addressing the legislature to set forth his or her agenda, issuing proclamations for various causes, and attending certain functions. These are major constraints on the governor's time, a commodity often in short supply.

Another is the actions by previous administrations which have begun projects or programs that cannot easily be stopped or modified. Major construction projects are often planned in one administration, built in the next, and dedicated in the third. Programs once in place are not easily dismantled.

Other constraints include the power of public opinion, which impacts the governor's ability to be reelected or to keep his or her political party in power, political demands that affect appointments, campaign commitments to follow a particular course, and, of course, the governor's personal set of values and ethics.

As stated at the outset, most folks are not aware of the constraints—they have expectations of the governor that often cannot be met even though the governor wishes to do so. This breeds disappointment, disillusionment, and cynicism among the electorate. It is surprising how many citizens are not even aware that an election has been held and a new governor has taken office. Witness the amount of mail coming to the capitol for six months or so addressed to the previous governor.

Demands on the governor continue after he or she leaves office. There is still mail to be answered, meetings to attend, requests for help to be considered. Once elected to office, one never really gets through being governor. But there is no staff, no driver, no mansion, and no authority. When the new governor takes the oath of office, the former governor becomes another citizen. That's the way it should be in a democracy.

Robert W. Scott,
governor of North Carolina, 1969–73

The State Capitol Building in Raleigh

ing their respective terms. Hunt became the state's top Democrat during his tenure as lieutenant governor from 1973 to 1977, the years that Republican James E. Holshouser Jr. served as governor. Hunt's multiple statewide political campaigns and personal campaign organization allowed him to remain the Democratic Party's acknowledged leader for a quarter of a century. Martin was committed to developing a two-party political system in North Carolina during his two terms as governor. He was the acknowledged leader of one of the GOP's two major factions, the other faction being led by U.S. senator Jesse Helms and the Conservative Club (formerly the Congressional Club). Greater party unity and growth were two of Martin's high priorities during 1985-93.

The Formal Powers of the North Carolina Governor

Although the governor is the central figure in North Carolina government, the formal powers of the office are weak compared to those of chief executive officers in other states. The major factors limiting the governor's ability to be a powerful administrative and policy leader for the executive branch are the large number of other administrative officials who are chosen by the voters in statewide elections; the large number of departments, boards, and commissions appointed by officials in the General Assembly and by officials other than

officials who as a group comprise the Council of State. These separately elected officials are the attorney general; auditor; commissioners of agriculture, insurance, and labor; lieutenant governor; secretary of state; superintendent of public instruction; and treasurer.

The governor oversees the execution of all state laws and is responsible for all phases of budgeting. He or she is empowered to convene the General Assembly in special session, deliver legislative and budgetary messages to that body, and, since 1997, veto legislation. The governor is chair of the

Council of State and may call upon that body for advice on allotments from the contingency and emergency fund and for the disposition of state property. The constitutional powers of the governor include the authority to grant pardons and commutations and issue extraordinary warrants and requests. The governor has extensive powers to reorganize the state bureaucracy, control state expenditures, and administer all funds and loans from the federal government.

Governors James B. Hunt and James G. Martin engaged in extensive party-building activities durthe governor; relatively modest powers to remove appointed executive officials from office; and weak veto power.

More than most states and far more than the national government, the executive branch of government in North Carolina is fragmented. Voters select in statewide elections ten executive officials: the governor and the nine officials who comprise the Council of State. Council of State members often are reelected to their respective offices and serve much longer than the governor; for example, Secretary of State Thad Eure served in that capacity for fifty-two years, from 1936 (when he shared the Democratic ballot with Franklin D. Roosevelt) to 1988. With the exception of Lieutenant Governor James Gardner, only Democrats have been elected to Council of State offices during this century, thus further complicating the leadership potential of Republican governors. Rooted in colonial practices, the Council of State has survived a declaration of independence from England, the adoption of new state constitutions in 1776, 1868, and 1971, and persistent attempts throughout the state's long history to reduce the number of separately elected statewide officials. A 1968 constitutional study commission appointed by Governor Dan K. Moore proposed a much shorter ballot of statewide officials and made the following critique of the Council of State:

Relatively few of the State's . . . voters have more than a faint idea of the duties of most of these offices; still fewer are in a position to know the qualities of the occupants of and candidates for these posts. . . . The fact is that for many decades, nearly all of these officers (other than the Governor and Lieutenant Governor) have reached their places by appointment by the Governor to fill a vacancy, have won nomination in a party primary without significant opposition, and have shared the success of the Democratic state ticket in the general election.

From the constitutional standpoint, these officers nevertheless hold their offices by gift of the voters, and so are only indirectly subject to supervision by the Governor. Thus, the Governor's ability to coordinate the activities of state government and to mount a comprehensive response to the problems of the day is handicapped if the elected department heads choose not to cooperate with him.

To many students of state government, this critique of the Council of State is as valid today as it was thirty-two years ago, and, as a consequence, initiatives to reduce the number of separately elected statewide officials continue to be introduced. The most recent initiative was the 1995 effort by Republicans in the North Carolina House to overhaul the state's governance structure for K-12 public education. The house effort failed by only two votes to achieve the three-fifths majority needed to submit a constitutional amendment to the voters calling for the superintendent of public instruction to be an appointive position. No other recent attempt to reduce the size of the Council of State has come so close to passage.

Whereas the trend in other states is toward fewer statewide elected officials, North Carolina legislators tend to be reluctant to enhance the power and authority of the governor, and they generally are unwilling to ask their constituents to give up the long-held right to vote for the occupants of the Council of State offices. Opponents of the long ballot argue that the state is not well served by electing so many officials, most of whom are invisible to the typical voter. But the current system is not likely to be changed due to the opposition of Council of State incumbents and their political supporters, as well as to the disinterest of the voters in this kind of constitutional reform. Also, if the Council of State offices remain popularly elected, occupants of these offices can use them as stepping stones to higher political office, as was the case when former superintendent of public instruction Bobby Etheridge won a seat in the U.S. House of Representatives in 1996. As a general rule, elected officials are loath to eliminate any pathway to higher office.

Freedom to appoint the heads of departments is an important measure of a governor's power and influence. Governors who have the sole authority to appoint these officials are more powerful than those who must share the appointive process with others. Governors who only approve appointments rather than initiating them have even weaker powers. Among various power rankings of the fifty state governors, the North Carolina governor is typically rated as having moderate-to-strong appointive powers. Of six major functional areas—corrections, education, health, highways, public utilities regulation, and welfare—the governor has strong appointive powers in four, the exceptions being education and public utilities regulation. The superintendent of public instruction is a separately elected official, but the governor appoints eleven of thirteen members of the state board of education, subject to the approval of the General Assembly. The governor's nominees to the seven-member North Carolina Utilities Commission, which oversees public utilities regulation, are subject to confirmation by the General Assembly.

The flip side of the power to appoint is the ability to remove officials from office. In North Carolina, the governor's removal powers are based on statutes, not the state constitution; such powers have been limited by court decisions related to cause, scope, and process. In some cases, even the power to remove officials appointed by previous administrations is restricted, and thus the removal powers of the governor are weak. As stated above, the governor shares executive authority with many independent policy-making advisory boards and commissions. Although the governor appoints the members of some of these boards and commissions, only nominal control over these individuals can be exercised following the appointment due to weak removal powers. This particular problem is compounded by the greatly increased number of state boards, commissions, and councils over the last two decades, which has further dispersed executive authority. All of these difficulties reaffirm the conclusion of numerous studies over the last thirty years that North Carolina's government is one of the least efficient and least accountable among the fifty states.

Former governor Robert W. Scott once observed that "North Carolina is not very effective in shaping regional and national policy as it affects our state because our state changes the team captain and key players just about the time we get the opportunity and know-how to carry the ball and score." With the approval of the gubernatorial succession amendment to the state constitution in 1977, the state's game plan for keeping the governor on the leadership team changed dramatically. James Hunt was the first governor to succeed himself, followed by James Martin who also served two terms, followed by Hunt who was elected to a third term in 1992 and a fourth term in 1996. For almost a quarter of a century only two men have served as governor, and thus the office of governor is now strong on length of tenure and succession potential.

Governors in all states have gained almost complete control over the budget development process. The Executive Budget Act of 1925 made the North Carolina governor the director of the budget, and the new state constitution in 1971 assigned the chief executive the role of budget formulator and administrator. The governor's budget role was enhanced as a result of the *Wallace v. Bone* decision in 1982, when the Advisory Budget Commission, a fifteen-person body with the governor, president of the senate, and speaker of the house each appointing five persons, was declared a strictly advisory body. The North Carolina Supreme Court ruled in that case that the separation-of-power principle in the state constitution prohibited legislators from exercising executive authority. Therefore, under the North Carolina Constitution only the governor is empowered to prepare and recommend to the General Assembly a comprehensive budget of anticipated revenues and proposed expenditures for the ensuing biennial session.

Once the governor delivers his or her budget message to the General Assembly, deliberations on the governor's budget in the house and senate initially occur within the appropriations and finance committees. These are large committees containing about half the membership of each chamber. It is at this stage of the review process that the governor's influence over the budget is seriously compromised. When voters began to elect Republican governors, the Democratic-controlled General Assembly started developing its own budget and often substituted its agenda for that of the governor. During the Holshouser and Martin administrations, it was common for budgets to be described as "dead on arrival" when submitted to the highly partisan, Democratic-controlled General Assembly. To a lesser degree, this practice continued even in the Hunt years. Subject only to statutory and constitutional requirements to balance revenues and expenditures, the General Assembly can make nearly unlimited changes in the governor's budget.

The one thing that school-aged children may have associated with the governor of North Carolina during most of the twentieth century was that he alone among the fifty state governors lacked the power to veto legislation. For at least six decades, the General Assembly debated the merits of a gubernatorial veto. Finally, largely due to the efforts of the Republican majority in the North Carolina House, the lawmakers in 1995 agreed to place the question on the ballot and allow the voters to decide. In the 1996 general election, the electorate gave Governor Hunt what every governor for half a century had coveted, the power to shape legislation through the use or threat of a veto.

The veto power designed by the North Carolina General Assembly and approved by the voters is relatively weak when compared with the veto power of other state governors. Forty-three governors enjoy some version of a line-item veto, and nine governors can even make reductions in budget lines. The governor of North Carolina is authorized to veto the total budget, not specific line items within it. Also, the governor is only empowered to veto bills that impact the whole state, not bills that appoint people to state boards or change legislative or congressional districts. He or she cannot veto local bills (those that apply to subunits of the state such as a county or municipality). The governor's veto can be overridden by a three-fifths majority in both the house and senate, a more modest hurdle to override than faced by many state legislatures and thus easier to achieve. Although Governor Hunt did not veto or even seriously threaten to veto legislation during the 1997 session of the General Assembly, advocates for the gubernatorial veto argued that it made the governor a more important player in the legislative process and allowed him to more forcefully represent the general public interest in legislative deliberations. Speaker Harold Brubaker acknowledged that the governor's newly acquired veto power caused him to communicate more often with Governor Hunt. Brubaker said, "I think it [the veto power] encouraged us to keep in touch, so he'd know what we were doing and why we were doing it."

For most members of the General Assembly, the governor's new veto power probably had little or no impact on behavior, but it is unnecessary that individual legislators know in advance whether the governor plans to block the passage of a controversial piece of legislation. The fact that the governor can stop a bill from becoming law, unless overridden by a three-fifths vote of both chambers, gives him or her a seat at the negotiating table when the house and senate leadership debate issues affecting the state's future. But the seat at the table has a price, for the governor now has to share responsibility for legislative outcomes. Armed with the power to veto legislation, the governor can no longer easily avoid accountability for what transpires in the General Assembly.

The Governor as a Political and Policy Leader

Even though the North Carolina governor has modest-to-weak formal powers, in the hands of a skillful political leader the informal powers of the office provide the opportunity for strong gubernatorial leadership. Thad L. Beyle observed: "A media-wise governor can . . . dominate a state's political and policy agenda if he or she is adept at handling the media and public appearances; by the same token, a governor's power can decline if the governor is inept at controlling the political agenda or communicating through television cameras." The North Carolina governor has other informal advantages not shared by many chief executive officers. Because no large metropolitan area dominates North Carolina's political landscape in the manner of an Atlanta or a Miami, there are no other highly visible political leaders in the state with whom the governor must compete for media attention. Captains of the state's dominant industries, such as banking, furniture, textiles, and tobacco, usually prefer to work behind-the-scenes and out of the public eye, and labor lacks sufficient political clout to field a serious challenge for public attention.

In the final analysis, the essence of the governor's power is personal suasion. To achieve legislative objectives and implement public policies, a governor must persuade department heads over whom he or she has limited control to support gubernatorial aspirations for the state, legislators who are fiercely independent and jealous to the extreme of their prerogatives, federal and local government officials who have their own political agendas and are beyond the governor's administrative reach, and a general public that views an office of limited formal powers as one of great authority and influence.

The Judicial Branch of State Government

The General Assembly rewrote the judicial article of the state constitution when it passed the Judicial Department Act of 1965. By this action, the legislators transformed North Carolina's court system from one developed through piecemeal change, and comprised of hundreds of courts specially created by statute that were widely dissimilar in form and jurisdiction, particularly at the local court level, to one that is highly centralized with primary responsibility and authority for the administration of justice residing in the office of the chief justice and the state supreme court. The state court system now consists of three tiers—district courts, superior courts, and appellate courts including the court of appeals and the supreme court. It is, with few exceptions, uniform across all counties and judicial districts in terms of jurisdiction, rules of procedure, personnel, and costs.

At the top of the North Carolina court system is the supreme court, the court of last resort. It is composed of the chief justice and six associate justices. The court of appeals, created in 1967 to relieve the caseload of the supreme court, consists of twelve judges who sit in panels of three to hear arguments and issue opinions and decisions. Superior courts are trial courts with general jurisdiction over civil and criminal cases. Many cases originate in superior courts, which use juries, formal hearings, witnesses, attorneys for the prosecution and defense, and a presiding judge. District courts also are trial courts but have more limited jurisdiction than superior courts. About half of the cases that come before district courts relate to motor vehicles; many others are civil cases involving domestic disputes that frequently focus on child support. The state constitution provides for the election of justices on the supreme court, court of appeals, and superior courts to eight-year terms; district court justices are elected to four-year terms.

At the national level, judges are appointed for life by the president and confirmed by the U.S. Senate. A central reason why federal judges are not elected to office is to insulate them from overt political pressure, including dependency on campaign contributors and the temporary and transitory mood swings of the electorate. In contrast, North Carolina judges have been chosen by the voters in partisan elections since 1868. Justices of the supreme court and the court of appeals are selected in statewide elections, whereas district and superior court judges are elected from judicial districts. Until 1994, superior court judges were nominated within districts but elected statewide. The Republican Party sued the state in federal district court over this arrangement, arguing that its purpose was to keep Republicans and African Americans off the bench. Since the voter registration ratio favored Democrats in statewide races, requiring superior court candidates to be elected statewide rather than from districts diluted Republican voting strength and usually ensured electoral victories for Democratic candidates. The GOP won the case in federal district court, but the court of appeals returned the case to the district court for rehearing. Late in the 1996 legislative session, the General Assembly resolved the issue by requiring superior court judges in the 1996 general election to be selected from districts in partisan elections and beginning in 1998 to be selected from districts in nonpartisan elections. This legislative action removed the need for continued legal action by the Republican Party.

Although the state constitution requires that judgeships be filled by election, in 1997 almost one-half—148 out of 307 sitting judges—were initially appointed to their posts by the governor. This oddity was due to judges dying, resigning, or retiring before the end of their terms, thus allowing the governor to fill the seat by appointment. From the turn of the century until the 1970s, judges who resigned or retired from the bench did so well in advance of the next election so that the Democratic governor could appoint an acceptable Democratic candidate to the vacancy. The newly appointed judge served until the next general election and then ran for the judicial seat as an incumbent, a distinct advantage since fewer than 10 percent of incumbent judicial candidates failed to be reelected, and many were returned to their posts without opposition. For seventy years, this was the primary pathway to the North Carolina bench. With the election of Republican governors in 1972, 1984, and 1988, and with the growing numbers of voters who identify with the Republican Party, GOP judicial candidates have become more competitive, the campaigns for judgeships more fierce and partisan, and the cost of winning a seat on the supreme court and court of appeals more daunting, costing as much as $300,000 to $500,000. Yet despite the changed circumstances surrounding the election of judges, almost half of the judicial seats in North Carolina continue to be initially filled by gubernatorial appointment rather than by election.

Although North Carolina judges officially gain office via partisan elections, the roles they play in the governance process are very different from those assumed by legislative and executive officials. As a result, judicial candidates must observe strict protocols described in the Code of Judicial Conduct. Until recently, they were prohibited from expressing personal views on disputed political and legal issues and from making campaign promises other than the faithful performance of duties. But in May 1997, the state supreme court removed the passage in the Code of Judicial Conduct that banned the expression of general philosophical views by candidates. Whereas most judicial elections in the past were dull affairs with the candidates largely restricted to a polite "no comment" when asked what they would do if elected to office, judicial contests beginning in 1998 have the potential to become more lively affairs as candidates share with the general public their personal preferences on such issues as abortion, driving while intoxicated, and other emotionally charged matters. Left intact, however, were bans on announcing how candidates would rule in specific cases, making speeches in which they supported a political party, and directly soliciting campaign funds.

The Role of Judges in the Political Process

Whereas members of the state legislature are expected to represent citizens who reside in their districts, a praiseworthy practice for a legislator, it is considered inappropriate behavior for a judge. Judges are supposed to approach disputes in an open, neutral manner and to apply settled principles of law so that equal justice under law is a reality for all citizens. Nevertheless, due to shifting attitudes within the electorate on matters concerning gender, politics, and race, there is growing interest in the "representativeness" of state courts as measured by the number of African Americans, Republicans, and women who serve on the bench. Among the state judges in 1995 were 35 African Americans/Native Americans (12 percent of the judiciary), 44 Republicans (15 percent), and 41 women (14 percent). Although demographics are theoretically unimportant in dispensing justice, African Americans, women's organizations, and certainly political parties are vitally interested in the demographic profile of the state's judiciary.

The courts are more passive and reactive than the other branches of government, mainly responding to issues brought to them in the form of specific cases, especially at the district and superior court levels. Appellate courts exercise limited discretion in determining the cases that will be heard, but even in the appeal format, judges have far less discretion over their agenda than legislators and executive officials. But it is important to remember that, within limits, judges do create common law, interpret statutes, and decide what the state constitution means in specific situations and under specific conditions. Judges thus have the potential to be major policymakers.

Nominating and Electing Judges

For decades, officeholders and citizens have debated how to choose judges—by popular election, by executive appointment, or by a screening arrangement that is commonly referred to as "merit selection." Many states were swept up in a wave of popular democracy during the administration of President Andrew Jackson, and one of the manifestations of Jacksonian democracy was the popular election of judges to make them more accountable to the people.

Over the last fifty years, however, there has been a shift toward appointing judges in combination with merit selection commissions and retention elections. Statistics compiled in 1997 by the American Judicature Society indicate that thirty-four states and the District of Columbia filled at least some judicial vacancies on the basis of merit. Focusing on North Carolina, Jack Betts summarized the arguments for and against merit selection of judges. The arguments for merit selection are "(1) the present, partisan system of election discourages qualified lawyers from running for judgeships; (2) the cost of running for office is too high; (3) politicking requires candidates to seek funds from lawyers who may subsequently have cases before that judge; (4) voters already are faced with an unusually long statewide ballot; (5) voters often lack information about candidates, and without the time or resources to become familiar with them, they are unable to make good choices; and (6) merit selection has worked well in some other states."

The arguments against merit selection are "(1) the system yanks power from its proper place—with the people—and deposits it in the hands of a select few; (2) North Carolina has had a good judiciary under the current system; (3) merit selection does not eliminate politicking, it just alters the way judicial candidates must run for office; and (4) merit selection has not worked well in some other states."

In 1994 Chief Justice James Exum appointed a twenty-seven-member nonpartisan panel of citizens known as the Commission for the Future of Justice and the Courts in North Carolina and charged it to "design the court system of the future and tell us how to get there." As part of the commission's inquiry, a statewide survey was conducted in 1995. The survey found that only 40 percent of the respondents knew that the state supreme court was an elected body. Sixty percent of the respondents stated they had participated in the 1994 general election, but only half of these voters recalled casting a ballot for any judicial candidate. Among those who recalled voting for a judge, 78 percent could not name a single judicial candidate on the ballot. These findings suggested that, with few exceptions, candidates for judicial offices were virtually invisible to the average voter, and it was a myth that judges were held accountable for their actions through popular election.

Among other things, the commission recommended appointing all judges and county clerks of court rather than choosing them by election; creating a state judicial council as a sort of board of directors to help advise a much stronger chief justice with power to set the rules of civil and criminal procedure and evidence; merging superior and district courts into a new circuit court; establishing a family court with trained judges and new personnel to handle cases involving divorce, child custody, and domestic violence; dropping the constitutional requirement for twelve-member unanimous juries in civil cases; instituting new case management procedures to streamline court dockets and the appeals process; and developing a plan to provide the technology and other resources the courts would need for the twenty-first century.

With some fanfare and high hopes, senate bills 834 and 835 and house bills 741 and 742, which called for replacing the existing system of electing judges with a merit system of nominating and appointing new judges to office, were introduced during the 1997 legislative session. But the General Assembly failed to consider these bills and instead referred the matter to a legislative research commission for further study. Some Democratic legislators worried that their constituents would object to giving up the opportunity to vote for judicial candidates, and many Republicans did not want to change the current system of selecting judges just when GOP candidates were beginning to win office at the trial court level.

In the past, campaign spending in judicial races has not been significant in the outcome of judicial contests. Partisan tides, such as in the election of 1994, were the only phenomena that produced meaningful change in the composition of the courts, except in those districts where there was almost a 50-50 partisan balance. But if judges continue to be elected to office in competitive races, especially at the appellate level, only higher levels of campaign spending will buy the name recognition required to win. Such an eventuality will force candidates for the appellate courts to seek large sums of money from the only people who will care enough about the outcome of these contests to bankroll the candidates—trial court attorneys and special interests that might have cases before that judge. Although up to now North Carolina has avoided most of the problems posed by "big-money politics" in judicial contests, this is no guarantee that it will always be so. Reformers who are concerned that big-money campaigns might eventually erode the integrity of the North Carolina judiciary will continue to work and lobby for changing the way state judges are selected for office.

Outlook

To be an elected state official in North Carolina as the twenty-first century opens is to confront a broad array of risky choices. At the beginning of the 1990s, a sluggish national economy, escalating health care costs, unrelenting public pressure for prison construction, and fierce voter resistance to new taxes forced North Carolina legislators, as well as state and local government officials everywhere, to slow spending and reduce services. With a sig-

nificant revenue shortfall during the 1991 legislative session, the General Assembly reduced the state budget by $576.3 million, approximately 6 percent of planned expenditures, and raised taxes by a similar amount to balance the budget.

Since 1991 North Carolina's booming economy has made it possible for the state to collect impressive amounts of tax revenue. For most of the 1990s, members of the General Assembly had the pleasant task of deciding what to do with a budget surplus—fund new spending programs, establish a rainy-day account and bank funds for future use, or return money to the taxpayers. The governor and legislators opted to do all three. From 1995 to 1998 the GOP majority in the house convinced the General Assembly to enact major tax reductions. These tax reductions included an increase in the individual income tax exemptions from $2,000 to $2,500 per person; a $60 child tax credit; elimination of the state's intangibles tax, sales tax on food, and soft drink tax; repeal of the inheritance tax; and a phased reduction in the corporate income tax from 7.75 percent to 6.90 percent by 2000. It has been estimated that by 2000 tax reductions will cost state government over $1.2 billion in lost revenues. Further, during the period of revenue reduction North Carolina's indebtedness escalated rapidly—from $750 million in 1993 to over $5 billion in 1999. The annual service cost for the new debt is almost $500 million.

Even with significant tax reductions, North

Carolina state government continued to grow. During the 1997-99 biennium it employed approximately 240,000 people, including public schoolteachers, and raised and spent over $40 billion from all sources (general and highway funds, federal funds and receipts). State spending and employment have been climbing steadily for decades, reflecting government's expanding responsibilities and continued growth in North Carolina's population. The constant increase in state spending is a product of many factors, including more students enrolled in the public schools, community colleges, and universities; more wastewater and trash to remove; more roads to build and maintain; more people living longer and receiving Medicaid payments; and more people occupying cells in the state's prisons. Also, a significant portion of state spending goes for state agencies that administer federal programs in such areas as welfare, health care, job training, education, and highway construction. During the 1997-99 fiscal biennium, for example, approximately 26 percent of the total North Carolina state budget was collected by the national government ($10.6 billion) but spent by state and local agencies (Fig. 11.15).

Since the 1980s there has been a fundamental change in federal-state relationships in the direction of a smaller role for Washington. This has been caused by a convergence of factors including the electoral success of GOP candidates at the presidential and congressional levels, the emer-

Figure 11.15. The Recommended North Carolina State Budget (in millions of dollars), 1997–1999

a. Income

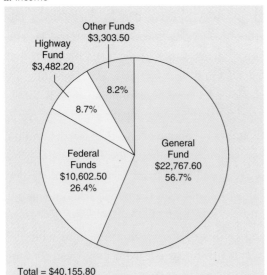

Other Funds
$3,303.50

Highway Fund
$3,482.20

8.2%

8.7%

Federal Funds
$10,602.50
26.4%

General Fund
$22,767.60
56.7%

Total = $40,155.80

b. Spending

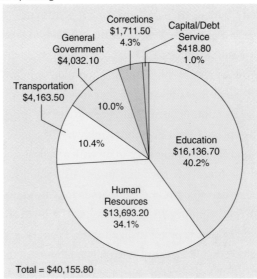

Corrections
$1,711.50
4.3%

General Government
$4,032.10

Capital/Debt Service
$418.80
1.0%

Transportation
$4,163.50

10.0%

10.4%

Education
$16,136.70
40.2%

Human Resources
$13,693.20
34.1%

Total = $40,155.80

Sources: North Carolina State Budget Summary of Recommendations, 1997-99; Office of State Budget and Management, Febuary 1997.

gence of the balanced budget concept as a potent political issue, and increasing citizen disillusionment with national efforts to solve public problems. The sweeping Republican victory in the 1994 congressional and state elections accelerated this shift of responsibility and authority away from Washington to Raleigh and other state capitols.

Perhaps the most dramatic manifestation of the new federalism is the transfer of responsibility for the welfare program from the national to the state level. In August 1996 Congress passed and President Clinton signed a measure ending a sixty-year-old, open-ended federal guarantee of income support for needy children and their parents, sub-stituting a fixed-sum block grant for each state to use largely as it sees fit. This transfer of responsibility is so recent that its effects on the state government and the people served by the welfare program cannot yet be judged. Predictions about how well it will work are based more on the ideology of the advocates and opponents of welfare reform than on evidence and experience. Whether welfare reform works well enough to make the case for transferring more responsibility from Washington to the states or turns out to be a policy disaster that brings devolution of the federal system to a halt is still unanswered.

Over the last few years welfare caseloads across the nation and in North Carolina have been declining. The strong economy is one obvious explanation for the reduction in the number of families on welfare, but perhaps just as important are the expectations of those served by welfare programs. When poor mothers go into state agencies to apply for welfare, they now find themselves confronting bureaucracies that perceive their task to be finding jobs for their clients, not writing checks. But many questions about welfare reform remain. Will private sector employers be willing to hire hard-core welfare recipients, who frequently require special attention and support in entry-level jobs? Will state government fund transportation assistance and child care programs to enable welfare mothers with children to take jobs outside of the home? Many state officials recognize that moving welfare recipients to work will require spending more money, not less, on health care, child care, transportation, and training. Coming to terms with the realization that simply cutting welfare spending will not solve human problems will not be easy and is sure to spark considerable debate in the General Assembly.

Other hard choices and daunting problems are waiting in the new century. Unlike the national government, state and local governments in North Carolina must function within the constitutional requirement that state revenues and expenditures must be balanced during every fiscal year, even during periods of economic recession. In addition, state statutes declare that the General Assembly's appropriations are "maximum, conditional and proportionate." Appropriations are maximum in that an agency may not spend more than is appropriated, conditional in that they are dependent on actual revenue collections, and proportionate in that the total amount agencies can spend is proportional to actual revenue collections. Further, the governor is required to monitor revenue collections and determine how much of the money appropriated by the legislature should be allocated each quarter. As a consequence of these balanced budget requirements, there is a "boom and bust" character to state spending cycles. When the economy is strong, the state budget develops surpluses, making it possible to cut taxes and increase spending. During periods of recession-induced fiscal crisis, such as in 1990-91, state government raises taxes and cuts spending (Fig. 11.16).

The obsession of house Republicans to reduce taxes and of senate Democrats and Governor Hunt to boost spending for schools, the environment, and human services has made large tax increases or large reductions in state programming a likely task for a future General Assembly. According to some observers, the tax-cutting spree of house Republicans during 1995-98 threatens the future of state programming even in the absence of a serious business downturn. The North Carolina Budget and Tax Center concluded that the tax relief adopted by the legislature since 1995 will produce over the 2000-2001 biennium annual deficits in excess of $200 million. Also contributing to the anxiety of state legislators in 1999 were two dramatic

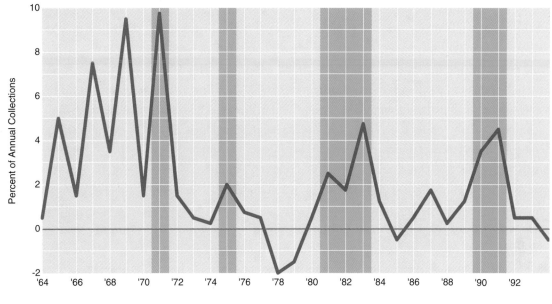

Figure 11.16. Economic Downturns and State Tax Increases in the United States, 1964–1994

━━━ Net state tax changes

▨ Recession

Sources: Center for the Study of the States, based on data from the Tax Foundation; National Conference of State Legislatures, 1997.

courtroom setbacks. In May 1998 the North Carolina Supreme Court ruled that the state had to repay $799 million to state government retirees whose pensions were illegally taxed. In December 1998 the state supreme court ordered that citizens be reimbursed for an unconstitutional tax on their stocks, a repayment that could cost the state up to $450 million.

If North Carolina begins to have revenue problems, future policymakers will confront some unenviable tasks. A fiscal crunch in health care spending looms with the coming tidal wave of babyboomer retirements around 2010, a demographic juggernaut that will place heavy pressure on state revenues and tax the ingenuity of the General Assembly. State legislatures around the country will have to set minimum care standards for an increasingly aging population, a politically sensitive task that may in the end inflate the cost of health care. Although rising health care costs slowed in recent years due to managed care trends, few believe that the problem is over.

At the other end of the age spectrum, school facilities and education budgets require attention. Between 1997 and 2007 North Carolina's public K-12 enrollment is expected to increase by 27 percent, a growth rate second only to California among the fifty states. To cope with the massive influx of new students crowding into the state's public schools, hundreds of new schools will have to be built and thousands of new teachers employed. The rising enrollments can be attributed to in-migration, a delay in marriage and child-bearing among the baby-boom generation, students staying in school longer, and higher birthrates among minorities, especially Hispanics, who will comprise a larger fraction of the school population in this century. Enrollment in the state's universities also is projected to expand by 41,800 students between 1995 and 2005, an increase roughly equivalent to twice the size of the student body of the University of North Carolina at Chapel Hill in 1998.

Despite North Carolina's record-breaking job growth and investment, not all working families are sharing in the prosperity. Current economic trends divide workers into two camps: those with more education and job skills are earning higher wages than ever before, but those who lack education and training have seen their income stagnate or decline. While per capita income for workers is rising and the state's unemployment rate continues to trail the national average, permanent layoffs in such sectors as textiles and apparel manufacturing also are rising. Jobs that pay moderate wages are disappearing while new jobs cluster around the top of the pay scale or around the minimum wage. Trapped in a changing economy, workers at the bottom of the pay scale will need a more sympathetic response from the probusiness General Assembly than they have received in the past.

State and local governments in North Carolina confront many challenges. If the U.S. Congress reduces its contributions for shared federal-state programs and if the national economy falters, thus reducing state revenues and generating fresh demands for government services, the governor and General Assembly will quickly confront a difficult agenda and unpleasant choices. Further, this worst-case scenario will have to be managed by elected officials within the context of a state trying to cope with problems that accompany both an aging population and exploding school enrollment.

Many, although not all, North Carolinians have benefited from the sustained good economic times of the 1990s. But unlike the story of Pharaoh and Joseph in ancient Egypt, where God revealed to Pharaoh through Joseph that seven years of great plenty throughout the land would be followed by seven lean years of famine, North Carolina's political and economic future is uncertain. Continuing prosperity will allow elected officials to expand services and to maintain or even further reduce current tax burdens on citizens and businesses. But if a serious and sustained downturn in the economy is part of the future, what will be the state's priorities under these new and more stressful conditions?

Selected References

Arrington, T. "When Money Doesn't Matter: Campaign Spending for Minor Statewide Judicial and Executive Offices in North Carolina." *Justice System Journal* 18/3 (1996): 257–66.

Fleer, J. *North Carolina Government and Politics*. Lincoln: University of Nebraska Press, 1994.

Key, V. "North Carolina: Progressive Plutocracy." In *North Carolina Focus: An Anthology on State Government, Politics, and Policy*. Raleigh: North Carolina Center for Public Policy Research, 1949.

Jacobson, G. "The 1994 House Elections in Perspective." *Political Science Quarterly* (Summer 1996): 203–23.

Luebke, P. *Tar Heel Politics*. Chapel Hill: University of North Carolina Press, 1990.

12. AIR QUALITY
Walter E. Martin

Expanding population, cities, transportation facilities, and industry have increased emissions that endanger the quality of the air. Ironically, greater prosperity threatens the well-being of the very people who are benefiting from newfound affluence. More people enjoy unprecedented mobility that is provided by the personal automobile, but their rapidly growing numbers threaten to offset the beneficial effects of better emission controls on their vehicles. As more people demand even more electricity to light or cool their homes, power-generating plants emit more particulates into the air despite the best efforts of utility companies to reduce such emissions. Nowhere is the tenuous balance between the benefits of growth and its costs more apparent or difficult to maintain.

Historically, cities in North Carolina have been spatially dispersed, but changes in the structure of the urban population are creating larger, more concentrated centers. Because of rapid urban growth, especially in the Charlotte and Raleigh metropolitan areas, the potential for higher concentrations of air pollution require vigilant air quality monitoring and attention to the efficacy of emission control strategies. Recent advances in air quality have resulted from aggressive and successful emission control strategies of the past.

In the last quarter of the twentieth century, the shift to unleaded motor fuels, catalytic converters, and other tailpipe emission controls brought such effective improvements in air quality that most North Carolina air pollutants were reduced from their 1980 levels despite dramatic rates of growth in population, road transportation, and economic activity. During the first years of the twenty-first century, however, the growth of population, energy use, and transportation threaten to cancel these gains and worsen air quality. As many cities in North Carolina continue to grow, the potential for concentrated emissions will increase. As prevailing winds transport urban air pollutants from larger- and higher-density cities, agriculture, forestry, and health within and downwind from those cities stand to be at greater risk.

Propelled by urban growth, many parts of North Carolina are currently threatened by summer ozone episodes. Although these episodes are infrequent by national standards, they suggest that air quality in the shadow of growing metropolitan areas is vulnerable and that continued or expanded emission controls will be required to maintain clean air for North Carolina's people, businesses, and industries. Until now, surface level oxidants such as ozone have been the most persistent threat to air quality. But as the state enters a new century, concern about the environmental and health effects of ozone is joined by concern about the concentration of small particles in the air that also may pose a risk to the public health.

Clean Air

The term "clean air" has various connotations when interpreted by residents in different environments. To most residents of eastern Europe, where long-term acid deposition from air pollution has produced soils as acidic as vinegar (pH of less than 2.5), the air quality in North Carolina would seem to be excellent. Residents in Mexico City, where smog levels can exceed World Health Organization standards every day from February until December, might be envious of the rare unhealthy day each year in Raleigh or Charlotte. But residents of Molokai, Hawaii, who are accustomed to the purity of midoceanic breezes, might find ambient air quality in North Carolina less than satisfactory.

Air pollution evokes images of coughing, choking, and eye irritation, but the total effect of polluted air is far worse. Adverse health effects such as asthma and cancer are associated with air pollutants. Acid deposition is linked with soil acidification and threatens the health of ecosystems, including forests and crops. Acid deposition and photochemical oxidants such as ozone, nitrogen deposition, and other nitrogen- and sulfur-derived pollutants contribute to plant stress and may be partly responsible for forest decline on Mount Mitchell and other high elevation sites in the Appalachian Mountains.

The U.S. Environmental Protection Agency (EPA) and state agencies are enforcing new emission standards for hundreds of chemicals collectively known as air toxics. Examples of these air pollutants that are particularly toxic or hazardous to human health include beryllium, mercury, asbestos, vinyl chloride, benzene, cadmium, carbon tetrachloride, chloroform, chromium trichloroethylene, radioactive isotopes, and arsenic. Methanol, toluene, and methyl ethyl ketone comprise the three most massive toxic air emissions emitted in North Carolina each year. In the industrial Piedmont counties the leading emissions are a reflection of the nature of local industry. Considerable effort is required to limit adverse effects from these and the more common atmospheric contaminants such as carbon monoxide, sulfur dioxide, and ozone. The intent of this effort would be to reduce the threat to public health or to wildlife, aquatic life, and other natural resources; protect local ecosystems; lessen impacts on populations of endangered or threatened species; and reduce significant degradation of environmental quality over broad areas.

Assessment of the risk posed to North Carolina's population and environment from air pollution is complex. Certainly photochemical oxidants such as ozone present a substantial health threat to a large number of people, because ozone and the other photochemical oxidants form across most reaches of the state every year between April and September. These oxidants have been monitored since the 1970s, and much is known about the hazards they present. In addition, recent studies suggest that risks from fine particulate matter may be greater than previously believed. Although epidemiological risk from air toxics has not been extensively explored, it is generally accepted that atmospheric dispersion from release points sufficiently reduces concentrations below the level where public health effects are measurable.

The principal technique employed to assess air quality has been to establish air quality standards and compare samples from a network of air quality monitors. Air quality monitors to detect carbon monoxide, nitrogen dioxide, particulates, and ozone are typically located within metropolitan areas where many emissions originate, but some air pollution monitors are also placed in suburban and rural areas (Fig. 12.1). Summaries of the monitored levels and trends are available through some county environmental protection departments and from the North Carolina Department of Environment, Health, and Natural Resources. Unfortunately, there is a substantial time lag between taking these observations and reporting the data. The data reported in this book are the most current that were available at press time.

Ambient Air Quality

"Ambient" means encompassing, and it is defined by the EPA as that portion of the atmosphere, external to buildings, to which the general public has access. Table 12.1 presents a summary of the national and North Carolina ambient air quality standards. The primary standards were established to provide an adequate margin of safety for public health. The secondary standards are designed to protect vegetation, materials, and visibility.

Particulates

The term "particulates" refers to any airborne particle, either solid or liquid (except pure water, mist, or steam), that is suspended in the air. Total suspended particulates (TSP) generally refers to all particulate matter smaller than 45 micrometers (mm) in diameter. Particulate matter less than or equal

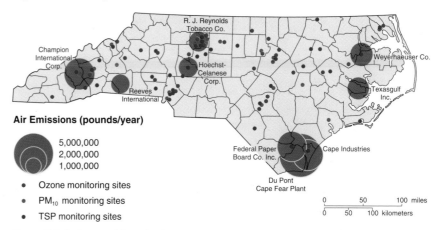

Figure 12.1. Principal Toxic Emissions Released to the Air

Air Emissions (pounds/year)

- 5,000,000
- 2,000,000
- 1,000,000

- Ozone monitoring sites
- PM$_{10}$ monitoring sites
- TSP monitoring sites

Source: U.S. Environmental Protection Agency, Toxic Chemicals Release Inventory, 1991.

to 10 micrometers (PM-10) is identified separately because these particles penetrate more deeply into the respiratory system, are more difficult to expel, and therefore pose a greater risk to public health. Recent epidemiologic studies have found an association between levels of fine particulate matter and effects such as premature mortality, hospital admissions, and respiratory illnesses at concentrations at or below the 1990 standards (Fig. 12.2a). Particulate matter less than or equal to 2.5 micrometers in diameter (PM-2.5), the smallest category of airborne particles, also has been implicated. The health effects of these particles are related in a minor way to the composition of the particles but mainly correspond to the density of particle concentration. Most of these particles form as sulfur dioxide and ammonia and combine to form ammonium sulfate, but other sources include diesel exhaust. Fine particles are associated with aggravation of existing lung and heart disease, effects on lung clearance, changes in the form and structure of organisms, and development of cancer.

The EPA has responded to these findings by adding a new annual PM-2.5 standard set at 15 micrograms per cubic meter ($\mu g/m^3$) and a new twenty-four-

Table 12.1. National and North Carolina Ambient Air Quality Standards

Pollutant	Mean Value	National Primary Standard	National Secondary Standard	North Carolina Standard
Total suspended particulates (TSP)	Ann. geo. mean	None	None	75 µg/m³
	24 hours	None	None	150 µg/m³
Particulate matter				
< 10 µm (PM-10)	Annual arithmetic	50 µg/m³	50 µg/m³	50 µg/m³
	24 hours	150 µg/m³	150 µg/m³	150 µg/m³
Sulfur dioxide (SO_2)	Annual arithmetic	80 µg/m³	None	80 µg/m³
	24 hours	365 µg/m³	None	365 µg/m³
	3 hours	None	1,300 µg/m³	1,300 µg/m³
Nitrogen dioxide (NO_2)	Annual arithmetic	0.053 ppm	0.053 ppm	0.053 ppm
Carbon monoxide (CO)	8 hours	9 ppm	None	9 ppm
	1 hour	35 ppm	None	35 ppm
Ozone (O_3)	1 hour	0.12 ppm	0.12 ppm	0.12 ppm
Lead (Pb)	Max. quart. arith.	1.5 µg/m³	1.5 µg/m³	1.5 µg/m³

hour PM-2.5 standard set at 65 µg/m³. Although North Carolina has not monitored PM-2.5 levels systematically, approximately forty new PM-2.5 monitors will be used to establish baseline data. The most recent published data show that the trend in particulate matter concentrations in North Carolina was downward between 1972 and 1996, indicating that emission controls and decreased open burning have been effective in improving particulate matter pollution (Fig. 12.2b).

Sulfur Dioxide

In North Carolina the primary sources of sulfur dioxide(SO_2), a colorless gas, are from coal-burning operations, usually for electricity generation. Concentrations of as low as 0.25 parts per million (ppm) have been shown to produce acute bronchoconstriction among hypersensitive individuals. Sulfur dioxide can aggravate existing cases of asthma, bronchitis, and emphysema. These responses may result less from the direct effects of the ambient gas exposures than from the highly irritant effects of sulfate aerosols (e.g., sulfuric acid) produced from sulfur dioxide. Cotton, sweet potatoes, wheat, cucumbers, alfalfa, peas, oats, apple trees, and several types of pine trees are susceptible to damage from sulfur dioxide pollution. Symptoms of injury to vegetation include bleached spots, bleached areas between veins, chlorosis, growth suppression, and reduction in yield. In the eastern United States, sulfur dioxide is responsible for approximately 65 percent of the acidity in precipitation.

Although sulfur dioxide levels in North Carolina have increased slightly during the period of record, levels are less than 15 percent of the ambient sulfur dioxide standard and are expected to remain low as a result of federal clean air legislation that encourages the use of low sulfur fuels (Fig. 12.3). Increased capacity for electricity generation from fossil fuels in North Carolina is shifting from coal to lower sulfur fuels like natural gas. Nationally, sulfur dioxide levels decreased by 30 percent between 1970 and 1996 as a result of significant regulatory attention and investment in pollution control at fossil fuel–fired electric power–generation facilities.

Nitrogen Dioxide

Nitrogen dioxide (NO_2) is less soluble than sulfur dioxide and consequently can penetrate deep into

Figure 12.2a. Average Second Maximum 24–Hour Total Suspended Particulates (TSP), 1972–1989

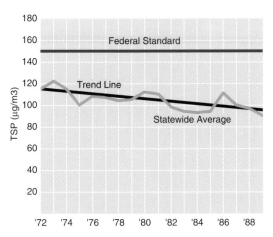

Note: These values represent the second most polluted day in terms of total suspended particulate matter.

Source: N.C. Department of Environment, Health, and Natural Resources, Division of Environmental Management, Air Quality Ambient Monitoring Section, *1996 Ambient Air Quality Report*, 1998.

Figure 12.2b. Average 24-Hour Particulate Matter (PM$_{10}$) Concentration, 1985–1996

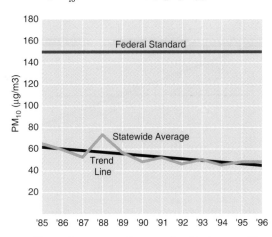

Note: These values represent the most polluted day in terms of fine dust suspended in the air.

Source: N.C. Department of Environment, Health, and Natural Resources, Division of Environmental Management, Air Quality Ambient Monitoring Section, *1996 Ambient Air Quality Report*, 1998.

Figure 12.3. Average Second Maximum 24-Hour Sulfur Dioxide (SO$_2$) Concentration, 1972–1991

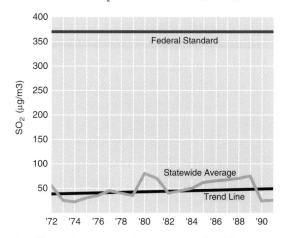

Note: These values represent the second most polluted day in terms of sulfur dioxide.

Source: N.C. Department of Environment, Health, and Natural Resources, Division of Environmental Management, Air Quality Ambient Monitoring Section, *1996 Ambient Air Quality Report*, 1998.

Figure 12.4. Average Annual Nitrogen Dioxide (NO$_2$) Level, 1972–1996

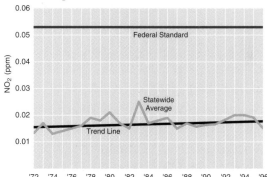

Note: These values represent the second most polluted day based on the highest eight-hour concentration of carbon monoxide.

Source: N.C. Department of Environment, Health, and Natural Resources, Division of Environmental Management, Air Quality Ambient Monitoring Section, *1996 Ambient Air Quality Report*, 1998.

the lungs where tissue damage can result. It is released from stationary sources such as coal- or natural gas–fired plants, but also from mobile sources. Tailpipe emissions tend to increase as vehicle speed increases, so higher speed limits result in greater emissions from automobile and truck transportation. Although a variety of epidemiological studies have failed to show any significant relationship between ambient levels of nitrogen dioxide and respiratory symptoms or diseases, both occupational and toxicological studies have demonstrated adverse effects at concentrations of 0.5 ppm, including destruction of cilia, alveolar tissue disruption, and obstruction of respiratory bronchioles. Respiratory damage from elevated exposures resembles emphysema in test animals. Crops sensitive to nitrogen dioxide include oats, alfalfa, tobacco, peas, and carrots. Approximately 25 percent of the acid in precipitation results from nitrogen oxides. Increases in levels of nitrogen dioxide increase the potential for higher levels of ozone pollution across North Carolina. Nitrogen dioxide levels in the state have declined very slightly during the period of record (Fig. 12.4).

Carbon Monoxide

This gas (CO) is colorless, odorless, and tasteless. Tailpipe emissions contribute the vast majority of carbon monoxide present in ambient air. Carbon monoxide levels peak in winter, when cold engine starts boost the level of tailpipe CO emissions. At concentrations greater than 1,000 ppm, carbon monoxide is highly toxic. Because it has an affinity for hemoglobin two hundred times greater than that of oxygen, breathing carbon monoxide produces carboxyhemoglobin in the blood which competes with oxygen for binding sites and deprives body tissues, including the brain, of oxygen. Frequently, fire victims who succumb to smoke inhalation actually die from carbon monoxide asphyxiation. Although no adverse health effects are associated with exposure equal to or less than 35 ppm for one hour, carboxyhemoglobin levels in the blood are directly proportional to the level of exposure. Beyond this threshold, which defines the ambient air quality standard, the results of increased carboxyhemoglobin levels include onset of angina and central nervous system effects such as increased reaction time. The effect of ambient carbon monoxide exposure is compounded in individuals burdened with elevated carboxyhemoglobin levels from other exposures such as active and passive cigarette smoking or from occupational exposures.

The statewide trend in carbon monoxide has been generally downward during the period of rec-

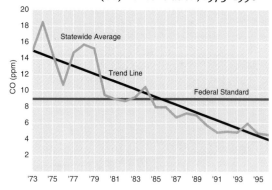

Figure 12.5. Average Second Maximum 8-Hour Carbon Monoxide (CO) Concentration, 1973–1996

Note: These values represent the second most polluted day based on the highest eight-hour concentration of carbon monoxide.

Source: N.C. Department of Environment, Health, and Natural Resources, Division of Environmental Management, Air Quality Ambient Monitoring Section, *1996 Ambient Air Quality Report*, 1998.

ord and suggests that vehicle emission controls have been very effective (Fig. 12.5). Vehicle emissions have been limited by the natural replacement of older vehicles with newer, cleaner models, improved traffic flow, better traffic signal coordination, and annual vehicle inspection and maintenance programs. Because carbon monoxide tends to be the principal air pollutant during the winter months, gasoline sold for highway use in Mecklenburg and Wake Counties between November and February contains oxygen-rich additives to reduce carbon monoxide emissions. Ethanol is a particularly effective additive in creating oxygenated fuel because of its high oxygen content. Gasoline blended with 10 percent ethanol produces a fuel

that contains 3.5 percent oxygen. Use of oxygenated fuels, however, are restricted to the winter months because they are ineffective in reducing levels of ozone, the major summer pollutant.

Lead

This is a common element in the environment, but lead (Pb) carries several health risks. Symptoms of lead poisoning vary from acute to chronic with the level and period of exposure. Symptoms of chronic lead exposure include brain damage, kidney damage, and damage to blood-forming systems, but there is also evidence that lead may cause sterility, spontaneous abortions, stillbirths, and neonatal deaths. Among the symptoms of acute lead poisoning are colic, shock, severe anemia, acute nervousness, kidney damage, brain damage, and death. Although other sources of lead persist in the environment, airborne lead has traditionally been the most pervasive source of exposure in the United States. The use of tetraethyl lead as an additive to motor fuel was phased out starting in 1974, an action that resulted in a 96 percent decrease in vehicle tailpipe lead emissions between 1970 and 1990. Because of the national shift to unleaded motor fuels, lead levels plummeted between 1977 and 1990, becoming almost zero by 1990, the latest year of record (Fig. 12.6).

Figure 12.6. Average Yearly Lead (Pb) Concentration, 1972–1990

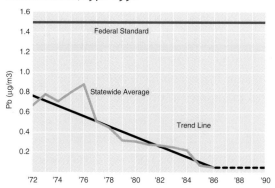

Note: No data available for 1987-1990. Dashed line is estimated.

Source: N.C. Department of Environment, Health, and Natural Resources, Division of Environmental Management, Air Quality Ambient Monitoring Section, *1996 Ambient Air Quality Report*, 1998.

Figure 12.7. Average Second Maximum Ozone (O_3) Concentration, 1973–1996

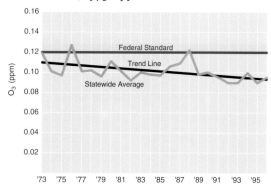

Note: These values represent the second most polluted day in terms of ozone concentration.

Source: N.C. Department of Environment, Health, and Natural Resources, Division of Environmental Management, Air Quality Ambient Monitoring Section, *1996 Ambient Air Quality Report*, 1998.

Figure 12.8. Ground-Level Ozone Concentrations in Mecklenburg County, 1981–1995

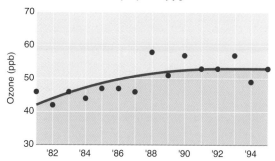

Sources: U.S. Environmental Protection Agency, 1997; Aerometric Information Retrieval System (AIRS).

Ozone

Tri-atomic oxygen (O_3) represents many other often unmeasurable oxidant pollutants. A pulmonary irritant, ozone is toxic to people, animals, and vegetation. Despite the useful role played by stratospheric ozone in shading the earth's surface from harmful solar ultraviolet radiation, surface ozone pollution threatens the public health in many of the nation's major cities. Unlike many other air pollutants, high levels of ozone are not emitted directly into the atmosphere from commercial or industrial sources but result from a series of photochemical processes supported by the simultaneous abundance of two precursors in the lower atmosphere: nitrogen dioxide and reactive hydrocar-

bons. Nitrogen dioxide is a by-product of high-temperature combustion and is emitted primarily from stationary sources such as coal-fired electricity-generation stations and motor vehicles. Hydrocarbons are released as volatile compounds from many sources, including evaporation from surface coatings and liquid fuels, but primarily as exhaust from motor vehicles and small engines.

Ozone is not generated in large quantities where abundant ultraviolet light (UV) from the sun is unavailable to drive photolytic chemical processes, and so ozone levels are lower at night and during the winter. The highest surface ozone levels are generated in cities such as Mexico City and Los Angeles where UV, oxides of nitrogen, and hydrocarbons are abundant. Declines in the level

of ozone pollution have been difficult to achieve. Ambient concentrations in North Carolina have persisted near or above the National Ambient Air Quality Standard (NAAQS) during the period of record (Fig. 12.7). Although the national standard for ground-level ozone concentrations has been based on the second highest annual observation, the long-term ozone trend is reflected in the time series of annual averages. Air quality from ozone pollution deteriorated in the mid- to late 1980s, but effective emission control strategies that targeted urban regions have stabilized air quality near 1990 levels.

Data for Charlotte illustrate the changing ozone levels that were typical across North Carolina during the 1981–95 period (Fig. 12.8). Pollution from photochemical oxidants has emerged as one of the most serious threats to regional air quality in North Carolina, and consequently it will be given special attention.

Ozone Pollution

Although emission controls are expensive, there are numerous costs associated with high levels of photochemical oxidants such as ozone. Antioxidants have been incorporated in rubber since 1960 to reduce its susceptibility to premature cracking from exposure to oxidants. During the 1980s when levels of photochemical oxidants were excessive in the Los Angeles Basin, some suggested that were it not for these antioxidants, women's hose would literally have disintegrated as their wearers walked down the streets of Los Angeles. Certainly crop yields and forest productivity are reduced because of exposure to oxidants. Much of the concern about ozone pollution, however, centers on human health.

Between 1980 and 1990 air quality was designated as not meeting federal standards in seven North Carolina counties: Mecklenburg and Gaston, Guilford and Forsyth, and Durham, Wake, and a small part of Granville. An inspection and maintenance (I/M) program was implemented in each of these counties as well as some of the neighboring counties, such as Union, Cabarrus, and Orange. Had air quality not improved throughout the state and specifically in the cities, emission control strategies such as I/M programs would have been implemented in additional counties such as Franklin, Lincoln, Rowan, Stokes, Yadkin, Randolph, and Cumberland.

Each of these counties is functionally linked with a North Carolina city. The preferred strategy to lower ozone levels within and downwind from urban areas has been to control emission levels within the urbanized area and within surrounding counties. Much of the functional relationship between cities and surrounding counties may not be obvious but must be considered in planning to maintain or improve air quality. Growing numbers of commuters driving greater distances add substantially to the regional emissions burden. One of the reasons that coal-fired electricity-generation stations are frequently sited in a surrounding county is to minimize the effect of smokestack emissions on air quality in urban counties. As emission controls are adopted by commuters and utilities in neighboring counties, air quality in the urban plume can be expected to improve, with benefits for all in the wind shadow of the city.

The EPA has replaced the previous 120 parts per billion (ppb), one-hour standard with a new eight-hour standard at 80.4 ppb; the agency defines the new standard as a "concentration-based" form, specifically the three-year average of the annual fourth highest daily maximum concentration of ozone during an eight-hour period. By the end of the twentieth century, the counties of North Carolina had nearly achieved compliance with federal clean air standards. Under new standards proposed in 1997 and recommended for the twenty-first century, seventeen North Carolina counties would not meet the standard for ozone (Fig. 12.9). During the three years between 1990 and 1992 a single monitor in Charlotte recorded 40 days with average maximum eight-hour concentrations greater than 80.4 ppb. Under the newly proposed standard, the fourth highest, eight-hour average in 1990 was 93.5 ppb, followed by 13 more days that exceeded the standard that year. As measured by the new standard, Charlotte's ozone concentrations would need to improve by approximately 10 percent beyond the levels observed during 1990. Between 1990 and 1995 the eight-hour average exceeded the new standard (80.4 ppb) a total of 79 times and within that group ranged from a minimum of 80.6 to 121.9 ppb. In the early summer of 1998, during a period of unusually hot weather, North Carolina was one of thirty states that exceeded the new federal ozone standard. In the Great Smoky Mountains National Park the new standard was exceeded during 11 of the last 18 days of May and a total of 17 days during the summer of 1998. The new standard was exceeded 441 times at the forty monitoring stations around the state during the first eight months of 1998. About

Figure 12.9. Counties with Ozone Levels Greater than 1997 Standards

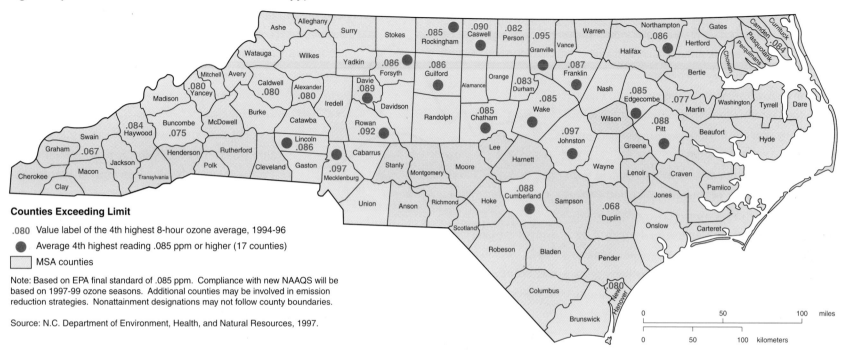

Counties Exceeding Limit

.080 Value label of the 4th highest 8-hour ozone average, 1994-96

● Average 4th highest reading .085 ppm or higher (17 counties)

▢ MSA counties

Note: Based on EPA final standard of .085 ppm. Compliance with new NAAQS will be based on 1997-99 ozone seasons. Additional counties may be involved in emission reduction strategies. Nonattainment designations may not follow county boundaries.

Source: N.C. Department of Environment, Health, and Natural Resources, 1997.

66 of those violations were recorded at Mecklenburg's three monitoring stations, and many of the other violations occurred throughout the rest of the Piedmont corridor.

The health effects of photochemical oxidants are primarily respiratory. Acute, short-term, reversible effects include reductions in one-second forced expiratory volume (FEV) and forced vital capacity (FVC). Reduced lung function at concentration levels less than 300 parts per billion, unsubstantiated before 1980, has been confirmed at levels between 120 and 240 ppb. Recent observations have found decreases in mean FEV between 7 and 13 percent in subjects performing moderate exercise for more than six hours at ozone concentrations between 80 and 120 ppb. The onset of symptoms—coughing and pain when breathing deeply—occurs in young healthy adults exercising heavily for one to three hours at concentrations as low as 120 ppb.

For unknown reasons, some individuals demonstrate an abnormally acute response to ozone.

The EPA estimates that between 5 and 20 percent of the population is ozone-sensitive. It has been postulated that asthmatics, children, the elderly, and people with a chronic obstructive pulmonary disease such as emphysema might have a heightened sensitivity to ozone.

Long-term effects of ozone on human health remain difficult to determine. Suspected potential effects of low-level exposure (80–250 ppb) include permanent changes in lung function and structure, effects on growth or aging of the lung, and increased response to bacterial and viral infections. Evidence that long-term low-level exposure is linked with disease does not exist; the long-term studies have not yet been done. Acute changes, especially among sensitive individuals, athletes, and outdoor workers, are well documented, and many researchers are concerned that permanent damage to the lungs may result from exposure over many years.

The National Ambient Air Quality Standard for ozone is now 120 ppb for the second highest average one-hour daily maximum between April 1 and October 31 each year. Although several studies suggest that levels as high as 120 ppb are unhealthful and levels between 80 and 120 ppb are potentially unhealthful, the issue of precisely where the health threshold for ozone may lie remains unresolved.

Except for those who work outdoors, exposure to higher concentrations of ozone in North Carolina may be avoided easily by remaining indoors. Indoor levels of ozone are less than 60 percent of the ambient level and as low as 25 percent in air-conditioned areas. Exposure can also be lessened by avoiding strenuous exercise during the peak ozone hours from 12:00 P.M. to 5:00 P.M. (Fig. 12.10). Ozone levels in Charlotte are only slightly higher but illustrate the same diurnal profile as those in other urban centers of North Carolina. Between April 1 and October 31, average ozone concentrations peak during the midafternoon but remain less than 60 ppb. Near the time of the sum-

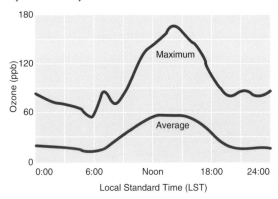

Figure 12.10. Typical Ozone Concentrations by Time of Day

Source: U.S. Environmental Protection Agency. Data reflect all observations recorded at the Plaza Rd. site in Charlotte, 1981-89.

mer solstice (ca. June 21), however, if high pressure systems such as the Bermuda-Azores high dominate atmospheric circulation across the state, ozone levels may rise substantially. Under these conditions, Charlotte experienced ozone levels of more than 170 ppb in 1988. These warm core highs may elevate ozone levels 10 percent or more throughout the Southeast by the third or fourth day of influence.

The effect in North Carolina, illustrated here by Greensboro, is less pronounced than in Atlanta but greater than in smaller southeastern places (Fig. 12.11). The worst ozone levels in North Carolina were experienced during 1988, a year when summer weather patterns were dominated by hot, dry atmospheric conditions. Whenever those weather patterns recur, as they did to some extent during

the summer of 1993, North Carolinians will again be at risk from high levels of ozone. Because peak levels of ozone pollution are a function of ambient levels of hydrocarbons and nitrogen oxides, reducing the number or severity of ozone pollution episodes relies on limiting or reducing the precursor emissions.

Unlike the risks to human health, the relationship between ozone exposure and crop yield has been well established through experiments that literally enclose the individual plant and observe the damage at varying levels of exposure. Walter Heck, former chair of the EPA's National Crop Loss Assessment Network, stated that cutting ozone levels by 50 percent would increase yields for four major crops—soybeans, corn, wheat, and peanuts—by up to $5 billion annually. Total ozone pollution is estimated to reduce annual crop yields by 5 to 10 percent.

Prevailing levels of ozone during the growing season in most U.S. agricultural regions are double the background level. At this level plants cannot repair cell damage quickly enough. Effects include yellowing, reduced growth, and decreased yield and quality. In North Carolina losses in crop productivity are estimated to exceed $100 million annually; twelve other states experience similar losses.

Studies in Germany and Sweden concluded that diebacks in the Black Forest and the North Rhine Westfalia were linked to ozone pollution. Tennes-

Figure 12.11. Progression of Ozone Levels during a Stagnating High-Pressure Episode

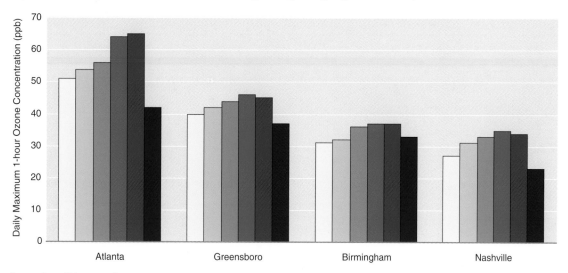

Ozone Level Progression

- Initial
- Day 1
- Day 2
- Day 3
- Day 4
- Day 5

Sources: Synoptic assessment based on National Weather Service surface- and upper-air observations, 1981-90; Ozone data from the U.S. Environmental Protection Agency; Synoptic events calculated by Lynda Ivey.

see, Virginia, and North Carolina contain 66,000 acres of spruce-fir forests. On a quarter of this land, more than 70 percent of the standing trees are dead. At elevations above 2,500 feet in the northeastern United States, half of the red spruce trees that appeared healthy in the early 1960s are now dead. The acute and chronic effects of oxidants on trees, especially those species with broad genetic susceptibility and low tolerance of oxidants, including white pine and others, may be significant factors in forest decline syndromes.

Air Toxics

In recent years some attention has been directed toward a group of primary pollutants known as air toxics. This includes a large number of chemically varied substances released into the atmosphere, generally from point sources as a by-product of industrial processes. State and local environmental protection agencies monitor stack emissions to ensure that releases from each site do not exceed the maximum annual permitted rate for each pollutant. The geographic pattern of air toxic emissions is defined by the location of population and manufacturing centers and as such reflects that of many other air pollutants (Figs. 12.12 and 12.13). Although the total number of air toxic emission sites across North Carolina is very small compared with the number of other air pollution sources and ambient concentrations are normally inconsequential, these sites are closely monitored because some air toxics are particularly hazardous. Examples include benzene, bromomethane, nickel, and arsenic, all of which are known cancer-causing toxins. Ethylene, methyl ethyl ketone, m-xylene, toluene, tetrachloroethylene, and mercury are known nerve-damaging toxics.

The degree to which these noxious substances are concentrated in the air above North Carolina is a function of two different controls: the rate at which effluents are injected into the atmosphere and the meteorological condition of the atmo-

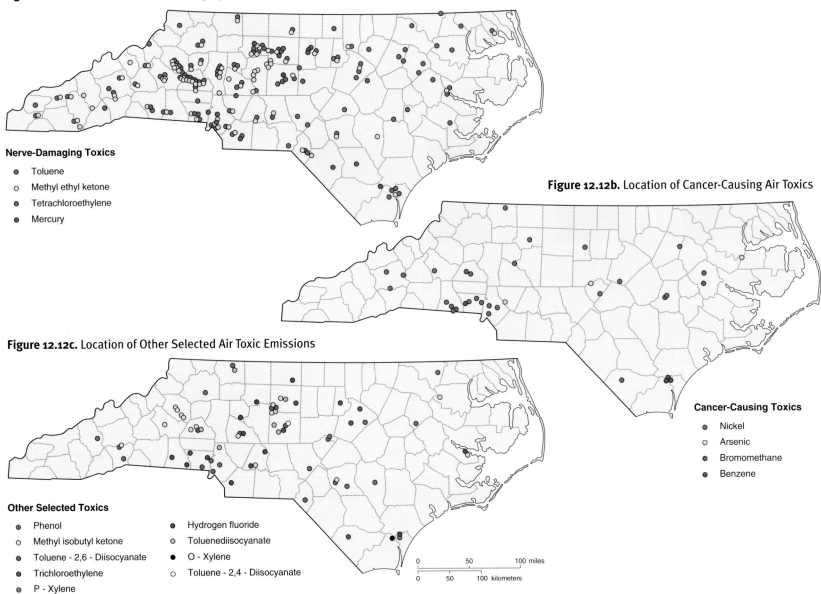

Figure 12.12a. Location of Nerve-Damaging Air Toxics

Nerve-Damaging Toxics

- Toluene
- Methyl ethyl ketone
- Tetrachloroethylene
- Mercury

Figure 12.12b. Location of Cancer-Causing Air Toxics

Cancer-Causing Toxics

- Nickel
- Arsenic
- Bromomethane
- Benzene

Figure 12.12c. Location of Other Selected Air Toxic Emissions

Other Selected Toxics

- Phenol
- Methyl isobutyl ketone
- Toluene - 2,6 - Diisocyanate
- Trichloroethylene
- P - Xylene
- Hydrogen fluoride
- Toluenediisocyanate
- O - Xylene
- Toluene - 2,4 - Diisocyanate

Source: U.S. Environmental Protection Agency, Toxic Chemicals Release Inventory, 1990.

Figure 12.13. Top Three Chemicals Released to the Air in North Carolina

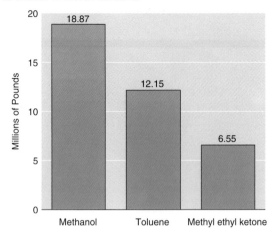

Source: U.S. Environmental Protection Agency, Toxics Chemicals Release Inventory, 1991.

Figure 12.14. Selected Upper-Limit Estimates of Volatile Organic Compound Emissions by SIC Employment

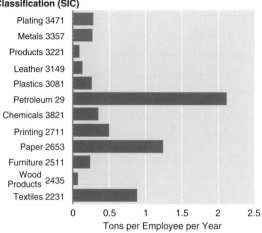

Source: U.S. Environmental Protection Agency, *Procedures for the Preparation of Emission Inventories for Carbon Monoxide and Precursors of Ozone,* 1991.

sphere. Emissions reach the atmosphere from both natural and human origins, but, in most instances, the capability to improve or maintain air quality is restricted to limiting or curtailing emissions from human sources.

Emissions

The atmosphere constantly receives a host of gases, particles, and droplets from the earth's surface. Except for volcanic eruptions, most particles fall quickly back to the surface, although smaller particulate matter can remain suspended for hours, days, weeks, or even longer. A major example was the heavy smoke from the Kuwaiti oil fires during the summer of 1991 that drifted hundreds of miles before being washed out by monsoonal rains over southern Asia. Regardless of their origin, whether human or natural, these substances threaten air quality whenever the emission rate exceeds the natural capacity of the atmosphere to cleanse itself.

Natural emission sources include material ejected during volcanic eruptions, sea salt, pollen, mold, spores, soil particles, hydrogen sulfide, ammonia, volatile organic compounds from trees, smoke from forest fires, nitrogen oxides and ozone from lightning, meteoric dust, and ozone that drifts downward from the stratosphere. Some volatile organic compounds such as terpenes from pines and isoprenes from deciduous tree species help to produce the occasional smoky appearance of the Great Smokies and the bluish hues of the air over the Blue Ridge Mountains.

Emissions that originate from human sources are usually grouped into three categories: point sources such as smokestacks; line sources such as busy highways, crop-dusting passes, or aircraft exhaust trails; and area sources that include forest fires, agricultural operations, or the aggregate emissions from hundreds or thousands of small singular sources spread across a metropolitan region. Emissions of nitrogen oxides, sulfur oxides, and carbon monoxide are generally by-products of combustion, whereas hydrocarbon emissions are associated with the use of fuels and solvents. Many of these area sources may be so commonplace that they are not usually recognized as sources of air

pollution. Hydrocarbon emissions, for example, occur when vapor-laden air in a partially empty fuel tank is displaced to the atmosphere while the tank is being refilled.

Area and small point source categories in North Carolina include surface coating operations such as printing, dyeing, or painting; bulk petroleum storage; degreasing operations; gasoline and jet kerosene distribution; incineration; and dry cleaning. Generally, major sources are defined as those with the potential to emit 100 tons per year or more of any regulated pollutant, but the total quantity of emissions from smaller, unregulated sources can be substantial. Consider the following examples: a single high-volume gasoline filling station in North Carolina can release 10 tons of evaporative emissions per year; an outboard motor emits as much in one hour as a new car driven 800 miles; and even gasoline-powered lawn mowers, leaf blowers, and chainsaws emit more pollution than driving a new car for the same period of time.

The 1990 amendments to the Clean Air Act require the establishment of local, often county-level, area source emission inventories for carbon monoxide and the precursors of ozone. Because many area and small point emission sources are too numerous to be measured directly, they must be estimated in one of several ways, including fuel or solvent consumption or employment in certain industry groups. The latter provides an estimate of the release of volatile organic compounds that are a precursor of ozone (Fig. 12.14). The 1990 amendments to the Clean Air Act updated many requirements for evaluating air quality, and as a result many previous surveys and emission inventories are currently being modernized to meet new regulations.

Climatic Controls on Air Pollution

Weather conditions affect air quality in several important ways. Extremes of temperature increase the quantity of fuel required for heating or air-conditioning and consequently increase emissions from coal-burning electric utilities. Of the energy

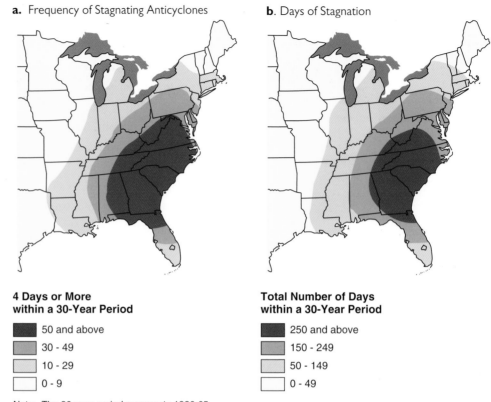

Figure 12.15. Stagnating Anticyclones in the Eastern United States

a. Frequency of Stagnating Anticyclones

b. Days of Stagnation

4 Days or More within a 30-Year Period

- 50 and above
- 30 - 49
- 10 - 29
- 0 - 9

Total Number of Days within a 30-Year Period

- 250 and above
- 150 - 249
- 50 - 149
- 0 - 49

Note: The 30-year period represents 1936-65.

Sources: J. Korshover, *Synoptic Climatology of Stagnating Anticyclones East of the Rocky Mountains in the United States for the Period 1936-1956, Rept. S.E.C. TR-A60-7*, Robert A. Taft Sanitary Engineering Center, Cincinnati, 1960. See also P. A. Leighton, "Geographical Aspects of Air Pollution," in *Man's Impact on Environment*, ed. T. Detwyler, pp. 113-130 (New York: McGraw-Hill, 1971).

used to generate electricity in North Carolina, the majority is generated at coal-fired plants, approximately one-third is produced from nuclear sources, and a small fraction comes from hydroelectric dams. During the winter, air quality in vulnerable locations, such as mountain valleys, can also be degraded by increased particulate emissions from wood-burning stoves and fireplaces. In summer, high temperatures increase the rate at which volatile pollutants evaporate from the surface into the atmosphere. Volatile organic compounds (VOCs) consist of hundreds of mostly hy-

Figure 12.16. Frequency of Nighttime Winds 7-Miles per Hour or Less

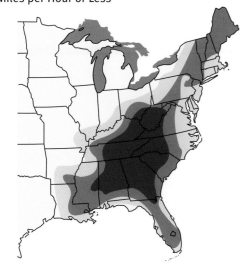

Percent of Frequency

- 70 and above
- 60 - 69
- 50 - 59

Source: S.C. Department of Health and Environmental Quality Control, Office of Environmental Quality Control, *1988 South Carolina Air Quality Report*, 1989.

Figure 12.17. Fall Season Average Daily Low-Level Inversion Frequency

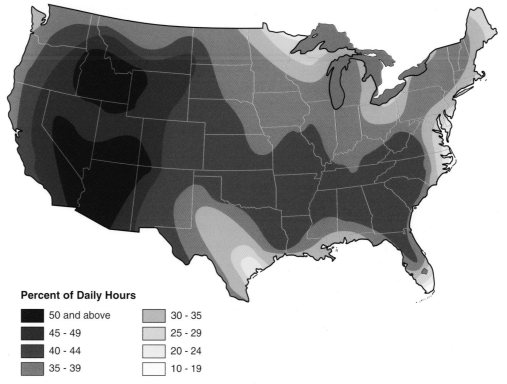

Percent of Daily Hours

- 50 and above
- 45 - 49
- 40 - 44
- 35 - 39
- 30 - 35
- 25 - 29
- 20 - 24
- 10 - 19

Source: D. H. Pack, "Meteorology of Air Pollution," *Science* 146 (November 1964): 119.

drocarbon compounds including methane, formaldehyde, benzene, and others from liquid fuels. As air temperatures rise, evaporation of VOCs accelerates and adds substantially to the total burden of air pollutants near the ground.

Fortunately, surface winds and vertical air currents normally disperse pollutants by mixing. The turbulent motion typical of horizontal winds and vertical air currents is essential in maintaining good air quality both in urban counties and in areas downwind from cities. Any reduction, however temporary, in the atmosphere's capacity to ventilate the surface poses a threat to air quality. Regions with frequent or extended periods of calm winds, stagnating high pressure cells (anticyclones), or temperature inversions are particularly vulnerable to episodic air pollution events. Unfortunately, much of North Carolina experiences extended periods of calm, relatively frequent anticyclones, and frequent low-level inversions that limit the ability of the atmosphere to disperse pollutants (Figs. 12.15, 12.16, and 12.17). Weather conditions across the latitudes of North America are alternately dominated by the eastward march of low-pressure systems with their cloudy, rainy weather and by high-pressure or anticyclonic systems with their clear and rainless skies.

For reasons that are not completely understood, strong anticyclonic systems may develop over the Southeast during the summer months of some years and block rain-producing low-pressure systems for an extended period. During the summer of 1993 this high-pressure system, sometimes known as the Bermuda high, stalled rain clouds over the upper Midwest and caused record flooding along the Mississippi Valley. Throughout the Southeast it contributed to high temperatures, drought, and reduced air quality. A large, persistent anticyclone during the summer of 1988 brought record high temperatures and record high ozone levels to many parts of the Southeast and the Midwest. The recurrence interval and magnitude of such systems represent a considerable uncertainty in evaluating the trend of ozone pollution in North Carolina and across the Southeast. Anticyclonic systems concentrate air pollution near the surface through reduced vertical and horizontal mixing or ventilation.

Vertical Mixing

Under normal conditions, temperature decreases as altitude increases for several kilometers above the surface. Air near the ground is heated during the day, lifts, and disperses pollutants both horizontally and vertically through a lower layer of the atmosphere called the mixing layer. Ascending air is replaced with cleaner air from above. A thick mixing layer provides greater volume through which pollutants are dispersed and results in improved air quality. Shallow mixing layers restrict dispersion and degrade air quality. Temperature inversions limit vertical mixing and trap air pollution close to the surface. Inversions occur frequently in the Piedmont and Mountain regions of North Carolina. They commonly develop overnight as the earth surface radiates energy and cools. The cooler surface forms a stable surface layer that is not readily mixed with the air immediately above until after sunrise, when surface heating reestablishes vertical mixing. Nighttime surface inversions usually break up by midmorning, but air quality at the surface may suffer temporarily. Pollutants that accumulate in the stable surface layer often remain aloft until they are drawn back to the surface as the vertical currents of early morning begin to develop. This fumigation process can degrade morning air quality for an hour or two until convective circulation deepens the mixing layer and provides a larger volume for dispersion.

The depth of the mixing layer in North Carolina is illustrated with data from Charlotte (Fig. 12.18). The mixing layer is typically shallowest during fall mornings and deepest during summer afternoons. This implies that air quality would be more vulnerable to emissions in the morning than in the afternoon and that it would be more vulnerable in winter than in summer, all other factors being equal. Fortunately, many pollution sources are greatly

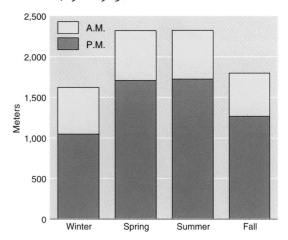

Figure 12.18. Average Depth of the Mixing Layer, Charlotte, 1981–1985

Source: National Climatic Data Center, Asheville.

reduced at night and only reach their maximum emission rate during the day.

Horizontal Mixing

In addition to vertical air currents, horizontal air motion as measured by wind speed and direction plays an important role in ventilating the lower atmosphere. Higher wind speeds indicate a greater volume of air moving past a given location and a greater dilution of the pollutants emitted from a stationary source. For most air pollutants with a constant emission rate, the concentration is an inverse function of wind speed. A doubling of wind speed, for example, will halve the pollutant con-

Figure 12.19. Wind Speed and Direction at Selected North Carolina Cities

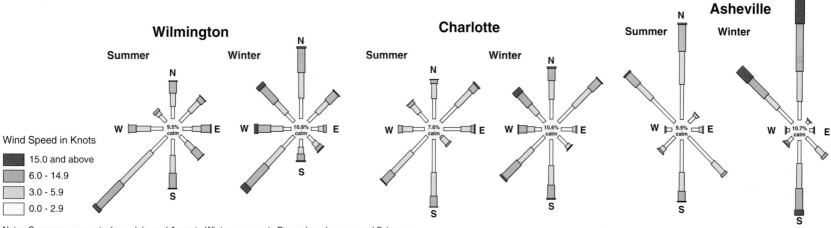

Note: Summer represents June, July, and August. Winter represents December, January, and February.

Source: Based on 3-hourly observations between 1985 and 1991, NOAA, National Climatic Data Center, Asheville.

centration. Although winds blow neither from a constant direction nor at a constant speed, the most frequently occurring wind direction and speed indicate prevailing conditions. From an air quality standpoint, wind speeds of less than three knots (nautical miles per hour) may be considered virtually calm, and even wind speeds of three or four knots may not provide adequate ventilation for dispersion of surface emissions. Knowledge of prevailing wind direction can provide useful clues about the transportation of pollutants both entering and leaving a populated area. Point, line, and area emission sources create plumes of air pollution that disperse as they drift downwind. The potential for dispersion of air pollutants across North Carolina is illustrated by wind speed and

wind direction data from Wilmington, the Raleigh-Durham airport, and Charlotte. These data, recorded by the National Weather Service and archived by the National Oceanic and Atmospheric Administration, represent all three-hour observations during the 1985–91 period.

Locations along the coast such as Wilmington typically experience prevailing winds from the southwest (Fig. 12.19). During both summer and winter months the most frequently occurring wind speeds are between six and nine knots. Stronger winds, especially between six and fifteen knots and greater than fifteen knots are much more frequent in winter. Periods of calm are common in the evening and at night during both seasons. Pollutants emitted into the air during the afternoon are

normally far less of a threat to air quality than those emitted into the more frequently calm nighttime air. Fortunately, few of the nighttime calms persist past 7:00 A.M. Prevailing winds are from the southwest in summer and bimodal from the north and southwest in winter.

With minor exceptions, a similar distribution of wind speed is typical in the Raleigh-Durham area. Winds greater than nine knots are less frequent in summer, however, and winds between three and six knots are more common, especially in winter. Despite somewhat slower winds, periods of calm are less frequent in the Raleigh-Durham area than along the coast. Prevailing winds are from the southwest during both summer and winter months. With only Sanford, Fayetteville, and

Two photographs taken from the same location on different days on the Blue Ridge Parkway near Linville Falls showing clear air (left) and haze (right)

Fort Bragg some thirty to fifty miles to the southwest, the Raleigh metropolitan area is relatively fortunate to not be in the shadow of a major urban air pollution plume.

With the state's largest population, Charlotte has a limited ability for dispersion of atmospheric pollutants. Charlotte is more likely to have light winds or calm than many other parts of the state (Fig. 12.19). The most frequently occurring wind speed is only three to six knots in both winter and summer, and although most calms take place at night, a significant number occur during the day when human activity and emission levels reach their peak. Charlotte, like the Raleigh-Durham area, receives prevailing airflow from the south, southwest, and northeast in both summer and winter; also like Raleigh, it is fortunate to not have large urban centers to the immediate southwest.

Winston-Salem, Greensboro, and Burlington, however, are less fortunate in this regard. Greensboro, for example, is situated along the prevailing wind vec-

tor almost precisely downwind from several urban areas including High Point, Thomasville, Lexington, Salisbury, Kannapolis, Concord, Charlotte, and Rock Hill. Although a blanket of emissions can be blown from one county down the prevailing wind vector to neighboring counties, both vertical and horizontal dispersion often diminish the effects of simple horizontal translocation of air pollutants.

Winds in Asheville prevail from the north and northwest in both summer and winter, but southerly winds are also frequent (Fig. 12.19). Like many other places in western North Carolina, Asheville is surrounded by mountains that can restrict air flow and trap air pollutants near the surface. Of the three-hour observations between 1985 and 1991, 9.5 percent were calm during the summer and 10.7 percent during the winter. Although air quality in Asheville is generally healthy, the combination of frequent calms, stagnating anticyclones, and the surrounding mountainous terrain combine to produce an environment that cannot support a heavy burden of emissions. With some prevailing winds from the northwest, the Mountain counties of North Carolina appear vulnerable to transported air pollutants from the Ohio and Tennessee Valleys.

Some might contend that North Carolina is the victim of imported air pollution from locations upwind, but most locations to the south and west, from which most North Carolina winds blow, are rural, agricultural, or forested expanses with lower rates of industrial and urban activity than are found in North Carolina. In contrast to New England, where elevated background levels of air pollution may be carried from sources in the Boston to Washington, D.C., corridor, North Carolina imports relatively clean air most of the time.

Evaluating Air Quality

The Pollution Standard Index (PSI) is the most commonly used method for evaluating air quality throughout the United States. It is used to describe the current pollutant concentration of the most concentrated pollutant in question. The National Ambient Air Quality Standard for each pollutant is indexed to be 100. A PSI of 100 with the offending pollutant being ozone means that measured levels of ozone are equal to the NAAQS. A PSI of 50 with the offending pollutant being ozone means that measured levels of ozone equal 50 percent of the NAAQS. PSI values less than 50 are used to classify

air quality as good. PSI values between 50 and 100 are used to classify air quality as moderate. PSI values greater than 100 indicate that the air is unhealthful and suggest that national air quality standards have been violated. Access to current air quality as measured by the PSI is available from television and radio broadcasts as part of the local weather information.

For regulatory purposes, counties and even sections of a county that do not meet NAAQSs are classified as nonattainment areas. Ozone nonattainment areas are further classified as marginal, moderate, serious, severe, or extreme. The 1990 amendments to the Clean Air Act require increasingly stringent emission controls for areas that carry higher levels of nonattainment. Serious nonattainment, for example, triggers measures to offset aggregate growth in the number of vehicle miles traveled. Other measures include a cutoff of highway funds; a complete ban on drinking water hookups, which effectively prevents new development; and felony charges for permit violations with sanctions of up to $25,000 and imprisonment up to one year with each day counting as a separate violation. Funding for major road construction projects is contingent on computer model projections that demonstrate improved future air quality or that, at least, no deterioration in air quality is likely to occur. These air quality models anticipate little or no improvement in emission levels to the middle of the next decade because of growth in population and vehicular traffic. Thus, as growth

continues, projected emission levels may not meet federally mandated standards. The effect is to provide industrial managers and state and local governments with strong incentives to protect or improve air quality. Otherwise, funding for planned road improvements may be delayed or canceled.

In addition to controlling highway funds, examples of future regulatory efforts intended to control volatile hydrocarbons for attainment of the ozone standard could include the following:

1. Tightening volatility requirements for gasoline in summer
2. Expanding the number of counties with motor vehicle inspection and maintenance programs
3. Adopting regulations to control emissions from treatment, storage, and disposal of hazardous wastes
4. Regulating volatile hydrocarbon emissions from small sources and consumer products such as paints
5. Requiring light-duty trucks to meet the same hydrocarbon exhaust standards as automobiles
6. Requiring controls to reduce evaporative emissions during motor vehicle refueling
7. Requiring emission controls on small engines such as those in lawn mowers, leaf blowers, and watercraft
8. Tightening regulations on nitrogen oxide emissions from major sources

9. Broadcasting zone forecasts to facilitate community-based action during high ozone episodes

10. Offering industry and individual incentives to reduce unnecessary trips and congestion.

Outlook

Impelled by the Clean Air Act and its subsequent amendments, much progress has been achieved during the past two decades in improving air quality in North Carolina. Technological advances have greatly helped to improve vehicle tailpipe emissions and avert more numerous or severe air pollution episodes.

The use of scrubbers or similar emission control technology to reduce point source emissions and the use of computers, catalytic converters, and vapor recovery systems to reduce emissions from transportation sources have played a significant role in maintaining or improving air quality statewide. Because of the vulnerability of air quality in North Carolina and across the Southeast, it will be necessary to monitor changes in emissions and air quality over the next few decades. Perhaps most important, the substantial effect of modern automobile emission controls such as computer-based ignition systems and catalytic converters has only recently been observed because of the long time lag between initial implementation and fleet turnover.

Although air quality today clearly benefits from these recent automotive improvements, there are no comparable innovations in place to further reduce emissions from the transportation sector. The threat to air quality during this century is that reductions in per capita emissions may be more than offset by increases in the number of those emission sources. That is, growth in population and employment, especially as it is concentrated in the larger metropolitan areas, poses a serious challenge to maintaining the quality of one of North Carolina's most precious resources, the very air that people breathe.

Selected References

Koch, K., and C. Ray. "Mesoanalysis of Summertime Convergence Zones in Central and Eastern North Carolina." *Weather Forecasting* 12, no. 1 (1997): 56.

Martin, W. "Identifying Surface Ozone Trends: A Case Study of Charlotte, North Carolina." *Southeastern Geographer* 31 (1991): 90–102.

Martin, W., D. Hartgen, and A. Reser. "Transportation-Related Air Quality and Economic Growth in American Cities." *Transportation Research Record*, no. 1444 (1994): 99–108.

North Carolina Department of Environment, Health, and Natural Resources. Division of Environmental Management/Air Quality Ambient Monitoring Section. *1996 Ambient Air Quality Report*, 1998.

Shprentz, D. *Breath-Taking: Premature Mortality Due to Particulate Air Pollution in 239 American Cities*. Washington, D.C.: Natural Resources Defense Council, 1996.

Tuttle, S. "Clearing the Air." *North Carolina* 56, no. 2 (February 1998): 37, 39–41, 43.

13. WATER RESOURCES

Randall D. Forsythe

Water is another basic resource that is critical to supporting life. More and more people need greater quantities of clean water to drink, cook with, or bathe. Greater numbers of stores and factories need more water to keep their businesses running. However, increasing rates of use and growing populations not only require more water for homes, factories, and farms, but they also lead to the discharge of greater quantities of waste and pollutants into the state's streams and groundwater. Thus, just as demand and use increases, some of the potential supply is lost. The draining of pocosins and other natural filtration systems diminishes the environment's ability to remove increasing loads of agricultural fertilizers. These fertilizers then wash into marine estuaries that are the nurseries for large populations of shellfish, poisoning their habitats.

North Carolina is blessed with an abundance of water resources that have supported the state's growth and development over the years. Today, there is sufficient water to meet its diverse domestic, agricultural, industrial, energy, and recreational needs. But the issue is becoming the future availability of water of sufficiently high quality. Water of adequate quantity and quality likely can be made available for future generations but only with proper management and planning.

Hydrologic Cycle

The movement of water between the atmosphere, land, and ocean is called the hydrologic cycle. An understanding of this cycle is necessary to determine whether water is present in usable and replenishable quantities for human use. Within the hydrologic cycle, water is constantly moving between a number of reservoirs. These are clouds (atmospheric water vapor), snow and ice fields, streams, lakes (or reservoirs), vegetation, soil moisture, groundwater, and the estuaries and oceans. The processes that transfer water between these reservoirs, or temporary sites of storage, can be divided into those that dominate during storm events such as precipitation, overland flow, and infiltration and those that dominate during nonstorm events such as evaporation, transpiration, interflow, and groundwater flow. A "pot" and "pipe" representation, such as that shown in Figure 13.1, is commonly used to model and manage water resources in a given region, as it clearly distinguishes between those terms that involve rates of movement and those that involve storage.

Water leaves the atmosphere as precipitation principally in the form of snow or rain. It varies from a high in the western Mountains, with values in excess of 80 inches per year, to values in the Piedmont of 44 to 48 inches, and to values of 46 to 54 inches on the Coastal Plain. Precipitation is evenly distributed throughout the year even though it tends to be higher in February–March and July–August. Lower levels are received in May–June and September–October.

Approximately two-thirds of precipitation in the state leaves the surface of the land and returns to the atmosphere by evaporation and by transpiration from plants. The importance of this process from the standpoint of water resources is that the combined evaporation and transpiration (evapotranspiration) leaves only one-third of precipitation for replenishing surface and groundwater supplies.

Runoff is the process by which rainfall is carried across the land surface and pulled by the force of gravity back to the ocean. The water that falls in the form of precipitation to the surface of the earth can fall over land or inland water

Figure 13.1. A "Pot" and "Pipe" Representation of the Hydrologic Cycle

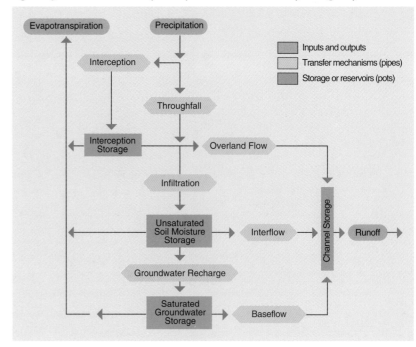

bodies such as streams, lakes, and reservoirs. Water that falls over land—such as on backyards, parking lots, streets, forests, fields, and rooftops—first runs in a sheetlike form downslope until it reaches a natural or human-made channel. The early, sheetlike runoff is referred to as overland flow. Once the water reaches a channel it is referred to as stream or channelized flow. Together they are the main inputs to our surface water reservoirs.

Dramatic variations in the runoff are experienced from year to year, month to month, and day to day. The variations in amounts of runoff at any single location in the state are the most important dynamic aspect of the environment for understanding the characteristics of flow in the natural waterways or river systems. Extreme periods of high precipitation in a particular region can bring the hazards of personal injury, loss of life, and dispossession of property associated with flooding. Extreme periods of low precipitation produce the economic and personal hardships that accompany prolonged droughts.

Effects of topography and geology on runoff are most easily understood in the context of the state's land regions. The Mountains have the most extreme variations in topography and are characterized by large, rapid changes in river flow. The Piedmont, though not having topography as high or rugged as the Mountains, is still moderately hilly and thus, overall, well drained. The region is underlain by rocks of low water–storing capacity, thus river flow responds quickly to precipitation. The Inner Coastal Plain is over 50 feet above sea level and slightly rolling. Because this region overlies rock formations that, generally speaking, have a higher water-bearing capacity than rocks of the Piedmont or the Mountains, the rivers do not respond as rapidly to events in precipitation and, on the whole, have a more moderate pattern of flow throughout the year.

The Tidewater portion of the Coastal Plain is formed of low-lying and gently sloping lands that are generally less than 30 feet above sea level. Here lie the major swamps, marshes, and estuaries that are separated from the open ocean by coastal sounds and barrier islands. These waters form several thousands of square miles in eastern North Carolina and collectively represent one of the largest wetlands resources of the Atlantic seaboard. The inner, western, extents of the creeks, streams, and rivers of the region are freshwater bodies that often are very dark in color due to drainage from swampy, organic-rich lands. Informally, these are sometimes called the "black water creeks."

An additional feature is the region's abundant elliptically shaped lakes and swamps, referred to as the Carolina Bays (Fig. 13.2). They occur as thousands of elliptical depressions, primarily in the southern part of the Coastal Plain. The term "bays" apparently derives from the evergreen bay tree, which commonly occurs in them. The Carolina Bays usually have sand rims, are located on sandy terraces, are filled with peat, and, most strikingly, are oriented in a northwestern-southeastern direction. Their origin is a matter of some mystery, with explanations ranging from such causes as ancient, high-speed winds to meteorite showers.

A small percentage of the water that reaches the land surface filters through the plants and organic matter and enters the underlying ground. The soils and rocks that sit under the land surface have varying physical attributes that determine their capacity to transmit and store water in their open spaces. These properties are commonly referred to as the *permeability* and *porosity* of the soil or rock. A soil with a high permeability transmits water easily from one location to another, essentially providing a pipeline for water flow, whereas a unit with low permeability transmits water very slowly, essentially retarding water flow. Porosity is a standard measure of the amount of water that soil or rock can hold in its open spaces. It is usually expressed as a percentage of the total volume. A sand with 30 percent porosity implies that up to 30 percent of its total volume could be filled with water. Together the permeability and porosity of the rocks and soils under yards, forests, and fields determine the amount of precipitation that can infiltrate the ground and seep downward.

Water that percolates downward to the water table (the boundary that separates unsaturated soil and rock from the deeper saturated zones) enters one of three types of saturated groundwater units: aquicludes, aquitards, and aquifers. *Aquicludes*, which are uncommon, essentially form layers through which water cannot be transmitted at appreciable rates. Most soils and rocks that have low permeabilities, such as clays and shales, in fact can transmit water, but only at very slow rates. These are *aquitards*, which retard the flow of water and generally have little storage capacity.

From a resource vantage point, the most important units are the *aquifers*, which both transmit and store water at rates that make it usable. Water moves constantly within the ground, albeit sometimes very slowly. Eventually the water, which is principally compelled to move under the forces of gravity, will intersect the land surface at a lower elevation, and here at the banks of a river or lake, it once again forms part of the surface flow (normally in a seep or spring). Water that enters streams and lakes from the underlying aquifers is referred to in the hydrologic cycle as baseflow.

The hydrologic cycle can also be viewed as a collection of reservoirs, each of which represents at any given instant a certain percentage of the total

Figure 13.2. Carolina Bays

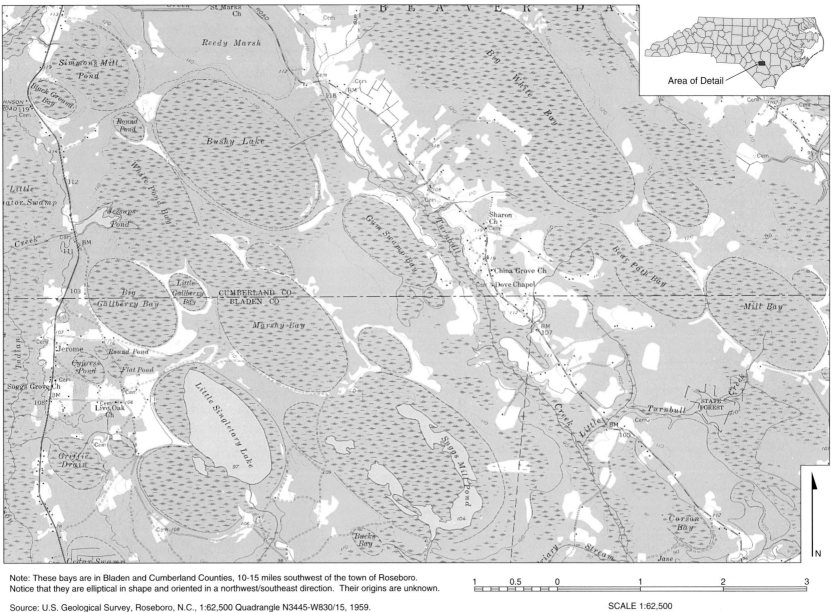

Note: These bays are in Bladen and Cumberland Counties, 10-15 miles southwest of the town of Roseboro.
Notice that they are elliptical in shape and oriented in a northwest/southeast direction. Their origins are unknown.

Source: U.S. Geological Survey, Roseboro, N.C., 1:62,500 Quadrangle N3445-W830/15, 1959.

SCALE 1:62,500

water in the system. Two major types of reservoirs are available for human use: surface water and groundwater. Surface water is represented by lakes, rivers, and human-made reservoirs, whereas groundwater is present in aquifers. Although both surface water and groundwater resources are inherently linked by the processes of infiltration, interflow, and baseflow, they are sufficiently different to be largely managed as distinct systems.

Surface Water Resources

Data provided by the U.S. Geological Survey (USGS) for 1995 indicate that surface water supplies more than 45 percent of North Carolina residents. Industries (including mining and thermoelectric facilities) that have their own intakes for water use 6,440 million gallons per day (Mgal/d), or 90 percent of the offstream surface water consumption. In 1995 another 65,400 Mgal/d were used instream, primarily by thirty-eight hydroelectric power facilities to generate 5,813 million kilowatt-hours of electricity. There is growing concern about protecting the quality of these surface waters, as they increasingly are threatened by various sources of pollution. The management of surface water resources depends on a thorough understanding of the state's river systems and how they respond to natural and human-induced changes in the environment.

Figure 13.3 illustrates the six major river sys-

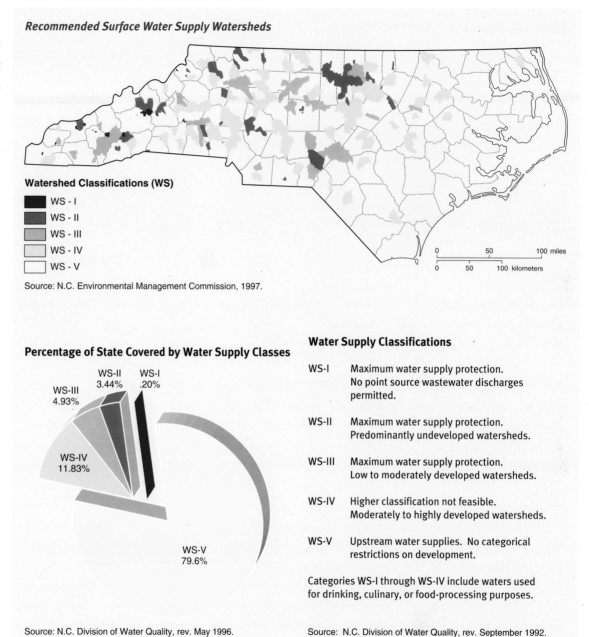

Recommended Surface Water Supply Watersheds

Watershed Classifications (WS)

- WS - I
- WS - II
- WS - III
- WS - IV
- WS - V

Source: N.C. Environmental Management Commission, 1997.

Percentage of State Covered by Water Supply Classes

WS-II 3.44%
WS-I .20%
WS-III 4.93%
WS-IV 11.83%
WS-V 79.6%

Source: N.C. Division of Water Quality, rev. May 1996.

Water Supply Classifications

WS-I   Maximum water supply protection. No point source wastewater discharges permitted.

WS-II   Maximum water supply protection. Predominantly undeveloped watersheds.

WS-III Maximum water supply protection. Low to moderately developed watersheds.

WS-IV   Higher classification not feasible. Moderately to highly developed watersheds.

WS-V   Upstream water supplies. No categorical restrictions on development.

Categories WS-I through WS-IV include waters used for drinking, culinary, or food-processing purposes.

Source: N.C. Division of Water Quality, rev. September 1992.

Figure 13.3. Lakes, Rivers, and River Basins

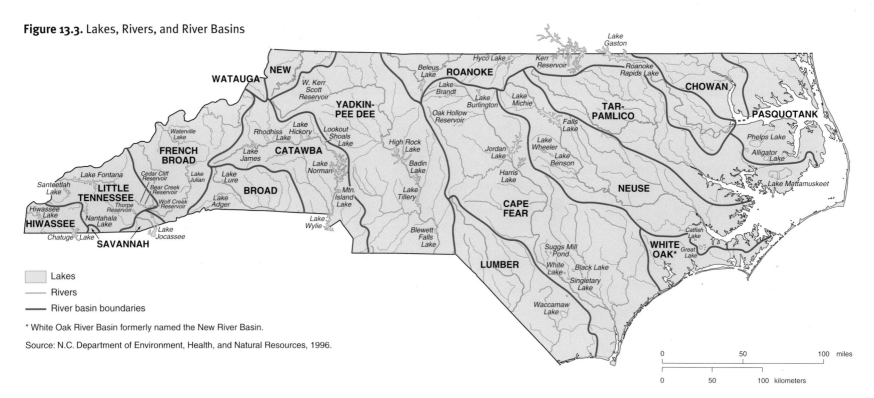

Lakes

—— Rivers

—— River basin boundaries

* White Oak River Basin formerly named the New River Basin.

Source: N.C. Department of Environment, Health, and Natural Resources, 1996.

0 50 100 miles

0 50 100 kilometers

tems, or watersheds, in North Carolina. Calculated on a daily basis, the combined rivers of the state carry 47,600 Mgal/d of water out of North Carolina. Of this total, 7,410 Mgal/d is carried by rivers into the state from adjacent lands, and the remaining is supplied largely by precipitation.

In the westernmost parts of North Carolina are located the Hiwassee, French Broad, Watauga, and New Rivers, all of which drain into the Mississippi River. These rivers are swift, rocky, wild, and scenic and provide one of the main foundations for the region's recreational resources. State and federal parks and forest preserves offer the state and region popular activities such as whitewater rafting and canoeing. Textile, wood, paper-manufacturing, and power-generation industries in the area also rely on substantial supplies of surface water. With increased development in the valley floors of this region, wetland and flood plain encroachment is a common problem.

To the east of the continental divide, the Blue Ridge Mountains, rivers drain into the Atlantic Ocean along either the North Carolina or South Carolina coasts. Those in the western region nearest the Blue Ridge are the Broad and Catawba Rivers. These two compose the upper part of the Edisto-Santee River Basin of North and South Carolina. The drainage area of the Broad River in North Carolina is 1,450 square miles and that of the Catawba is 3,250 square miles; together they comprise 10 percent of the land surface of North Carolina. The Catawba is the most developed watershed, with eight major dams and reservoirs that are used primarily for hydroelectric power generation. The dams provide more than 510,000 kilowatts of generating capacity in North Carolina alone, earning the Catawba its reputation as the "most electrified river in the United States." It also supplies water for many of the largest cities in North Carolina, including Charlotte and Gastonia. Approximately 10 percent of the state's population lies in this watershed. For this reason, as well as the river's heavy use for recreation, water quality in the Catawba is a major concern.

To the east of the Catawba River system is the Pee Dee Basin, which drains parts of Virginia, North Carolina, and South Carolina. In North Carolina it covers 9,300 square miles (19 percent of the land surface). The river is known as the Yadkin to the north of the Uwharrie River and the Pee Dee south of it. It reaches the Atlantic Ocean at Georgetown, South Carolina. The Yadkin River Basin in the north is one of the most developed basins in North Carolina, with approximately 17 percent of the state's population. Several major dams were built initially for hydroelectric power, but now they serve as multipurpose impoundments providing limited flood control, hydroelectric power generation, and water for cooling, recreation, and municipal supply. The river has one of the largest suspended sediment loads (for a given volume of water) of rivers that drain to the Atlantic coast.

The three river systems that drain into the Atlantic Ocean along the North Carolina coast are the Cape Fear, Neuse, and Pamlico. The southernmost of the three is the Cape Fear, which is the largest river entirely within North Carolina. It includes 9,010 square miles (18 percent of the land surface). The inner parts of the Cape Fear include tributaries such as the Haw and Deep Rivers, which have numerous falls and rapids, steep narrow banks, and narrow flood plains. These characteristics make them popular for canoeing. A major reservoir on the Haw River, the B. Everett Jordan Lake, completed in 1981, is used for flood control, water supply, and recreation.

The Neuse River Basin includes 5,710 square miles, or approximately 12 percent of the state's land surface. About 14 percent of North Carolina residents (and the state capital) reside in the Neuse watershed. Within the watershed are forty-eight human-made lakes and large ponds, such as Falls Lake, which provides flood control, water supply, low flow augmentation, and recreation. The lower, coastal, portions of this watershed include significant agricultural lands with increasing water quality concerns.

The Tar-Pamlico River originates in the Piedmont and flows southeastward across the Coastal Plain and enters Pamlico Sound. The basin encompasses 4,302 square miles. The river is swift in its headwater regions but slows and broadens as it nears the sound. A number of municipalities obtain water from the Tar-Pamlico River, including Rocky Mount, Greenville, and Tarboro.

Each river in North Carolina has its own distinctive patterns of flow. Only after monitoring these patterns for decades do sufficient data emerge on which to base scientifically sound policy decisions. The observations are made at carefully placed and calibrated hydrographic stations. Records for rivers throughout the state provide a basis for understanding their comparative discharges (Fig. 13.4). Important here are the dramatic

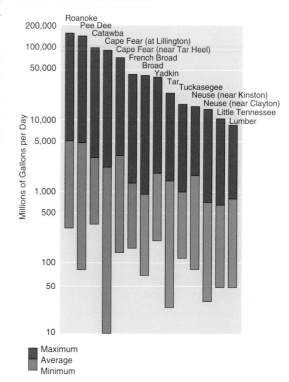

Figure 13.4. Characteristic Discharge of Selected Streams in North Carolina

Source: J. W. Clay, D. M. Orr Jr., and A. W. Stuart, eds., *North Carolina Atlas: Portrait of a Changing Southern State* (Chapel Hill: University of North Carolina Press, 1975).

ranges in the minimum and maximum flows recorded for all of these rivers. River management strategies must take into account both extremes in the flow of the rivers across the state.

Equally as important as the flow of water in rivers is water quality. There are four classes of water quality indices: suspended sediment, biological content, chemical characteristics, and temperature. As these indices vary with natural and human-related factors, the quality of water needed for various uses is affected by, and provides impetus for, a multitude of efforts to protect water quality.

Groundwater Resources

Groundwater in North Carolina provides 55 percent of the population with water supplies. These waters are extracted by private and municipal wells that pump from underground freshwater-saturated rock and soil formations. Underground aquifers, like rivers or lakes, have a constant flow of water in and out of their boundaries. New water percolates into the underground formations from the infiltration of surface water. Eventually, with time that ranges from a few hours to tens of thousands of years, it returns to the earth's surface in the form of springs and seeps along the banks of a river, where it contributes once again to stream discharge as baseflow unless, of course, it is intercepted first by a pumping well.

Aquifers are generally named after their hosting geologic formations, but they are regionally grouped into groundwater regions by the U.S. Geological Survey. Each of the fifteen groundwater regions across the United States has distinctive climatic, physiographic, and geologic attributes. North Carolina aquifers fall into one of two groups. Those west of the Fall Line lie within the Piedmont–Blue Ridge groundwater region and those to the east of it lie within the Atlantic Coastal Plain groundwater region.

Encompassing the two land regions from which it gets its name, the Piedmont–Blue Ridge Groundwater Region consists of unconfined, near-surface aquifers. Between the rocks that underlie the surface and the surface itself is a layer of weathered rock and clay-rich soil that is of variable thickness, typically between 10 and 100 meters. Under some of the mountain valley floors lie well-sorted, stratified river deposits. When the water table is encountered before reaching intact rock formations, the water resides in these poorly consolidated deposits as a diffuse-flow, unconfined aquifer. If the water table is deeper in the underlying rock formations, then water must continue downward toward the water table following narrow cracks and fissures in the rocks. This makes flow nondiffuse, or occurring along the discrete, sheetlike fractures within the rocks. The upper soils can have porosities near 20 to 30 percent, but the underlying rocks have porosities rarely in excess of 2 percent. These combined attributes lend this region its distinctive groundwater characteristics.

Wells typically are finished at 100 meters, as below this depth fractures tend to be closed or less numerous. In general, two wells drilled to 100 meters will yield substantially more water than one drilled to 200 or even 400 meters. As water is pumped from aquifers in this region, water must be replenished from the surrounding and overlying zones of rock and soil. The overlying soils, because of their higher porosities, often form important storage for the deeper wells of the province. The yields for any given well are largely determined by the number and size of fractures that the well intercepts. In choosing a location for a well, it is important to realize that the fractures are not uniform.

Erosion of the landscape in the Mountains and Piedmont by the forces of water and wind preferentially act on weaker zones of highly fractured rocks. The result is that the topography of the modern landscape partly reflects the internal weaknesses in the rocks. The surface is characterized by a complex network of linear depressions crossing the landscape. Undoubtedly, many of these areas are underlain by more intensely fractured rocks with high porosities and permeabilities. They are areas of potentially high-yielding wells. Also important for a good well in this province is the proximity of the well location to nearby recharge. For these reasons, wells drilled at the base of hill slopes or near surface water bodies tend to have higher sustainable, "safe" yields.

Wells drilled in either the Piedmont or the Blue Ridge Province will likely yield water only in quantities sufficient for domestic use (Fig. 13.5). Typical yields are 75 to 150 gallons per minute. Well interference and recharge are two related issues to determining yields. It has been estimated that recharge of these aquifers in some areas may be around 6 to 17 inches per year. With a recharge of 12 inches per year and a 10 percent porosity, one would expect a

Figure 13.5. Well Yields by Aquifer Type

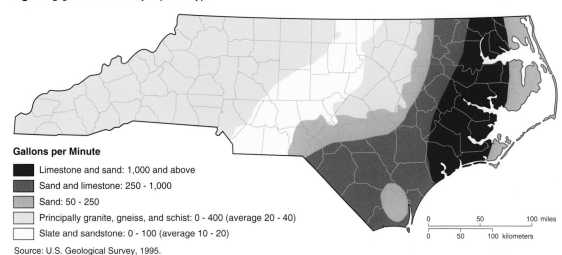

Gallons per Minute

- ⬛ Limestone and sand: 1,000 and above
- ⬛ Sand and limestone: 250 - 1,000
- ⬛ Sand: 50 - 250
- ⬜ Principally granite, gneiss, and schist: 0 - 400 (average 20 - 40)
- ⬜ Slate and sandstone: 0 - 100 (average 10 - 20)

Source: U.S. Geological Survey, 1995.

Figure 13.6. Diagram Illustrating Where a Confined Coastal Aquifer Is Recharged in Its Area of Outcrop

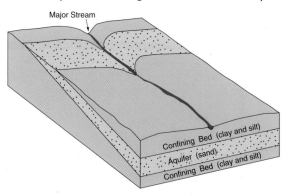

Source: D. Walters, *Estimated Water Use in North Carolina, 1995.*
U.S. Geological Survey, Fact Sheet FS-087-97, 1997.

seasonal change in the water table of 10 feet. The porosities typically are much lower, thus water tables can fluctuate by several factors larger.

The aquifers of the Coastal Plain are composed generally of unconsolidated to poorly consolidated beds of sand, gravel, and limestone that are separated by beds (layers) and lenses of clay and clayey silt. The series of beds dip eastward from the Fall Line and compose a gigantic wedge of layered sediment lying over the eastward extension of the harder rocks of the Piedmont. Figure 13.6 shows, schematically, the manner in which these beds are disposed and how water is held in the various porous layers within the sequence. The individual aquifers have modifying names after their hosting rock units. Some of these aquifers are near the surface and have the water table as their upper surfaces. These unconfined aquifers receive their recharge by direct vertical percolation of water from the surface.

The upper and lower boundaries of the lower aquifers consist of less permeable layers that force the water in the aquifers to move along the layer. Water is fed (recharged) into the layer principally to the west, where the aquifer layer breaches the earth's land surface. Wells that are drilled seaward of this zone encounter the water under a pressurized state in which the water will rise through the well to a level that defines what is referred to as the hydraulic head for that point in the aquifer. As water is extracted from confined aquifers, over and above the amount of recharge from the recharge zone, the aquifer becomes depressurized. The loss of pressure may be accompanied by ground sub-sidence as the hosting formation is allowed to collapse when the internal water pressure is reduced.

The unconfined, surficial aquifers of the Coastal Plain lie in three areas: the Sandhills, the area around the eastern portions of Pamlico Sound, and the barrier islands of the Outer Banks. In all three areas they represent important sources of freshwater. In the Pamlico Sound area the surficial units are 50 to 200 feet thick, and individual wells can yield up to 1 million gallons per day. The deeper levels of this surficial aquifer are transitional to confined conditions and are said to be semiconfined.

The Yorktown aquifer is present at shallow depths in the northern Coastal Plain. It is an important aquifer for a number of municipalities such as Elizabeth City, in Pasquotank County, which draws 1.3 million gallons per day from one well field alone. By far the most productive aquifer in the Coastal Plain is the Castle Hayne aquifer: wells with yields over 1,000 gallons per minute can be developed readily. It is the principal aquifer used for freshwater in the southeastern Coastal Plain, where nearly all other potential units have waters too saline for practical uses. The lowermost of the confined aquifers is the Cretaceous aquifer of the central and southern Coastal Plain. Although the units here have only moderate permeabilities, the thickness of the units permits yields up to 1,400 gallons per minute in some wells.

In all of the confined aquifers, and those surficial aquifers that border the Atlantic Ocean, eventually there is a seaward boundary where freshwater becomes first brackish and turns to salt water. The boundary is constantly maintained by the influx of freshwater from the land.

Freshwater Use

A common perspective on water use is that of an engineer or resource manager who seeks to quantify the volumes of water physically used, or bypassed, through some human-made facility. Water that is used in this manner includes water that is derived from pumping groundwater as well as by diverting surface water.

Groundwater can be pumped to the surface from a well to supply irrigation water to farms, processing water for industry, and potable water for municipalities and households. It is also pumped on occasion merely to control the water table in a specific manner. Two activities that require a controlled water table are open and underground mining and the containment and remediation of sites of groundwater pollution.

Surface water likewise is used in a variety of ways. In addition to the obvious water intakes required to divert the water needed by municipalities and industries, surface water is used instream for power generation. Some of the power-related uses are coal and hydrocarbon fuel-fired stream generation, the cooling of nuclear reactors, and hydroelectric power generation. Most of this water is not consumed and stays in the river system. Water consumption by the other offstream uses is largely represented by losses to the atmosphere. In some respects this water is not lost, as it increases the atmospheric moisture that may return once again to the surface or groundwater reservoirs through precipitation.

In 1995 an estimated 7,730 million gallons per day of freshwater were withdrawn from surface and groundwater sources. Figure 13.7 shows withdrawals, uses, and dispositions for surface water and groundwater. The 7,730 Mgal/d constitute approximately 18 percent of the total stream outflow in the state. Although this may seem excessive, the majority of that amount is used only in a tempo-rary capacity and is returned to the stream. Only 713 Mgal/d, or 9 percent of total withdrawals, are actually consumed or not returned to the surface water system. The differences in the way water is used and its final disposition underscore the complexities, and sometimes confusion, that surround water use statistics.

In addition to the engineered uses of water for various activities of humankind, water is used in a number of other ways that have important impacts economically, aesthetically, and ecologically. The creation of major reservoirs for water storage, power generation, flood control, and recreation represents an instream use of water that affects the economics, quality of life, and ecology of surrounding areas. Though historically reservoirs have been viewed as having a major benefit to a given region, they are often built with some controversy. A central issue, of course, centers on land ownership in the areas to be flooded. A second concern is that these dams be environmentally sound and consistent with the land use needs of the surrounding communities. Most North Carolina dams or reservoirs were built for flood control or power generation. The areas surrounding the reservoirs generally have benefited in a variety of economic ways and have gained in recreational resources. An additional benefit is that reservoirs temporarily slow the flow of water in the river, thus helping remove suspended particles and improving aspects of water quality.

Figure 13.7. Source, Use, and Disposition of Freshwater in North Carolina, 1995

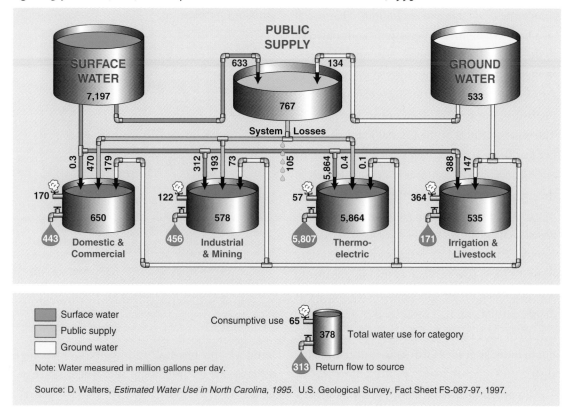

Surface water
Public supply
Ground water

Note: Water measured in million gallons per day.

Consumptive use **65**
378 Total water use for category
313 Return flow to source

Source: D. Walters, *Estimated Water Use in North Carolina, 1995.* U.S. Geological Survey, Fact Sheet FS-087-97, 1997.

to evapotranspiration. Only in the off-season (late fall, winter, and early summer) are the water needs of plants diminished sufficiently to promote large amounts of runoff and infiltration to recharge groundwater systems. In many ways plants can be regarded as competing with humankind for water resources.

Marine and Estuarine Water Resources

The coastal waters of North Carolina represent one of the most important natural resources in the state. These waters are composed of the nearshore open ocean, the sounds, and estuaries (Fig. 13.8). The marine estuaries and sounds, such as the Pamlico River Estuary and Pamlico Sound, yield the majority of the commercial and recreational fisheries catch taken statewide. The coastline of North Carolina is one of the most important resources along the Atlantic coast, and, as such, it serves as a base for an important, long-standing recreation and tourism industry. It also represents one of the most valuable ecological resources on the east coast of the United States.

These waters, including the intracoastal waterway, also provide a valuable navigation corridor, and the seaports at Wilmington and Morehead City provide the state access to important national and international shipping routes. These collective waters and their surrounding lands are today, in

Beyond the large reservoirs and other faster-moving segments of the state's river systems, thousands of smaller impoundments have been constructed for local purposes. In the Piedmont particularly, these dot the landscape. Here farmers created small ponds to feed livestock and provide a source of irrigation water during interstorm periods in growing seasons. Today, however, they are a common part of a civil engineer's plan to manage storm water runoff and mitigate potential water pollution. In some cases they are built as a recreational or aesthetic resource that enhances the general quality of community life.

By far the biggest user of water in North Carolina is the vegetation that is found in natural ecosystems and agricultural crops. In the growing season most precipitation that reaches the land surface during small and moderate storms is lost

Figure 13.8. Extent of Important Estuarine Zones in Atlantic Coastal States

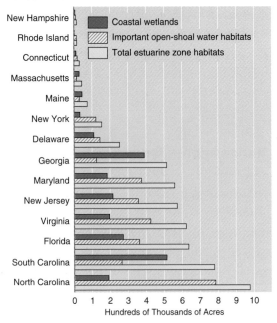

Source: G. P. Spinner, ed., *Serial Atlas of the Marine Environment* (New York: American Geographical Society, 1969).

many peoples' eyes, experiencing the beginnings of a new wave of agricultural, commercial, and recreational development. To minimize potential adverse effects of development, and thus optimize potential benefits, an understanding must first be acquired of the physical, chemical, and biological processes that operate in what can only be regarded as one of the most dynamic and complex natural environments in the state.

The physical setting of the coastal waters of North Carolina is a product of past and present geologic processes that have shaped the coastal and submarine landscape and sea bottom. The coastal area has been uplifted progressively and subjected to the erosive forces of runoff. Naturally, the areas farthest inland have been subjected to these forces for a longer period and sit at higher elevations than the lands closest to the open ocean. Much of the Tidewater portions of the Coastal Plain sit only a few feet above sea level, have been little affected by erosion, and are in fact poorly drained. Much of the poorly drained, or wetland, areas are salt marshes that directly border and provide a transitional wetland fringe to the coastal estuaries and sounds. The gradual decrease in the land surface from the Inner Coastal Plain to the salt marshes of the Tidewater to the gradually increasing water depths offshore on the continental shelf is part of a pattern that continues tens of miles offshore, out to the edge of the North American continental shelf.

This gradual pattern is shown in the bathymetric map of the coastal water (Fig. 13.9). An important interruption of this overall pattern is the narrow, linear bed of barrier islands that has been constructed by the winds, waves, and currents seaward of the sounds and coastal salt marshes from Cape Fear north. The form and character of the coast and coastal waters are a complex function of continuing sea-level changes, sediment buildup from rivers, ocean currents, and wave energy. The balance of forces that shapes the coastline also de-

Figure 13.9. Bathymetry of the North Carolina Coastline

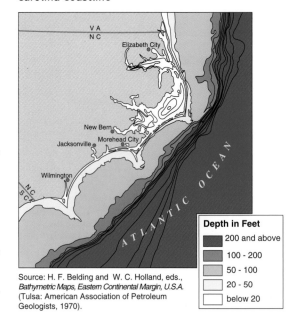

Source: H. F. Belding and W. C. Holland, eds., *Bathymetric Maps, Eastern Continental Margin, U.S.A.* (Tulsa: American Association of Petroleum Geologists, 1970).

termines the physical and chemical hydrologic foundations of the marine and estuarine ecosystems.

An *estuary* is the lower course of a river whose flow and chemical characteristics are affected by ocean tides. An estuary is a complex physical, chemical, and biological system. It does not function independently of the streams entering it, the land that surrounds it, the sounds connected to it, or the ocean waters that bound it. A *sound* is formally defined as a relatively narrow passage of water, but too wide and extensive to be called a strait, that connects two water bodies, or it can be a channel between the mainland and an island. It is also thought of as an inlet or arm of the sea. The latter sense is perhaps closest to describing the characteristics of Albemarle and Pamlico Sounds.

The fundamental aspect of the estuarine waters is in the regular, periodic, fluctuations of saltwater influences. The driving forces behind the periodic influxes of salt water into the estuaries are the diurnal ocean tides. Other forces that also influence water motions in the estuarine environment are winds, runoff in the tributaries feeding into the estuaries, and regional barometric pressure. A measure of the changes brought about by these forces in the estuaries is seen in the records of water levels that are registered at tide or gauge stations throughout the coastal area. Estuaries that are not well protected from the open ocean, such as the Cape Fear Estuary, are strongly and most directly influenced by tides. Those that lie inboard of the sounds, behind the barrier islands, such as the Pamlico River, Neuse River, and Albemarle Sound, have changes in water levels that are more strongly affected by winds. Here tidal influences are commonly only one-half foot or so, whereas typical wind influences are two to four times the tidal ranges. The combined diurnal and wind effects operate at different scales and time periods.

Although water fed into the estuarine environment from tributaries is fresh in character, this freshwater mixes with the marine waters of the sounds as it reaches the inner limits of the estuary.

The concentrations of chloride, as measured upstream in the estuaries, change as the tides and winds push ocean waters into these inner reaches. As water recedes from the estuary during low tide, the salt concentrations will also drop, as the estuary becomes more influenced by the discharges of freshwater from the upstream tributaries.

The Pamlico River Estuary and adjacent Sound constitute one of the most important estuarine ecological resources on the Atlantic coast. This portion of North Carolina's coastal waters covers approximately 2,000 square miles and is second in size, along the Atlantic coast, only to Chesapeake Bay. About 70 percent of the fish and shellfish taken by North Carolina fishers come from this area and its tributaries. Because of the region's large size, isolation, and sparse population, it remains among the least polluted and potentially most valuable estuaries on the Atlantic coast for a variety of migrating fish species.

The lack of a thorough understanding of the relationship between various types of development on the land surrounding the estuaries and productivity in the nursery areas constitutes a potential threat to the future well-being of this important ecosystem. The Neuse Estuary to the south is more extensively developed and more polluted; it experiences buildups of algal blooms in the upper estuary, which are in part induced by municipal and other effluent discharges into the tributaries that feed the estuary. The Albemarle Sound to

the north of the Pamlico Sound contains waters with lower salt (higher freshwater contents) concentrations. Here, the waters support predominantly nonmigratory species.

Managing North Carolina's Water Resources

Water management issues can be discussed in the context of water as a natural hazard or as a natural resource. The issues are complex and impact substantially on humankind's efforts to develop a sound and sustainable socioeconomic infrastructure. Some of the major natural hazards represented by water are floods, droughts, naturally occurring chemical contaminants in drinking water, and the suspended sediments that pose hazards to power generation, water supplies, riparian and wetland ecosystems, and navigation. Depending on the climate, geology, and human land and water use, each of these natural hazards may represent significant management changes. The U.S. Geological Survey, U.S. Corps of Engineers, Federal Emergency Management Agency, Environmental Protection Agency, and National Oceans and Atmospheric Administration—specifically the National Weather Service (NWS)—are some of the federal agencies that provide technical assistance in assessing, predicting, and mitigating the impacts of these hazards. Between 1995 and 1997 there were five presidentially declared natural disaster areas that affected ninety-one of North Carolina's one hundred counties.

Water is a natural resource that ideally should be used in a sustainable or renewable manner. Its quality should be protected from deterioration, and it should be shared in some equitable way to meet not only the array of human demands but also those of ecosystems. The last century of growth in the country's agricultural and industrial economies has in many regions been at the expense of water resources. Large extents of groundwater resources have been overpumped and show continuing declines in water levels, large areas have been chemically contaminated by various agricultural and industrial chemicals, and surface waterways have taken on a highly engineered character, often at the sacrifice of their original ecological and aesthetic characteristics.

These changes represent an intangible accrued environmental debt that is rarely factored into regional economic models. Water law, though undergoing a constant process of reinterpretation to meet new circumstances, was formulated long before modern technical understanding of the hydrologic cycle and largely before society's ingenuity in managing and altering watersheds to serve specific ends was understood. There are few issues less controversial today than water resources and watershed management.

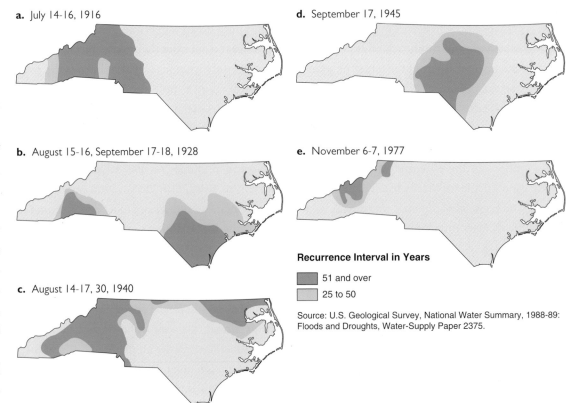

Figure 13.10. Areal Extents of Floods

a. July 14-16, 1916

b. August 15-16, September 17-18, 1928

c. August 14-17, 30, 1940

d. September 17, 1945

e. November 6-7, 1977

Recurrence Interval in Years

51 and over

25 to 50

Source: U.S. Geological Survey, National Water Summary, 1988-89: Floods and Droughts, Water-Supply Paper 2375.

Droughts and Floods

North Carolina can expect to experience major droughts and floods every five to twenty-five years. About 90 percent of the estimated damages caused by natural disasters nationally (except droughts) are due to flooding. The North Carolina Department of Environment, Health, and Natural Resources calculated that between 1956 and 1981 flooding caused an average of $10 million per year in damage. Droughts, though historically linked to widespread famine, are largely associated in the United States with periods of economic and personal hardship. Most economic losses are in the agricultural sector. But as the demands for water increase due to population and economic growth, the socioeconomic impacts of future droughts likely will be magnified.

Figure 13.11. Areas Subject to Flood Inundation Caused by Wind Tides

a. 50% chance of being equaled or exceeded in any one year

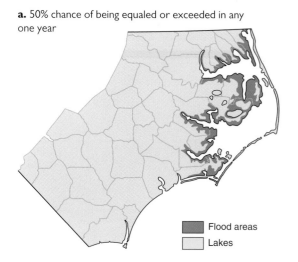

b. 1% chance of being equaled or exceeded in any one year

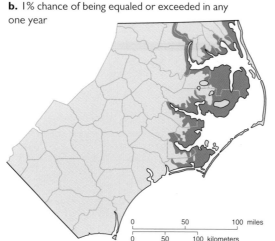

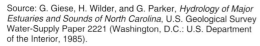
Flood areas

Lakes

Source: G. Giese, H. Wilder, and G. Parker, *Hydrology of Major Estuaries and Sounds of North Carolina*, U.S. Geological Survey Water-Supply Paper 2221 (Washington, D.C.: U.S. Department of the Interior, 1985).

Figure 13.12. Relationship of Discharge of the 100-Year Flood to Drainage Area

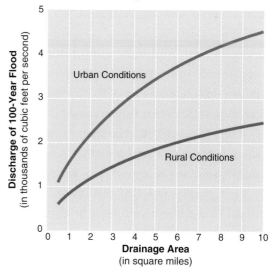

Note: This chart is based on an impervious cover of 25%.

Source: J. W. Clay, D. M. Orr Jr., and A. W. Stuart, eds., *North Carolina Atlas: Portrait of a Changing Southern State* (Chapel Hill: University of North Carolina Press, 1975).

In North Carolina, floods have been linked largely to major precipitation events such as those that accompany tropical storms, hurricanes, or major frontal systems. Figure 13.10 shows the areal extent and date of some significant floods that have occurred in North Carolina. These can be regarded as either inland or coastal floods. Those on or near the coast are typically associated with hurricanes in the late summer to early fall or with large winter and early spring storms (Fig. 13.11). Inland floods can be related to the intense rainfall that accompanies tropical storms as they move inland or to major frontal systems such as that associated with the November 1977 flood in the Blue Ridge Mountains (Fig. 13.10c).

A similar event occurred in July 1997, when the remnants of Hurricane Danny brought over 10 inches of rain within a twenty-four-hour period to portions of the southern Piedmont, including Charlotte. Ironically, this storm came at the end of three weeks of hot, dry weather that approached drought conditions.

Besides the obvious role of weather and climate, the preexisting state of the land surface can exacerbate or buffer the impact of flooding. For example, the development of retention basins and reservoirs in a given drainage basin can mitigate rapid stream level changes downstream from the impoundment areas. However, urbanization can accelerate or accentuate runoff due to the increase in impervious land cover by potentially producing flooding where previously it would not have occurred or would have occurred rarely (Fig. 13.12). During the growing season much rainfall can be absorbed by soils and vegetation, thus buffering the extremes of flooding. From late fall to early spring, runoff is usually rapid and storms are typically associated with high flows in streams and rivers.

Droughts are essentially periods when less precipitation is delivered to the land surface than usual. Periods of major droughts tend to be measured in years and thus represent the longer-term cumulative deficits in rainfall. Whereas floods are regarded as short-term weather anomalies, droughts are longer-term climate anomalies. There are many definitions of a drought, but common to all of them is the notion that a drought is a water deficit that has some longevity related to the time scale of humankind's expected water needs. It is not always obvious by inspection of a rainfall record for a given period that there is or is not a drought. Groundwater levels could be high, for example, in winter months when there have been few rainfall events of any significant duration, or levels could be lower than normal even when rainfall has been higher than normal, particularly if that rainfall came down in a few large rainfall events. In North Carolina there were seven major droughts in the twentieth century; five of these are shown in Figure 13.13.

The impacts of these droughts, which reoccured with an average frequency of one every twelve to thirteen years, varied. During the 1930–34 drought, the Red Cross had to provide basic food, water, clothing, and livestock feed from August 1930 to June 1931. In 1954 the city of Greensboro was down to a three-day water supply when Hurricane Hazel came through and refilled the city reservoirs. In 1980 the governor declared sixty-seven of one hundred counties to be disaster areas. In 1986 ten cities had mandatory water use restric-

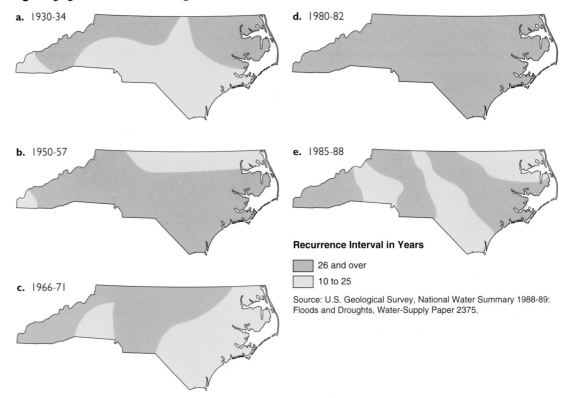

Figure 13.13. Areal Extent of Droughts

a. 1930-34

b. 1950-57

c. 1966-71

d. 1980-82

e. 1985-88

Recurrence Interval in Years

■ 26 and over
□ 10 to 25

Source: U.S. Geological Survey, National Water Summary 1988-89: Floods and Droughts, Water-Supply Paper 2375.

tions and thirty had voluntary conservation measures. The 1985–88 drought left eighty-one counties as federal disaster areas; agricultural damages were estimated at $330 million. In the summer of 1999 one of the worst droughts of the twentieth century struck the eastern United States, including parts of North Carolina.

Today, federal, state, and local governments all play a role in society's attempt to predict, cope with, and mitigate the effects of floods and droughts. In each state, responsibility for forecasting and issu-

ing warnings of floods is vested in the National Weather Service Forecast Offices. They are supported by thirteen NWS Regional River Forecast Centers. Thousands of weather and stream-gauging stations are telemetered into these centers to provide the timely data needed to forecast and provide advance warnings to communities of flooding. It is estimated that timely forecasts save $1 billion annually.

But forecasts of stream flow are important for more than just hazard avoidance, disaster preparedness, and damage mitigation. Forecasts of river stages help manage rivers that are used for navigation, hydroelectric power generation, and water supplies to meet agricultural, municipal, industrial, and ecological needs. At present, the NWS does not have the capacity to predict droughts. But its new Water Resource Forecasting System can provide hydrologic forecasts that, in turn, provide state, local, or other water management authorities a basis on which to support risk-based decision-making regarding the continued probability of drought conditions and the assessment of alternative strategies to cope with near- and long-term water shortages.

The U.S. Army Corps of Engineers has been the federal agency with the greatest vested role in structural modifications of the nation's waterways to cope with flooding and flood control problems. In addition, several major reservoirs in western North Carolina are operated by the Tennessee Valley Authority. Although the state's larger reservoirs serve a multitude of uses, all provide for flood control and low-flow augmentation.

The primary authority regarding the imposition of restrictions over the use and management of land in the flood plains lies with the local governments that have flood plains within their jurisdictions. State laws call for the local authority but do not require that localities adopt, administer, or enforce flood plain ordinances except in coastal areas. Incentives for local management are furnished by eligibility criteria established for mu-

nicipal or county participation in the National Flood Insurance Program (NFIP). Approximately 80 to 90 percent of North Carolina communities that have Special Flood Hazard Areas participate in the NFIP, which is administered by the Federal Emergency Management Administration (FEMA). State agencies such as the Department of Environment, Health, and Natural Resources, the Department of Crime Control and Public Safety, and the Department of Emergency Management help local governments draft appropriate flood plain regulations that typically include zoning ordinances and building restrictions and codes.

Finally, plans for water management during droughts generally are developed and implemented at the local level. The first measure is usually the imposition of water use restrictions. As conditions worsen, local governments enter into emergency contracts to buy water from nearby systems with more plentiful sources. The North Carolina Division of Water Resources monitors the state's water resources for potential shortages and notifies communities of potential problems. It also provides technical assistance in the writing of local ordinances to deal with water shortages and in the assessment of alternative water sources during drought, and it can arrange for emergency hauling or pumping of water during a water shortage.

Water Quality Problems

The presence of substantial quantities of suspended fine-grained sediment in surface water is considered one of the most widespread water quality problems in North Carolina. Sediment lowers the aesthetic quality of the water, clogs channels and increases flood potential, creates hazards to river navigation, reduces reservoir storage capacity, is costly to filter from water supplies, lowers the amount of light that penetrates water bodies to reach aquatic plants, smothers fish eggs, and generally reduces the diversity of aquatic life. One benefit, however, of suspended sediment in reservoirs is that particles tend to attract other chemical contaminants, thus providing an instream treatment process for contaminated runoff.

Sediment is always transported by rivers, but under a natural forest cover, only 5 to 58 tons per square mile per year ($t/mi^2/yr$) likely would be removed from the North Carolina landscape. But estimates indicate that 180 $t/mi^2/yr$ of sediment are carried off the landscape in the Cape Fear Basin, 280 $t/mi^2/yr$ in the Catawba Basin, and 300 $t/mi^2/yr$ in the Yadkin–Pee Dee Basin. The increase in the North Carolina population necessarily is at the expense of forest and agricultural lands as cities grow outward. Thus, the amount of soil erosion and suspended sediment is likely to remain a major problem.

Management of suspended sediment or sediment erosion problems takes two forms. One is to

Sediment plume from a construction site entering Lake Wylie from Dutchman Creek in Gaston County

promote best management practices in forestry and agriculture, which are efforts organized through the U.S. Department of Forestry and the Soil Conservation Service. The Soil Conservation Service has a Small Watershed Program to offer technical and financial assistance to farmers for the construction of impoundments, which, while providing for flood control and irrigation, also help to trap sediment in headwater regions. Second, the North Carolina Sedimentation and Control Act of 1973 provides that "an erosion and sedimentation control plan shall be prepared prior to the commencement of any land-disturbing activity whenever the proposed activity is to be undertaken on a tract comprising more than one acre if more than one continuous acre is to be uncovered." In most cases, these plans involve trapping sediment on site during the construction or uncovering phase and reestablishing vegetation cover soon afterward. No one argues against the importance of mitigating soil erosion or stopping sediment from being carried into surface waters. Once it is in the stream system, however, one of the most effective means for its removal is the construction of upstream dams that can impound runoff. There are about four thousand privately owned dams at least 15 feet high with storage capacities exceeding 10 acre-feet.

Any water body with a capacity equal to or greater than the annual inflow volume will trap 95 to 100 percent of the suspended sediment. Even reservoirs with capacities as small as 0.02 percent of the annual runoff can potentially trap 20 to 60 percent of the suspended sediment. Without the presence of upstream retention basins to help trap sediment in urban areas with clayey soils, such as in and around Charlotte, small basins can have sediment yields as great as 1,500 tons per square mile per year. Decreases in existing reservoir capacity (due to siltation) and a decreasing pool of prospective sites for future new reservoirs present challenges for managing sediment pollution in this century. The state of North Carolina has assumed many responsibilities for meeting national guidelines under the Clean Water Act, the Safe Drinking Water Act, and subsequent amendments of these acts. These activities are coordinated with a number of branches within the North Carolina Department of Environment, Health, and Natural Resources. The activities can be organized roughly into (1) statewide programs of water and water quality assessments that involve monitoring and regional planning, (2) stream classification and issuance of permits for both point and nonpoint source activities that have a potential impact on drinking water supplies, and (3) oversight of the new water supply watershed protection program whereby local government is authorized (required) to set up ordinances that restrict or control land use within areas designated by the state as protected water supply watersheds.

Each biennium, the state's water quality division must submit a report of surface water quality conditions, which is then compiled with reports from all states by the EPA and submitted to the U.S. Congress. These are referred to as the CWA Section 305(b) reports. The 1994 report for North Carolina indicated that 70 percent of surveyed freshwater rivers and streams had good water quality that fully supported aquatic life uses. About 25 percent had fair water quality that only partially supported aquatic life uses, and 5 percent had poor quality that did not support aquatic life uses. Another 18 percent did not support swimming. Some 56 percent of impaired streams had been harmed by agricultural sources, 13 percent by nonpoint urban runoff, 12 percent by point sources, and 11 percent by construction sites.

The 1990–91 water quality summary report of the U.S. Geological Survey indicated that upward trends in nitrogen were seen in the Tar-Pamlico, Neuse, Cape Fear, and Yadkin–Pee Dee Basins. Both EPA and USGS sampling protocols for defining surface water quality are best used for establishing conditions averaged over time; these protocols thus miss low-frequency and low-duration events of water impairment due to accidental releases and spills. They also poorly characterize some biological (e.g., bacterial) hazards. In the coastal rivers during 1995 and 1996, 10 million fish were killed in only five spills, which also closed over 356,000 acres of coastal wetlands to shellfish harvesting and commercial fishing. In the first eight months of 1997, thirty-seven fish kills were reported statewide. These events reflect inherent inadequacies in current monitoring protocols that seek to protect aquatic ecosystems or public health.

Normally, fish kills have been linked to excessive nutrient and organic loads that deoxygenate waters and thus suffocate fish, but permitted nutrient loads in North Carolina streams and rivers are 10 to 100 times over natural conditions. These elevated levels of nutrients are potentially linked to outbreaks of toxic microorganisms such as Pfiesteria, which has also been linked to fish kills, and threaten other uses of surface water. Regardless of the specific pathologic mechanism, there is little doubt that nutrient levels, particularly dissolved forms of nitrogen, are too high and need to be reduced. Nitrogen sources in coastal rivers have seen unprecedented rises largely due to an explosive growth in hog farm operations using waste lagoons that are highly susceptible to failure during winter and spring storms.

Outlook

In the 1990s the North Carolina legislature took some rather dramatic steps to protect surface waters. These actions are needed to stem the increasing negative impacts of agricultural land use and urban growth on surface water quality. The North Carolina Water Supply Watershed Protection program, for example, seeks to curtail sources of contamination that could threaten drinking water supplies. The North Carolina Clean Water Fund has multiple funding options for grants to state and local government agencies and nonprofit organizations for water quality improvements. And in 1997 the General Assembly passed a water quality regulatory act to further limit nutrient releases from both agricultural nonpoint pollution and public water treatment facilities. As the new century opens, the state will likely see vigorous efforts to bring a new generation of waste and waste water treatment systems into both agricultural and urban facilities.

In 1998 the North Carolina Clean Water Management Trust Fund, established in the previous year, allocated $6.5 million to buy 1,300 acres of shoreline along Mountain Island Lake. That lake, on the Catawba River, is a major water source for Gaston and Mecklenburg Counties. The land will be set aside for preservation, possibly as a regional park, rather than developed as sites for as many as 3,600 homes. The expectation is that its removal from development will significantly lessen the deposition of sediment and various pollutants into this vital supply of freshwater.

Beyond the established state programs that focus primarily on the removal and prevention of point and nonpoint sources of contaminants in surface waters, the Army Corps of Engineers, in cooperation with the state and the EPA, administers Section 404 of the Clean Water Act, which requires a permit for dredging and filling of surface water bodies. It is through this regulatory program that wetlands and riparian habitats are presently safeguarded.

The North Carolina Department of Environment, Health, and Natural Resources, through its Division of Environmental Management, implements many of the oversight functions of the state to protect groundwater resources. These are in part administered through the department's seven regional offices. Oversight activities include, for example, required permits for well construction and well water withdrawal for public or industrial water supplies. No waste water injection is allowed in the state. Well drillers must be registered annually and comply with the reporting requirements for well completions (installations) or well abandonments (closings). The state's Environmental Management Commission provides oversight of the permitting processes and can also designate special groundwater Capacity Use Areas within which special restrictions on groundwater withdrawals may apply.

In addition to issuing permits for wells and designating Capacity Use Areas, the state also allows underground storage tanks and manages these in a manner similar to wells. For each tank, permits must be obtained and the installations and closings

Fish kill in the Roanoke River

must be reported. Despite these protective measures, the quality of groundwater remains in serious question. There are, in practice, two different groundwater management challenges in North Carolina. The first relates to problems of increasing water demand in coastal areas with very limited groundwater supplies, and the second is the statewide threat of contamination of groundwaters from point and nonpoint sources of biological and chemical agents.

In regions near the coast, overpumping of the surficial and deeper confined aquifers (Fig. 13.14)

and the incursion of salt water into aquifers from the east represent serious management problems. To help restore declining water levels in portions of the coastal areas (vicinity of the Pamlico Estuary), the state has designated the first special Capacity Use Area, which establishes the authority to restrict groundwater withdrawal from certain categories of wells. Future development in the coastal areas will likely create groundwater problems, but wetland regulations may restrict some areas from agricultural or urban invasion. Expansions and additional Capacity Use Areas may have to be designated to

Figure 13.14. Coastal Aquifers

a. Depth to Saltwater in the Coastal Aquifers

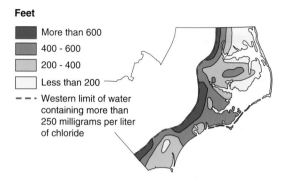

Feet

- More than 600
- 400 - 600
- 200 - 400
- Less than 200
- – – – Western limit of water containing more than 250 milligrams per liter of chloride

Source: R. Heath, *Basic Elements of Ground-Water Hydrology with Reference to Conditions in North Carolina*, U.S. Geological Survey Water-Resource Investigations Open-File Report 80-44 (Washington, D.C.: Department of the Interior, 1980).

b. Conditions of Saltwater Encroachment in Association with a Pumping Well

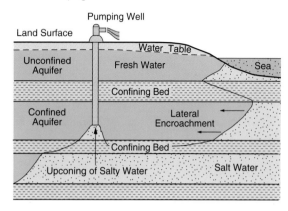

c. Freshwater Lens under a Barrier Island

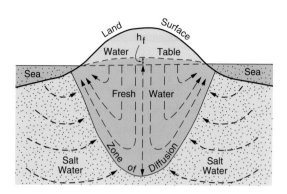

protect resources from overconsumption in the next two decades.

Point sources of potential groundwater contamination are represented by hundreds of old industrial sites, landfills, accidental spills, and ruptured underground tanks (Fig. 13.15). North Carolina, in cooperation with the EPA, is co-administering provisions of the Comprehensive Environmental Responsibilities and Liabilities Act (Superfund) and the Resource Conservation and Recovery Act, or the state's equivalent of these acts, to both remediate and control point source contaminants. These actions are diverse but include oversight of the generators, storers, transporters, and disposers of hazardous waste; the permitting of underground storage tanks; and, in some cases,

the assessment and remediation of potentially contaminated sites that pose threats to existing water supplies. Nonpoint sources are most controllable through the implementation of best management practices, but also by land use planning and in some cases by regulating access to, and use of, specific compounds (such as DDT). Despite protective measures, groundwater resources in North Carolina will remain significantly threatened into this century, as the following statistics illustrate.

As of 1996 there were 10,562 public groundwater supply systems in the state, of which 2,575 were registered community public water supply systems that fell under the testing requirements of the U.S. Safe Drinking Water Act. There were approximately 700,000 individual household water supply

Figure 13.15. Groundwater Contamination Sources

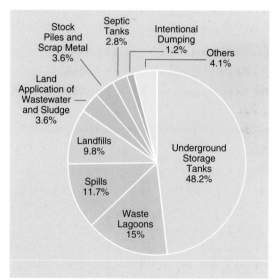

Source: Modified from H. B. Mew, N.C. Department of Natural Resources and Community Development, written communication, 1985.

wells, the locations of which were largely unknown and thus difficult to integrate into state-promulgated risk assessment strategies. Less than 1 percent of groundwater supply sources in North Carolina were under any regulatory monitoring program. Of the estimated 220,000 underground storage tanks in the state, 84,000 were registered and only 13,500 were covered under the state's Leaking Underground Storage Tank Fund. Approximately 50 percent of the tanks were older than sixteen years with no secondary containment or leak-detection system. It was estimated that 25–30 percent of the tanks might be leaking. In 1994 leaking underground tanks had been the primary cause of new sources of contamination that affected 276 public water supply systems in North Carolina.

In agricultural areas, there are growing concerns of contamination from herbicides and pesticides. The results from a seven-year study (1987–95) of 55 ambient (nonpumping) wells and 97 percent shallow supply wells from thirty-seven North Carolina counties revealed contamination in 13 percent of the ambient wells and 27 percent of the shallow wells. These data indicate that groundwater resources are significantly threatened, with a high probability that 5 to 15 percent of the wells statewide (serving approximately 150,000 to 500,000 persons) have been impacted by some form of chemical contaminant. In addition to the chemical contamination of groundwater, the state's 1.2 million septic systems are aging, with over 50 percent likely to be more than twenty years old. These older systems represent biological threats to groundwater and will likely increase failure rates in the first quarter of this century. Though not easily monitored, their failures may be recorded in rural disease statistics of cholera, typhoid, and similar water-transmitted diseases.

In addition to human sources of chemical and biological contamination, natural contaminants must be dealt with. Radon, a naturally occurring gas that is produced by the decay of naturally occurring radioactive isotopes of uranium in the underlying rocks of the state, poses a tangible risk in many areas. There have been many incidences where municipal waters have exceeded standards for radon as set by the EPA under the Safe Drinking Water Act. Only the continued and expanded monitoring and regulation of groundwater in North Carolina will likely protect this resource, on which slightly over 50 percent of the population relies for its water supply.

The increasing regulation of the state's water supply has improved the availability of this precious resource. The nature of the physical environment ensures that the supply will be abundant. The issue for the twenty-first century is whether the quality of the water supply will remain adequate in the face of growing demand from increased population and economic activities. Along with maintaining air quality, this may be one of the most pressing issues that future policymakers will have to face.

Selected References

Barnes, C., and M. Davenport. "North Carolina Stream Water Quality." In *National Water Summary, 1990–91—Hydrologic Events and Stream Water Quality*, edited by R. Paulson, pp. 421–28. Washington, D.C.: U.S. Geological Survey, Water Supply Paper 2400, 1993.

Giese, G., and R. Mason. *Low-Flow Characteristics of Streams in North Carolina.* Washington, D.C.: U.S. Geological Survey, Water Supply Paper 2403, 1993.

Giese, G., R. Mason, A. Strickland, and M. Bailey. "North Carolina Groundwater Quality." In *National Water Summary 1996—Hydrologic Events and Groundwater Quality*, pp. 393–400. Washington, D.C.: U.S. Geological Survey, Water Supply Paper 2325, 1988.

Heath, R. *Basic Elements of Groundwater Hydrology with Reference to Conditions in North Carolina.* Washington, D.C.: U.S. Geological Survey, Water Resources Investigations Open File Report 80-44, 1980.

North Carolina Department of Environment, Health, and Natural Resources. Division of Environmental Management. Water Quality Section. *North Carolina Lake Assessment Report.* Report 92-02, June 1992.

Simmons, C. *Sediment Characteristics of North Carolina Streams, 1970–79.* Washington, D.C.: U.S. Geological Survey, Water Supply Paper 2364, 1993.

Terziotti, S., T. Shrader, and M. Treese. *Estimated Water Use, by County, in North Carolina, 1990.* Washington, D.C.: U.S. Geological Survey, Open File Report 94-522, 1994.

U.S. Geological Survey. "Hydrologic Events and Floods and Droughts." *National Water Summary, 1988–89*, pp. 425–34. Water-Supply Paper 2375, 1991.

Walters, D. *Estimated Water Use in North Carolina, 1995.* Washington D.C.: U.S. Geological Survey, Fact Sheet FS-O87-97, 1997.

14. CRIME

Richard C. Lumb

Paralleling North Carolina's growth and increasing prosperity has been a precipitous rise in crime. More and more people have personal encounters with crime, and both individuals and institutions are compelled to invest heavily in security systems. The results are fear, political attention, and, ultimately, the cost of crime in fiscal and emotional terms.

Escalating crime rates are a national trend, but it comes as a surprise to many that North Carolina's crime rate is higher than that of the nation as a whole. The factors associated with crime are not thoroughly understood. Poverty, lack of opportunity, perceptions of an unfair socioeconomic system, undereducation, drug habit costs, emotional instability, and many other reasons have been suggested as general causes of crime. Why crime rates are higher in North Carolina than in the country generally is something of a mystery. One factor that does stand out is the great number of affluent newcomers to the state who make compelling targets for criminals. As shown in Chapter 4 ("Population"), this in-migration—a relatively new phenomenon—is the primary driver of the state's strong population growth. In-migration not only brings in great numbers of affluent newcomers but it also creates communities of strangers. The loss of social controls in neighborhoods composed of strangers is one of the consequences of rapid growth.

In any case, without dealing realistically with the factors that seem to be the basis for criminal behavior, including racism and other forms of prejudice, it is unlikely that crime will diminish in this century. There is little evidence that the current emphasis on incarceration, though expensive, is an effective solution.

Crime statistics appear in *Uniform Crime Reports* (*UCR*), published by the Federal Bureau of Investigation, and in *Crime in North Carolina*, published by the North Carolina State Bureau of Investigation (SBI). Combined, the two sources report on twenty-nine categories of crime. Both have been criticized for alleged inaccuracies. In some cases crime rates are understated because some crimes go unreported, whereas in other instances recent improvements in data collection have led to an exaggeration of crime rates. Despite such flaws, these reports are virtually the only comprehensive sources of crime data that are available.

Statewide Crime Rates

In 1996 North Carolina recorded 399,381 Index Crimes at a rate of 5,650 per 100,000 population (Table 14.1); the national rate was 5,079 Index Crimes per 100,000 population. Put another way,

Table 14.1. Crime Rates in North Carolina and the United States, 1986–1996

	Total Index Crimes*	Rate per 100,000
1986		
United States	13,210,800	5,480
North Carolina	266,415	4,399
1996		
United States	13,473,614	5,079
North Carolina	399,381	5,650
Change, 1986–96 (%)		
United States	+2.0	-7.3
North Carolina	+49.9	+28.4

Sources: Federal Bureau of Investigation, *Uniform Crime Reports*, 1986–96; State Bureau of Investigation, *Crime in North Carolina*, 1986–96.
*Index crimes include murder, rape, robbery, aggravated assault, burglary, larceny, and motor vehicle theft.

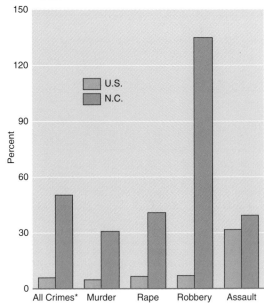

Figure 14.1. Percentage Change in the Number of Crimes in North Carolina and the United States, 1986–1995

*Percentage change in crime nationwide is based on 1994 data.

Source: State Bureau of Investigation, Report for the Law Enforcement Committee of the N.C. General Assembly, November 1996.

with 2.65 percent of the nation's population, North Carolina accounted for 2.96 percent of the recorded Index Crimes in the United States. Moreover, between 1986 and 1996 the state's Index Crime rate increased by 28.4 percent, whereas the national rate declined by 7.3 percent. The total number of Index Crimes rose a scant 2.0 percent nationally, whereas the North Carolina total shot up by a whopping 49.9 percent. As a result, the statewide

rate rose from considerably below the national rate in 1986 to well ahead of it by 1996. This sharp jump gives credence to the idea that rising crime is associated with the state's recent growth in population, driven largely by in-migration from across the country and from abroad.

Index offenses include murder, nonnegligent manslaughter, rape, burglary, aggravated assault, motor vehicle theft, and larceny. All four catego-

Figure 14.2. Crime Rate per 100,000 Population, 1997

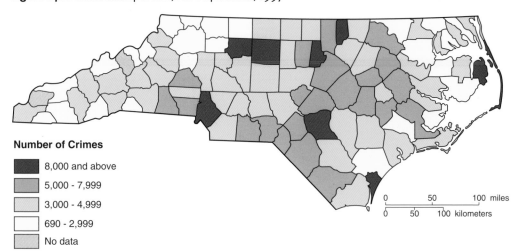

Number of Crimes

■ 8,000 and above
▨ 5,000 - 7,999
▢ 3,000 - 4,999
□ 690 - 2,999
▨ No data

0   50   100 miles
0   50   100 kilometers

Source: State Bureau of Investigation, *Crime in North Carolina*, 1997.

Figure 14.3. Trends in North Carolina, by Category of Crime, 1988 and 1997

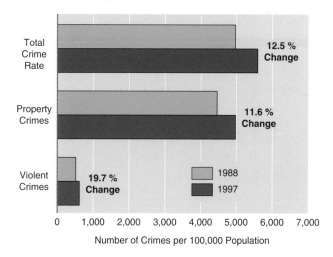

Number of Crimes per 100,000 Population

Note: Property crimes include burglary, larceny, and motor vehicle theft. Violent crimes include murder, rape, robbery, and aggravated assault.

Source: State Bureau of Investigation, *Crime in North Carolina*, 1988, 1997.

ries of Part I violent crimes (murder, rape, robbery, and aggravated assault), displayed in Figure 14.1, occurred at higher rates in North Carolina than in the United States as a whole.

County Patterns

Figure 14.2 shows the overall crime rate in North Carolina, by county, in 1997. The most obvious feature is the association of high crime rates with more urban counties. The counties that contain the cities of Charlotte, Durham, Henderson, Wilmington, and Winston-Salem appear in the highest category on the map: 8,000 or more crimes per 100,000 population. The next highest level is represented by a greater number of counties, including urban areas

such as Raleigh, Greensboro, and Asheville; some suburban counties; and an array of counties between Raleigh and the coast. The lowest crime rates are clustered mainly in the northwestern, western, and northeastern parts of the state, predominantly in rural counties.

The North Carolina statistics published by the SBI indicate that between 1988 and 1997 total reported crime increased by 12.5 percent (Fig. 14.3). Violent crimes rose by 19.7 percent and nonviolent crimes by 11.6 percent.

Clearance Rates

An offense is considered cleared (solved) when at least one offender is arrested for the crime. In 1997 violent crimes experienced a moderately high clearance

Figure 14.4. Percentage of North Carolina Index Crimes Cleared, 1997

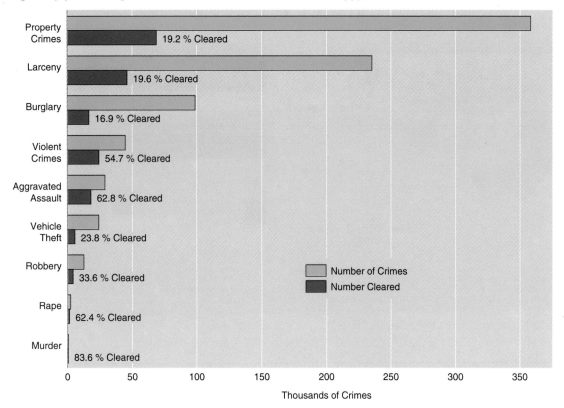

Property Crimes — 19.2 % Cleared
Larceny — 19.6 % Cleared
Burglary — 16.9 % Cleared
Violent Crimes — 54.7 % Cleared
Aggravated Assault — 62.8 % Cleared
Vehicle Theft — 23.8 % Cleared
Robbery — 33.6 % Cleared
Rape — 62.4 % Cleared
Murder — 83.6 % Cleared

Number of Crimes
Number Cleared

Thousands of Crimes

Source: State Bureau of Investigation, *Crime in North Carolina*, 1997.

rate of 54.7 percent (Fig. 14.4). Robberies were cleared at the rate of 33.6 percent, whereas Part I property crimes (burglary, larceny, and motor vehicle theft) were pursued less successfully, sustaining a clearance of only 19.2 percent.

It is clear that the frequency of criminal acts has increased rapidly in recent years. Although many of these offenses are being cleared, specific categories of crime (robbery, burglary, larceny, and motor

vehicle theft) do not result in substantial case closures. The overall clearance rate for all 1997 Part I crimes was 23.1 percent. Clearance of violent crimes (54.7 percent) was substantially higher than for property crimes (19.2 percent), which is generally attributable to police resource allocation to those more visible crimes, the ones most associated with citizens' fear.

The accuracy of these data is inevitably open to

question, for several reasons. For instance, some crimes go unreported. When they are reported, information on arrests is dependent on investigation by the police and prosecutorial acceptance of cases for submission to the court system; some cases are not investigated or prosecuted. On the other hand, improvements in record keeping, including the computerization of reports, may reflect a rise in crime rates that is more apparent than real.

Illegal Drugs

Illegal drugs are often cited as a cause of crime and social disorder in North Carolina. An examination of arrests for either illegal possession or illegal sales of drugs paints a rather bleak picture (Table 14.2). In 1997 4,198 individuals were charged with selling opium, cocaine, or their derivatives (morphine, heroin, and codeine). An additional 2,182 people were charged with selling marijuana. Add to these figures the 261 charged with selling synthetic narcotics (e.g., Demerol and methadone) and other dangerous drugs (e.g., barbiturates), and the problem quickly exacerbates. Those charged with possession of these substances numbered 34,894, for a combined sales/possession total of 41,535 drug arrests. This represents a 12.2 percent increase over the previous year. Of the total arrests made, 4,778 were under age eighteen and 36,757 were eighteen or older.

Specific data linking drug use with the commis-

Table 14.2. Drug Arrests in North Carolina, 1997

	Total	Male	Female
Illegal sales			
Under age	653	578	75
18 or older	5,988	5,060	928
Subtotal	6,641	5,638	1,003
Illegal possession			
Under age	4,125	3,631	494
18 or older	30,769	25,426	5,343
Subtotal	34,894	29,057	5,837
Totals			
Under age	4,778	4,209	569
18 or older	36,757	30,486	6,271
Total	41,535	34,695	6,840

Source: State Bureau of Investigation, *Crime in North Carolina*, 1997.

Figure 14.5. Part I Crimes Reported in Urban and Rural North Carolina, 1985 and 1997

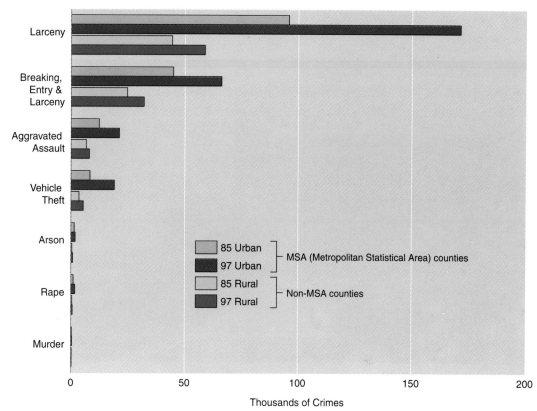

Note: Part I offenses include criminal homicide, rape, robbery, aggravated assault, burglary, larceny, motor vehicle theft, and arson.

Source: State Bureau of Investigation, *Crime in North Carolina*, 1985, 1997.

sion of crimes are unavailable. Estimates of individuals arrested for committing a crime while under the influence of illegal drugs vary between 50 and 85 percent, depending on the source of information.

Urban and Rural Patterns

Violent crimes increased fastest in North Carolina's urban areas. Between 1985 and 1997 murders, rapes, and aggravated assaults rose in those areas by 72 percent, compared with a 21 percent increase in rural areas (Fig. 14.5). With the single exception of arson, not only did urban crime rates increase faster but also the rates already were higher than the rural rates. Even the sharp rural climb in arson left the actual rate lower than for urban areas.

Violent crime rates in both rural and urban North Carolina were higher than those for the United States as a whole. Nevertheless, the rates in larger U.S. cities were far greater than the North Carolina rates. The leading crimes in larger cities include murder, rape, aggravated assault, and robbery. Increased mobility, within and between cities,

A crime scene after a break-in in the Orange County Courthouse in Hillsborough

Overall, however, assaults against police officers decreased through 1993, but then they rose slightly in 1994 and 1995. Some 2,652 officers were assaulted in 1993, 2,691 in 1994, 2,725 in 1995, 2,603 in 1996, and 2,678 in 1997. In 1997 circumstances associated with the greatest number of assaults were disturbance calls (30 percent) and attempted arrests (19 percent). Of the total assaults that year, 82 percent were by hand, fist, and feet, and 10 percent were by other dangerous weapons; 8 percent resulted in injuries to the officers. The most dangerous time of day was between 6:00 P.M. and 2:00 A.M., when 1,480 officers were injured. The murder of two police officers in conjunction with a routine traffic stop outside Fayetteville in September 1997 and the murder of Mecklenburg County deputy captain Anthony Stancil by a robber in late 1998 are indications that such assaults have been a serious problem in North Carolina.

enables individuals intent on committing crimes to move from place to place more readily. The increasingly transient nature of communities, in which more people are away from home at work, makes it easier for criminals to move in and out of areas undetected. Many people who live in rural areas work in larger urban centers, resulting in long absences from home, leaving them unprotected and vulnerable to criminal activity. Thus, increased freedom of mobility has come at a price.

Police Officer Assaults and Deaths

Crime threatens not only the general public but also the police officers who are trying to control it. During the 1988–97 period, a total of twenty-three officers were killed in the line of duty in the United States. Of that number, four were killed in 1991, four in 1993, and five in 1997. The four most frequent fatal situations were disturbance calls (five), attempts to arrest (four), ambushes—no warning (four), and traffic violations (four).

Offender Profiles and Arrest Trends

In 1997, 403,587 males and 120,336 females were arrested in North Carolina. Female arrests for Part I crimes accounted for 22 percent of the total and males for 79 percent. As shown in Figure 14.6, even though female arrests increased substantially, far more males were arrested in both 1981 and 1997. Combining the two groups, a total of 523,923 arrests were made, an increase of 46 percent over 1981.

Figure 14.6. Arrests in North Carolina by Gender, 1981 and 1997

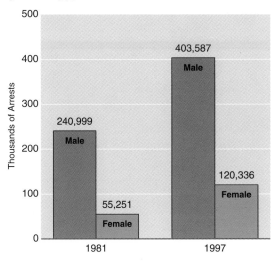

Source: State Bureau of Investigation, *Crime in North Carolina*, 1981, 1997.

Figure 14.7. Arrests in North Carolina by Ethnic Group, 1981–1997

Part I Offenses

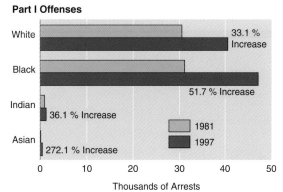

Part II Offenses

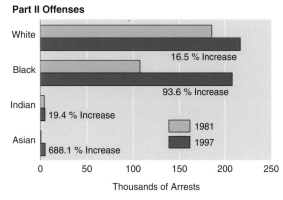

Note: Part I offenses include criminal homicide, rape, robbery, aggravated assault, burglary, larceny, motor vehicle theft, and arson. Part II offenses include other (simple) assaults, forgery, and counterfeiting, fraud, embezzlement, stolen property, vandalism, weapons, prostitution and commercialized vice, all other sex offenses, drug laws, gambling, offenses against the family or children, driving under the influence, liquor laws, disorderly conduct, vagrance, all other offenses, curfew and loitering laws, and running away (juveniles).

Source: State Bureau of Investigation, *Crime in North Carolina*, 1981, 1997.

Figure 14.8. Increase in Arrests in North Carolina by Age, 1981–1997

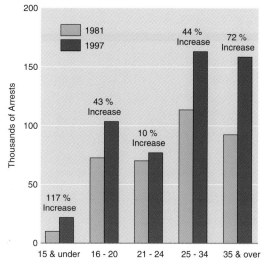

Note: All ages increased by a total of 46.1%.
Source: State Bureau of Investigation, *Crime in North Carolina*, 1981, 1997.

Figure 14.7 displays increases in arrest rates by ethnic group between 1981 and 1997. The percentage of arrests for all other ethnic groups rose much faster than it did for whites. Blacks, who comprised 22 percent of the state's population, accounted for slightly less than one-half (48.6 percent) of all arrests in 1997, up from 38 percent in 1981. Of concern is the sharp upturn in arrests of Asians during the sixteen-year period. A sixfold increase in arrests for Part I and Part II offenses can partially be explained by the expansion of these ethnic groups in North Carolina, but the arrest numbers are disproportionately high in relation to growth of the general population.

Significant changes also occurred in the age of persons arrested between 1981 and 1997. As shown in Figure 14.8, the second greatest increase was among those persons 35 and older, followed by those between 25 and 34. Those persons aged 15 or under represented the highest category of persons arrested, and this rate more than doubled over the 1981 level.

Figure 14.9 illustrates the spread between the number of violent crimes that occurred in both 1985 and 1997 and the number of resulting arrests. While violent crimes increased by 75 percent during the twelve-year period, the number of arrests for these crimes rose by 83 percent. Arrests were

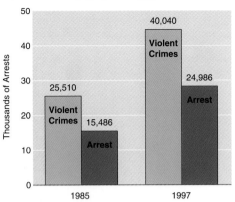

Figure 14.9. Violent Crimes and Arrests in North Carolina, 1985 and 1997

Note: Arrests include murders, rapes, robberies, and aggravated assults. Arrests listed in 1997 would include offenses occurring in other years and during 1997.

Source: State Bureau of Investigation, Crime in North Carolina, 1985, 1997.

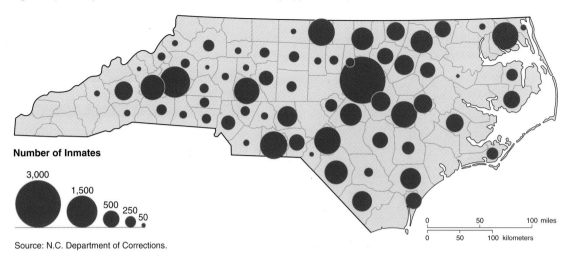

Figure 14.10. Population in State Prison Facilities, July 1998

Number of Inmates

Source: N.C. Department of Corrections.

made in approximately one-third of the rape and robbery offenses and in three-quarters of the aggravated assault cases. Not all arrests were made in 1997, as some would be from previous years that were solved during the subsequent year.

Correctional Facilities

Soaring arrest totals have produced a similar rise in the prison population, creating a serious problem of overcrowding. North Carolina has a total of 106 facilities housing inmates throughout the state; the largest is Central Prison in Raleigh with a prisoner population of 1,309. Figure 14.10 indicates the total population incarcerated in state prisons in each

county in 1998. The capacity for imprisoning criminals was substantial, yet there was insufficient space for the great numbers of offenders awaiting sentencing or recommitment.

In 1985 some 16,370 persons were admitted to North Carolina state prisons. In 1997 this figure jumped to 24,972, an increase of 53 percent. As of December 1997, violent crimes accounted for 48 percent of the prison population; another 26 percent had been incarcerated for property crimes and the balance for a variety of other crimes. Males represented 94 percent of the prison population. Most prisoners were between 20 and 34 years old. In the case of women, those 25–39 years old represented the largest group that was incarcerated. In 1996 blacks accounted for 63 percent of

the prison population, whites 33 percent, and other ethnic groups (Indians, Asians, etc.) comprising the rest.

Prison releases for all offenders (felons and misdemeanants) totaled 24,025 in 1997. As of December 31, 1997, the probation population had committed the following types of crimes: 16,464 (15 percent), violent crimes; 35,683 (33 percent), property crimes; and 56,511 (52 percent), public order crimes. Of those on supervision, 9,536 were placed on Intensive Probation and 837 on Electronic House Arrest.

These statistics make it abundantly clear that North Carolina is experiencing a crisis in prison space availability and in the caseload of people on parole or probation. The 1991 General Assembly ratified Senate Bill 886, an act to appropriate the balance of funds from a previously authorized general obligation bond issue for $200 million to build more state prison and youth services facilities. Since 1985 a total of 11,262 new prison beds were authorized for construction, in addition to the existing 20,182 beds. This would bring the total bed space in state prisons to 31,844. In 1995 estimated prison construction costs approved by the State Construction Office totaled $73,766,200. These expenditures are summarized in Table 14.3.

Criminal Justice Expenditures

Funding for the police comes from state, county, and municipal revenues. Per capita spending for police protection in 1993–94 amounted to $111.42 (compared to $142.27 nationwide), up sharply from $76.67 in 1988. Overall expenditures by state and local governments for the North Carolina justice system are massive. In 1993–94 they came to just over $1.8 billion. About 42 percent of that amount went for police protection, 42 percent for correctional programs, and 16 percent for courts and legal services (Fig. 14.11). These expenditures do not reflect the cost of crime in terms of injury, medical care, lost work time, stolen property, insurance rates, security expenses, and emotional suffering. Police protection accounted for 16 percent of state expenditures for the justice system and 74 percent of local expenditures. Corrections rep-

Table 14.3. Prison Construction Expenditures, 1995

Boot camp (female), 60-bed dorm	$2,041,100
Female minimum security, 104-bed dorm	$2,183,000
624-bed dorm and 40-cell segregation unit	$26,335,300
Warren Correctional Institution expansion, 208 cells	$9,628,300
Metro single-cell facility, 376 cells	$33,578,500
Total	$73,766,200

Source: State Construction Office.

The Durham County detention facility

Figure 14.11. Justice System Expenditures in North Carolina, 1993–1994

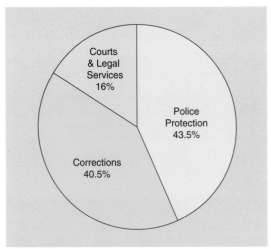

Source: U.S. Department of Justice, Bureau of Justice Statistics, *Sourcebook of Justice Statistics, 1997.*

resented the greatest proportion of justice expenditures at the state level: 59 percent of all costs.

In 1994, after hearing testimony from representatives of government, law enforcement, public and private institutions, and private citizens, the North Carolina General Assembly in special session authorized a new system for sentencing and punishing criminals. The new system, called *structured sentencing*, intends to help the state improve the criminal justice system, strengthen credibility in the sentencing of criminals, and prioritize the use of correctional resources. Under the new act, conviction for violent and career offenders carries mandatory prison sentences, and nonviolent of-

fenders with a minimal or no prior record will be sentenced into intermediate and community-based facilities.

The new law created a need for increased prison capacity. When current or authorized prison construction is completed, North Carolina will have space for over thirty thousand inmates. Whereas "truth in sentencing" mandates the availability of a prison bed for each prison sentence that is handed down, nonprison sentences must have sufficient probation and community resources available to imprison offenders. To handle the increase in community-based and probation sentences, the state is adding several hundred new probation officer positions. In addition, each prosecutorial district will receive a staff position and computer equipment linking them to the state's prior criminal record database.

Community Policing

One of the most promising developments in fighting crime has been the introduction of community policing. This involves closer day-to-day contact between the police and neighborhoods. It means building partnerships with citizens to seek out and solve persistent problems. Substantial progress has been made in reducing crime and social disorder when approached by the total community, including police working in conjunction

Terms Used in Crime Statistics

Urban: *As used by the North Carolina State Bureau of Investigation (SBI): a core city of 50,000 population or more that is in a Metropolitan Statistical Area (MSA); a suburban city that is within an MSA exclusive of core cities; any suburban county within an MSA.*

Rural: *As used by the SBI: any city with a population of 10,000 or more not within an MSA; a rural city of less than 10,000 not within an MSA; any non-MSA county.*

Violent crimes: *Murder, rape, robbery, and aggravated assault.*

Clearance rates: *The difference between the number of reported offenses and the number of offenses that have been cleared by the police (a) by arrest, (b) by declaring unfounded, or (c) by exception. Cases not cleared remain open for further police investigation.*

Part I crimes: *Criminal homicide, rape, robbery, aggravated assault, burglary, larceny, motor vehicle theft, and arson.*

Part II crimes: *Simple assaults, forgery, counterfeiting, fraud, embezzlement, stolen property, vandalism, weapons, prostitution, commercial vice, all other sex offenses, drug laws, gambling, offenses against the family or children, driving under the influence, liquor laws, disorderly conduct, vagrance, all other offenses, curfew and loitering laws, and juvenile runaways.*

Richard C. Lumb

with other governmental services. This change in the style of policing alone promises to make more headway in reducing crime than have years of emphasizing incarceration.

Outlook

It is apparent that growth and change in North Carolina have come at a heavy cost. Both economic development and population increases seem to correlate with rising crime rates, particularly in the state's burgeoning metropolitan areas.

The shift from stable rural, small-town communities to growing, transient cities has brought with it a decline in community social controls that typically are more effective crime deterrents than the police. The factors associated with criminal behavior are complex and not always well understood. However, an almost total reliance on enforcement seems to be doing little to stem the rising wave of crime, including illegal drug use. Community policing may be a more effective tool than simple enforcement.

Little in the current situation offers much assurance that criminal activity can be expected to decline substantially in the foreseeable future. Ironically, the best hope may lie in slowing down the very growth that is due to the state's many assets and to aggressive economic development policies. The state and its institutions must come to grips with this alarming issue if the benefits of increasing affluence are not to be negated by society's lawless element. This may well be one of the most pressing and difficult issues facing state policymakers as North Carolina enters the new century.

Selected References

Bursik, R., and H. Grasmick. *Neighborhoods and Crime*. New York: Lexington Books, 1993.

Kelling, G., and C. Coles. *Fixing Broken Windows*. New York: Free Press, 1996.

North Carolina Department of Justice. State Bureau of Investigation. *Crime in North Carolina, 1997*.

Reiss, A., and M. Tonry. *Communities and Crime*. Chicago: University of Chicago Press, 1986.

U.S. Department of Justice. Bureau of Justice Statistics. *Justice Expenditure and Employment Extract*, NCJ-163068, 1993.

———. Federal Bureau of Investigation. *Uniform Crime Reports*. Annually, 1976–97.

15. PUBLIC EDUCATION

Rex Clay and H. William Heller

Compared to the rest of the nation, North Carolina made significant advances in its public schools during the last quarter of the twentieth century. On most performance indicators the state no longer ranks near the bottom. But because other states made notable improvements as well, North Carolina is challenged just to maintain its current ranking among the states. Unfortunately, this is made more difficult by the state's historical and persistent rural poverty.

The American economy, including North Carolina's, is in the midst of a profound transformation, driven by the twin engines of rapid technological change and increasing global competition. In this century new jobs created by the labor market will require more than a high school education, and 30 percent of workers will need a college degree. North Carolina is struggling to increase its rate of educational attainment fast enough to keep pace with those demands so that its citizens can share fully in the new economic opportunities.

Figure 15.1. North Carolina General Fund Expenditures, 1996–1997

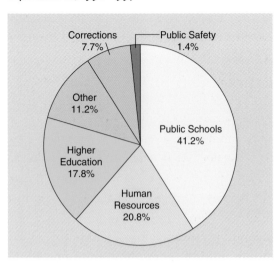

Source: State Budget Office, *The N.C. State Budget: Post-Legislative Budget Summary, 1996-97.*

Figure 15.2. Public School Share of the General Fund

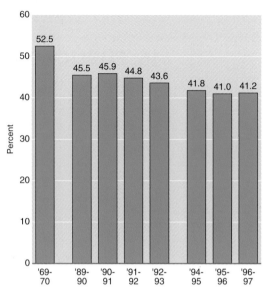

Note: Data were unavailable for the years 1971-88 and the 1993-94 school year.

Source: State Budget Office.

Figure 15.3. Sources of North Carolina's Public School Funds, 1994–1995

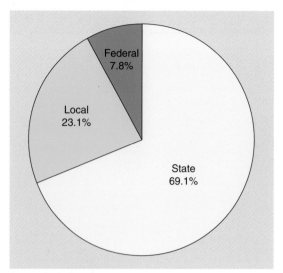

Source: N.C. Department of Public Instruction, *Statistical Profile, 1996.*

Public School Expenditures

A measure of the importance of public education is the amount a state invests in this area in relation to per capita income. As reported by *Education Week* (1997), in 1996 North Carolina spent $41 on education for every $1,000 in personal income, which was just at the national average, for a ranking of twenty-eighth among the fifty states. In fiscal year 1996–97, 41.2 percent of its total expenditures went for public education (Fig. 15.1). Although that percentage represented the largest categorical expenditure, it nonetheless continued a long-term decline in the public schools' share of the General Fund (Fig. 15.2).

North Carolina's public education system is funded by state, local, and federal dollars. Figure 15.3 shows the relative contribution of each of these sources. The state, by far, is the major source, contributing 69.1 percent of the 1994–95 total. Underscoring the importance of state funding, Figure 15.4 indicates that in 1995–96 North Carolina tied with Kentucky for fifth in the nation in school spending. The state's role will increase significantly in the future, as voters in 1996 approved a $1.8 billion bond issue, the largest ever, to build schools, a task borne mainly by local school systems in the past.

State money is allocated on a formula based on average daily attendance for a portion of the preceding school year. State support in 1994–95 ranged from a high of $5,797 per pupil in Hyde County to a low of $3,070 in Onslow County. Local funding provided 23.1 percent of expenditures for schools (Fig. 15.3).

Figure 15.4. Percentage of Revenue for Public Schools from State Governments, 1995–1996

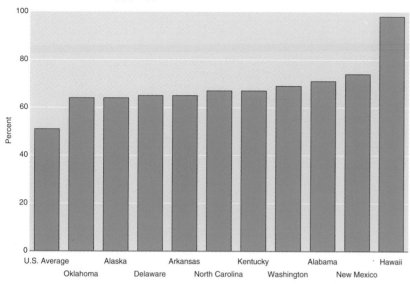

Source: National Education Association, *Ranking of the States, 1996.*

Figure 15.5. Per Pupil Expenditures for Public Education in North Carolina, 1994–1995

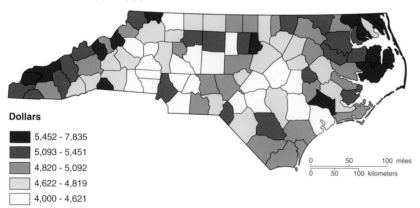

Dollars

- 5,452 - 7,835
- 5,093 - 5,451
- 4,820 - 5,092
- 4,622 - 4,819
- 4,000 - 4,621

Source: N.C. Department of Public Instruction, *Statistical Profile, 1996.*

Local funds are used to build and maintain school buildings, supplement teacher salaries, purchase supplemental materials, and generally enhance instructional program quality. Local support, at an average of $1,130 per pupil statewide in 1994–95, ranged from a high of $2,363 per pupil in the Chapel Hill–Carrboro city system to a low of $540 in Bertie County.

The remaining 7.8 percent of school funding came from the federal government. This money was targeted largely for vocational education, school lunch programs, textbooks and library materials, aid to disadvantaged students, and support to school districts that were impacted by large numbers of military or other federal employees. Federal support, at an average of $382 per pupil statewide, ranged from a high of $948 per pupil in Swain County to a low of $194 in Chapel Hill–Carrboro. Federal support is relatively high in North Carolina because of the presence of a number of military facilities.

The aggregate of state, local, and federal funds is expressed in terms of expenditures per pupil in Figure 15.5, which presents such expenditures for 1994–95 by city and county school districts. Average per pupil expenditures (based on final daily membership) for public education in North Carolina were $4,893, ranging from a high of $7,833 in Hyde County to a low of $4,068 in Onslow County, a difference of $3,765 (52 percent). This disparity indicates a major problem in school funding, as poorer districts simply cannot match the wealthier districts in local expenditures. According to the Public School Forum of North Carolina, in 1995–96 the average difference was $1,514 a year per student between the ten wealthiest and ten poorest counties.

Figure 15.6 shows that in recent years per pupil expenditures in North Carolina increased from state and local funds while remaining almost constant from federal funds. On the national level (where average daily attendance rather than final daily attendance is used as the basis for per pupil expenditures), North Carolina lags in per pupil expenditures, ranking thirty-seventh in 1995–96 (Fig. 15.7). Figure 15.8 indicates a fairly steady increase in per pupil expenditures in North Carolina, the Southeast, and the nation throughout the 1980–96 period, with North Carolina's per pupil expenditures

Figure 15.6. Per Pupil Expenditure in North Carolina, 1991–1995

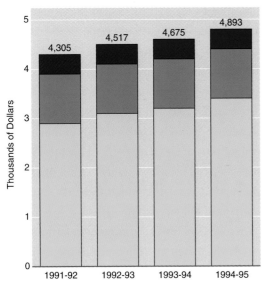

Source

- Federal
- Local
- State

Source: N.C. Department of Public Instruction, *Statistical Profile, 1996*.

Figure 15.7. Per Pupil Expenditure in the United States, 1995–1996

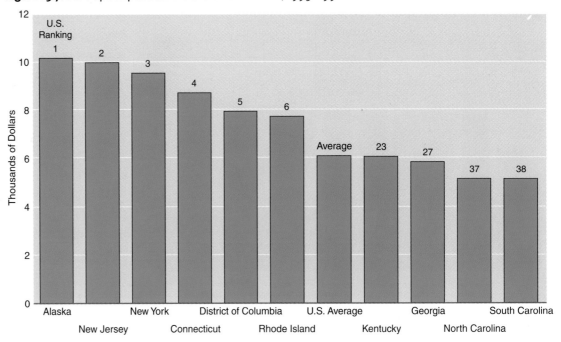

Note: Expenditures are based on average daily attendance.

Source: N.C. Department of Public Instruction, *Statistical Profile, 1996*.

being less than the national average but greater than the southeastern average.

There is a universal tendency to compare what is being spent on public education today with what was spent in the past. That comparison leads to the contention that there is no need to spend more money, because it appears that increased spending in the past made little or no difference. This would be a false conclusion. According to research reported in *The Kappan*, a journal published by the educational honorary society Phi Delta Kappa, most of the increased spending was absorbed by federally mandated special education for students with physical, emotional, and mental disabilities. Also, *Education Week* reported in 1997 that "too few of the additional dollars have reached classrooms and that most of the increased spending has been spent on the approximately 12 percent of students in special education, on trying to keep up with enrollment growth, and on raising salaries for an aging teaching force." The bulk of the remaining funds was consumed by higher transportation costs, liability and health insurance, construction of new schools, and other essential administrative overhead needs. These expenditures, though necessary, were unlikely to yield significant, short-term improvements in student performance.

Another important index of a state's financial support of the public school system is teacher salaries. In North Carolina, the state pays the base salary for most teachers and other professional personnel. More than two-thirds receive local pay supplements as well. According to the National Education Association, in 1995–96 the average salary for North Carolina teachers was $30,411, 83 percent of the national average of $36,605. In this category North Carolina ranked fortieth among the fifty states and eighth among the eleven southeastern states. Throughout the 1982–96 period, the North Carolina average stayed close to that for the Southeast but was well below the national level (Fig. 15.9). Governor James B. Hunt and the 1997 General Assembly committed the state to raising teacher salaries to the national average by the beginning of this century. To that end, the legislature funded salary increases for 93 percent of all teachers; those increases ranged between 6 and 11 percent per year for both 1996–97 and 1997–98.

Special Programs

Kindergarten

Most educational authorities agree that the availability of kindergarten programs for five-year-olds greatly enhances their chances for academic success in later years. As long ago as 1964, Benjamin Bloom at the University of Chicago advanced strong evidence that more than half of a child's intelligence develops prior to his or her enrollment in the first grade. He estimated that 50 percent of

Clayton High School students hurry through crowded hallways

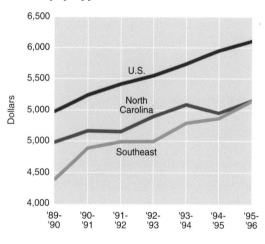

Figure 15.8. Per Pupil Expenditure Trends in North Carolina, the Southeast, and the United States, 1989–1996

Note: Expenditures are based on average daily attendance.

Source: National Education Association, *Ranking of the States, 1996.*

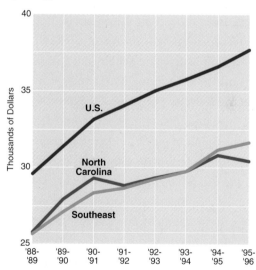

Figure 15.9. Average Teacher Salaries in North Carolina, the Southeast, and the United States, 1988–1996

Source: National Education Association, *Ranking of the States, 1996.*

measurable intelligence developed by age four, another 30 percent between ages four and eight, and another 20 percent between eight and seventeen. Although Bloom did not suggest that these estimates were infallible or irreversible, he did emphasize the crucial importance of each child having at an early age the most intellectually stimulating environment possible to maximize school achievement in later years. Numerous other studies support Bloom's findings.

Enrollments in kindergarten climbed steadily in North Carolina from 1985–86 through 1994–95 (Fig. 15.10). This was due in large part to an increase in the number of working mothers. A 1988 study reported that about 64 percent of North Carolina mothers of four-year-olds were employed. With 95 percent of all five-year-olds enrolled in kindergarten, the state ranks among the national leaders on this measure. A benchmark moment in the North Carolina kindergarten movement occurred with the publication in 1992 of a study commissioned by the Frank Porter Graham Child Development Center at the University of North Carolina at Chapel Hill. That study found that only 20 percent of a random sample of public kindergarten classes met or exceeded criteria of developmental appropriateness and that far too many students were retained. Since then, considerable effort has been made to reverse that situation by introducing developmentally appropriate curricula into the kindergarten program. A highly promising initiative that com-

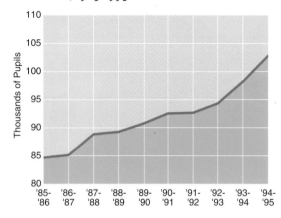

Figure 15.10. North Carolina Kindergarten Enrollment, 1985-1995

Source: N.C. Department of Public Instruction, *Statistical Profile, 1996.*

plements kindergarten is the Smart Start early childhood program. Launched in 1993 with strong support from Governor Hunt, Smart Start combines state and private money for improved day care, health services, parent education, and other aids for preschool children.

Math and Science

When compared to the nation as a whole and to other southeastern states, the percentage of North Carolina students taking math and science courses is impressive (Table 15.1). The percentage taking algebra in 1992 and upper-level math in 1994 was above the average for the Southeast and the United States. The proportion taking upper-level science courses in 1994 was above the average for the Southeast and only slightly below the national average.

The state has made two notable efforts to improve mathematics and science programs. First and foremost was the establishment of the North Carolina School of Science and Mathematics, a model for the nation. Located in Durham, the school enrolls about 550 students in grades 11 and 12 and offers a vigorous curriculum and rich content. In 1995–96 the school produced sixty-seven national merit scholars, the third largest number among all U.S. high schools, and the largest per capita number of semifinalists.

The second major initiative in science and math education has been the development of a statewide network of mathematics and science education centers. Constituting the North Carolina Mathematics and Science Education Network, eleven centers are located at state universities and colleges. Their primary purpose is to conduct in-service and related programs for public school teachers to improve the quality of science and mathematics instruction.

Advanced Placement

The Advanced Placement (AP) program provides a way for high schools to offer college-level course work to talented, motivated students. Students take

Table 15.1. Public School Students Taking Selected Science and Math Courses, 1992 and 1994

State	Taking Algebra, 1992 (%)	Students Taking Upper-level Math, 1994 (%)	Students Taking Upper-level Science, 1994 (%)
Alabama	15	32	22
Arkansas	15	38	18
Florida	23	—	—
Georgia	18	—	—
Kentucky	16	40	29
Louisiana	12	44	21
Mississippi	13	43	41
North Carolina	22	45	24
South Carolina	17	—	—
Tennessee	11	36	22
Virginia	19	—	—
Southeast (median)	16	40	22
United States	19	39	26

Source: "Quality Counts," *Education Week*, 1997.

an annual examination to assess their performance and to earn college credits in a particular subject or subjects. This program is an indicator of high-quality curricula content and student performance, and it establishes a national standard for judging outcomes. With eighty-eight public high schools offering AP courses in 1996, North Carolina ranked seventh in the nation in this regard. North Carolina students performed slightly below the national average in the proportion of eleventh and twelfth graders who took AP examinations

and ranked fourth among southeastern states. A score of 3 to 5 is required to obtain college credit; 50.7 percent of North Carolina students achieved this score, compared to 60.5 percent nationally. North Carolina ranked fifth among the southeastern states in this indicator.

School Personnel

Figure 15.11 shows that both instructional and support personnel employed full-time by public

schools increased annually from 1989–90 through 1994–95. The number of classroom teachers rose from 62,947 in 1990 to 70,657 in 1997, an increase of 12 percent; the number of administrators went up less than 1 percent. Overall school employment increased 11 percent between 1990 and 1995, to a total of 135,189. In 1995, 53 percent of school personnel were teachers, 37 percent were nonprofessionals, 6 percent were other professionals, and 4 percent were administrators.

The increase in personnel over this period was accompanied by an increase of 65,691 (6 percent) in average daily membership and thus did not substantially reduce the student-teacher ratio. In Fall 1990 the number of students per teacher was 17.0; in 1995–96 it was 16.3. In 1995–96 North Carolina ranked twenty-third lowest in student-teacher ratios nationally and fourth in the Southeast.

An important indicator of the quality of a state's public schoolteachers is the proportion possessing at least a master's degree, based on the assumption that the higher the teacher's educational level, the more effective she or he is likely to be in the classroom. North Carolina lags far behind the national average in this regard. Among the teachers employed in North Carolina public schools in 1995–96, only 34.5 percent held a master's degree or higher, compared with a national mean of 47.2 percent in 1987–88; however, teacher deficiencies at the undergraduate level have increasingly been eliminated as the proportion holding a bachelor's de-

Figure 15.11. Full-Time School Personnel by Major Activity Group, 1989–1996

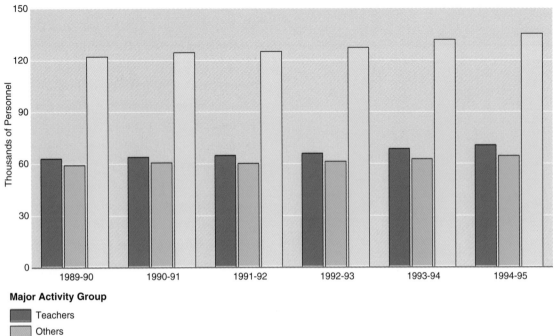

Major Activity Group

▮ Teachers
▮ Others
▯ Total

Source: N.C. Department of Public Instruction, *Statistical Profile, 1996*.

gree rose from 92.9 percent in 1969–70 to 98.6 percent in 1990–91 and 99.3 percent in 1995–96.

Indicators of Student Progress

NAEP Exams

To assess achievement in public schools nationwide, Congress established the National Assessment of Educational Progress (NAEP), which in 1969 began monitoring student achievement in reading, writing, math, science, and other areas in grades 4, 8, and 12. Exam results are encouraging in that solid gains are evident throughout the nation and especially in North Carolina. Between 1992 and 1996 both fourth- and eighth-grade students in North Carolina made impressive gains in math. Fourth-graders made an eleven-point gain, tying Texas for the highest gain in the nation and ranking twentieth nationally on total score. Eighth-graders made a nine-point gain, the second high-est in the nation, and ranked twenty-fifth on total score.

North Carolina also performed well on the NAEP's 1994 reading exam given to the nation's fourth-graders. It ranked seventeenth on total performance and showed an increase of two points on the numeric score, in contrast to a two-point decline nationally and a three-point decline among the southeastern states.

Figure 15.12 compares North Carolina with the nation and the Southeast in the percentage of fourth- and eighth-graders performing at or above a proficient level in reading and math on NAEP exams. As shown, North Carolina consistently outperformed the rest of the Southeast in reading and math. North Carolina fourth-graders performed better in reading than the national average in 1994 and performed at the national level in math in 1996; eighth-graders scored just slightly below the national average in 1996. Fourth-graders ranked sixteenth among the 39 participating states in reading in 1994 and seventeenth among the 43 participating states in math in 1996; eighth-graders ranked twenty-fifth among the 40 participating states in math in 1996.

Compared to the nation, North Carolina's performance on NAEP exams is respectable, and its improvement is impressive. But the NAEP results are discouraging in that the vast majority of students—both nationally and in North Carolina—still are not proficient in math and reading (70 percent in fourth-grade reading, 81 percent in

Figure 15.12. Percentage of Students Performing at an Advanced or Proficient Level in Reading and Math on NAEP Exams

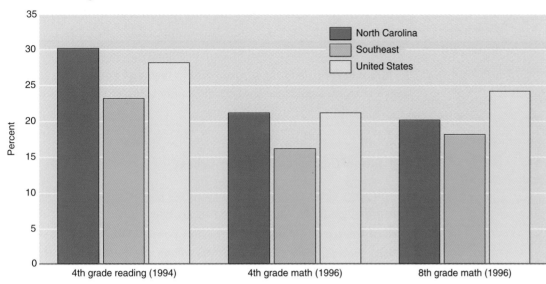

Source: National Center for Educational Statistics, *NAEP 1994 Reading: A First Look* and *NAEP 1996 Mathematics*.

Figure 15.13. Scholastic Aptitude Test Scores, 1986–1996

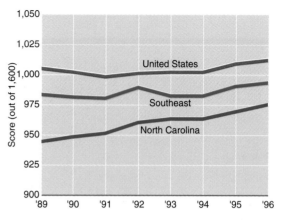

Source: Educational Testing Service.

fourth-grade math, and 80 percent in eighth-grade math). Regarding similar national results, *Education Week* in 1997 observed: "Our public school systems are riddled with excellence but rife with mediocrity."

Scholastic Aptitude Test (SAT)

Most colleges and universities in the United States require applicants to take the nationally standardized Scholastic Aptitude Test (SAT) as a condition of admittance. It is also used widely to compare states and school systems at a point in time and as an indicator of student achievement over time.

Compared to the nation and other southeastern states, North Carolina students historically have performed poorly on this test. But as with the NAEP scores, the state's SAT scores have improved considerably in recent years and at a pace greater than the national or southeastern average. From 1989 (when North Carolina ranked last among all the states) to 1996, SAT scores rose from 945 to 976, an increase of 31 points, while SAT scores nationally increased by only 7 points and in the Southeast by only 10 (Fig. 15.13). In 1996 the state ranked ninth among eleven southeastern states in mean scores and forty-seventh nationally. Thus, although good progress has been made on SAT per-

formance, the state has a long way to go. On an encouraging note, the 1996 SAT scores were the highest ever in North Carolina.

The SAT results require careful interpretation because the proportion of students sitting for the exam varies from state to state. As the proportion rises, the greater is the possibility that the test will be taken by less able students, including some who do not intend to go to college. Thus, it seems appropriate to compare only states with similar percentages of students taking the SAT. Table 15.2, which presents such a comparison, shows that in 1996 59 percent of seniors in North Carolina took the SAT. Only thirteen other states had a higher

Table 15.2. Scholastic Aptitude Test Scores, 1996

	Score			Percentage of Seniors
State	Verbal	Math	Total	Taking SAT
North Carolina	490	485	976	59
Georgia	484	477	961	63
Maryland	507	504	1,011	64
Delaware	508	495	1,003	66
Maine	504	498	1,002	68
Virginia	507	496	1,003	68
Rhode Island	501	491	992	69
New Jersey	498	503	1,003	69
Vermont	506	499	1,006	70
New Hampshire	520	514	1,034	70
Pennsylvania	498	492	990	71
New York	497	499	996	73
Connecticut	505	504	1,009	79
Massachusetts	507	504	1,011	80

Source: Educational Testing Service.

percentage taking the exam. When North Carolina's scores are compared to the average SAT scores of states with 59 percent or more of seniors sitting for the exam, North Carolina rates poorly. All states (except Georgia) with a higher percentage of seniors taking the exam had a higher average score.

High School Graduation Rates

Another important indicator of student progress is the proportion of students that graduate from high school. Dropping out before graduation has serious consequences for the student and the state. For the most part, dropouts enter menial, low-wage jobs and reduce the quality of the state's labor supply. In 1993, 85 percent of eighteen- to twenty-four-year-olds in North Carolina had earned a high school diploma, which was just below the national average of 86 percent; North Carolina ranked fifth among the eleven southeastern states on this measure. The statewide dropout rate in 1996 was 3.45 percent, ranging from a low of 0.49 percent in Mitchell County to a high of 6.39 percent in Vance County.

High School Graduates Attending College

The corollary of the percentage of high school graduates is the percentage of high school graduates who go on to college. When student progress is measured in these terms, North Carolina fares poorly. With 51 percent of 1994 graduates enrolling in a two- or four-year college, the state was well below the national average of 62 percent and ranked last among southeastern states.

The Socioeconomic Context of Public Education

The relatively poor socioeconomic standing of North Carolina contributes greatly to the poor academic achievement of its public school students. Table 15.3 presents ten indicators of this status. The national rank on the indicators varies from twenty-third to forty-eighth, with a national composite rank of thirty-ninth. Between 1985 and 1993 North Carolina improved in five of the indicators but recorded worsening conditions for the other five. Particularly striking were a 148 percent increase in juvenile crime and a 24 percent rise in the number of families headed by a single parent.

One of the greatest barriers to academic achievement is living in poverty. The adverse effects of poverty on children's scholastic performance is illustrated by the fact that as family income falls so do SAT scores. Children from poor homes generally lack adequate preparation for elementary school learn-

Table 15.3. Indicators of Low Socioeconomic Status of Children in North Carolina and the United States, 1993

Indicator	N.C.	U.S.	N.C. Rank
Low-weight babies	8.6%	7.2%	44
Infant mortality			
(deaths per 1,000 live births)	11.6	10.5	48
Child death rate			
(ages 1–14, deaths per 100,000)	29	30	23
Teen violent death rate			
(ages 15–19, deaths per 100,000)	76	69	33
Teen birthrate			
(ages 15–17, births per 1,000 females)	43	38	38
Juvenile violent crime arrest rate			
(ages 10–17, arrests per 100,000)	429	506	36
Teen high school dropout rate			
(ages 16–19)	11%	9%	38
Teens not working or in school			
(ages 16–19)	10%	10%	26
Children in poverty	20%	21%	31
Single-parent families with children	26%	26%	29
Composite national rank	—	—	39

Source: Anne E. Casey Foundation, *Kids Count Data Book*, 1996.

ing and, therefore, usually need more school services than do other children. Thus, it is important to track the number and proportion of poor children as a measure of the challenge that faces the schools. Figure 15.14 presents, by county, the proportion of children between age five and seventeen who were living below the poverty level in 1990. North Carolina has a slightly lower percentage of children in poverty than the nation as a whole.

Another significant factor is ethnicity, which affects the makeup of the school system and levels of performance. Largely because a high proportion of minority students come from poor families, research shows, the presence of a large minority student population is associated with reduced levels of achievement and the necessity for using different instructional approaches. Figure 15.15 depicts enrollment by race in 1995–96. Total enrollments by white students declined between 1977 and 1996, while those of other ethnic groups increased. In 1977 white enrollment was 68.9 percent of the total but fell to 64.7 percent in 1996.

In addition to the growth of the nonwhite population, another factor that accounts for the drop in white enrollments is that more white students now attend private schools. While public schools experienced an 8 percent increase in enrollments between 1985–86 and 1996, private school enrollments rose by over 28 percent. Even as the nonwhite school population has increased, there has not been a concomitant rise in the proportion of nonwhite teachers. In 1995–96 only 17.3 percent of public school teachers were nonwhite, compared to 35 percent of the student body.

Students' scores on the SAT are positively related to the level of parental education. The proportion of North Carolina adults who graduated from high school has increased significantly in recent years, but the state continues to rank low compared to other states. In 1950 Tar Heels placed forty-eighth, with only 20.5 percent of the population aged twenty-five and older completing at least four years of high school, against a national level of 33.3 percent. In 1990 the North Carolina proportion that finished high school had reached 70.0 percent, closer to the national mean of 75.2 percent, ranking the state forty-second. Thus, despite a substantial absolute increase, North Carolina still trailed most other states.

Figure 15.16 depicts this pattern geographically as of 1990. Typically the proportion of adults who received a high school diploma was higher in the more urban counties and in counties with large military bases. In the more rural counties, especially those with large black populations, fewer residents had completed high school.

Figure 15.14. Percentage of Related Children Age 5–17 in Poverty, 1990

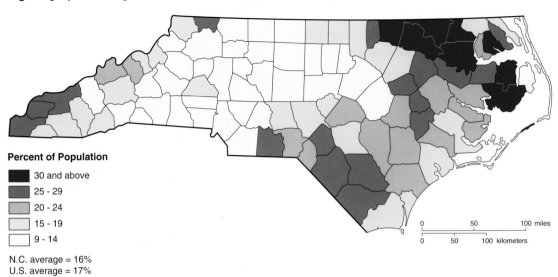

Percent of Population

- 30 and above
- 25 - 29
- 20 - 24
- 15 - 19
- 9 - 14

N.C. average = 16%
U.S. average = 17%

Source: U.S. Census of Population and Housing, 1990.

Figure 15.15. Enrollment by Race in North Carolina Public Schools, 1996

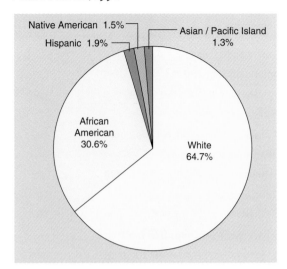

Native American 1.5%
Hispanic 1.9%
Asian / Pacific Island 1.3%
African American 30.6%
White 64.7%

Source: N.C. Department of Public Instruction, *Statistical Profile, 1996.*

Figure 15.16. Percentage of Population Age 25 and Over with High School Degrees, 1990

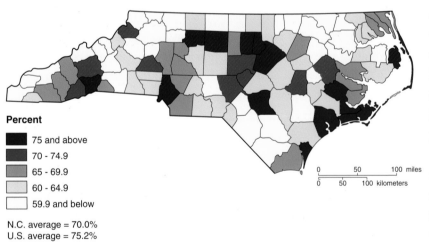

Percent

- 75 and above
- 70 - 74.9
- 65 - 69.9
- 60 - 64.9
- 59.9 and below

N.C. average = 70.0%
U.S. average = 75.2%

Source: U.S. Census of Population and Housing, 1990.

It is instructive to compare Figure 15.16 with Figures 15.17 and 15.5, which depict the percentage of households headed by females and per pupil school expenditures, respectively. Clearly, the proportion of high school graduates is smallest in those counties with high proportions of female-headed households and where per pupil school expenditures are low. The proportion of female-headed households in 1990 (Fig. 15.17) ranged from a low of 9 percent in Clay County to a high of 28.5 percent in Edgecombe County. The statewide proportion (16.5 percent) slightly exceeded the national rate of 15.9 percent.

Income levels largely determine a state's ability to finance education. In this regard North Carolina is at a considerable disadvantage. Whereas in 1994 it ranked tenth nationally in average daily school attendance, it placed thirty-fifth nationally and fourth in the Southeast in per capita personal income. Over past decades North Carolina has remained a relatively poor state even though its relative economic position, as indicated in Chapter 6, has improved

Figure 15.17. Percentage of Households Headed by Females with No Husband Present, 1990

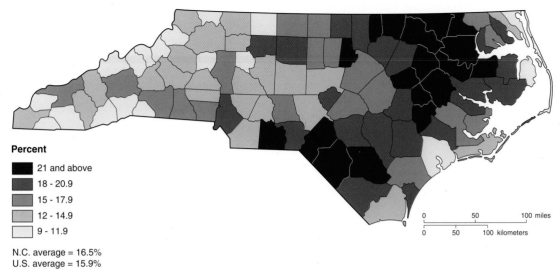

Percent

- 21 and above
- 18 - 20.9
- 15 - 17.9
- 12 - 14.9
- 9 - 11.9

N.C. average = 16.5%
U.S. average = 15.9%

Source: U.S. Census of Population and Housing, 1990.

considerably. It is clear that relatively low incomes correlate with low SAT scores and with the capacity to fund education.

Outlook

In relation to the nation, North Carolina has made significant advances in important educational indices such as SAT scores, performance on the national assessment of reading and mathematics proficiency, high school graduation rates, and others. The state is by no means at the bottom, in large part due to expenditures to raise teacher salaries, to

reduce class size, and to restructure the educational system generally. Even though other states were doing the same things, North Carolina posted gains greater than most of them.

Certainly, other states can be expected to spend to improve their educational systems, requiring North Carolina to make an even greater financial commitment just to maintain its relative standing. Additionally, even though the state has performed well recently compared to the country as a whole, there is strong evidence that, in an absolute context, the majority of students are not performing at their grade level. North Carolina recognizes this deficiency. The governor's office adopted the six

national goals (America 2000 Goals) that were devised by the nation's governors in conjunction with the national administration and added three goals of its own. Together, these nine goals specify that

- All children will start school ready to learn
- The high school graduation rate will be at least 90 percent
- Students in grades 4, 8, and 12 will demonstrate competency in English, math, science, history, and geography
- American students will be "first in the world" in math and science achievement
- Every adult will be literate
- Every school will be free of drugs and violence
- All educators will meet established standards to ensure that they are the most qualified in their field
- North Carolina will be first in the nation in the effective use of technology for teaching, learning, and administration
- Every community and every school in North Carolina will have a comprehensive parent involvement and assistance program with every parent actively involved in their children's education.

Obviously it has been difficult to meet these lofty goals. First, the most challenging tasks lay ahead. The easy victories have already been won, in that those students most responsive to the existing educational reforms have already boosted their performance, leaving behind the hard-core disadvantaged, the most difficult population to treat. Second, the socioeconomic context of the educational system is a great handicap, as characterized by a large number of poor students, a greater-than-average illiteracy rate, a large proportion of adults who did not finish high school, and relatively low income levels. North Carolina ranks thirty-ninth nationally on a composite measure of the condition of children. Third, it is likely that the state may not have as much money in the near future to devote to education as it did in the 1980s. Already it has struggled to fully fund its reform legislation. The Basic Education Program, launched in 1984 to provide essentials such as textbooks, equipment, supplies, clerical help, teaching assistants, and programs for dropouts, is now millions of dollars behind schedule and its status is uncertain. The same problems confront the School Improvement and Accountability Act, passed in 1989. Finally, as shown in Figure 15.18, unlike the declining enrollments of the 1980s, the number of students increased in the 1990s and is expected to continue increasing, making additional demands on available funds.

Despite these difficulties, reorganization reform efforts will continue, because the public and government perceive that the public school system is not yet meeting the state's needs. The main theme of the reform movement will be flexibility with accountability. Based on a belief that top-down regulatory policies have not served the state well,

Figure 15.18. Enrollment Trends and Projections in North Carolina Public Schools, 1986–2001 (Final Average Daily Attendance)

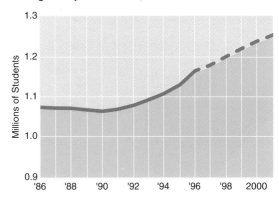

Source: N.C. Department of Public Instruction, *Statistical Profile, 1996.*

schools will be given more flexibility in developing ways to achieve state-imposed goals.

Primarily through the "ABC" program, which measures performance through growth standards (improvement over time) and performance standards (achievement at a point in time), schools will be held accountable for how much their students learn. Under the ABC program, much is at stake. Top-performing schools can win funds for teacher bonuses or new or enhanced school programs. Struggling schools could come under state oversight. Or the State Board of Education could remove teachers and principals from consistently low-performing schools. Additionally, standards are significantly higher. In March 1997 Charlotte-Mecklenburg school officials announced that 61 of

its 105 elementary and middle schools would have failed to meet the ABC test score standard for "growth" if the state system had been in place that year. Growth is defined as at least a year's worth of academic improvement.

Accountability will be heightened by fine-tuning the current report card system that measures school district performance. Also, the state has developed new end-of-course and grade tests that go far beyond rote memorization, and it is likely that a state report card will be developed (as specified by the School Accountability and Improvement Act of 1989) to compare North Carolina's performance with that of the United States and the world.

Students also will be subject to more accountability. Already, they must pass a competency test to graduate from high school, and standards for this test will be raised. This mood is reflected in the March 1993 report of the national Competitiveness Policy Council, which stated that educational restructuring/reform cannot succeed unless students assume responsibility for their own learning. The report argued that students must pass qualifying exams for colleges and for better jobs and that their school achievement record must become a more important consideration in admission to college, in obtaining financial aid, and in obtaining employment.

School reform will also alter the curriculum, which likely will become increasingly outcome-based. That is, a set of competencies will be speci-

Raleigh's Ligon School students take a trip to Africa via the Internet in the school's computer lab

fied for successful completion of a course. Moreover, the curriculum will be much more concerned with developing reasoning skills. To teach the curriculum, more sophisticated technology will be used, making use especially of computers and distance learning techniques. In response to the widely held belief that expectations of students are too low, curricula will become more demanding and requirements for graduation will become more rigorous.

Another reform will cause the school year to lengthen. There is an awareness that North Carolina must compete not only with other states but with other countries as well. The average school year in some industrialized countries lasts 197 days and in Japan, 243 days, but in North Carolina it is only 182 days long.

Teachers will be greatly affected by the reform movement. One of the most significant trends is the growing pressure to make teacher training programs five years in length, with the first four years focusing on a strong liberal arts/

subject area preparation and the fifth year on teacher training. This will include a strong clinical supervision component leading to a master's degree in education. Certified teachers would, in effect, receive teacher training only after earning the equivalent of a bachelor's degree. It is also likely that requirements for admission to teacher education programs will become more rigorous, continuing a ten-year movement in that direction.

The fundamental structure of public education itself, to some unknown extent, will change. Commenting on the poor performance of public school students, *Education Week* in 1997 asserted that "Despite 15 years of earnest efforts to improve public schools and raise student achievement, states haven't made much progress." It went on to speculate that perhaps "Alternative forms of education will emerge to replace public schools as we have known them."

Already the North Carolina legislature has authorized the establishment of thirty-seven charter schools, public schools existing independently of state and school system regulations that can be attended tuition-free by children from anywhere in the school district. Charter schools are typically endorsed or chartered by a public agency and have specific academic targets to achieve as part of their contract with the chartering entity. They generally focus on a new curriculum approach, a new school organization, or other features that set them apart from what a regular public school would offer. It is argued that competition created by charter schools will improve public schools, that deregulation afforded by charter schools will foster innovation, and that such schools will provide public school choice without resulting in private schools or private school vouchers. It should be noted that there also are calls for a voucher system, in which the state or school system would pay the tuition of public school students at private schools.

Finally, reform efforts will bear in mind that schools increasingly must contend with students who come to school not ready to learn, that schools must provide many social services, including feeding children, protecting them from illegal drugs and violence, and meeting their health needs. Realizing that schools mirror the larger society and that the efforts of schools are to a great extent negated by the failures of society, reforms will address broader socioeconomic problems.

One initiative in particular, Smart Start, has tremendous promise for addressing the impact of social conditions on the schools. Recognizing the importance of a child's youngest years, Governor Hunt in 1993 implemented a systematic approach to providing all children with quality preschool care by creating a public/private partnership rooted in the local community whose mission is to ensure that every child enters kindergarten healthy and prepared to learn. Counties are responsible for first determining their needs and the availability of local resources, then creating a plan of action. Public and private funds help to support the initiatives, which vary greatly from county to county. Over $250 million in state funds went into Smart Start between 1994 and 1998, and the likely allocation for 1998–99 was $50 million.

Given the presence of efforts such as Smart Start, the reform movement will bring many changes to public education in North Carolina. Such reforms will alter the fundamental structure of public education, change curricula and scheduling, involve personnel changes, produce enlightened legislation, and generate meaningful appropriations for public education. Together, these efforts will help North Carolina keep pace with other states and the continually rising requirements of the workplace.

Selected References

Batten, J. *Public Education in North Carolina, 1839 to 1955.* Greenville: J. W. Batten, 1962.

National Education Association. *Ranking of the States.* Washington, D.C.: National Education Association, 1996.

North Carolina Department of Education. *Restructuring Education in North Carolina: A Synthesis of Eight Education Reform Reports.* Raleigh: North Carolina Department of Education, 1991.

North Carolina Department of Public Instruction. *Statistical Profile.* Raleigh: North Carolina Department of Public Instruction, annually.

North Carolina Office of the State Auditor. *Special Report on Smart Start, the Early Childhood Initiative Program: Summary Information from the 1997 and 1996 Financial Statement Audits of the North Carolina Partnership for Children, Inc., and the Local Partnerships for Children.* Raleigh: Office of the State Auditor, 1998.

Peek, W. *The History of Education in North Carolina.* Raleigh: North Carolina Department of Education, 1993.

16. HIGHER EDUCATION

Roy Carroll

The economic and social landscape of North Carolina has been transformed in the last half century. Colleges and universities have played a core role in that transformation. Through their teaching, research, and public service, they have enabled the state to respond to profound changes—a rapidly growing population, the increased mobility of capital, the globalization of the economy, the explosive combination of electronic communications and the computer—and to take advantage of the opportunities spawned by scientific and technological advances.

Since World War II, higher education has been one of the growth industries in the state. Today, at the start of a new century, total enrollments, the number of degrees conferred annually, the volume of research and service activities, and the level of support for higher education are at all-time highs. The growing demand for access to higher educational opportunities and the growing support, both public and private, indicate clearly that North Carolinians see higher education as a wise investment.

Among the personal or private benefits to be derived from higher education are increased income, greater opportunity, the fulfillment of individual potential, and an improved quality of life. The social and economic benefits include a better-prepared and more highly trained workforce, employment for thousands of citizens, greater equalization of opportunity and attainment, and a more active, better-informed citizenry.

The basic contributions of colleges and universities to the state and to the nation are made through students and their individual contributions as citizens and in their jobs. Beyond that, the research conducted in North Carolina universities has made substantial and enduring contributions in a wide range of areas—agriculture, biotechnology, marine resources, forestry, health, life sciences, education, energy, communications, transportation, and the environment. Both basic and applied research are of fundamental importance to society, and despite resource limitations, it is essential to sustain the academic research enterprise.

Public service activities extend the resources of higher educational institutions—their faculties' expertise, their research findings, their public events, and their libraries and other facilities—to a wider constituency. Some of the public service entities, particularly within the University of North Carolina (UNC) system, are designed to reach across the state. Among those organizations are UNC Hospitals at Chapel Hill, the North Carolina Cooperative Extension Service, the North Carolina School of Science and Mathematics, Area Health Education Centers (AHECs), the UNC Center for Public Television, the North Carolina Center for the Advancement of Teaching, and the North Carolina Arboretum. Each of these organizations plays a vital educational role in the state.

History

Higher education has long served a crucial function in the economic, political, and social life of North Carolina. One of the first actions of the state after declaring independence in 1776 was to adopt a constitution that directed in part that "all useful Learning shall be duly encouraged and promoted in one or more Universities" (Constitution of North Carolina, Sec. 41 [1776]). The General Assembly of 1789 responded to that mandate by chartering the University of North Carolina and endowing it with the escheats to which the state as sovereign was entitled. The arrival of the first student at the university in 1795 marked the opening of the nation's first operating, state-supported institution of higher education.

In 1868 the new state constitution gave more explicit recognition to the university, as did an 1873 constitutional amendment. Throughout that period, the university at Chapel Hill was the only state-supported institution of higher education in North Carolina.

In the first half of the nineteenth century additional higher educational opportunities were provided by a growing number of private colleges. Some had been created as academies in the eighteenth century and began to offer collegiate-level instruction later. Salem College was founded as an academy in 1772, and Louisburg College evolved from Franklin Academy, which was chartered in 1787 and reopened its doors in 1805. During the 1830s the principal religious denominations in the state initiated a number of colleges of their own, including the institutions now known as Davidson College and Guilford College (both in 1837), Duke University and Greensboro College (both in 1838), and Wake Forest University (1844).

The common school movement, the land-grant college initiative, and a growing recognition of the importance of higher education to the further development of the state led North Carolina to establish and provide increased appropriated support for the University of North Carolina as well as for additional public institutions. Between 1877 and 1923 the General Assembly created or acquired for the state eleven other organizations that are today part of the University of North Carolina. Those institutions, identified by their current titles and the dates when they became were acquired by the state, are Fayetteville State University (1877), North Carolina State University at Raleigh (1887), the University of North Carolina at Pembroke (1887), the University of

A Pivotal Plan for Higher Education

It was a sunny afternoon early on in Terry Sanford's term as governor. He had invited the Honorable Dallas Herring, chairman of the Board of Higher Education, and me to meet with him to talk over his hopes and dreams for educational opportunities for all qualified youth in North Carolina.

The conversation ran well into the afternoon. At its conclusion, a plan had been developed and the most comprehensive study and overhaul of the post-secondary structure of North Carolina ever in the history of the state was about to be under way.

John Sanders, an able servant of the state, was asked to direct the enterprise under the splendid chairmanship of Irving Carlyle. When the work ended, the community college system as we know it today was launched, the expansion of the university into metropolitan areas of the state set in motion, and a new and stronger emphasis on post-secondary education was firmly in place.

The consolidation was completed early in the 1970s with the merger of the existing Board of Higher Education, all remaining independent publicly funded institutions, and the School of the Arts into the University of North Carolina.

The process that began in the 1930s with Governor O. Max Gardner and Frank Porter Graham was now complete through the initiative and leadership of Governor Sanford, the wisdom of Dallas Herring and John Sanders, and the putting in place of the new comprehensive University of North Carolina by Governor Robert Scott.

Few events in the history of our state have proved so beneficial to the commonwealth as has this evolution of the university in its service to North Carolina.

William Friday, president of the University of North Carolina system, 1956–86

North Carolina at Greensboro (1891), North Carolina Agricultural and Technical State University (1891), Elizabeth City State University (1891), Western Carolina University (1893), Winston-Salem State University (1897), Appalachian State University (1903), East Carolina University (1907), and North Carolina Central University (1923).

Throughout that period, however, thirty or so small, denominational colleges and a dozen state colleges and universities with low tuition were not sufficient to make higher education accessible to many citizens in North Carolina. In 1900 the total enrollment in the state's public and private colleges was fewer than 5,000 students and in 1920 was still fewer than 8,000.

By 1940 the enrollment had risen to slightly more than 30,000 students, but it was the GI Bill following World War II that changed the entire tradition of who attended college. Higher education enrollments began to grow at unprecedented rates in North Carolina and elsewhere. Between 1946 and 1956 fall head-count enrollment in North Carolina colleges and universities grew by 25 percent; by 1966 enrollment increased another 125 percent and by 1976 yet another 99 percent. Older institutions expanded rapidly, and new institutions, both public and private, were established to meet enrollment demands. Institutional ambitions and the cost of supporting them were rising sharply. The competition for students and for resources became keen.

In an effort to bring about better coordination of the numerous elements of the state's fast-growing higher education enterprise, the General Assembly of 1955 established the North Carolina Board of Higher Education and gave it general planning and coordinating authority for public institutions of higher education. Until then the various institutions operated almost totally independently of one another, duplicating programs and competing for dollars. During the crisis of the Great Depression, the General Assembly in 1931 had consolidated the three largest state-supported institutions. The University of North Carolina at Chapel Hill, the North Carolina State College of Agriculture and Engineering at Raleigh, and the North Carolina College for Women at Greensboro were brought together under one president and a single board of trustees as the "Consolidated University."

The Belk Tower in the heart of the UNC Charlotte campus at dusk

By 1963 the higher education landscape contained public and private senior colleges, private junior colleges, and public community colleges, technical institutes, and industrial education centers. That year was a pivotal one in the history of higher education in North Carolina. In 1963 a Commission on Higher Education beyond the High School presented a set of sweeping recommendations to the General Assembly. In response, the legislature enacted the Community Colleges Act of 1963. A Department of Community Colleges was established under the State Board of Education to administer a new North Carolina Community College System, which included all twenty industrial education centers and three existing community colleges.

Between 1964 and 1968 all of the industrial education centers became technical institutes or community colleges. The development of the Community College System gave strong impetus to the expansion of educational opportunities. The dispersal of these community colleges and technical institutes across the state, offering open admissions and low cost, enabled many first-time college students to live at home and work part-time for two years before transferring to a senior college. These new institutions trained thousands of persons to enter a wide array of occupations and opened college doors to growing numbers of adults.

The 1963 session of the General Assembly also created the North Carolina School of the Arts to train students in the performing arts and passed the Higher Education Act of 1963 by which the former local community colleges at Asheville, Charlotte, and Wilmington were elevated to senior college status and made state institutions. In 1965 the college at Charlotte became a fourth campus of the University of North Carolina, and in 1969 those at Asheville and Wilmington became the fifth and sixth campuses of the Consolidated University. By action in the 1967 and 1969 sessions, the General Assembly designated the other nine independent public senior institutions (excluding the School of the Arts) as "regional universities" and broadened their missions to include, in all cases, undergraduate-, master's-, and doctoral-level programs, subject to the approval of the Board of Higher Education and the availability of funds.

In 1970 the electorate adopted a new constitution that took effect the following year. Whereas the Constitution of 1868 had merely acknowledged the existence of the University of North Carolina, the Constitution of 1971 commanded it, providing: "The General Assembly shall maintain a public system of higher education, comprising the University of North Carolina and such other institutions of higher education as the General Assembly may deem wise" (Constitution of North Carolina, Art. IX, Sec. 8 [1971]).

The coordination and governance of public higher education was a matter of increasing concern to state policymakers. The State Board of Higher Education had been assigned the responsibility to "allot the functions and activities" of the public colleges and universities, but it was not given authority sufficient to match that responsibility, nor did the General Assembly place any restraints on itself in the 1955 legislation creating that board. Thus from 1955 to 1969 institutional ambitions and program proliferation proceeded almost unimpeded by any major restraints.

More rigorous review and screening procedures were established in 1969. But shortly thereafter the state entered a lengthy debate on restructuring public higher education. Growing concern over rising costs and the appropriateness of increased legislative involvement in educational decisions led Governor Robert W. Scott to appoint a special committee in late 1970 to study and make recom-

The historic Old Well on the UNC Chapel Hill campus

mendations to him concerning the structure and organization of the system of public higher education.

The report of that committee led to the Higher Education Reorganization Act of 1971. This act (1) "redefined" the University of North Carolina to comprise sixteen institutions, including the six that were then a part of the University of North

Carolina, the nine "regional universities," and the North Carolina School of the Arts, (2) "redesignated" the constitutional Board of Trustees of the University of North Carolina as the "Board of Governors of the University of North Carolina," and (3) granted to the Board of Governors extensive governing powers over the sixteen constituent institutions. The Board of Higher Education was abolished and its functions were absorbed by the Board of Governors, a thirty-two-member body of citizens elected by the General Assembly. Among the duties assigned to the new Board of Governors were the responsibilities to plan and develop a co-ordinated system of higher education in North Carolina and to prepare and submit to the General Assembly a single, unified budget request for all sixteen institutions of the University of North Carolina. Separate institutional boards of trustees were provided for, but with virtually all their powers to be delegated by the Board of Governors. The University of North Carolina remains today the same legal entity that was created in 1789, despite changes in the name of its governing board, the number of its campuses, its size and scope, and almost every other particular aspect of the institution.

The North Carolina Community College System remained under the State Board of Education until 1979, when the General Assembly established the State Board of Community Colleges as a separate governing board for the Community College System. The president heads the system and reports to the State Board. The board's function is to provide services and assistance to institutions in the statewide system in a number of areas. As the fifty-eight institutions are governed locally by individual boards of trustees, the functions of the department tend to be limited to those activities deemed appropriate for the department to perform. The powers and duties of the local boards include the appointment of the institutional president, subject to the approval of the State Board, and the appointment of other personnel, subject to standards set by the State Board.

The private colleges are all independent of state control and regulation except that they must be chartered and licensed to grant degrees and are subject to special state licensing requirements in certain academic program areas such as nursing and education. The private colleges and universities work together through North Carolina Independent Colleges and Universities, Inc., in the areas of education and public information, research, and policy development.

The establishment of the Board of Governors of the University of North Carolina and of the State Board of Community Colleges brought more comprehensive, orderly, and rational planning for the development of public higher education in North Carolina. The result has been a quarter century of stability and restrained academic program development in higher education.

Types and Locations of Institutions

In 1972 North Carolina had 113 nonproprietary, postsecondary educational institutions operating within its boundaries. Of these, 41 were technical institutes that did not offer college-transfer curricula. The remaining 72 institutions included 15 public community colleges, 12 private junior colleges, the 16 public senior institutions that comprise the University of North Carolina, and 29 private senior colleges and universities. There were also 2 Bible colleges and 1 autonomous theological seminary. In 1997 the corresponding numbers were 112 institutions, including community and technical colleges, 3 private junior colleges, 16 public senior institutions, and 35 private senior colleges and universities. There were also 6 Bible colleges and 1 autonomous theological seminary.

The two most striking changes in the types of institutions over the past two decades have been (1) the significant increase in the number of public two-year institutions offering college-transfer programs, and (2) the reduction in the number of private junior colleges. In the early 1970s, two of the twelve private junior colleges closed, and one was converted into a public community college. Since then, six others have become senior institutions, leaving only three private junior colleges in the state. In 1986 one private senior institution (Sacred Heart College) closed.

All of the senior colleges offer baccalaureate

programs. Forty-one of the senior institutions offer the master's degree, and fifteen of them also offer first professional (law, medicine, dentistry, etc.) or doctoral-level programs. The private junior colleges and public community and technical colleges offer two-year college programs leading to associate degrees. In addition, the community and technical colleges provide a variety of technical and vocational programs leading to diplomas and certificates.

Figure 16.1 gives the locations of the higher educational institutions. The institutional distribution corresponds generally to the distribution of population. The senior institutions tend to be clustered in the Piedmont region. Only 28 of the state's 100 counties have neither a two-year nor a four-year institution; however, 25 of those 28 counties are adjacent to one or more counties in which postsecondary institutions are located (and some of the community and technical colleges were established to serve more than one county). Moreover, a number of them have satellite campuses operating in a neighboring county. It is therefore apparent that reasonable geographic access to college-level work has been provided to the vast majority of North Carolinians.

Students share a quiet moment on the Warren Wilson College campus

The Percy H. Sears Applied Technologies Center at Guilford Technical Community College

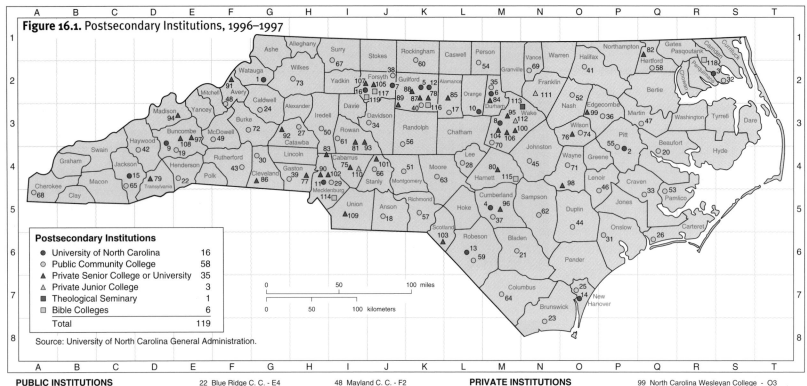

Figure 16.1. Postsecondary Institutions, 1996–1997

Postsecondary Institutions

●	University of North Carolina	16
○	Public Community College	58
▲	Private Senior College or University	35
△	Private Junior College	3
■	Theological Seminary	1
◻	Bible Colleges	6
	Total	119

Source: University of North Carolina General Administration.

PUBLIC INSTITUTIONS

● University of North Carolina

1 Appalachian State University - G2
2 East Carolina University - P4
3 Elizabeth City State University - R2
4 Fayetteville State University - M5
5 North Carolina Agricultural and
   Technical State University - K2
6 North Carolina Central University - M2
7 North Carolina School of the Arts - J2
8 North Carolina State University - M3
9 University of North Carolina at Asheville - D3
10 University of North Carolina at Chapel Hill - L3
11 University of North Carolina at Charlotte - H4
12 University of North Carolina at Greensboro - K2
13 University of North Carolina at Pembroke - L6
14 University of North Carolina at Wilmington - O7
15 Western Carolina University - C4
16 Winston-Salem State University - I2

○ Community and Technical Colleges

17 Alamance C. C. - L3
18 Anson C. C. - J5
19 Asheville-Buncombe Technical C. C. - E4
20 Beaufort County C. C. - Q4
21 Bladen C. C. - M6

22 Blue Ridge C. C. - E4
23 Brunswick C. C. - N8
24 Caldwell C. C. and Technical
   Institute - G3
25 Cape Fear C. C. - O7
26 Carteret C. C. - Q6
27 Catawba Valley C. C. - H3
28 Central Carolina C. C. - L4
29 Central Piedmont C. C. - I4
30 Cleveland C. C. - G4
31 Coastal Carolina C. C. - P6
32 College of the Albemarle - S2
33 Craven C. C. - Q5
34 Davidson County C. C. - J3
35 Durham Technical C. C. - M2
36 Edgecombe C. C. - P3
37 Fayetteville Technical C. C. - M5
38 Forsyth Technical C. C. - J2
39 Gaston College - G4
40 Guilford C. C. - K3
41 Halifax C. C. - O2
42 Haywood C. C. - D4
43 Isothermal C. C. - F4
44 James Sprunt C. C. - O5
45 Johnston C. C. - N4
46 Lenoir C. C. - P5
47 Martin C. C. - Q3

48 Mayland C. C. - F2
49 McDowell Technical C. C. - F3
50 Mitchell C. C. - H3
51 Montgomery C. C. - J4
52 Nash C. C. - O2
53 Pamlico C. C. - Q5
54 Piedmont C. C. - L2
55 Pitt C. C. - P4
56 Randolph C. C. - J3
57 Richmond C. C. - K5
58 Roanoke-Chowan C. C. - Q2
59 Robeson C. C. - L6
60 Rockingham C. C. - K1
61 Rowan-Cabarrus C. C. - I3
62 Sampson C. C. - N5
63 Sandhills C. C. - K4
64 Southeastern C. C. - M7
65 Southwestern C. C. - C4
66 Stanly C. C. - J4
67 Surry C. C. - I1
68 Tri-County C. C. - A5
69 Vance-Granville C. C. - N2
70 Wake Technical C. C. - M3
71 Wayne C. C. - O4
72 Western Piedmont C. C. - F3
73 Wilkes C. C. - H2
74 Wilson Technical C. C. - O3

PRIVATE INSTITUTIONS

▲ Senior Colleges and Universities

75 Barber-Scotia College - I4
76 Barton College - O3
77 Belmont Abbey College - H4
78 Bennett College - K2
79 Brevard College - D4
80 Campbell University, Inc. - M4
81 Catawba College - I3
82 Chowan College - Q1
83 Davidson College - H4
84 Duke University - M2
85 Elon College - L2
86 Gardner-Webb University - G4
87 Greensboro College - K2
88 Guilford College - K2
89 High Point University - J3
90 Johnson C. Smith University - H4
91 Lees-McRae College - F2
92 Lenoir-Rhyne College - G3
93 Livingstone College - I3
94 Mars Hill College - E3
95 Meredith College - M3
96 Methodist College - M5
97 Montreat College - E3
98 Mount Olive College - O4

99 North Carolina Wesleyan College - O3
100 Peace College - M3
101 Pfeiffer University - J4
102 Queens College - H4
103 St. Andrews Presbyterian College - K6
104 St. Augustine's College - M3
105 Salem College - J2
106 Shaw University - M3
107 Wake Forest University - I2
108 Warren Wilson College - E3
109 Wingate University - I5

△ Junior Colleges

110 Cabarrus College of Health Sciences - I4
111 Louisburg College - N2
112 Saint Mary's College - M3

■ Theological Seminary

113 Southeastern Baptist Theological Seminary - N3

◻ Bible Colleges

114 East Coast Bible College - I5
115 Heritage Bible College - M4
116 John Wesley College - K3
117 Piedmont Bible College - J2
118 Roanoke Bible College - R1
119 Winston-Salem Bible College - I2

Enrollments

In North Carolina, as in the nation, higher education enrollments have grown significantly in the past four decades. Although the rate of growth has fallen in successive decades since the boom years of the 1960s, enrollments have continued to increase substantially in both the state and the country generally. Further, the enrollment growth in North Carolina has exceeded that of the nation for the past three decades. The rate of enrollment growth in higher education has also exceeded the rate of population growth in the state. The accompanying tables and figures focus on notable enrollment trends in North Carolina since 1976.

Table 16.1 shows that between 1976 and 1996 total fall enrollments increased by 51 percent—from 240,936 to 362,713. All three higher education sectors (UNC, Community College System, and private colleges and universities) shared in the growth. In that twenty-year period, increases in enrollments were as follows: the UNC system, 45 percent; community colleges, 69 percent; and private colleges, 45 percent. Clearly, community colleges have increased their share of total college enrollments.

It should be noted, however, that the number of students in private colleges and universities continues to rise. Indeed, private college enrollments increased 16 percent from 1986 to 1996, compared to only a 12 percent increase in the preceding decade. The drop in enrollments at private junior

Table 16.1. Profile of Higher Education in North Carolina

	1976	1986	1996
Number of postsecondary institutions			
Community colleges*	57	58	58
Private 4-yr. colleges and universities	29	32	35
Private 2-yr. colleges	9	6	3
UNC system (4 yrs.)	16	16	16
Total	111	112	112
Number of fall enrollments			
Community colleges**	86,789	127,446	146,459
Private 4-yr. colleges and universities	43,550	51,411	63,086
Private 2-yr. colleges	5,790	3,766	817
UNC system (4 yrs.)	104,807	129,880	152,351
Total	240,936	312,503	362,713
Number of degrees conferred	1975–76	1985–86	1995–96
Sub-baccalaureate certificate	4,849	5,451	10,904
Associate degree	9,794	10,433	13,750
Baccalaureate degree	23,356	24,887	32,819
Master's degree	4,911	5,646	7,859
Doctoral degree	734	730	1,042
First professional degree	1,114	1,352	1,609
Law	614	701	836
Dentistry	83	72	74
Pharmacy	—	7	86
Medicine	327	430	424
Veterinary medicine	—	43	65
Theology	90	99	124
Total	44,758	48,499	67,983
*College transfers	20	25	58
**College transfers	10,427	19,027	39,391

Source: University of North Carolina General Administration, Planning/LRP.AT001A/5-8-97.

Figure 16.2. Fall Enrollment of Women in North Carolina Colleges and Universities, 1972–1996

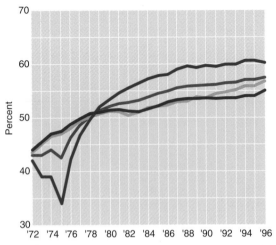

College System Type

—— University of North Carolina
—— Community College System
—— Private
—— All sectors

Source: University of North Carolina General Administration.

colleges reflects the decline in the number of such institutions. Correspondingly, the increase in private senior college enrollments reflects, in part, the elevation of six junior colleges to senior-college status.

Stimulating the increases in enrollments and degrees conferred over the 1976–96 period was a greater rate of participation in higher education by women, minorities, nontraditional students, and college graduates returning for postgraduate study. A disproportionate number of those students, particularly nontraditional students who faced com-

peting demands on their time at work and home, chose to attend college on a part-time basis. These trends are charted in Figures 16.2 through 16.5. Figure 16.2 conveys the striking increase in female enrollments from 43.4 percent of total environments in 1972 to 57.4 percent in 1996. The number of female students first surpassed the number of males in 1978. There was little variation in this trend among sectors, except for the dramatic increase in the enrollment of women in community colleges following the recession of 1975–76.

Figure 16.3 reveals that the increase in minority enrollments was somewhat erratic between 1982 and 1996. Enrollment of African Americans, North Carolina's largest minority group, decreased from 17.9 percent of total enrollment in 1986 to 17.3 percent in 1988, and then rose to 20.1 percent in 1996. In absolute numbers, however, black enrollments increased from 51,996 in 1972 to 73,032 in 1996.

Figure 16.4 shows an overall increase in the enrollment of students aged twenty-five and older from 31.4 percent of total enrollment in 1976 (when data on the age of students were first collected) to 38.5 percent in 1996. In private institutions the proportion of nontraditional students has begun to approach that of public universities. The percentage of students aged twenty-five and older in community colleges ranged from 49 to 52 percent over the same period.

Figure 16.5 plots the percentage of enrollments at the graduate and first professional degree level. UNC enrollments at this level increased from 16.4

Figure 16.3. Fall Enrollment of Minorities in North Carolina Colleges and Universities, 1982–1996

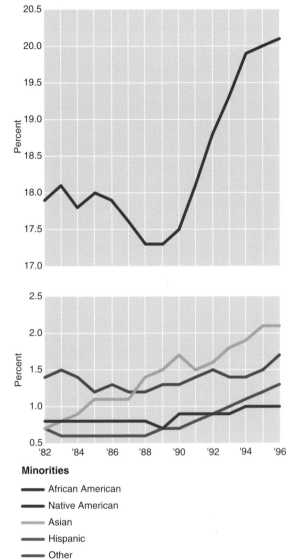

Minorities

—— African American
—— Native American
—— Asian
—— Hispanic
—— Other

Source: University of North Carolina General Administration.

Figure 16.4. Fall Enrollment of Students Age 25 and Older in North Carolina Colleges and Universities, 1976–1996

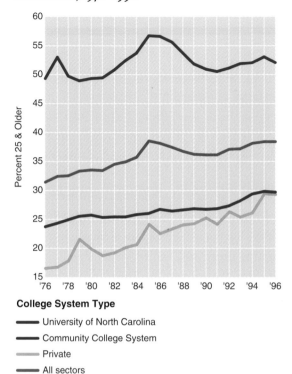

College System Type

—— University of North Carolina
—— Community College System
—— Private
—— All sectors

Source: University of North Carolina General Administration.

percent of total enrollment in 1972 to 18.2 percent in 1975 and then to 18.9 percent in 1996. The increases in the private sector have exceeded those at public universities largely because a growing number of private institutions are offering master's-level programs, and Campbell University has added professional programs in law and pharmacy. In the fall of 1996 total graduate enrollment at the

UNC campuses was 25,901, compared to 7,624 in the private institutions. Doctoral-level enrollments, largely concentrated at UNC institutions, have been restrained, as an overproduction of doctorates nationwide was corrected during the 1980s. Projections of faculty shortages in response to projections of record numbers of faculty retirements in the late 1990s appear to be stimulating doctoral-level enrollments. There was also an increase in enrollment of part-time students from 19.2 percent of total enrollment in 1972 to 35.1 percent in 1996. Increases were greatest in the community colleges, where almost two out of three students attended part-time in 1985. Since then, part-time enrollments have grown more slowly than full-time enrollments.

Another significant trend has been the drop in the percentage of out-of-state students enrolled. At UNC institutions the percentage fell from 14.6 in 1972 to 11.7 in 1976, rose gradually to 15.9 in 1986, and then dropped steadily to 14.0 in 1996. This decline reflects a decrease in the number of high school graduates in neighboring states, a limitation on the percentage of out-of-state students admitted as freshmen, and the rapid increases in out-of-state tuition at UNC campuses. In the private sector, the percentage dropped about three points in the 1970s but stood at 47.4 in 1996.

The large increase in higher education enrollments in North Carolina over the past decade has come in the face of significant declines in the number of high school graduates and of 18–24-year-

Figure 16.5. Fall Enrollment in Graduate and First Professional Degree Programs, 1972–1996

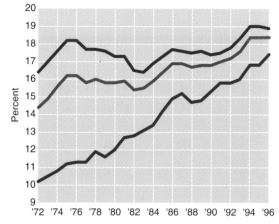

College System Type

—— University of North Carolina
—— Both sectors
—— Private

Source: University of North Carolina General Administration.

olds in the general population. This divergence between enrollments and the traditional source of enrollment growth is due not only to the higher participation rates of groups traditionally underrepresented in higher education, but also to a marked improvement in the college participation rates of 18–24-year-olds. Between 1986 and 1996 the participation rate for that age group rose from 31.8 percent to 43.4 percent. Although the number of such persons declined by 12.2 percent, their enrollment in higher education rose by 20 percent. Further analysis of the data reveal that each percentage point increase in the college participation rate of the 18–24-year-old pool adds more than four thousand students to postsecondary enrollments in North Carolina.

The pool of potential students aged 25 and older increased sharply during the 1980s and early 1990s, in contrast to a decrease in the pool of 18–24-year-olds. If past trends in the participation rates of persons aged 25 and older continued through the 1990s, and if the given population projections for this group have been realized, then the number of nontraditional students enrolled in North Carolina's postsecondary institutions will have increased by more than 27,000 students by the year 2000. Even if the participation rate for this group has not changed from its 1996 value, enrollments of older students will have increased by more than 2,000 per year throughout the 1990s.

Enrollment levels are determined by participation rates of pools of potential students. Those pools depend on the size of the population and the number of high school graduates—variables influenced by the demography and economy of the state. But participation rates are influenced by more complex variables ranging from the educational preparation of high school graduates, to the financial benefits and costs associated with college attendance, to social forces affecting attendance.

There is considerable evidence that recent high school graduates are better prepared for postsecondary course work than were those in the 1970s and early 1980s. Average Scholastic Aptitude Test (SAT) scores in North Carolina increased during the 1980s and early 1990s concurrently with a substantial rise in the percentage of high school graduates taking the test. The difference between average SAT scores for the state and for the nation has fallen steadily over the past twenty-five years. Another indication of improved preparation for college comes from course membership data collected by the State Department of Public Instruction. Those data show a significant upward trend in course enrollments in Algebra I, Geometry, Algebra II, Chemistry, and Physics. Whereas enrollments in grades nine through twelve have declined overall, the enrollments in these key college preparatory courses have *increased*.

These improvements stem from a number of state-level initiatives including increases in high school graduation requirements, establishment of the University of North Carolina Minimum Admissions Requirements, formulation and revision of the state's Standard Course of Study and End-of-Course tests, state funding (since discontinued) for a "free" administration of the Preliminary Scholastic Aptitude Test (PSAT) for every public school student who chooses to take it, and various efforts to strengthen mathematics and science education.

Although North Carolina and the Southeast remain below the national average in some areas of educational opportunity, they have made important advances and narrowed or closed many gaps. Rising literacy rates and improved participation and completion rates at every level of education have characterized the state and the region since 1900, but particularly over the past four decades.

Between 1950 and 1980 the median years of schooling completed by residents of North Carolina aged 25 and older rose from 7.9 years to 12.2 years. In other words, by 1980 half of the adult population had some education beyond high school—in sharp contrast to thirty years earlier, when half of the adult population had completed less than the eighth grade. The 1980 census was the first to show that more than half the residents 25 aged or older of every state had completed at least four years of high school. For North Carolina, the proportion was 54.8 percent, compared to only 38.5 percent in 1970. By 1990 the proportion had risen to 70 percent and by 1995 to 76.3 percent.

The increased participation and completion rates are equally impressive in higher education. The percentage of persons in North Carolina aged 25 and older who have completed four or more years of college climbed from 8.5 percent in 1970, to 13.2 percent in 1980, to 17.4 percent in 1990, to 20.6 percent in 1995. Substantial progress has been made in improving the state's relatively low college-going rates. Figure 16.6 compares freshman college-going rates for North Carolina and the nation since 1986, when national data on residence and migration first made this calculation possible. The rate for North Carolina rose from 51.8 percent in 1986 to 62.9 in 1996, but fluctuated between 90 and 99 percent of the national rate over that period.

Another measure of completion rates for higher education is the marked

Figure 16.6. Percentage of Recent High School Graduates Attending College in North Carolina and the United States, 1986–1996

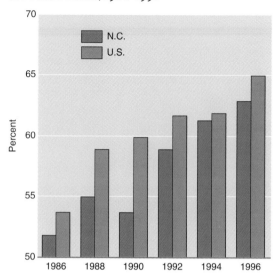

Source: University of North Carolina General Administration.

increase in the number of degrees conferred. Table 16.1 shows the degrees conferred for the period 1976 to 1996. In 1975–76 North Carolina colleges and universities awarded a total of 23,356 baccalaureate, 4,911 master's, 1,114 first professional, and 734 doctoral degrees. In 1995–96 the number of baccalaureate and master's degrees had risen to 32,819 and 7,859 respectively, first professional degrees reached 1,609, and doctorates increased to 1,042. The number of sub-baccalaureate certificates more than doubled, and the number of two-year associate degrees increased 40 percent in the same period. Given the strong correlation between levels of education and income, and given the growing demand for a more highly trained and better-educated workforce, there is still a compelling need for North Carolina to raise the educational level of its citizens.

The Community College System provides most of the vocational and technical training for North Carolina workers. Senior institutions of higher education offer the education and training required for the state's advanced and professional workforce. Except in the case of law and theology, most professional training is provided in UNC institutions. For example, in nursing, UNC institutions conferred 88 percent of baccalaureate and 93 percent of master's degrees in 1995–96. The medical schools at the University of North Carolina in Chapel Hill and at East Carolina University granted 53 percent of the degrees awarded in medicine that year. In dentistry, veterinary medicine, and library science, UNC institutions conferred all of the degrees, and in pharmacy, at all degree levels, it conferred 73 percent of the degrees. Other calculations, based on degrees conferred at all levels in 1995–96, show the UNC share in selected fields:

- Agriculture and natural resources— 77 percent
- Architecture and environmental design— 96 percent
- Biological and physical sciences— 71 percent
- Business—56 percent
- Computer science and mathematics— 71 percent
- Education—83 percent
- Engineering—89 percent
- Physical therapy—78 percent

Enrollment Growth during the Next Decade

Institutions in all three of North Carolina's higher education sectors (the University of North Carolina, the Community College System, and private colleges and universities) have experienced substantial growth in enrollments in the last two decades, with total enrollment increasing from 241,000 in 1976 to 363,000 in 1996. In part this was driven by increased attendance rates for women, minorities, older students, and college graduates returning for postgraduate study, although enrollments slowed during the first half of the 1990s because there were fewer high school graduates. In contrast, enrollments in the higher education sectors will accelerate over the next decade largely due to an upward trend in North Carolina high school graduates, whose numbers are expected to jump from 56,770 in 1996 to approximately 73,000 in 2006.

Based on Department of Public Instruction projections of high school graduates and on population projections by the state demographer, the University of North Carolina has anticipated a growth of about 33,000 students on its sixteen campuses during the period 1996–2005, with enrollment steepest during the last half of the decade. Community colleges are projecting large enrollment increases from 146,000 in 1996 to 186,000 in 2005 (including degree, certificate, and diploma programs as well as occupational continuing education, business and industry services, and basic skills programs). Based on enrollment capacity estimates from the North Carolina Independent Colleges and Universities, Inc., private colleges and universities (total enrollments of 63,086 in 1996) anticipate growth of about 9,000 students between 1996 and 2005. Overall, head-count enrollments in the three sectors could increase by about 228,000 by 2005.

One factor that may dramatically affect higher education enrollments is the increasing availability of college courses and degrees via distance education either to off-campus sites or provided directly in the home or workplace. As information technology becomes more sophisticated and dispersed, higher education during the next decade will become available to a greatly expanded audience of potential students.

Financial Considerations

Enrollments and participation/completion rates in higher education ultimately depend on access,

both geographic and financial. There is a direct relationship between level of educational attainment and level of income: as one goes up, the other also rises. The public sector has sought to keep tuition charges to North Carolina students low both to broaden access and to achieve a goal of the state Constitution of 1971, which directed that the General Assembly "provide that the benefits of the University of North Carolina and other public institutions of higher education, as far as practicable, be extended to the people of the State free of expense." In keeping with that mandate, tuition and required academic fees for in-state students have been held to relatively modest levels at the public colleges and universities. Nevertheless, these charges have risen steadily over the past twenty-five years.

Figure 16.7 shows the average cost of tuition and required fees for both public and private institutions for the period 1972–73 through 1996–97. During those years, the average cost for in-state students rose by 268 percent in the public senior institutions and by 295 percent in the public two-year institutions. The costs for out-of-state students increased by 356 percent in the public senior institutions and by 946 percent in the community college system.

Throughout the same period, the average tuition and required fees were higher and increased at a faster rate in private colleges than in public institutions. The increases for in-state students were

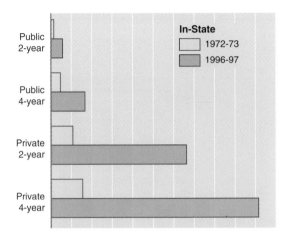

Figure 16.7. Average Tuition and Required Academic Fees of North Carolina Colleges and Universities, 1972–1973 and 1996–1997

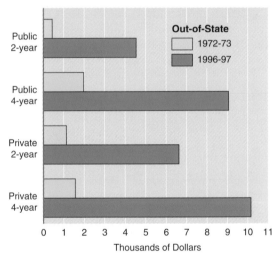

Source: University of North Carolina General Administration.

556 percent at private senior institutions and 530 percent at private junior colleges. The percentage increases for out-of-state students were roughly parallel to those for North Carolina residents in both levels of private institutions.

Tuition and required fees constitute only a part of the cost of attending a college or university. There are also special fees, such as departmental service fees and health fees, as well as expenses for food, housing, books, transportation, and other necessities. Table 16.2 shows the average costs for tuition, required fees, and room and board and the ratio of those costs to median family incomes in North Carolina and the nation for the period 1977–78 through 1995–96. In terms of increases in costs and their relationship to median family income, North Carolina compares favorably to the rest of the nation.

Low tuition is one of the most crucial forms of student financial aid. It is a key element in North Carolina's efforts to improve access to higher education. Because there are additional costs beyond tuition, however, low tuition does not solve the problem of access. Comprehensive programs of student financial aid must be available if higher educational opportunities are to be provided for large numbers of citizens.

Various federal programs of grants and guaranteed loans are the largest source of student financial aid for undergraduates in North Carolina and the nation. The amount of assistance available per full-time undergraduate in North Carolina through Pell Grants and federal campus-based aid peaked in 1979–80 after passage of the Middle-Income Assistance Act. Subsequent restrictions on eligibility in the 1980s led to declines in the aid available per full-time undergraduate in both current and constant dollars. The sharpest drops were in the per student amounts available for undergraduates enrolled in the public senior institutions. Over the past decade another disturbing trend has been the marked shift from grants and scholarships to an increasing reliance on student loans. These trends have generated a growing concern over the debt burden accumulated by students during their undergraduate experience.

The state's principal approach to financial aid has been the maintenance of relatively low tuition for in-state students in the public sector. For North

Table 16.2. College Costs and Median Family Income for North Carolina and the United States, 1977–1978 to 1995–1996

	1977–78	1984–85	1991–92	1995–96
United States				
Public 4-yr.	$2,038	$3,682	$5,714	$7,013
Private 4-yr.	4,240	8,451	14,351	17,613
Public 2-yr. (tuition only)	306	584	962	1,245
Median family income	18,723	31,097	43,056	49,687
North Carolina				
Public 4-yr.	1,696	2,754	4,018	5,119
Private 4-yr.	3,352	6,292	10,912	15,428
Public 2-yr. (tuition only)	137	174	506	581
Median family income	16,252	27,995	39,934	47,367
Ratio of cost to median family income				
United States				
Public 4-yr.	10.9	11.8	13.3	14.1
Private 4-yr.	22.6	27.2	33.3	35.4
Public 2-yr.	1.6	1.9	2.2	2.5
North Carolina				
Public 4-yr.	10.4	9.8	10.1	10.8
Private 4-yr.	20.6	22.5	27.3	32.6
Public 2-yr.	0.8	0.6	1.3	1.2

Sources: University of North Carolina General Administration; National Center for Educational Statistics; U.S. Census Bureau.
Notes: Median family income is for a 4-person family. Board plan is a 7-day or 19–21 meal plan. Room is double occupancy. Student costs are for in-state tuition plus required fees, room, and board. The cost ratio is tuition as a percentage of median family income.

Carolina undergraduates in private colleges, the General Assembly has provided two programs: the State Contractual Scholarship Fund (SCSF), established in 1972–73, and the Legislative Tuition Grant (LTG) program, begun in 1975–76. The SCSF is a need-based program, and the LTG is nonneed-based. Each program was initiated on the basis of $200 per North Carolina undergraduate enrolled in a private college in the state.

Figure 16.8 shows the growth of these two programs since they were established. The 1997–98 per student basis for SCSF allocations was $750, and the legislative tuition grants were $1,450 per full-time North Carolina undergraduate. The combined appropriations for the two programs for 1997–98 totaled $52.8 million. This substantial assistance from the state, combined with federal aid, has helped to offset the tuition differential between the public and private sectors of higher education and has contributed to enrollment stability in the private sector.

The higher tuition and fees of the private institutions reflect their heavier dependence on those two revenue sources for educational and general (E&G) operating expenses. In 1995–96 tuition and fees were the leading source of E&G revenues for the private senior (39 percent) and junior colleges (58 percent). The corresponding percentages twenty-four years earlier, in 1971–72, were 33 and 69, respectively. Tuition and fees are also a substantial source of income for all of the public institutions and one that is anticipated in their budgets. It

is significant that the percentages of revenue from these two sources in North Carolina are below the national level for both the private and public sectors.

State appropriations for the UNC institutions and state and local funds for the community/technical colleges were the major sources of E&G revenues for the public sector—in 1994–95, 53 percent for senior institutions and 69 percent for two-year colleges. Those percentages have changed little since 1971–72, when the corresponding percentages were 54 and 82. These percentages are higher than those for public institutions nationwide. State support for higher education remains strong, as demonstrated by the sizable increase in state appropriations for higher education. Nevertheless, higher education's share of the state's General Fund appropriations for current operations has declined from 17.4 percent in 1986–87 to 13.0 percent in 1996–97. The appropriations for senior institutions shown in Figure 16.9 include the indirect support that the state provides to private senior and junior colleges through student financial aid programs.

Funds for higher education from federal sources have risen substantially. North Carolina has consistently ranked high among the fifty states in receipt of total federal obligations each year. A 1996 report from the National Science Foundation (NSF) (*Science and Engineering State Profiles*) indicates that the state has been continuing to achieve high rankings in funding for academic research

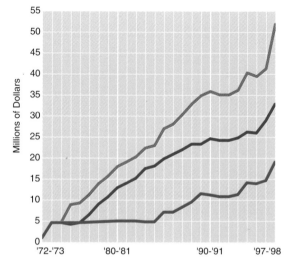

Figure 16.8. Budgeted State Appropriations for Aid to In-State Undergraduates in North Carolina Private Colleges and Universities, 1972–1973 to 1997–1998

Budgeted State Appropriations

— Combined programs
— Legislative Tuition Grants
— State Contractual Scholarship Fund

Source: University of North Carolina General Administration.

and development (R&D). Although ranked eleventh in population and in gross state product, North Carolina ranked ninth in academic R&D expenditures and seventh nationally in federal R&D funds provided for academic R&D (Table 16.3). According to a 1997 report of the Association of American Universities (*Employment Impacts of Academic R&D, Fiscal Year 1995*), R&D expenditures by doctorate-granting institutions in North Carolina supported 26,846 jobs.

Figure 16.9. North Carolina General Fund Operating Appropriations for Community Colleges and Senior Institutions, 1982-1983 to 1996-1997

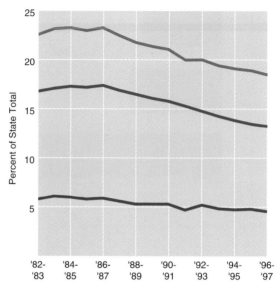

Institution Type

⎯⎯ Combined

⎯⎯ Senior institutions

⎯⎯ Community colleges

Source: *Post-Legislative Summary*, 1995-97.

Table 16.3. North Carolina Science and Engineering R&D Profile

	North Carolina	United States	Rank
Population, 1995 (thousands)	7,195	262,755	11
Gross state product, 1992 ($ billions)	160	5,994	11
Higher education expenditures, 1993 ($ millions)	5,012	163,994	9
Total R&D, 1993 ($ millions)	2,745	161,427	18
Industry R&D, 1993 ($ millions)	1,929	117,622	17
Academic R&D, 1994 ($ millions)	658	20,573	9
Federal funds for academic R&D, 1994 ($ millions)	449	11,956	7

Source: National Science Foundation, *Science and Engineering State Profiles*, Fall 1996.

The four major research and doctorate-granting institutions in North Carolina—Duke University, North Carolina State University (NCSU), UNC Chapel Hill, and Wake Forest University—account for the vast majority of the state's academic R&D expenditures. As shown in Figure 16.10, annual R&D expenditures increased from $363 million in FY 1988 to $676 million in FY 1995, the latest year for which national statistics were available from NSF. Each of the four institutions approximately doubled its annual R&D expenditures over the eight-year period. For FY 1995, total R&D expenditures and corresponding national rankings were as follows: Duke, $219 million, 26th; UNC Chapel Hill, $209 million, 29th; NCSU, $180 million, 37th; and Wake Forest, $68 million, 106th. Federally financed R&D expenditures were the principal source (63 percent) of these funds. Specifically, federal R&D expenditures and corresponding national rankings for the four institutions in FY 1995 were as follows: UNC Chapel Hill, $157 million, 21st; Duke, $149 million, 22d; NCSU, $69 million, 65th; and Wake Forest, $51 million, 79th.

The University of North Carolina has steadily improved its position among all university systems nationally with respect to federal funds received for research and development. In the early 1980s UNC ranked seventh behind the California, Texas, District of Columbia, Wisconsin, Illinois, and Georgia systems. By FY 1995, however, it had achieved third place behind only the California and Texas systems. This improved national ranking reflects the gain in the UNC "market share" of federal R&D funds awarded to academic institutions. In 1985 the University of North Carolina received 1.3 percent of the available federal funds; by 1995 it was awarded 2.3 percent of the federal funds. Success in obtaining external funds for research and other sponsored projects also is reflected in the growing importance of these funds to the total UNC budget. For example, 1986-sponsored program funding was equivalent to 21 percent of the state General Fund appropriations to UNC. By 1995 this ratio had increased to 39 percent.

Expenditures are the other side of the financial profile of higher educational institutions. Exclud-

Figure 16.10. R&D Expenditures at North Carolina Institutions of Higher Education, FY 1984–1995

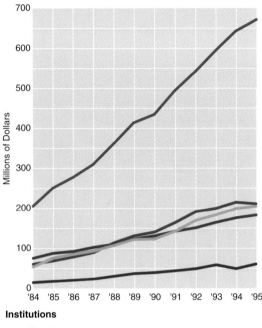

Institutions

—— Total
—— Duke
—— NCSU
—— UNC Chapel Hill
—— Wake Forest

Note: UNC Chapel Hill, NCSU, Duke, and Wake Forest collectively comprise the largest portion of R&D expenditures in North Carolina.

Source: National Science Foundation, *Science and Engineering State Profiles*, 1996.

ing capital expenditures and the sums spent by the four teaching hospitals, the total current operating expenditures for North Carolina colleges and universities in FY 1994–95 exceeded $5 billion. Of that amount, $1.7 billion was spent by private institu-

tions and $3.4 billion by public institutions. However, the public total does not include expenditures for either UNC General Administration or the North Carolina School of Science and Mathematics, an affiliated school of the University of North Carolina.

Most of these expenditures were for faculty salaries, libraries, and other academic support activities related to instruction, but substantial amounts also were spent for research and public service. Figure 16.10 presents the total R&D expenditures from federal and nonfederal sources by North Carolina higher educational institutions from FY 1984 through FY 1995. During that period R&D expenditures almost doubled. The total expenditures for public service by the sixteen constituent institutions of the University of North Carolina total more than $500 million annually. These data indicate the generous support given to higher education in North Carolina and suggest the extent to which higher education directly affects the social, economic, and political well-being of the state.

Faculty

The ability of an institution to contribute needed programs of instruction, research, and public service depends on the quality of its human resources —students, faculty, and administrative and

Figure 16.11. Number of Full-Time Faculty in North Carolina Colleges and Universities, Fall 1995

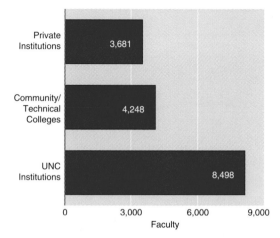

Source: University of North Carolina General Administration.

support staff. A university's quality and character rests on the qualifications, industry, and commitment of its faculty. A primary obligation of each higher educational institution, therefore, is to recruit and retain the best-qualified faculty possible.

Figure 16.11 gives the number of full-time faculty in North Carolina colleges and universities in the fall of 1995. Of 16,427 full-time faculty members, 77.6 percent were in the public sector and 22.4 percent were in the private sector. With 82 percent of the students enrolled in the public sector and 18 percent in the private sector, the ratios of students to full-time faculty were higher in public institutions.

One measure of the quality of the faculty is the earned degrees of its members. Figure 16.12 reveals

Figure 16.12. Percentage of Full-Time Faculty Holding the Doctorate or First Professional Degree at North Carolina Four–Year Institutions, 1972–1996

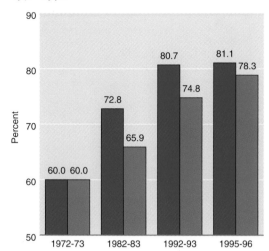

Institution Type
- University of North Carolina
- Private senior colleges and universities

Source: University of North Carolina General Administration.

that, in terms of highest earned degree, there has been significant improvement in North Carolina senior colleges and universities since 1972. Not shown is the striking advancement in the five historically black institutions in the UNC system. The percentage of faculty holding earned doctorates or first professional degrees in those institutions in 1972–73 ranged from 27 to 36 percent, whereas by 1996–97 the range was 67 to 76 percent.

Figure 16.13. Percentage of Full-Time Female Faculty at North Carolina Four-Year Institutions, 1972–1997

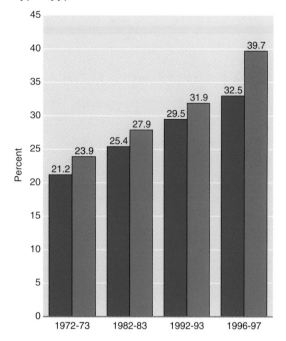

Institution Type
- University of North Carolina
- Private senior colleges and universities

Source: University of North Carolina General Administration.

Steady progress has also been made in recruiting and retaining a more diverse faulty. Figure 16.13 shows the rising number and percentage of women faculty members in North Carolina's public and private senior institutions since 1972.

Libraries and Facilities

Libraries are an indispensable resource for every major function of a higher educational institution. They support all of its instructional, research, and public service programs. The collections and services of academic libraries are a recognized measure of the quality of the institution and are an essential information resource for the state and the region.

Table 16.4 gives the number of volumes (books, bound serials, and government documents) in the libraries of the public and private colleges and universities in North Carolina in 1995–96. In addition to the 27.9 million bound volumes shown in the table, the collections included another 3.6 million books on microfilm. Among the senior institutions, almost half (46.3 percent) of the bound volumes were in the libraries of the three major research universities: the University of North Carolina at Chapel Hill, 4.6 million volumes; Duke University, 4.5 million volumes; and North Carolina State University, 2.5 million volumes. The combined unduplicated holdings of these three libraries linked within the Triangle Research Libraries Network create North America's second largest research library, surpassed only by Harvard University's. Other libraries in North Carolina reporting more than 1 million volumes each were at Wake Forest University (1.3 million) and East Carolina University (2.4 million).

Table 16.4. Number of Bound Volumes in North Carolina College and University Libraries, 1995–1996

Type of Institution	Number of Volumes*
Public 4-year (UNC)	15,403,305
Public 2-year	2,139,587
Private 4-year	9,981,507
Private 2-year	428,147
Total	27,952,546

Source: University of North Carolina General Administration.
*Includes books, bound serials, and government documents

Figure 16.14. University of North Carolina Educational Computing Service Library Network Managed by Network Services

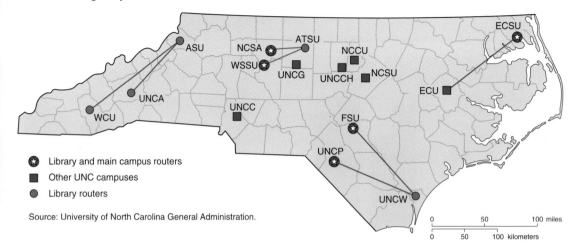

★ Library and main campus routers
■ Other UNC campuses
● Library routers

Source: University of North Carolina General Administration.

0   50   100 miles
0   50   100 kilometers

The explosion of knowledge in the late twentieth century, coupled with a rapid escalation of the real cost of acquiring books and serial publications, has seriously strained library resources. Total operating expenses for North Carolina college and university libraries in 1995–96 amounted to $142.4 million, an increase of 69 percent since 1985–86. But devaluation of the dollar and unprecedented inflation in the cost of printing materials during the 1980s, particularly since 1986, have meant a drastic loss of purchasing power and a serious erosion of library collections in the state.

Fortunately, advances in information technology enable libraries to cope with some of the problems they face. Networking and telecommunications have evolved in conjunction with dependence on computing facilities to alter dramatically the means by which libraries provide access to

their holdings. Electronic (on-line) catalogs can be accessed not only locally but also from sites throughout the world.

Library networking is provided by a combination of network services. The eleven constituent institutions of the University of North Carolina whose libraries participate in shared on-line catalog arrangements are connected by a network administered by the Network Services group in the University of North Carolina General Administration (Fig. 16.14). They include Appalachian State, East Carolina, Elizabeth City State, Fayetteville State, N.C. A&T, the School of the Arts, UNC Asheville, UNC Pembroke, UNC Wilmington, Western Carolina, and Winston-Salem State. In

addition, each of the sixteen constituent institutions of the UNC system has Internet access to the on-line catalogs of all other UNC institutions. Faculty, staff, student, and public access to the catalogs is provided by a combination of Internet access and terminals available in the libraries. Network Services works with all of the UNC libraries to provide access to other on-line information resources, such as the Encyclopedia Britannica. Databases of the American Psychological Association and the Educational Resources Information Center (ERIC) of the U.S. Department of Education are accessible through OVID search services.

North Carolina's university libraries have also been linked with hundreds of libraries throughout the world. The Internet, a network of networks to which all UNC institutions as well as many other public and private colleges and universities are connected, links most colleges and universities worldwide. Participation in the Internet is growing, with a total global user base estimated at over 35 million people.

Although such networking is costly to develop and maintain, it can lead to significant savings through the sharing of catalogs and resources, the cooperative development of library collections, the avoidance of unnecessary duplication of some expensive items in the holdings, and the facilitation and encouragement of greater use of interlibrary loans. Most important, these technological advances are increasing exponentially the information available to North Carolinians.

The libraries and other facilities located on college campuses constitute an enormous investment and immense asset for North Carolina. They serve the instructional and research needs of the students and faculty, but many buildings were also designed to meet a broader range of community, regional, and statewide public service needs. Figure 16.15 shows the gross area by age of the existing structures in each sector of higher education. Figure 16.16 indicates the original cost and the estimated replacement value of those buildings.

A survey completed in 1999 reported that UNC and the community colleges need $7 billion for new and renovated facilities to accommodate projected enrollment growth. The 1999 General As-

Figure 16.15. Percentage Distribution of Gross Area by Age of Buildings, 1995–1996

a. UNC Campuses and UNC Hospitals at Chapel Hill

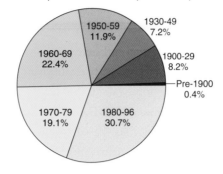

b. Community Colleges

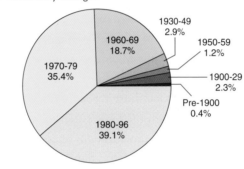

c. Private Institutions

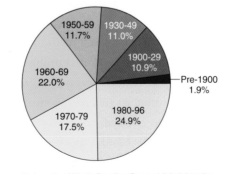

Source: University of North Carolina General Administration.

Figure 16.16. Value of Physical Plant in North Carolina Higher Education Institutions, FY 1982–1983 vs. FY 1995–1996

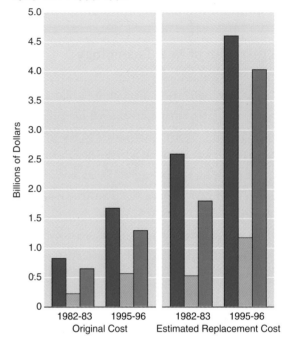

Institution Type

- Public senior
- Public (2-year)
- Private (4- and 2-year)

Source: University of North Carolina General Administration.

sembly failed to approve a $3 billion bond issue that would have met the most critical of those needs.

Utilization of New Technology

Extensive modification of existing facilities, new construction, and major investment in equipment are required if higher education is to take full advantage of new technology. The effective use of emerging information technologies enhances a university's performance of its instructional, research, and service roles.

Dramatic technological changes have occurred in higher education since the 1970s. In that decade the few universities that had mainframe computers used them primarily, if not exclusively, for administrative functions. Today most senior institutions of higher education have mainframe and other central computers that are used by both administrative and academic computing and that play a substantial role in distributed computing. Institutions have invested heavily in microcomputers and workstations for student, faculty, and staff use in classrooms, laboratories, libraries, and offices. Client-server computing is common in administrative computing applications. Campus networks have been developed and are being expanded and upgraded to link persons and functions for a wide variety of purposes encompassing administration, research, instructional, and public services.

Network linkages beyond the individual campuses are crucial, and North Carolina is much further along in statewide networking than most other states. In 1993 planning was begun for a joint venture among the providers of telecommunication in North Carolina and state agencies, including colleges and universities, to establish an "Information Highway" for the state. The North Carolina Information Highway (NCIH) is being designed to provide an optical fiber–based public network with the potential to deliver access to distance learning and to high-performance computing for students at the elementary school, secondary school, college, and university levels.

The University of North Carolina, assisted by MCNC (formerly the Microelectronics Center of North Carolina), has established a means for participating in distance learning across a number of campuses. Through microwave transmission and leased public telecommunications lines, the North Carolina Research and Education Network (NC-REN) provides two channels linking the sixteen UNC campuses and General Administration. A third channel is reserved for the exclusive use of the state's four public and private medical schools. NC-REN interfaces with the North Carolina Information Highway, which also serves UNC institutions plus the community colleges, public schools, and state agencies. Telemedicine is already being utilized extensively by health practitioners in cooperation with numerous health care facilities, medical school sites, and Area Health Education Centers. NC-REN, NCIH, and the telephone network are all used in the provision of telemedicine.

The NC-REN network allows two or more sites to revive and transmit simultaneously full motion video and audio instruction in a fully interactive manner. The network has also been used extensively for seminars and video conferences, reducing the expense and travel time for participants. Usage of the facilities averages over one hundred hours per week during the fall and spring semesters. NC-REN also provides universities not in the Research Triangle Park locale access to the facilities of the North Carolina Supercomputer Center (NCSC). In 1988 the General Assembly provided funds to purchase a supercomputer for use by educational institutions and by government and business for the economic advantage of the state. After careful testing and study, a Cray YPM supercomputer was installed. Several upgrades and replacements have been accomplished, leading to a current array of High Performance Computing equipment including a CRAY TO916/4256 vector supercomputer with an attached massively parallel CRAY T3E, an IBM SP2 parallel supercomputer, and a cluster of superscalar workstations. These computers are used by public and private universities, colleges, and secondary schools statewide under a contract between MCNC and the University of North Carolina.

The tremendous potential of the new technology cannot be realized unless an adequate networking and communications infrastructure is provided. The existing infrastructure is an excellent start, but it will require expansion and enhancement as technology improves and use increases. North Carolina's colleges and universities are playing and will continue to play a key role in that task.

Outlook

Education is, by definition, unfinished business. For two centuries North Carolina has endeavored to raise the educational level of its people through schools, colleges, and universities. The University of North Carolina at Chapel Hill held its Bicentennial Convocation on October 12, 1993. In approaching its third century, the university faces a dilemma that it has faced frequently in the past: (1) a growing demand for educational opportunities and for programs and services that are responsive to the needs of the state, and (2) continuing limitations on resources available to meet those needs. That same dilemma confronts all North Carolina colleges and universities as they seek to fulfill traditional commitments to access, quality, and institutional diversity. North Carolina higher education has succeeded in attracting large numbers of students from within and beyond the state. The most recent data on student residence and migration show that in 1988 North Carolina ranked sixth among the fifty states in the percentage of freshmen choosing to remain in the state to attend college and ranked second as a net importer of students. The explanation for this attraction lies in the presence of a wide array of large and small, public and private institutions, in the relative affordability of those institutions, and in their reputation for quality. Continued access to higher educational opportunities and an effective response to the state's needs will depend on the same three inter-related factors: cost, quality, and institutional diversity.

Among the major needs to be met by institutions of higher education as North Carolina enters the twenty-first century are the following:

- *Responsiveness to issues confronting North Carolina and the nation.* Institutions of higher education will continue to offer supportive campus environments that sustain and promote the self-directed scholarly pursuits of students and faculty among a wide range of disciplines. But increasingly, higher education is called upon to evaluate the process and outcomes of the academic enterprise in light of the economic, environmental, and social needs of the state and the nation—both traditional needs related to the economic prosperity, health, and well-being of North Carolina's citizens and new needs emerging from the transition to the knowledge-based economy of the Information Age. This responsibility must address both the required skills and attributes of educated citizens who will manage the change inherent in this new era and the specific societal issues that demand disciplinary and interdisciplinary responses in teaching, research, and public service.

- *Interinstitutional and intersector collaboration.* For higher education to address successfully these challenges, increased levels of coordination and cooperation are required among higher educational institutions and between higher education and other sectors such as the public schools, business and industry, state and federal agencies, and governmental entities at all levels. Increasingly, educational consortia and alliances will be required to meet the educational and economic development needs of the state, and each higher educational institution must examine carefully which of its strengths can be leveraged with those of other institutions to address those needs.

- *Extending the benefits of higher education to all citizens with appropriate learning needs.* No demographic subpopulation or geographic area should be educationally disadvantaged or left behind economically as North Carolina enters the twenty-first century. Given the possibilities offered by information technology and the necessity for all of the state's workers to be competitive in a global economy, higher education faces the need and the opportunity to extend its services to under-served age groups, minority populations, and various geographic areas of the state. This potential for greatly expanding the benefits of higher education will require careful assessment of the state's needs and coordinated efforts among institutions and sectors in response to those needs.

- *Accountability and quality.* Throughout the 1990s there was an emphasis in North Carolina and the nation on documenting the benefits of higher education and on ensuring the highest quality both of traditional educational activities and new educational services made possible by information technology. During the previous decade the General Assembly indicated interest in higher education's response to predicted increases in enrollments, access to education by nontraditional learners, equity and mission differentiation among educational institutions, efficiency and economy in delivery of education and graduation of students, and careful assessment of needs of the state in planning new programs and initiatives. Higher education's response in each of these areas must be based on a fundamental and widely held commitment to quality and accountability to the state's citizenry.

Ultimately, the continuing goal for North Carolina must be to maintain a cost effective system of higher education while ensuring quality, affordability, and the ability to serve a diversity of student needs.

Selected References

Aspen Institute. *American Higher Education: Purposes, Problems, and Public Perceptions.* Queenstown, Md.: Aspen Institute, 1992.

Association of Independent Colleges and Universities. *Annual Report.* Raleigh: AICU, annually.

Evans, T., and D. Nation, eds. *Open Education: Policies and Practices from Open and Distance Education.* Routledge Studies in Distance Education. New York: Routledge, 1996.

Jennings, J., ed. *National Issues in Education: The Past Is Prologue.* Bloomington, Ind., and Washington, D.C.: Phi Delta Kappa International and Institute for Educational Leadership, 1993.

King, A. *The Multicampus University of North Carolina Comes of Age, 1956–1986.* Chapel Hill: University of North Carolina Press, 1987.

Levine, A., ed. *Higher Learning in America, 1980–2000.* Baltimore: Johns Hopkins University Press, 1993.

Link, W. *William Friday: Power, Purpose, and American Higher Education.* Chapel Hill: University of North Carolina Press, 1995.

Powell, W. *Higher Education in North Carolina.* Raleigh: North Carolina Department of Archives and History, 1964.

University of North Carolina. General Administration. Communications Division. *Cornerstone of Public Higher Education: The Multi-Campus University of North Carolina.* Chapel Hill: UNC General Administration, 1993.

17. HEALTH AND HEALTH CARE
Gerald R. Pyle

One of the most important issues facing the people of North Carolina is the state of their health and the availability of health care resources. The good news is that both generally have improved in recent years. However, reflecting the general trend toward the concentration of growth in urban areas, this progress has advantaged metropolitan areas more than the rural counties. For example, some of the most modern medical technologies available anywhere are found in the larger Piedmont urban centers, whereas many rural parts of the Mountains and Coastal Plain remain isolated from such services. There are also diverse geographic patterns of death and disease. Some of these patterns are comparable with urban-rural differences, whereas others seem to be associated with east-to-west cultural contrasts. Over time elements of change in the distribution of diseases and in national trends in the supply of primary care physicians, hospital facilities, and managed care programs can also be observed when North Carolina patterns are examined.

Patterns of Disease

Heart Disease

In 1994, 2.25 million people died in the United States from all causes. About one-third of this mortality was due to some form of heart disease. Indeed, for much of the twentieth century such deaths were on the increase. By the mid-1980s, however, heart disease rates had begun to fall nationally. This decline continued into the mid-1990s among both males and females of all races. A combination of factors, including changing lifestyles, early detection and prevention, and improved medical care, seems to have contributed to this shift.

A historical perspective helps to understand the geography of heart disease in North Carolina. Patterns of heart disease mortality for the periods 1972–76, 1986–90, and 1991–95 reveal North Carolina's version of national trends (Fig. 17.1). In the early 1970s, for example, pockets of counties in the western Mountains, one area in the southern Piedmont, and a concentration of counties in the northeast reported the highest rates of heart disease mortality. Conversely, some of the lowest rates were in many of the more urbanized counties. The patterns shown in Figure 17.1 demonstrate how geographic differences in mortality have changed little from the early 1970s to the mid-1990s in spite of an overall decline in rates. By the mid-1990s the heart disease mortality rate for North Carolina,

about 275 per 100,000 persons, had dropped below the U.S. rate of 288 per 100,000. However, there continued to be a clustering of somewhat higher-than-average rates in northeastern counties and the western Mountains, while the urbanized Piedmont maintained its lower-than-average rates.

Cancer

About 16 percent of all deaths in the United States during the 1990s were attributed to some form of cancer, and the same was true for North Carolina. In 1995 the mortality rate for cancer both nationwide and in North Carolina was about 206 per 100,000 persons. As a general disease, cancer is second to only heart disease as a leading cause of death. Just as there are many forms of heart disease, there are also different kinds of cancer.

Cancers are uncontrolled new growths that invade and destroy living tissue. These growths are made up of cancerous cells that differ from normal cells in size, shape, rate of growth, and many other ways. Malignant tumors are, of course, different from benign types and are characterized by growth beyond the body organ of origin. The patterns shown in Figure 17.2 represent the distribution of malignant neoplasms as a cause of death in the state for the periods 1972–76, 1986–90, and 1991–95. Unlike heart disease, which has declined, cancer as a leading cause of death is on the rise, and this aspect of disease geography is quite pronounced

Figure 17.1. Rate of Death from Heart Disease, 1972–1995

a. 1972-1976

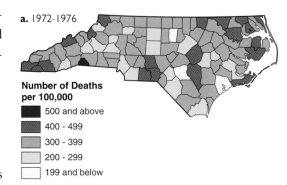

Number of Deaths per 100,000

- 500 and above
- 400 - 499
- 300 - 399
- 200 - 299
- 199 and below

b. 1986-1990

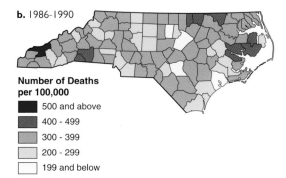

Number of Deaths per 100,000

- 500 and above
- 400 - 499
- 300 - 399
- 200 - 299
- 199 and below

c. 1991-1995

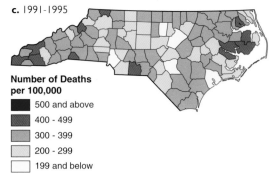

Number of Deaths per 100,000

- 500 and above
- 400 - 499
- 300 - 399
- 200 - 299
- 199 and below

Source: N.C. Department of Environment, Health, and Natural Resources, State Center for Health Statistics.

when examining distributions within North Carolina.

As shown in Figure 17.2, the pattern of cancer deaths from 1972 to 1976 contains several distinct regional clusters. As with heart disease mortality, there was a heavy concentration of higher-than-average cancer deaths in the northeast and another cluster in the western Mountains. In contrast, death rates for the 1986–90 period show that the incidence of cancer had become more widespread. The mortality rate had increased from about 145 per 100,000 persons in the mid-1970s to 190 per 100,000 persons by the mid-1980s. By the mid-1990s the rate was in excess of 200. Concentrations of higher-than-average rates on the northeastern Coastal Plain persisted into the 1990s. There were also several other pockets of high cancer incidence: one appeared on the southern Coastal Plain, and another large cluster was found in the western Mountains. The advanced age of the population in these areas is a probable explanation for these clusters.

Cerebrovascular Disease

Cerebrovascular disease, or stroke, can be manifested by the abrupt onset of multiple conditions. A stroke results from a disturbed blood supply that leads to an inadequate flow to the brain. Loss of speech and/or the use of all or part of the arms and legs often occurs. A mild stroke may result only in short-term disability, but a severe stroke can lead

Figure 17.2. Rate of Death from Cancer, 1972–1995

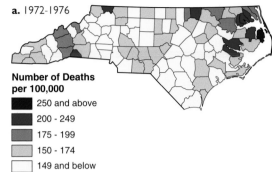

a. 1972-1976

Number of Deaths per 100,000
- 250 and above
- 200 - 249
- 175 - 199
- 150 - 174
- 149 and below

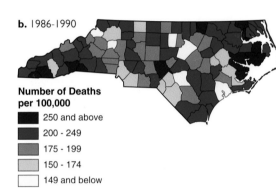

b. 1986-1990

Number of Deaths per 100,000
- 250 and above
- 200 - 249
- 175 - 199
- 150 - 174
- 149 and below

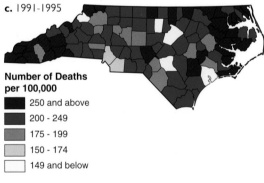

c. 1991-1995

Number of Deaths per 100,000
- 250 and above
- 200 - 249
- 175 - 199
- 150 - 174
- 149 and below

Source: N.C. Department of Environment, Health, and Natural Resources, State Center for Health Statistics.

Figure 17.3. Rate of Death from Cerebrovascular Disease, 1972–1995

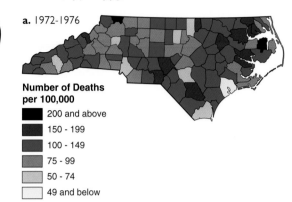

a. 1972-1976

Number of Deaths per 100,000
- 200 and above
- 150 - 199
- 100 - 149
- 75 - 99
- 50 - 74
- 49 and below

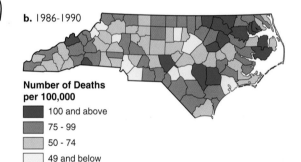

b. 1986-1990

Number of Deaths per 100,000
- 100 and above
- 75 - 99
- 50 - 74
- 49 and below

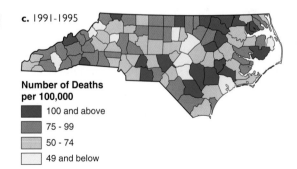

c. 1991-1995

Number of Deaths per 100,000
- 100 and above
- 75 - 99
- 50 - 74
- 49 and below

Source: N.C. Department of Environment, Health, and Natural Resources, State Center for Health Statistics.

to permanent disability or even death. A stroke can begin with loss of consciousness, but sometimes early symptoms only include blurred vision and dizziness. Strokes often happen between midnight and 6:00 A.M. Frequently, either the right or the left side of the body is affected, depending on which half of the brain suffers damage.

As in the case of heart disease, deaths due to stroke have declined over the past several decades. Nevertheless, stroke deaths in North Carolina continue to be above the national average. The U.S. rate during the mid-1990s was about 58 per 100,000 persons, whereas the North Carolina rate was closer to 70 per 100,000. The heaviest geographic concentrations of stroke mortality in the United States have traditionally been in the South. High stroke death rates have been found in the Mountains as well as the Coastal Plain of North Carolina, South Carolina, and Georgia. As the patterns in Figure 17.3 indicate, there were definite geographic variations in the incidence of cerebrovascular disease mortality in North Carolina from 1972 to 1995. These patterns were a microcosm of some known national distributions. Historically, there have been heavy concentrations of stroke mortality in the Coastal Plain and pockets of higher concentration in the Mountains. Once again, some of the more urbanized Piedmont counties continued to report lower-than-average rates.

Health Resources

In 1970, 7.1 percent of the U.S. gross domestic product (GDP) was devoted to health care expenditures. By 1994 this figure had nearly doubled, to 13.7 percent. Hospital and physician costs accounted for the largest share of those expenditures. In 1991 total per capita health expenditures were $2,245 for North Carolinians and $2,648 for the country as a whole. Per capita costs for hospital services were $973, in contrast to $1,109 nationwide. Per capita payments for physician services were $468 for North Carolina and $596 nationwide. Interestingly, the supply of physicians and hospitals demonstrated different trends in the latter part of the twentieth century. In 1994 there were more than twice as many licensed physicians (684,400) in the United States as in 1970 (334,000) but fewer hospitals—7,061 in 1972 but only 6,374 in 1994. These trends are a testimony to the changing nature of health care delivery. Examination of the distribution of physicians and hospital beds in North Carolina help to explain this phenomenon.

Physicians

Physicians continue to be the keystone of the health care system for most of the U.S. population. Most of the time the doctor is the first person to whom people turn for care when faced with unusual medical conditions or ailments. Doctors will continue to be central in the medical care delivery process for the foreseeable future. Historically, the South has lagged behind the national average in doctors per 100,000 persons. Recent growth trends and changes in the nature of health care delivery have offset this deficiency to some extent. As urban-rural differences in the geographic distribution of physicians continue to be pronounced, researchers have attributed this trend to the attraction of large cities and other places with higher income potential. By the early 1970s there were about 300,000 nonfederal practicing physicians in the United States. At that time North Carolina ranked about thirtieth nationally in physicians per 100,000 persons, and by the mid-1990s it was close to the national average.

The distribution of physicians in North Carolina in 1980, 1990, and 1995 continued to reflect the nature of urbanization in the state. Physicians have clustered in larger cities, which offer more hospitals and other medical facilities as well as the opportunity to earn a higher income. Figure 17.4 shows the heavy concentrations of physicians that have persisted in the most urbanized parts of the state. In addition, counties with the largest numbers of physicians in 1995 have seaside golf or mountain resort amenities or medical schools or contain larger cities. Another pattern of change that is revealed by these maps is that the number of physicians increased not only in urban counties but also in the adjacent suburban counties.

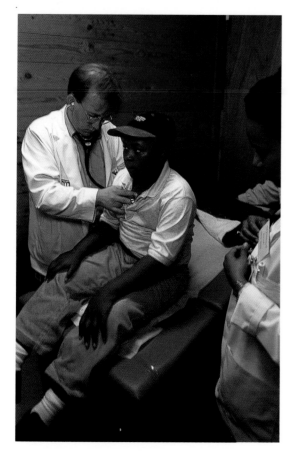

A medical clinic in Halifax County

Hospitals

Initial indications are that the story of hospital supply is just the opposite of that of physicians. Historically, hospitals have been associated with the status of many communities. To many people, they also are viewed as the pinnacle of available medical care. But the rising cost of health care de-

Figure 17.4. Number of Physicians, 1980–1995

a. 1980

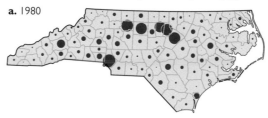

b. 1990

c. 1995

500 250 150 50 1

Source: N.C. Department of Environment, Health, and Natural Resources, State Center for Health Statistics.

livery and rapid technological change have altered that impression. More and more community hospitals can no longer afford to exist as single entities as outpatient care has replaced inpatient care for many routine hospital functions. Further, much local duplication has been eliminated through mergers of hospitals and health care groups. Thus, patterns of hospital use have also changed drasti-

cally even within the past fifteen years. Many surgical procedures that only a few years ago required a stay of several days in the hospital are now performed as outpatient surgery. And some forms of treatment that often took weeks now only take a few days. Figure 17.5 displays the pattern of hospital bed distribution per 1,000 persons in 1980, 1990, and 1996. As North Carolina follows the nation in decreasing dependence on hospitals for many forms of health care, urban settings continue to have the largest number of available beds. In fact, the number of North Carolina counties that do not have a hospital at all increased from fifteen to eighteen between 1980 and 1996. All of these counties are rural, either in the Mountains or on the northeastern Coastal Plain.

What the maps do not show is the strong trend toward the formation of extensive health care networks by larger urban health care systems through the acquisition or merger of a number of smaller facilities over a multicounty region. Many smaller hospitals are being converted to primary care units, and more specialized care and facilities are being centralized in large urban hospitals. Increasingly, therefore, management of larger shares of hospital resources are directed from the offices of regional systems in the major cities.

Hospital mergers can leave a city with only one hospital. Such is the case in Asheville, where Memorial Mission and St. Joseph's Hospitals combined into a single entity with no significant local competition. In 1998 Blue Cross and Blue Shield of

Figure 17.5. Number of Hospital Beds, 1980–1996

a. 1980

b. 1990

c. 1996

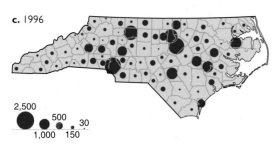

2,500
500   30
1,000   150

Source: N.C. Department of Environment, Health, and Natural Resources, State Center for Health Statistics.

North Carolina reported that the cost of hospital services for its Health Maintenance Organization (HMO) members in Asheville was 80 percent or more higher than for those in Charlotte, Durham, Greensboro, Hickory, Raleigh, and Winston-Salem. Although a host of factors may have accounted for the higher cost in Asheville, presumably a major cause was the lack of competition. In any case, the cost differential was so great that Blue Cross and Blue Shield discontinued offering HMO coverage to state employees in Buncombe County, effective October 1, 1998.

Many hospitals serve as medical education centers as well as care facilities. The state has four medical schools, each associated with a university: Duke University, East Carolina University, University of North Carolina at Chapel Hill, and Wake Forest University (formerly Bowman Gray Medical School). In addition to the medical schools, a number of hospitals have residency programs for the further training of beginning physicians. Large programs are offered in several areas that have no medical school, such as Asheville and Charlotte.

Medical and Information Technology

The tendency to concentrate major health care facilities in either large urban centers or medical schools is largely a result of the development of expensive medical technologies. The North Carolina Department of Health and Human Services controls the acquisition of expensive equipment through a "Certificate of Need" program that requires requesting hospitals to justify the need for the item. The department seeks to reduce redundancy of linear accelerators, magnetic resonance imaging machines (MRIs), and other sophisticated technologies. Additionally, it is felt that the largest and more medically important locations that exist already are best prepared to support highly specialized super-regional treatment centers for specific ailments and the expensive equipment that typically is required. The best examples of this approach, referred to as the "focused factory" model, are seen in the several university hospitals in the Raleigh-Durham area. Another approach, the "integrated delivery systems" model, offers a full range of health care services from primary care to specialized treatment. In this case the larger urban hospitals expand and incorporate other facilities into a network within the metropolitan region. It is the larger hospitals in the network that provide specialized treatment and that have the sophisticated equipment that is required. This model is best exemplified in the Charlotte and Greensboro–Winston-Salem areas.

Advancements in medical information technology support both models. In the past such technology tended to involve the use of mainframe computers by hospitals and larger group practices, primarily to handle billing. Today, information technology has expanded to include more interactive record keeping and diagnostic/treatment information. Regional networks extend the benefits of this technology to many urban and rural parts of the state. But the acquisition of newer technologies, staff training, budget management, and implementation of performance measures are led by

The UNC Memorial Hospital complex in Chapel Hill

the larger urban-based medical centers and institutions such as the new School of Information Technology at UNC Charlotte and North Carolina State University, with its long tradition in information programs.

Some Net Gains in Health Care Resources

As recent trends indicate an increased number of physicians and a changing role for hospitals, it is useful to examine just where some of these changes are taking place. The patterns in Figure 17.6 show the counties that experienced net gains in primary care physicians and hospitals from 1991 to 1995. In spite of decreasing numbers of hospital beds in 25 percent of North Carolina's counties during this period, seventeen other counties have demonstrated sustained increases in the number of hospital beds. As indicated on the map (Fig. 17.6), these seventeen counties are mostly nonurban, except for Wake and Durham, and many are just beginning to take on a suburban nature. Increases in the number of primary care physicians are more striking. Counties with such

Figure 17.6. Changes in Number of Physicians and Hospital Beds, 1991–1995

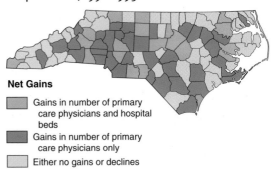

Net Gains

- ▨ Gains in number of primary care physicians and hospital beds
- ▨ Gains in number of primary care physicians only
- ▨ Either no gains or declines

Source: N.C. Department of Environment, Health, and Natural Resources, State Center for Health Statistics.

increases cut across North Carolina's geographic spectrum: they were coastal, in the mountains, urban, suburban, and rural. The counties that demonstrated no gains in the number of physicians or hospitals from 1991 to 1995 had small populations and were mostly rural. Many had never had a single hospital.

Social Dimensions of Mortality and Morbidity

Two medically different but geographically similar patterns of health care problems continue to plague North Carolina and can be placed into the general category of lingering social issues. The first of these problems is infant mortality. Although tremendous progress has been made nationally, as well as in the state, to decrease the rate of infant mortality, North Carolina still has severe difficulties in this area. The second health problem of a social nature that will continue to burden North Carolina's health care system in the future is the current HIV/AIDS epidemic. Although these health problems seem very different in nature, there are some striking geographic similarities due to increasing associations of HIV/AIDS rates with lower-income groups. Infant mortality has long been identified with populations at or below poverty levels.

Infant Mortality

Infant mortality is defined as the number of children who are born alive but who die within the first year. Infant mortality rates often are considered to be a general indicator of both the health and socioeconomic conditions of a population as the rates are affected by a host of factors, including access to prenatal and postnatal care. In the United States there has been a direct relationship between lower income and educational levels and higher rates of infant mortality. Consequently, regional differences in infant mortality patterns seem to endure because of differences in these socioeconomic conditions. In 1995 the U.S. infant mortality rate was about 8 deaths per 1,000 live births, whereas the North Carolina figure was just over 10 infant deaths per 1,000 live births.

Figure 17.7a displays patterns of annual average infant mortality for the period 1991–95. In recent decades the North Carolina rate has fallen sharply from the more than 20 infant deaths per 1,000 live births recorded for 1972–76 (Fig. 17.7b). Fifteen counties had rates in excess of 25 deaths per 1,000 live births during this earlier period, mostly on the northeastern Coastal Plain, but also in rural counties in the Piedmont and Mountain regions. The rates in three of these counties (Hyde, Northampton, and Polk) exceeded 30 deaths per 1,000. The drop to 11.7 deaths per 1,000 recorded for the 1986–90 period was spread across the state, and only Washington County had a rate over 20. By the 1991–95 period, the North Carolina average was about half that of the 1972–76 level. Yet geographic patterns of distribution remained similar from one period to the next. In spite of decreasing rates, the 1986–90 distribution contained clusters in northeastern North Carolina as well as on the southern Coastal Plain and in parts of the Mountains. These concentrations also had shown up during the earlier period. By the mid-1990s, counties with the highest rates were even more concentrated in the east. In general, the Coastal Plain counties have had persistently higher infant mortality rates than the state average even though those rates have fallen. Conversely, some of the more urbanized parts of the Piedmont normally have had lower-than-average mortality rates.

When placed within the overall context of the proportion of the population living at the poverty level, the geography of infant mortality in North

Figure 17.7. Infant Mortality Rates

a. 1991-1995

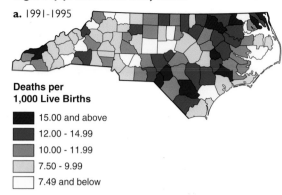

Deaths per
1,000 Live Births

■ 15.00 and above
■ 12.00 - 14.99
■ 10.00 - 11.99
□ 7.50 - 9.99
□ 7.49 and below

b. Statewide

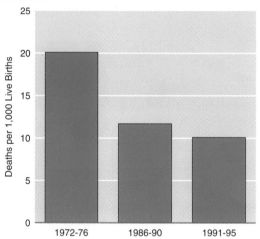

Source: N.C. Department of Environment, Health, and Natural Resources, State Center for Health Statistics.

Carolina can be more readily understood. Figure 17.8 depicts the percentage of county populations at federally defined poverty levels in 1970, 1980, and 1990. Though it is indeed encouraging that overall levels of poverty have decreased, patterns of infant

Figure 17.8. Percentage of Population at Poverty Level, 1970–1990

a. 1970

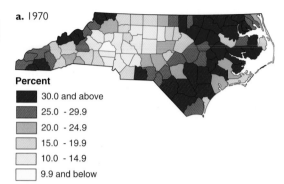

Percent

■ 30.0 and above
■ 25.0 - 29.9
■ 20.0 - 24.9
□ 15.0 - 19.9
□ 10.0 - 14.9
□ 9.9 and below

b. 1980

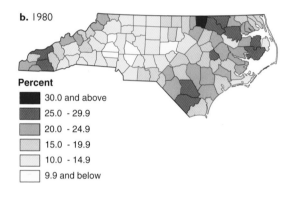

Percent

■ 30.0 and above
■ 25.0 - 29.9
■ 20.0 - 24.9
□ 15.0 - 19.9
□ 10.0 - 14.9
□ 9.9 and below

c. 1990

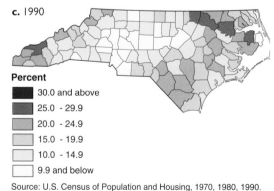

Percent

■ 30.0 and above
■ 25.0 - 29.9
■ 20.0 - 24.9
□ 15.0 - 19.9
□ 10.0 - 14.9
□ 9.9 and below

Source: U.S. Census of Population and Housing, 1970, 1980, 1990.

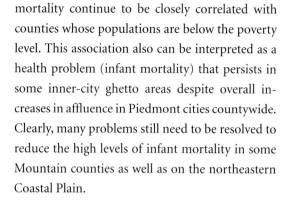

mortality continue to be closely correlated with counties whose populations are below the poverty level. This association also can be interpreted as a health problem (infant mortality) that persists in some inner-city ghetto areas despite overall increases in affluence in Piedmont cities countywide. Clearly, many problems still need to be resolved to reduce the high levels of infant mortality in some Mountain counties as well as on the northeastern Coastal Plain.

HIV/AIDS Epidemic

The dominant public perception of HIV/AIDS in the United States as a problem for persons living deviant, socially unacceptable lifestyles has changed as the epidemic has diffused into the general population. Many people still view HIV/AIDS as an issue only for socially marginalized populations. But the data tell a different story. With the spatial diffusion of HIV/AIDS, the risk of contracting the disease has spread from earlier geographic clusters into virtually all strata of society. In fact, HIV/AIDS has already become a serious problem for the economically deprived. The spread of this dangerous disease illustrates the downside of a society becoming more mobile as well as perhaps more deviant in its behavior.

As the disease has progressed during the past decade, the linkage between HIV/AIDS and poor and socially disadvantaged people has become stronger. The spread of HIV/AIDS into and among disadvantaged populations comes as no surprise to anyone familiar with the geography of disease and health care systems. Disadvantaged populations living in urban ghettos or rural areas of North Carolina have greater medical and health problems and less access to medical services than more affluent segments of the population.

Although the disease, Acquired Immune Deficiency Syndrome (AIDS), entered the United States during the 1970s, it did not start spreading through North Carolina until the mid-to-late 1980s. The diffusion of AIDS within the United States has been well documented. That expansion followed an ascertainable sequence of events. During its early phase, HIV infection was spread by individuals who frequently used international air travel. Clusters of HIV infections and AIDS cases initially appeared within very specific neighborhoods of large cities. Outbreaks of AIDS among homosexual and bisexual males residing in or frequenting these particular neighborhoods of New York, San Francisco, Los Angeles, Miami, and Houston made for spectacular media coverage. Epidemic reconstruction has led to the conclusion that the HIV epidemic had circulated from these urban core nodes much more quickly than had been initially surmised. By the mid-1980s, a major regional core area and secondary diffusion nodes developed in the United States.

Clearly, some of these regional nodes of HIV/AIDS diffusion were more extensive than others.

The largest were contained in New York, San Francisco, and Los Angeles, and they were referred to as "incubator districts." Other regional nodes included an area extending outward from southern Florida to eventually spread into Georgia and South Carolina. As these AIDS core areas expanded, a well-defined fringe and periphery could be identified by the late 1980s. By 1985 North Carolina was still on the periphery of the major AIDS epidemic in the country. In other words, no national AIDS diffusion core area had developed in North Carolina during the 1980s.

The diffusion of HIV/AIDS within North Carolina can be reconstructed by examining cumulative cases reported from 1986 to 1990. The first part of the epidemic, including 1986 and 1987, is referred to as the "infusion stage." During this period, HIV infection and AIDS had become "seeded" in some counties of the state. By the end of 1987, nodal areas for the future proliferation of the disease had been established. The sequence of maps in Figure 17.9 shows this progression. Few cases were reported in 1985, and these appeared to have been somewhat scattered except that most counties with larger cities were represented in the early data. Cumulative HIV/AIDS reporting per 100,000 residents by 1986 indicated geographic patterns that continued for several years. By 1988 some of the state's larger counties—Mecklenburg and Wake, for example—had manifested the formation of certain nodes of diffusion.

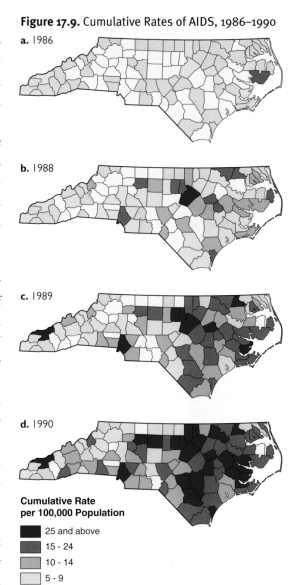

Figure 17.9. Cumulative Rates of AIDS, 1986–1990

a. 1986

b. 1988

c. 1989

d. 1990

Cumulative Rate per 100,000 Population

- 25 and above
- 15 - 24
- 10 - 14
- 5 - 9
- 0.001 - 4
- None reported

Source: N.C. Department of Environment, Health, and Natural Resources, State Center for Health Statistics.

The subsequent period of HIV/AIDS diffusion is referred to here as the "second wave." As depicted in Figure 17.9, this second wave included the continued growth of HIV/AIDS reporting within major metropolitan areas as well as the formation of an HIV/AIDS corridor essentially mirroring the Piedmont Urban Crescent extending from Charlotte to Raleigh. The cumulative AIDS reporting for 1988 reflects this pattern. By 1989 it was clear that another phenomenon had begun to show up: many coastal counties in eastern North Carolina had reported rates that were somewhat higher than counties in the more western parts of the state. By 1990 this pattern became even more pronounced as the heaviest reporting of AIDS cases in the state included not only the previously defined Piedmont Urban Crescent, but many more rural eastern counties as well.

The assumption is made here that during the first several years of the infusion stage of AIDS in North Carolina, the disease was spread primarily by bisexual and homosexual males. Thus, scattered counties, parts of larger cities, and resort areas such as Wilmington and the area around Asheville showed up in early reporting. During the second wave, more and more cases of AIDS could be attributed to needle sharing during HIV–drug abuse as well as to prostitution. The disease subsequently became more and more of a problem in some ghetto portions of the larger cities. Such a sequence of events appears to have taken place in the Charlotte metropolitan area. Mecklenburg County contains the city of Charlotte, where most of the early AIDS cases were located. The disease spread quickly to some poverty pockets in Charlotte as well as to York County, South Carolina, ghetto areas. In many respects, a geographic distance-decay relationship can be identified in Mecklenburg County. This HIV/AIDS decline with distance from Charlotte is similar to that reported in many metropolitan areas of the United States as early as 1989. The pattern seen in the Charlotte area underscores broader aspects of the infectious disease complex in the state.

In North Carolina generally, the second wave of HIV/AIDS diffusion included all of the phenomena identified in Charlotte within the broader context of the entire Piedmont urbanized corridor. The basic difference between North Carolina and some other states, however, was the tremendous diffusion of AIDS into poor rural counties in the eastern part of the state. By 1990, a broad band of eastern rural counties had AIDS rates equal to or in some instances higher than the rates found in the Piedmont. Among them were some of the poorest and most disadvantaged counties in the state, including Bladen, Halifax, and Hertford.

To those familiar with the region, the spread of HIV/AIDS into rural eastern North Carolina was not unexpected—a consequence of traditional economic and social relationships in this largely agricultural area. Historically, the promise of higher-wage jobs and economic opportunities in the urban centers of the Piedmont and the smaller urban areas of the Coastal Plain have attracted the rural poor. Although they lived and worked in cities such as Raleigh, Charlotte, Norfolk, Elizabeth City, or Wilmington, many out-migrants continued to have strong family ties "back home." With relatively short travel distances and an excellent highway system, regular movement between rural and urban areas is easy.

Since the mid-1990s, the annual new case rate for HIV/AIDS has tapered off and the intrastate distribution of the disease has not changed substantially. The AIDS epidemic is by no means over, but it does not appear to be spreading as rapidly as in the past and, indeed, may have leveled off.

Risks of Dying in North Carolina

It is especially useful to use the tools of the epidemiologist in determining probabilities of dying in the counties of North Carolina. Recent information is based on comparisons of "expected" death rates with actual rates that are standardized by race result in the patterns shown in Figure 17.10. These maps show age, race, and gender-specific mortality rates adjusted to 1980 and 1990 "standard" populations for the entire state and help determine overall health conditions. They indicate where death rates vary from what would be expected after

Figure 17.10. Risk of Dying

a. White

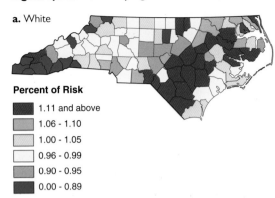

Percent of Risk

- 1.11 and above
- 1.06 - 1.10
- 1.00 - 1.05
- 0.96 - 0.99
- 0.90 - 0.95
- 0.00 - 0.89

b. Nonwhite

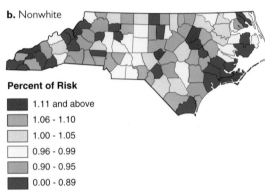

Percent of Risk

- 1.11 and above
- 1.06 - 1.10
- 1.00 - 1.05
- 0.96 - 0.99
- 0.90 - 0.95
- 0.00 - 0.89

Note: Values of less than 1.0 indicate a lower-than-projected chance of dying. Values above 1.0 indicate a higher-than-expected chance of dying.

Source: N.C. Department of Environment, Health, and Natural Resources, State Center for Health Statistics, 1997.

taking age, race, and gender into account. Values greater than 1.0 indicate a higher-than-expected rate of dying. Values of less than 1.0 indicate a lower-than-expected rate of dying.

The most pronounced pattern of higher-than-expected rates of dying is displayed by the white population in eastern North Carolina (Fig. 17.10a). This is also the part of the state that has fewer-than-average numbers of hospitals and physicians. Conversely, counties that have higher-than-average health care resources generally show a lower-than-expected risk of dying.

The risk-of-dying pattern is less variable in the state's nonwhite population, but some clusters are familiar (Fig. 17.10b). In some of the lowest-income counties of the Coastal Plain, for example, the nonwhite population has a higher-than-average risk of dying. Yet in parts of the Charlotte area, including Mecklenburg, Cabarrus, and Gaston Counties, the nonwhite population has a higher-than-average risk of dying despite the region's relative wealth of health care facilities.

As with the distribution of health care resources, there is a dual pattern of risk of dying in North Carolina. The strong east-west contrast that dominates health care conditions in general is clear. The lower risk for whites in metropolitan areas and their higher risk in the more rural east correspond with the distribution of physicians and hospitals, as well as with economic conditions. The urban-rural contrast is different for nonwhites, with many groups demonstrating a higher risk of dying regardless of the distribution of health care resources and programs that provide medical care to the indigent. In these cases, it seems that poorer socioeconomic conditions for this population segment are more decisive than proximity to health care resources. Future changes in the Medicaid program may help these people, but many of them are ineligible for funds under current guidelines. In any event, it will take decades to reverse general health conditions in a population that has a long history of relatively poor health and health care.

The Managed Care Phenomenon

Managed care, especially that provided by Health Maintenance Organizations, is a phenomenon with a long history but a relatively short existence in terms of widespread use. About half of the states, including North Carolina, now have legislation pertaining to managed care. A little over 15 percent of North Carolina's population is enrolled in HMOs. In December 1997 the North Carolina Department of Insurance reported that eighteen full service HMOs were operating in the state, with a total enrollment of over 1.1 million people. Consistent with the trend toward consolidating health care administration in the larger metro areas, nine of these HMOs were headquartered in Charlotte, six in the Raleigh-Durham area, and three in the Triad.

Regional coverage by HMOs varies, and in some instances plans are part of larger, nationally based insurance coverage. Whereas some HMOs have opted to own, locate, and operate their own group practices, others have followed more traditional insurance plans with physicians already in practice. Some HMOs are owned by physician investment groups and local health authorities.

It is too soon to determine the impact of HMOs on the general health status of the population. In North Carolina, oversight is the domain of the commissioner of the Department of Insurance. As a result, public health authorities do not maintain patient treatment records. At this juncture, the best aspect of HMOs appears to be in such areas of health promotion as smoking cessation, diet, and healthier lifestyles generally.

Outlook

When it comes to personal health, the state's more affluent residents have an obvious advantage. Not only are they more healthy, but also most of them live in and around cities where increasing concentrations of health care resources are found. Poor inner-city residents and those living in many rural areas have experienced real improvements in health care, but it appears that the gap between the health of the affluent and the poor will continue to be a chronic problem.

This gap may widen in the future, especially in remote Mountain and eastern counties. It could be alleviated somewhat by the expansion of information technologies to assist rural physicians and smaller hospitals in staying abreast of advancing knowledge, but the related development of expensive medical technologies will likely reinforce the concentration of more specialized treatment centers in urban centers and teaching hospitals associated with medical schools. As a result, North Carolinians will have access to increasingly more effective health care if they can afford it and can access the major treatment centers.

Selected References

Meade, M. "Landscape and Disease in the Carolinas." In *Snapshots of the Carolinas: Landscapes and Culture*, edited by G. Gordon Bennette, pp. 135–40. Washington, D.C.: Association of American Geographers, 1996.

Pyle, G. "AIDS Comes to the Carolinas—And Stays." In *Snapshots of the Carolinas*, pp. 141–48.

Pyle, G., and O. Furuseth. "The Diffusion of AIDS and Social Deprivation in North Carolina." *North Carolina Geographer* 1 (Summer 1993): 1–10.

Shannon, G., and G. Pyle. *Atlas of Disease and Health Care in the United States.* New York: MacMillan, 1993.

Shannon, G., G. Pyle, and R. Bashshur. *The Geography of AIDS.* New York: Guilford Press, 1991.

State Center for Health Statistics. Division of Health Services. Vital Statistics. *North Carolina Vital Statistics.* Raleigh: Division of Health Services, 1997.

18. CULTURAL ARTS AND HISTORIC PRESERVATION

Jack Claiborne

Interest in both the cultural arts and historic preservation has grown at an explosive pace. Between 1967 and 1997 the number of state and local arts establishments rose from 242 to 2,224. Among them were 106 arts councils, 331 artist organizations, 83 arts service organizations, 52 literary magazines, 108 dance companies, 525 music groups, 142 arts centers, 292 arts festivals or concert series, 13 arts publications, 5 cinemas, 256 galleries and museums, and 311 theater groups.

In the same period, the state's catalog of identified historic properties grew from a few dozen to more than 35,000, including 2,000 listings on the National Register of Historic Places. Among the 35,000 properties were Indian sites, shipwrecks, log houses, homes of ordinary farmers and townspeople, and mansions of wealthy planters, merchants, and industrialists; a wide variety of churches, courthouses, schools, and other public buildings; and an increasing number of mills and industrial sites, transportation facilities, and commercial buildings.

In both the arts and historic preservation, the stimulus for such growth was the onset of federal funding in the late 1960s. Almost overnight limited, elitist movements were democratized into popular enterprises. The arts moved beyond the museums, symphony halls, and opera houses of the socially prominent and into public parks, abandoned storefronts, and neighborhood centers to serve ordinary citizens as well. To the restoration of homes of the rich and famous were added the preservation of cotton mills, mill villages, fire houses, and other places that represented the lives of working people.

In that change came a redefinition of what is art and what is history. What many citizens had earlier dismissed as social frills began to be recognized as economic assets. Art and history were increasingly seen as tourist attractions, tools for downtown revitalization, complements to urban or rural development, instruments of neighborhood restoration, and enrichments to education.

With federal assistance also came a dramatic increase in state, local, and private support. A dollar of federal aid was often matched many times over by state and local governments and by private foundations and corporations. In her tenure as director of the National Endowment for the Arts (NEA), Jane Alexander estimated that every federal dollar spent on the arts stimulated an investment of eleven dollars from other sources.

In North Carolina, that ratio might have been higher. As the U.S. Congress withdrew support for the arts in the 1980s and 1990s, the North Carolina General Assembly increased its arts funding. Legislative support for state arts agencies grew from $10.1 million in 1991 to $14.1 in 1996. In that period, the legislature's direct grants to local arts groups grew from $48,500 to $3 million. At the same time, public and private funding also expanded.

Yet in the second half of the 1990s, all was not well. Controversies at federal, state, and local levels clouded the outlook. Federal support had been sharply diminished. State funding was increasingly being questioned by taxpayers and threatened by tax-cutting legislators. Local support was endangered by rising competition from other demands on the public purse.

In response, some national and state lawmakers sought to replace government grants with private incentives. Between 1976 and 1995 a federal tax credit for expenditures made to restore historic properties created a total investment of $319 million. In 1997 the North Carolina legislature voted unanimously to expand that tax credit program, allowing state tax write-offs of up to 30 percent of the cost of improving both commercial and non-commercial historic properties. Faced with growing controversies over what is art and what art is in the public interest, members of Congress and state legislators began discussing similar tax credits to support the arts.

Beyond maintaining their financial bases, historic preservation and the arts also faced sensitive cultural issues. In response to a population that was growing more and more diverse, they explored ways to broaden their programs to appeal to Native Americans, African Americans, and a rising population of Hispanics and Asians whose history in the United States and whose concepts of art might be considerably different from those of people in the cultural and political mainstream. The definition of art and history appeared to be open to further debate and revision.

History of the Cultural Arts

As the twentieth century dawned, North Carolina had a rich history to preserve but relatively little to celebrate in the cultural arts. Widespread poverty, illiteracy, and isolation had left much of the citizenry untutored in literature, music, drama, painting, sculpture, or dance. There were opera houses and concert halls in many cities but few artists to perform in them except those on regional or national tours.

Even before H. L. Mencken seared southern sensitivities by condemning the region as the "Sahara of the Bozart," a departing native son had looked back at North Carolina and pronounced it "the laughingstock among the States." The native was Walter Hines Page of Cary. In going to New York in 1886 to launch his career as a distinguished editor and commentator on American culture, he wrote a shocking letter to his former newspaper in Raleigh comparing North Carolina's leaders to

Egyptian mummies and dismissing North Carolina writers, editors, and thinkers as intellectually cowed and artistically barren. If his purpose was to shame the state into remedial action, Page succeeded. The immediate object of his scolding was the General Assembly, which had just defeated a bill to create a land-grant college to teach the agricultural and mechanical arts. At its next meeting two years later the legislature established the institution that is now North Carolina State University.

When published in the *State Chronicle* at Raleigh, Page's letter stirred outrage. But among those who privately cheered it was Charles B. Aycock, of Goldsboro, a young lawyer and editor who wrote Page that "fully three fourths of the people are with you" in the effort to motivate the state. Aycock was elected governor in 1900 and launched a vigorous campaign for public schools and universal education. From the inauguration of Aycock in 1901 until the Great Depression, North Carolina made significant progress, not only in industrialization, education, and the establishment of libraries, but also in the arts. In those years Walter Hines Page achieved international prominence, as did William Sidney Porter, of Greensboro, writing under the name "O. Henry." Charles W. Chesnutt of Fayetteville became the first African American writer of fiction to gain national attention. Many of his stories were based on his experiences in North Carolina.

Other famous writers of the period included Thomas Dixon of Shelby, author of *The Clansman*, a novel that became the movie *Birth of a Nation*. Wilbur Daniel Steele of Greensboro began his prolific writing career in that period. Francis Fisher Tiernan of Salisbury published eleven of the forty-two books she wrote under the name "Christian Reid." She is best known for a novel about mountain life entitled *Land of the Sky*, which gave the highlands around Asheville their picturesque name.

Another chronicler of mountain life was Olive Tilford Dargan, a transplanted Kentuckian who made her home in Swain County and wrote plays, poems, and short stories under the name "Fielding Burke." Among the state's celebrated poets were John Henry Bonner of Salem and John Charles McNeill

of Laurinburg. A flourishing crafts tradition led to the founding of the Penland School of Crafts at Spruce Pine.

Despite the depression—indeed, perhaps because of it—the 1930s and 1940s saw an unprecedented outpouring of North Carolina's contributions to the arts, including the novels of Thomas Wolfe of Asheville, the essays of Gerald W. Johnson of Greensboro, Wilbur J. Cash's celebrated critique, *The Mind of the South*, and the novels and short stories of transplanted Mississippian James Street of Chapel Hill and of North Carolina native Frances Gray Patton of Durham. Between 1935 and 1938 the federal Works Progress Administration (WPA) paid artists to paint murals in public buildings, perform and compose music for concerts, write and perform dramas, record folklore, preserve recollections of senior citizens, and write local histories and guidebooks for the state.

In the second half of the twentieth century, North Carolina built upon depression-era tradition by producing a wealth of nationally and internationally renowned poets, writers, novelists, and commentators, many of whom were associated with the colleges and universities where they taught writing and criticism. Their names included A. R. Ammons, Maya Angelou, Doris Betts, Fred Chappell, Orson Scott Card, Patricia Cornwell, Tony Earley, Clyde Edgerton, John Ehle, Charles Frazier, Kaye Gibbons, Allan Gurganus, Randall Kenan, Charles Kuralt, Jill McCorkle, Tim McLaurin, Robert Morgan, Reynolds Price, Lee Smith, Tom Wicker, and many more.

Though it rarely published poetry or fiction, the University of North Carolina (UNC) Press encouraged the development of literary talent by publishing informed commentaries on national, southern, and state history, culture, and social conditions, all of which fed the imaginations of rising generations of writers. Its publications also helped create a market for books that fostered the establishment of other printing ventures, such as the Algonquin Press in Chapel Hill, John F. Blair in Winston-Salem, Heritage Printers in Charlotte, and other specialty printing and publishing companies.

Writers and literary commentators also had their imaginations stirred by

A Literary Renaissance

In the thirties, when Richard Walser was a graduate student at UNC Chapel Hill, he wanted to write his dissertation on North Carolina literature, but a professor discouraged him on the ground that "there isn't any."

Walser went on to make his academic career for the next fifty years in that very subject at North Carolina State University in Raleigh. His Literary North Carolina (North Carolina Department of Cultural Resources, 1986) remains the place to start for readers who want to trace literary development from explorers like John Lawson and Thomas Hariot through a giant like Thomas Wolfe and on to contemporary writers with national reputations like Lee Smith, Clyde Edgerton, Charles Frazier, Fred Chappell, Reynolds Price, Kaye Gibbons, and many others who were leading the North Carolina renaissance by the end of the century.

By 1998 the North Carolina Writers Network, established by Marsha Warren on a shoestring and then led by Linda Hobson, had a membership of over 1,700 published or aspiring writers, with biannual conferences and a newsletter. The North Carolina Writers Conference, established by popular historical novelist Inglis Fletcher, continued to function but on a small scale. In a few decades, too, the North Carolina Poetry Society had climbed from two dozen to more than 300 members.

Graduate and undergraduate creative writing programs in many of the state's colleges have helped nourish this explosion of new talent. Writing teachers such as William Blackburn (Duke), Jessie Rehder and Max Steele (UNC Chapel Hill), and John Foster West (Appalachian) have sent forth a younger generation of writer-teachers (Marianne Gingher, Chappell, Price) with graduate programs in writing established at UNC Greensboro, UNC Wilmington, North Carolina State University, and Warren Wilson College and lively writers' groups operating in most of the state's counties and encouraged by local arts councils.

Not only are prizes awarded annually for outstanding North Carolina books (the Sir Walter Raleigh Award, the Rowan-Chowan Poetry Award, the Parker Award, etc.), but the state is unusual in that its governor and legislature also present a North Carolina Medal in Literature, Fine Arts, and other fields to honor lifelong achievement.

At Weymouth in Southern Pines, the North Carolina Literary Hall of Fame recognizes a tradition of writers while simultaneously honoring the former Weymouth owner, the late novelist James Boyd. Residencies are offered on-site for developing writers.

The North Carolina Literary Review, published at East Carolina University, the North Carolina Historical Review, Brightleaf (a private literary magazine published in Durham), a host of high school and campus literary magazines, and a growing number of independent small presses and literary quarterlies offer opportunities for publication and recognition. The North Carolina Collection at Wilson Library, UNC Chapel Hill, collects many manuscripts and reviews of North Carolina books. Among the most successful of regional publishers has been Algonquin Press, in Carrboro, founded by Louis Rubin with Shannon Ravenel as editor, which has introduced such writers as Jill McCorkle to a national audience.

Interesting, too, is the strong interaction of the state's writers with other artists and educators. Whether in Poets-in-the-Schools Programs, in recording their work for the state's library for the blind, writing about art works for the North Carolina Art Museum's popular Store of Joys volume, gathering for the 1998 North Carolina Literary Festival in Chapel Hill where 100 writers read, or interacting with Friends of the Library groups in many counties, Tar Heel writers have a vivid public life reading for lively audiences.

These growing audiences have, especially during the 1990s, attracted large national bookstore chains to the already strong independent bookstores scattered across the state.

Doris Betts, Alumni Distinguished Professor of English, University of North Carolina at Chapel Hill, and novelist

the presence of major libraries and literary collections in the state, including the State Archives in Raleigh, the Wilson Library at Chapel Hill, the Perkins Library at Duke, and their various manuscript collections, including the Southern Historical Collection and the North Carolina Collection at Chapel Hill.

The same impetus that writers felt was apparent among other artists and cultural groups. It was in the depths of the depression that Charlotteans salvaged the century-old building that had housed the U.S. Mint, moved it to a new site, and, with help from the Works Progress Administration, rebuilt it as the Mint Museum of Art, one of the first local art museums in the state. It was also in the depths of the depression that private interests established the North Carolina Symphony, which in 1943, when the state began to contribute to its funding, became the nation's first state-supported symphony orchestra.

In 1936 friends of music founded the privately financed Brevard Music Center, which has trained generations of young musicians. A year later, with the depression still hanging on, playwright Paul Green's symphonic drama *The Lost Colony* opened at a specially built theater on Roanoke Island, reenacting English efforts to plant a colony in America. It still draws crowds of spectators to its annual summer productions at the theater in Manteo. In the process, the *Lost Colony* created a new genre of theater, the outdoor drama, that has since been emulated in many other parts of the state and nation, including ten other such productions in North Carolina (Fig. 18.1). Collectively, the state's outdoor dramas generated over $71 million in tourist expenditures in 1995.

In 1947 North Carolina became the first state to fund a public art collection, now the North Carolina Museum of Art. In 1949 it became the first state to have a local arts council, one privately organized by citizens of Winston-Salem. The Winston-Salem example prompted residents of other cities—Charlotte, Greensboro, High Point, and Raleigh—to take similar action.

Throughout the 1930s and 1940s North Carolina produced musicians for national orchestras, painters for state and national galleries, soloists for opera companies, actors and actresses for motion pictures, writers for national magazines, syndicated columnists for newspapers, performers and commentators for radio networks, composers and arrangers for jazz bands, and banjo pickers, guitarists, and falsetto singers for a new, indigenous genre of music called "bluegrass." It also turned out regionally and nationally admired weavers, woodworkers, quilters, potters, and other native artisans for fairs and exhibitions across the South and the country.

But the real burgeoning of art in North Carolina began in the 1960s. In 1963, at the urging of Governor Terry Sanford, the General Assembly created

Figure 18.1. Outdoor Dramas and Major Craft Festivals

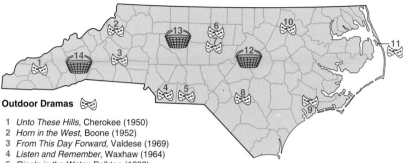

Outdoor Dramas

1 *Unto These Hills*, Cherokee (1950)
2 *Horn in the West*, Boone (1952)
3 *From This Day Forward*, Valdese (1969)
4 *Listen and Remember*, Waxhaw (1964)
5 *Ripple in the Water*, Polkton (1993)
6 *Sword of Peace*, Snow Camp (1973)
7 *Pathway to Freedom*, Snow Camp (1993)
8 *Micajah*, Autryville (1980)
9 *Worthy Is the Lamb*, Swansboro (1987)
10 *First for Freedom*, Halifax (1976)
11 *The Lost Colony*, Manteo (1937)

Craft Festivals

12 Carolina Designer Craftsmen, Raleigh
13 Piedmont Craftsmen, Winston-Salem
14 Southern Highland Handicraft Guild, Asheville

Source: N.C. Arts Council, 1997.

the North Carolina School of the Arts, the nation's first state-supported, residential college for the performing arts. A year later, in an executive order, Sanford positioned the state to make rapid progress in democratizing the arts by organizing the first state Arts Council in the country. Later the legislature converted the Arts Council into a statutory body with cabinet rank.

As those developments were taking root at the state level, President Lyndon Johnson was urging Congress to create the National Endowment for the Arts, an agency to counterbalance the National Science Foundation. With the endowment came federal funding to both the state Arts Council and a proliferation of local arts groups (Fig. 18.2). Almost overnight, arts councils were formed in ninety of the state's one hundred counties (some counties had more than one). From 242 arts groups of all kinds in 1967, the state's arts community expanded to more than 2,200 by 1997.

Factors other than money contributed to that growth. Public officials dis-

Figure 18.2. NEA Grants in North Carolina, 1980–1995

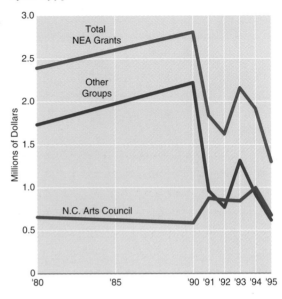

Note: Data were not provided for the years between 1980 and 1990.

Source: National Endowment for the Arts.

covered that art had more than aesthetic value. By the mid-1960s the urban flight to the suburbs had depopulated downtowns in most of the state's largest cities, leaving empty storefronts, vacant churches, and darkened movie houses. Revitalization efforts and many historic preservation projects encouraged arts groups to move into those spaces and stimulate new activity in the inner city. The same thing happened in middle-sized and small towns, where new highways changed traffic patterns and diverted customers from central business districts. In many communities, industries moved to new locations, leaving abandoned mill villages to be salvaged by arts groups. Expanding communication systems, especially television and the advertising industry, made the arts more utilitarian.

Suddenly, exposure to the arts, once limited to the privileged, was available to ordinary citizens, rich or poor, rural or urban. People who in earlier generations might never have known anyone who made a living as an artist had an opportunity to know artists on a first-name basis. The museums, symphony orchestras, and opera companies remained, but they were tailoring their programs to appeal to wider audiences. The arts community was expanding to include many more participants: actors, poets, folk singers, jazz musicians, mimes, painters, dancers, sculptors, silk-screeners, choral groups, cloggers, and steel-drum bands. In 1995 more than 10 million people participated in one or more North Carolina arts programs.

The federal money, the proliferation of arts groups, the rising numbers of artists and arts consumers—and a grudging recognition that the arts have economic value—strengthened support for the arts among state legislators, county commissioners, city council members, leaders of private foundations, and executives in corporate suites. The federal assistance was not lavish. The peak of federal aid came in the early 1990s, when grants to the North Carolina Arts Council climbed to $883,000. But each federal dollar generated additional spending at state, county, and city levels.

Woodworker John Hillyer

In the first five years of the 1990s, local governments doubled their support of the arts. The North Carolina General Assembly increased its aid by 38 percent.

In 1996, when the Arts Council received $794,000 in federal assistance, its appropriation from the state legislature was $5.4 million, making North Carolina the twenty-third most generous

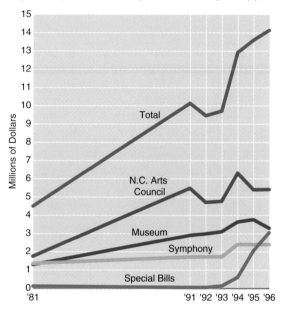

Figure 18.3. State Funding for the Arts, 1980–1996

Millions of Dollars

Total

N.C. Arts Council

Museum

Symphony

Special Bills

'81 '91 '92 '93 '94 '95 '96

Note: Data were not provided for the years between 1981 and 1991.

Source: N.C. Department of Cultural Resources.

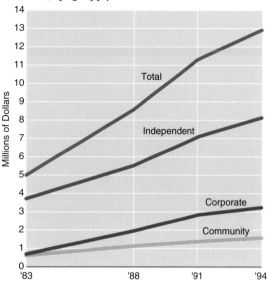

Figure 18.4. Private Foundations Giving to the Arts, 1983–1994

Millions of Dollars

Total

Independent

Corporate

Community

'83 '88 '91 '94

Note: Data were not provided for the years between 1981 and 1991.

Source: N.C. Department of Cultural Resources.

patron of the arts among the fifty states. But the $5.4 million represented only 38 percent of the legislature's total spending for the arts. An additional $3.3 million went to the North Carolina Museum of Art, $2.4 million to the North Carolina Symphony, and $3 million to local arts groups by way of direct appropriations (Fig. 18.3).

In addition, North Carolina arts groups received money from local arts councils that functioned not only as promoters of the arts and clearinghouses for arts events but also as fund-raising agencies, much like United Way organizations. In

1994 funds raised in local drives across the state totaled $6.4 million. The 1998 campaign by the Arts and Science Council of Charlotte and Mecklenburg County reaped $6.5 million—the fourth-highest total raised in the country. Campaigns by similar councils in Winston-Salem and Raleigh also were in the top twenty-five nationally.

About 56 percent of the money raised by local arts councils and fund drives came from corporations and foundations. Individuals contributed another 42 percent. As well as giving to local arts fund-raisers, corporations and other enterprises

often made direct contributions to local arts groups. So did 290 of North Carolina's 750 private foundations. In 1994 gifts to the arts from private foundations amounted to $12.9 million, up 14 percent from 1991 (Fig. 18.4).

Though the arts in North Carolina are a bigger business than they have ever been in the past, they are not rolling in money, nor are they free of political threat. Stimulating the eyes, ears, and minds of 10 million arts patrons is an expensive undertaking—and fraught with potential controversy. A state public arts program calling for the investment in art of one-half of 1 percent of the construction cost of a new or renovated building was killed after seven years because of a dispute over what constitutes art. Some taxpayers dismissed the proposed art as graffiti or junk. The program died before many construction projects were completed or art purchased.

One problem is that contemporary art is no longer simply beautiful; often it is meaningful as well. And art no longer confines itself to one medium; frequently it is a mixture of several media, which may confuse or annoy critics. More significant, art is also political. When artists are most true to their craft, their work makes statements about life as seen by the artists. When those statements offend many members of the public and provoke controversy, they can endanger state and local financing.

To continue public support in an increasingly multicultural society, the arts face the challenge of further expanding their activities to include all elements of society—old and young, white and black, urban and rural, native-born and foreign, male and female, straight and gay—while at the same time retaining the firm support of the political mainstream. That promises to create opportunities for even greater criticism. But it is the kind of art and public dialogue that would make Walter Hines Page proud of his home state.

Historic Preservation

In October 1939, in the well of the North Carolina House of Representatives in the old capitol at Raleigh, tall, distinguished Archibald Henderson, a mathematics professor at UNC Chapel Hill and an associate of Albert Einstein and George Bernard Shaw, summoned all his erudition in imploring other North Carolinians to join him in forming a private agency to preserve the state's historic landmarks. To underscore the need for such an organization, he quoted a former governor's estimate of the number of historic shrines that remained standing in the state. "There ain't any," the governor had said.

Henderson and members of the North Carolina Garden Club knew better. They had just surveyed the entire state to identify places of historic and architectural significance for a book, *Old Homes and Gardens in North Carolina*, published later that year by the UNC Press. The book contained photos of 450 structures worthy of preservation, including remnants of the Tryon Palace in New Bern. Even so, the former governor's flinty assessment probably reflected prevailing public opinion.

As the site of the first English colony in America, the scene of crucial battles in the American Revolution and the Civil War, and the birthplace of two, maybe three, American presidents, North Carolina was an old state with a rich history. Yet it lagged behind New England, Virginia, and South Carolina in promoting its heritage. The voluntary preservation group that Henderson advocated was modeled after similar bodies in New England and Virginia. Like theirs, it was to be called "The Society for the Preservation of Antiquities."

The society was organized as Henderson had suggested and was active for about thirty-five years. Its good works are chronicled in *A Lasting Gift of Heritage* by David L. S. Brook, administrator of the North Carolina Historic Preservation Office. The book also traces the efforts of historic preservation movements in the United States and North Carolina. In both jurisdictions, preserving history has had an uphill climb.

Among the U.S. preservation movement's earliest expressions was an 1813 petition by Philadelphians to prevent the destruction of Independence Hall. In 1858 a group of women led by South Carolinian Ann Pamela Cunningham saved George Washington's home at Mount Vernon from being demolished to make room for a hotel. The success at Mount Vernon led to the organization of the Virginia Antiquities Association in 1889 and subsequently the preservation of Jefferson's Monticello, Robert E. Lee's birthplace at Stratford, John Marshall's home at Richmond, and the site of Jamestown.

But it was not until 1924 and the commitment of John D. Rockefeller Jr. to restore colonial Williamsburg that preservation stirred the national imagination. The Williamsburg project led to passage of the National Historic Sites Act of 1935, making historic preservation a federal policy and empowering the secretary of the interior to preserve historic properties of national significance.

The Williamsburg project also introduced a new idea. In preserving an entire community, it saved not only the homes of the wealthy, but also those of working people to give visitors a sense of how all Americans once lived. In the 1930s and 1940s the Williamsburg example was emulated in the restoration of Deerfield Village in Massachusetts and Henry Ford's Greenfield in Michigan and at Old Salem in North Carolina, beginning in 1948.

The earliest preservation efforts in North Carolina were limited to erecting monuments, preserving cemeteries, and collecting and publishing colonial and state records, the latter of which proved a great benefit to future historians. In 1896, the same year that the first ten volumes of North Carolina's colonial records were published, a private group purchased Fort Raleigh, the site of the first English settlement in America, and gave it to the state. But North

Wilmington's Thalian Hall

By the mid-nineteenth century, Wilmington was secure in its cultural and economic preeminence in North Carolina. The development and expansion of the port, the railroad, and river trade built on the Lower Cape Fear area's historical significance, and Wilmington enjoyed a midcentury population boom. Wilmington's educated and moneyed elite fostered a cultured society like that in other southern port cities. Scions of wealthy Wilmington families received classical educations and toured Europe. At home, they formed literary and philosophical societies and entertained themselves with amateur dramatic and musical productions. Many gentlemen (women did not participate in such activities) belonged to the Wilmington Thalia Association, the most famous of the amateur theater societies that sprang up throughout North Carolina from the late eighteenth century until the Civil War. Named after the Greek muse of comedy, Thalia, the society presented educational and inspirational plays. The Thalians wanted a new theater for their productions, and the city sought to build a civic hall and opera house. A partnership between the city and the Thalians was formed in the early 1850s to construct and furnish such a structure.

On Tuesday, October 12, 1858, the combination City Hall and Opera House (later named Thalian Hall) opened. Its architect was John Trimble, the premier architect of the day. Thalian Hall was one of more than forty theaters and concert halls throughout the country designed by Trimble, and it is the last surviving example of his work in the United States. The theater was a model of modern theater construction. It seated an audience of 950, was lit by 188 gas burners, and featured state-of-the art special effects equipment. Most notable among these is a "thunder roll"—a long wooden trough in which small cannon balls rumble along to replicate the sound of thunder. It is the only one of its kind still in existence in the country and is still used on occasion. The original stage curtain was painted by Philadelphia artist Russell Smith with classical scenes, and the lower half hangs in the lobby. The theater remained popular until the early twentieth century, when the advent of movies hastened the demise of professional touring companies.

Thalian Hall continued to offer a stage to community theater and important classical musicians, but the city's financial difficulties during the depression meant that little money was available to maintain the building. It slipped into neglect, despite a grant from the WPA in 1938, until fire in 1973 almost destroyed it completely. Realizing how close the community had come to losing a cherished landmark, citizens acted quickly to repair and restore Thalian Hall. In 1975 the theater was reopened, the fire damage repaired, and the auditorium restored to its former splendor.

The 1970s also saw the burgeoning of the Wilmington arts community, as well as increasing activity in restoring the historic district. In the 1980s nearly $5 million was raised to complete the restoration and expansion of the theater and municipal offices. In 1990 Thalian Hall once again took its place as the cultural center of Wilmington. Within its walls the city still conducts its business, and professional and amateur theater has a home, much as its builders envisioned nearly a century and a half ago.

Sarah Park Rankin, former Wilmington resident and student of historic preservation

---

Carolina did little with it and ultimately passed it on to the U.S. Park Service, which developed it as a national historic site.

In the fall of 1900, a group of concerned citizens formed a Literary and Historical Association to stimulate public interest in state history and literature. In 1903 that association encouraged the legislature to establish the North Carolina Historical Commission, only the third state historical agency in the nation. The commission was assigned to collect and maintain records and documents related to state history. Four years later its mission was expanded to include "the preservation of battlefields, houses, and other places celebrated in the history of the state." In time, the commission became the North Carolina Division of Archives and History, now the state's lead agency for historic preservation.

The 1903 legislature also appropriated money for the preservation of Revolutionary War battlefields at Moores Creek Bridge and the Guilford Courthouse. In 1909 it added the Alamance Battleground to that list. Appropriation for all three projects totaled $103,000, about $1.5 million in contemporary dollars.

Subsequent legislatures assisted groups like the Daughters of the American Revolution and the

Colonial Dames in preserving structures such as Constitution House in Halifax, the Joel Lane House in Raleigh, the Lincolnton Academy in Lincolnton, and Buck Spring, the Warrenton home of Nathaniel Macon, an early speaker of the U.S. House of Representatives.

During the depression of the 1930s, the federal Works Progress Administration put historians to work cataloging state archives and courthouse records as well as restoring historic landmarks such as the John Wright Stanly House in New Bern. But as the North Carolina Garden Club survey cited by Archibald Henderson showed, many of North Carolina's most valuable historic places were falling into ruin. It was about their urgent need for restoration that Henderson spoke.

The North Carolina Society for the Preservation of Antiquities, composed largely of the wealthy and privileged, had ambitious plans, but the outbreak of World War II diverted public attention and dashed hopes for more WPA-styled public works funding. After the war the society, abandoning hopes of buying and restoring major properties, narrowed its focus and created a revolving fund for assisting local projects. It was that revolving fund that in 1976 fueled the establishment of the Historic Preservation Foundation of North Carolina, Inc., the first statewide revolving fund in the nation.

The foundation's success since then is measured in big numbers. Operating as Preservation North Carolina, it has restored more than 275 properties representing a private investment of more than $70 million. Its voice was influential in persuading the 1997 legislature to expand the state program of tax credits for restoring historic properties.

Beginning in the 1920s, the General Assembly created special commissions to oversee specific historic sites. The first site, in 1923, was the Bennett Place in Durham, where General Joseph Johnston surrendered to General William Sherman, ending the Civil War. Others included the birthplace of Civil War governor Zebulon B. Vance at Weaverville, funded in 1943; Tryon Palace in New Bern, funded in 1945; and the birthplace of Charles B. Aycock in Wayne County, funded in 1949.

Meanwhile, through the North Carolina Division of Archives and History and its predecessor agencies, state taxpayers were increasingly involved in the preservation of other elements of state and local history. In 1914 the state established the Hall of History, now the Museum of History. In 1915 it began collecting and cataloging county records. In 1924 it launched the quarterly *North Carolina Historical Review*, and in 1935 it began a state highway marker program. It also assisted preservation efforts by private agencies.

A more direct state intervention in historic preservation began in 1953, when the legislature created a Historic Sites Commission to establish criteria for state aid to historic and archaeological properties. Two years later the legislature created a historic sites office within Archives and History and gave it authority over seven properties, including the Bennett Place and the three others listed above, previously operated by the Department of Conservation and Development.

In 1964 Archives and History called for a statewide survey of historic sites to serve as a guide to future programs. A 1967 grant from the Smith Reynolds Foundation in Greensboro helped get the survey under way. But it was congressional enactment of the National Historic Preservation Act of 1966 that brought federal funding and put the North Carolina Division of Archives and History into historic preservation in a big way. Federal assistance began in 1969 with a grant of $4,181, but by 1980 its annual support had reached a high of $1.6 million. It has since stabilized at about $450,000 a year.

Federal funding encouraged a statewide survey of historic properties (Fig. 18.5) and stimulated the establishment of 18 local commissions for preserving historic landmarks, 24 local commissions for preserving historic districts, and 31 local commissions for overseeing both landmarks and districts (Fig. 18.6). Each commission was supported by public and private grants. Expenditures for restoring and preserving historic properties ran into the hundreds of millions of dollars.

The National Historic Preservation Act created a partnership with the states to identify and preserve properties significant to national, state, and lo-

Figure 18.5. Architectural Survey Status, 1997

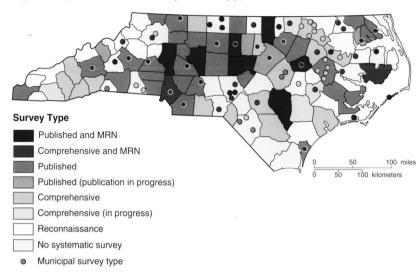

Survey Type

- Published and MRN
- Comprehensive and MRN
- Published
- Published (publication in progress)
- Comprehensive
- Comprehensive (in progress)
- Reconnaissance
- No systematic survey
- ● Municipal survey type

Note: MRN = Major Nomination Work.

Source: N.C. State Historic Preservation Office, Surveying and Planning Branch.

Figure 18.6. Local Governments with Landmark, District, or Preservation Commissions

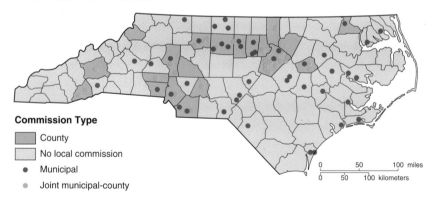

Commission Type

- County
- No local commission
- ● Municipal
- ● Joint municipal-county

Source: N.C. State Historic Preservation Office, Survey and Planning Branch, 1997.

cal history. It also encouraged preservation by local governments and private interests. In carrying out its purposes, it established the National Register of Historic Places.

Federal assistance enabled Archives and History to accelerate its county-by-county survey. By 1997 it had completed research in two-thirds of the one hundred counties and had surveys under way in twenty-one others (Fig. 18.5). A dozen counties, mostly in remote areas, had yet to be studied. As a result of that research, 2,000 sites had been listed on the National Register. Figure 18.7 locates some of the major historic sites in the state. On those 2,000 sites were situated more than 35,000 individual structures. So much for the "there ain't any" estimate of Archibald Henderson's former governor!

In addition, federal grants-in-aid permitted the establishment of seventy-three local historic landmarks commissions. Each commission is locally supported, usually by a city or county government, and often receives additional support from private foundations or corporations. One exemplary commission was established in an unlikely locale, Charlotte and Mecklenburg County, where economic development had wiped out many historic structures. By 1997 the area's Historic Landmarks Commission had identified, researched, and designated 213 historic properties, twice as many as any other county. Further, with the approval of voters and the Board of County Commissioners, the landmarks commission maintained a $1.5 million revolving fund, the largest of any landmarks commission in the state, with which to buy and resell endangered properties.

The Mecklenburg landmarks commission's greatest success, however, might have been in finding, restoring, and operating vintage trolleys in a project so popular that over time it persuaded city and corporate leaders to restore trolley service through the midtown area, connecting the Charlotte Convention Center to a historic district south of midtown and to an arts community to the north.

In addition to those public agencies, numerous private historic preservation groups are operating in the state, building public awareness of history

Figure 18.7. Major Historic Sites

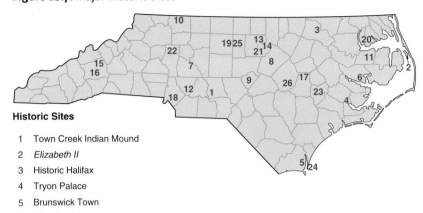

Historic Sites

1   Town Creek Indian Mound
2   *Elizabeth II*
3   Historic Halifax
4   Tryon Palace
5   Brunswick Town
6   Historic Bath
7   North Carolina Transportation Museum
8   North Carolina State Capitol
9   House in the Horseshoe
10   Horne Creek Living History Farm
11   Somerset Place
12   Reed Gold Mine
13   Stagville Preservation Center
14   Duke Homestead
15   Zebulon B. Vance Birthplace
16   Thomas Wolfe Memorial

17   Charles B. Aycock Birthplace
18   James K. Polk Memorial
19   Charlotte Hawkins Brown Memorial
20   James Iredell House
21   Bennett Place
22   Fort Dobbs
23   Confederate Ship Neuse/Caswell Memorial
24   Fort Fisher
25   Alamance Battlefield
26   Bentonville Battlefield

Source: N.C. Division of Parks and Recreation, Natural Heritage Program, 1997.

and preserving places of local, state, and national significance. Among them were Old Salem, the Hope Plantation in Windsor, Historic Edenton, Old Beaufort by the Sea in Carteret County, and the nationally acclaimed Biltmore Estate near Asheville. One of the best examples of a local private preservation agency is Historic Salisbury, which made that city, once the most important urban place in the Piedmont, one of the state's most history-conscious communities. Fittingly, Salisbury was the hometown of Archibald Henderson.

A 1997–98 study commissioned by the Carolina Power and Light Company showed that, since 1976, federal tax incentives for investing in historic preservation had benefited 732 private-sector, income-producing development projects representing a private investment of $325 million. When the impact of nonfederal incentives, including investments in private homes and public projects, was added, the total funding swelled to more than $1.5 billion. Old Archibald Henderson would be astounded to know what his plea had wrought.

Festivals

Much of the money raised by arts groups supports a variety of local arts and cultural festivals celebrating the season, the harvest, or some other event of community significance. Since the 1930s, the number of festivals in North Carolina has increased about 5 percent a year, and like historic preservation and cultural arts, they have been promoted by local governments and chambers of commerce as tourist attractions and stimulants to the economy.

The festival cycle begins on New Year's Eve with "First Night," an alcohol-free celebration in central business districts featuring music, entertainment, and exhibits appealing to families. A concept that originated in Boston, First Night festivals spread to Raleigh, Charlotte, Asheville, and other cities. Spring is greeted by St. Patrick's Day parades in Charlotte and elsewhere, the Azalea Festival in Wilmington, the Biltmore Estate's Festival of Flowers, Springfest and its imitators in Charlotte and other cities, and Mayfests in a variety of communities, including Durham's Hispanic-flavored "Cinco de Mayo." With summer come Junefests and other summer festivals, such as the Hollerin' Contest at Spivey's Corner, Mule Day in Benson, Hog Day in Hillsborough, and Fourth of July celebrations, watermelon festivals, flower shows, and arts and crafts exhibitions in many cities. Among the more notable summer celebrations are the Grandfather Mountain Highland Games, the Gathering of Scottish Clans at Linville, and the North Carolina Folk Festival at Asheville. In the fall, barbecues add spice to a variety of festivals celebrating the harvest

The Swannanoa Gathering

One summer, a bassoon player from the Hong Kong Symphony came to study Irish flute. Another season, a couple who run a bed and breakfast in New South Wales, Australia, traveled in for Old-Time Music and Dance Week, and a mandolin player from Japan enrolled to learn blues guitar. Since 1992, growing numbers of people from around the world and from just down the road have followed the sounds of pipes, fiddles and mountain dulcimers to the campus of Warren Wilson College, just outside of Asheville, for The Swannanoa Gathering.

The series of week-long workshops, which begin in July and run through early August, has become a summer home of sorts for an extended family of kindred spirits—spirits who are drawn to the idea of celebrating and passing on tradition. "We explore the musical and folk heritage of these mountains," says Gathering director Jim Magill. That translates into classes in Southern Appalachian clogging, Scottish folklore, advanced tin whistle, and most everything in between. Participants come in at all levels, from those who stop off in nearby Black Mountain on their way to class to purchase their first dulcimer, to semi-pros in the Performance Lab, which becomes its own traveling road show.

Farmers, physicians, college professors, stone masons, and CPAs, as well as whole families, attend the Gathering. Students range from 12-year-olds to retirees, and many who make the pilgrimage live daily lives that have little to do with music, dance, or storytelling. That's exactly the audience Doug Orr, president of Warren Wilson College and the visionary behind the Gathering, had in mind.

"It's long been a part of the culture of Asheville and Western North Carolina to honor and preserve its musical heritage, and here is the perfect setting for a summer program built around the connection between Appalachian music and folklore and that of Scotland, Ireland and England," says Orr. "Additionally, we are witnessing a growing trend for people from all walks of life to get in touch with their artistic souls, so there is a resurgence of music workshops and festivals throughout our state and on a national level."

An impressive roster of instructors finds its way to this musical venue in the Blue Ridge Mountains' Swannanoa Valley, filled with legends from both sides of the Atlantic. National Heritage Award and North Carolina Folk Heritage Award recipients sign on as well as All-Ireland Fiddle Champions. Balladeers who got their starts in Irish pubs take their places alongside an 83-year-old dancer from Jackson County and a seventh-generation storyteller from just north of Asheville. Students like Becky Mojica, a school nurse from Northern California, come back year after year for what she calls "the mountaintop experience." At a time when headlines and self-help books remind us how much we're craving community, Mojica and other Gathering regulars say they've found it among a set of traditions passed on, not by sheet music and books, but through other people.

It is a place where "community happens"—sometimes in a big way. A couple who met at Celtic Week were married in the college's formal garden, just outside the dance hall, during Celtic Week of the next year. They return the same week each summer to celebrate their anniversary with friends and, of course, with music.

Then there are the literal mountaintops, the gentle, rolling peaks that have safeguarded those traditions for generations. They're the same mountains that, at The Swannanoa Gathering, provide the backdrop for an informal jam session here, a group of buckdancers practicing under an evergreen over there. "I find the Gathering to be a magical place," says Paul Brown, program director at WFDD Public Radio in Winston-Salem and, along with his wife, Terri McMurray, a regular instructor at the Gathering. "With the college's old dance hall right there in the center of things, it feels like a small musical village."

It's this mingling of special new traditions with those that have been handed down for generations that lies at the heart of a folk gathering. At a vibrant 80 years of age, Ralph Blizard is a three-time first-place winner of the Old-Time Fiddle Contest at North Carolina's Mt. Airy Fiddlers' Convention, and he's been recognized internationally for his distinctive Appalachian long bow playing. He returns to teach at the Gathering each year, he says, because he likes the singing and the dancing, the callers and the storytellers. He also likes watching beginners develop their talents from day to day and year to year. And he's always interested in picking up a new tune.

Most of all, though, he feels it's important to share what he knows with "the younger people coming up." That's the true value, he says, of musical events such as The Swannanoa Gathering. "If people don't have a real connection to something, it goes by the wayside. At some point, we all need to make sure we're passing on our heritage."

Paige G. Blomgren, Our State: Down Home in North Carolina (Greensboro: Mann Media, Inc., June 1997).

of apples, peanuts, pumpkins, sweet potatoes, collards, cotton, and other crops.

Handmade in America

An example of the arts as economic stimulus is celebrated in the twenty-two westernmost counties of North Carolina. A consortium of communities, colleges, craft guilds, public agencies, and private companies have joined to form HandMade in America, an entrepreneurial arm that intends to make western North Carolina the center of the nation's crafts industry.

When mountain leaders looked for an organizing idea around which to build a stable economy that would support their population and unite their splintered society, they knew it was not going to be agriculture or manufacturing and they believed mining and timbering were environmentally destructive. With a grant from the Pew Partnership for Civic Change, they took soundings and discovered the handicrafts industry that had been a part of mountain life and lore for generations. An economic survey by Appalachian State University showed that crafts were a $122-million-a-year economic stimulus, four times what burley tobacco had generated in its prime.

From that economic reality they arrived at an ambitious goal: to make a hardheaded business out of what had been a discrete and isolated cottage enterprise, to make visible through marketing, education, and public relations what traditionally had been indigenous and invisible. Within twenty years HandMade in America hopes to have expanded western North Carolina's crafts industry until it dominates the national handicrafts market. The idea has excited imaginations from the coves and hollows of Ashe and Allegheny Counties hard by the Virginia line to the peaks and valleys of rugged Clay and Cherokee Counties down by the Georgia border.

The mountains are dotted with institutions that have signed on to assist in teaching and promoting craft enterprises: the John C. Campbell Folk School at Brasstown in Clay County, the Qualla Arts and Crafts Mutual at Cherokee, the Penland School for Crafts and Mayland Community College in Mitchell County, Haywood Community College in Haywood County, Appalachian State University in Boone, Warren Wilson College near Asheville, the Tryon Arts Center in Polk County, and many others. The intent is not to make western North Carolina "the Santa Fe of the East" but to overtake Santa Fe and render western North Carolina supreme in the crafts industry.

A Coalescing of the Arts and History

The rapid expansion of the cultural arts and historic preservation has been fueled in part by increased public recognition that both have economic value. Often arts and history groups have joined forces to help revitalize deserted downtowns, stabilize declining neighborhoods, or preserve rural communities—objectives that have attracted both public and private support.

In Charlotte, Bank of America purchased a vacant but historically significant downtown building previously occupied by a retailer of upscale women's apparel whose clientele had moved to the suburbs. In an effort to build an arts community in the inner city, the bank gave the building to the Mint Museum of Art as a place to exhibit pottery and craft collections. A few blocks away the bank bought a burned-out church building and converted it into a warren of artist workshops.

Other such projects abound across the state. The following are important examples:

- In Durham, the Hayti Heritage Center is housed in the restored St. Joseph's AME Zion Church, an 1891 structure listed on the National Register of Historic Places.
- In Rocky Mount, the Arts Council is housed in what once was a city water tank.
- In Salisbury, the Waterworks Visual Arts Center is housed in the former waterworks.
- In Fayetteville and Shelby, local arts councils are housed in downtown buildings previously used as U.S. Post Offices.
- In New Bern, the Craven County Arts Council and Gallery operates out of a former First Citizens Bank and Trust Company building dating from the early 1900s.

The Pack Place Education, Arts, and Science Center on Pack Square in Asheville, an example of the revitalization of an old community downtown building for a new arts center

• In Wilson, the local Arts Council operates a multidisciplinary arts center in a 25,000 square-foot building that housed a bank from 1903 to 1985.

• In Hickory, a 1925 high school building has been preserved as the home of the Arts and Science Center of the Catawba Valley, housing the Catawba County Council for the Arts, the Catawba Science Center, the Hickory Choral Society, the Hickory Museum of Art, and the Western Piedmont Symphony.

• In Winton, the C. S. Brown Cultural Center and Museum is located in a structure that originally housed North Carolina's first public high school for African Americans.

• Asheville's downtown revitalization has been stimulated by Pack Place, on historic Pack Square, which houses a performing arts theater, the Asheville Art Museum, the Rock and Mineral Museum, and Health Adventure.

Selected References

Bishir, C. *North Carolina Architecture.* Chapel Hill: University of North Carolina Press, 1990.

Brook, D. *A Lasting Gift.* Raleigh: Preservation North Carolina and the North Carolina Division of Archives and History, 1997.

Buckner, S. *Our Words, Our Ways: Reading and Writing in North Carolina.* Durham: Carolina Academic Press, 1995.

Cannon, R., E. Cotton, and M. Latham, eds. *Old Homes and Gardens of North Carolina.* Chapel Hill: University of North Carolina Press, 1939.

Crow, J., ed. *Public History in North Carolina, 1903–1978: Proceedings of the 75th Anniversary Celebration, March 7, 1978.* Raleigh: North Carolina Department of Cultural Resources, Division of Archives and History, 1979.

Foushee, O. *Art in North Carolina: Episodes and Developments, 1585–1970.* Chapel Hill: University of North Carolina Press, 1972.

Johnson, B., and T. Waterman, eds. *The Early Architecture of North Carolina: A Pictorial Survey.* Chapel Hill: University of North Carolina Press, 1941.

Lefler, H., and A. Newsome. *North Carolina: The History of a Southern State.* Rev. ed. Chapel Hill: University of North Carolina Press, 1954.

Romine Powell, D. *Parting the Curtains: Interviews with Southern Writers.* Winston-Salem: John F. Blair, 1994.

Walser, R. *Literary North Carolina: A Historical Survey.* Raleigh: North Carolina Department of Cultural Resources, Division of Archives and History, 1986.

19. OUTDOOR RECREATION
Woodward S. Bousquet

North Carolina's varied landscape and rich natural resource base support an outstanding array of outdoor recreation activities. Its four land regions—Mountains, Piedmont, Inner Coastal Plain, and Tidewater—each give outdoor pursuits within their boundaries a distinctive character.

In the past three decades, demand for outdoor recreation has grown and changed. The state's population has become larger, more urban, better educated, more mobile, and older. Now that baby boomers are parents, the percentage of young children is also on the rise. In addition, the proportion of two-wage-earner families and single-parent families has increased significantly. New residents from other parts of the country, including a high percentage of retirees, have added their interests and values to the state's cultural setting. For many North Carolinians, outdoor recreation has become an integral part of their lives. Not surprisingly, attendance figures and statewide surveys reveal increased participation in outdoor recreation activities.

Counties and municipalities have often been the first to feel the pressure from these expanding and changing needs. Urban residents, low-income families, persons who are physically challenged, and single-parent families depend especially heavily on nearby facilities. In response, cities such as

Raleigh and Charlotte have increased their budgets for capital improvements, programs, and staffing. For those living in rural areas, however, recreation services frequently lag behind those provided in the growing cities and suburbs.

The two-week family vacation across the country in a station wagon has largely been replaced by shorter breaks closer to home. Consequently, North Carolina parks and other outdoor recreation facilities operated by the state and federal government also face an upsurge in demand—an upsurge with which they are not always able to keep pace. The private sector has filled in some of the gaps, particularly in the case of such intensive and expensive recreational developments as ski areas, golf courses, and four-season resorts. Other needs remain unmet.

The desires of a growing population for housing, transportation, employment, goods, and services have threatened the natural environment responsible for much of North Carolina's perceived quality of life. Green spaces are being lost as cities and their suburbs expand. Both rural and metropolitan areas are experiencing the degradation of natural areas, the species they protect, and the human amenities they provide. Paradoxically, these problems have increased in intensity at the same time that public concern for the state of the environment also has risen. Outdoor recreation in the state is thus a tapestry, richly woven with opportunities but challenged in many ways by the snarls of changing needs, tight budgets, and resource impairment.

The Scope of Outdoor Recreation in North Carolina

North Carolina's outdoor recreation picture is complex. The opportunities are extensive, and many people take advantage of them. But how many residents actually participate in outdoor pursuits, in what kinds of activities do they engage, and how often do they take part? To better understand recreation in the state, the North Carolina Division of Parks and Recreation mailed questionnaires to 3,100 randomly selected North Carolina households. As Figure 19.1 shows, the five most popular types of outdoor recreation for North Caro-

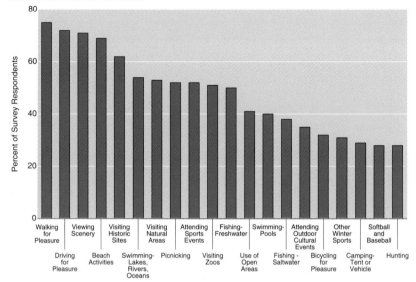

Figure 19.1. The Twenty Most Popular Outdoor Recreation Activities in North Carolina

Source: N.C. Department of Environment, Health, and Natural Resources, Division of Parks and Recreation, *Outdoors North Carolina, 1990-1995* (Raleigh, 1989).

linians are walking for pleasure, driving for pleasure, viewing scenery, beach activities, and visiting historic sites. In addition to these five activities, over 50 percent of the state's households have members who engage at least once a year in the next six activities on the list: swimming, visiting natural areas, picnicking, attending sports events, visiting zoos, and fishing at freshwater sites.

Another measure of present-day demand for outdoor recreation is people's level of participation in various outdoor pursuits. Table 19.1 shows household participation rates and total annual participation by respondents to the Division of Parks and Recreation study. A single "outdoor recreation occasion" occurs when one household member spends a day or any portion of a day taking part in an activity. Among the top five activities based on participation levels, three are fitness-related: walking, jogging, and bicycling. These activities are often a part of regular exercise routines and do not involve special sites or prohibitively expensive equipment. On the other hand, activities with the

Table 19.1. Household Participation Rates and Total Participation in Outdoor Recreation, by Activity

Rank	Activity	Participation Rate*	Annual Occasions**	Rank	Activity	Participation Rate*	Annual Occasions**
1	Walking for pleasure	49.97	114,631,180	24	Visiting historical sites	3.30	7,570,200
2	Driving for pleasure	32.69	74,990,860	25	Using motorcycles, dirt bikes, ATVs	3.10	7,111,400
3	Viewing scenery	31.39	72,008,660	26	Using four-wheel-drive vehicles	2.98	6,836,120
4	Jogging or running	14.12	32,391,280	27	Target shooting	2.81	6,446,140
5	Bicycling for pleasure	11.17	25,623,980	28	Waterskiing	2.49	5,712,060
6	Beach activities	10.78	24,729,320	29	Horseback riding	2.46	5,643,240
7	Swimming (in pools)	10.10	23,169,400	30	Trail hiking	2.46	5,643,240
8	Fishing (freshwater)	9.97	22,871,180	31	Playing football	1.96	4,486,240
9	Nature study	8.79	20,164,260	32	Attending outdoor cultural events	1.82	4,175,080
10	Attending sports events	8.59	19,705,460	33	Playing soccer	1.78	4,083,320
11	Swimming (in lakes, rivers, ocean)	8.31	19,063,140	34	Playing volleyball	1.72	3,945,680
12	Use of open area	7.53	17,273,820	35	Skateboarding	1.53	3,509,820
13	Visiting natural areas	6.75	15,484,500	36	Engaging in other winter sports	1.43	3,280,420
14	Playing basketball	6.68	15,323,920	37	Visiting zoos	1.24	2,844,560
15	Playing golf	6.58	15,094,520	38	Camping (primitive)	0.87	1,995,780
16	Playing softball or baseball	6.40	14,681,600	39	Canoeing and kayaking	0.66	1,514,040
17	Hunting	6.27	14,383,380	40	Skiing (downhill)	0.64	1,468,160
18	Using play equipment	6.09	13,970,460	41	Sailing	0.54	1,238,760
19	Power boating	5.54	12,708,760	42	Windsurfing	0.12	275,280
20	Fishing (saltwater)	5.28	12,112,320	43	Skiing (cross-country)	0.08	183,520
21	Picnicking	4.26	9,772,440				
22	Playing tennis	3.84	8,808,960		Total	298.44	684,621,360
23	Camping (tent or vehicle)	3.35	7,684,900				

Source: N.C. Division of Parks and Recreation, *Outdoors North Carolina, 1990–1995*
(Raleigh: N.C. Department of Environment, Health, and Natural Resources, 1989).
*Participation rate: The average number of times per year that one or more
households engaged in an activity
**Annual occasions: The participation rate multiplied by the 2.294 million
households in North Carolina

lowest rates—canoeing and kayaking, downhill and cross-country skiing, sailing, and windsurfing—generally require substantial investments in equipment. Nevertheless, they represent significant elements of North Carolina's commercial outdoor recreation industry. Skiing and whitewater sports are especially popular in the Mountains, whereas sailing and windsurfing are more prevalent in the Piedmont and Tidewater regions.

These participation rates show that North Carolinians are active. When their separate activities are totaled, the result is 684.6 million outdoor recreational occasions for all state residents over an entire year (Table 19.1). The average household reported participating nearly three hundred times per year in the forty-three outdoor recreation activities listed in the survey.

Comparing the responses in Figure 19.1 with those in Table 19.1 reveals other important aspects of the state's outdoor recreation picture. Certain activities, such as visiting historic sites or picnicking, are several times more popular than, for example, motorcycling or riding all-terrain vehicles (ATVs). But participation rates for all four of these activities are nearly identical—an average of between three to five occasions per household per year. Thus, although many state residents (52 percent of all households) go picnicking, the average household picnics only a few times a year. In contrast, North Carolina's small group of four-wheel-drive enthusiasts (13 percent of all households) engages in their sport much more frequently.

Results of this survey reflect, to a large degree, the current demand for each type of activity. They also demonstrate the significant contribution that outdoor recreation makes to the quality of life in North Carolina.

Selected Outdoor Activities

It is impossible to address in this chapter all of the outdoor recreation activities that take place in North Carolina. Although the extensive survey conducted by the Division of Parks and Recreation listed over forty types of outdoor recreation, even it omitted hang gliding, bungee jumping, caving, rock

climbing, and, no doubt, other recreational endeavors that are important to at least some residents of this state. The activities described below, though not inclusive, illustrate the scope of outdoor recreation in North Carolina.

Outdoor recreation can be divided into two categories by the settings and developments required. *Natural resource–dependent activities*, like backpacking and river rafting, must occur at specific places such as lakes, mountains, or beaches. To a large extent the characteristics of the natural setting shape these recreational experiences. On the other hand, *facility-dependent activities* are centered on human-built structures such as tennis courts, playground equipment, or swimming pools. These facilities can provide similar recreational experiences even when constructed in different settings. Several activities—jogging, alpine skiing, and golf, for example—lie somewhere between the two categories; they are affected by the nature of both the resource and the facility. In this discussion, those activities that are natural resource–based are considered first, followed by activities more dependent on developed facilities.

Camping

Camping in a tent, a tent trailer, or a recreational vehicle is especially popular with retirees and families with children. It can provide an inexpensive way for travelers to spend the night and have a natural setting just outside the trailer door or tent flap. Much of camping's popularity can be attributed to recreationists' interest in nature study and visiting natural areas, which ranked ninth and thirteenth, respectively, in terms of the frequency with which they are undertaken (Table 19.1).

Approximately three hundred campgrounds operate in North Carolina. As shown in Figure 19.2, the vast majority are privately owned. Amenities provided range widely. Only pit toilets and cleared tenting areas may be available at primitive campsites. At the other end of the spectrum, commercial campgrounds may include a playground, recreation hall, grocery store, laundromat, electrical outlets, plumbing hookups, showers, and even cable television. Although state and federal facilities usually have spaces for both tents and recre-

Figure 19.2. North Carolina Campground Ownership

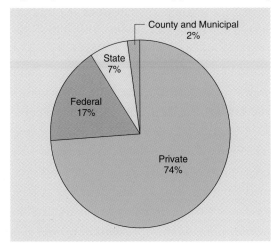

Note: Total = 278 campgrounds

Sources: *Woodall's Campground Directory*, 1997;
U.S. Forest Service, 1997.

ational vehicles, few provide individual electrical, water, or sewer hookups. Some federal campgrounds have showers and most provide flush toilets. All state campgrounds in North Carolina have hot showers and flush toilets.

Heavily developed campgrounds have become recreation destinations in themselves, offering swimming, hiking, square dancing, or other activities on the property. Interpretive programs presented at many state and federal camping areas can help vacationers develop a deeper appreciation of North Carolina's natural and cultural heritage.

Hunting

Animal species large and small have long been objects of human pursuit, first for sustenance and then primarily for sport. After the first English landing on Roanoke Island in 1584, Captain Arthur Barlowe reported to Sir Walter Raleigh that he found "many goodly woods, fulle of Deere, Conies [rabbits], Hares, and Fowle, even in the middest of Summer, in incredible aboundance."

Today big-game hunters in North Carolina seek black bear, wild boar, white-tailed deer, and wild turkey. The most popular small-game animals are fox, rabbit, gray squirrel, grouse, raccoon, opossum, mourning dove, quail, and nearly forty species of waterfowl. Almost 2 million acres of land stand open to hunting through the state's Game Lands Program. Much of this land is private, leased for public use through cooperative agreements negotiated by the North Carolina Wildlife Resources Commission with private companies and nonprofit organizations. Additional arrangements for game lands have been made with various state and federal agencies.

Black bears are found today in twenty-four Mountain counties and twenty-eight eastern counties. Because they roam widely, bears need large tracts of land, preferably uninhabited swamps or forests with dense cover. Large expanses of mixed hardwoods and an understory of rhododendron and laurel meet this habitat requirement in the Mountains, and the Coastal Plain provides swamps, pocosins, and tracts of lowland hardwoods. Bear populations declined as the state became more settled, because of logging, wetland drainage, the chestnut blight, and unrestricted hunting and trapping.

Alarmed by results of a population survey in 1967, the Wildlife Resources Commission established bear sanctuaries in 1970 covering approximately 800,000 acres. Twelve sanctuaries lie in the coastal region, and eleven more, plus the Great Smoky Mountains National Park, protect some bear populations in the Mountains. Bear hunting is prohibited on sanctuary lands. This measure helps prevent overharvesting by ensuring a core of breeding bears that can provide an overflow for sport hunting. The season usually opens in mid-October, with about 50 days of hunting in the Mountains and from about 6 to 30 days in the eastern counties. Although the statewide average total as recently as the mid-1980s was slightly over 300 bears, hunters in 1996 reported a total bear kill of 1,010. Hunting with dogs remains a tradition and accounts for a major portion of the bear harvest.

With the success of North Carolina's bear management program, some animals have become a nuisance, feeding on crops, destroying beehives, and visiting garbage containers. On the other hand, human activities continue to threaten bear habitats in many parts of the state. Resort and second-home developments, highway construction, and other land-clearing operations divide and reduce bear ranges.

Habitat destruction and unrestricted hunting also have reduced wild turkeys in the state. Diseases from domestic poultry may have played an additional role in the rapid decline of the original turkey flocks. In 1970 the estimated North Carolina population was down to 2,000. Live trapping and relocation of wild birds, coupled with stricter hunting regulations, proved to be the only reliable way to begin restoring the turkey's numbers. By 1995 the population had grown to over 80,000 and the occupied range had more than doubled, allowing the hunters to take over 1,000 birds across the state. That number exceeded 2,500 in 1996 and 1997.

Turkey hunting requires careful stalking, a camouflaged shotgun and clothing, and precise shooting. Hunters enter the range at dawn. When a male turkey gobbles, the hunter quickly moves into position and tries to lure the bird closer with an artificial call. Only a spring season is currently permitted in North Carolina, because none of the state's flocks has yet reached the level that would warrant a fall hunt.

European wild boars escaped from a Graham County hunting preserve in the early 1920s. The hogs established breeding populations in Graham and neighboring counties, and the first open season took place in the Nantahala National Forest in 1937. They are now considered a pest in the Great Smoky Mountains National Park, where their rooting destroys native wildflowers. Most boar hunters work in teams and use dogs to herd a hog within shooting range. Over one hundred wild boar kills from nine western North Carolina counties were reported by hunters for the 1996–97 season.

Deer hunting has always been part of the sporting tradition in North Carolina, and the white-tailed deer remains the state's primary big-game species today. Unlike black bears and several other species, deer populations can benefit from human settlement. When cleared areas are left fallow for a few years or allowed to revert to forest, plants on which deer feed often take over. Pastureland, the forested edges of croplands, and logged areas also produce browse for deer.

European colonists, like their Native American predecessors, quickly recognized deer as an important meat source. Deer also provided clothing and tools and served as a medium of exchange. Market hunting for deer and other game species grew rapidly in the nineteenth century. New gun technology, the absence of bag limits, and unrestricted baiting and night hunting sped up the slaughter. After deer populations reached a nationwide low in the early 1900s, Congress ended market hunting and North Carolina enacted its first bucks-only law. Combined with habitat management and restoration efforts, game regulations helped the white-tails rebound. This adaptable species is now found in every North Carolina county. Today, the statewide deer population is at an all-time high, and in about one-third of the state the deer herds have reached or exceeded carrying capacity (Fig. 19.3). That is, their numbers have equaled or exceeded the maximum number that the land can sustain over the long term without being damaged.

Excess deer fall victim to diseases and automobile collisions, and they can damage agricultural crops, young forests, native plant communities, and gardens. The deer that remain in overpopulated habitats are often undernourished or malnourished. Now that wolves and cougars have been extirpated from the state, humans are the primary limiting factor on deer. Thus, the Wildlife Resources Commission attempts to regulate the number of bucks and does killed by hunters each year to control the state's deer herds. The estimated white-tail harvest from sport hunting has risen dramatically since World War II (Fig. 19.4). It surpassed 100,000 in 1983 and has exceeded 200,000 in recent years.

The annual small-game harvest by recreational hunters in North Carolina dwarfs the figures for the state's four big-game animals. For instance, hunters usually take a few million quail, gray squirrels, and mourning doves each year. Such high numbers, however, appear to have little effect on long-term population trends for these three prolific species. Raccoon and opossum hunting are also popular in the state. Hounds are almost always employed in these two sports, and canine field trials and other organized competitions have become important recreation activities themselves.

Figure 19.3. Distribution of Deer

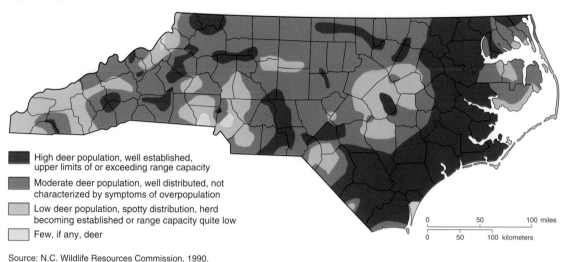

- High deer population, well established, upper limits of or exceeding range capacity
- Moderate deer population, well distributed, not characterized by symptoms of overpopulation
- Low deer population, spotty distribution, herd becoming established or range capacity quite low
- Few, if any, deer

0   50   100 miles

0   50   100 kilometers

Source: N.C. Wildlife Resources Commission, 1990.

Figure 19.4. Estimated Deer Harvest in North Carolina, 1949–1996

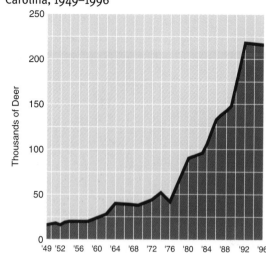

Source: N.C. Wildlife Resources Commission surveys.

Sport Fishing

From brook trout to bluefin tuna, North Carolina's varied environments support fishing that many enthusiasts contend is difficult to match anywhere in the East (Fig. 19.5). Rainfall in the Mountains cascades down thousands of miles of cold, fast-flowing streams. Over one thousand miles of designated trout waters are stocked regularly from state fish hatcheries. The upper reaches are home to native brook trout, while brown and rainbow trout dominate pools farther downstream. Anglers working the bigger creeks and river-dammed lakes in the Mountain region's valleys find largemouth and smallmouth bass, bream (bluegill), crappie, walleye, and the introduced white bass.

In the Piedmont, large rivers and their chains of hydroelectric-power lakes create warmer fish habitats. They support largemouth bass, landlocked striped bass, catfish, and several kinds of panfish. The Catawba River, for instance, features 30,000-acre Lake Norman north of Charlotte as well as Lakes James, Rhodhiss, Hickory, and Wylie. Other popular impoundments include Kerr Reservoir on the Virginia line, along with Jordan Lake and Falls-of-the-Neuse Lake in the Raleigh-Durham area. Smaller reservoirs that serve primarily as drinking water supplies also provide sport for anglers. Slow-moving rivers in the western Coastal Plain are another home to many southern warmwater species and to the annual spring spawning runs of shad and striped bass.

The march of progress once severely diminished fish populations in this midstate region, but numerous species have made comebacks and others have been introduced. Although fishing in the area is at its best during the late spring and early fall, knowledgeable summer anglers and hardy winter fishers can make good showings in off-peak times as well.

In the eastern Coastal Plain's Tidewater region lie North Carolina's natural lakes, including Phelps, Mattamuskeet, and Waccamaw. These lakes, and the swamp creeks and canals that feed them, are well known for panfish, pickerel, and bass. Fish also prowl the sluggish blackwater rivers and nutrient-rich estuaries that fringe the coastal sounds. The state has over 2,000 square miles of these sounds, where fresh and salt water merge. The two largest are Albemarle

Figure 19.5. Principal Bodies of Water

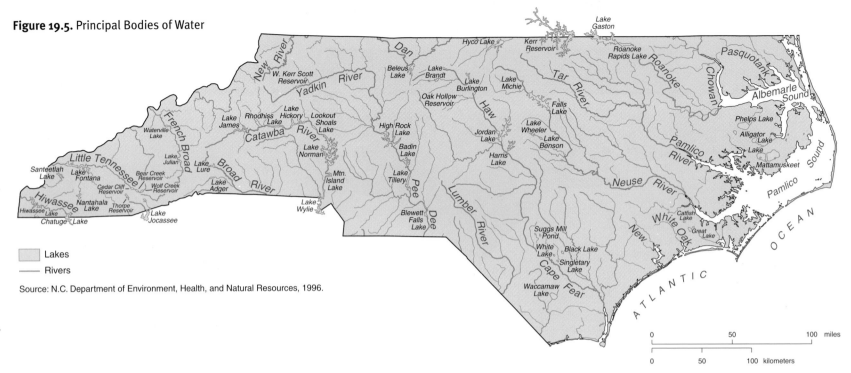

Lakes

Rivers

Source: N.C. Department of Environment, Health, and Natural Resources, 1996.

and Pamlico. Here, species such as channel bass, bluefish, and Spanish and king mackerel make periodic runs from offshore waters. Most fishing in the sounds—as well as most inshore and inlet fishing—is done by trolling from watercraft.

At Cape Hatteras, cold waters from the Virginia shoreline collide with warm tropical waters of the Gulf Stream, which lie only twelve miles offshore. At this "game fish junction" meet northern and southern saltwater species—tautog, striped bass, dolphin, barracuda, wahoo, sailfish, and marlin. The Outer Banks are a base for angling in the surf, inlets, and sounds. Piers extend fishing a thousand feet or more away from shore, providing access to certain species such as bluefish and spot that are not restricted to feeding in the surf. Beyond, offshore waters lure fishing parties in pursuit of the magnificent king mackerel, sailfish, and blue marlin.

The saltwater fishing season depends on annual migration and feeding pat-

terns. Surf and offshore seasons, for example, normally extend from March through mid-December. Inlet fishing runs through the warm months. But one fish species or another can be caught in the salty waters of North Carolina's coast and sounds in almost any month of the year.

Other Water-Based Activities

North Carolina is generously endowed with water. It covers over 2 million acres of the state, and some form of water recreation is readily available to nearly all of North Carolina's dispersed populace. As Figure 19.1 and Table 19.1 show, many water-related pursuits, especially swimming and beach activities, are in particularly high demand. Annual participation levels run in the tens of millions of occasions.

Within or straddling the state's borders lie 135 lakes and reservoirs of 100 or

A surf fisherman on the South Core Banks of North Carolina's Outer Banks

185,000 people enjoying whitewater rafting in 1994. Probably the most popular whitewater river is the Nantahala, where more than a half-dozen outfitters guide enthusiasts through the boulder mazes and rapids. Other challenging western rivers include the Green, French Broad, Nolichucky, and New. Farther east, flatwater paddlers find many suitable streams and rivers.

Bicycling

Bicycling can be an unsteady spin around a suburban neighborhood block on a hand-me-down sixteen-inch model fitted with training wheels. It could involve a thirty-minute daily workout on a bicycle path in a linear park. Bicycling may be a rugged jeep trail descent on a mountain bike with knobbed tires and a heavy-duty frame. It can also mean a two-week camping trip across the state on a touring bike.

Whatever the equipment, the purpose, or the length of the journey, bicycling has become one of North Carolinians' most frequent outdoor recreation activities. The only off-season for lengthy or vigorous outings is midsummer, often unbearably hot and humid for cycling in the eastern and central parts of the state. But winters tend to be mild, and the spring and fall feature warm days and cool evenings—ideal weather for riding a bicycle. Prevailing winds are not a major factor, except along the coast.

The state's urban areas are scattered, connected

more acres in size. River networks dissect the western and central regions. Fast-flowing currents with rapids up to whitewater Class III and IV slice through the Mountains, while larger but gentler thoroughfares cross the Piedmont. Much of the eastern third of the state is marshland. However, sluggish rivers thread the Coastal Plain and empty into the sounds, which contain over half of North Carolina's total surface waters. Farther east stretch barrier islands and the Atlantic Ocean.

From the South Carolina line north to Corolla on the Outer Banks, beaches lure swimmers, anglers, sunbathers, runners, and people who come just to relax, watch birds, or read a book. Inland lakes and larger rivers also provide these recreational opportunities. Boating and waterskiing are popular in the state. By 1996 the number of registered North Carolina power boaters had exceeded 300,000. The number of canoeing, kayaking, and rafting adherents is increasing as well. Whitewater sports in the western counties have grown dramatically in the past three decades, with nearly

to small towns not only by interstate highways but also by lightly traveled rural roads. It is along the quieter routes that the North Carolina Department of Transportation (DOT) has designated ten "bicycle highways." Initiated in 1975, the biking routes cover 3,000 miles and virtually all types of landscapes and terrain. The longest is the 700-mile Mountains to Sea run from Murphy to Manteo. Several other routes lead from or intersect this one. Another route, the Carolina Connection, serves as part of the East Coast Bicycle Trail that will eventually lead from Maine to Florida. From the DOT's Bicycle Program office, bike-touring enthusiasts can obtain maps, planning tips, and lists of campgrounds on or adjacent to each route.

In addition to these state-designated routes, the Blue Ridge Parkway and Route 12 through the Outer Banks from Ocracoke northward draw significant numbers of recreational cyclists. Several counties and municipalities also promote bicycling. For example, the cities of Greensboro, Charlotte, and Swansboro and Macon, Moore, and Onslow Counties have identified cycling options that connect major points of interest in their respective jurisdictions. Many of these routes are marked by special highway signs, and all have accompanying maps or interpretive brochures.

Yet the demand for designated cycling lanes on highways and for bicycle paths separated from automobile traffic in local recreation areas is high and far exceeds the supply. Only fifteen miles of the state's roads have separate lanes for bicycles.

Snow Skiing

Although skiing in the South means waterskiing to many recreationists, wintertime skiing has spread southward along the Appalachian chain over the past few decades. In some years weather patterns and high elevations can leave a total of over sixty inches of snow above the 5,000-foot level. North Carolina's first ski area, Cataloochee, opened in 1961. Eight areas currently operate in the state (Fig. 19.6), with four clustered in the Boone–Banner Elk–Blowing Rock area of Watauga County. In addition, cross-country skiing has made a modest start.

Ski resort development in the southern mountains has differed considerably from that in other parts of the country. Generally, ski areas in the Northeast and West were the first recreation facilities built at a given location. Their success prompted sales of surrounding property. Nightclubs, condominiums, and four-season outdoor centers with tennis courts and golf courses followed. In the upland South, most vacation real estate developments began as second-home and resort complexes. They were designed primarily for spring, summer, and fall activities. Investors from Florida, New York, and other areas outside southern Appalachia spurred land speculation in the 1960s. Ski facilities were added to existing mountain developments to provide year-round recreational opportunities and stimulate further real estate sales.

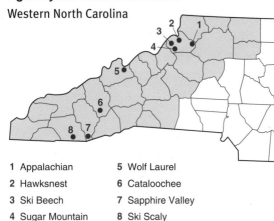

Figure 19.6. Downhill Ski Areas in Western North Carolina

1 Appalachian	5 Wolf Laurel
2 Hawksnest	6 Cataloochee
3 Ski Beech	7 Sapphire Valley
4 Sugar Mountain	8 Ski Scaly

Sources: R. Johnson, *Southern Snow: The Winter Guide to Dixie* (Boston: Appalachian Mountain Club, 1987); N.C. Ski Areas Association.

Skiing as a commercial venture has experienced good and bad years in North Carolina. During the recession of the early 1970s, failing real estate developments owned by ski area investors siphoned off the profits that some ski centers were just beginning to make. Many of the founding corporations faced foreclosure or bankruptcy. Rising gasoline prices and warm winters contributed to the fledgling industry's woes. By the end of the decade, however, colder weather and improved management had revitalized the industry.

Snowmaking, a multimillion-dollar expenditure, improves skiing conditions on the key weekends that can make or break a season. The winter of 1986–87 brought a record 600,000 skiers to North Carolina's slopes. But that figure fell to 390,000 three years later, when not even snowmaking could overcome the season's high temperatures and ill-timed rains. A study by Appalachian State University for the North Carolina Ski Areas Association demonstrated the economic impact of the ski business. Skiing brought $55.8 million into the state during the winter of 1989–90, the survey showed, yet only 27 percent of that money went directly to the ski resorts. The remainder was spent on meals, lodging, equipment, and transportation. Out-of-state skiers accounted for 53 percent of total ski expenditures. That season was unusually warm, so the North Carolina Division of Travel and Tourism estimates that the industry has a potential to generate $100 million in a good year.

Cross-country skiing arrived even more recently on North Carolina's outdoor recreation scene. Favorable winters in the late 1970s encouraged Nordic enthusiasts to try their long skis on snow-covered roads and hiking trails. Regional sports shops began to add cross-county equipment to their sales and rental departments. Today Mount Mitchell State Park, the Blue Ridge Parkway, and the grassy balds of Roan Mountain draw the most cross-country ski traffic when the snow flies in North Carolina. Plowed state and federal roads that cross mountain ranges at high elevations provide access that is generally reliable. Lessons and groomed trails are available in the Beech Mountain area, and more such business ventures may spring up if conditions warrant.

Golf

North Carolina claims to have given golfing to the United States in 1728, when an early resident of Fayetteville reputedly whacked a feather ball across an open field near town. The state's modern golfing era began in 1895 with the initial development of its largest and most famous golf course, Pinehurst. Today the Pinehurst Country Club boasts seven separate golf courses, the nucleus of Sandhills golfing that consists of nearly thirteen courses within a fifteen-mile radius. Golf brings money into North Carolina from expenditures that vacationers make, not only at the golf establishments, but also on accommodations, meals, entertainment, transportation, and the like.

Nearly five hundred courses dot the state. They meander next to the

The first hole at the Mt. Mitchell Golf Course

beaches, across the Piedmont, and throughout the Mountains. Their abundance, plus the presence of several major tournaments including the U.S. Open at Pinehurst in 1999, allow North Carolina to advertise itself as "Golf State U.S.A." Few dispute the title. Though many golf courses are run by city or county recreation departments, the majority are privately operated as parts of country clubs or resort complexes.

Recreation Areas

Federal Areas

A substantial component of North Carolina's mix of outdoor recreational opportunities is the system of federally owned lands in the state (Fig. 19.7). North Carolina boasts one of the nation's widest and most visited arrays of national parks, forests, parkways, seashores, historic sites, wildlife refuges, and scenic trails. The principal agencies that manage federal recreation areas are the National Park Service and the U.S. Forest Service.

Congress created the National Park Service in 1916 to protect the country's natural, scenic, and historic resources and to provide for their enjoyment by the public. In North Carolina, the Park Service administers nine areas, including five historic and cultural sites. Outstanding among this state's recreation resources are four National Park System units: the Great Smoky Mountains National Park, the Blue Ridge Parkway, and two national seashores, Cape Hatteras and Cape Lookout.

One of the largest protected land areas east of the Rockies, Great Smoky Mountains National Park straddles the Tennessee–North Carolina border. Its half-million acres were declared an International Biosphere Reserve by the United Nations in recognition of the diversity of plants and animals found within its borders. Recreational opportunities are extensive; they range from nature study and picnicking to horseback riding, camping, fishing, and bicy-

cling. The Appalachian Trail runs along the Smokies' crest for 170 of its 2,100 miles. Hundreds of miles of other trails probe the coves and mountain slopes.

The Great Smokies ranks among the most popular parks in the United States, attracting over 9.2 million visits in 1996, for instance. Recreationists searching for solitude can usually find it on the Smokies' less-frequented walkways and hiking trails. Or they can try places like Cataloochee that are situated away from the park's main roads and the clusters of commercial attractions outside its boundaries.

From the Great Smoky Mountains to Virginia's Shenandoah National Park, the Blue Ridge Parkway winds through the southern Appalachians. In 1987 the last segment was opened around Grandfather Mountain, fifty-two years after construction began. Renowned for its ever-changing natural vistas, 252 of this motor route's 469 miles lie within North Carolina. The parkway also traverses a variety of cultural landscapes such as farmsteads edged by split-rail fences and the Moses Cone manor and estate. Local, state, and U.S. highways provide access points at frequent intervals.

Although the Blue Ridge Parkway links two other units of the National Park System, few motorists drive the route from one end to the other. Instead, they incorporate portions of the parkway into their visits to the general area. In addition to recreational driving and sightseeing, park activities include camping, picnicking, hiking, and fishing. Ease of access and diverse recreational opportunities drew 19.1 million visits in 1996, making the Blue Ridge Parkway the most frequently visited federal property east of California.

At the opposite end of the state stretch Cape Hatteras and Cape Lookout National Seashores. Together they cover nearly 130 miles of open beach along North Carolina's Outer Banks. Four lighthouses, coastal fishing villages, remains of shipwrecks, and other points of historic interest preserve slices of the country's maritime heritage. Cape Hatteras, the nation's first national seashore, is reached by bridge or ferry. In addition to swimming, surfing, and other beach-based activities, Hatteras provides opportunities for boating, fishing, camping, and waterfowl hunting. Both Cape Hatteras and Cape Look-

Figure 19.7. Selected Federal and State Outdoor Recreation Areas

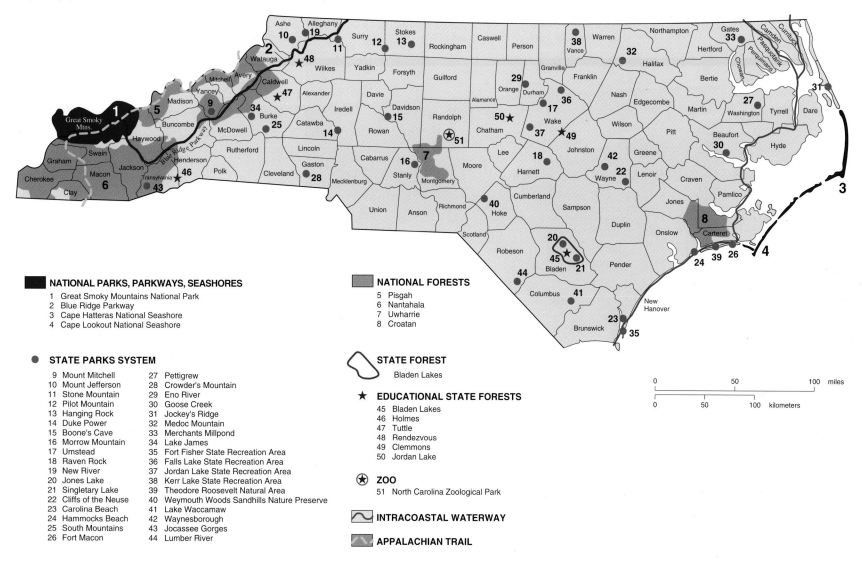

NATIONAL PARKS, PARKWAYS, SEASHORES

1 Great Smoky Mountains National Park
2 Blue Ridge Parkway
3 Cape Hatteras National Seashore
4 Cape Lookout National Seashore

● **STATE PARKS SYSTEM**

9 Mount Mitchell
10 Mount Jefferson
11 Stone Mountain
12 Pilot Mountain
13 Hanging Rock
14 Duke Power
15 Boone's Cave
16 Morrow Mountain
17 Umstead
18 Raven Rock
19 New River
20 Jones Lake
21 Singletary Lake
22 Cliffs of the Neuse
23 Carolina Beach
24 Hammocks Beach
25 South Mountains
26 Fort Macon

27 Pettigrew
28 Crowder's Mountain
29 Eno River
30 Goose Creek
31 Jockey's Ridge
32 Medoc Mountain
33 Merchants Millpond
34 Lake James
35 Fort Fisher State Recreation Area
36 Falls Lake State Recreation Area
37 Jordan Lake State Recreation Area
38 Kerr Lake State Recreation Area
39 Theodore Roosevelt Natural Area
40 Weymouth Woods Sandhills Nature Preserve
41 Lake Waccamaw
42 Waynesborough
43 Jocassee Gorges
44 Lumber River

NATIONAL FORESTS

5 Pisgah
6 Nantahala
7 Uwharrie
8 Croatan

STATE FOREST

Bladen Lakes

★ **EDUCATIONAL STATE FORESTS**

45 Bladen Lakes
46 Holmes
47 Tuttle
48 Rendezvous
49 Clemmons
50 Jordan Lake

⊛ **ZOO**

51 North Carolina Zoological Park

INTRACOASTAL WATERWAY

APPALACHIAN TRAIL

Sources: N.C. Division of Parks and Recreation; National Park Service; U.S. Forest Service; N.C. Department of Transportation.

The Linn Cove Viaduct of the Blue Ridge Parkway winding around Grandfather Mountain

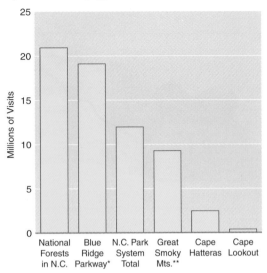

Figure 19.8. Recreational Visits to Government-Operated Areas, 1996

* N.C. and Virginia combined.
**N.C. and Tennessee combined.

Sources: U.S. Forest Service, National Forests in North Carolina; National Park Service units; N.C. Division of Parks and Recreation.

out have sections open to four-wheel drive vehicles. Cape Lookout, however, offers a more remote and primitive recreational experience. Accessible only by private boat or ferry, it receives fewer visitors than the other federal units in the state (Fig. 19.8). The park, plus nearby offshore areas, comprise the South Atlantic International Biosphere Reserve.

The federal government's water impoundment projects offer additional recreational opportunities. The Tennessee Valley Authority (TVA) is responsible for Fontana Lake, located at the southern border of the Great Smoky Mountains National Park. Negotiations with TVA have been aimed at securing higher water levels during the May–October recreation season at Fontana and other hydro-electric projects in the western part of the state. Three water resource developments built by the U.S. Army Corps of Engineers contain recreation facilities leased to the North Carolina Division of Parks and Recreation. Kerr Reservoir is the largest. Along its 800-mile shoreline, which crosses the state line into Virginia, sit seven separate park developments and two commercial marinas.

The U.S. Forest Service, which is responsible for over 1.2 million acres of national forests in North Carolina, manages about two-thirds of the government-owned land in the state. This acreage is dis-

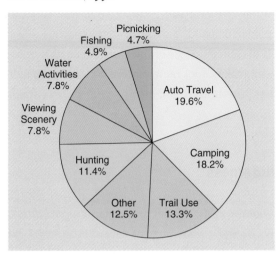

Figure 19.9. Recreation in the National Forests in North Carolina, 1996

Picnicking 4.7%
Fishing 4.9%
Water Activities 7.8%
Viewing Scenery 7.8%
Hunting 11.4%
Other 12.5%
Trail Use 13.3%
Camping 18.2%
Auto Travel 19.6%

Source: U.S. Forest Service, National Forests in North Carolina.

tributed among four national forests: Pisgah and Nantahala in the Mountains, Uwharrie in the Piedmont, and Croatan on the coast. Under terms of the Multiple Use–Sustained Yield Act of 1960, the Forest Service is required to administer all national forests for a variety of purposes, including recreation, over the long term. Although timber production is an important management objective in many areas, recreational use is diverse and substantial, as Figure 19.9 illustrates.

Eleven national forest tracts covering over 100,000 acres have been set aside as wilderness areas in North Carolina. Other significant recreational lands in the state's national forests include the Appalachian Trail, Joyce Kilmer Memorial Forest, Uwharrie Trail, and numerous hunting, fishing, camping, and swimming areas. The Forest Service also has designated "scenic byways" along several routes to encourage recreational driving.

State Areas

North Carolina acquired its first state park, Mount Mitchell, in 1916 in response to citizens' concerns over destructive logging practices there. Since then the State Parks System has grown to thirty-six operating units: thirty parks, four recreation areas, and two natural areas (Fig. 19.7). Additional management units without budgets or staff include several state natural areas. Park environments range from mountains, forests, and open cliff faces to reservoirs, bay lakes, cypress swamps, waterfalls, and ocean beaches. Many include historic sites.

Visitor traffic at state parks exceeds that of the Great Smoky Mountains National Park (Fig. 19.8) yet covers only one-quarter of the acreage. Fort Macon State Park has attracted the most use in recent years, primarily due to its oceanside location. The four state recreation areas—Kerr Lake, Fort Fisher, Falls Lake, and Jordan Lake—also rank among the system's most popular units. Morrow Mountain and Umstead State Parks are visited heavily as well because of their proximity to urban areas. Thus, these parks are an especially important part of North Carolina's overall recreation picture. Situated closer to population centers than national forests or national parks, state parks often provide North Carolina residents with convenient access to outdoor recreational opportunities in natural settings. In addition, many units of the state system protect areas of ecological or historic significance.

State forests in North Carolina are limited in number. On the Coastal Plain, Bladen Lakes State Forest consists of over 37,000 acres and surrounds Jones Lake and Singletary Lake State Parks. The North Carolina Division of Forest Resources has also developed a series of small educational state forests with picnic areas and interpretive trails that explain forest ecology and management practices.

County and Municipal Areas

Local governments in North Carolina differ greatly in their commitment and their ability to finance outdoor recreation. Large metropolitan jurisdictions in the Piedmont, for example, offer high levels of service, whereas a study by the North Carolina Division of Parks and Recreation found that fourteen rural counties have neither municipal (i.e., city or town) nor county park and recreation departments. In these latter instances, support is often limited to maintaining a few picnic areas or boat ramps. In twenty-eight more counties municipal programs exist, but the local county governments provide no additional services.

Fifty-eight of North Carolina's one hundred counties have established county-level recreation programs and departments. Typically they provide resource-based recreational opportunities such as swimming, boat access, picnic grounds, and scenic areas. Playgrounds, athletic fields, tennis courts, and other outdoor facilities also are common.

Municipal park departments tend to concentrate their efforts more on intense, facility-based recreation activities that require comparatively little space in proportion to their use. The usual outdoor recreation facilities at city and town parks include playgrounds, swimming pools, ball fields, tennis courts, and picnic areas. Several cities even provide golf courses. In North Carolina, 128 municipalities operate parks. They vary considerably. Larger jurisdictions employ salaried staff, whereas smaller towns often depend more heavily on local school systems, counties, or private organizations to administer recreation programs.

Private Areas

The private sector also provides a variety of outdoor recreational opportunities in North Carolina. Groups such as the Southern Appalachian Highlands Conservancy, the North Carolina Nature Conservancy, Audubon Society, and historic preservation organizations help protect the state's ecological and cultural heritage by purchasing natural areas or historic sites. Private nonprofit organizations and agencies—including the YWCA, YMCA, scout councils, church groups, and 4-H—sponsor recreation programs to achieve their varied goals. Numerous hunting and fishing areas are privately owned and leased for limited public use as part of the state's Game Lands Program.

Whereas states like Kentucky have established publicly operated resort parks, North Carolina has left these more extensive and expensive recreational developments to private enterprise. Private corporations, for example, operate all of the state's downhill ski areas and theme parks. In addition, commercial enterprises are responsible for the vast majority of North Carolina's campgrounds and golf courses and a sizable portion of its tennis courts, swimming pools, and horseback riding areas. Whitewater rafting companies, charter boat operations, and hunting guides represent other contributions of the private sector to outdoor recreation within the state's borders.

These options are not equally accessible to all residents, however. Profit-making ventures charge admission or membership fees, and they usually cluster around vacation destinations. Nevertheless, commercial operators can respond more quickly to public demand, and some can finance projects involving the large amounts of capital that government may be unable or unwilling to allocate. Nonprofit groups, too, can act more rapidly than public agencies when opportunities arise to purchase historic properties or fragile natural sites.

Natural Areas and Wilderness

From barrier islands to mountain crests, North Carolina hosts a profusion of native plant and animal species and a wide range of natural ecosystems. But only remnants of the once vast forests, wetland areas, and marine habitats remain unaltered by human activities. As a result, more than half the state's major natural community types are considered at risk in North Carolina or worldwide, according to the state's Natural Heritage Program. Many of these places face an uncertain future, especially in light of North Carolina's dispersed and growing population. Among the potentially harmful activities are land development, highway construction, logging, and wetland drainage. The demand for new or expanded outdoor recreation facilities also threatens to destroy natural habitats or overwhelm them with visitors.

Of the state's native species, many are listed as endangered or threatened, and the survival of several hundred other types of flora and fauna is believed to be imperiled within the state. These vulnerable species represent a sizable share of North Carolina's total kinds of animals and plants.

Natural areas help protect water supplies, air quality, and soil productivity, and they are refuges for both common and rare organisms. They can serve as outdoor classrooms and "living laboratories," where students, citizens, and scientists can learn about native species and natural processes in intact surroundings. For many people they provide relaxation and a renewal of the hu-

Threatened and Endangered Species in North Carolina

The U.S Fish and Wildlife Service has classified 49 species of plants and animals in North Carolina as either endangered or threatened. *Endangered* species are defined in the Endangered Species Act of 1973, as amended, as "in danger of extinction throughout all or a significant portion of its range." A *threatened* species is one "which is likely to become an endangered species within the foreseeable future throughout all or a significant portion of its range."

ENDANGERED

ANIMALS

Bat, Indiana (Myotis sodalis)

Bat, Virginia big-eared (Corynorhinus [=Plecotus] townsendii virginianus)

Butterfly, Saint Francis' satyr (Neonympha mitchellii francisci)

Elktoe, Appalachian (Alasmidonta ravenliana)

Falcon, American peregrine (Falco peregrinus anatum)

Heelsplitter, Carolina (Lasmigona decorata)

Manatee, West Indian (Trichechus manatus)

Pearlymussel, littlewing (Pegias fabula)

Shiner, Cape Fear (Notropis mekistocholas)

Spider, spruce-fir moss (Microhexura montivaga)

Spinymussel, Tar River (Elliptio ssteinstansana)

Squirrel, Carolina northern flying (Glaucomys sabrinus coloratus)

Wedgemussel, dwarf (Alasmidonta heterodon)

Wolf, red (Canis rufus)

Woodpecker, red-cockaded (Picoides borealis)

PLANTS

Small-anthered bottercress (Cardamine micranthera)

Smooth coneflower (Echinacea laevigata)

Spreading avens (Geum radiatum)

Rock gnome lichen (Gymnoderma lineare)

Roan Mountain bluet (Hedyotis purpurea var. montana)

Schweinitz's sunflower (Helianthus schweinitzii)

Pondberry (Lindera melissifolia)

Rough-leaved loosestrife (Lysimachia asperulaefolia)

Canby's dropwort (Oxpolis canbyi)

Harperella (Ptilimnium nodosum[=fluviatile]

Michaux's sumac (Rhus michauxii)

Bunched arrowhead (Sagittaria fasciculata)

Green pitcher-plant (Sarracenia oreophila)

Mountain sweet pitcher-plant (Sarracenia rubra ssp.jonesii)

American chaffseed (Schwalbea americana)

White irisette (Sisyrinchium dichotomum)

Cooley's meadowrue (Thalictrum cooleyi)

THREATENED

ANIMALS

Chub, spotfin (=turquoise shiner) (Cyprinella [=Hybopsis] monacha)

Eagle, bald (Haliaeetus leucocephalus)

Plover, piping (Charadrius melodus)

Shrew, Dismal Swamp southeastern (Sorex longirostris fisheri)

Silverside, Waccamaw (Menidia extensa)

Snail, noonday (Mesodon clarki nantahala)

Tern, roseate (Sterna dougallii dougallii)

Turtle, loggerhead sea (Caretta caretta)

PLANTS

Sensitive joint-vetch (Aeschynomene virginica)

Seabeach amaranth (Amaranthus pumilus)

Swamp pink (Helonias bullata)

Dwarf-flowered heartleaf (Hexastylis naniflora)

Mountain golden heather (Hudsonia montana)

Small whorled pogonia (Isotria medeoloides)

Heller's blazingstar (Liatris helleri)

Blue Ridge goldenrod (Solidago spithamaea)

Virginia spiraea (Spiraea virginiana)

Source: U.S. Fish and Wildlife Service, Division of Endangered Species, December 1998

man spirit. Some larger or less vulnerable locations can support passive outdoor recreation activities such as nature study, hiking, backpacking, and photography. Others may require restricted access because of their delicate nature or landowner preferences.

Although undisturbed places make up only a small percentage of the state's area, over 850 locations have been identified by the North Carolina Natural Heritage Program as possessing national, statewide, or regional significance. They range from the size of a suburban backyard to the 23,000-acre Roan Mountain highlands and the half-million-acre Great Smoky Mountains. Protection has been arranged for only about one-third of the 850 areas. Consequently, nearly half of the state's endangered and threatened species lack even one secure population site.

A variety of measures helps to preserve natural areas in North Carolina. National or state programs can protect wild and scenic rivers, following field evaluation and legislative approval. Congress can designate wilderness areas on federally held land. The state's Natural Heritage Program, described below, involves both public agencies and private owners in acquiring or otherwise preserving natural areas. Nonprofit organizations such as the Nature Conservancy and the Trust for Public Land purchase significant parcels, often with the aim of eventually turning them over to a public agency. Through its North Carolina branch, the Nature Conservancy has protected almost 300,000 acres across the state. In 1998 it bought and resold to the state nearly 18,000 acres next to the South Mountains State Park in Burke County. These and several other adjacent and publicly owned tracts encompass 53 square miles of unbroken forest. Similarly, the Nature Conservancy acted as an intermediary between Canal Wood Products, the landowner, and the state Wildlife Resources Commission in the purchase of 7,800 acres around Suggs Mill Pond in Bladen County. The property will become part of a wildlife preservation corridor in Bladen and Cumberland Counties that also includes the Bushy Lake State Park natural area.

Private individuals, too, may elect to keep portions of their property in a natural state. Grandfather Mountain's 5,000 acres of backcountry in Avery and Watauga Counties are an outstanding example. In addition, many tracts of de facto wilderness exist on both public and private land where, although no formal legislation or declaration has occurred, the land retains much of its undisturbed character intact. Such areas, of course, are subject to future change unless further steps are taken to protect them.

Sections of five free-flowing rivers in North Carolina that add up to over 150 miles have been designated as wild or scenic rivers (Fig. 19.10). The protected segments of the Linville and Chattooga Rivers, situated largely on federal land, are relatively secure. Tracts surrounding much of the Horsepasture River have been acquired from Duke Power Company for addition to the Nantahala National Forest and as part of the new Jocassee Gorges State Park. The New River and the Lumber River may pose greater challenges. Proposed land purchases and easements for state parks along these two rivers encompass only small portions of their watersheds, although the areas targeted for acquisition lie primarily in and adjacent to the critical riparian zones.

Linville Gorge and Shining Rock, both located in the Pisgah National Forest, were two of the first four eastern areas set aside by Congress under the Wilderness Act of 1964. Subsequently, ten other parcels of federal land have been protected in North Carolina as part of the nation's Wilderness Preservation System. These twelve areas total almost 110,000 acres. The U.S. Forest Service manages all but Swanquarter Wilderness, which is under the jurisdiction of the U.S. Fish and Wildlife Service. Wilderness studies are also under way or pending on several other Forest Service tracts. Beyond these areas are about three dozen roadless parcels in North Carolina's national forests that the Wilderness Society, a national organization, recommended be considered for wilderness or low impact–use status.

In the national parks, wilderness status has been proposed for the Shackleford Banks section of Cape Lookout National Seashore and for the majority of the Great Smoky Mountains National Park. Controversy surrounds the latter designation because of a 1943 agreement between the federal

Figure 19.10. Designated Wilderness Areas and Protected Rivers

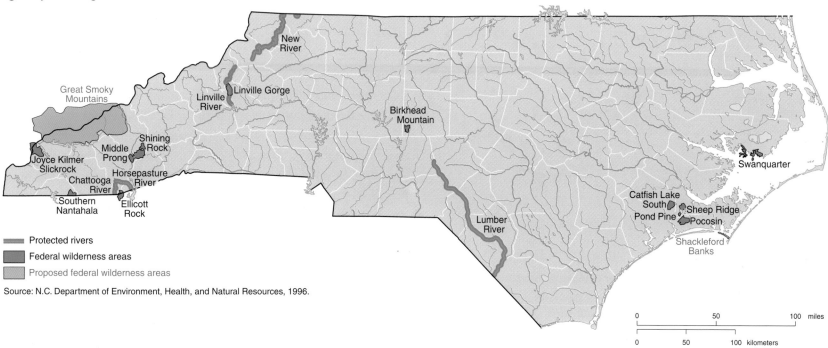

New River

Linville Gorge

Great Smoky Mountains

Linville River

Birkhead Mountain

Shining Rock

Middle Prong

Joyce Kilmer Slickrock

Horsepasture River

Chattooga River

Southern Nantahala

Ellicott Rock

Swanquarter

Catfish Lake South

Sheep Ridge

Pond Pine

Pocosin

Lumber River

Shackleford Banks

— Protected rivers
▮ Federal wilderness areas
▮ Proposed federal wilderness areas

Source: N.C. Department of Environment, Health, and Natural Resources, 1996.

| 0 | 50 | 100 | miles |

| 0 | 50 | 100 | kilometers |

government and Swain County to construct a road along the Smokies' flanks parallel to Fontana Lake that would replace a state highway flooded by the Fontana project.

The North Carolina Natural Heritage Program

The North Carolina Natural Heritage Program was established in 1976 by the state's Department of Environment, Health, and Natural Resources with the assistance of the Nature Conservancy. Administered within the Division of Parks and Recreation, the program's objectives are to identify and help protect North Carolina's most significant natural areas. Program staff conduct a state-wide inventory to locate areas that best represent the state's natural heritage and determine if they are adequately safeguarded.

Once these areas are identified, the Natural Heritage Program can employ a variety of protection techniques. Its Registry of Natural Heritage Areas, for example, honors the owners and administrators of recognized public or private natural areas who declare their intent to protect their land. An eligible natural area is entered on the registry only after the owner voluntarily agrees to its designation. The registry thus represents a nonbinding, nonregulatory approach. However, land acquisition may be considered for particularly important tracts. Protection can be effected through purchase, donation, or conservation easements. In addition, natural areas in either public or private

Figure 19.11. Dedicated Nature Preserves and Registered Natural Heritage Areas, 1997

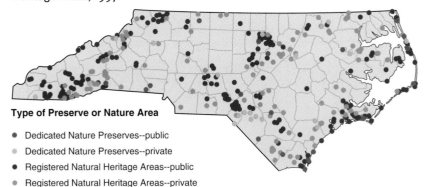

Type of Preserve or Nature Area

● Dedicated Nature Preserves--public
● Dedicated Nature Preserves--private
● Registered Natural Heritage Areas--public
● Registered Natural Heritage Areas--private

Source: N.C. Division of Parks and Recreation, Natural Heritage Program, 1997.

ownership can be protected from misuse or damaging changes by designating them as Dedicated Nature Preserves. As of 1997, the Natural Heritage Program had arranged protection for over four hundred public and private lands in the state (Fig. 19.11). Not all are open for visitation, but Charles E. Roe's *Directory to North Carolina's Natural Areas* lists more than a hundred places where the public can experience North Carolina's natural heritage firsthand.

Maintaining Recreational Resources

Outdoor recreation in North Carolina is changing and growing. The demand for more facilities and space comes up against efforts to preserve and protect our natural heritage. Today, as the twentieth century and millennium have drawn to a close, the challenges of maintaining and protecting the outdoor resource base while also meeting present and future needs have never been greater.

Addressing the Increasing Demand

Many local governments confronting increased demand have constructed new facilities and added programs and staff. Several municipalities have also recognized the need for new and innovative approaches. To provide close-to-home recreation where space is often at a premium, for example, communities have developed or proposed linear parks. These include trail networks, parkways, protected river corridors, bike paths, and greenways. They help link existing recreation facilities and protect open space, especially in urban and suburban settings. Some recent projects have been supported through North Carolina's Parks and Recreation Trust Fund, described below. Raleigh, the first city in the state to initiate a greenway program, is regarded as a national leader in communitywide open space protection. But as the human population and development projects in metropolitan areas increase, green space across the state continues to decline.

The need for hiking trails is also acute in the more heavily settled portions of the state. *Hiking Trails in North Carolina* identifies nearly eight hundred hiking trails totaling 2,400 miles. More than 80 percent, including such well-known pathways as the Appalachian Trail and the trail networks at Grandfather Mountain and Shining Rock, are located in the Mountain region, however. The Piedmont, where more than half of North Carolinians live, contains only 5 percent of the state's public trail mileage.

The state parks are, in several respects, unable to handle the heavy influx of visitors they receive. Maintenance of some existing parks is barely at the custodial level, with facilities marginal or unusable because of the lack of repairs. Their educational potential has yet to be fully realized. Several comprehensive plans and a succession of legislative study committees have consistently reported on the need for land acquisition, physical plant development, adequate staffing, and increased and stable funding. The estimated cost of the most important land purchases, repairs, and capital improvements exceeds $225 million.

The annual budget for operating and maintaining the North Carolina State

Parks System for the 1997–98 fiscal year was approximately $15 million. The state ranks close to last in the nation in terms of its per capita operating budget for state park and recreation facilities. Figure 19.12 provides comparative data for the Southeast. Annual expenditures by Charlotte and Raleigh for their city parks generally exceed the state's parks budget. Yet North Carolina's $15 million allocation represented a 60 percent increase since 1992–93. Staffing has been added to the point where each park has at least one full-time maintenance staff member and one full-time office assistant, freeing up park rangers for their intended responsibilities.

Appropriations, gifts, and matching grants from the federal Land and Water Conservation Fund supported numerous local projects and more than doubled state park acreage in the 1970s. Since then, the level of funding has diminished substantially. Land and Water Conservation Fund grants dropped from a high of over $7 million in the late 1970s to less than $300,000 in the early 1990s.

A number of strategies for increasing park funding are available. For example, a cigarette tax in Texas provides over $15 million annually for state and local parks. Florida passed a $250 million bond issue to acquire undeveloped beaches. Missouri's 0.1 percent tax increase on retail sales generates about $20 million annually—above and beyond the operating budget—for state parks. Another approach, once proposed in North Carolina, is to sell some park acreage where land values are

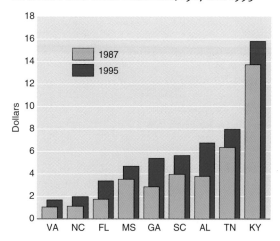

Figure 19.12. Per Capita Operating Expenditures for State Parks in the Southeast, 1987 and 1995

Sources: N.C. Department of Environment, Health, and Natural Resources; National Association of Park Directors.

especially high and use the proceeds to endow the remainder of the system. A special appropriation from the North Carolina General Assembly in 1985 and a $35 million bond issue approved by voters in 1993 helped support capital improvements and land acquisition.

The Parks and Recreation Trust Fund and Other Options

In 1994 the General Assembly established the Parks and Recreation Trust Fund, supported by 75 percent of the state's share of the land transfer tax. The fund is distributed to three programs: 65 percent to the State Parks System, 30 percent as matching grants to local parks and recreation programs, and 5 percent for the coastal beach access

program. The Parks and Recreation Trust Fund is expected to generate more than $18 million annually. It represents an attempt to find a long-term approach to many of North Carolina's most pressing outdoor recreational needs.

Other options for augmenting parks and recreation budgets include further raising the real estate deed transfer tax and enacting a severance tax on the extraction of nonrenewable mineral resources. In the face of budget cuts, many government agencies such as the U.S. National Park Service have instituted admission fees and other charges to boost park revenues. In North Carolina's State Parks System, only Falls Lake State Recreation Area and Jordan Lake State Recreation Area require an entrance fee. It has also been suggested that North Carolina could follow Kentucky's lead in building a system of state resort parks to generate income. But private resort development in North Carolina is already extensive in traditional vacation areas, and many people argue that state parks should remain in a more natural condition.

In addition to private contributions, private-public partnerships offer opportunities for outdoor recreation. For instance, the Carolina Power and Light Company became the country's first corporate sponsor of an entire State Parks System in 1991, when it initiated a program to support environmental education and volunteer programs and a challenge grant project to involve other industries in adopting North Carolina state parks. In Jackson County, the U.S. Forest Service, Duke

Power Company, and The Nature Conservancy co-operated in a planning project and land swap to minimize the impact of power lines through the Panthertown Valley and preserve the remainder in its natural state. The Park Fund, a nonprofit organization founded by parks and recreation professionals and concerned citizens, formed in 1987 to raise supplementary funds for local and state parks and recreation areas in North Carolina.

Twelve local citizen task forces are working with various government entities on the Mountains-to-Sea Trail (Fig. 19.13). This trail is actually a corridor from the Tennessee border to the Outer Banks. It is projected to have a network of land and water routes that will link major population centers with national forests, national parks, and state parks. By 1997 about half of the main hiking trail in the Mountains-to-Sea corridor had been completed or officially designated as part of existing trail networks.

Recognizing the Economic Impacts

Inadequate funding of recreation may stem in large part from the belief that parks and their associated facilities, although enjoyable, are nonessential and a drain on tax dollars. However, studies of the state parks, the Blue Ridge Parkway, and wildlife-related leisure activities illustrate the impact that recreation has on the state's economy and appeal as a tourist destination.

Figure 19.14 shows the distribution of visitor ex-

Figure 19.13. Mountains-to-Sea Trail Corridor

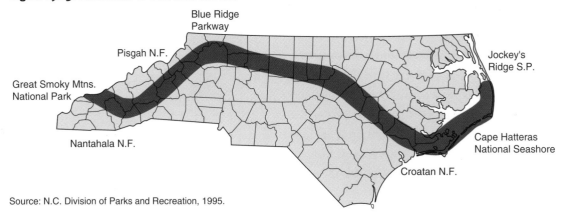

Source: N.C. Division of Parks and Recreation, 1995.

penditures at state parks. (Although the figures are based on 1986 spending, the patterns today are likely to be similar and the impacts even greater.) The information reveals two important points. First, visitors' spending affects numerous businesses—grocery stores, motels, gift shops, restaurants, service stations, and amusements. Because these expenditures are diffused, their economic effects tend to be unrecognized and undervalued. Nevertheless, all have an effect on the tax base and employment, although the latter may be low-wage and seasonal in many cases. Second, expenditures by individual state park users are modest. It is only when the average number of dollars spent is multiplied by the millions of annual participants that the significant effects can be appreciated. Besides these direct impacts, there are the secondary benefits of the money as it recirculates through local and regional economies. Typically, this mul-

Figure 19.14. Distribution of Expenditures by North Carolina State Park Visitors, 1986

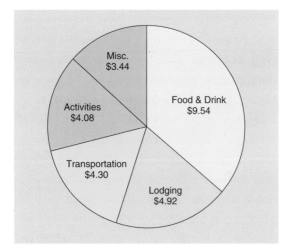

Note: Figures indicate average dollars spent per 12 hours of on-site recreation activity.

Source: Outdoor Wilderness Assessment Group; Southeastern Forest Experiment Station.

tiplier effect doubles or even triples the impact of each outdoor recreation dollar.

A 1980 study by the U.S. Fish and Wildlife Service estimated that participants in wildlife-related recreation activities spent $580 million that year in North Carolina: $266 million on fishing, $167 million on hunting, and $147 million on observing, feeding, and photographing wildlife. These expenditures also generated about $23 million in state and local taxes, which represented a return of approximately $50 annually for each dollar spent by the North Carolina Wildlife Resources Commission. This figure is even more impressive when one considers that fishers and hunters pay most of their own way: 90 percent of Wildlife Resources Commission funds come from licenses, permits, and excise taxes.

In 1995–96 researchers from North Carolina State University studied the economic impact of travel to the Blue Ridge Parkway. Stays by out-of-state visitors to the parkway's North Carolina segment averaged three days and two nights. Each visiting group spent an average of $500, contributing a total of $1.9 billion to the economies of adjacent counties after the entire impact of their purchases during the twelve-month research period was analyzed. These expenditures supported 63,782 jobs in the state and added $105.5 million to state and local revenues. The findings represent a 280 percent rise in the number of jobs created and a 66 percent increase in revenues since a similar study done in 1987. Not surprisingly, outdoor recreation was the most common purpose for going to the Blue Ridge Parkway, accounting for 42 percent of the visits.

Protecting Recreational Resources

A 1972 amendment to the Constitution of North Carolina and the State Parks Act of 1987 charge the North Carolina Division of Parks and Recreation with managing the state's parks for the present and future. As the parks system's mission statement declares: "The North Carolina state parks system exists for

Rafters on the Nantahala River

the enjoyment, education, health and inspiration of all our citizens and visitors. The mission of the state parks system is to conserve and protect representative examples of the natural beauty, ecological features, and recreational resources of statewide significance; to provide outdoor recreational opportunities in a safe and healthy environment; and to provide environmental education opportunities that promote stewardship of the state's natural heritage."

Similarly, in establishing the National Park Service in 1916, the U.S. Congress stated that the purpose of the parks is to "conserve the scenery and the natural and historic objects and the wild life therein and to provide for the enjoyment of the same in such manner and by such means as will leave them unimpaired for the enjoyment of future generations."

Although these goals appear to be appropriate and straightforward, their implementation as a new century begins poses some critical challenges. How can North Carolina's natural heritage be protected for tomorrow while it is being enjoyed today? How can increasing numbers of recreationists be accommodated in the same amount of space? The expansive vistas of the Great Smoky Mountains National Park are deceptive. This destination receives over 9 million visits each year, but the vast majority of users remain within a half mile of their automobiles. North Carolina's State Parks System attracts even more visitors to tracts of land that add up to less than one-third of the Smokies' acreage. The Blue Ridge Parkway is the most-visited federal property east of California. Such demand can impair not only the visitors' enjoyment but also the ecological integrity and scenic beauty that parks were established to protect.

Park managers have attempted to resolve the conflicts in this pair of mandates in a variety of ways. For instance, to limit crowding and vegetation damage on hiking trails in the backcountry, Great Smoky Mountains National Park has instituted a permit system for all trail campsites. Several vehicle campgrounds in the Smokies have become so popular that campers now arrange for sites through nationwide ticket reservation centers. State park facilities damaged by heavy use have had to be closed in several cases. In other instances,

some visitors complain about overdevelopment—the paved paths and fenced-in overlooks intended to safeguard the public interfere with the natural settings they came to enjoy.

Because park boundaries rarely encompass an entire ecosystem or view shed, changes on neighboring property may be ecologically or visually incompatible. Adjacent housing developments, resorts, commercial establishments, logging operations, highway construction, and waste disposal all constitute potential threats to park integrity. For instance, over five thousand individual, corporate, or governmental land holdings border the Blue Ridge Parkway's narrow protected corridor. Though many cooperative agreements have been negotiated, some recent developments have altered the landscape that the parkway traverses. At White Lake—a state park that protects an outstanding example of the freshwater ecosystem known as a Carolina bay—criticism has arisen over lakefront construction projects. Neighboring property holders have been permitted to build piers and retaining walls on state land to protect their holdings and provide private access.

Additional environmental problems originate at locations far removed from park boundaries. According to a 1996 report by the North Carolina Department of Environment, Health, and Natural Resources, the water quality of at least 17 percent of the state's freshwater streams and rivers did not support intended uses. Although point-source pollution from municipal and industrial waste was

partly responsible, the majority of the impairment was from a variety of nonpoint sources. These included farms, cities, and construction projects.

Air pollutants from factories, power plants, and automobiles threaten Mount Mitchell, the Great Smoky Mountains, Grandfather Mountain, and other areas. Wind-borne or rain-deposited substances are blamed for the decreased visibility from scenic viewpoints in these popular destinations and have been identified as factors in the death of evergreen trees at higher elevations.

Outlook

Outdoor recreation in North Carolina is rich and diverse. Viewed as an amenity by some, recreational opportunities are more essential than most people realize to physical fitness, mental health, and human relationships. Recreation areas also play important roles in protecting natural resources and supporting local economies in the state. They affect business relocations and the localities in which people choose to live and work. Outdoor recreation can foster important psychological bonds with a state's ecological and cultural heritage.

The degree to which these values are recognized will determine the future quality of outdoor recreation in North Carolina. The state's economic, social, and physical well-being is strongly connected to the protection of its natural heritage.

Selected References

Biggs, W., and J. Parnell. *State Parks of North Carolina*. Winston-Salem: John F. Blair, Publisher, 1989.

Brothers, G., and R. Chen. *1995–96 Economic Impact of Travel to the Blue Ridge Parkway*. Raleigh: Department of Parks, Recreation and Tourism Management, North Carolina State University, 1997.

DeHart, A. *North Carolina Hiking Trails*. Boston: Appalachian Mountain Club, 1996.

Drake, D., and P. Bromley. *1997 Natural Resources Inventory of North Carolina*. Raleigh: North Carolina Cooperative Extension Service, North Carolina State University, 1997.

Flournoy, W. "Vigilantes, the Neuse, and Sure Salvation: Evolving Advocacy for Greenways." In *Parkways, Greenways, Riverways: The Way More Beautiful: Proceedings of the Third International Biennial Linear Parks Conference*, edited by Woodward S. Bousquet. Boone: Appalachian Consortium Press, 1993.

Jackson, L. *Mountain Treasures at Risk: The Future of the Southern Appalachian National Forests*. Washington: Wilderness Society, 1989.

Johnson, R. *Southern Snow: The Winter Guide to Dixie*. Boston: Appalachian Mountain Club, 1987.

Jolley, H. *Blue Ridge Parkway: The First Fifty Years*. Boone: Appalachian Consortium Press, 1985.

McClure, T. *North Carolina's Mountain Treasures: The Unprotected Wildlands of the Nantahala and Pisgah National Forests*. Atlanta: Wilderness Society, 1992.

North Carolina Division of Parks and Recreation. *Outdoors North Carolina, 1990–1995*. Raleigh: North Carolina Department of Environment, Health, and Natural Resources, 1989.

———. *North Carolina Outdoor Recreation Plan, 1995–2000*. Raleigh: North Carolina Department of Environment, Health, and Natural Resources, 1995.

Roe, C. E. *A Directory to North Carolina's Natural Areas*. Raleigh: North Carolina Natural Heritage Foundation, 1987.

We have traditions which are precious

to us—and a destiny worthy of the best

in our powers as in our past. We shall not

find the way into the future easily—I find

no easy roads for most people running

through the past.

—Jonathan Daniels

20. RETROSPECT AND PROSPECT

Douglas M. Orr Jr. and Alfred W. Stuart

At the close of the twentieth century North Carolina is undergoing not only sustained growth but also fundamental change in many aspects of the state's life. There are many reasons for these changes and widespread consequences.

Economic Change

The primary impetus for change resides in the economy, and for the most part the factor most responsible is the trend toward regional, national, and global economies. First, the emergence of a global economy has, on the one hand, disadvantaged many of the more labor-intensive manufacturing industries that have for so long been the backbone of North Carolina's economy. Imports of clothing and cloth have cost many textile and apparel firms large parts of their markets, and many jobs went with them. But the surviving textile companies have invested heavily in new technology, raising productivity and profits in the process. Thus, although employment is down, the industry has responded in a way that should protect it from large downturns in the future.

435

The other side of the internationalization coin is that there were 738 for-eign-owned businesses in North Carolina in 1998 and exports increased, reaching $18 billion in 1997. The passage of the North American Free Trade Agreement (NAFTA) is expected to provide yet new markets for North Caro-lina companies. Canada is already the leading market for North Carolina's ex-ports, and exports to Mexico have been increasing at an average of 38 percent a year since 1987, moving that country into third place among the state's ex-port markets.

A second major reason for the state's economic growth is that manufactur-ing has increased in North Carolina while it has been declining in the rest of the nation, at least in employment. Even as measured by value of output, North Carolina's industrial sector has increased faster than the other states'. Value added per employee in manufacturing, typically well below the national mean, has now moved close to that average, indicating that the state's factories are moving away from their traditional emphasis on low-skill, labor-intensive industries.

Third, the national shift toward information processing, coupled with the computer-based revolution in communications, has given rise to new indus-tries and the rapid growth of office occupations. Symptomatic of this devel-opment, multi-tenant office space in Charlotte mushroomed from about 2 million square feet in 1970 to nearly 30 million square feet by the end of the century. During the same period, Charlotte emerged as the nation's second largest banking center in terms of assets controlled by banks that are head-quartered there. Also related is the continuous expansion of the Research Tri-angle Park in the Raleigh-Durham area as a major national center for innova-tive, high-technology industries. These trends are symptomatic of an even broader one: most of the state's economic growth, whether in high-tech facto-ries or in office towers, is focusing on metropolitan areas, especially the larger ones.

Fourth, improvements in national transportation systems have given North Carolina better access to national and global markets, making it easier for companies to take advantage of the state's competitive operating costs.

The interstate highway system, the presence of a major airline hub, two com-mercial ports, and location along major railroad lines make it possible to real-ize the benefits of being positioned strategically in a mid-Atlantic location between the urban centers of the Northeast and the rapidly expanding Deep South.

Finally, North Carolina has a favored environment, both cultural and natural. People are attracted to a benign climate, wide beaches, and mountain scenery. The ease of modern transportation and rising levels of affluence al-low thousands of people to take advantage of these resources, whether as tourists or as retirees. Coupled with a prized natural environment is a way of life that others see as "laid back," open, and friendly. Both are part of a quality of life that includes honest government, low taxes, and moderate living costs.

Population Change

Throughout most of its modern history North Carolina barely was able to maintain its proportion of the national population as thousands left every year, primarily in search of better economic opportunities elsewhere. This be-gan to change in the 1960s as the economy started to expand and diversify and as the constraint of racial segregation was removed. In the 1970s—for the first time in the twentieth century—North Carolina experienced net population in-migration, which increased in the 1980s. Currently and according to future projections, about two-thirds of the state's net growth is occurring through net in-migration. This in-migration has two important elements: (1) it is comprised not just of African Americans and whites but also of Asians and Hispanics, diversifying the ethnic mix of the population (though the Asian and Hispanic components are still relatively small, these two groups are the most rapidly growing segments of the North Carolina population), and (2) hundreds of thousands of people, of whatever ethnic character, are moving into the state from all over the country. The new arrivals bring with them diverse cultures that range from various cuisines to interest in sports such as ice hockey. Roman Catholicism, once a minority among religious groups, is now one of the fastest-growing denominations in the state. Parochial attitudes of native North Carolinians are being challenged by this change.

North Carolina is now considered to be a high-growth state generally and has risen to fifth place among the states as one of the most popular destinations for retirees. The North Carolina Office of State Planning projects that the state's population will reach 9.3 million by the year 2020, only two decades into the future. Given the 6.6 million total in 1990, this would mean the addition of 2.7 million people in thirty years. It was only in 1920 that North Carolina had a population of 2.5 million. As with economic growth and strongly related to it, population growth is increasingly concentrated in and around metropolitan areas, principally the larger ones. An exception to this are the clusters of new residents in recreation and retirement areas along the coast or in the mountains. Regional centers such as Wilmington and Asheville have economies that depend on serving the patrons of these more rural areas.

Urban/Rural Balance

Economic growth and change have driven the steady shift away from a rural, small-city pattern of living for most North Carolinians. It was only with the 1990 census that the majority of the population was classified as living in urban places of at least 2,500 population. In that year Charlotte, the largest city, accounted for a little more than 6 percent of the state's population. Only 41 percent of the North Carolina population lived in a federally delineated metropolitan area in 1960, as then designated, and that proportion reached two-thirds in 1990, mainly because the number of metropolitan areas increased, as did the number of counties that were included in the earlier areas. Still, the two-thirds proportion was below the level for the rest of the South and the nation. Meanwhile, even though the rural nonfarm population increased, the proportion classified as rural farm fell by 86 percent between 1960 and 1990, comprising only 1.8 percent of the state total in 1990. Continued suburban sprawl is suggested by the fact that, despite decades of urban growth, the 536 active municipalities in the state in 1997 still contained barely half of the state's population within their corporate limits.

Political Change

These numbers provide a measure of the extent to which North Carolina has moved away from its heritage as a rural, small-town state. This dramatic shift has created major tensions within the political body. Rural areas long dominated the state's politics, the allocation of resources, and the implementation of state policies. Rural legislators and corporate sympathizers used a tightly controlled, single-party political system to prevail in the General Assembly. The increase in urban populations, the institution of one man–one vote districting, and the entry of women, Republicans, and blacks into the process all weakened this monopoly and create a more open, unpredictable legislative system. As yet, however, urban representatives have been unable to act in concert to promote an urban agenda.

Metropolitan Shift

The population statistics also mask a perhaps more fundamental alteration in growth patterns. The expansion of high-technology and research-oriented industries, the addition of thousands of jobs in office towers, the emergence of nationally prominent banks, and the accessibility gained via hub airports have not occurred uniformly throughout the state but primarily within a few metropolitan areas. In general, all metro areas are growing rapidly compared with most of rural North Carolina. Their income and wage levels are higher, and they contain most of the increasingly diverse ethnic population. The greater part of the in-migrant flow to the state is headed for the metropolitan areas, and most particularly its largest ones—a trend seen in many Sunbelt growth areas.

Environmental Impacts

Growth and change, whether in metropolitan or rural areas, are having serious consequences for the state's prized natural environment. The *Charlotte Observer* in December 1997 offered a list of the state's most serious environmental problems:

1. Sprawling growth, which threatens to overwhelm both urban and rural recreation areas
2. Water pollution in streams, lakes, and groundwater
3. Overdevelopment of coastal areas
4. Air pollution, which is choking the air in cities and killing trees in forests
5. Destruction of wetlands that act as filters to remove increasing levels of farm chemicals (their loss also removes habitats that are crucial to wildlife populations)
6. Hog farm waste that fouls the air and water in large areas of eastern North Carolina (a moratorium placed on further growth of hog farms by the 1997 General Assembly momentarily checked the spread of this problem, but further regulation, especially of waste ponds, may be required)
7. Removal of forest resources faster than they can be replenished by new growth (based on long-term projections)
8. Overexploitation of shell- and finfish, which reduces harvests (this problem is compounded by wetland removals that allow critical nursery areas to become polluted and no longer productive)
9. Overdevelopment of mountain areas, which threatens to destroy the environmental beauty that more and more people are seeking to enjoy
10. Billboards, cellular telephone towers, satellite dishes, and similar structures, which—though seemingly inevitable consequences of growth— take away from the state's scenic splendor (the number of cellular towers is expected to more than double over the next few years)

Clearly these problems will require serious, aggressive treatment if North Carolina's future is not to be jeopardized.

Regionalism and Planning

Today the world seems to be reorganizing itself as old boundaries and economic/political units give way to new geographic groupings. City limits have become just that—too restrictive. County lines, designed for and in another century, are often irrelevant, and states are too extensive to offer a coordinated community. The nation-state, a creation of Middle Ages Europe, is often bypassed in the present global commerce, as transactions of all kinds occur among the urban regions of the world, and Americans more frequently question the federal approach to local problems and needs. A rising tide of regionalism is reshaping old alliances and rivalries as new technologies tie together geographic areas that are similar to the old Greek city-states that predated the nation-state phenomenon of the last five hundred years. Author and syndicated columnist Neal Pierce writes: "Across the United States and the globe, the age of the citistate is upon us as regions—not cities, states or even nation-states—are emerging as the world's most influential players."

Although the mega "citistates" receive most of the headlines as the new players on the global stage, with interchanges involving London, New York, Hong Kong, Tokyo, and the like, the relevance of regionalism extends to a variety of geographic settings. The Seattle area developed a model mass transit program out of a regional compact created to clean up Lake Washington and Puget Sound; the Denver-area chambers of commerce came together to form a computerized economic development recruiting program that has ended old rivalries among communities; the Portland area has developed a coordinated cultural arts planning effort; a regional commission in south-central Missouri is addressing the area's high illiteracy rate; and five Alabama counties developed a coordinated waste management authority to negotiate a landfill contract. Other smaller regional groups have much to gain as well. For example, leaders in Missoula, Montana, have identified a region of 200,000 people bound together by newspaper circulation, television market, retailing, medical services, and environmental issues.

The regional phenomenon focuses on collaboration among several sectors—business, education, service organizations, elected officials—rather than governmental reorganization. In getting started, there is an emphasis on specific projects with achievable goals. As ad hoc coalitions come together, thousands of citizens have turned out for regional forums to address the regional agenda. And regional issues run the gamut: cultural arts distinctiveness, transportation, economic cohesiveness, land and water use, education, and the impact of commuter flows. These issues also help to define the boundaries of the region. The Carolinas Issues Academy at the University of North Carolina at Charlotte typifies this trend. Since the late 1980s it has sponsored an annual workshop—attended by hundreds of regional elected officials, business leaders, and government professionals—to examine similar issues.

Planning to deal with growth is seriously out of synch with the nature of recent and probable future change. The primary engines of growth in North Carolina are its multicounty urban regions, many of which are even more extensive than the federally designated Metropolitan Statistical Areas

(MSAs). Though the MSAs are useful for statistical purposes, they bear no relation to legal jurisdictions. In North Carolina, planning, for example, is largely a local matter. All but one of the one hundred counties report having a planning agency, although in thirty-seven, mostly rural, counties the "planning agency" is in the office of the county manager rather than a separate planning department. This probably means only that there is a clerk who handles zoning compliance or subdivision approvals. In fact, not even zoning is an issue for some, as nearly thirty counties do not have countywide zoning. Actually, planning is more local than that. Some 167 cities and towns report having a planning agency, but, again, 41 are housed in the town manager's office, suggesting that planning is not a high priority in those communities. On the other hand, 126 cities and towns do have separate planning departments. They range from the large, relatively sophisticated staff of the Charlotte-Mecklenburg Planning Commission to the lone planner fresh out of college who works primarily with zoning and similar issues.

North Carolina has eighteen multicounty planning agencies, most of them councils of governments, that were authorized by the General Assembly in 1972 (Fig. 20.1). These agencies do provide planning services to their constituent communities, often small towns that lack planning expertise of their own. This service is limited by the fact that 100 of the state's 615 local governments have

elected not to have members on their respective regional councils. These regional councils frequently provide regionwide data and programmatic services, along with forums that bring together community leaders from across their regions. Unfortunately, discussions are not always followed by actions, and the councils are reluctant to take on controversial issues that might offend member governments. In any case, these agencies have no authority to implement zoning or any of the other enforcement tools that are used to implement land use planning. They can advise, but implementation is left to the individual communities, and predictably the latter perspectives will be local, not regional. Moreover, the regional councils are typically underfunded, and in some instances their boundaries do not fit with those of the functioning region or even the MSA of which they are a part.

Another significant view of regionalism in North Carolina is expressed in Figure 20.2, which identifies nine functional urban regions that were designated, with advice from local economic development officials, by the North Carolina Department of Commerce in the early 1980s. Broader than the federal MSAs, these regions contain sixty-five of the state's one hundred counties but account for 90 percent of its population, employment, and personal income and over 93 percent of the total value added by North Carolina manufacturers. Future economic and demographic expansion will take place within these kinds of broad,

Figure 20.1. Multicounty Planning Regions

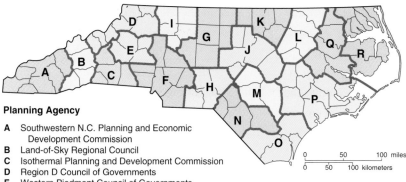

Planning Agency

A Southwestern N.C. Planning and Economic
    Development Commission
B Land-of-Sky Regional Council
C Isothermal Planning and Development Commission
D Region D Council of Governments
E Western Piedmont Council of Governments
F Centralina Council of Governments
G Piedmont Triad Council of Governments
H Pee Dee Council of Governments
I Northwest Piedmont Council of Governments
J Triangle J Council of Governments
K Kerr-Tar Regional Council of Governments
L Region L Council of Governments
M Region M Council of Governments
N Lumber River Council of Governments
O Cape Fear Council of Governments
P Neuse River Council of Governments
Q Mid-East Commission
R Albemarle Regional Planning and Development Commission

Source: N.C. Department of Administration, Division of Policy Development, 1998.

functional regions that are based on North Carolina's historically dispersed population patterns. Given such expansion, it will be necessary to act on a more consciously regional scale.

This was recognized initially in the state's larger urban areas and led to the establishment of several regional groups. The Charlotte-area Carolinas Partnership, the Piedmont Triad Partnership, and the Raleigh-Durham Regional Association are broad-based, multicounty associations that were organized to promote economic development and to more generally advance a regional perspective on growth. Collateral groups, such as the Carolinas Counties Coalition, a voluntary association of public officials in the Charlotte area, and the Carolinas Transportation Compact, have been formed to promote regional cooperation in government and in transportation planning. And some plan-

Figure 20.2 Urban Regions

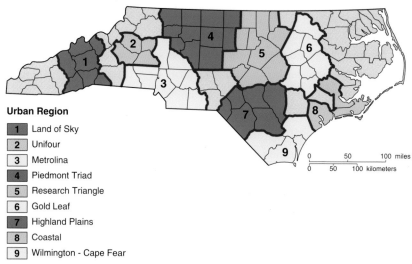

Urban Region

1 Land of Sky
2 Unifour
3 Metrolina
4 Piedmont Triad
5 Research Triangle
6 Gold Leaf
7 Highland Plains
8 Coastal
9 Wilmington - Cape Fear

Source: J. W. Clay, D. M. Orr Jr., A. W. Stuart, *N.C. Urban Regions: An Economic Atlas* (Charlotte: Urban Institute, UNC Charlotte, 1983).

ning assistance is provided by state agencies, especially the North Carolina Division of Coastal Management and the Division of Community Assistance.

In 1993 the North Carolina Economic Development Board initiated a major reorganization of economic development programs in the state by establishing a series of new economic development regions (Fig. 20.3). The three multicountry associations already existing in the three largest urban areas (Carolinas Partnership, the Piedmont Triad Partnership, and Research Triangle Regional Partnership) are included. Others focus on the new Global Transpark Region, southeastern North Carolina counties (Southern Economic Commission), a group of counties in the northeast (Northeastern Economic Region), and the western mountain counties with Asheville as the regional core (Western Economic Commission). The Department of Commerce coordinates the economic development efforts of these groups, including the funneling of incentive and infrastructure funds to counties that are

Figure 20.3. Economic Development Regions

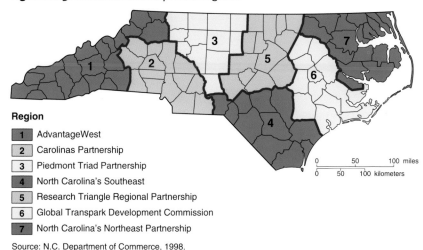

Region

1. AdvantageWest
2. Carolinas Partnership
3. Piedmont Triad Partnership
4. North Carolina's Southeast
5. Research Triangle Regional Partnership
6. Global Transpark Development Commission
7. North Carolina's Northeast Partnership

Source: N.C. Department of Commerce, 1998.

designated as distressed. Some analysts are concerned that these regions will weaken the unified face of North Carolina currently provided by the Division of Business and Industry Development and that there will be an undue deflection of resources into poor rural counties in which few modern businesses have any interest, whether promoted on a single or multicounty scale. This concern is reinforced by recent initiatives such as the multibillion-dollar *intrastate* highway program and the William States Lee economic incentives act, which is oriented heavily toward struggling rural areas.

It is in the area of transportation that some of the most significant regional planning is beginning to take place. The most advanced example of this is the Triangle Transit Authority, authorized by the General Assembly in 1989 to plan for and operate transit systems for Durham, Orange, and Wake Counties. Included in that act and subsequent actions was the authorization to collect a $5-per-vehicle registration tax and a 5 percent tax on the gross receipts of rental vehicles. These funds, plus federal and state grants, are used to integrate and expand regional transit systems, including planning for a possible light rail transit network. Preliminary efforts have been made to establish a similar

authority in the Triad (Winston-Salem, High Point, Greensboro). In the Charlotte area, transit planning to this point is confined to Mecklenburg County, and efforts to develop coordination among the several Metropolitan Planning Organizations (MPOs) in the region are only in the preliminary stages.

The formation of loose, general regions comes at a time when strong regions have a central core around which the region is organized. Much of the growth of the entire region is driven by what happens in the core cities. The suburban parts of the region are able to attract businesses, in part, because their locations provide them access to the core while also allowing them to take advantage of whatever benefits the suburban county can offer. For example, the core may contain a major airport, financial services, and distribution services. The suburban county may have lower taxes and cheaper land and labor. Together the two areas create a synergy that exists only when both situations are present. On the other hand, a grouping of similar counties does not offer this synergy, only more of the same features that each county offers individually.

Nowhere is the strong centrality of regional core areas more apparent than in Charlotte and Raleigh-Durham. The three large counties that are central to these two regions—Mecklenburg, Durham, and Wake—collectively accounted for fully one-third of the state's net population gain between 1980 and 1990, compared with 16.8 and 23.9 percent shares of population and employment, respectively. Charlotte has two nationally prominent bank headquarters, and Raleigh-Durham is home to the Research Triangle Park. Both contain the state's two busiest airports. The two urban cores are anchors along a corridor that flanks Interstate 85 between Raleigh and Atlanta, one that the Ernst and Young accounting firm predicted would be "the preferred megacorridor for business" in the 1990s and that *Business Week* magazine described as "The Boom Belt."

Mecklenburg, Durham, and Wake Counties received 48 percent of the state's total net in-migration between 1980 and 1990. The North Carolina

Office of State Planning has projected that they will account for 42 percent of the net population growth between 1990 and 2020, reaching a population of 2.3 million, or 24 percent of the statewide total. Mecklenburg, Durham, and Wake lead the state in wage levels and incomes; between 1970 and 1997 per capita income levels in the three counties continued to increase faster than the statewide average.

A group of the state's most rural areas also has achieved gains in income statewide, primarily because some of the constituent counties are significant recreation and retirement locales. Moore and Polk Counties, for example, have per capita income averages that are well above the statewide mean, but most of this income was brought in by retirees, as the average wage of the people who work in both counties is, by contrast, rather low. A similar situation persists in Dare, one of the state's leading coastal recreation counties and one of the fastest growing in population, where in 1997 income levels were above 90 percent of the state average but average private sector wages were less than two-thirds of the North Carolina mean. This suggests that although retirement and recreation specializations bring significant economic benefits to the areas affected, in terms of construction, retail sales, and the demand for services, they also drive an economy of generally low-wage, often seasonal service jobs for the resident labor force.

In great measure, the future of North Carolina's cities, and therefore of the entire state, will be determined by the ability to direct growth—as it relates to transportation, land use, infrastructure, and environmental quality—in a positive way. Yet the state and its communities seem to be poorly organized to do this. Controls on developments are one thing, but it is also necessary to have planning carried out on the appropriate geographic scale. Increasingly, that scale is the urban-based, multicounty region, not the counties and towns that for so long have been the usual formats.

Sustainable Development and Smart Growth

As the problems of a rapidly growing and urbanizing state continue to mount, there is increasing concern that North Carolina's greatest assets—viable communities with a sense of place, a prized environment, accelerated economic growth—may not be sustainable to the next generation. More and more, leaders of all political persuasions are calling for a new economic paradigm.

One such person is Paul Hawken, whose book, *The Ecology of Commerce*, placed the sustainable challenges in the context of a new societal revolution. He maintains that a true paradigm shift has occurred only a few times in human history, as exemplified by transitions from the hunter-gatherer era to the agricultural period to the Industrial Revolution. Referring to the rapidly emerging communications and technology revolution as the "Age of Discontinuity," he believes that we are entering a new era not unlike the first reverberations of the Industrial Revolution.

Hawken contends that every leading city is beginning to address the sustainability issue with a shared sense of destiny, some due to a circumstance of crises (Detroit, Philadelphia) and others out of the momentum of success (Seattle, Minneapolis). He builds a case that the future of business depends on restoring balance to natural systems and that "to create an enduring society, we will need a system of commerce and production where each and every act is inherently sustainable and restorative." Hawken documents highly inefficient business practices regarding energy, transportation, land use, and waste disposal; he argues that a sustainability approach can lead to higher profitability and efficiencies in the private and public sectors if the emerging technologies of the new era are seized upon. As for North Carolina, out of a $14 billion energy expenditure, $6 million is "leakage" that could be saved by the opportunities of new technology and sustainability. The same applies to other states and cities, with the United States wasting $220 billion each year.

In effect, Hawken's thesis addresses an American drift toward a throwaway society that too often is transitory and insists on immediate gratification. It is an alarming tendency, from the local to the national level. To live for the short haul and the quick fix has unfortunate consequences: bankrupting budget deficits, jobs and products with built-in obsolescence, a diminished natural environment, deteriorated core cities, and fragmented neighborhoods and families.

The President's Council on Sustainable Development has drawn upon the definition of sustainable development by the World Commission on Environment and Development: "To meet the needs of the present without compromising the ability of future generations to meet their own needs." Many states and communities are part of this initiative that calls for sustainable communities, where "people are encouraged to work together so that natural and historic resources are preserved, jobs are created, sprawl is contained, neighborhoods are viable and secure, education is lifelong, transportation and health care are accessible, and all citizens have opportunities to improve the quality of their lives." Basically, the sustainable community movement is built on the tripartite pillars of economic success, environmental stewardship, and social equity.

In North Carolina, a Sustainable Development program has been fostered through the UNC Chapel Hill School of Public Health and Environmental Resource Program, which has highlighted case studies of successful sustainability efforts among selected businesses, utilities, and nonprofit agencies throughout the state. It also has identified nineteen "Indicators of Sustainability" under the categories of the economy, environment, and community.

An approach similar to sustainable development is smart growth, in which the fundamental idea is to preserve green space and encourage new construction in areas already developed, particularly those close to public transit lines. There is a groundswell of smart growth initiatives under way at the federal, state, and community levels. The U.S. House and Senate have created smart growth or livability task forces to examine every aspect of federal policy that encourages runaway growth. Both are receiving significant bipartisan support.

A number of states have adopted smart growth programs, and there is a general consensus that state and local initiatives will make the difference. North Carolina's Department of Environment, Health, and Natural Resources is cooperating with the state's Department of Commerce in this effort. Meanwhile, a growing number of local smart growth organizations are forming throughout North Carolina, as well as the nation, with continuous information being shared through E-mail, newsletters, and the media.

Additionally, a number of North Carolina communities, including Asheville and Charlotte, have incorporated the sustainability concept into a community visioning process. And in the report of the North Carolina Progress Board, "Measuring Our Progress: Targets for the Year 2010," specific targets are set for maintenance and improvements in such areas as land use planning, air and water quality, solid waste disposal, and transportation.

Several common threads run through each of these sustainability and smart growth concepts and programs. They include an emphasis on public-private partnerships, with business leadership especially critical, creating a spirit of compromise and win-win outcomes, reaching out to grassroots community initiatives and visioning, finding a regional context for land use agendas, and consistently focusing results toward stewardship for the next generation.

New Geographic Divisions Entering the Twenty-First Century

The emerging technology and communications era is bringing potent forces of change to North Carolina and the national landscape. The twin phenomena of globalism and information technology are driving a new geography that is still in flux, with the eventual land use patterns not yet played out. These new geographic divisions are more subtle and complex than the state's traditional Coastal/Piedmont/Mountain subdivisions of the past but very real nonetheless. And North Carolina's traditional character of a widely dispersed population among small and medium-sized towns seems to be reconfiguring more in line with the rest of the country, moving away from the unique qualities and paradoxes that made North Carolina so difficult to understand by John Herbers and other national observers.

This unfolding twenty-first century landscape seems to be divided into four categories: the core cities of the major metropolitan centers; the "edge cities" of swollen suburbanism on the outskirts of core cities; small towns, which in many cases are bedroom communities of core-city commuters and in other settings self-standing towns that harken back to an earlier time; and the increasingly "empty spaces" of rural counties, often out of range of the urban economic and amenity orbit.

Americans seem ambivalent about their living preferences within these options, and the shifting patterns over the last three decades of the twentieth century have conveyed a mixed message. This ambivalence seems especially prevalent in North Carolina and the South, where there is a traditional attachment to a human scale sense of place on one hand and yet a pent-up hunger for growth as well. The previous pages have documented a significant gravitation toward the state's three major metropolitan centers, one that presently shows no sign of abating. In this trend North Carolina is becoming more like the traditional American urban model, which brings with it the economic opportunities and greater amenities of American cities as well as the often out-of-control urban ills. Technology and globalism tend to fuel this momentum toward urban mass.

Yet America's cities are also governed by centrifugal forces that sprawl the urban outreach across outdated political boundaries, often to the detriment of the core city. The resulting edge cities have enough suburban residents and employers to

Activity around Charlotte's extensive South Park mall, one of the state's largest regional malls creating the edge city phenomenon

feel themselves autonomous. The decentralization of the American economy due to technology is also feeding this trend. During the last several years of the 1990s, the ten fastest-growing centers in the United States were on the outer edge of metropolitan centers. North Carolina's major metropolitan areas are classic examples of this pattern, and while the state's progressive annexation laws help ameliorate the "doughnut effect" that afflicts many major American core cities, the tentacles of the edge-city expansion readily spread across county and municipal boundaries, centerless and endlessly elastic. At the same time, the giant car parks next to monolithic and soulless shopping malls are becoming increasingly unfulfilling to citizens everywhere. There is a growing disaffection for suburban life among young professionals and a fundamental discomfort with the notion of urban life among many Americans, especially in a southern state like North Carolina.

Not surprisingly, urban sprawl, which reaches its full expression throughout the nation's edge cities, is becoming a lively issue in the voting booth. In the twentieth century's last nationwide election in November 1998, voters approved nearly two hundred state and local ballot initiatives on curbing urban sprawl. A grassroots movement within neighborhoods and communities crosses party lines and ideologies, as a clamor for smart growth indicates a significant suburban frustration with congestion, dwindling open spaces, and higher property taxes. Indeed, survey polls show that runaway suburban sprawl ranks as voters' top priority in rapidly growing metropolitan areas.

Consequently, there is a countervailing trend at work on the American and state landscape as well, as people flee suburbia for the small towns that have a true identity and a sense of place. In the past decade, 2 million more people have moved from metropolitan centers to more rural locales than have made the customary small-town to big-city journey. This trend, which began with the back-to-nature 1970s, slowed considerably in the 1980s and accelerated again in the 1990s. Fully 75 percent of rural counties grew in the 1990s, as opposed to losing 1.4 million people in the 1980s. This is sometimes referred to as the "neo-classical" movement, with a diminishing popularity of shopping malls, faceless suburbia, and bigness in general.

Many small towns in North Carolina are enjoying such a revitalization with refurbished storefronts, art centers in downtown historic buildings,

Historic Cherry Street in Black Mountain, exemplifying the revitalization of small downtowns

restaurants, and community theaters, sometimes called the "boutiquing" of small-town America. Frequently, there is still a commute to work in the nearby core or edge city. But information technology now permits the option of telecommuting by mobile entrepreneurs, who are geographically footloose and thereby choose the quality of life offered by small towns, of which North Carolina has an abundance. This is particularly prevalent in scenic mountain and coastal towns, as well as Piedmont towns within a convenient driving distance to a larger city. Examples are numerous through-

out the breadth of the state: Black Mountain, Hendersonville, Salisbury, Shelby, Edenton, and New Bern.

These trends underscore a longtime sentiment among people to want the best of both worlds—the human face of small-town living and an easy commute to the cultural opportunities of the large metropolitan core. The nine North Carolina urban regions portrayed in Figure 20.2 thus become of paramount consideration in planning for the future living preferences of the citizenry.

There remain the largely vacant spaces of ap-

Challenges for a New Century

I remember, in December 1941, sitting on my father's lap in front of a stand-up radio listening to H. V. Kaltenborn talk about Pearl Harbor. The nation was at war and I was about six-and-one-half years old. Around our living room walls we had maps of the war. Every day my father would update the movement of American troops in Europe and the Pacific.

I grew up in Bennettsville, South Carolina. During the war my friends, brothers, and I went around town with our little wagons picking up metal (pipes, bottle-tops, old tin cans) to take to the drives to make weaponry. With all of the money we made, we bought war bonds. Once you accumulated $18.75 you had a bond worth $25 with a picture. When I got married, I had $225 worth of bonds from when I was a kid. I used that to buy Jane's wedding ring.

I went to segregated schools throughout my childhood, and I didn't think anything was wrong with that. In fact, I thought it was quite normal. The society was segregated. The black people that I knew were maids, our nurses, the cooks and their children who came sometimes and played with us.

In my teens, I worked on my father's farm. There were about 120 African American workers who lived on our farm and sharecropped, growing corn and cotton. I learned to pick and weigh cotton. I learned early that some of the black people had a distrust of the young white boys who weighed the cotton at the end of the day. Eventually, I was found to be trustworthy. It was a very simple society. Our entertainment came from playing football, hunting, fishing, and camping out. We knew nothing about girls. Even when we tried to learn about them, we learned very little. So, we grew up in a very sheltered way. For those of us in the white middle class, it was a very pleasant way to grow up. We were unaware of the limitations we had placed on our own society, limitations created by the deliberate holding back of a large group of our own people. We did not see lack of opportunity or unfairness.

When I went off to Chapel Hill, I suddenly found myself in a liberal school where we had a couple of famous communists, and we were preparing to accept our first black student. There were many who could not decide which of these developments was the greater evil. It was still a white man's world. The young women at Chapel Hill numbered about 400, the men about 5,000. The girls liked it. The boys did not.

When I got out of college in 1957, I went into the Marine Corps; all of us were going into the service. In many ways, our lives were planned for us. After the marines, I came back and got a job. As a white man with a college degree, there was very little competition for jobs. It was not until the early 1960s, about the time President Kennedy was killed, that we integrated our schools. We did it under court order and, to a large degree, under protest.

proximately one-third of the counties that are outside of any urban shadow. Commuting distances are too inconvenient. Part of the dilemma is that North Carolina created far too many counties in the first place, ranking third nationally (after Texas and Georgia) in the number of counties. Some of them have little prospect of future development; they have long been places of dwindling populations, left behind in the state's rapid economic ascent.

These several categories of North Carolina's population spread, somewhat mirroring national trends, raise significant public policy considerations as the state enters a new century. What should be the priorities for investment in infrastructure? One approach would be to invest much more in the major urban centers, where the preponderance of growth is occurring and infrastructure needs are accelerating, and anticipate that the enhanced economic and urban base will generate a stronger revenue pool to benefit other corners of the state. This would create a sort of metropolitan trickle-down effect.

Some contend that state policies often seem to be more concerned with rural areas than with cities, the apparent assumption being that the cities are prospering and do not need as much help from the state. Urban areas are burgeoning with economic growth and amenities, but whether this will continue is by no means assured. Their postindustrial economies tend to be two-tiered, with a small proportion of high-paying jobs for well-educated and technically trained people supported by a bevy of lower-range service jobs. Urban economist Wilbur Thompson once remarked in reference to the Sunbelt that "they are not building new cities but old cities on new sites." His chilling statement suggests that someday the same problems that haunt older American cities

I date the change in my part of the world to that time. We threw off the yoke of segregation, a yoke we had gone out of our way to create and spent tremendous resources to maintain. In one stroke, we made possible a southern future where the talents, creativity, and energy of all our people would be set free, to the great benefit of all our people. Almost immediately after we integrated our schools, the southern economy took off like a wildfire in the wind. Some will say this is because we had no labor unions, lots of good clean water, and affordable electricity. All of which is true. But I believe that integration made the difference. I believe that integration, and the diversity it began to nourish, became a source of economic, cultural, and community strength.

I used to think that if we could bring jobs, any jobs, into economically depressed neighborhoods, things would be O.K. I was wrong about that. Most of these jobs—the manual, unskilled labor—have long since gone to Latin America, Asia, and Africa. They are not coming back. We cannot re-create those jobs and pay a wage that will allow people to live in dignity in this much more productive society that we have. Education has brought us this far. And education is our only hope for the future.

The year 2000 will be another turning point. Are we serious about providing educational, and by extension, economic, opportunity to every southerner? Will we find ways to achieve parity in terms of preparedness for education? Will we create positive learning environments for our children? Will we find a way to start with three-year-olds to get everyone on an even intellectual playing field? Will we move toward equality of opportunity and resources as a doctrine, and trust that fairness will be the result?

These are the questions that come to mind when my grandchildren climb up on my lap, as I climbed up on my father's lap a half century ago. I know they will have every advantage my family can provide—but what about all the other six-year-olds across the Carolinas sitting on their fathers' laps, wondering what life has in store? Will they all get an opportunity to pursue their dreams? Will they get a fair shot? Asking these questions, and starting to answer them, has moved us from a community of slavery to a community of freedom, and from Jim Crow to the civil rights movement. Whether we persist, and find real answers to these questions, will determine our success in the century to come.

*Hugh L. McColl Jr., chairman of the board and CEO,
Bank of America Corporation*

will come to burden newer ones in North Carolina and elsewhere unless some lessons are learned from the mistakes of our urban history. Inner-city decay, suburban sprawl, environmental degradation, neglected infrastructure, crime and traffic gridlock, among other problems, plague older cities, and North Carolina is not immune from them. Much of the state's present and future prosperity depends on its ability to deal successfully with these issues.

Meanwhile, the edge cities of North Carolina, like their national counterparts, may be veering out of control with their overdependence on the automobile and little in the way of effective mass transit. Clearly better transportation planning and infrastructure investment will be critical for these spreading metropolitan footprints that represented an American urban growth story during the last quarter of the twentieth century. The signals seem mixed as to the future direction of these spaces, as mall shopping diminishes and sense of place remains elusive. North Carolina will need to develop a more proactive public policy approach to this volatile and expansive element of its urban geography.

At the same time, a foundation stone of the state's traditional living patterns rests on the identity of the small and medium-sized towns, which began as agricultural market centers, were thereafter transformed into textile or furniture towns, and today seem to be reinventing themselves in keeping with a growing national trend. Public investment in the infrastructure of the core of these smaller communities can often serve as the kernel that revitalizes the legacy of small-town North Carolina.

It may be that those very rural counties, outside of the state's nine urban regions (Fig. 20.2), will need to reduce their populations and economic activities to a level that realistically reflects the market. Despite periodic state subsidies, these areas will not attract significant business investment from the outside, as they are too far removed from the needed complementary services of the urban areas. They are not conveniently located for easy access to urban amenities, an ongoing priority for most rural dwellers. In the early 1970s North Carolina public policy attempted without much success to identify and support 368 "job clusters" throughout the state's far-flung 100 counties, a clearly unrealistic goal.

But overall, it is not simply a matter of rural versus urban. The economy that will provide the resources needed to deal with health care and educational deficiencies in rural areas will come mainly from urban areas. Thus, it is imperative for the entire state that its cities function soundly and that they not be overcome by the problems that have sapped the health of their counterparts in other areas of the country. The rebirth of one of North Carolina's historic treasures—its small towns—should be facilitated as a matter of ongoing state investment. And public policy must increasingly be oriented toward the regional context

and all the interrelationships that ensue: from the complex urban core, to the edge cities with their unconcern with political boundaries, to the ubiquitous small towns, scattered like fireflies across the North Carolina landscape.

The challenge of thinking and planning in this twenty-first century context, in a new technological age played out on the world map, will call for creative thinking within a whole new paradigm. As Jonathan Daniels observed, there will be "no easy roads" for this paradoxical, changing, and colorful state.

Selected References

"America's Cities: They Can Yet Be Resurrected." *Economist*, January 10, 1998.

Hass, S., and B. Williams. *A Profile of North Carolina: Indicators of Sustainability*. Chapel Hill: University of North Carolina at Chapel Hill, Environmental Resource Program, 1995.

Hawkin, P. *The Ecology of Commerce*. New York: Harper Business, 1993.

Herbers, J. *The New Heartland*. New York: Times Books, 1986.

Kennedy, P. *Preparing for the Twenty-first Century*. New York: Random House, 1993.

Newbold, M., and S. Newbold. *Sustainable Development in North Carolina*. Chapel Hill: University of North Carolina at Chapel Hill, Environmental Resource Program, 1995.

"Our Worst Nightmare." *Charlotte Observer*, December 14, 1997.

Peirce, N. "Regionalism and American Citistates." *Asheville Citizen-Times*, May 15, 1996.

———. "Citistates: Cash Cows of the American Economy." *Charlotte Observer*, April 18, 1998.

CONTRIBUTORS

John F. Bender is professor of earth sciences at the University of North Carolina at Charlotte.

Andy R. Bobyarchick is associate professor of earth sciences at the University of North Carolina at Charlotte.

Woodward S. Bousquet is professor of environmental studies and biology at Shenandoah University in Winchester, Virginia.

Harrison S. Campbell Jr. is assistant professor of geography at the University of North Carolina at Charlotte.

Roy Carroll is senior vice president and vice president for academic affairs at the University of North Carolina General Administration in Chapel Hill.

Jack Claiborne is associate vice chancellor for public relations at the University of North Carolina at Charlotte.

Rex Clay is director of research and planning at Gaston College in Dallas, North Carolina.

Arthur W. Cooper is professor of forestry at North Carolina State University in Raleigh.

John A. Diemer is associate professor of earth sciences at the University of North Carolina at Charlotte.

Randall D. Forsythe is associate professor of earth sciences at the University of North Carolina at Charlotte.

David R. Goldfield is Robert Lee Bailey Professor of History at the University of North Carolina at Charlotte.

Larry D. Gustke is associate professor in the Office of Parks, Recreation, and Tourism Management at North Carolina State University in Raleigh.

David T. Hartgen is professor of geography and director of the Interdisciplinary Center for Transportation Studies at the University of North Carolina at Charlotte.

H. William Heller is dean and executive director of the St. Petersburg Campus at the University of South Florida.

Gerald L. Ingalls is professor of geography at the University of North Carolina at Charlotte.

Sallie M. Ives is associate professor of geography at the University of North Carolina at Charlotte.

J. Dennis Lord is professor of geography at the University of North Carolina at Charlotte.

Richard C. Lumb is director of the Research, Planning, and Analysis Bureau, Charlotte-Mecklenburg Police Department.

Schley R. Lyons is dean of the College of Arts and Sciences and professor of political science at the University of North Carolina at Charlotte.

Walter E. Martin is assistant professor of earth sciences at the University of North Carolina at Charlotte.

Douglas M. Orr Jr. is president of Warren Wilson College in Asheville.

Gerald R. Pyle is professor of health promotion and kinesiology at the University of North Carolina at Charlotte.

Robert Reiman is adjunct professor of geology and geography at the University of North Carolina at Pembroke.

Peter J. Robinson is professor of geography at the University of North Carolina at Chapel Hill.

Tom Ross is department chair and professor of geology and geography at the University of North Carolina at Pembroke.

Donald Steila (dec.) was professor of earth sciences at the University of North Carolina at Charlotte.

Alfred W. Stuart is professor of geography at the University of North Carolina at Charlotte.

Wayne A. Walcott is associate provost and associate professor of geography at the University of North Carolina at Charlotte.

PHOTOGRAPH CREDITS

INDEX

Italic page numbers refer to photos.

253–54, 277; and economy, 62; during World War II, 71; and civil rights era, 72–74; and population, 80, 436; and urbanization, 108, 446–47; and crime, 328; and public education, 349, 350 (fig. 15.15); and health care, 389, 390

Raleigh: and transportation, 55, 56, 200, 201 (fig. 9.1), 203, 211, 212, 213, 220; population of, 61; and history, 70, 72; and urbanization, 111, 112, 113, 114–15; and employment, 129; and economy, 139; and air quality, 283, 284; and crime, 329, 334; and health care, 384, 389; and cultural arts, 394–95, 396, 397, 399, 404; and historic preservation, 400, 402; and recreation, 410, 428, 429

Raleigh-Durham: and urbanization, 67, 118; and economy, 87, 137, 140, 142; and housing, 98; population of, 101, 102; and manufacturing, 186, 189; and transportation, 199, 211, 215, 216; and television, 240; and air quality, 299; and health care, 384, 390; and recreation, 415; and regional planning, 440, 441

Raleigh–Durham–Chapel Hill, 140, 228

Randolph County, 88, 101, 186, 210, 290

Recreation: and population, 91, 99, 101, 102; and employment, 129, 135; and forest resources, 160; and fishing industry, 167, 410, 415–16; and banking, 237; and tourism, 240; and water resources, 303, 309, 312, 313, 314; and environmental protection, 410, 413–14, 424–28, 431–32, 436; types of, 410 (fig. 19.1), 412–20, 413 (fig. 19.2), 415 (fig. 19.4), 416 (fig. 19.5), 418 (fig. 19.6); scope of, 410–12; and deer distribution, 415 (fig. 19.3); areas, 420–24, 421 (fig. 19.7), 422 (fig. 19.8), 423 (fig. 19.9); natural areas and wilderness, 424–28, 427 (fig. 19.10), 428 (fig. 19.11); and resource maintenance, 428–31, 429 (fig. 19.12), 430 (figs. 19.13, 19.14); and

resource protection, 431–32; outlook for, 433. See also Tourism

Regional areas: and history, 1, 2; land regions, 2, 3 (fig. 1.1), 10; and population, 86–87; and economy, 145–47, 438–42; and government and politics, 246, 247, 266; and health care, 384; and planning, 438–42, 440 (figs. 20.1, 20.2), 441 (fig. 20.3)

Regulators, 51

Research Triangle Park: and technology, 1, 376; history of, 75; and population, 88, 99; and urbanization, 112; and manufacturing, 188, 190, 194, 195; and government and politics, 246; and economy, 436; and regional planning, 440, 441

Retail trade: and economy, 127, 224–30, 224 (fig. 10.1), 226 (fig. 10.2), 228, 230 (figs. 10.3, 10.4), 231 (fig. 10.6), 244; and employment, 128, 129; and tourism, 240

Reynolds, Richard, 69

Rhode Island model, 63–64

Richland Mountains, 38

Richmond County, 88, 170, 188

Roan Mountain, 38, 419, 426

Roanoke Island, 49, 397, 413

Roanoke River, 20, 200, 322

Robeson County, 93, 158, 183, 188

Robinson, Jackie, 73

Rockingham County, 172

Rocky Mount, 86, 87, 140, 189, 214, 309, 406

Rowan County, 194, 210, 290

Rural areas: poverty in, 1, 3, 63, 75, 111, 339; and lack of economic growth, 4, 5, 70; and employment, 4, 84; and tourism, 24; and population, 61, 63 (fig. 3.13), 65, 79, 83 (fig. 4.4), 84–106 passim, 85 (fig. 4.5), 445; and transportation, 67, 209, 220; history of, 104–7; and government and politics, 105, 120, 437; and economy, 124, 136, 137, 139, 447–48; and manufacturing, 183–96 passim; and

utilities, 218; and air quality, 285, 301; and crime, 329, 331–32, 331 (fig. 14.5), 336; and public education, 349; and health care, 379, 383, 386, 388, 389, 390, 391; and cultural arts, 400; and recreation, 410, 423; and environmental protection, 438; and regional planning, 439, 442

Salem, 395

Salisbury, 213, 229, 300, 395, 404, 406, 445

Sampson County, 153, 158

Sandhills district: and Fall Line, 11 (fig. 2.1), 16; and Coastal Plain region, 13; and soils, 16, 40, 42; and vegetation, 34; and economic growth, 69; and mining industry, 170; and water resources, 311; and recreation, 419

Sanford, Terry, 75, 250, 397

Sanford, 299

Sanford Basin, 18

Sauratown Mountains, 17

Savannah River, 20

Schenck, Michael, 63

Scotland County, 93, 209

Scott, Robert W., 274, 359

Scott, W. Kerr, 67, 71

Sea Islands, 31

Services sector: growth in, 3–4; and employment, 4, 127, 128, 129, 130, 135, 180; and population, 93, 96, 99; and urbanization, 111, 112, 113, 114; and economy, 124, 125–26, 144, 244; and newspapers, 238–39; and television, 239–40, 239 (fig. 10.11); and telephone service, 240, 240 (fig. 10.12). See also Finance; Retail trade; Wholesale trade

Shackleford Banks, 426

Shelby, 213, 395, 445

Shining Rock, 426, 428

Singletary Lake State Park, 423

Slaveholding, 1, 50, 54, 56 (fig. 3.8), 57–58, 78

Smith Island, 31

Snowbird Mountains, 20

Soils: and wetlands, 13; and pocosins, 15; and Sandhills, 16, 40, 42; and vegetation, 30–42 passim; quality of, 39; characteristics of, 40–41, 43 (fig. 2.22); classification of, 41, 42; and agriculture, 42, 44; and urban uses, 44–45; and forest resources, 160; and air quality, 284; and water resources, 305, 317, 319, 320

South Atlantic International Biosphere Reserve, 422

South Carolina, 47, 49, 50, 52, 120, 214, 231–32, 382, 400

South Mountains, 18

South Mountains State Park, 426

Spruce Pine, 169, 213, 395

Stanly County, 194

Stokes County, 89, 172, 210, 226, 290

Suggs Mill Pond, 426

Surry County, 170

Swain County, 87–88, 89, 93, 138, 244, 341, 395, 427

Swannanoa Gap, 20

Swannanoa River, 21

Swannanoa Valley, 2

Swanquarter Wilderness, 426

Swansboro, 418

Tarboro, 309

Tar-Pamlico Basin, 321

Tar-Pamlico River, 309

Tar River, 18, 200

Technology. See High-technology industry

Textile and apparel industries: and population patterns, 2; history of, 56, 63–64, 66 (fig. 3.15), 69, 70, 71, 74; mills, 64, 182; and urbanization, 108, 121; and economy, 123, 124, 136, 179–91 passim, 435; and employment, 129, 179, 181, 183,